The Law of Marketing

SECOND EDITION

Lynda J. Oswald

Professor of Business Law and Michael R. and Mary Kay Hallman Fellow
Stephen M. Ross School of Business at the University of Michigan

SOUTH-WESTERN
CENGAGE Learning

Australia • Brazil • Japan • Korea • Mexico • Singapore • Spain • United Kingdom • United States

SOUTH-WESTERN
CENGAGE Learning™

The Law of Marketing, 2e
Lynda J. Oswald

Vice President of Editorial, Business:
Jack W. Calhoun

Editor-in-Chief: Rob Dewey

Acquisitions Editor: Vicky True

Developmental Editor: Krista Kellman

Marketing Manager: Jennifer Garamy

Marketing Coordinator: Heather McAuliffe

Associate Marketing Communications
Manager: Suzanne Istvan

Editorial Assistant: Nicole Parsons

Production Manager: Jennifer Ziegler

Content Project Management:
PrePress PMG

Senior Media Editor: Kristin Meere

Production Technology Analyst: Starratt
Alexander

Senior Manufacturing Buyer: Kevin Kluck

Production Service: PrePress PMG

Copyeditor: Deborah Bader

Senior Art Director: Michelle Kunkler

Senior Text Acquisition Manager:
Katie Huha

Image Permissions Acquisitions Manager:
Deanna Ettinger

Cover Designer: Ramsdell Design

Cover Image: © Siede Pries/Getty Images,
Inc.

For product information and technology assistance, contact us at
Cengage Learning Customer & Sales Support, 1-800-354-9706

For permission to use material from this text or product,
submit all requests online at **www.cengage.com/permissions**
Further permissions questions can be emailed to
permissionrequest@cengage.com

Library of Congress Control Number: 2009936769

ISBN-13: 978-1-4390-7924-9

ISBN-10: 1-4390-7924-2

South-Western Cengage Learning
5191 Natorp Boulevard
Mason, OH 45040
USA

Cengage Learning products are represented in Canada by
Nelson Education, Ltd.

For your course and learning solutions, visit **www.cengage.com**

Purchase any of our products at your local college store or at our
preferred online store **www.CengageBrain.com**

Printed in Canada
1 2 3 4 5 6 7 13 12 11 10 09

To Brad, Rhiannon, Nathaniel, & Kiernan

Brief Contents

Table of Cases   xi

Preface   xvii

About the Author   xxi

PART 1   Introduction to Marketing Law   1

CHAPTER 1   Overview of the Legal Environment of Marketing Activities   3

PART 2   Legal Issues Relating to Product Development   21

CHAPTER 2   Protection of Intellectual Property Assets: Patent and Copyright Law   23

CHAPTER 3   Protection of Intellectual Property Assets through Trade Secret Law, Contractual Agreements and Business Strategies   71

PART 3   Legal Issues Relating to Product Distribution   107

CHAPTER 4   Antitrust Law   109

CHAPTER 5   The Franchisor-Franchisee Relationship   155

PART 4   Legal Issues Relating to Product Promotion   189

CHAPTER 6   Trademark Law   191

CHAPTER 7   Commercial Speech and the Regulation of Advertising   231

CHAPTER 8   Consumer Protection Law   275

PART 5   Legal Issues Relating to Product Sale   313

CHAPTER 9   Contracts and Sales of Goods Law   315

CHAPTER 10   Warranties and Products Liability   355

Glossary   393

Index   409

Contents

Table of Cases xi

Preface xvii

About the Author xxi

PART 1   Introduction to Marketing Law

CHAPTER 1
Overview of the Legal Environment of Marketing Activities 3

Introduction   3

Classifications of the Law   3

Sources of the Law   5
Primary Sources of the Law   5
Secondary Sources of the Law   6

The American Legal System   7
Common Law and Equity   7
Court Structure   8

Jurisdiction   11
Subject Matter Jurisdiction   11
Jurisdiction Over the Parties   12
Jurisdiction on the Internet   12

Discussion Case 1.1 Jurisdiction   13

Discussion Case 1.2 Jurisdiction   17

PART 2   Legal Issues Relating to Product Development

CHAPTER 2
Protection of Intellectual Property Assets: Patent and Copyright Law 23

Overview   23
Categories of Intellectual Property Law   23
Underlying Policy Considerations   25

Patent Law   25
Standards for Patent Issuance   26
Ownership of Patents   29
Patent Application Procedures   30
Rights Granted by a Patent   31
Infringement   32
Remedies for Patent Infringement   34
Filing for Foreign Patents   35

Copyright Law   37
Sources of Copyright Law   37
Subject Matter of Copyrights   38
Rights Provided by Copyright   40
Ownership of the Copyright   41

Copyright Procedures   41

Copyright Infringement   43

Defenses to Copyright Infringement   45

Remedies for Copyright Infringement   47

Copyright Law on the Internet   49

International Copyright Law Issues   50

Discussion Case 2.1 Patent Law—Patentable Subject Matter   51

Discussion Case 2.2 Patents—Novelty, On-Sale Bar   53

Discussion Case 2.3 Copyright—Work for Hire   55

Discussion Case 2.4 Copyright—Infringement, Copyrightable Subject Matter   58

Discussion Case 2.5 Copyright—Fair Use   61

Discussion Questions   65

CHAPTER 3

Protection of Intellectual Property Assets through Trade Secret Law, Contractual Agreements and Business Strategies 71

Trade Secret Law   71

Definition of "Trade Secret"   71

Patent Protection versus Trade Secret Protection   73

Ownership of Trade Secrets Created by Employees   74

Misappropriation of a Trade Secret   75

Remedies for Trade Secret Misappropriation   77

Protection of Trade Secrets   79

International Aspects of Trade Secret Protection   80

The Law of Unsolicited Ideas   80

From the Inventor's Perspective   80

From the Company's Perspective   81

Business Strategies for Protecting Intellectual Property Assets   82

Contractual Agreements   82

Intellectual Property Audits   86

Discussion Case 3.1 Trade Secrets—Definition   89

Discussion Case 3.2 Trade Secrets—Required Elements   91

Discussion Case 3.3 Noncompete Covenant, Trade Secrets—Required Elements   92

Discussion Case 3.4 Covenants Not to Compete   96

Discussion Case 3.5 Protection of Unsolicited Ideas   100

Discussion Questions   103

PART 3   Legal Issues Relating to Product Distribution

CHAPTER 4

Antitrust Law 109

Overview   109

Common Law Contracts in Restraint of Trade   110

The Federal Antitrust Statutes   111

The Sherman Act   111

The Clayton Act   112

The Federal Trade Commission Act   113

The Robinson-Patman Act   114

The Antitrust Statutes Generally   114

The Rule of Reason Versus *Per Se* Violations   115
Remedies for Antitrust Violations   116

Horizontal Restraints Among Competitors   118
Price-Fixing   121
Group Boycotts and Concerted Refusals to Deal   122
Horizontal Market Allocations   123
Agreements to Restrict Advertising   123
Joint Ventures   123

Vertical Restraints Against Competition   124
Resale Price Maintenance Agreements   124
Nonprice Agreements Between a Manufacturer and a Dealer   127
Tying Arrangements   127

Monopolization and Attempts to Monopolize   128
Monopolization by a Single Firm   128
Attempted Monopolization   131
Conspiracy to Monopolize   131

Price Discrimination   131
Elements of Price Discrimination   132
Defenses   133

Antitrust and the Internet   135

State Antitrust Enforcement   135

International Implications of Antitrust Laws   136

Discussion Case 4.1 Horizontal Price-Fixing, Horizontal Market Allocation   137

Discussion Case 4.2 Vertical Price Restraints, Rule of Reason   138

Discussion Case 4.3 Rule of Reason, Vertical Maximum Resale Price Maintenance   142

Discussion Case 4.4 Monopolization, Attempted Monopolization   145

Discussion Case 4.5 Monopolization, Attempted Monopolization, Definition of Market, Essential Facility, State Antitrust Law   148

Discussion Questions 150

CHAPTER 5
The Franchisor-Franchisee Relationship 155

Overview   155

Types of Franchises   156

Definition of a "Franchise"   156

Creation of a Franchise   159

Regulation of the Franchise Relationship   160
Disclosure   161

Legal Issues Arising from the Franchise Relationship   162
Existence of a Franchise Relationship   163
Vicarious Liability of a Franchisor   163
Franchise Antitrust Issues   165
Co-Branding   168
Encroachment   168
Termination Issues   170
Multi-Level Marketing   170

Franchising and the Internet   170
"Offering" Franchises on the Internet   171
Franchisor Control Over Franchise Internet Activities   171
Internet "Encroachment" Issues   172

International Issues in Franchising   172

Discussion Case 5.1 Constitutionality of Local Ordinances Restricting Franchise
    Location   173

Discussion Case 5.2 Existence of Franchise Relationship   175

Discussion Case 5.3 Existence of Franchise Relationship   177

Discussion Case 5.4 Vicarious Liability of Franchisor   179

Discussion Case 5.5 Franchise Antitrust Issues   182

Discussion Questions   184

PART 4   Legal Issues Relating to Product Promotion

CHAPTER 6
Trademark Law 191

Overview   191
  Origins of Trademark Law   192
  Types of Marks   192

Creating and Protecting a Mark   193
  Distinctiveness of the Mark   193
  What May Constitute a Mark?   194
  Trademark Searches   197
  Creation and Ownership of the Mark   199
  U.S. Customs Service Assistance   202

Trademark Infringement and Dilution   203
  Infringement   203
  Dilution   209

International Trademark Law Issues   212

Trademarks on the Internet   213
  Cybersquatting   213
  Typopiracy   214
  Portals, Banner Advertising, and Metatags   214
  Linking Issues   215
  Internet Strategies for Business   215

  Discussion Case 6.1 Trademark Protection—Color as a Mark   216

  Discussion Case 6.2 Trade Dress Protection—Functionality   218

  Discussion Case 6.3 Trademark Infringement, Dilution, Defenses, First Amendment   221

  Discussion Case 6.4 Trademarks—Infringement, Metatags, Remedies   224

  Discussion Questions 227

CHAPTER 7
Commercial Speech and the Regulation of Advertising 231

Commercial Free Speech   231

Common Law Causes of Action   234
  Right of Publicity   234

Statutory and Regulatory Causes of Action   236
  State Statutes   236
  The Lanham Act   237
  The Federal Trade Commission Act   241
  General Principles of FTC Regulation of Business Acts and Practices   243
  Specific Advertising Practices   247

The National Advertising Division   250

Advertising on the Internet   250
  On-line Advertising   251
  Privacy Issues   251

International Advertising Law   252

  Discussion Case 7.1 Commercial Speech   253

  Discussion Case 7.2 Commercial Speech   256

  Discussion Case 7.3 Lanham Act—False Advertising   259

  Discussion Case 7.4 Commercial Speech: FTC Act—Deceptive Advertising   264

  Discussion Questions   271

CHAPTER 8
Consumer Protection Law 275

Overview   275

Direct Marketing Activities   275
  Telemarketing   276
  Electronic Retailing and Advertising   278
  Home Solicitations   280
  Unsolicited Merchandise, Merchandise on Approval, and Negative Option Plans   282
  900 Numbers   283
  Warranties and Guarantees   283

Labeling and Packaging Regulation   283
  "Made in USA" Labeling   284
  "Green" Marketing   285
  International Labeling Considerations   286

Health and Safety Regulation   287
  Food, Drug, and Cosmetic Laws   287
  Consumer Product Safety Law   291

Consumer Credit Protection   293
  The Truth-in-Lending Act   293

  Discussion Case 8.1 First Amendment Challenge to the Do-Not-Call Registry   296

  Discussion Case 8.2 CAN-SPAM Preemption   300

  Discussion Case 8.3 Home Solicitations   303

  Discussion Case 8.4 Fair Debt Collections Practices Act   306

  Discussion Questions 309

PART 5   Legal Issues Relating to Product Sale

CHAPTER 9
Contracts and Sales of Goods Law 315

Overview   315

Sources of Contract Law   315
  The Common Law of Contracts   316
  Uniform Commercial Code   316

Elements of a Contract   317
  Mutual Assent   317
  Consideration   322
  Legality/Unenforceability on Public Policy Grounds   323
  Capacity   324

Promissory Estoppel   324

The Statute of Frauds   325

Parol Evidence Rule and Contract Interpretation   325

Special UCC Rules   326
Definiteness and the UCC's "Gap-Filler" Provisions   326
Performance of the Contract   326
Transfer of Title and Risk of Loss   328

Breach of Contract and Contract Remedies   331
Actual and Anticipatory Breach   331
Remedies Generally   331
Remedies in Sales Contracts   332

Contract Law and E-Commerce   335

Contracts in the International Environment   336
Discussion Case 9.1 Advertisements as Offers, Statute of Frauds   337
Discussion Case 9.2 UCC Battle of the Forms   341
Discussion Case 9.3 Promissory Estoppel, Contract Remedies   345
Discussion Case 9.4 Convention on the Sale of Goods   347
Discussion Questions   349

CHAPTER 10
Warranties and Products Liability 355

Overview   355

Warranties   356
Warranty of Title   356
Express Warranties   357
Privity   359
Warranty Disclaimers   361
The Buyer's Obligations in Warranty Actions   363
Remedies and Defenses   363
The Magnuson-Moss Federal Warranty Act   364

Products Liability Law   365
Negligence   365
Strict Products Liability   367
Discussion Case 10.1 Warranties—Express and Implied; Warranties—Remedies   379
Discussion Case 10.2 Warranties—Disclaimers; Magnuson-Moss Federal Warranty Act   382
Discussion Case 10.3 Products Liability—Negligence, Strict Liability   384
Discussion Case 10.4 Strict Liability—Consumer Expectations; Risk-Utility Test   386
Discussion Questions   389

Glossary 393
Index 409

Table of Cases

21st Century Concepts, Inc., Rossi v., 303–306

44 Liquormart, Inc. v. Rhode Island, 232–233

AAA Abachman Enterprises, Inc. v. Stanley Steemer International, Inc., 169

Abbott Laboratories, Sindell v., 372

A.B. Dick Co., Henry v., 182

Abood v. Detroit Board of Education, 258

Acuff-Rose Music, Inc., Campbell v., 47, 48

A. E. Staley Mfg. Co., FTC v., 135

Akkaoui, Toys "R" Us, Inc. v., 211

Albrecht v. Herald Co., 14, 144

Al Minor & Associates, Inc. v. Martin, 89–91

Alpo PetFoods, Inc. v. Ralston Purina Co., 243

Aluminum Co. of America, United States v., 128, 130, 137

Alyeska Pipeline Service, Reeves v., 81

American Automobile Association, Inc. v. Darba Enterprises Inc., 17–20

American Football League v. National Football League, 130

American Home Products Corp., McNeilab, Inc. v., 263

American Tel. & Tel. Co., MCI Communications Corp. v., 131

Ames Publishing Co. v. Walker-Davis Publications, 243

Amestoy, International Dairy Foods Association v., 289

Anderson v. Owens-Corning Fiberglas Corp., 376

Andy's Sportswear, Inc., Anheuser-Busch, Inc. v., 211

Angus v. Shiley, Inc., 372

Anheuser-Busch, Inc. v. Andy's Sportswear, Inc., 211

The Antioch Co. v. Western Trimming Crop., 198

Applied Anagramics, Inc., Futuredontics, Inc. v., 215

Arnold, Schwinn & Co., United States v., 143

Asis Internet Services v. Vistaprint USA, Inc., 280

Associates Commer Corp., Trailer Leasing Co. v., 94

Augusta National Inc., Bancroft & Masters, Inc. v., 15

Auto-By-Tel, LLC, Jerome-Duncan, Inc. v., 158

A.V. v. iParadigms, LLC, 61–65

Baby Food Antitrust Litigation, In re, 120–121

Baker v. Burlington Coat Factory, 362

Bancroft & Masters, Inc. v. Augusta National Inc., 15

Barazzotto v. Intelligent Sys., Inc., 383

Baxter Healthcare Corp., Vassallo v., 376

Bay State Harness Horse Racing & Breeding Assoc. Inc., Famous Music Corp. v., 44

Beech v. Outboard Marine Corp., 375

Bell Sports, Inc. v. Yarusso, 365

Bilski, In re, 27–28

Blockbuster, Inc., Harris v., 323

Bloomfield Motors, Inc., Henningsen v., 359, 360

Board of Trustees of State University of New York v. Fox, 232

Boston Duck Tours, LP v. Super Duck Tours, LLC, 195

Bottling Group, LLC, Green County Food Market, Inc. v., 148–150

BRG of Georgia, Inc., Palmer v., 137–138

Brinkman v. Shiley, Inc., 372

Bristol-Myers Squibb Co., Strategic Directions Group, Inc. v., 91–92

Brooke Group, Ltd. v. Brown & Williamson Tobacco Corp., 130

Brown & Williamson Tobacco Corp., Brooke Group, Ltd. v., 130

Brown Shoe Co. v. United States, 110

BSH Home Appliances Corp., Detroit Radiant Prods. Co. v., 334–335

Buick Motor Co., MacPherson v., 366

Burck v. M Mars, Inc., 235

Burlington Coat Factory, Baker v., 362

By Rite Distributing, Inc. v. The Coca-Cola Co., 238

Caddy, Pebble Beach Company v., 13–17

CAL Circuit Abco, NEC Electronics v., 207

Calder v. Jones, 14, 16

California Auth. of Racing Fairs, ITSI T.V. Prods., Inc. v., 44

California Closet Co. v. Space Organization Systems, Inc., 172

Campbell Soup Co., In re, 246, 249

Campbell v. Acuff-Rose Music, Inc., 47, 48

Campbell v. Gala Indus., Inc., 377

Capital Cities/ABC, Inc., Hoffman v., 224

Capital City Foods, United States v., 288

Carson v. Here's Johnny Portable Toilets, Inc., 236

Cascade Auto Glass, Inc., CIM Insurance Corp. v., 319

Case, Inc., McAnany v., 368

Casper Corp., Donsco, Inc. v., 243

Casper Corp., John Wright, Inc. v., 243

Cass County Music Co. v. Vineyard County Gold Corp., 44

Central Hudson Gas & Electric Corp. v. Public Service Commission of New York, 232–233, 253, 254, 256, 289, 297

Chakrabarty, Diamond v., 27, 51–53

Chiquita Brands Int'l Inc., Del Monte Fresh Produce, N.A., Inc. v., 92–96

Chordiant Software, Inc., Netbula, LLC v., 46

Christy Sports, LLC v. Deer Valley Resort Co., Ltd., 145–147

Ciaramelli, Curran v., 357

CIM Insurance Corp. v. Cascade Auto Glass, Inc., 319

Clomon v. Jackson, 307–308

Clorox Co., S.C. Johnson & Son v., 240–241

CMG Worldwide, Inc., Shaw Family Archives Ltd. v., 236

Cohen, Ticor Title Insurance Co. v., 96–100

Colgate & Co., United States v., 125

Collins v. International Dairy Queen, 167

Columbia Pictures Industries, Inc., Moore v., 60

Community for Creative Non-Violence v. Reid, 41, 55–58

Continental Inc. Co., Oakley Fertilizer, Inc. v., 341–344

Continental T.V., Inc. v. GTE Sylvania Inc., 143, 144

Coors Brewing Co., Rubin v., 253–256

Copperweld Corp. v. Independence Tube Corp., 112, 116

Cory Int'l Corp., Kolarik v., 358

Country Walkers, Inc., Tour Costa Rica v., 345–347

Crinkley v. Holiday Inns, Inc., 181

Crossroads Cogeneration Corp. v. Orange & Rockland Utilities, Inc., 133

Curran v. Ciaramelli, 357

Curtis 1000 v. Suess, 95

Daimler Chrysler Corp., Flax v., 377

Darba Enterprises Inc., American Automobile Association, Inc. v., 17–20

Dash, Weil Ceramics & Glass, Inc. v., 207

Deer Valley Resort Co., Ltd., Christy Sports, LLC v., 145–147

Del Monte Fresh Produce, N.A., Inc. v. Chiquita Brands Int'l Inc., 92–96

Deltek, Inc. v. Iuvo Systems, Inc., 215

Detroit Board of Education, Abood v., 258

Detroit Radiant Prods. Co. v. BSH Home Appliances Corp., 334–335

Diamond v. Chakrabarty, 27, 51–53

DirecTV, Inc., Time Warner Cable, Inc. v., 259–264

Diversified Prod. Industries, SEMA Construction, Inc. v., 329–330

Dolphin World, Inc., Snuba International, Inc. v., 33

Domino's Pizza, Inc., Queen City Pizza, Inc. v., 167

Donsco, Inc. v. Casper Corp., 243

Dr. Miles Medical Co. v. John D. Park & Sons Co., 138, 139, 142, 143

Dumex Medical Surgical Products, Inc., Molnlycke Health Care A.B. v., 13

Dunkin' Donuts, Inc., Wu v., 164–165

Dunleavey v. Paris Ceramics USA, Inc., 379–381

Dycho Co., Whitehead v., 378

Eastern Tube Co., Nat'l Tube Co. v., 89

Eastman Kodak Co. v. Image Technical Services, Inc., 129, 149

Ebay, Inc., Tiffany (NJ) Inc. v., 205

Edenfield v. Fane, 232, 254, 255

Emanuel Lutheran, Themins v., 180

Estate of Presley v. Russen, 235

Ezell, The Plantation Shutter Co. v., 318

Falstaff Brewing Co., United State v., 119

Famous Music Corp. v. Bay State Harness Horse Racing & Breeding Assoc. Inc., 44

Fane, Edenfield v., 232, 254, 255

Farsian v. Pfizer, 372

Feist Publications, Inc. v. Rural Telephone Service Co., 39–40, 59

Fenton, Fibreboard Corp. v., 376

Fibreboard Corp. v. Fenton, 376

Flax v. Daimler Chrysler Corp., 377

Ford Motor Co., Midler v., 236

Fort Bridger Rendezvous Ass'n., Gregory v., 122–123

Fox, Board of Trustees of State University of New York v., 232

Francis, In re, 163

Fred Martin Motor Co., Schwarzenegger v., 16

Free Speech Coalition, Inc. v. Shurtleff, 280

Frisby v. Schultz, 297

Frito-Lay, Inc., Waits v., 236

FTC, Kraft, Inc. v., 264–271

FTC, Mainstream Marketing Services, Inc. v., 296–300

FTC, Novartis Corp. v., 244

FTC, Orkin Exterminating Co. v., 276

FTC, Warner-Lambert Co. v., 243

FTC v. A. E. Staley Mfg. Co., 135

FTC v. Global Marketing Group, Inc., 279

FTC v. Motion Picture Advertising Service Co., 113

Futuredontics, Inc. v. Applied Anagramics, Inc., 215

Gaines-Tabb v. ICI Explosives, USA, Inc., 384–386

Gala Indus., Inc., Campbell v., 377

Gizzi v. Texaco, Inc., 181

Glickman v. Wileman Brothers & Elliott, Inc., 256, 257, 258

Global Marketing Group, Inc., FTC v., 279

Gonzalez v. Kay, 306–309

Graco Children's Products, Inc., Thongchoom v., 388

Great Minneapolis Surplus Store, Lefkowitz v., 339–340

Greco v. Trauner, Cohen & Thomas, LLP, 308

Green County Food Market, Inc. v. Bottling Group, LLC, 148–150

Gregory v. Fort Bridger Rendezvous Ass'n., 122–123

Grinnell Corp., United States v., 129

Grokster, Ltd., MGM Studios, Inc. v., 44

GTE Prods. Corp., Tasca v., 378

GTE Sylvania Inc., Continental T.V., Inc. v., 143, 144

Haelan Labs, Inc. v. Topps Chewing Gum, Inc., 235

Hamlin v. Motel 6, 166

Hanover Insurance Co., Kelley v., 367

Harlow Meyer Savage, Inc., Maltby v., 99–100

Harris, Service Sys. Corp. v., 100

Harris v. Blockbuster, Inc., 323

Hasbro, Inc. v. Internet Entertainment Group, Ltd., 211

Heinz W. Kirchner, In re, 245

Henningsen v. Bloomfield Motors, Inc., 359, 360

Henry v. A.B. Dick Co., 182

Herald Co., Albrecht v., 14, 144

Here's Johnny Portable Toilets, Inc., Carson v., 236

Higgins v. Intex Recreation Corp., 386–389

Hirsch v. S. C. Johnson & Son, Inc., 236

Hoffman, Telxon Corp. v., 93

Hoffman v. Capital Cities/ABC, Inc., 224

Hogg Wyld, LTD, Jordache Enterprises, Inc. v., 206

Holiday Inns, Inc., Crinkley v., 181

Hyatt v. Toys "R" Us, Inc., 359

ICI Explosives, USA, Inc., Gaines-Tabb v., 384–386

Illinois Tool Works, Inc. v. Independent Ink, 128

Image Technical Services, Inc., Eastman Kodak Co. v., 129, 149

Incase, Inc. v. Timex Corp., 73

Independence Tube Corp., Copperweld Corp. v., 112, 116

Independent Ink, Illinois Tool Works, Inc. v., 128

Intelligent Sys., Inc., Barazzotto v., 383

International Dairy Foods Association v. Amestoy, 289

International Dairy Queen, Collins v., 167

Internet Entertainment Group, Ltd., Hasbro, Inc. v., 211

Intex Recreation Corp., Higgins v., 386–389

iParadigms, LLC, A.V. v., 61–65

Isbell, Mary Kay, Inc. v., 177–179

Islamorada, Island Silver & Spice, Inc. v., 173–175

Island Silver & Spice, Inc. v. Islamorada, 173–175

ITSI T.V. Prods., Inc. v. California Auth. of Racing Fairs, 44

Iuvo Systems, Inc., Deltek, Inc. v., 215

IWI, Inc., Nettis Environment, Ltd. v., 215

Jackson, Clomon v., 307–308

Jacobson Products Co., Qualitex Co. v., 197, 216–217

JCW Investments, Inc. v. Novelty, Inc., 58–61

Jerome-Duncan, Inc. v. Auto-By-Tel, LLC, 158

John D. Park & Sons Co., Dr. Miles Medical Co. v., 138, 139, 142, 143

Johnson, Kamposek v., 281–282

John Wright, Inc. v. Casper Corp., 243

Jones, Calder v., 14, 16

Jordache Enterprises, Inc. v. Hogg Wyld, LTD, 206

Joseph E. Seagram & Sons, Inc., Kiefer-Stewart Co. v., 143

Jostens, Inc. v. Nat'l Computer Sys., Inc., 92

Kamposek v. Johnson, 281–282

Kay, Gonzalez v., 306–309

Keller v. State Bar of California, 258

Kelley v. Hanover Insurance Co., 367

Khan, State Oil Co. v., 116, 142–144, 167

Kiefer-Stewart Co. v. Joseph E. Seagram & Sons, Inc., 143

KMD Media, LLC, Market Access International, Inc. v., 84

Kolarik v. Cory Int'l Corp., 358

Kraft, Inc. v. FTC, 264–271

L'Anza Research Int'l, Inc., Quality King Distributors, Inc. v., 208

Leegin Creative Leather Products v. PSKS, Inc., 116, 125, 135, 138–142, 168

Lefkowitz v. Great Minneapolis Surplus Store, 339–340

Leonard v. PepsiCo., Inc., 337–341

Lever Bros. Co. v. United States, 208

Lipton v. Nature Co., 262

MacPherson v. Buick Motor Co., 366

Mailcoups, Inc., Nagrampa v., 159

Mainstream Marketing Services, Inc. v. FTC, 296–300

Maltby v. Harlow Meyer Savage, Inc., 99–100

Marathon Petroleum Co., LLC, Sheridan v., 182–184

Market Access International, Inc. v. KMD Media, LLC, 84

Marketing Displays, Inc., TrafFix Devices, Inc. v., 218–220

Marquette Electronics, Inc., T. Harris Young & Associates, Inc. v., 129

Mars Snackfood U.S., LLC, Vent v., 100–103

Martin, Al Minor & Associates, Inc. v., 89–91

Mary Kay, Inc. v. Isbell, 177–179

Mathews v. University Loft Co., 370–371

Mattel, Inc., In re, 249

Mattel, Inc. v. MCA Records, Inc., 221–224

McAnany v. Case, Inc., 368

MCA Records, Inc., Mattel, Inc. v., 221–224

McCance, Venderwerff Implement, Inc. v., 333–334

McDonald's Corp., Miller v., 179–182

McGills Glass Warehouse, Venture Tape Corp. v., 224–227

MCI Communications Corp. v. American Tel. & Tel. Co., 131

McNeilab, Inc. v. American Home Products Corp., 263

Mecurio v. Nissan Motor Corp., 375

Metropolitan Life Insurance Co. V. Neaves, 15

MGM Studios, Inc. v. Grokster, Ltd., 44

Michel Co., Rolex Watch, U.S.A. v., 209

Micro Center, Thomas v., 382–384

Microflock Textile Group Corp., Zhejiang Shaoxing Yongli Printing & Dyeing Co., Ltd. v., 347–349

Midler v. Ford Motor Co., 236

Miller v. McDonald's Corp., 179–182

Mitchell v. Reynolds, 98

Mitsubishi Caterpillar Forklift America, Inc., To-Am Equipment Co., Inc. v., 175–177

M Mars, Inc., Burck v., 235

Mobil Oil Corp., Wilson v., 167

Molnlycke Health Care A.B. v. Dumex Medical Surgical Products, Inc., 13

Monsanto Co. v. Spray-Rite Service Corp., 126

Montana Siversmiths, Inc., Todd v., 47

Moore v. Columbia Pictures Industries, Inc., 60

Motel 6, Hamlin v., 166

Motion Picture Advertising Service Co., FTC v., 113

Mummagraphics Inc., Omega World Travel Inc. v., 280, 300–303

Nagrampa v. Mailcoups, Inc., 159

National Computer Sys., Inc., Jostens, Inc. v., 92

National Football League, American Football League v., 130

Nat'l Tube Co. v. Eastern Tube Co., 89

Nature Co., Lipton v., 262

Neaves, Metropolitan Life Insurance Co. v., 15

NEC Electronics v. CAL Circuit Abco, 207

Netbula, LLC v. Chordiant Software, Inc., 46

Netscape Communications Corp., Playboy Enterprises v., 215

Nettis Environment, Ltd. v. IWI, Inc., 215

Newspapers of New England, Inc., Union Leader Corp. v., 130

Nissan Motor Corp., Mecurio v., 375

Northern Pacific Railway Co. v. United States, 112, 115, 167

Northrup King Co., Widmark v., 92

Novartis Corp. v. FTC, 244

Novelty, Inc., JCW Investments, Inc. v., 58–61

Oakley Fertilizer, Inc. v. Continental Inc. Co., 341–344

Office of Disciplinary Counsel, Zauderer v., 267

Ohio Dept. of Ins., State ex rel The Plain Dealer v., 90

Omega World Travel Inc. v. Mummagraphics Inc., 280, 300–303

Orange & Rockland Utilities, Inc., Crossroads Cogeneration Corp. v., 133

Original Appalachian Artworks, Inc. v. Granada Electronics, Inc., 207

Orkin Exterminating Co. v. FTC, 276

Outboard Marine Corp., Beech v., 375

Owens-Corning Fiberglas Corp., Anderson v., 376

Paine Webber, Inc. v. wwwpainewebber.com, 214

Palmer v. BRG of Georgia, Inc., 137–138

Panavision Int'l v. Toeppen, 15

Paris Ceramics USA, Inc., Dunleavey v., 379–381

Pebble Beach Company v. Caddy, 13–17

PepsiCo., Inc., Leonard v., 337–341

Perez v. Wyeth Laboratories, Inc., 378

Perrin, Landry, deLaunay & Durand, Taylor v., 307–308

Pfaff v. Wells Electronics, Inc., 53–55

Pfizer, Farsian v., 372

Pfizer, Inc., Walus v., 372

The Plain Dealer, State ex rel v. Ohio Dept. of Ins., 90

The Plantation Shutter Co. v. Ezell, 318

Playboy Enterprises v. Netscape Communications Corp., 215

The Procter & Gamble Co. v. Ultreo, Inc., 239–240

PSKS, Inc., Leegin Creative Leather Products v., 116, 125, 135, 138–142, 168

Public Service Commission of New York, Central Hudson Gas & Electric Corp. v., 232–233, 253, 254, 256, 289, 297

Qualitek Int'l, Inc., Roberge v., 93

Qualitex Co. v. Jacobson Products Co., 197, 216–217

Quality King Distributors, Inc. v. L'Anza Research Int'l, Inc., 208

Queen City Pizza, Inc. v. Domino's Pizza, Inc., 167

Ralston Purina Co., Alpo PetFoods, Inc. v., 243

Reeder-Simco GMC, Inc., Volvo Trucks North Am., Inc. v., 134

Reeves v. Alyeska Pipeline Service, 81

Reid, Community for Creative Non-Violence v., 41, 55–58

Reynolds, Mitchell v., 98

Rhode Island, 44 Liquormart, Inc. v., 232–233

Rio Int'l Interlink, Rio Properties, Inc. v., 15

Rio Properties, Inc. v. Rio Int'l Interlink, 15

Roberge v. Qualitek Int'l, Inc., 93

Rolex Watch, U.S.A. v. Michel Co., 209

Rossi v. 21st Century Concepts, Inc., 303–306

Ross-Simmons Hardwood Lumber Co., Weyerhaeuser Co. v., 130, 131

Rubin v. Coors Brewing Co., 253–256

Rural Telephone Service Co., Feist Publications, Inc. v., 39–40, 59

Russen, Estate of Presley v., 235

Samara Brothers, Inc., Wal-Mart Stores, Inc. v., 197

Schultz, Frisby v., 297

Schwarzenegger, Video Software Dealers Ass'n v., 233–234

Schwarzenegger v. Fred Martin Motor Co., 16

S. C. Johnson & Son, Inc., Hirsch v., 236

S.C. Johnson & Son v. Clorox Co., 240–241

SEMA Construction, Inc. v. Diversified Prod. Industries, 329–330

Service Sys. Corp. v. Harris, 100

Shaw Family Archives Ltd. v. CMG Worldwide, Inc., 236

Sheridan v. Marathon Petroleum Co., LLC, 182–184

Shiley, Inc., Angus v., 372

Shiley, Inc., Brinkman v., 372

Shiley, Inc., Spuhl v., 372

Shurtleff, Free Speech Coalition, Inc. v., 280

Signature Financial Group, Inc., State Street Bank & Trust Co. v., 27

Sindell v. Abbott Laboratories, 372

Snuba International, Inc. v. Dolphin World, Inc., 33

Socony-Vacuum Oil Co., United States v., 121, 137, 143

Sony Corp. of America v. Universal City Studios, 44, 45

South Park Cigar, Inc., In re, 199

Space Organization Systems, Inc., California Closet Co. v., 172

Spray-Rite Service Corp., Monsanto Co. v., 126

Spuhl v. Shiley, Inc., 372

Standard Oil Co. of California v. United States, 128

Standard Oil Co. of New Jersey v. United States, 112

Stanley Steemer International, Inc., AAA Abachman Enterprises, Inc. v., 169

The Stanley Works, United States v., 284

State Bar of California, Keller v., 258

State ex rel The Plain Dealer v. Ohio Dept. of Ins., 90

State Oil Co. v. Khan, 116, 142–144, 167

State Street Bank & Trust Co. v. Signature Financial Group, Inc., 27

Staub v. Toy Factory, Inc., 374

Strategic Directions Group, Inc. v. Bristol-Myers Squibb Co., 91–92

Suess, Curtis 1000 v., 95

Super Duck Tours, LLC, Boston Duck Tours, LP v., 195

Taco Cabana, Inc., Two Pesos, Inc. v., 197

Tasca v. GTE Prods. Corp., 378

Taylor v. Perrin, Landry, deLaunay & Durand, 307–308

Telephone Cases, The, 54–55

Telxon Corp. v. Hoffman, 93

Texaco, Inc., Gizzi v., 181

T. Harris Young & Associates, Inc. v. Marquette Electronics, Inc., 129

The Coca-Cola Co., By Rite Distributing, Inc. v., 238

Themins v. Emanuel Lutheran, 180

Thomas v. Micro Center, 382–384

Thongchoom v. Graco Children's Products, Inc., 388

Ticor Title Insurance Co. v. Cohen, 96–100

Tiffany (NJ) Inc. v. Ebay, Inc., 205

Time Warner Cable, Inc. v. DirecTV, Inc., 259–264

Timex Corp., Incase, Inc. v., 73

To-Am Equipment Co., Inc. v. Mitsubishi Caterpillar Forklift America, Inc., 175–177

Todd v. Montana Siversmiths, Inc., 47

Toeppen, Panavision Int'l v., 15

Topco Assoc., Inc., United States v., 109, 137

Topps Chewing Gum, Inc., Haelan Labs, Inc. v., 235

Tour Costa Rica v. Country Walkers, Inc., 345–347

Toy Factory, Inc., Staub v., 374

Toys "R" Us, Inc., Hyatt v., 359

Toys "R" Us, Inc. v. Akkaoui, 211

TrafFix Devices, Inc. v. Marketing Displays, Inc., 218–220

Trailer Leasing Co. v. Associates Commer Corp., 94

Trauner, Cohen & Thomas, LLP, Greco v., 308

Two Pesos, Inc. v. Taco Cabana, Inc., 197

Ultreo, Inc., The Procter & Gamble Co. v., 239–240

Union Leader Corp. v. Newspapers of New England, Inc., 130

United Foods, Inc., United States v., 256–259

United States, Brown Shoe Co. v., 110

United States, Lever Bros. Co. v., 208

United States, Northern Pacific Railway Co. v., 112, 115, 167

United States, Standard Oil Co. of California v., 128

United States, Standard Oil Co. of New Jersey v., 112

United States, White Motor Co. v., 143

United States v. Aluminum Co. of America, 128, 130, 137

United States v. Arnold, Schwinn & Co., 143

United States v. Capital City Foods, 288

United States v. Colgate & Co., 125

United States v. Grinnell Corp., 129

United States v. Socony-Vacuum Oil Co., 121, 137, 143

United States v. The Stanley Works, 284

United States v. Topco Assoc., Inc., 109, 137

United States v. United Foods, Inc., 256–259

United States v. Women's Sportswear Manufacturers Assoc., 115

United State v. Falstaff Brewing Co., 119

Universal City Studios, Sony Corp. of America v., 44, 45

University Loft Co., Mathews v., 370–371

Vassallo v. Baxter Healthcare Corp., 376

Venderwerff Implement, Inc. v. McCance, 333–334

Venture Tape Corp. v. McGills Glass Warehouse, 224–227

Vent v. Mars Snackfood U.S., LLC, 100–103

Video Software Dealers Ass'n v. Schwarzenegger, 233–234

Vineyard County Gold Corp., Cass County Music Co. v., 44

Virginia Citizens Consumer Council, Inc., Virginia State Board of Pharmacy v., 232, 254

Virginia State Board of Pharmacy v. Virginia Citizens Consumer Council, Inc., 232, 254

Vistaprint USA, Inc., Asis Internet Services v., 280

Volvo Trucks North Am., Inc. v. Reeder-Simco GMC, Inc., 134

Waits v. Frito-Lay, Inc., 236

Walker-Davis Publications, Ames Publishing Co. v., 243

Wal-Mart Stores, Inc. v. Samara Brothers, Inc., 197

Walus v. Pfizer, Inc., 372

Warner-Lambert Co. v. F.T.C., 243

Weil Ceramics & Glass, Inc. v. Dash, 207

Wells Electronics, Inc., Pfaff v., 53–55

Western Trimming Crop., The Antioch Co. v., 198

Weyerhaeuser Co. v. Ross-Simmons Hardwood Lumber Co., 130, 131

Whitehead v. Dycho Co., 378

White Motor Co. v. United States, 143

Widmark v. Northrup King Co., 92

Wileman Brothers & Elliott, Inc., Glickman v., 256, 257, 258

Wilson v. Mobil Oil Corp., 167

Women's Sportswear Manufacturers Assoc., United States v., 115

Wu v. Dunkin' Donuts, Inc., 164–165

wwwpainewebber.com, Paine Webber, Inc. v., 214

Wyeth Laboratories, Inc., Perez v., 378

Yarusso, Bell Sports, Inc. v., 365

Zauderer v. Office of Disciplinary Counsel, 267

Zhejiang Shaoxing Yongli Printing & Dyeing Co., Ltd. v. Microflock Textile Group Corp., 347–349

Preface

Instructors want to educate their students to become knowledgeable consumers of legal services. Students want to become successful managers, capable of planning to avoid legal problems and of making more informed decisions when confronted with legal issues regarding the marketing of goods and services. This textbook is designed for both audiences.

Experienced marketing managers know that the law affects marketing activities in a multitude of ways. In the course of carrying out marketing duties, a manager may deal with such diverse issues as intellectual property, antitrust, franchise agreements, health and safety regulation, and products liability. Business students benefit immeasurably from a course that focuses on the many areas in which law and marketing intersect. *The Law of Marketing* is the book that will help you achieve your educational goals in a marketing law course.

Business students cannot assume that a single book or course on marketing law will make them an expert in the legal issues that might arise in their careers; nor can they assume that a single lawyer will be able to fully address all the legal concerns that they might encounter. However, by developing an understanding of the complexity and relevance of the various types of law that impact the marketing function, the informed student can meet these challenges head-on and be better prepared to meet his or her career challenges.

Through a unique design that intertwines marketing principles, legal cases, and current business examples, *The Law of Marketing* focuses specifically and in detail on those legal principles of particular relevance to marketing activities. It addresses the pivotal topics necessary for understanding the impact that law has upon marketing activities and how law affects current marketing trends. The book also highlights the personal liability issues that students, as future managers, might face.

Subject Matter and Organization of the Book

This textbook is designed to take the student through the legal aspects of the marketing function. It covers the initial legal issues related to product development, such as protection of intellectual property assets, legal issues relating to distribution and promotion of the product or service, and ultimately legal issues pertaining to the sale of the product or service, including attendant issues such as products liability and warranties. Structuring the book according to these marketing practices and functions creates a logical progression for students to use as a framework for real-life experiences.

This book is designed for both those students who have had a legal environment prerequisite and those who are new to the study of business law. Thus, each individual chapter can stand alone. Students already possessing an understanding of the legal environment or who have previously taken courses addressing specialized legal topics will benefit from being able to jump almost immediately into the various marketing law topics covered in Chapters 2 through 10. For students who are new to the study of business law, Chapter 1 provides a very brief overview of the legal environment of marketing law.

The book covers the following marketing law topics:

- *Part Two: Legal Issues Relating to Product Development*
  - **Chapter 2: Protection of Intellectual Property Assets through Patent and Copyright Law:** This chapter examines two of the four areas of law that protect intellectual property assets: patent law and copyright law.

- **Chapter 3: Protection of Intellectual Property Assets through Trade Secret Law, Contractual Agreements, and Business Strategies:** This chapter addresses the third area of intellectual property law—trade secrets—as well as the law relating to the protection of unsolicited ideas, and business strategies for protecting and maximizing the value of intellectual property assets, including the use of contractual agreements.
- *Part Three: Legal Issues Relating to Product Distribution*
  - **Chapter 4: Antitrust Law:** This chapter addresses the major federal antitrust statutes, horizontal and vertical restraints of trade, monopolization, price discrimination, and the international implications of antitrust laws.
  - **Chapter 5: The Franchisor-Franchisee Relationship:** This chapter provides an overview of typical franchise agreements, the types of legal issues that commonly arise in franchise relationships, and state and federal regulation of franchises.
- *Part Four: Legal Issues Relating to Product Promotion*
  - **Chapter 6: Trademark Law:** This chapter covers trademark law, including issues pertaining to international protection of marks and to the use of marks on the Internet.
  - **Chapter 7: Commercial Speech and Regulation of Advertising:** This chapter focuses on First Amendment restrictions on advertising and other forms of commercial speech, common law actions for deceptive or false advertising, and statutory causes of action for deceptive or false advertising arising under the Lanham Act and the Federal Trade Commission Act.
  - **Chapter 8: Consumer Protection Law:** This chapter addresses the regulation of direct marketing activities, labeling and packaging regulation, health and safety regulation, and consumer credit protection statutes.
- *Part Five: Legal Issues Relating to Product Sale*
  - **Chapter 9: Contracts and Sales of Goods Law:** This chapter focuses on the fundamental common law contract principles, the basic provisions of UCC law pertaining to the sale of goods, and the Convention on the International Sale of Goods.
  - **Chapter 10: Warranties and Products Liability:** This chapter examines the law pertaining to warranties on sales of goods and to products liability.

Key Features

The chapters consist of textual discussion of the relevant issues and rules of law, with cases and problems for discussion.

Cases

Several tools are used to convey the ideas of each chapter. Each chapter contains two types of cases: "Case Illustrations" and "Discussion Cases." The Case Illustrations are short summaries of cases that illustrate a particular legal point discussed in the text. These cases are mostly paraphrased. When the original language of the court is used, it is indicated through quotation marks or through block quotes.

At the end of each chapter there are several "Discussion Cases." These cases have been edited for length, but the language appearing on the page is entirely that of the court. Ellipses (…) have been used to indicate where a portion of a sentence has been omitted. Three asterisks (* * *) are used to indicate where a complete sentence or more has been omitted from a paragraph or where a complete paragraph or more has been omitted.

The Discussion Cases are somewhat longer than the cases found in most legal environment texts. Depending upon how the course is structured and how the text is used, instructors may assign all or just some of the cases, picking and choosing those that are most relevant to their own teaching objectives.

Why the long cases? In my two decades of teaching, I have noticed a trend toward cases being more and more heavily edited, often with the facts, issue, legal rule, and analysis being specifically labeled for the students. I am a firm believer in developing the student's ability to "brief" cases, which enables the student to acquire the skill of analyzing a court's reasoning process and to hone his or her own reasoning skills. There is a real value in a student seeing the factual background of a case and the court's reasoning process and to working through the language used by the court. The longer cases provided within this textbook allow the students to engage in this process.

The Case Illustrations and the Discussion Cases have been selected based upon their relevance to the function of marketing, their appeal to business students, and their effectiveness in highlighting key legal ideas. Recent cases, including *In re Bilski, A.V. v. iParadigms, LLC; Leegin Creative Leather Products v. PSKS, Inc.;* and *Time Warner Cable, Inc. v. DirecTV, Inc.,* have been incorporated to address current legal issues.

Internet and International Coverage

Coverage of international and Internet legal issues are integrated into chapters, as appropriate. Scattered throughout the text are numerous Web addresses to websites of particular relevance to the topics being discussed throughout the book. These sites can be visited for additional background on topics of particular interest to the reader.

Discussion Questions

At the end of each chapter are several Discussion Questions. Most of these problems are based on real cases and give the students an opportunity to apply the concepts discussed in the chapter to real-life scenarios. Case citations for these questions appear in the Instructor's Manual.

Supplements

Instructor's Manual with the Test Bank

www.cengage.com/blaw/oswald

Prepared by the author, the Instructor's Manual provides a succinct chapter summary and outline, lecture considerations, notes on the cases and answers to the discussion case questions and end-of-chapter exercises (including case citations). The Test Bank questions include multiple-choice and essay questions crafted for use on quizzes, tests, and exams. Available online at www.cengage.com/blaw/oswald.

Text Companion Website

www.cengage.com/blaw/oswald

The website for this edition includes access to the Instructor's Manual and Test Bank as well as access to the Court Case Updates.

Business Law Digital Video Library Online Access

www.cengage.com/blaw.dvl

The Business Law Digital Video Library has 25 videos that address marketing law topics (such as intellectual property, antitrust, privacy, free speech, and contracts, etc.) in addition to other topics. Access to these videos is FREE for your students when bundled with a new textbook. Please be sure to let your sales representative know if you would like temporary access to demo this product, which offers a total of over 65 clips with instructor resources (such as discussion questions).

Court Case Updates

www.cengage.com/blaw/cases

South-Western's Court Case Updates provide monthly summaries of the most important legal cases happening around the country.

Business Law Case Database

www.textchoice.com

Wondering what happened to your favorite case? The Business Law Case Database is a robust case library that houses over 700 cases. You can now hand-pick the cases you want, making it easy to create customizable casebook. Start by searching the Business Law Custom Case Database by state or topic for a complete list of offerings.

Westlaw® Access

www.westlaw.com

Westlaw®, West Group's vast online source of value-added legal and business information, contains over 15,000 databases of information spanning a variety of jurisdictions, practice areas, and disciplines. Qualified instructors may receive 10 complimentary hours of Westlaw® for their course (certain restrictions apply; contact your South-Western sales representative for details).

Business Law Community Website

www.cengage.com/community/blaw

Visit South-Western's Community website for a wealth of resources to help you deliver the most effective course possible, including our "Great Ideas in Teaching Business Law" section. Our Community website offers teaching tips and ideas for making the subject interesting and appealing to your students. Ideas include class presentations, discussion topics, research projects, and more.

Acknowledgments

The second edition of *The Law of Marketing* reflects many comments from colleagues, all of which are deeply appreciated. In particular, the author would like to thank the following:

Malcolm Abel
Western Carolina University

Craig Andrews
Marquette University

Robert C. Bird
University of Connecticut

Dr. William N. Bockanic
John Carroll University

Judy Gedge
Quinnipiac University

Joseph Gordon
Davis Applied Technology College

James Gould
Pace University

Patricia Greer
Berkeley College

Norman Hawker
Western Michigan University

Silvia Hodges
Emerson College

Jack E. Karns
East Carolina University

Arlen Langvardt
Indiana University

Tim Lemper
Indiana University, Bloomington

Ross D. Petty
Babson College

Kiana Pierre-Louis, Esq.
Bentley University

Dr. Joanie Sompayrac
University of Tennessee, Chattanooga

Gregory L. Young
California State University, Northridge

And special thanks to Vicky True and Krista Kellman of South-Western Legal Studies in Business/Cengage Learning for their invaluable assistance and support in the preparation of this edition.

About the Author

Lynda J. Oswald is a Professor of Business Law and Michael R. and Mary Kay Hallman Fellow at the Stephen M. Ross School of Business at the University of Michigan. She received her A.B., M.B.A., and J.D. degrees from the University of Michigan. While at the Michigan Law School, she served on the editorial board of the *Michigan Law Review*. She clerked for the Honorable Cornelia G. Kennedy of the U.S. Court of Appeals for the Sixth Circuit before joining the faculty of the Ross School of Business in 1988. Professor Oswald is also a Past President of the Academy of Legal Studies in Business, and served on its Executive Committee from 2003 to 2008.

Professor Oswald has received numerous awards for her research, including the Hoeber Memorial Award and the Holmes-Cardozo Award for Research Excellence from the *American Business Law Journal*. Her work has been cited by numerous courts, including the U.S. Supreme Court in *United States v. Bestfoods*.

Professor Oswald is currently the Editor of the *Michigan Real Property Review*. She has served as the Louis and Myrtle Moskowitz Research Professor of Law and Business and as a Contributing Editor to the *Real Estate Law Journal*, as well as serving as a special editor for the *American Business Law Journal* and the *Journal of Legal Studies Education*. She has also served as a Contributing Editor of Environmental Law for the *Real Estate Law Journal*.

Professor Oswald has taught at the University of Florida Law School and the University of Michigan Law School. She was a visiting scholar at China University of Political Science and Law in Beijing, PRC, and at Lviv State University in Lviv, Ukraine; a visiting professor at the University of Sydney in Sydney, Australia; and a Visiting Professor of Law at the Hopkins-Nanjing Center in Nanjing, PRC.

PART 1

Introduction to Marketing Law

Chapter 1
Overview of the Legal Environment of Marketing Activities

Overview of the Legal Environment of Marketing Activities

Introduction

This chapter is intended to provide you with a brief overview of the legal environment in which marketing activities occur. As is shown throughout the remainder of the book, many types of law impact marketing activities. Some of this law is statutory, while some arises under court opinions, the U.S. Constitution, or the rules and regulations of administrative agencies. Some of the law is found at the federal level, some at the state, or even local, level. Some types of law impose duties upon marketers in an effort to promote free competition, protect consumers, or foster fair business relationships. Other types of law grant rights to marketers, such as providing legal protection for patents, copyrights, and trademarks or protection from unfair business tactics of competitors.

This chapter provides you with a framework within which you can start to analyze the various legal issues discussed in the following chapters. The topics touched upon briefly here appear in specific contexts throughout the book. In many respects, then, this chapter is a preview of coming attractions and is intended to help orient you as you begin your study of the law of marketing.

In light of this goal, this chapter begins by providing several classifications of the law so that you can understand the larger picture of the various types of law that exist within the American legal system. It then discusses the primary and secondary sources of the law and describes the American legal system, including the structure of the state and federal court systems. Finally, the chapter concludes with a short discussion of jurisdiction issues.

Classifications of the Law

The law has two main purposes: (1) it provides guidelines for decision making, and (2) it creates and enforces legal rights and duties. When we start to classify the law, we can see these two objectives come into play. Classifications also provide snapshots of the organization of the legal system and provide a sense of the wide variety of interests and activities that the law affects.

Law can be classified in many different ways. The first classification provided here is based upon the type of law involved. (See Exhibit 1.1.) The broad category of "law" can be divided into two basic areas: criminal law and civil law. *Criminal law* deals with a violation of the public order; i.e., it involves a wrong against the whole community. The purpose of a

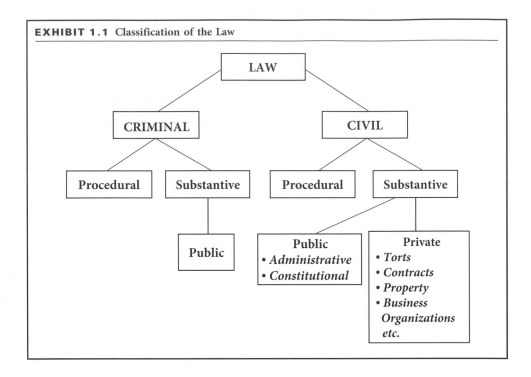

EXHIBIT 1.1 Classification of the Law

criminal prosecution is to punish the wrongdoer and to deter the wrongdoer and others from committing similar acts in the future. *Civil law*, on the other hand, deals with private relations between individuals or between individuals and the government and establishes the rights and responsibilities arising out of those relationships. The objective of a civil lawsuit is to obtain relief for the injured party, most commonly in the form of monetary damages and/or an injunction. Most of the law discussed in this book is civil law.

Each of these two basic categories can be further divided into procedural and substantive law. *Substantive law* actually defines, creates, and governs legal rights and duties. *Procedural law*, by contrast, defines the method by which people can enforce the rights given to them by the substantive law. For example, procedural law tells us the steps that must be taken to move a lawsuit through the legal system from its initial filing to its final judgment.

Substantive law can be further classified into public and private law. *Public law* deals with the relationship between the government as a sovereign and the individual and is typically enacted or created by a governmental body. Criminal law, for example, is public law, as is constitutional and administrative law. *Private law* deals with the rights and duties that arise as the result of a relationship between individuals, including legal entities such as corporations. Private law encompasses a wide variety of topics, including tort law, contract law, property law, and the law of business organizations.

Law can also be classified based upon political jurisdictions. In the United States, there are essentially three levels of political and legal jurisdictions: (1) federal; (2) state; and (3) local. All three jurisdictions can affect marketing activities, although our discussion in this book focuses primarily on federal and state regulation of these activities.

The *federal government* is the national government and is comprised of the legislative, executive, and judicial branches. Each of these has the ability to create law. Within its sphere, the federal government is superior to the state and local governments. Under the U.S. Constitution, however, the federal government is a government of limited powers. The federal government has no power to act in areas not granted to it under the Constitution. In the specific areas in which the federal government is authorized to act, such as patents and copyrights, the federal government is superior to the state and local governments.

The *state governments* also have legislative, executive, and judicial branches. The states retain all of the governmental power not explicitly granted to the federal government under the U.S. Constitution. This means that the states retain authority to regulate in a number of areas that implicate marketing activities, including trade secrets, contracts, warranties, and products liability. Some areas of the law—such as trademark law, which is discussed in Chapter 6—are regulated by both the federal and state governments.

Each state has the power to create its own state law. Thus, state laws can vary substantially from state to state. Marketers engaged in interstate or national marketing efforts need to be aware of the ramifications of differences in state laws. In some areas, such as sales of goods, the states have undertaken measures to foster uniformity among state laws, thus easing the burden on interstate businesses. These efforts are discussed at various points throughout the book.

Local governments, such as cities, towns, villages, and counties, can also regulate business activities, including marketing activities. The powers of local governments are delegated to them by their state legislatures and may be limited or modified by the states. To the extent that they are authorized to act, local governments can create local laws, such as municipal ordinances and regulations. Although local regulations can impact certain types of marketing activities (for example, issues relating to consumer protection), local regulation is of considerably less significance than federal or state regulation in the marketing law arena.

Finally, law can be classified based upon the branch of government that created it. At both the state and federal levels, each of the three branches can create law. The legislative branch enacts statutes; the judicial branch creates common law through its opinions; and the executive branch creates administrative rules and regulations through its power over administrative agencies. Numerous examples of all three types of law are found throughout this book.

Sources of the Law

The "law" can be found in many places. We look to *primary sources* when we want to find out what the legal rules "really are." We look to *secondary sources* when we want assistance in finding and interpreting the "law." There are numerous references to both primary and secondary sources throughout the book, both in the chapter discussions and in the judicial opinions.

Primary Sources of the Law

As already noted, there are two parallel legal systems in the United States: the federal system and the state systems. (And, in fact, there are 50 separate state systems, plus a system for the District of Columbia, making a total of 52 legal systems in the United States.)

Primary Sources of Federal Law   At the federal level, there are a number of primary sources of law: the U.S. Constitution, treaties, federal statutes, federal court opinions, and administrative rules and regulations.

The *U.S. Constitution* is said to be the "supreme law of the land." It establishes the three branches of the federal government—legislative, judicial, and executive—and addresses the powers and limitations of each of those branches. It restricts the power of the federal government and guarantees the rights and liberties of the people.

No law—whether created by the legislative, judicial, or executive branch or by the federal or a state government—is permitted to conflict with the U.S. Constitution. In addition, under the Constitution, federal statutes and treaties are superior to state constitutions and statutes. The U.S. Supreme Court, by virtue of its power of *judicial review*, has the authority to determine the constitutionality of all laws, federal or state.

A *treaty* is an agreement between or among nations. Under the U.S. Constitution, the President, with the advice and consent of the Senate, has sole authority to enter into treaties. A valid treaty has the legal force of a federal statute. If a treaty and a federal statute conflict, the last to have been adopted prevails.

In addition, as noted earlier, each of the three federal governmental branches can create law. First, Congress can enact *statutes*. We look at a number of such statutes in later chapters, including the Patent Act, the Copyright Act, the Sherman and Clayton Antitrust Acts, the Federal Trade Commission (FTC) Act, and the Lanham Act. Second, the courts can create *common law* through their judicial opinions. We examine many federal court opinions throughout the book. Third, administrative agencies are part of the executive branch and have the power to enact *administrative agency rules and regulations*. Later chapters examine the regulatory activities of several federal administrative agencies, such as the FTC and the Consumer Product Safety Commission.

Primary Sources of State Law   To a large extent, the primary sources of state law parallel those found at the federal level. The major exception is that treaties are found only at the federal, and never the state, level. Similarly, local government regulation is found only at the state, and never the federal, level.

Each state has its own *constitution*. Although often patterned upon the language of the federal Constitution, state constitutions are frequently more detailed than the federal Constitution. State constitutions cannot deprive individuals of federal constitutional rights, but they can give individuals additional rights beyond those found in the federal Constitution.

Each of the three branches of the state governments can create law, just as with the three branches of the federal government. The state legislatures can enact state *statutes*. Trade secrets and the right of publicity, for example, are governed by statute in many states, as are sales of goods. The executive branches of the state governments can enact state *administrative agency rules and regulations*. For example, state administrative agencies have undertaken several measures to protect consumers from unscrupulous marketing practices. Finally, the state courts can create *common law* through their opinions. Contract and tort law, for example, are still largely matters of state common law, which means that judicial opinions are an important primary source of state law in these areas.

Secondary Sources of the Law

Numerous secondary sources of the law exist. Among the most influential of these are the *Restatements of the Law* compiled by the American Law Institute (ALI).[1] The ALI was formed in 1923 and consists of a group of distinguished lawyers, judges, and professors who compile authoritative statements of the common law in particular areas, including contracts, torts, and unfair competition. While the Restatements are not law themselves, the courts frequently look to and adopt the Restatements' positions on various points. Once adopted by a court, the Restatement language becomes a part of the common law of that jurisdiction. We will see numerous references to various Restatements in later chapters.

As noted earlier, each state creates its own legal rules. Historically, the growth of interstate businesses was hampered by the fact that the laws could differ substantially from state to state, making planning and compliance difficult for businesses operating across state lines. In an effort to reduce some of the variation in state laws, the National Conference of Commissioners on Uniform State Laws (NCCUSL) was created in 1892 to prepare uniform state legislation for presentation to and possible adoption by the state legislatures.[2] Until adopted by a state legislature, these model laws have no binding legal effect and so are considered secondary sources of the law. Once adopted by a state legislature, of course, the model statute becomes a state statute and hence a primary source of

---

[1]For general information on the ALI, see www.ali.org

[2]For general information on the NCC, see www.nccusl.org

law. The most widely adopted of the uniform laws is the *Uniform Commercial Code (UCC)*, which was jointly created by the NCCUSL and the ALI and which provides uniform rules regarding commercial transactions. The UCC has been adopted by all of the 50 states (although Louisiana has adopted only part of it) and the District of Columbia. The UCC is discussed in Chapter 9 and Chapter 10 in the context of sales of goods and warranties. The NCCUSL is still active in drafting model uniform laws.

The courts may refer to legal encyclopedias, legal dictionaries, treatises, law review articles, and other secondary sources when trying to identify and interpret the legal rules contained within the primary sources of the law. Numerous examples of such secondary sources appear in the cases presented throughout this book.

The American Legal System
Common Law and Equity

The American legal system is a *common law*, or *Anglo-American*, legal system. This type of legal system is also found in other English-speaking countries, such as England, Canada (with the exception of Quebec), and Australia. In a common law system, much of the law is created by the judiciary and is found within court opinions. By contrast, much of the world, including Western Europe, Quebec, Scotland, Latin America, and parts of Africa and Asia, has a *civil law system*, in which the bulk of the law is found within legislative codes.

The American legal system is also an *adversary system*, which means that the parties, not the court, initiate and conduct litigation and gather evidence. The parties present their dispute to a neutral fact finder, the court. The theory behind the adversary system is that the two interested parties are most likely to vigorously litigate a case. Civil law systems, by contrast, often depend upon an *inquisitorial system*, in which the judiciary assists in initiating litigation, investigating facts, and presenting the evidence.

Because of the way that the common law developed in England historically, the primary form of legal relief available is monetary damages. Because money is not necessarily an appropriate form of relief in all cases, an additional system of judicial relief evolved that was known as *equity*. A court of chancery, sitting in equity, could award nonmonetary relief in instances where the monetary remedy available at law was inadequate. Among the primary forms of equitable relief found today are *injunctions*, which are court orders requiring a party to undertake an act or refrain from an act, and *specific performance*, which is an order to a party to fulfill its contractual obligations.

Today, virtually all jurisdictions in the United States have merged their courts of equity and law so that a single court can administer both forms of justice. Nonetheless, important distinctions remain. While a jury may be available in cases at law, only judges decide equity cases. In addition, equitable relief is available only at the discretion of the judge. In order to obtain equitable relief, the party seeking such relief must typically show that he or she has "clean hands," i.e., that he or she acted fairly and honorably toward the other party. There are numerous examples of courts acting in equity throughout this book. Preliminary injunctions, for example, are a commonly requested form of equitable relief in disputes involving marketers.

Within the American legal system, the operative doctrine is **stare decisis**, also known as the *doctrine of precedent*. Stare decisis is a Latin term that means "to stand by a decision." Essentially, this doctrine tells us that each court is bound by its own "precedents," i.e., that each court must decide subsequent cases in the same way that it or a superior court decided earlier cases with similar facts. A court can overrule its own precedents, however, if it determines that a precedent was wrongly decided or that social or technological advances have rendered the precedent obsolete.

A court is not bound by *every* case that was decided earlier. As noted earlier, there are 52 court systems within the United States—the federal system, 50 state systems, and a system for the District of Columbia. In general, decisions of one court are binding only on that court and on *lower* courts within the *same system*. Thus, a Michigan trial court is bound by a decision of the Michigan Supreme Court but not by a decision of the Texas Supreme Court, which is outside its system. Similarly, the Michigan Supreme Court is not bound by a decision of the Michigan trial court, which is a lower court within its system. A decision of the U.S. Supreme Court on a *federal question* (i.e., a question involving the U.S. Constitution, a federal statute, or a treaty) is binding on all state and federal courts. Within the federal system, however, a decision of a specific circuit court of appeals is binding on that court and on all district (lower) courts within that circuit, but not on other circuit courts or upon the district courts outside its circuit.

Court Structure

The doctrine of precedent means that it is important to understand how the court systems are arranged. All courts fulfill one of two basic types of judicial functions. First, some courts exercise *trial* functions and are said to have *original jurisdiction*. Cases originate in these courts, and the judges or juries (in appropriate cases) in these courts determine the facts of the case and take the first stab at applying the law to those facts.

In the American legal system, the person who starts a civil lawsuit is known as the *plaintiff*. The person who is being sued is known as the *defendant*. The plaintiff has the burden of proof, which means that the plaintiff must show, usually by a *preponderance of evidence*, that it should prevail. The most common remedies for a civil action are monetary damages and/or an injunction.

In a criminal case, the government, in its role as *prosecutor*, prosecutes an individual, known as the *defendant*, for a wrong that the individual allegedly committed against the whole community. The government bears the burden of proving that the defendant is guilty *beyond a reasonable doubt*. The punishment for crimes usually consists of imprisonment and/or fines.

The second type of court is said to have *appellate jurisdiction*. Appellate courts generally review only the lower court's theory and application of the law, not the trial court's findings of fact. Appellate courts do not conduct trials, hear evidence or testimony, or determine facts. Rather, appellate courts must accept the facts as determined by the trial court unless the trial court's decision is "clearly erroneous," which is a very difficult standard to meet. An appellate court reviews the factual *record* created by the trial court (e.g., the trial transcript and physical evidence introduced at trial). The appellate court's job is to resolve questions of law, i.e., to determine whether the trial was conducted in a procedurally proper manner and whether the appropriate law was applied correctly to the facts as determined by the trial court.

At the appellate level, the person who lost below and who is bringing the appeal is known as the *appellant* or the *petitioner*. The person who won below and who is defending the appeal is known as the *appellee* or the *respondent*. If the appellate court finds no prejudicial error in the lower court's determination, it will *affirm* the decision. If the court finds a prejudicial error, it will either *reverse* or *modify* the decision. If necessary, the appellate court can also *remand* the case back to the lower court for further proceedings.

We first examine the typical state court structure; then we examine the federal court structure.

State Court Structure   As already noted, each state has its own court system. There is great variety in state court systems. The most common state court structure is a four-tier

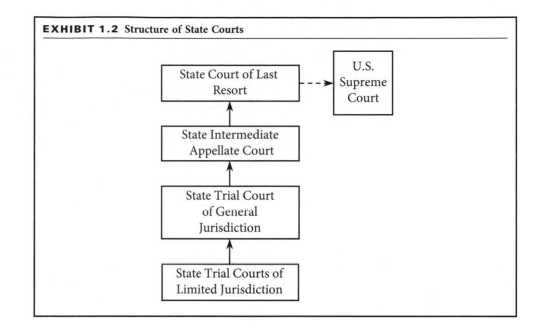

EXHIBIT 1.2 Structure of State Courts

judicial system, although some states use a three- or even two-tier system. (See Exhibit 1.2.) The first, or lowest, tier consists of *trial courts of limited jurisdiction*. These courts have jurisdiction over specific subject matters, such as minor criminal offenses and civil cases up to a specified sum (e.g., $10,000). *Small claims courts* are found at this level. These are courts that hear civil cases involving relatively small sums of money. In most small claims courts, neither side is represented by an attorney, there is no jury, and the legal procedures are relaxed.

The second tier consists of *trial courts of general jurisdiction*. These courts conduct the trials on all cases not heard by the first tier courts, such as major crimes and civil cases involving larger sums of money. Juries are available in these courts in appropriate types of cases.

The third tier consists of *intermediate appellate courts*. Generally, the losing party in a case before the trial court is entitled to appeal to the intermediate appellate court provided that it can point to an alleged error of law (e.g., that the judge allowed evidence in that should have been excluded, that the jury instructions were incorrect, or that the wrong legal rule was applied). This is known as an *appeal of right* because if the losing party can point to an alleged error of law, the appellate court must hear the appeal. Generally, a panel of three judges hears appeals at this level and a party must persuade two of the three in order to prevail.

Finally, the fourth tier consists of the *appellate court of last resort*, generally known as the supreme court in most (but not all) states. Usually, there are five to nine judges found on this court (they are generally referred to as justices) and all of them hear and decide each case. In most instances, the appealing party must ask the court's permission to appeal; there is usually no appeal of right at this level as there is with the intermediate appellate court. A party generally must persuade a majority of the justices in order to prevail. The decision of this court is usually final. A very few types of cases can be appealed from this court to the U.S. Supreme Court, but those cases must involve a federal question as discussed below. For the most part, cases that reach this level stop here.

Federal Court Structure   The federal court structure parallels the state court system in many ways. (See Exhibit 1.3.) The main distinction between the two is that federal

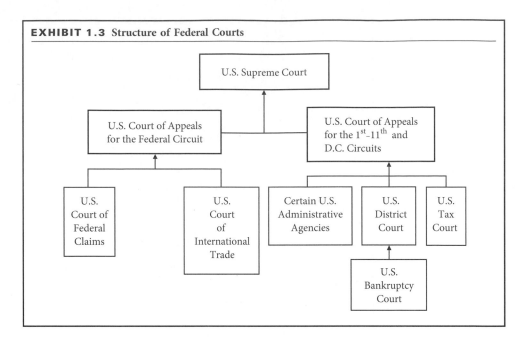

EXHIBIT 1.3   Structure of Federal Courts

courts are courts of limited jurisdiction. They can hear cases only in areas granted to them under the U.S. Constitution. All other cases must go to state court.

The first tier in the federal court system consists of the *trial courts*. These courts include *specialty tribunals*, such as the Patent and Trademark Office (PTO), which we discuss in Chapter 2 and Chapter 6. These tribunals have very limited jurisdiction over specific subject matter. The trial courts also include the *U.S. District Courts*. The district courts hear all cases not heard by the specialty tribunals, including general civil and criminal courts. Generally, one judge hears the case and juries are available in appropriate cases.

The second tier consists of the *U.S. Courts of Appeals*. These are reviewing courts with appellate jurisdiction, like the intermediate appellate courts in the states. Parties who can point to an alleged error of law have an appeal of right to these courts. Typically, a panel of three judges hears each case (and a party must convince two of the three in order to prevail), although in some instances all of the judges of the circuit may sit *en banc* to hear a case.

There are 12 judicial circuits (the First through Eleventh Circuits, plus the D.C. Circuit). (See Exhibit 1.4.) They hear appeals from the district courts as well as decisions of certain administrative agencies, the Tax Court, and the Bankruptcy Court. Certain appeals, including those from the Court of Federal Claims, the PTO, the United States Court of International Trade, and patent cases decided by a U.S. District Court, are heard by the Court of Appeals for the Federal Circuit (CAFC).

The final tier consists of the *U.S. Supreme Court*. Nine Justices sit on the Supreme Court, and typically all of them hear each case. The U.S. Supreme Court typically reviews federal appellate decisions, although the Court does have original jurisdiction in a very few specific types of cases. In addition, a state court case can end up before the Supreme Court if it raises a federal question (i.e., if it contains an issue involving a federal statute, a treaty, or the federal Constitution).

For all practical purposes, there is no appeal of right to the U.S. Supreme Court. Rather, a party wishing to have its case heard by the Supreme Court must file a petition for a *writ of certiorari*. The Court may either grant the writ and agree to hear the case or, more likely, deny the writ, which means that the lower court's decision stands. The Court typically hears only a very small percentage of the cases presented to it each year. Usually, the Court selects cases that involve a federal question of significant importance or a conflict among the U.S. Circuit Courts of Appeal.

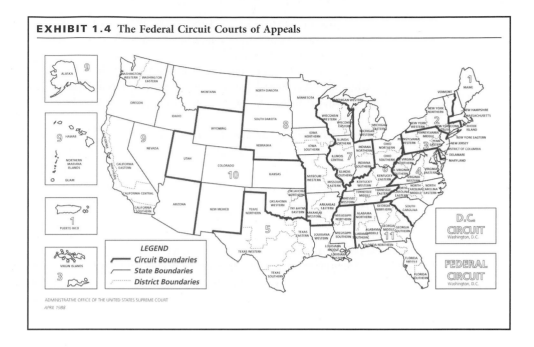

EXHIBIT 1.4 The Federal Circuit Courts of Appeals

Jurisdiction

Jurisdiction refers to the power or right of a court to hear or decide a case. The court must have two types of jurisdiction in order to have the power to resolve a case: (1) subject matter jurisdiction and (2) jurisdiction over the parties.

Subject Matter Jurisdiction

Subject matter jurisdiction refers to the power of a court to resolve a lawsuit involving a particular type of issue. The federal courts have limited subject matter jurisdiction, as set forth in Article III, Section 2 of the U.S. Constitution. That means that the federal courts can hear cases only where Congress or the Constitution has granted them the power to do so. The state courts have exclusive jurisdiction over all remaining cases.

The federal courts have exclusive jurisdiction over those areas where Congress has explicitly or implicitly so provided. These areas include certain admiralty issues, antitrust, bankruptcy, copyright and patent, federal criminal prosecutions, and suits against the United States.

The federal and state courts have *concurrent jurisdiction* in two instances. Concurrent jurisdiction means that both the state and the federal courts have jurisdiction to hear the case (although ultimately the case will be heard by one court or the other, not both). First, the state and federal courts have concurrent jurisdiction over *federal questions* in which the federal courts have not been given exclusive jurisdiction.

Second, the state and federal courts have concurrent jurisdiction in *diversity* cases. By definition, diversity cases involve state law issues that nonetheless are heard in federal court. Diversity jurisdiction arises where there is: (1) "diversity of citizenship" between the two parties (e.g., when all of the plaintiffs are residents of a state or states different from the state or states of residence of all of the defendants or when the lawsuit is between citizens of the United States and citizens of a foreign country), and (2) the amount in controversy is more than $75,000. A party's place of residence is the state in which it resides or is domiciled. A corporation, however, is a resident of both the state in which it is incorporated and the state in which it has its principal place of business.

If a federal court hears a diversity case, it must apply state substantive law. (*Conflict of laws rules* determine which state's law applies.) The federal court generally applies federal procedural law, however.

In a concurrent jurisdiction case, the plaintiff has the option of bringing the case in either state or federal court. If the plaintiff files in state court, however, the defendant may usually have the case *removed* to federal court.

Jurisdiction over the Parties

In addition to subject matter jurisdiction, a court must also have jurisdiction over the parties to the lawsuit, that is, the court must have the power to bind the parties involved in the dispute. This jurisdictional requirement can be satisfied in one of several ways.

First, the court has jurisdiction over a person who voluntarily comes before it and subjects himself to the court's jurisdiction. In a contract, for example, one party may agree that in the event of a lawsuit, the courts of the state of residence of the other party will have jurisdiction over the dispute.

Second, the court can exercise *in personam* jurisdiction, or *personal jurisdiction*, either over parties located within the state or over parties located outside the state to whom a "long-arm statute" applies. A *long-arm statute* is a state statute that allows a state court to exercise jurisdiction over nonresident defendants who have sufficient contacts (known as *minimum contacts*) with the state such that the exercise of jurisdiction does not offend "traditional notions of fair play and substantial justice."[3] Long-arm statutes typically apply to defendants who: (1) have committed a tort within the state and the tort is the subject matter of the lawsuit; (2) own property within the state and the property is the subject matter of the lawsuit; (3) have entered into a contract within the state and the contract is the subject matter of the lawsuit; or (4) have transacted business within the state and the lawsuit involves that transaction.

Finally, the court can exercise *in rem jurisdiction*, which refers to the power of a state court to hear cases involving property situated within the state.

Jurisdiction on the Internet

The Internet raises special types of jurisdiction issues. Does a marketer located in Maine, for example, subject itself to the jurisdiction of the Hawaii courts simply because it has a website that is accessible to Hawaii residents? Or, must the marketer undertake more direct activities in Hawaii, such as selling to Hawaiian residents or shipping goods to Hawaii, before it becomes subject to such jurisdiction?

The law is not yet settled regarding jurisdiction on the Internet. Courts generally have held that merely having a website that is accessible by residents in another state is insufficient to subject a defendant to the jurisdiction of that other state. Rather, courts generally look to see whether a defendant website owner has "purposefully availed" itself of the privilege of doing business in that state. Often, the courts have found this requirement is satisfied where a resident of the state has accessed the contents of the site or purchased goods or services offered on it. A recent court decision summarized the law thus:

> The likelihood that personal jurisdiction can be constitutionally exercised is directly proportionate to the nature and quality of commercial activity that an entity conducts over the Internet…. At one end of the spectrum are situations where a defendant clearly does business over the Internet. If the defendant enters into contracts with residents of a foreign jurisdiction that involve the knowing and repeated transmission of computer files over the Internet, personal jurisdiction is proper. At the opposite end are situations

---

[3] *International Shoe Co. v. Washington*, 326 U.S. 310, 316 (1945).

where a defendant has simply posted information on an Internet Web site which is accessible to users in foreign jurisdictions. A passive Web site that does little more than make information available to those who are interested in it is not grounds for the exercise [of] personal jurisdiction. The middle ground is occupied by interactive Web sites where a user can exchange information with the host computer. In these cases, the exercise of jurisdiction is determined by examining the level of interactivity and commercial nature of the exchange of information that occurs on the Web site.[4]

Several state courts have held that successful solicitation of local residents is also sufficient to establish personal jurisdiction over the website owner. Websites that are purely local in nature, however, generally do not support exercise of jurisdiction, especially where the website contains conspicuous disclaimers to that effect.

DISCUSSION CASES

1.1 Jurisdiction

Pebble Beach Company v. Caddy, 453 F.3d 1151 (9th Cir. 2006)

Pebble Beach Company ("Pebble Beach"), a golf course resort in California, appeals the dismissal for lack of jurisdiction of its complaint against Michael Caddy ("Caddy"), a small-business owner located in southern England. * * * Because Caddy did not expressly aim his conduct at California or the United States, we hold that the district court determined correctly that it lacked personal jurisdiction. * * * Thus, we affirm.

I

Pebble Beach is a well-known golf course and resort located in Monterey County, California. The golf resort has used "Pebble Beach" as its trade name for 50 years. Pebble Beach contends that the trade name has acquired secondary meaning in the United States and the United Kingdom. Pebble Beach operates a website located at www.pebblebeach.com.

Caddy, a dual citizen of the United States and the United Kingdom, occupies and runs a three-room bed and breakfast, restaurant, and bar located in southern England. Caddy's business operation is located on a cliff overlooking the pebbly beaches of England's south shore, in a town called Barton-on-Sea. The name of

Caddy's operation is "Pebble Beach," which, given its location, is no surprise. Caddy advertises his services, which do not include a golf course, at his website, www.pebblebeach-uk.com. Caddy's website includes general information about the accommodations he provides, including lodging rates in pounds sterling, a menu, and a wine list. The website is not interactive. Visitors to the website who have questions about Caddy's services may fill out an on-line inquiry form. However, the website does not have a reservation system, nor does it allow potential guests to book rooms or pay for services on-line.

Except for a brief time when Caddy worked at a restaurant in Carmel, California, his domicile has been in the United Kingdom.

On October 8, 2003, Pebble Beach sued Caddy under the Lanham Act and the California Business and Professions Code for intentional infringement and dilution of its "Pebble Beach" mark. Caddy moved to dismiss the complaint for lack of personal jurisdiction .... On March 1, 2004, the district court granted Caddy's motion on personal jurisdiction grounds .... * * * Pebble Beach timely appealed to the Ninth Circuit.

---

[4]*Molnlycke Health Care A.B. v. Dumex Medical Surgical Products, Inc.,* 64 F. Supp. 2d 448, 451 (E.D. Pa. 1999) (quoting *Zippo Mfg Co. v. Zippo Dot Com, Inc.,* 952 F. Supp. 1119, 1124 (W.D. Pa. 1977)).

II

* * *

A. Personal Jurisdiction

The arguments are straightforward. Caddy contends that the district court may not assert personal jurisdiction over him, and, consequently, that the complaint against him was properly dismissed. Pebble Beach argues in return that Caddy is subject to specific personal jurisdiction in California, or, alternatively, in any forum in the United States, because he has expressly aimed tortious conduct at California and the United States. * * *

* * *

The general rule is that personal jurisdiction over a defendant is proper if it is permitted by a long-arm statute and if the exercise of that jurisdiction does not violate federal due process. Here, both the California long-arm statute and Rule 4(k)(2)—what is often referred to as the federal long-arm statute—require compliance with due process requirements. Consequently, under both arguments presented by Pebble Beach, resolution turns on due process.

For due process to be satisfied, a defendant, if not present in the forum, must have "minimum contacts" with the forum state such that the assertion of jurisdiction "does not offend traditional notions of fair play and substantial justice."

In this circuit, we employ the following three-part test to analyze whether a party's "minimum contacts" meet the Supreme Court's directive. This "minimum contacts" test is satisfied when,

> (1) the defendant has performed some act or consummated some transaction within the forum or otherwise purposefully availed himself of the privileges of conducting activities in the forum, (2) the claim arises out of or results from the defendant's forum-related activities, and (3) the exercise of jurisdiction is reasonable.

"If any of the three requirements is not satisfied, jurisdiction in the forum would deprive the defendant of due process of law." * * * Here, Pebble Beach's arguments fail under the first prong. Accordingly, we need not address whether the claim arose out of or resulted from Caddy's forum-related activities or whether an exercise of jurisdiction is reasonable ....

Under the first prong of the "minimum contacts" test, Pebble Beach has the burden of establishing that Caddy "has performed some act or consummated some transaction within the forum or otherwise purposefully availed himself of the privileges of conducting activities in the forum." We have refined this to mean whether Caddy has either (1) "purposefully availed" himself of the privilege of conducting activities in the forum, or (2) "purposefully directed" his activities toward the forum. * * *

Thus, in order to satisfy the first prong of the "minimum contacts" test, Pebble Beach must establish either that Caddy (1) purposefully availed himself of the privilege of conducting activities in California, or the United States as a whole, or (2) that he purposefully directed its activities toward one of those two forums.

1. Purposeful Availment

Pebble Beach fails to identify any conduct by Caddy that took place in California or in the United States that adequately supports the availment concept. Evidence of availment is typically action taking place in the forum that invokes the benefits and protections of the laws in the forum. All of Caddy's action identified by Pebble Beach is action taking place outside the forum. * * * Accordingly, we reject Pebble Beach's assertion that Caddy has availed himself of the jurisdiction of the district court and proceed only to determine whether Caddy has purposefully directed his action toward one of two applicable forums.

2. Purposeful Direction: California

In *Calder v. Jones,* [465 U.S. 783 (1984)], the Supreme Court held that a foreign act that is both aimed at and has effect in the forum satisfies the first prong of the specific jurisdiction analysis. We have commonly referred to this holding as the "*Calder* effects test." To satisfy this test the defendant "must have (1) committed an intentional act, which was (2) expressly aimed at the forum state, and (3) caused harm, the brunt of which is suffered and which the defendant knows is likely to be suffered in the forum state." However, referring to the *Calder* test as an "effects" test can be misleading. For this reason, we have warned courts not to focus too narrowly on the test's third prong—the effects prong—holding that "something more" is needed in addition to a mere foreseeable effect. Specifically we have stated,

> Subsequent cases have struggled somewhat with *Calder's* import, recognizing that the case cannot stand for the broad proposition that a foreign act with foreseeable effects in the forum state will

always give rise to specific jurisdiction. We have said that there must be "something more" .... We now conclude that "something more" is what the Supreme Court described as "express aiming" at the forum state.

Thus, the determinative question here is whether Caddy's actions were "something more"—precisely, whether his conduct was expressly aimed at California or alternatively the United States.

We conclude that Caddy's actions were not expressly aimed at California. The only acts identified by Pebble Beach as being directed at California are the website and the use of the name "Pebble Beach" in the domain name. These acts were not aimed at California and, regardless of foreseeable effect, are insufficient to establish jurisdiction.

In support of its contention that Caddy has expressly aimed conduct at California, Pebble Beach identifies a list of cases where we have found that a defendant's actions have been expressly aimed at the forum state sufficient to establish jurisdiction over the defendant. Pebble Beach asserts that these cases show that Caddy's website and domain name, coupled by his knowledge of the golf resort as a result of his working in California, are sufficient to satisfy the express aiming standard that it is required to meet. We disagree. If anything, these cases establish that "something more"—the express aiming requirement—has not been met by Pebble Beach.

In *Panavision* [*Int'l v. Toeppen,* 141 F.3d 1316 (9th Cir. 1998)], the defendant, a cybersquatter, registered the plaintiff's trademark as part of a domain name. The use of the domain name by the defendant prevented the plaintiff from registering its own domain name and was part of a plan to obtain money from the plaintiff in exchange for the rights to the domain name. The court found personal jurisdiction, not merely because of the domain name use, but because the plan was expressly aimed at the plaintiff:

[The Defendant] did considerably more than simply register Panavision's trademarks as his domain names on the Internet. He registered those names as part of a scheme to obtain money from Panavision. Pursuant to that scheme, he demanded $13,000 from Panavision to release the domain names to it. His acts were aimed at Panavision in California, and caused it to suffer injury there.

Here, Caddy has hatched no such plan directed at Pebble Beach. He is not a cybersquatter trying to obtain money from Pebble Beach. His operation is legitimate and his website relates directly to that end.

In *Metropolitan Life Insurance Co. v. Neaves,* [912 F.2d 1062 (9th Cir. 1990)], the defendant's alleged plan to defraud the insurance company involved direct interaction with the forum state. We held that the action at issue satisfied *Calder's* "effects test" because the defendant sent a letter to the forum state addressed to the plaintiff, thereby defrauding a forum state entity.

In *Bancroft & Masters, Inc. v. Augusta National Inc.,* [223 F.3d 1082 (9th Cir. 2000)], a dispute over the domain name www.masters.org was triggered by a letter sent by Augusta that required Bancroft & Masters, a computer corporation in California, to sue or lose the domain name. We stated that the "expressly aiming" standard was satisfied when "individualized targeting was present." We reasoned that specific jurisdiction was proper and that the expressly aiming requirement was satisfied because the letter sent by Augusta constituted "individualized targeting."

The defendant in both *Bancroft* and *Metropolitan Life* did "something more" than commit a "foreign act with foreseeable effects in the forum state." In both cases this "individualized targeting" was correspondence that was a clear attempt to force the plaintiff to act. Here, Caddy engaged in no "individualized targeting." There is no letter written by Caddy forcing Pebble Beach to act. The only substantial action is a domain name and non-interactive informative website along with the extraneous fact that Caddy had worked, at some point in his past, in California. This does not constitute "individualized targeting." Indeed, to hold otherwise would be contrary to what we have suggested in earlier case law.

In *Rio Properties, Inc. v. Rio Int'l Interlink,* 284 F.3d 1007 (9th Cir. 2000), we [stated] that when a "website advertiser [does] nothing other than register a domain name and post an essentially passive website" and nothing else is done "to encourage residents of the forum state," there is no personal jurisdiction. Similarly, in *Panavision* we stated, "We agree that simply registering someone else's trademark as a domain name and posting a website on the Internet is not sufficient to subject a party domiciled in one state to jurisdiction in another." Why? Because "the objectionable webpage simply was not aimed intentionally at the [forum state] knowing that harm was likely to be caused there," and "[u]nder the effects doctrine, 'something more' was required to indicate that the defendant purposefully directed its activity in a substantial way to the forum state."

These cases establish two salient points. First, there can be no doubt that we still require "something more" than just a foreseeable effect to conclude that personal jurisdiction is proper. Second, an internet domain name and passive website alone are not "something more," and, therefore, alone are not enough to subject a party to jurisdiction.

In contrast to those cases where jurisdiction was proper because "something more" existed, the circumstances here are more analogous to *Schwarzenegger v. Fred Martin Motor Co.,* 374 F.3d 797 (9th Cir. 2004). In *Schwarzenegger,* we determined that personal jurisdiction based solely on a non-interactive print advertisement would be improper. In *Schwarzenegger,* the former movie star and current California governor, brought an action in California alleging that an Ohio car dealership used impermissibly his "Terminator" image in a newspaper advertisement in Akron, Ohio. The federal district court in California dismissed the complaint for lack of personal jurisdiction. Applying the *Calder* "effects test," we affirmed, concluding that even though the advertisement might lead to eventual harm in California this "foreseeable effect" was not enough because the advertisement was expressly aimed at Ohio rather than California. We concluded that, without "something more" than possible effect, there was simply no individualized targeting of California, or the type of wrongful conduct, that could be construed as being directed at the forum state. We held that Schwarzenegger had not established jurisdiction over the car dealership.

Pebble Beach, like Schwarzenegger, relies almost exclusively on the possible foreseeable effects. Like Schwarzenegger, Pebble Beach's arguments depend on the possible effects of a non-interactive advertisement here, Caddy's passive website. Notably absent in both circumstances is action that can be construed as being expressly aimed at California. The fact that Caddy once lived in California and therefore has knowledge of the Pebble Beach golf resort goes to the foreseeable effect prong of the "effects test" and is not an independent act that can be interpreted as being expressly aimed at California. [W]e reject also any contention that a passive website constitutes expressed aiming. * * * As with the print advertisement in *Schwarzenegger,* the fact that Caddy's website is not directed at California is controlling.

3. Purposeful Direction: United States

Even if Pebble Beach is unable to show purposeful direction as to California, Pebble Beach can still establish jurisdiction if Caddy purposefully directed his action at the United States. This ability to look to the aggregate contacts of a defendant with the United States as a whole instead of a particular state forum is a product of Rule 4(k)(2). Thus, Rule 4(k)(2) is commonly referred to as the federal long-arm statute.

The exercise of Rule 4(k)(2) as a federal long-arm statute requires the plaintiff to prove three factors. First, the claim against the defendant must arise under federal law. Second, the defendant must not be subject to the personal jurisdiction of any state court of general jurisdiction. Third, the federal court's exercise of personal jurisdiction must comport with due process. Here, the first factor is satisfied because Pebble Beach's claims arise under the Lanham Act. And, as established above, the second factor is satisfied as Caddy is not subject to personal jurisdiction of California, or any state court.

That leaves the third factor—due process. The due process analysis is identical to the one discussed above when the forum was California, except here the relevant forum is the entire United States. And, as with the foregoing analysis, our resolution here depends on whether Caddy's actions were purposefully directed at the United States. Pebble Beach contends that the "purposeful direction" requirement is satisfied under the *Calder* "effects test" because Caddy's operation is expressly aimed at the United States. Pebble Beach makes four arguments.

First, Pebble Beach claims that because Caddy selected a ".com" domain name it shows that the United States was his "primary" market and that he is directly advertising his services to the United States. Second, Pebble Beach asserts that his selection of the name "Pebble Beach" shows the United States is his primary target because "Pebble Beach" is a famous United States trademark. Third, Pebble Beach asserts that Caddy's intent to advertise to the United States is bolstered by the fact that Caddy's facilities are located in a resort town that caters to foreigners, particularly Americans. Finally, Pebble Beach asserts that a majority of Caddy's business in the past has been with Americans.

As before, Pebble Beach's arguments focus too much on the effects prong and not enough on the "something more" requirement. First, … we conclude that the selection of a particular domain name is insufficient by itself to confer jurisdiction over a non-resident defendant, even under Rule 4(k)(2), where the forum is the United States. The fact that the name "Pebble Beach" is a famous mark known worldwide is of little practical consequence when deciding whether action is directed at a particular forum via the world wide web. Also of minimal importance is

Caddy's selection of a ".com" domain name instead of a more specific United Kingdom or European Union domain. To suggest that ".com" is an indicator of express aiming at the United States is even weaker than the counter assertion that having "U.K." in the domain name, which is the case here, is indicative that Caddy was only targeting his services to the United Kingdom. Neither provides much more than a slight indication of where a website may be located and does not establish to whom the website is directed. Accordingly, we reject these arguments.

This leaves Pebble Beach's arguments that because Caddy's business is located in an area frequented by Americans, and because he occasionally services Americans, jurisdiction is proper. These arguments fail for the same reasons; they go to effects rather than express aiming. Pebble Beach's arguments do have intuitive appeal—they suggest a real effect on Americans. However, as reiterated throughout this opinion, showing "effect" satisfies only the third prong of the *Calder* test—it is not the "something more" that is required. The "something more" additional requirement is important simply because the effects cited may not have been caused by the defendant's actions of which the plaintiff complains. Here, although Caddy may serve vacationing Americans, there is not a scintilla of

evidence indicating that this patronage is related to either Caddy's choice of a domain name or the posting of a passive website. Accordingly, we find no action on the part of Caddy expressly directed at the United States and conclude that an exercise of personal jurisdiction over Caddy would offend due process.

* * *

III

Caddy did not expressly aim his conduct at California or the United States and therefore is not subject to the personal jurisdiction of the district court. A passive website and domain name alone do not satisfy the *Calder* effects test and there is no other action expressly aimed at California or the United States that would justify personal jurisdiction. * * *

AFFIRMED.

QUESTIONS FOR DISCUSSION FOR CASE 1.1

1. Why is it necessary for Pebble Beach to try to assert the long-arm statutes in this case?
2. The court analyzes only one part of the three-part test for minimum contacts. Why?
3. How does the court apply precedent in deciding this case?

1.2. Jurisdiction

The American Automobile Association, Inc. v. Darba Enterprises Inc., 2009 U.S. Dist. LEXIS 37564 (N.D. Cal. 2009)

* * *

Background

This case arises out of the allegedly infringing use by defendants Darba Enterprises, Inc. and Darren Bagnuolo of plaintiff American Automobile Association's ("AAA") trademarks. AAA is a non-profit corporation that provides services and products to consumers, such as roadside assistance packages, auto insurance and health insurance. AAA has used its "famous and distinctive" AAA trademarks (the "AAA Marks") for over 100 years, and has registered more than 70 of these marks with the United States Patent and Trademark Office. Defendant Darba Enterprises is a corporation that operates several websites that purport to match consumers seeking auto insurance quotes with third-party insurers. Defendant

Darren Bagnuolo is the President, Secretary, Treasurer, and Director of Darba Enterprises.

Plaintiff alleges that defendants' websites, including "aaa-insurance-website.com" and "insurance-website .com" displayed the AAA Marks without authorization for the purpose of tricking internet users into believing that the site was affiliated with AAA. Plaintiff also alleges that defendants have used the AAA Marks in pay-per-click advertisements hosted by search engines such as Google and Yahoo!, and have used those marks to act as "keywords" when typed into these search engines. When an internet user clicks on one of defendants' web pages, the user is invited to enter her zip code to get an auto insurance quote. Once the user clicks through several screens and enters information about her car and driving record, the user comes to a screen that asks her to enter her contact information, including name, address, and phone number. The information entered is submitted to a third-party vendor who apparently distributes it to insurance companies, none of which are AAA and many of which are AAA's direct competitors. Plaintiff has received at least two complaints from consumers in California who mistakenly reached defendants' websites while trying to find AAA on the internet.

When plaintiff discovered defendants' websites, it sent several cease and desist letters to defendants via certified mail. Although defendants did not answer the letters, the websites were modified to remove reference to AAA. However, defendants did not remove the "insurance-website.com" site nor did they discontinue the infringing pay-per-click advertisements. On February 4, 2009, plaintiff filed the instant suit, alleging trademark infringement and dilution, false designation of origin, and unfair competition.

* * *

Legal Standards

I. Motion to Dismiss for Lack of Personal Jurisdiction

Personal jurisdiction over a non-resident defendant may exist if the defendant has either a continuous and systematic presence in the state (general jurisdiction), or minimum contacts with the forum state such that the exercise of jurisdiction "does not offend traditional notions of fair play and substantial justice" (specific jurisdiction). * * *

* * *

Discussion

* * *

II. Personal Jurisdiction

Defendant Bagnuolo argues that this case should be dismissed for lack of personal jurisdiction. Plaintiff responds that defendant's forum-related activities make personal jurisdiction appropriate. Because plaintiff argues only that specific jurisdiction is warranted, the Court does not address whether general jurisdiction would be appropriate here.

California law requires that the exercise of personal jurisdiction comply with federal due process requirements. To satisfy due process, a nonresident defendant must have "'minimum contacts' with the forum state such that the assertion of jurisdiction 'does not offend

traditional notions of fair play and substantial justice.'" The Ninth Circuit employs a three-part test to determine whether the defendant has such minimum contacts with a forum state. First, the "nonresident defendant must do some act or consummate some transaction with the forum or perform some act by which he purposefully avails himself of the privilege of conducting activities in the forum," thereby invoking the benefits and protections of the forum state. Second, the claim must "arise [] out of or result [] from the defendant's forum-related activities," and third, the exercise of personal jurisdiction over the defendant must be reasonable. The plaintiff bears the burden of proving the first two prongs. If the plaintiff carries this burden, "the defendant must come forward with a 'compelling case' that the exercise of jurisdiction would not be reasonable."

A. Purposeful Availment

The "purposeful availment" prong of the specific jurisdiction test "ensures that a nonresident defendant will not be haled into court based upon 'random, fortuitous or attenuated' contacts with the forum state." This prong is satisfied if the defendant has either "(1) 'purposefully availed' himself of the privilege of conducting activities in the forum, or (2) 'purposefully directed' his activities toward the forum."

A defendant has not "purposefully availed" himself of the privilege of conducting activities in a forum state merely because he operates a website which can be accessed there. Rather, in the context of the internet, courts use a sliding scale approach to assess purposeful availment. At one end of the scale are "passive" websites which merely display information, such as an advertisement. Personal jurisdiction is "not appropriate when a website is merely … passive." At the other end of the scale are "interactive" websites which function for commercial purposes and where users exchange information. Personal jurisdiction is appropriate "when an entity is conducting business over the internet." Where a website is somewhere between the two extremes, "the likelihood that personal jurisdiction can be constitutionally exercised is directly proportionate to the nature and quality of commercial activity that an entity conducts over the internet."

Defendant argues that his websites were passive. He stresses that because he did not sell anything directly to consumers, his website cannot be considered commercial. But this argument ignores the fact that users who searched for "AAA insurance" and found defendant's website were brought to a web-page where they were instructed to enter their names and contact information to get a "free rate quote." Contrary to defendant's assertions, this is not an example of a website that merely provides information to consumers. In fact, the websites provided *no* information to consumers unless and until they entered their contact information. Plaintiff alleges, and provides circumstantial evidence, that defendant sold this contact information to a third party. Because the defendant has not contradicted or denied this allegation, the Court accepts it as true. Defendant thus profited when California users entered their contact information in his website, even though he did not sell anything to them directly. Therefore, the Court finds that defendant's websites were interactive and commercial.

By maintaining a commercial website, defendant has "reached out beyond [his] home state of [Nevada] to avail [himself] of the benefits of the California forum." Plaintiff received at least two complaints from California residents who had mistakenly entered their information into defendant's website thinking it was an AAA website. Defendant presumably benefitted from these actions by selling the contact information of these California residents. Although the actual number of California residents who entered their contact information into defendant's website may be small, "the critical inquiry in determining whether there was a purposeful availment of the forum state is the quality, not merely the quantity, of the contacts." Nor may defendant "escape jurisdiction by claiming that its contacts with California are merely fortuitous." Defendant's website required users to enter their zip codes to get "insurance quotes." It is reasonable to infer that the third parties to whom defendant sold this contact information targeted potential customers based on their geographic location. Moreover, by utilizing pay-per-click advertisements to ensure that its name would come up when internet users searched for "AAA insurance," defendant intended to lure internet users to its website, including California residents. He "is not being haled into a court in some unexpected location where the Internet is not commonly available, but into a court in California, where a large portion of the world's Internet users presumably reside."

The Court therefore finds that defendant purposefully availed himself of the privilege of conducting activities in California and that therefore that plaintiff has satisfied the first prong of the minimum contacts analysis.

B. Forum-Related Activities

The second prong of the minimum contacts analysis requires that "the claim asserted in the litigation arises out of defendant's forum related activities." The Court must determine whether plaintiff would not have been injured but for defendant's forum-related activities.

This prong is satisfied here. Defendant's allegedly trademark-infringing website harmed plaintiff in California. Indeed, plaintiff received complaints from at least two California residents who had mistakenly entered their contact information into defendant's website thinking it was an AAA site. Plaintiff alleges harm directly related to such consumer confusion. But for defendant's conduct, this harm would not have occurred. Plaintiff's claims therefore arise out of defendant's forum-related activities.

C. Reasonableness

Finally, the Court must determine whether the exercise of jurisdiction would be reasonable here. Even if the first two prongs of the test are satisfied, "the exercise of jurisdiction must be reasonable" in order to satisfy due process. Once the plaintiff carries its burden by proving the first two prongs of the test, the defendant "must present a compelling case that the presence of some other considerations would render jurisdiction unreasonable."

In deciding whether the exercise of jurisdiction would be reasonable, the Court considers seven factors: "(1) the extent of a defendant's purposeful interjection; (2) the burden on the defendant in defending in the forum; (3) the extent of conflict with the sovereignty of the defendant's state; (4) the forum state's interest in adjudicating the dispute; (5) the most efficient judicial resolution of the controversy; (6) the importance of the forum to the plaintiff's interest in convenient and effective relief; and (7) the existence of an alternative forum." The Court balances all seven factors and no one factor is dispositive.

1. Purposeful Interjection

"Even if there is sufficient 'interjection' into the state to satisfy the purposeful availment prong, the degree of interjection is a factor to be weighed in assessing the overall reasonableness of jurisdiction under the reasonableness prong."

Although defendant has not come forward with any affirmative evidence that the degree of intrusion was small (e.g., by providing the Court with information regarding how many California residents versus how many non-California residents entered their information into his website), the evidence so far before the Court does not show a high degree of interjection in California. The Court has evidence only that two California residents … were confused by defendants' website. This factor weighs in favor of defendant.

2. Defendant's Burden in Litigating

"A defendant's burden in litigating in the forum is a factor in the assessment of reasonableness, but unless the 'inconvenience is so great as to constitute a deprivation of due process it will not overcome clear justifications for the exercise of jurisdiction.'"

Here, defendant has not argued to the Court that his burden in litigating in California would be so great as to deprive him of due process. Even if he had, advances in technology and discounted airfare do not make it unreasonable for defendant to litigate in California. This factor does not favor defendant.

3. Sovereignty

This factor "concerns the extent to which the district court's exercise of jurisdiction in California would conflict with the sovereignty" of Nevada, defendants' home state. Defendant has not pointed to any conflict of law between California and Nevada or other issues which would adversely impact Nevada's sovereignty interests. This factor therefore does not weigh in favor of defendant.

4. Forum State's Interest

California has "a strong interest in protecting its residents from torts that cause injury within the state, and in providing a forum for relief." Defendant has not pointed to any compelling interest that Nevada has in adjudicating the dispute. This factor therefore does not weigh in favor of defendant.

5. Efficient Resolution

This factor "focuses on the location of the evidence and the witnesses. It is no longer weighed heavily given the modern advances in communication and transportation." Even if the Court were to weigh this factor, defendant has not come forward with any evidence that resolution of this matter would not [be] efficient in California. Therefore, this factor does not weigh in favor of defendant.

6. Convenient and Effective Relief for Plaintiff

Plaintiff's inconvenience is not weighed heavily in this analysis. AAA is a nation-wide non-profit organization. It is unlikely that convenient and effective relief for plaintiff would be hindered by litigating in Nevada. Plaintiff might be slightly burdened by having to retain local counsel. This factor therefore weighs slightly in favor of plaintiff.

7. Alternative Forum

Plaintiff has not shown that an alternative forum is not available. Nevada is an alternate forum. This factor therefore weighs in defendants' favor.

* * * In balancing these factors, the Court finds [defendant] "failed to present a compelling case that the district court's exercise of jurisdiction in California would be unreasonable."

* * *

Conclusion

For the foregoing reasons and for good cause shown, the Court hereby DENIES defendants' motion to dismiss.

* * *

QUESTIONS FOR DISCUSSION FOR CASE 1.2

1. Why was it necessary for AAA to try to assert the long-arm statute in this case?
2. Does the court conclude that it does or does not have personal jurisdiction over the defendant? Why?
3. This opinion does not resolve the underlying dispute between the parties. Why not? What will happen next in this case?

PART 2

Legal Issues Relating to Product Development

Chapter 2

Protection of Intellectual Property Assets Patent and Copyright Law

Chapter 3

Protection of Intellectual Property Assets Through Trade Secret Law, Contractual Agreements, and Business Strategies

Protection of Intellectual Property Assets: Patent and Copyright Law

When a firm or an individual develops a new product or service, one of the very first legal issues that arises is protection of that new asset from competitors. If the firm waits until later in the product development or marketing process to consider this issue, it may find that it has lost the right to protect the asset. Thus, those creating a new product or service need to budget for and obtain legal advice on this issue very early in the development process. This chapter discusses ways in which patent and copyright law protect intellectual property assets and the steps that firms must take to obtain those protections.

Overview

Although managers often think of intellectual property issues as arising primarily in the context of high-technology ventures, all firms need to be concerned with intellectual property protection. Intellectual property law can be used to protect assets as sophisticated as computer software or as simple as soft drink formulas or customer databases.

Categories of Intellectual Property Law

Intellectual property assets consist of property rights in intangible products of investment, creative intellect, or labor. "Intellectual property law" is a broad legal term that is used to refer to a number of separate, but related, legal doctrines that relate to these assets. We examine the four basic categories of intellectual property law: (1) patent law; (2) copyright law; (3) trade secret law; and (4) trademark law. These doctrines provide overlapping protection. It is possible, for example, to protect different aspects of a single product through a combination of some or all of these four categories (see Exhibit 2.1). The decision as to which type or types of protection to pursue is a matter of both business and legal strategy and so requires the active participation of both management and its legal counsel.

Patent, copyright, and trade secret law comprise one major branch of intellectual property law. Each of these three mechanisms may be used to prevent others from making or selling protected products or services. The second main branch of intellectual property law, which includes trademark and unfair competition law, allows firms to take action to prevent others from providing false and misleading information to consumers or to protect famous marks (see Exhibit 2.2).

This chapter addresses patent and copyright law. Trade secret law is addressed in Chapter 3, as is the law relating to covenants not to compete, nondisclosure agreements, and other contractual agreements and business strategies used to protect intellectual property assets. Trademark law and unfair competition law are discussed in Chapter 6, Chapter 7, and Chapter 8, which address legal issues related to the promotion of products and services.

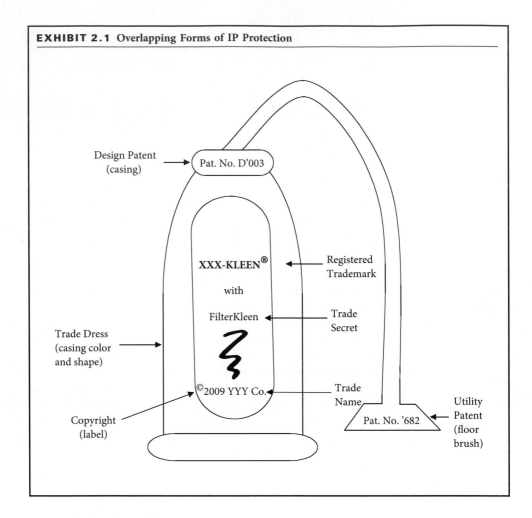

EXHIBIT 2.1 Overlapping Forms of IP Protection

Design Patent (casing) → Pat. No. D'003

XXX-KLEEN®

with

FilterKleen ← Trade Secret

← Registered Trademark

©2009 YYY Co. → Trade Name

Trade Dress (casing color and shape)

Copyright (label)

Pat. No. '682

Utility Patent (floor brush)

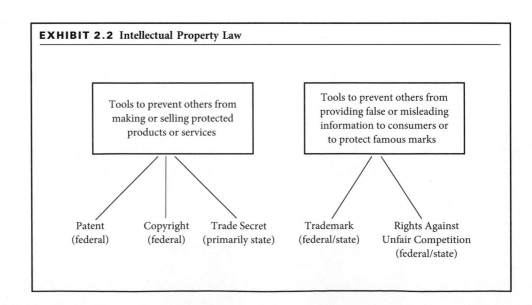

EXHIBIT 2.2 Intellectual Property Law

Tools to prevent others from making or selling protected products or services	Tools to prevent others from providing false or misleading information to consumers or to protect famous marks

Patent (federal)   Copyright (federal)   Trade Secret (primarily state)

Trademark (federal/state)   Rights Against Unfair Competition (federal/state)

Managerial interest in intellectual property issues has increased dramatically in recent years as a result of a stunning increase in the value of intellectual property over the past few decades. A number of "pure knowledge" companies, such as Microsoft, now derive much of their value from intellectual property rather than from tangible assets.

The federal government has also devoted much more attention to the international aspects of intellectual property law in recent years. The government wants to protect U.S. intellectual property rights overseas as much as possible. It also wants to harmonize intellectual property laws between the United States and other countries as much as possible to reduce transaction costs for global businesses and to provide a level playing field for American companies competing in foreign countries.

As a result of these initiatives, U.S. intellectual property law is currently changing very rapidly. Although every manager should have an understanding of the basic parameters of intellectual property law, firms should seek the expert advice of legal counsel before undertaking activities in this area.

Underlying Policy Considerations

Intellectual property law hinges on a fundamental policy conflict. The ultimate goal of intellectual property law is to provide a diverse, competitive marketplace. Thus, on the one hand, intellectual property law tries to promote creativity in an effort to encourage the provision of a wide variety of goods and services to the market. By giving inventors, writers, or artists property rights in their intangible creations, the law gives them an opportunity to recoup their investment in the creative process and to earn a profit. On the other hand, the law wants to provide the freest possible public access to new products and services. Intellectual property law represents compromises between the goal of encouraging creativity and that of promoting public access. The net result is that intellectual property law is constantly changing as legislators attempt to strike a balance between these two competing goals.

Patent Law

A **patent** is a grant of an exclusive monopoly for a limited time period from the federal government to an inventor. The theory behind patent law is that the opportunity to obtain such an exclusive monopoly encourages investment in research and development. To receive a patent, the inventor must reveal to the public information about the invention. In return, the inventor may exclude others from making, using, selling, or offering to sell in the United States the patented invention or from making, using, selling, or offering to sell a substantial portion of components that, if combined, would infringe the patent. In addition, federal law prohibits the importation to the United States of products made from any process covered by a U.S. patent.

Patents are issued exclusively by the federal government. Article I, Section 8 of the U.S. Constitution provides:

> The Congress shall have power ... To promote the Progress of Science and useful Arts, by securing for limited Times to Authors and Inventors the exclusive Right to their respective Writings and Discoveries.

States therefore may not issue patents.

Patents are issued under the auspices of the federal Patent and Trademark Office (PTO), in accordance with the provisions of the federal Patent Act.[1] In addition, Congress

---

[1] 35 U.S.C. §§ 1 *et seq.*

created the U.S. Court of Appeals for the Federal Circuit (CAFC) in 1982. The CAFC is a specialized appellate court with limited jurisdiction over certain types of legal issues, including patent law. All patent appeals are heard by this court, which has developed expertise in this area of the law, rather than by the 12 regular circuit courts. As a result, patent law is now much more uniform than it was in the past.

Standards for Patent Issuance

There are three kinds of patents in the United States: (1) utility patents; (2) design patents; and (3) plant patents. As Exhibit 2.3 indicates, utility patents are by far the most common. When people use the term "patent," they usually are referring to a utility patent.

Utility patents protect the function of articles or processes. *Design patents* protect the ornamental features of articles. *Plant patents* may be issued for asexually reproducible plants that are novel, nonobvious, and distinct. Because plant patents are such a narrow niche, our discussion focuses primarily on utility patents and secondarily on design patents.

An inventor can have only one patent per invention. If the item involved incorporates two or more inventions, however, the inventor can receive separate utility patents for each invention. In Exhibit 2.1, for example, separate utility patents could be obtained for the floor brush and the motor. In addition, an inventor can obtain both design and utility patents on different aspects of a single item. Suppose a company invents a new kind of no-spill cup for children that is unusually effective at preventing spills and leaks and that has a unique and attractive shape. The company could obtain a utility patent on the no-spill lid and a design patent on the shape of the cup.

Utility Patents   Utility patents cover *useful* inventions that fall into one of five categories: processes (such as a gene-splicing procedure), machines, articles of manufacture (such as a tire or a chair),[2] a composition of matter (such as a new chemical compound), or improvements upon existing ideas that fall into any one of these categories. Utility patents protect only processes or tangible products. Patents may not be used to protect expressions of ideas (that is the function of copyright law), nor may patent law be used to obtain a

---

EXHIBIT 2.3 2008 Patent Statistics

PATENT DOCUMENTS GRANTED (CALENDAR YEAR)	
Utility Patents	157,772
Design Patents	25,565
Plant Patents	1,240
Reissue Patents	647
TOTAL - 2008	185,224

Source: *www.uspto.gov/web/offices/ac/ido/oeip/taf/us_stat.htm*

---

[2]"Articles of manufacture" are generally simple objects without moving parts, as opposed to "machines," which generally have moving parts or electronic circuits.

monopoly on laws of nature, naturally occurring substances, mathematical formulas, or abstract ideas, for such a monopoly would stifle scientific inquiry and advancement.

The distinction between man-made and naturally occurring organisms has important implications for the biotechnology industry in particular. In *Diamond v. Chakrabarty,*[3] decided in 1980, the Supreme Court determined that while naturally occurring microorganisms cannot be patented, man-made microorganisms may be.

◆ *See Discussion Case 2.1.*

The PTO has since interpreted *Chakrabarty* as authorizing patents on higher forms of genetically engineered mammals, such as mice and rabbits. The United States tends to be more liberal on this issue than most countries. Man-made organisms patentable in the United States may well not receive patent protection elsewhere in the world.

The categories of patentable subject matter can shift over time as courts respond to changing technology and circumstances. Recent significant changes involve the patentability of *business methods* (i.e., patents that pertain to a method of doing or conducting business). In a 1998 decision, *State Street Bank & Trust Co. v. Signature Financial Group, Inc.,*[4] the CAFC held that business methods could be patented provided the method involved a practical application (i.e., produced a "useful, concrete and tangible" result). After *State Street Bank,* business method patent applications grew dramatically, though they are still only a small fraction of the total number of patent applications filed each year. In fiscal year 2008, the PTO received 9,563 business method patent applications and issued 1,643 patents.[5]

The issuance of business method patents has been very controversial, as many commentators feel that the PTO is issuing patents for obvious inventions. In particular, many argue that the PTO is issuing patents for ways of doing business on the Internet that are common in the non-Internet business world. They fear that the growth in business method patents will hamper the development of the Internet as a commercial medium.

The *State Street Bank* decision has created problems as well as opportunities for businesses. Many businesses that had treated their business methods as trade secrets and had not attempted to patent them suddenly found themselves facing patent infringement claims from inventors who filed for business method patents long after the method had already been in use by others. Congress responded to this unexpected consequence in the American Inventors Protection Act of 1999,[6] which created the "first inventor defense." This defense allows a person who invented and used commercially a method of doing business at least one year before the date another person filed a business method patent application on it to continue using the method without infringing on any patent that might be granted.[7]

In 2008, the Federal Circuit issued a decision in *In re Bilski,*[8] in which the court significantly reined in the scope of business method patents. The *Bilski* court held that the "useful, concrete and tangible" result test of *State Street Bank* was insufficient to judge patentability of business methods. The inventors in *Bilski* had applied for a patent for a method of hedging certain commodity transactions. The PTO denied their application on the grounds that it lacked patentable subject matter. The inventors appealed the denial. The Federal Circuit, sitting *en banc,* affirmed the denial. The Federal Circuit stated that the test

---

[3]447 U.S. 303 (1980).

[4]149 F.3d 1368 (Fed. Cir. 1998).

[5]See www.uspto.gov/web/menu/pbmethod/applicationfiling.htm

[6]Pub. L. No. 106-113, as amended by Pub. L. No. 107-273.

[7]35 U.S.C. § 273.

[8]545 F.3d 943 (Fed. Cir. 2008).

to be applied to determine the patentability of any process, including business methods, is whether the process: (1) is tied to a particular machine or apparatus, and (2) transforms a particular article into a different state or thing. This "machine-or-transformation test," as it is known, has created its own questions about patentability of business methods, and the PTO and the lower courts are still determining how it applies in specific situations. The U.S. Supreme Court will hear oral argument in *In re Bilski* in November, 2009. So the future of business method patents is still uncertain as this edition goes to press.

A utility patent gives its owner a monopoly of limited duration in an invention in return for full public disclosure of the invention's details (so that the public may learn from it). Patents currently have a term of 20 years from the date the application was filed. This term can be extended if the PTO fails to grant a patent within three years after filing because of administrative delay. Patent terms cannot otherwise be extended or renewed, however; and, once the term has expired, all members of the public (including competitors) are free to make or use the invention as they wish.

An inventor will not receive a patent merely because he has invented something. Rather, the inventor must show that the invention is worthy of a patent. The Patent Act requires that in order for a utility patent to issue, the invention must be: (1) novel; (2) nonobvious; and (3) useful.

Novelty is covered in Section 102 of the Patent Act. Although Section 102 has numerous provisions covering a variety of types of circumstances, two are particularly important. Section 102(a) provides that a patent must be denied:

> if the invention was known or used by others in this country or patented or described in a printed publication in this or a foreign country, before the invention thereof by the applicant for a patent ….

The focus in Section 102(a) is on the actions of persons other than the applicant prior to the date that the applicant made the invention. Prior to that date, did other persons cause the invention to be known or used in the United States? Did they cause it to be patented or make it the subject of a printed publication anywhere else in the world? The policy behind Section 102(a) is to prevent a second inventor from obtaining a patent if a previous inventor has already placed the invention in the public domain before the second inventor made his invention.

Section 102(b) provides that a patent must be denied:

> if the invention was patented or described in a printed publication in this or a foreign country or in public use or on sale in this country, more than one year prior to the date of application for patent in the United States ….

Section 102(b) focuses on the actions of the applicant and others more than one year before the application was filed. Essentially, once one of the listed events has occurred, the inventor has one year in which to file an application for patent, or the inventor loses the right to do so. There are several policy reasons behind this provision. First, it ensures that inventions in the public domain for one year remain there. Second, it allows the inventor one year in which to test market reaction before going to the considerable expense of filing for a patent. Third, it prevents the inventor from marketing the product for several years before applying for a patent in an effort to extend the effective patent time.

◆▶ *See Discussion Case 2.2.*

The *nonobviousness* standard asks whether the invention would have been obvious to someone skilled in the particular field as of the date of invention. If so, the invention is not patentable.

The *usefulness* standard requires that there be a current, significant, beneficial use for the invention. This is not a particularly high bar, and most inventions have no problem in meeting this requirement.

Design Patents   Design patents protect the *ornamental* features of an article of manufacture. As you can imagine, design patents are of great importance to many manufacturers, particularly manufacturers of consumer goods. Many goods—such as athletic shoes, coffeemakers, or chairs—may be virtually indistinguishable from each other except for their design, which then becomes critical to the marketing function.

To receive a design patent, the inventor must show that her design is: (1) novel; (2) nonobvious; and (3) ornamental. With a few exceptions, the novelty requirement applies to design patents just as it does to utility patents. The test for nonobviousness of design patents is whether a professional designer of ordinary skill, viewing the overall appearance of the design as compared to prior designs, would consider the new design obvious. The ornamentality standard requires that the design be primarily ornamental and not dictated by functional considerations. If there are a variety of ways in which the article could be designed and still perform its function, the design is most likely ornamental and not functional. If the design affects the invention's function or performance, however, it must be protected, if at all, through a utility patent, not a design patent. Design patents are valid for a term of 14 years from the date of patent issuance—a much shorter term than that granted to utility patents.

Ownership of Patents

Under U.S. law, the **first to invent** is the only person who can file for and obtain a patent. In virtually every other country of the world, however, the *first to file* is entitled to the patent.

Very often, employees create inventions while at work. This situation raises two issues: (1) Who owns the invention—the inventor or the employer? and (2) Who may file for the patent—the inventor or the employer?

If the employee creates the invention in the context of fulfilling his specific job duties (i.e., the employee was "hired to invent"), the invention belongs to the employer and the employee is obligated to assign all rights to the invention to the employer. It is best, from the employer's perspective, to have a specific employment agreement in place providing that the employee will make such an assignment. In the absence of an explicit agreement, the common law will reach the same result.

If the employee does not create the invention as part of his official job duties but nonetheless invents something closely related to his duties or uses company resources in doing so, the employee will "own" the invention, but the employer will have *"shop rights"* in the invention. Shop rights are an irrevocable, nontransferable, royalty-free license to use the invention. The theory behind shop rights is that the employer, whose resources contributed to the invention, should have the right to use the invention in its business, although the employee retains the right to exploit the invention for all other purposes.

Employers generally are not satisfied with obtaining shop rights, however. Rather, they want to own the invention. Thus, employers often use "invention assignment agreements," in which the employee agrees in advance to assign all rights in an invention to the employer. (Invention assignment agreements are discussed in more detail in Chapter 3.)

Ownership of the *invention* does not resolve the question of who can apply for the *patent,* however. Recall that under U.S. law, only the *inventor* (i.e., the person who conceived of the invention) is entitled to apply for a patent. Thus, even if the employer has an invention assignment agreement transferring ownership of the invention to it, the inventor must still file for the patent; ownership of the patent can then be assigned to the employer by the inventor. Thus, the invention assignment agreement should contain a provision obligating the employee/inventor to cooperate in the application for the patent.

Patent Application Procedures

Applications for patents are made to the PTO in Washington, D.C. The PTO will examine the application and, if all of the statutory standards have been met, will issue a patent.

Inventors may represent themselves before the PTO. As a practical matter, however, because of the complexity and technicality of the documents required, it is usually advisable to seek the services of a patent agent or patent attorney who is skilled in drafting an application that is broad enough to protect the invention yet narrow enough to pass the scrutiny of the PTO examiner. Both patent lawyers and patent agents are individuals licensed to practice in patent cases before the PTO. The major distinction between the two is that patent agents cannot represent clients outside the PTO (for example, in litigation resulting from patent infringement), while patent lawyers, of course, can. Both patent lawyers and patent agents must have a degree in a technical or scientific field, such as engineering or physics, and both must pass a PTO exam that tests knowledge of patent laws and rules and the ability to write a patent claim.

The process of obtaining a patent from the PTO is known as a *prosecution.* The application must describe the invention in detail and include diagrams or illustrations. The Patent Act requires that patent applicants fully disclose their inventions to the public as part of the "price" of obtaining a patent. The patent applicant is required to describe how to make and use the invention with sufficient clarity, precision, and detail to enable a person skilled in the relevant art to make and use it without undue experimentation. Failure to do so will result in either denial of the patent or, if the patent has already issued, invalidation of the patent.

The application must set forth the *claims*—statements that describe the invention in a very formal and stylized manner and that articulate the basis for the monopoly that is to be granted to the inventor. Typically, a number of negotiations take place between the patent examiner and the patent lawyer or agent, which often result in the patent application being rewritten to result in a narrower monopoly being granted to the inventor. On average, it takes eighteen months to two years to obtain a patent, although the process can take much longer for complex or disputed patents.

Before filing an application, the applicant should conduct a *prior art search.* "Prior art" refers to any printed publication, prior patent, or other document, or prior invention that references or makes use of the invention that is the subject of the patent application. The PTO may find that such prior art renders the applicant's invention obvious or nonnovel, making the issuance of a patent improper. A careful search for prior art helps the applicant to avoid the expense of filing an application that the PTO is unlikely to grant and helps the applicant to prepare responses in advance to issues likely to be raised by the PTO examiner. The applicant must disclose to the PTO all of the prior art of which it is aware. There are a number of professional firms that specialize in searching for prior art; there are a number of online databases available as well. Because the consequences of an improper prior art search can be both expensive and time-consuming, it is wise to seek professional assistance in this area. The PTO examiner also conducts a search for prior art in the course of evaluating the application.

The filing fee for a patent is relatively modest—typically, $330.[9] Of course, the filing fee is only one small part of the entire process. The PTO charges additional examination and maintenance fees as well. The largest expense the applicant is likely to face, however,

---

[9]For a complete and current PTO fee schedule, see the PTO's webpage at www.uspto.gov/

is for expert counsel throughout the prosecution process. If the inventor hires a patent agent or patent lawyer to represent the inventor in the preparation of the patent application and in the negotiations with the PTO examiner, the inventor is likely to spend several thousand dollars to obtain his patent.

Historically, U.S. patent applications were kept secret and were not released to the public. That practice differed significantly from practices in the rest of the world, in which patent applications are typically published, or "laid open" to the public, within a specified time period (usually 18 months after filing). The American Inventors Protection Act of 1999, however, changed the U.S. practice of holding patent applications secret. Now, all U.S. utility patent applications that are also foreign-filed and published abroad are published 18 months from their first effective filing date. The PTO will still hold utility patent applications that are filed solely in the United States and not abroad secret if the applicant so requests. If the patent application is made public, the inventor gains several advantages, including enhanced damages for infringement. The inventor loses the opportunity to treat the invention as a trade secret in the event that the PTO does not issue the patent, however. (This topic is discussed further in Chapter 3.) Therefore, the inventor should discuss the implications of publishing the application versus holding it secret with legal counsel before proceeding with the application.

If a patent is issued, the patent is summarized and published in the *Official Gazette,* which is an official U.S. government publication.[10] At this point, the patent becomes a public document and anyone can examine it to determine the details of the invention. The theory is that, in return for receiving the limited monopoly granted by the patent, the patentee must make the invention available to the public so that others can make technological improvements upon it. At the end of the patent period, the invention is available to the public as a whole and anyone can make or use it without incurring liability.

If the patent examiner determines that the invention is not patentable, the applicant may take an administrative appeal to the PTO Board of Appeals. If the Board provides no relief, the applicant may appeal on the administrative record directly to the CAFC or may file suit against the Commissioner of Patents and Trademarks in the U.S. District Court, where a *de novo* review of patentability will be made. Appeals go to the CAFC (see Exhibit 2.4).

It is important to realize that issuance of the patent does not guarantee that the patentee has a valid patent. The PTO's issuance of a patent provides a *presumption* of validity, but this presumption can be overcome. For example, if the patentee attempts to enforce the patent in an infringement action, the alleged infringer can raise patent invalidity as a defense. A party can also challenge the validity of a patent through a *declaratory judgment action* before it has been charged with infringement by the patentee.

The standards for obtaining a valid patent are strict. The PTO denies many applications for patents, and, of the ones granted, a significant percentage are later invalidated by a court. A patentee cannot be complacent just because a patent has issued.

Rights Granted by a Patent

A patent grants the patentee an exclusive monopoly (for a limited time period) to prevent others from making, using, selling, offering to sell, or importing the invention, even if those others independently create the invention. In most instances, the patentee may "work" the invention (i.e., put it into commercial use), license others to work the invention, or simply hold the patent and refuse to make the invention (or allow others to make it) during the patent period. Firms may use this latter tactic as a strategic measure to prevent competitors from entering specific markets.

---

[10]Recent issues of the *Patent Official Gazette* are available online on the PTO's webpage at www.uspto.gov/

EXHIBIT 2.4 Patent Prosecution Procedure

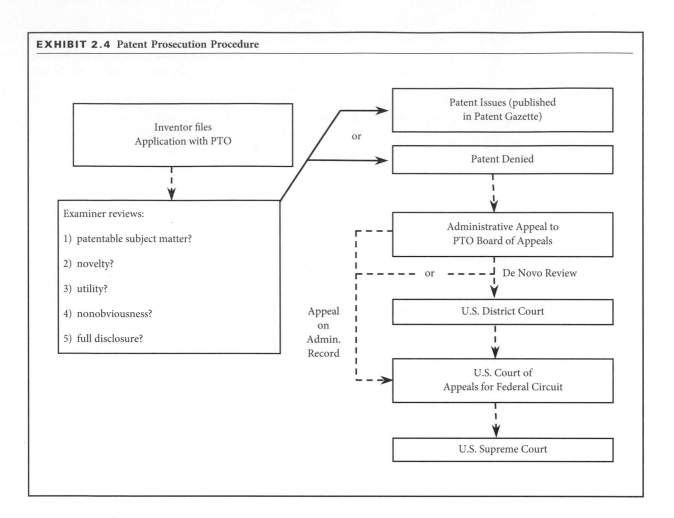

Patentees do not automatically have a right to "work" their inventions in every in-stance, however. A patent does not grant the inventor the right to make, use, or sell the invention; rather, it grants the patentee the right to exclude others from doing so. Sup-pose that Inventor A holds a patent on a new type of widget that will revolutionize the widget-using industries. To make the widget, however, Inventor A must use a specific manufacturing process that has already been patented by Inventor B. Inventor A there-fore cannot manufacture her widgets without infringing upon Inventor B's patent. Inven-tor B's patent is known as a *blocking patent,* and it will have the effect of preventing Inventor A from commercializing her widget invention. Inventor A will have the right to prevent others from making her patented widget, but will be unable to make the wid-get herself unless she is able to negotiate a license with Inventor B for the use of the patented manufacturing method.

Infringement

There are two dimensions of patent infringement issues that are relevant to marketers. First, a marketer may find that its patent has been infringed by another and may want to pursue legal remedies to protect the patent. Second, a marketer may find itself defending against an infringement action brought by a competitor. The marketer may have unintentionally in-fringed upon another's patent. Alternatively, a marketer may deliberately infringe a patent, believing that if its actions are challenged in court, the patent will be declared invalid.

Types of Infringement   The Patent Act provides that a person can be held liable for infringement if she: (1) directly infringes a patent; (2) induces another to infringe a patent; (3) contributorially infringes a patent; (4) manufactures or sells certain components of a patented invention to be assembled abroad; or (5) imports, sells, offers to sell, or uses a product made abroad through a process protected by a U.S. patent.

The last provision prevents a business from avoiding a patentee's U.S. process patent by using the process abroad to manufacture products, then importing the products into the United States to sell or use. The use of the *process* abroad is not infringement, because U.S. patent laws do not have extraterritorial reach; however, the subsequent importation, offer for sale, or use of the *products* in the United States is infringement. Theoretically, retailers and noncommercial users are subject to liability under this provision. However, the Patent Act provides that retailers and noncommercial users are held liable only if there is no adequate remedy against the primary manufacturers, importers, distributors, or wholesalers on the theory that the most culpable parties should be held liable first.

Direct infringement is most common. It occurs when the defendant makes, uses, sells, or imports the patented invention in the United States during the patent term. For example, in *Snuba International, Inc. v. Dolphin World, Inc.*,[11] Snuba International held a patent on a diving system. Snuba's invention consisted in part of a lightweight raft that carried compressed air tanks and that was attached to the diver by a harness and towline. Dolphin World sold a competing product called the "Free Diver," which used a "pod" and harness mechanism. Although Dolphin World attempted to argue that a "pod" was not a "raft" and that its system therefore did not infringe, the CAFC disagreed and found that Dolphin World had directly infringed Snuba's patent.

Inducement to infringe occurs when the defendant actively, intentionally, and knowingly solicits or assists a third party in directly infringing a patent. Direct infringement by a third party is a prerequisite to finding inducement to infringe. In *Snuba International,* for example, the CAFC found that the use of the Free Diver system by Dolphin World's customers constituted direct infringement and that Dolphin World had induced this infringement by disseminating sales information and promotional materials that encouraged consumers to purchase its Free Diver system.

Contributory infringement occurs when the defendant sells, offers to sell, or imports a material component of the patented invention that has no substantial use aside from use in the patented invention, provided that: (1) the defendant knows that the component he sold was specially made or adapted for use in the patented invention, has no other substantial use, and is likely to be used to infringe the patent; and (2) his actions contribute to another's direct infringement. Direct infringement is a prerequisite to finding contributory infringement. In *Snuba International,* the CAFC found that Dolphin World had notice of the Snuba patent and admitted that its Free Diver pod had no noninfringing use. Because the use of the Free Diver system by Dolphin World's customers was direct infringement, Dolphin World was liable for contributory infringement (in addition to inducement to infringement and its own direct infringement).

Finally, managers should be aware that the courts have held corporate officers—but not non-management employees—personally liable for the infringing activities of their corporations in certain instances. While a corporate officer is not automatically held personally liable merely because of her status as an officer of the corporation, an officer may be held personally liable in instances in which she personally took part in the commission of the infringing act or specifically directed other officers, agents, or employees of

---

[11]2000 U.S. App. LEXIS 16946 (CAFC, July 11, 2000).

the corporation to infringe the patent of another.[12] Often, officers can avoid this personal liability by showing that they obtained the advice of legal counsel and relied in good faith on that advice in structuring their behavior. Failure to obtain such advice or to heed it may well result in personal liability.

Defenses to Infringement Claims   A defendant charged with patent infringement can raise four basic defenses. First, the defendant can raise *patent invalidity*. If the defendant can show by clear and convincing evidence that the invention was not novel, nonobvious, and useful (for a utility patent) or not novel, nonobvious, and ornamental (for a design patent), the court will find the patent invalid and the defendant will not be liable for infringement.

Second, the defendant can raise *patent misuse* by the patentee. The patentee has misused his patent if he uses it to obtain more market power than Congress intended the patent to convey. Generally, this involves some sort of antitrust violation. Where patent misuse is shown, the patentee is denied enforcement of the patent until the misuse ceases; the defendant is not liable for infringement. Antitrust issues are discussed in more detail in Chapter 4.

Third, the defendant is relieved of liability for infringement if the defendant can show *inequitable conduct* on the part of the patentee. For example, if the patentee intentionally made a misrepresentation or withheld material information about the patentability of the invention during patent prosecution, the patent is unenforceable.

Finally, the defendant can raise the *experimental use defense.* This is a very narrow defense that permits a person to make or use a patented invention if that person's purpose is only to satisfy her scientific curiosity or to engage in an intellectual exercise. The experimental use defense does not apply if the defendant has any commercial motivation.

Remedies for Patent Infringement

Two basic forms of remedies are available for patent infringement: injunctions and monetary damages. In addition, patentees may recover attorney fees and treble damages under certain circumstances.

Injunctions   An *injunction* is a court order to a party requiring that party to either do something or to refrain from doing something. When infringement is found, the court usually awards the patentee both monetary damages and a *permanent injunction* against further infringement.

The patentee often seeks a *preliminary injunction* as well, which is harder to obtain. This is a court order issued during the lawsuit that prevents the defendant from continuing its alleged infringing activities until the lawsuit is resolved. Courts traditionally have been reluctant to grant preliminary injunctions because they fear that if the defendant is ultimately found not to be infringing the plaintiff's patent, the defendant's market position might have been impaired or lost altogether. However, the CAFC has become much more liberal in recent years in granting preliminary injunctions. Generally, to receive a preliminary injunction, the patentee must show that: (1) the patentee has a reasonable likelihood of success on the merits; (2) irreparable harm to the patentee will occur if the injunction is not granted; (3) the balance of hardships tips in the patentee's favor; and (4) the impact of the injunction is in the public interest.

Monetary Damages   The Patent Act requires the court to award monetary damages to a prevailing patentee in an amount "adequate to compensate for the infringement."

---

[12]See, e.g., *Orthokinetics, Inc. v. Safety Travel Chairs, Inc.,* 806 F.2d 1565 (Fed. Cir. 1986).

The preferred measure of damages is the patentee's *lost profits* attributable to the infringement. To recover under this measure of damages, the patentee must demonstrate a reasonable probability that, but for the defendant's infringement, the patentee would have made the sales that the defendant made. Thus, the patentee generally must show: (1) sufficient demand for the patented invention, and (2) an absence of noninfringing substitutes.

For example, suppose that Inventor A has a patent for a telephone answering machine. Several of Inventor A's competitors sell comparable, noninfringing answering machines. Inventor B infringes Inventor A's patent. Inventor A must show that, absent Inventor B's infringement, Inventor B's customers would have bought from Inventor A, not Inventor A's competitors.

Obviously, many patentees find it difficult to meet this standard. In such instances, the patentee may still recover damages in the form of a *reasonable royalty*. This is the amount that a prospective licensee seeking a license to make, use, sell, or import the patented invention would be willing to pay and a reasonable patentee would be willing to accept in an arm's-length transaction at the time of the infringement.

The Patent Act requires the patentee to give *notice* to the public of its patent. Notice is given by putting the word "patented" or the abbreviation "Pat.," along with the patent number, on the items being marketed. If the patentee fails to provide notice, the patentee may still obtain injunctive relief against infringers. However, the patentee will receive monetary damages only if the defendant had specific notice that the defendant was being charged with infringement. In addition, damages will be limited to the infringement that occurred after the defendant received the notice. Thus, patentees should be careful to place the required notice on their goods.

While damages for infringement traditionally have been measured from the date of patent issuance, under the American Inventors Protection Act of 1999, an inventor may collect "reasonable royalties" for infringement that occurred during the period after publication of the application but before issuance of the patent. To take advantage of this remedy, though, the patentee must bring the published application to the infringer's attention.

Attorneys Fees and Treble Damages   Generally, under U.S. law, each side must bear its own legal costs in litigating a case. Thus, even a winning party is ordinarily required to pay for its own attorneys fees. Some statutes, such as the Patent Act, alter this rule by allowing the winning party to recover its legal fees from the losing party. The Patent Act authorizes the court to award *attorneys fees* to the prevailing party in exceptional cases, such as those in which: (1) the patentee has won and there was willful or deliberate infringement by the defendant, or (2) the defendant has won and there was bad faith conduct by the patentee in obtaining the patent or in suing for infringement. A few statutes also provide for increasing the damage award in certain circumstances. Under the Patent Act, the court may award up to *treble damages* to the patentee if the defendant willfully infringed or acted in bad faith.

Filing for Foreign Patents

No single patent protects an invention in every country around the world. Rather, the inventor must obtain a patent in each country in which the inventor wants to protect her intellectual property asset. Because of the expense and effort involved in filing for patent protection, the inventor generally must choose the countries in which patent protection makes the most commercial sense. To a large extent, this is determined by the inventor's assessment of potential markets and potential competitors and depends upon the inventor's plans for future marketing of the product.

The United States adheres to the Convention for the Protection of Industrial Property, more commonly known as the *Paris Convention*.[13] This is a multilateral treaty to which over 170 countries, including most industrialized countries, belong. The key provision of the Paris Convention is that it requires each country to grant "national treatment" to foreign patent applicants. This means that foreign applicants must be treated the same as domestic applicants and cannot be discriminated against. However, the Paris Convention provides little in the way of substantive rights to inventors, and no enforcement mechanisms apply if a member state does not comply with its obligations.

Inventors thus must look to the specific laws of the countries in which they seek patent protection. In general, all countries grant patents to new inventions and give the patentee some sort of limited monopoly in the invention. The length of the patent term varies from country to country, although 20 years is becoming the norm, at least in industrialized countries. Patentable subject matter also varies from country to country. As noted earlier, the United States tends to be more liberal than most countries. An inventor cannot assume that, just because a patent issues in the United States, the same invention is patentable elsewhere. The process of obtaining a patent varies from country to country as well. It is always important that an inventor have, in addition to whatever U.S. legal counsel the inventor may hire, a local legal representative who is familiar with the language, laws, customs, and procedures of the country in which the inventor wants to seek a patent.

U.S. patent law is different from that found in most of the rest of the world in several key respects. First, the United States has a first-to-invent system, not a first-to-file system as exists in virtually every other country around the world. (The United States is considering legislation that would implement a first-to-file system, however.) Second, applications in the United States that are not also filed abroad may be held secret unless and until a patent issues. As we see in Chapter 3, if the PTO denies a patent application that is held secret, the inventor still has the option of treating the invention as a trade secret. In most countries, however, all patent applications are made public, either immediately or within 18 months after filing, making trade secret protection impossible if a patent is not issued. Third, in many countries, the inventor is required to "work" the invention within a certain time period. Some countries also impose "compulsory licensing," in which the inventor is required to license other parties within the country to produce the item at reasonable royalty rates. The United States does not require either "working" or compulsory licensing of inventions.

An inventor wishing to obtain patents in foreign countries can follow one of two paths. First, the inventor can file directly in each country in which the inventor wants patent protection. This process can be expensive, as the inventor must pay filing fees, translation costs, and prosecution costs in each country in which the inventor applies. However, the inventor can target specific countries. Depending upon the nature of the invention, such targeting may be the best business strategy.

Second, the inventor can seek patent protection indirectly through a *convention filing*. The two most widely known conventions are the *European Patent Convention* and the *Patent Cooperation Treaty*. The European Patent Convention permits an inventor to file a single patent application with the European Patent Office. If the patent is granted, patent rights arise in all member countries designated by the inventor in her application.[14]

---

[13]Information on the Convention can be found at www.wipo.int/treaties/en/ip/paris/summary_paris.html

[14]For information on the European Patent Convention, see www.epo.org/patents/law/legal-texts/epc.html

The Patent Cooperation Treaty has over 140 member countries, including the United States.[15] Under this treaty, the inventor can file an international application with one of several specified receiving offices (which include the PTO and the European Patent Office). A patent examination is conducted and the results sent to all member countries designated by the inventor. At that point, the inventor has to hire translators and local attorneys to complete the patent application in each country and has to pay local filing fees.

Using a convention filing tends to be cheaper up front than directly filing in foreign countries, although the registration fees at the end can be very high. Filings can generally be done in English, however, which makes the examination process quicker and cheaper.

Copyright Law

Copyright law gives the owner of a creative work of authorship the right to keep others from using the work without the owner's permission. The purpose of copyright law is similar to that of patent law: to encourage creativity. Specifically, copyright law seeks to encourage creation of works of art, literature, music, and other "works of authorship."

We find the same type of fundamental policy tension in copyright law as in patent law. On the one hand, the law wants to encourage creativity by giving creators exclusive rights in their works through copyright protection. On the other hand, the law wants to foster a competitive marketplace by giving the public the freest possible access to works of authorship and the ideas they express.

Copyright law balances these two interests by limiting the author's property rights to the author's particular method of expressing an idea or information. The author can copyright only the *expression* of an idea and not the idea itself, facts, or information.

This is a key distinction between copyright and patent. Patent law gives the inventor an exclusive monopoly in an invention. In return for that monopoly, patent law imposes very strict substantive standards in the form of rigorous application procedures and standards. Copyright law, on the other hand, gives the author a monopoly in one way of expressing an idea—and even that monopoly is limited, because copyright law does not prohibit independently created works, as does patent law. As a result, the requirements for obtaining a copyright are much less stringent than those for obtaining a patent.

Sources of Copyright Law

Like patent law, the foundation of copyright law is the U.S. Constitution. The first copyright statute was passed in 1790 and underwent several major revisions. The current statute was adopted in 1976 but has been amended numerous times since then. Many of the most recent amendments resulted from the United States joining the *Berne Convention*[16] in 1988 and as a result of the *Trade-Related Aspects of Intellectual Property Rights (TRIPS)*[17] agreement of the Uruguay Round of the General Agreement on Tariffs and Trade (GATT), which was completed in December 1993. The Berne Convention is an 1886 international treaty that standardizes basic copyright protection among its 160-plus member countries.

Prior to the Copyright Act of 1976, the United States had a dual system of copyright. Unpublished works were protected under state common law copyright. Once the works were published, state protection ceased and federal copyright law applied, provided that proper copyright notice was affixed to the works.

---

[15]For information on the Patent Cooperation Treaty, see www.wipo.int/treaties/en/registration/pct/

[16]See www.wipo.int/treaties/en/ip/berne/index.html

[17]See www.wto.org/english/tratop_e/trips_e/trips_e.htm

In the 1976 Copyright Act, Congress provided that federal copyright protection attaches automatically as soon as a work is fixed in tangible form. Thus, federal law now covers unpublished as well as published works. Today, very little, if any, state copyright law survives.

Generally, copyrighted works today are covered by one of three laws, depending upon when the work was copyrighted and the issues involved: (1) the Copyright Act of 1909; (2) the Copyright Act of 1976, as originally enacted; or (3) the Copyright Act of 1976, as amended. Our discussion focuses on the latter category as it is applicable to the most recently copyrighted works.

The U.S. Copyright Office[18] registers copyrights, issues certificates of registration, keeps records of assignments and licenses, and regulates deposit of copyrighted material. It does not engage in the extensive, comprehensive review that the PTO undertakes in a patent application, however. Rather, the Copyright Office looks merely to see if the submitted work falls within a copyrightable subject matter area and whether the formal registration requirements have been met. As we will see below, works do not need to be registered in order to be protected by copyright. Rather, copyright arises automatically once the work is created and fixed in a tangible form. Registration merely provides additional rights to the copyright owner.

Subject Matter of Copyrights

The Copyright Act provides for a long list of works that may be copyrighted, including literary works (which include computer programs, flowcharts, and advertising items such as catalogues, product labels, and directories); musical works; dramatic works; pantomimes and choreographic works; pictorial, graphic, and sculptural works; motion pictures and other audiovisual works; sound recordings; and architectural works. This is not an exclusive list, and the courts can extend copyright protection to new forms of work if the legislative history of the Copyright Act suggests that Congress would have intended to cover those works had it known of them at the time it passed the Act. Thus, the Copyright Act adjusts quite well to advances and changes in technology.

Section 102 of the Copyright Act defines copyrightable subject matter. It states that copyright exists

> in original works of authorship fixed in any tangible medium of expression, now known or later developed, from which they can be perceived, reproduced, or otherwise communicated, either directly or with the aid of a machine or device.

Thus Section 102 contains two important requirements: the work must be: (1) "original" and (2) "fixed" in a tangible medium.

Originality   *Originality* simply means that the author must have created the work herself (as opposed to merely copying from someone else). Copyright law, unlike patent law, does not protect against independent creation. If a second person independently creates an identical form of work, the second person is entitled to a copyright as well as the first (provided there truly is no copying going on).

Originality also requires that the work contain some minimal amount of creativity, although the work does not have to be unique, novel, or of high quality. Thus, even product descriptions or labeling directions can qualify for copyright protection. There must be *some* level of creativity involved, however. For example, a person could not copyright the word "the" because there is no creativity on the part of the purported author. Moreover,

---

[18]The webpage of the Copyright Office can be found at www.copyright.gov

granting such a copyright would remove an important word from common usage and make it difficult, if not impossible, for others to engage in normal expression.

According to a rule issued by the Copyright Office, words and short phrases (such as names, titles, and slogans), listings of ingredients or contents, and familiar symbols or designs are not copyrightable. Some of these things may be protected by trademark law, however, as discussed in Chapter 6.

The U.S. Supreme Court addressed the originality requirement in *Feist Publications, Inc. v. Rural Telephone Service Co.*[19] (see Case Illustration 2.1). The Court's decision that a phone company's compilation of names, addresses, and telephone numbers in its white pages was not entitled to copyright protection caused a great deal of consternation in the business world. Databases are a multibillion-dollar industry in the United States. **Feist** is viewed as leaving the industry with little, if any, protection for these valuable assets. Data itself may not be protected by copyright. Rather, only the selection and

---

CASE ILLUSTRATION 2.1

FEIST PUBLICATIONS, INC. v. RURAL TELEPHONE SERVICE CO., 499 U.S. 340 (1991)

FACTS Rural Telephone Service published a standard telephone directory, with "white pages" listing Rural's subscribers in alphabetical order, and "yellow pages" listing business subscribers by category and offering classified advertisements. Feist Publications, a publishing company specializing in area-wide telephone directories, sought a license to use Rural's white pages listings. When Rural refused permission, Feist used the listings without Rural's consent. Rural sued for copyright infringement, arguing that Feist was not permitted to copy Rural's information, but rather had to obtain the information directly via telephone surveys or door-to-door solicitations of Rural's subscribers. Feist argued that the information that it copied was not protected by copyright law. The lower courts ruled in Rural's favor; Feist appealed.

DECISION The U.S. Supreme Court noted that "[t]his case concerns the interaction of two-well established propositions. The first is that facts are not copyrightable; the other, that compilations of facts generally are." The Court went on to explain:

*The key to resolving the tension lies in understanding why facts are not copyrightable. * * * To qualify for copyright protection, a work must be original to the author. Original, as the term is used in copyright, means only that that the work was independently created by the author (as opposed to copied from other works), and that it possesses at least some*

*minimal degree of creativity. * * * [E]ven a slight amount will suffice. * * * Originality does not signify novelty; a work may be original even though it closely resembles other works as long as the similarity is fortuitous, not the result of copying.*

By contrast, compilations of facts (as opposed to facts themselves) may have sufficient originality to be copyrightable material: "The compilation author typically chooses which facts to include, in what order to place them, and how to arrange the collected data so that they may be used effectively by readers. These choices as to selection and arrangement, so long as they are made independently by the compiler and entail a minimal degree to creativity, are sufficiently original that Congress may protect such compilation through the copyright laws." But, as the Court emphasized, "[i]n no event may copyright extend to the facts themselves."

Here, Feist had copied the names, towns, and telephone numbers of Rural's subscribers. These were merely uncopyrightable facts, however. Moreover, Rural had arranged this information in alphabetical order by last name within its own white pages. This arrangement was not original and creative, but rather "is an age-old practice, firmly rooted in tradition and so commonplace that it has come to be expected as a matter of course." Because Rural's white page listings were not copyrightable material, Feist's copying of those listings was not copyright infringement.

---

[19]499 U.S. 340 (1991).

arrangement of data may be so protected and only then if that selection and arrangement contain sufficient creativity.

Congress has several times considered legislation that would close the gap on the protection of databases caused by **Feist** but no legislation has been enacted. The European Union, by contrast, passed a Database Directive in 1996 that provides for a 15-year protection period for databases created "through substantial investment."[20]

Fixation   The *fixation* requirement prevents works that are not put into a tangible form—such as oral statements or unrecorded, unwritten musical improvisations—from receiving copyright protection. For example, if you hear jazz improvisation, those works are neither copyrighted nor copyrightable unless and until they are written down or recorded. The Copyright Act permits works to be fixed in a wide variety of tangible media, including paper, floppy disks, fabrics, records, tapes, and compact discs.

Rights Provided by Copyright

The Copyright Act sets forth several exclusive *economic rights* that are granted to the copyright owner. Section 106 provides that the author, or the person to whom the author has transferred the copyright, has the exclusive right to do or authorize the following:

1. reproduce the copyrighted work;[21]
2. prepare derivative works based upon the copyrighted work;
3. distribute copies or phonorecords of the copyrighted work to the public;
4. publicly perform certain types of copyrighted works;
5. publicly display certain types of copyrighted works; and,
6. in the case of sound recordings, perform the copyrighted work publicly by means of a digital audio transmission.

In addition to these economic rights, Congress amended the Copyright Act in 1990 to provide for protection of *moral rights*. Many nations, especially civil law nations, view a work of authorship as an extension of the author's personality. These nations grant the author: (1) *the right of attribution* (i.e., the right to prevent others from claiming authorship in the work, the right to be known as the author, and the right to avoid having others' works falsely attributed to an individual); and (2) *the right of integrity* (i.e., the right to prevent others from distorting, mutilating, or misrepresenting the author's work).

The United States traditionally did not recognize the moral rights of attribution and integrity. The Berne Convention requires member countries to provide protection for such rights, however, so the United States amended the Copyright Act so that it would be in compliance with its treaty obligations. Section 106A of the Copyright Act now provides that, in the case of works of visual art (which are narrowly defined as works of fine art but not objects of utility or mass production), the artist (not the copyright owner, who may be a different individual or entity) has the moral rights of attribution and integrity. Specifically, the artist has the right to:

1. claim authorship in the work;
2. prevent the use of her name as the author of any work she did not create;

---

[20]The Directive can be found on the EU Law webpage of the European Union Publications Office, available at http://publications.europa.eu/eur_lex/index_en.htm

[21]This right is subject to certain exceptions. For example, the lawful owner of a copy of a copyrighted computer program may make a backup copy. In addition, public libraries and archives are permitted to copy in many instances that would constitute infringement if done by a private party.

3. prevent the use of her name as the author of the work if the work has been distorted, mutilated, or otherwise modified such that the work would be prejudicial to her honor or reputation;
4. prevent any additional distortion, mutilation, or other modification of her work that would be prejudicial to her honor or reputation; and
5. prevent any intentional or grossly negligent destruction of her work, if the work is of recognized stature.

Ownership of the Copyright

Initially, the copyright is owned by the author of the work. If there are two or more authors, they are considered joint owners of a single copyright in the work. Unless the authors have agreed otherwise, each has an equal ownership share.

The author can transfer some or all of the economic rights in the copyright to others. Transfers of exclusive rights must be made in writing and signed by the author. Transfers of nonexclusive rights may be made through oral agreements. (As a practical matter, however, oral agreements are seldom a wise business practice.)

The exception to the rule that the author is the owner of the copyright involves two categories of works known as *works for hire*. First, when a work is prepared by an employee within the scope of his employment, the employer owns the copyright. Second, when a work is created by an independent contractor, the copyright belongs to the hiring party, provided that: (1) the parties expressly agree in a written, signed agreement that the work will be considered a work for hire, and (2) the work fits within one of nine broad categories listed in Section 101 of the Copyright Act. It can often be difficult to determine whether an individual is an employee or an independent contractor. The Supreme Court addressed this issue in *Community for Creative Non-Violence v. Reid,*[22] in which it set forth the types of factors a court should consider in making this critical determination.

◆ *See Discussion Case 2.3.*

As a practical matter, a firm should always require anyone who creates copyrighted works for it (whether an employee or an independent contractor) to sign an agreement assigning any intellectual property rights that that individual might have in the works to the firm. This topic is discussed in further detail in Chapter 3.

Copyright Procedures

Copyright Creation   As previously noted, copyright arises automatically once an original work is expressed in a tangible form. This distinguishes copyrights from patents, which involve a lengthy and detailed application process.

Although an author need not do anything to obtain a copyright, there are certain steps that the author should take to strengthen the copyright protection he receives under the law. In particular, the author can provide a *copyright notice* on the work and can *register* the work with the Copyright Office.

Copyright Notice   Before 1989, the United States, unlike most of the rest of the world, had very strict requirements regarding the use of copyright notices. If the author failed to place the correct notice on his work, he lost his copyright protection.

Once the United States joined the Berne Convention, however, it was required to redraft its copyright laws in order to meet its treaty obligations. For works published after 1989, U.S. copyright arises automatically and attaches to the work without any formal

---

[22]490 U.S. 730 (1989).

action being required on the part of the author. Thus, the author is not required to register the work or place a copyright notice upon it in order to obtain copyright protection. Nonetheless, it is a good idea for authors to include a copyright notice on their works, as the notice tells the public who owns the copyright in a particular work. In addition, some foreign countries do not protect works that do not contain a copyright notice.

To encourage authors to include notices on their works, the Copyright Act provides a special remedy: where a proper copyright notice has been affixed to a work, a defendant may be barred from claiming an innocent infringement defense to mitigate actual or statutory damages. This defense is discussed in more detail below.

The form of copyright notice required is very simple. For example, an author named Jane Smith who created an original work in 2010 would place one of the following notations on her work:

"Copyright, 2010, Jane Smith" **or**

"Copyr. 2010, Jane Smith" **or**

"© 2010 Jane Smith."

The notice should be placed on the first page or on a visible part of the work or copy.[23]

Deposit and Registration   Under the Copyright Act, the copyright owner of a published or unpublished work may register the work with the Copyright Office at any time. The purpose of this provision is to create a comprehensive record of U.S. copyright claims. The registration procedure is very simple:

1. the copyright owner fills out a very short application form;
2. the copyright owner mails the form and a filing fee ($50 for paper filing; $35 for online filing) to the Copyright Office; and
3. the copyright owner deposits one copy of an unpublished work or two copies of a published work with the Copyright Office.

Copyright application forms and a current fee schedule may be obtained from the Copyright Office's webpage.

The Copyright Office reviews the application only for obvious errors or lack of copyrightable subject matter and then issues a certificate of registration. The process is relatively simple and can be accomplished by most individuals without the assistance of a lawyer.

Prior to adopting the Berne Convention, the United States required all copyright owners to register their works before suing for infringement. However, the Berne Convention prohibits member states from imposing formalities such as registration as a prerequisite to copyright protection. As a result, U.S. law now provides that only authors of works whose country of origin is the United States must register before they can bring suit for infringement. A work's country of origin is the United States if: (1) the work was first published in the United States; (2) the work was simultaneously published in the United States and another country; or (3) if unpublished, the work was created entirely by U.S. authors. Authors of works whose country of origin is another Berne Convention member state need not preregister.

Note that registration need not occur prior to the infringement but, rather, only prior to filing of the lawsuit. If the copyright owner waits to register until after infringement

---

[23]Although in the past it was customary to add the words "all rights reserved" as well in order to obtain complete protection around the world under a specific international copyright treaty, current international agreements have made the phrase unnecessary.

EXHIBIT 2.5 Copyright Duration

PRE-1/1/78 WORKS	POST-1/1/78 WORKS	MORAL RIGHTS IN VISUAL WORKS CREATED AFTER 6/1/91
95 years	Life of Author + 70 years	Life of Author
	Work for Hire: 95 years after first publication or 120 years after creation, whichever expires first	

has occurred, however, she may be barred from receiving certain remedies. This is discussed more below. As a practical matter, then, a copyright owner who wants to ensure that she will have access to the greatest range of potential remedies in the event of an infringement should register her work promptly.

Copyright Duration   Prior to the 1976 Copyright Act, federal copyright protection began when the work was published, assuming proper notice had been affixed. Under the 1976 Copyright Act, copyright protection begins when the work is created and fixed in a tangible medium. Publication or registration is not necessary.

Moreover, Congress has extended copyright terms significantly through the Sonny Bono Copyright Term Extension Act.[24] This Act extended all existing copyrights by 20 years, thus harmonizing U.S. law with European Union law. Copyright duration for pre-1978 copyrighted works is now 95 years. For works created after January 1, 1978, copyrights now generally last for the life of the author plus 70 years. If there are joint authors, the copyright is measured by the life of the last to die plus 70 years. If the work is published anonymously or under a pseudonym or is a work for hire, copyright protection lasts for 95 years after first publication or 120 years after creation, whichever expires first. Moral rights in visual works created after June 1, 1991, last for the life of the author or, in the case of joint authors, for the life of the last to die (see Exhibit 2.5).

Copyright Infringement

Direct Infringement   An individual becomes liable for *direct infringement* if the individual violates any of the exclusive rights of the copyright owner or illegally imports copies of a copyrighted work into the United States. The most common form of violation is an infringement of the copyright owner's exclusive right to reproduce a work.

To prove copyright infringement, the plaintiff generally must show that the defendant's work was: (1) copied from the plaintiff's work, and (2) "substantially similar" to the plaintiff's copyrighted work. The alleged infringer can then attempt to demonstrate one of the defenses discussed later in the chapter.

Copying is usually shown in one of two ways. First, the plaintiff may have direct evidence of the defendant's copying. This is relatively rare, as it requires an eyewitness or documentary evidence showing that the defendant copied or an admission of copying by the defendant. Second, the plaintiff may produce circumstantial evidence that the

---

[24]Pub. L. No. 105-298.

defendant had access to the copyrighted work and that the defendant's work is similar to the plaintiff's work. This is known as the *access plus similarity test*.

◆ *See Discussion Case 2.4.*

Vicarious and Contributory Infringement   With one narrow exception,[25] the Copyright Act does not specifically provide for liability for infringement based on acts committed by another. Nonetheless, the courts have determined that a defendant may be liable for vicarious or contributory infringement (collectively known as *secondary liability*).

Vicarious liability attaches in cases in which the defendant: (1) had the right and ability to supervise the infringing acts of another, and (2) had an obvious and direct financial interest in the exploitation of the copyrighted materials. For example, owners of nightclubs have been held vicariously liable for unauthorized public performances by bands that they had hired, even though they did not direct the bands to engage in infringing behavior.[26]

Contributory infringement occurs when the defendant: (1) knew or had reason to know of someone else's directly infringing activity, and (2) actively participated by inducing, materially contributing to, or furthering that other person's directly infringing acts. As with patent law, however, contributory infringement does not attach in situations in which the products or materials supplied are capable of "substantial noninfringing uses." The Supreme Court clarified this rule in a 1984 decision, *Sony Corp. of Am. v. Universal City Studios*, in which the Court held that the manufacturer of a VCR could not be held liable for contributory infringement even if some (or many) of the users used the product to infringe because the VCR was capable of commercially significant noninfringing uses (such as time-shifting for personal viewing) (see Case Illustration 2.2).

In 2005, the U.S. Supreme Court, in *MGM Studios, Inc. v. Grokster, Ltd.*,[27] again considered secondary liability for copyright infringement, but this time in the more complex context of the Internet and digital technology. Advances in technology make it possible for infringing copies to now be made very rapidly and inexpensively. In *Grokster,* the Supreme Court held that "one who distributes a device with the object of promoting its use to infringe copyright, as shown by clear expression or other affirmative steps taken to foster infringement, is liable for the resulting acts of infringement by third parties."[28]

Corporate officers should be aware that they can be held personally liable for the copyright infringement of their employees even if they had no knowledge of the infringing activities. For example, the courts have held corporate officers vicariously liable in situations in which: (1) the officer personally participated in the actual infringement; (2) the officer derived financial benefit from the infringing activities, either as a major shareholder in the corporation or through some other means such as receiving a percentage of the revenues from the activity giving rise to the infringement; (3) the officer used the corporation as an instrument to carry out a deliberate infringement of copyright; or (4) the officer was the dominant influence in the corporation and determined the policies that resulted in the infringement.[29] A corporate officer who fails to adequately monitor the activities of employees may well find herself personally liable for copyright infringement (see Case Illustration 2.3).

---

[25]This exception involves semiconductor mask works. See 17 U.S.C. § 905(3).

[26]See, e.g., *ITSI T.V. Prods., Inc. v. California Auth. of Racing Fairs,* 785 F. Supp. 854 (E.D. Cal. 1992); *Cass County Music Co. v. Vineyard Country Golf Corp.,* 605 F. Supp. 1536 (D. Mass. 1985).

[27]545 U.S. 913 (2005).

[28]**Id.** at 919.

[29]See *Famous Music Corp. v. Bay State Harness Horse Racing & Breeding Assoc, Inc.,* 423 F. Supp. 341 (D. Mass. 1976), *aff'd,* 554 F.2d 1213 (1ˢᵗ Cir. 1977).

CASE ILLUSTRATION 2.2

SONY CORP. OF AM. v. UNIVERSAL CITY STUDIOS, 464 U.S. 417 (1984)

FACTS Universal City Studios and Walt Disney Productions, which owned the copyrights on a number of television programs broadcast on the public airwaves, sued Sony Corp., the maker of Betamax, a brand of VCR. The plaintiffs alleged that individuals directly infringed upon their copyrights by using Betamaxes to copy some of plaintiffs' copyrighted works that had been aired on commercially sponsored television. Because it would be impossible to find and sue those anonymous people, the plaintiffs sued Sony for con tributory infringement for marketing a product that makes such direct infringement possible. The trial court ruled for Sony. The appellate court reversed and Sony appealed to the U.S. Supreme Court.

DECISION The Supreme Court noted that the Copyright Act does not specifically address liability for acts committed by others, but found that the Act's silence on this issue was not conclusive:

> *The absence of such express language in the copyright statute does not preclude the imposition of*

liability for copyright infringements on certain parties who have not themselves engaged in the infringing activity. For vicarious liability is imposed in virtually all areas of the law, and the concept of contributory infringement is merely a subspecies of the broader problem of identifying the circumstances in which it is just to hold one individual accountable for the actions of another.

While the Court held that the Copyright Act does allow recovery for contributory infringement, it determined that contributory infringement of a copyright does not exist where the item in question has some substantial noninfringing use as well. Betamaxes could be used for home "time shifting" (e.g., recording a broadcast program for private, noncommercial viewing at a later date or time), which the Court found to be a fair use. Because Betamaxes had a substantial non-infringing use, Sony's sale of them did not constitute contributory infringement (even though some purchasers of Betamaxes may have put them to illegal uses).

Defenses to Copyright Infringement

A defendant charged with copyright infringement can raise a number of defenses, including that: (1) the later work was independently created; (2) the use of an earlier work was permitted by statute; or (3) the earlier work was not copyrightable (e.g., because it did not contain sufficient originality (see Case Illustration 2.4).

The most common defense, however, is the *fair use defense.* Because this is an equitable doctrine, it is purposely vague and must be applied on a case-by-case basis, depending upon the facts before the court. Essentially, the defense states that, although technically infringement did occur, it should be excused under the circumstances.

A court evaluating a fair use defense is to consider all of these factors and is not to treat any of them as conclusive. In addition, these factors are not exclusive and a court should consider whatever other factors are relevant under the circumstances before it.

◆ *See Discussion Case 2.5.*

Parodies are a special category of fair use. Parody is considered an important form of social commentary within U.S. society. Because the authors of serious works are unlikely to authorize others to parody their work, the courts have recognized that the fair use doctrine is important in ensuring that parodies will be created.

In determining whether a parody is a fair use, the courts consider: (1) whether the defendant's purpose was at least in part to parody the plaintiff's work; (2) the amount

CASE ILLUSTRATION 2.3

NETBULA, LLC v. CHORDIANT SOFTWARE, INC., 2009 U.S. DIST. LEXIS 25372 (N.D. CAL. MAR. 20, 2009)

FACTS Plaintiffs Dongxiao Yue and Netbula, LLC sued Defendants Chordiant Software, Inc., Steven R. Springsteel, and Derek P. Witte, alleging that Defendants infringed Plaintiffs' copyrights by reproducing copyrighted computer programs.

Plaintiffs sued Springsteel and Witte in their individual capacities for vicarious copyright infringement, alleging that Springsteel, as CEO of Chordiant, had the right and ability to supervise Chordiant's infringing activities and that Witte, as Vice President and General Counsel, had the right and ability to supervise the infringing activity by giving advice to other Chordiant officers and employees and directing others as their superior officer. Each had a compensation package under which they personally profited from Chordiant's profits.

Defendants Springsteel and Witte moved to dismiss the claims against them on the grounds that Plaintiffs failed to state a claim for vicarious copyright infringement.

DECISION The court granted Springsteel's and Witte's motion to dismiss. The court reasoned: "To state a claim for vicarious copyright infringement, a plaintiff must sufficiently allege that a defendant has (1) the right and ability to supervise the infringing conduct and (2) a direct financial interest in the infringing activity. Knowledge of the infringing activity is not a requirement of vicarious liability."

Individual officers of a corporation can be liable for vicarious copyright liability if their actions meet this two-prong test. Here, however, neither prong was met.

First, Plaintiffs failed to adequately allege that that Springsteel and Witte had a direct financial interest in the infringing activity. The court stated:

> The essential aspect of the direct financial benefit inquiry is whether there is "a causal relationship between the infringing activity and any financial benefit a defendant reaps," irrespective of the magnitude of the benefit. There must be an obvious and direct financial interest in the exploitation of copyrighted materials. The mere fact that a defendant is an officer and shareholder of an infringing corporation is "too

attenuated" to show a "'direct' financial interest in the exploitation of copyrighted materials."
>
> * * * However, where a defendant is a high ranking executive with majority ownership, or receives payments directly related to the infringing activity, he can be held vicariously liable.

While Plaintiffs alleged that Springsteel personally owned shares in Chordiant and that both Springsteel and Witte were compensated in part based on Chordiant's performance, Plaintiffs did not allege "a direct relationship between [Springsteel's and Witte's] compensation and Chordiant's acts of primary infringement." Thus, Plaintiffs did not adequately plead that Springsteel and Witte had a *direct* financial interest that was causally related to Chordiant's alleged direct infringement.

Second, Plaintiffs failed to adequately allege that Springsteel and Witte had the right and ability to supervise the alleged infringement:

> Vicarious copyright liability—even of corporate officers—does not require knowledge that the conduct is infringing. Corporate officers, shareholders and employees have the right and ability to supervise a corporation's infringing activities when they are "a moving active conscious force behind the corporation's infringement." However, a plaintiff must allege more than an officer's mere right and ability to supervise the corporation's conduct generally. A plaintiff must allege that the defendant had supervisory power over the infringing conduct itself.

Here, Plaintiffs' allegations against Springsteel and Witte were directed against their general ability to supervise arising from their respective corporate positions, and was not directed toward any particular oversight or participation that either individual had in the allegedly infringing conduct.

The court thus dismissed Plaintiffs' complaint against Springsteel and Witte "with leave to amend" (thus giving Plaintiffs the opportunity to cure the defects in their allegations and file a new complaint against the individual officers).

CASE ILLUSTRATION 2.4

TODD v. MONTANA SILVERSMITHS, INC.,
379 F. SUPP. 2D 1110 (D. COLO. 2005)

FACTS Plaintiff Kathleen Todd designed, manufactured, and sold "western-themed" jewelry, as did Defendant Montana Silversmiths. Todd created a barbed-wire style bracelet and a set of matching earrings. She filed for and received copyright registrations on these items.

After Montana Silversmiths began selling similar bracelets and earrings, Todd filed suit for copyright infringement. Montana Silversmiths moved for summary judgment, arguing that Todd's jewelry lacked sufficient originality to be the subject matter of a valid copyright.

DECISION The court granted Montana Silversmith's motion for summary judgment.

The court first set forth the general legal rules governing the dispute:

> *To prove copyright infringement, Plaintiff must show that: (1) she held a valid copyright, and (2) that Defendants copied protectable elements in her work. Possession of a copyright registration certificate creates a presumption of validity, although that presumption is rebuttable. Defendants may rebut the presumption ... by presenting evidence which casts doubt on the copyrightability of the work in question.*

The court further explained, "[f]or an item to be copyrighted, it must exhibit some form of originality. * * * Novelty is not required for originality, but the author must have made some contribution to the work which is irreducibly his own." In addition:

> *Copyright protection only extends to expression, never the underlying idea. Even an item that possesses a valid copyright may contain both protectable and unprotectable types of expression. The former consists of the author's original creative contributions, while the latter consists of (among other things): purely functional elements, public domain elements, scenes a faire, forms of expression which are inextricably linked to the underlying idea, and simple changes of medium.*

The court found that Todd's barbed-wire jewelry lacked sufficient originality to be copyrightable subject matter: "While Plaintiff is no doubt a skilled artist capable of making jewelry with a certain aesthetic appeal, she has failed to show what copyrightable feature(s) she has added to her work to separate it from ordinary public domain barbed-wire. * * * [F]or all her aesthetic choices, the final arrangement of the elements in her jewelry still corresponds to the arrangement of public domain barbed-wire." As the court explained: "when dealing with items derived from the public domain, a work is copyrightable only if the creator has added "some substantial, not merely trivial, originality." Thus, Todd did not hold a valid copyright and Montana Silversmiths was not liable for copyright infringement.

of the copyrighted material taken; and (3) the effect of the parody on the plaintiff's market (including the effect on the market for derivative works). The Supreme Court addressed these issues in a 1994 case, *Campbell v. Acuff-Rose Music, Inc.* (see Case Illustration 2.5).

Remedies for Copyright Infringement

Copyright law, like patent law, provides for two basic forms of remedies: (1) injunctions and (2) monetary damages. The Copyright Act also allows infringing materials to be impounded and destroyed under certain circumstances.

Injunctions   Preliminary and permanent injunctions are available against both copyright infringement and violation of moral rights.

Impoundment   Under Section 503 of the Copyright Act, the court may impound allegedly infringing materials prior to judgment and may destroy them if a final judgment is entered against the defendant.

CASE ILLUSTRATION 2.5

CAMPBELL v. ACUFF-ROSE MUSIC, INC.,
510 U.S. 569 (1994)

FACTS 2 Live Crew, a popular rap music group, released a parody of Roy Orbison's rock ballad, "Oh, Pretty Woman." Acuff-Rose Music, Inc., which held the copyright to Orbison's song, sued for copyright infringement. 2 Live Crew defended on the grounds that its parodic use was a fair use under § 107 of the Copyright Act. The District Court granted summary judgment to 2 Live Crew. The Court of Appeals reversed. 2 Live Crew appealed to the U.S. Supreme Court.

DECISION The Supreme Court reversed the decision of the Court of Appeals. The Court noted first that 2 Live Crew's song would clearly infringe Acuff-Rose's rights absent a finding of fair use through parody.

The Court examined the role of § 107's four-factor test in fair use cases:

> It is uncontested that 2 Live Crew's song would be an infringement of Acuff-Rose's rights in "Oh, Pretty Woman" but for a finding of fair use through parody. The task [of evaluating fair use] is not to be simplified with bright-line rules, for [Section 107] calls for case-by-case analysis. Nor may the four statutory factors be treated in isolation, one from another. All are to be explored, and the results weighed together, in light of the purposes of copyright.

The Court thus found that the appellate court had erred in treating the first factor, the purpose and character of the use, as determinative. Although 2 Live Crew's use was commercial, the commercial character of the use is but one factor to consider under § 107.

The Court then stated that the second factor, "the nature of the copyrighted work," is "not much help in this case, or ever likely to help much in separating the fair use sheep from the infringing goats in a parody case, since parodies almost invariably copy publicly known, expressive works."

The third factor, which "asks whether 'the amount and substantiality of the portion used in relation to the copyrighted work as a whole,' are reasonable in relation to the purpose of the copying," looks not only to the quantity of the material copied from the original, but to its quality and importance as well. This factor requires careful application in a parody case. As the Court noted:

> Parody's humor, or in any event its comment, necessarily springs from recognizable allusion to its

> object through distorted imitation. Its art lies in the tension between a known original and its parodic twin. When parody takes aim at a particular original work, the parody must be able to "conjure up" at least enough of that original to make the object of its critical wit recognizable. What makes for this recognition is quotation of the original's most distinctive or memorable features, which the parodist can be sure the audience will know. Once enough has been taken to assure identification, how much more is reasonable will depend, say, on the extent to which the song's overriding purpose and character is to parody the original or, in contrast, the likelihood that the parody may serve as a market substitute for the original. But using some characteristic features cannot be avoided.

The fourth fair use factor examines "the effect of the use upon the potential market for or value of the copyrighted work." Under this factor, the court must consider not only harm to the market for the original work but also harm to the market for derivative works.

Parody can affect market demand in ways that do not violate the Copyright Act. The Court stated:

> [A]s to parody pure and simple, it is more likely that the new work will not affect the market for the original in a way cognizable under this factor, that is, by acting as a substitute for it. This is so because the parody and the original usually serve different market functions.
>
> We do not, of course, suggest that a parody may not harm the market at all, but when a lethal parody, like a scathing theater review, kills demand for the original, it does not produce a harm cognizable under the Copyright Act. Because "parody might quite legitimately aim at garroting the original, destroying it commercially as well as artistically," the role of the courts is to distinguish between "biting criticism [that merely] suppresses demand [and] copyright infringement[, which] usurps it."

Because 2 Live Crew's parody was also rap music, the lower court should have considered the impact of the parodic rap song on the market for a nonparodic rap version of "Oh, Pretty Woman." Thus, the Supreme Court remanded the case to the lower court for further proceedings.

Monetary Damages   Section 504 of the Copyright Act gives the copyright owner the choice of recovering either: (1) actual damages and any additional profits of the infringer or (2) statutory damages.

The plaintiff can recover any actual damages she incurred as a result of the defendant's actions, plus any of the defendant's profits attributable to the infringement that are not taken into account in calculating actual damages. Actual damages are usually measured by either: (1) the *lost sales* that the plaintiff suffered as a result of the defendant's infringement, or (2) the *reasonable royalty* that the plaintiff would have received had the defendant purchased a license to carry out its infringing activities.

In situations in which it is too difficult to prove actual damages, the plaintiff may elect instead to receive statutory damages, provided that the copyright owner registered the work within the proper time frame (i.e., before infringement occurred for unpublished works or within three months after first publication for published works). Statutory damages are set by the court and must be between $750 and $30,000. If the defendant willfully infringed, the court may increase the statutory damages up to $150,000. If the defendant can show that its infringement was innocent (i.e., that it did not know and had no reason to think that it was infringing), the court may reduce the statutory damages to not less than $200. However, the defendant may not use this defense if a proper copyright notice appeared on the copy of the work to which the defendant had access.

Attorneys Fees and Costs   Section 505 of the Copyright Act provides that the court, in its discretion, may award costs to either side if the opposing side acted in bad faith. In addition, prevailing parties may receive attorneys' fees, although copyright owners who failed to register their works in a timely manner are barred from this relief.

Criminal Penalties   Section 506 of the Copyright Act also allows for criminal penalties for willful infringement: (1) for commercial advantage or private financial gain or (2) "by the reproduction or distribution, including by electronic means, during any 180-day period, of 1 or more copies or phonorecords of 1 or more copyrighted works, which have a total retail value of more than $1,000." The Act provides for fines and imprisonment for up to 10 years, depending upon the nature of the offense (e.g., how many copies were made or whether it was a first offense), as well as forfeiture and destruction of the infringing works and all equipment used to produce them. Section 506 also provides for criminal sanctions (of fines of up to $2,500) for fraudulent copyright notice, fraudulent removal of copyright notice, and false representations in applications for copyright registrations. Criminal sanctions are not provided for violations of moral rights, however.

PRO-IP Act of 2008   A new federal statute, The Prioritizing Resources and Organization for Intellectual Property Act of 2008 (PRO-IP Act),[30] seeks to improve federal enforcement of intellectual property rights by increasing penalties for violating U.S. copyright and trademark rights and by allowing trademark and copyright owners to respond to infringements faster. The Act enhances existing forfeiture penalties by providing that property subject to forfeiture includes not only the infringing goods, but also the property used to facilitate the infringement and property derived from proceeds directly or indirectly obtained as result of infringement.

Copyright Law on the Internet

The Internet, with its ability to enable millions of people to instantaneously access, reproduce, and disseminate information, including copyrighted material, is having a significant impact on copyright law. While the Internet makes distribution of copyrighted

---

[30]Pub. Law 110-403.

works much easier and cheaper, it also makes it far more difficult for a copyright owner to protect its copyright and prevent piracy of its works. Commentators are currently debating whether copyright law will, or should, survive the Internet. Some argue for the free and unhindered flow of information; others maintain that individuals who engage in creative endeavors should continue to be rewarded for their efforts through the use of copyrights. This debate is a complex and highly controversial one and is beyond the scope of this book. Several types of webpage-related activities, such as linking, framing, and the use of metatags, can have very real effects upon businesses and their marketing activities. These topics also implicate trademark law and so are addressed in Chapter 6.

Several new technologies are available to assist businesses in identifying and halting copyright and/or trademark infringement on the Internet. In particular, several providers now offer online business intelligence services that use specialized software to track trademark and copyright infringement, counterfeited goods, and bootlegged videos and music.

International Copyright Law Issues

There is no "international copyright" that automatically protects a work around the world. Copyright protection within a specific country depends upon the laws of that country. The United Nations' World Intellectual Property Organization (WIPO) has been working to harmonize national copyright laws, and there is a substantial amount of international cooperation in this area. Nonetheless, some countries provide little or no copyright protection to foreign works, and foreign piracy of copyrighted works can be hard to combat.

There are two principal international copyright conventions: (1) the Berne Union for the Protection of Literary and Artistic Property (*Berne Convention*), initiated in 1886,[31] and (2) *the Universal Copyright Convention* of 1952 (UCC).[32] The United States was initially a member of the UCC and became a signatory of the Berne Convention in 1989. Even if a work is not protected under one of these two conventions, it may be protected by a bilateral agreement between the United States and the other country or under the other country's national laws.

International copyright issues are particularly relevant to copyrighted materials appearing on the Internet. While the Internet is global in reach, copyright law is inherently national. The Berne Convention provides some protection in this area, however, because it states that member countries must provide at least the same protection to citizens of other member countries as they do to their own. In addition, once copyright protection is obtained in one Berne Convention country, it is automatic in all other member countries as well. The Berne Convention has few substantive restrictions and weak enforcement provisions, however. Its only enforcement mechanisms are nonmandatory provisions for the seizure of infringing materials.

Generally, an author should check to see what protection is available for foreign authors in each country in which the author wants copyright protection. The author should do this before the work is published anywhere because in some countries copyright protection depends upon the facts existing at the time of first publication, regardless of where that publication occurred.

In 2008, global software piracy alone was estimated to exceed $50 billion.[33] Obviously, international intellectual property piracy is a major concern for companies and managers. Although there are practical steps a company can take to protect its intellectual property, companies are often limited to seeking remedies for such piracy in the country

---

[31]See www.wipo.org.int/treaties/en/ip/berne/index.html

[32]The text of The Universal Copyright Convention can be found on the website of The United Nations Educational, Scientific and Cultural Organization, http://portal.unesco.org/

[33]See http://global.bsa.org/globalpiracy2008/studies/globalpiracy2008.pdf

or countries where such activities are taking place. These countries may not have copyright protections equivalent to those of the United States. In addition, pursuing these remedies in distant lands may prove too time-consuming, difficult, and/or expensive for many companies. As a result, much international intellectual property piracy goes on unhindered.

If pirated goods that violate U.S. patents, copyrights, mask works, trade secrets, or trademarks are being imported, the injured party can file a complaint with the International Trade Commission (ITC) under Section 337 of the U.S. Tariff Act. If the ITC determines that the imported goods do violate U.S. intellectual property rights, it can direct the U.S. Customs Service to prevent importation of the infringing goods. Section 337 does not provide for monetary damages to injured intellectual property owners, however.

If the piracy is occurring completely overseas—for example, a foreign company is making bootlegged copies of copyrighted books or films and is selling them in foreign markets—the aggrieved copyright owner often finds it difficult to obtain a meaningful remedy. At the governmental level, the U.S. government can bring pressure to bear upon countries in which piracy is rampant. Thus, companies and industry groups can lobby the United States Trade Representative (USTR) for trade sanctions against countries that fail to take effective action against intellectual property piracy within their jurisdictions. Similarly, the U.S. government can (and has) opposed membership in the World Trade Organization (WTO) by countries who fail to adequately protect intellectual property.

At the firm level, intellectual property owners faced with international piracy can directly pursue certain types of measures abroad. For example, some foreign countries have censorship offices that may require a marketer to demonstrate title to a copyrighted work before the marketer can obtain a license to sell the product. Some countries also require duplication licenses for copyrighted works. For example, in China, the central government requires that all copies have a certification sticker.

DISCUSSION CASES

2.1 Patent Law—Patentable Subject Matter

Diamond v. Chakrabarty, 447 U.S. 303 (1980)

OPINION: MR. CHIEF JUSTICE BURGER We granted certiorari to determine whether a live, human-made micro-organism is patentable subject matter under 35 U.S.C. §101.

I

In 1972, respondent Chakrabarty, a microbiologist, filed a patent application, assigned to the General Electric Co. The application asserted 36 claims related to Chakrabarty's invention of "a bacterium from the genus *Pseudomonas* ...." This human-made, genetically engineered bacterium is capable of breaking down multiple components of crude oil. Because of this property, which is possessed by no naturally occurring bacteria, Chakrabarty's invention is believed to have significant value for the treatment of oil spills.

Chakrabarty's patent claims were of three types: first, process claims for the method of producing the bacteria; second, claims for an inoculum comprised of a carrier material floating on water, such as straw, and the new bacteria; and third, claims to the bacteria themselves. The patent examiner allowed the claims falling into the first two categories, but rejected claims for the bacteria. His decision rested on two grounds: (1) that micro-organisms are "products of nature," and (2) that as living things they are not patentable subject matter under 35 U.S.C. § 101.

* * *

[Chakrabarty appealed to the Patent Office Board of Appeals, which affirmed the patent examiner's decision. Chakrabarty then appealed to the Court of Customs and Patent Appeals, which reversed. (Today, the appeal would go to the CAFC.) The Commissioner of Patents and Trademarks appealed to the Supreme Court.]

II

The Constitution grants Congress broad power to legislate to "promote the Progress of Science and useful Arts, by securing for limited Times to Authors and Inventors the exclusive Right to their respective Writings and Discoveries." Art. I, § 8, cl. 8. The patent laws promote this progress by offering inventors exclusive rights for a limited period as an incentive for their inventiveness and research efforts. * * *

The question before us in this case is a narrow one of statutory interpretation requiring us to construe 35 U.S.C. § 101, which provides:

> Whoever invents or discovers any new and useful process, machine, manufacture, or composition of matter, or any new and useful improvement thereof, may obtain a patent therefore, subject to the conditions and requirements of this title.

Specifically, we must determine whether respondent's micro-organism constitutes a "manufacture" or "composition of matter" within the meaning of the statute.

III

In cases of statutory construction we begin, of course, with the language of the statute. And "unless otherwise defined, words will be interpreted as taking their ordinary, contemporary, common meaning." We have also cautioned that courts "should not read into the patent laws limitations and conditions which the legislature has not expressed." * * * In choosing such expansive terms as "manufacture" and "composition of matter," modified by the comprehensive "any," Congress plainly contemplated that the patent laws would be given wide scope.

The relevant legislative history also supports a broad construction. The Patent Act of 1793, authored by Thomas Jefferson, defined statutory subject matter as "any new and useful art, machine, manufacture, or composition of matter, or any new or useful improvement [thereof]." * * * Subsequent patent statutes in 1836, 1870, and 1874 employed this same broad language. In 1952, when the patent laws were recodified, Congress replaced the word "art" with "process," but otherwise left Jefferson's language intact. The Committee Reports accompanying the 1952 Act inform us that Congress intended statutory subject matter to "include anything under the sun that is made by man."

This is not to suggest that § 101 has no limits or that it embraces every discovery. The laws of nature, physical phenomena, and abstract ideas have been held not patentable. Thus, a new mineral discovered in the earth or a new plant found in the wild is not patentable subject matter. Likewise, Einstein could not patent his celebrated law that $E = mc^2$; nor could Newton have patented the law of gravity. Such discoveries are "manifestations of … nature, free to all men and reserved exclusively to none."

Judged in this light, respondent's micro-organism plainly qualifies as patentable subject matter. His claim is not to a hitherto unknown natural phenomenon, but to a non-naturally occurring manufacture or composition of matter—a product of human ingenuity "having a distinctive name, character [and] use." * * * [T]he patentee has produced a new bacterium with markedly different characteristics from any found in nature and one having the potential for significant utility. His discovery is not nature's handiwork, but his own; accordingly it is patentable subject matter under § 101.

IV

* * *

B

The [petitioner argues] that micro-organisms cannot qualify as patentable subject matter until Congress expressly authorizes such protection. His position rests on the fact that genetic technology was unforeseen when Congress enacted § 101. From this it is argued that resolution of the patentability of inventions such as respondent's should be left to Congress. The legislative process, the petitioner argues, is best equipped to weigh the competing economic, social, and scientific considerations involved and to determine whether living organisms produced by genetic engineering should receive patent protection. * * *

It is, of course, correct that Congress, not the courts, must define the limits of patentability; but it is equally true that once Congress has spoken it is "the province and duty of the judicial department to say what the law is." Congress has performed its constitutional role in defining patentable subject matter in § 101; we perform ours in construing the language Congress has employed. In so doing, our obligation is to take statutes as we find them, guided, if ambiguity appears, by the legislative history and statutory purpose. Here, we perceive no ambiguity. The subject-matter provisions of the patent law have been cast in broad terms to fulfill the constitutional and statutory goal of promoting "the Progress of Science and the useful Arts" with all that means for the social and economic benefits envisioned by Jefferson. Broad general language is not necessarily ambiguous when congressional objectives require broad terms.

* * *

To buttress his argument, the petitioner … points to grave risks that may be generated by research endeavors such as respondent's. The briefs present a gruesome parade of horribles. Scientists, among them Nobel laureates, are quoted suggesting that genetic research may pose a serious threat to the human race, or, at the very least, that the dangers are far too substantial to permit such research to proceed apace at this time. We are told that genetic research and related technological developments may spread pollution and disease, that it may result in a loss of genetic diversity, and that its practice may tend to depreciate the value of human life. * * *

It is argued that this Court should weigh these potential hazards in considering whether respondent's invention is patentable subject matter under § 101. We disagree. The grant or denial of patents on microorganisms is not likely to put an end to genetic research or to its attendant risks. * * *

What is more important is that we are without competence to entertain these arguments—either to brush them aside as fantasies generated by fear of the unknown, or to act on them. The choice we are urged to make is a matter of high policy for resolution within the legislative process after the kind of investigation, examination, and study that legislative bodies can provide and courts cannot. That process involves the balancing of competing values and interests, which in our democratic system is the business of elected representatives. Whatever their validity, the contentions now pressed on us should be addressed to the political branches of the Government, the Congress and the Executive, and not to the courts.

* * * Our task, rather, is the narrow one of determining what Congress meant by the words it used in the statute; once that is done our powers are exhausted. Congress is free to amend § 101 so as to exclude from patent protection organisms produced by genetic engineering. Or it may choose to craft a statute specifically designed for such living things. But, until Congress takes such action, this Court must construe the language of § 101 as it is. The language of that section fairly embraces respondent's invention.

Accordingly, the judgment of the Court of Customs and Patent Appeals is affirmed.

QUESTIONS FOR DISCUSSION FOR CASE 2.1

1. What are the limits of patentable subject matter?
2. What are the relative roles of the courts and the legislature in making and interpreting law?
3. What steps does a court take when it engages in statutory interpretation? What sources does it look to in determining what a statute means?

2.2 Patents—Novelty, On-Sale Bar

Pfaff v. Wells Electronics, Inc., 525 U.S. 55 (1988)

OPINION: JUSTICE STEVENS delivered the opinion of the Court.

Section 102(b) of the Patent Act of 1952 provides that no person is entitled to patent an "invention" that has been "on sale" more than one year before filing a patent application.[1] We granted certiorari to determine whether the commercial marketing of a newly invented product may mark the beginning of the 10-year period even though the invention has not yet been reduced to practice.[2]

I

On April 19, 1982, petitioner, Wayne Pfaff, filed an application for a patent on a computer chip socket. Therefore, April 19, 1981, constitutes the critical date

---

[1]"A person shall be entitled to a patent unless— …

"(b) the invention was patented or described in a printed publication in this or a foreign country or in public use or on sale in this country, more than one year prior to the date of the application for patent in the United States, …."

35 U.S.C. § 102.

[2]"A process is reduced to practice when it is successfully performed. A machine is reduced to practice when it is assembled, adjusted and used. A manufacture is reduced to practice when it is completely manufactured. A composition of matter is reduced to practice when it is completely composed."

for purposes of the on-sale bar of 35 U.S.C. § 102(b); if the 1-year period began to run before that date, Pfaff lost his right to patent his invention.

Pfaff commenced work on the socket in November 1980, when representatives of Texas Instruments asked him to develop a new device for mounting and removing semiconductor chip carriers. In response to this request, he prepared detailed engineering drawings that described the design, the dimensions, and the materials to be used in making the socket. Pfaff sent those drawings to a manufacturer in February or March 1981.

Prior to March 17, 1981, Pfaff showed a sketch of his concept to representatives of Texas Instruments. On April 8, 1981, they provided Pfaff with a written confirmation of a previously placed oral purchase order for 30,100 of his new sockets for a total price of $91,155. In accord with his normal practice, Pfaff did not make and test a prototype of the new device before offering to sell it in commercial quantities.

The manufacturer took several months to develop the customized tooling necessary to produce the device, and Pfaff did not fill the order until July 1981. The evidence therefore indicates that Pfaff first reduced his invention to practice in the summer of 1981. The socket achieved substantial commercial success before Patent No. 4,491,377 (the '377 patent) issued to Pfaff on January 1, 1985.[4]

After the patent issued, petitioner brought an infringement action against respondent, Wells Electronics, Inc., the manufacturer of a competing socket. Wells prevailed on the basis of a finding of no infringement. When respondent began to market a modified device, petitioner brought this suit, alleging that the modifications infringed six of the claims in the '377 patent.

[The District Court found that four of Pfaff's six patent claims were valid, and that three of the four were infringed by Wells' device. The District Court rejected Wells' § 102(b) on-sale defense on the basis that Pfaff had filed his patent application less than one year after reducing his invention to practice. On appeal, the CAFC reversed, finding that as long as the invention is "substantially complete at the time of sale," the one-year period of 102(b) begins to run and the four patent claims at issue were thus invalid.]

---

[4]Initial sales of the patented device were:

    1981 $350,000

    1982 $937,000

    1983 $2,800,000

    1984 $3,430,000

* * *

Because other courts have held or assumed that an invention cannot be "on sale" within the meaning of § 102(b) unless and until it has been reduced to practice, and because the text of § 102(b) makes no reference to "substantial completion" of an invention, we granted certiorari.

II

The primary meaning of the word "invention" in the Patent Act unquestionably refers to the inventor's conception rather than to a physical embodiment of that idea. The statute does not contain any express requirement that an invention must be reduced to practice before it can be patented. * * *

* * *

It is well settled that an invention may be patented before it is reduced to practice. In 1888, this Court upheld a patent issued to Alexander Graham Bell even though he had filed his application before constructing a working telephone. Chief Justice Waite's reasoning in that case [The Telephone Cases] merits quoting at length:

It is quite true that when Bell applied for his patent he had never actually transmitted telegraphically spoken words so that they could be distinctly heard and understood at the receiving end of his line, but in his specification he did describe accurately and with admirable clearness his process, that is to say, the exact electrical condition that must be created to accomplish his purpose, and he also described, with sufficient precision to enable one of ordinary skill in such matters to make it, a form of apparatus which, if used in the way pointed out, would produce the required effect, receive the words, and carry them to and deliver them at the appointed place. * * * A good mechanic of proper skill in matters of the kind can take the patent and, by following the specification strictly, can, without more, construct an apparatus which, when used in the way pointed out, will do all that it is claimed the method or process will do ….

The law does not require that a discoverer or inventor, in order to get a patent for a process, must have succeeded in bringing his art to the highest degree of perfection. It is enough if he describes his method with sufficient clearness and precision to enable those skilled in the matter to understand what the process is, and if he points out some practicable way of putting it into operation.

When we apply the reasoning of *The Telephone Cases* to the facts of the case before us today, it is evident that Pfaff could have obtained a patent on his novel socket when he accepted the purchase order from Texas Instruments for 30,100 units. At that time he provided the manufacturer with a description and drawings that had "sufficient clearness and precision to enable those skilled in the matter" to produce the device. * * *

III

* * *

As we have often explained, … the patent system represents a carefully crafted bargain that encourages both the creation and the public disclosure of new and useful advances in technology, in return for an exclusive monopoly for a limited period of time. The balance between the interest in motivating innovation and enlightenment by rewarding invention with patent protection on the one hand, and the interest in avoiding monopolies that unnecessarily stifle competition on the other, has been a feature of the federal patent laws since their inception. * * *

We originally held that an inventor loses his right to a patent if he puts his invention into public use before filing a patent application. * * * A similar reluctance to allow an inventor to remove existing knowledge from public use undergirds the on-sale bar.

Nevertheless, an inventor who seeks to perfect his discovery may conduct extensive testing without losing his right to obtain a patent for his invention—even if such testing occurs in the public eye. The law has long recognized the distinction between inventions put to experimental use and products sold commercially. * * *

* * *

We conclude … that the on-sale bar applies when two conditions are satisfied before the critical date. First, the product must be the subject of a commercial offer for sale. An inventor can both understand and control the timing of the first commercial marketing of his invention. * * * In this case the acceptance of the purchase order prior to April 8, 1981, makes it clear that such an offer had been made, and there is no question that the sale was commercial rather than experimental in character.

Second, the invention must be ready for patenting. That condition may be satisfied in at least two ways: by proof of reduction to practice before the critical date; or by proof that prior to the critical date the inventor had prepared drawings or other descriptions of the invention that were sufficiently specific to enable a person skilled in the art to practice the invention. In this case the second condition of the on-sale bar is satisfied because the drawings Pfaff sent to the manufacturer before the critical date fully disclosed the invention.

The evidence in this case thus fulfills the two essential conditions of the on-sale bar. * * *

* * * When Pfaff accepted the purchase order for his new sockets prior to April 8, 1981, his invention was ready for patenting. The fact that the manufacturer was able to produce the socket using his detailed drawings and specifications demonstrates this fact. Furthermore, those sockets contained all the elements of the invention claimed in the '377 patent. Therefore, Pfaff's '377 patent is invalid because the invention had been on sale for more than one year in this country before he filed his patent application. Accordingly, the judgment of the Court of Appeals is affirmed.

QUESTIONS FOR DISCUSSION FOR CASE 2.2

1. At what point in time could Pfaff have applied for a patent on his invention?
2. What rule does the Supreme Court set forth for determining when the on-sale bar applies?
3. What could Pfaff have done differently in order to avoid this outcome?

2.3 Copyright—Work for Hire

Community for Creative Non-Violence v. Reid, 490 U.S. 730 (1989)

OPINION: MARSHALL, J. In this case, an artist and the organization that hired him to produce a sculpture contest the ownership of the copyright in that work. To resolve this dispute, we must construe the "work made for hire" provisions of the Copyright Act of 1976 and in particular, the provision in § 101, which defines as a "work made for hire" a "work prepared by an employee within the scope of his or her employment."

I

Petitioners are the Community for Creative Nonviolence (CCNV), a nonprofit unincorporated association dedicated to eliminating homelessness in America, and Mitch Snyder, a member and trustee of CCNV In the fall of 1985, CCNV decided to participate in the annual Christmastime Pageant of Peace in Washington, D.C., by sponsoring a display to dramatize the plight of the homeless. As the District Court recounted:

> Snyder and fellow CCNV members conceived the idea for the nature of the display: a sculpture of a modern Nativity scene in which, in lieu of the traditional Holy Family, the two adult figures and the infant would appear as contemporary homeless people huddled on a streetside steam grate. The family was to be black (most of the homeless in Washington being black); the figures were to be life-sized, and the steam grate would be positioned atop a platform "pedestal," or base, within which special-effects equipment would be enclosed to emit simulated "steam" through the grid to swirl about the figures. They also settled upon a title for the work—"Third World America"—and a legend for the pedestal: "and still there is no room at the inn."

Snyder made inquiries to locate an artist to produce the sculpture. He was referred to respondent James Earl Reid …. In the course of two telephone calls, Reid agreed to sculpt the three human figures. CCNV agreed to make the steam grate and pedestal for the statue. * * * Reid … suggested, and Snyder agreed, that the sculpture would be made of a material known as "Design Cast 62," a synthetic substance that could meet CCNV's monetary and time constraints, could be tinted to resemble bronze, and could withstand the elements. The parties agreed that the project would cost no more than $15,000, not including Reid's services, which he offered to donate. The parties did not sign a written agreement. Neither party mentioned copyright.

After Reid received an advance of $3,000, he made several sketches of figures in various poses. At Snyder's request, Reid sent CCNV a sketch of a proposed sculpture showing the family in a crechelike setting: the mother seated, cradling a baby in her lap; the father standing behind her, bending over her shoulder to touch the baby's foot. Reid testified that Snyder asked for the sketch to use in raising funds for the sculpture. Snyder testified that it was also for his approval. Reid sought a black family to serve as a model for the sculpture. Upon Snyder's suggestion, Reid visited a family living at CCNV's Washington shelter but decided that only their newly born child was a suitable model. While Reid was in Washington, Snyder took him to see homeless people living on the streets. Snyder pointed out that they tended to recline on steam grates, rather than sit or stand, in order to warm their bodies. From that time on, Reid's sketches contained only reclining figures.

Throughout November and the first two weeks of December 1985, Reid worked exclusively on the statue, assisted at various times by a dozen different people who were paid with funds provided in installments by CCNV. On a number of occasions, CCNV members visited Reid to check on his progress and to coordinate CCNV's construction of the base. CCNV rejected Reid's proposal to use suitcases or shopping bags to hold the family's personal belongings, insisting instead on a shopping cart. Reid and CCNV members did not discuss copyright ownership on any of these visits.

On December 24, 1985, … Reid delivered the completed statue to Washington. There it was joined to the steam grate and pedestal prepared by CCNV and placed on display near the site of the pageant. Snyder paid Reid the final installment of the $15,000. The statue remained on display for a month. In late January 1986, CCNV members returned it to Reid's studio in Baltimore for minor repairs. Several weeks later, Snyder began making plans to take the statue on a tour of several cities to raise money for the homeless. Reid objected, contending that the Design Cast 62 material was not strong enough to withstand the ambitious itinerary He urged CCNV to cast the statue in bronze at a cost of $35,000, or to create a master mold at a cost of $5,000. Snyder declined to spend more of CCNV's money on the project.

In March 1986, Snyder asked Reid to return the sculpture. Reid refused. He then filed a certificate of copyright registration for "Third World America" in his name and announced plans to take the sculpture on a more modest tour than the one CCNV had proposed. Snyder, acting in his capacity as CCNV's trustee, immediately filed a competing certificate of copyright registration.

Snyder and CCNV then commenced this action…, seeking return of the sculpture and a determination of copyright ownership. The District Court granted a preliminary injunction, ordering the sculpture's return. After a 2-day bench trial, the District Court declared that "Third World America" was a "work made for hire" under § 101 of the Copyright Act and that Snyder, as trustee for CCNV, was the exclusive owner of the copyright in the sculpture. The court reasoned that

Reid had been an "employee" of CCNV within the meaning of § 101(1) because CCNV was the motivating force in the statue's production. Snyder and other CCNV members, the court explained, "conceived the idea of a contemporary Nativity scene to contrast with the national celebration of the season," and "directed enough of [Reid's] effort to assure that, in the end, he had produced what they, not he, wanted."

The Court of Appeals … reversed and remanded, holding that Reid owned the copyright because "Third World America" was not a work for hire. * * *

We granted certiorari to resolve a conflict among the Courts of Appeals over the proper construction of the "work made for hire" provisions of the Act. We now affirm.

II

A

The Copyright Act of 1976 provides that copyright ownership "vests initially in the author or authors of the work." As a general rule, the author is the party who actually creates the work, that is, the person who translates an idea into a fixed, tangible expression entitled to copyright protection. The Act carves out an important exception, however, for "works made for hire." If the work is for hire, "the employer or other person for whom the work was prepared is considered the author" and owns the copyright, unless there is a written agreement to the contrary. * * *

Section 101 of the 1976 Act provides that a work is "for hire" under two sets of circumstances:

(1) a work prepared by an employee within the scope of his or her employment; or

(2) a work specially ordered or commissioned for use as a contribution to a collective work, as a part of a motion picture or other audiovisual work, as a translation, as a supplementary work, as a compilation, as an instructional text, as a test, as answer material for a test, or as an atlas, if the parties expressly agree in a written instrument signed by them that the work shall be considered a work made for hire.

Petitioners do not claim that the statue satisfies the terms of § 101(2). Quite clearly, it does not. Sculpture does not fit within any of the nine categories of "specially ordered or commissioned" works enumerated in that subsection, and no written agreement between the parties establishes "Third World America" as a work for hire.

The dispositive inquiry in this case therefore is whether "Third World America" is "a work prepared by an employee within the scope of his or her employment" under § 101(1). * * *

* * *

* * * To determine whether a work is for hire under the Act, a court first should ascertain, using principles of general common law of agency, whether the work was prepared by an employee or an independent contractor. After making this determination, the court can apply the appropriate subsection of § 101.

B

* * * In determining whether a hired party is an employee under the general common law of agency, we consider the hiring party's right to control the manner and means by which the product is accomplished. Among the other factors relevant to this inquiry are the skill required; the source of the instrumentalities and tools; the location of the work; the duration of the relationship between the parties; whether the hiring party has the right to assign additional projects to the hired party; the extent of the hired party's discretion over when and how long to work; the method of payment; the hired party's role in hiring and paying assistants; whether the work is part of the regular business of the hiring party; whether the hiring party is in business; the provision of employee benefits; and the tax treatment of the hired party. No one of these factors is determinative.

Examining the circumstances of this case in light of these factors, we agree with the Court of Appeals that Reid was not an employee of CCNV but an independent contractor. True, CCNV members directed enough of Reid's work to ensure that he produced a sculpture that met their specifications. But the extent of control the hiring party exercises over the details of the product is not dispositive. Indeed, all the other circumstances weigh heavily against finding an employment relationship. Reid is a sculptor, a skilled occupation. Reid supplied his own tools. He worked in his own studio in Baltimore, making daily supervision of his activities from Washington practically impossible. Reid was retained for less than two months, a relatively short period of time. During and after this time, CCNV had no right to assign additional projects to Reid. Apart from the deadline for completing the sculpture, Reid had absolute freedom to decide when and how long to work. CCNV paid Reid $15,000, a sum dependent on "completion of a specific job, a method by which independent contractors are often compensated." Reid had total discretion in hiring and paying assistants. "Creating sculptures was hardly 'regular business' for CCNV." Indeed, CCNV is not a business at all. Finally, CCNV did not pay payroll or Social Security taxes, provide any employee benefits, or contribute to unemployment insurance or workers' compensation funds.

* * * Thus, CCNV is not the author of "Third World America" by virtue of the work for hire provisions of the Act. * * * However, … CCNV nevertheless may be a joint author of the sculpture if, on remand, the District Court determines that CCNV and Reid prepared the work "with the intention that their contributions be merged into inseparable or interdependent parts of a unitary whole." In that case, CCNV and Reid would be co-owners of the copyright in the work.

For the aforestated reasons, we affirm the judgment of the Court of Appeals ….

QUESTIONS FOR DISCUSSION FOR CASE 2.3

1. Was Reid an independent contractor or an employee? What "test" did the Court apply in deciding this issue?
2. What is the legal effect of classifying Reid as an independent contractor or an employee for purposes of the Copyright Act?
3. What issue did the Court remand to the trial court for further determination?

2.4 Copyright—Infringement, Copyrightable Subject Matter

JCW Investments, Inc. v. Novelty, Inc., 482 F.3d 910 (7th Cir. 2007)

Meet Pull My Finger® Fred. He is a white, middle-aged, overweight man with black hair and a receding hairline, sitting in an armchair wearing a white tank top and blue pants. Fred is a plush doll and when one squeezes Fred's extended finger on his right hand, he farts. He also makes somewhat crude, somewhat funny statements about the bodily noises he emits, such as "Did somebody step on a duck?" or "Silent but deadly."

Fartman could be Fred's twin. Fartman, also a plush doll, is a white, middle-aged, overweight man with black hair and a receding hairline, sitting in an armchair wearing a white tank top and blue pants. Fartman (as his name suggests) also farts when one squeezes his extended finger; he too cracks jokes about the bodily function. Two of Fartman's seven jokes are the same as two of the 10 spoken by Fred. Needless to say, Tekky Toys, which manufactures Fred, was not happy when Novelty, Inc., began producing Fartman, nor about Novelty's production of a farting Santa doll sold under the name Pull-My-Finger Santa.

Tekky sued for copyright infringement, trademark infringement, and unfair competition and eventually won on all claims. The district court awarded $116,000 based on lost profits resulting from the copyright infringement, $125,000 in lost profits attributable to trademark infringement, and $50,000 in punitive damages based on state unfair competition law. The district court then awarded Tekky $575,099.82 in attorneys' fees. * * * [W]e affirm.

I

Somewhat to our surprise, it turns out that there is a niche market for farting dolls, and it is quite lucrative. Tekky Toys, an Illinois corporation, designs and sells a whole line of them. Fred was just the beginning. Fred's creators, Jamie Wirt and Geoff Bevington, began working on Fred in 1997, and had a finished doll in 1999. They applied for a copyright registration on Fred as a "plush toy with sound," and received a certificate of copyright on February 5, 2001; later, they assigned the certificate to Tekky. In the meantime, Tekky sent out its first Fred dolls to distributors in 1999. By the time this case arose, in addition to Fred, Tekky's line of farting plush toys had expanded to Pull My Finger® Frankie (Fred's blonde, motorcycle-riding cousin), Santa, Freddy Jr., count Fartula (purple, like the Count on Sesame Street), and Fat Bastard (character licensed from New Line Cinema's "Austin Powers" movies), among others. By March 2004, Tekky had sold more than 400,000 farting dolls.

Novelty, a privately held Indiana corporation, is owned by Todd Green, its president. Green testified in his deposition, "any time we'd create an item, okay, we try to copy—or try to think of some relevant ideas." Novelty personnel go to trade shows and take pictures of other companies' products, seeking "ideas" for their own. In early 2001, Green visited the Hong Kong showroom of TL toys, a manufacturer of Tekky's Fred doll, and he spotted Fred. In his deposition, Green testified that he might have photographed Fred since "[i]t wouldn't be unusual for us to photograph everything we see." Green admits that his idea for Fartman was based on Fred and that he described his idea to Mary Burkhart, Novelty's art director, who prepared a drawing based on Green's description. According to Burkhart, Green wanted "a plush doll that would … fart and shake …. And make a sound … a hillbilly-type guy, sitting in a chair that would fart and be activated by actually pulling his finger." Typically, Novelty would assign the job of drawing a new product to an artist, such as Burkhart, and the artist would then take her drawing to Green for his approval. That was the procedure it followed for Fartman. Novelty began to manufacture plush farting dolls around October 8, 2001; the first doll it released was the one it called Pull-My-Finger Santa. Fartman hit the stores one month later, on November 5, 2001.

Tekky first learned of Fartman in March 2002; three months later it filed this suit. In September 2002, the district court granted a preliminary injunction, halting Novelty's sales of Fartman and his smaller relative Fartboy. [Tekky won at trial, and Novelty filed this appeal.] * * *

II

A

We begin with the district court's finding that Novelty violated Tekky's copyright when it created Fartman. * * *

To establish copyright infringement, one must prove two elements: "(1) ownership of a valid copyright, and (2) copying of constituent elements of the work that are original." What is required for copyright protection is "some minimal degree of creativity," or "the existence of … intellectual production, of thought, and conception." Generally, copyright protection begins at the moment of creation of "original works of authorship fixed in any tangible medium of expression," including "pictorial, graphic, and sculptural" works and sound recordings. A work is "fixed" in a tangible medium of expression "when its embodiment in a copy … is sufficiently permanent or stable to permit it to be perceived, reproduced, or otherwise communicated for a period of more than transitory duration." The owner of a copyright, may obtain a certificate of copyright, which is "*prima facie* evidence" of its validity.

Once it is established that a party has a valid copyright, whether registered or not, the next question is whether another person has copied the protected work.

Copying may be proven by direct evidence, but that is often hard to come by. In the alternative, copying may be inferred "where the defendant had access to the copyrighted work and the accused work is substantially similar to the copyrighted work." It is not essential to prove access, however. If the "two works are so similar as to make it highly probable that the later one is a copy of the earlier one, the issue of access need not be addressed separately, since if the later work was a copy its creator must have had access to the original." "The more a work is both like an already copyrighted work *and*—for this is equally important—unlike anything that is in the public domain, the less likely it is to be an independent creation." If the inference of copying is drawn from proof of access and substantial similarity, it can be rebutted if the alleged copier can show that she instead "independently created" the allegedly infringing work. "A defendant independently created a work if it created its own work without copying anything or if it copied something other than the plaintiff's copyrighted work."

Novelty contends that the district court protected too much of Tekky's toy—not just the expression but the idea or common elements known as *scenes a faire,* which we defined in [an earlier case] as "incidents, characters or settings which are as a practical matter indispensable or at least standard, in the treatment of a given topic." Novelty also takes issue with the district court's finding that it had access to Fred, that Burkhart copied rather than independently created Fartman, and that Fred and Fartman were substantially similar. As we explain below, we are unpersuaded. Tekky had a valid copyright in Fred, Novelty (the company) indisputably did have access to Fred, and the two dolls are so similar that the inference of copying even without access is irresistible.

Novelty does not argue that Tekky lacks a valid copyright in Fred or that Fred is so lacking in creativity that a copyright could not attach. Indeed, Fred is a far cry from a noncreative compilation of facts such as the telephone book in [*Feist Publications, Inc. v. Rural Telephone Service Co.,* 499 U.S. 340 (1991)]. Here, we have a creative doll and a valid copyright registration. There is no doubt that there is a valid copyright. How much creativity Fred reflects and what ideas he embodies (as opposed to the way he expresses those ideas) merely help us to decide whether we can infer copying from substantial similarity.

It is notable that Green, Novelty's president, admits that he saw and perhaps photographed Fred, and that Fred gave him the idea for Fartman. While Burkhart denies having seen Fred or even a picture of him, she drew the model for Fartman at Green's direction. Moreover, Fred was already on the market in the United States at the time Fartman was created. In *Moore v. Columbia Pictures Industries, Inc.,* 972 F.2d 939, 942 (8th Cir. 1991), the Eighth Circuit found that a "reasonable possibility of access can be established under the 'corporate receipt doctrine,'" under which:

> if the defendant is a corporation, the fact that one employee of the corporation has possession of plaintiff's work should warrant a finding that another employee (who composed defendant's work) had access to plaintiff's work, where by reason of the physical propinquity between the employees the latter has the opportunity to view the work in the possession of the former.

In this case, Novelty's president saw Fred, directed that the artist draw a figure that looks like Fred, and from that drawing approved the manufacture of Fartman. On those facts, the corporate receipt doctrine may just be icing on the cake; the fact that Green directed Burkhart as she created the drawing, rather than taking pencil in hand and sketching it himself, is immaterial. Novelty plainly had access to Fred and used that access in the manufacture of Fartman.

Even if access existed, Tekky had to show substantial similarity between the two items in order to support an inference of copying. The test for substantial similarity is an objective one. We look at the dolls themselves to determine substantial similarity…. The … similarities between Fred and Fartman go far beyond the fact that both are plush dolls of middle-aged men sitting in armchairs that fart and tell jokes. Both have crooked smiles that show their teeth, balding heads with a fringe of black hair, a rather large protruding nose, blue pants that are identical colors, and white tank tops. On the other hand, Fartman has his name emblazoned in red across his chest, his shoes are a different color from Fred's, as is his chair, and Fartman wears a hat. In the end, despite the small cosmetic differences, the two dolls give off more than a similar air. The problem is not that both Fred and Fartman have black hair or white tank tops or any other single detail; the problem is that execution and combination of features on both dolls would lead an objective observer to think they were the same. We conclude that no objective person would find these dolls to be more than minimally distinguishable. To the contrary, they are substantially similar. That, in combination with Green's access, compels an inference of copying. Indeed, the dolls are so similar that an inference of copying could be drawn even without the evidence of access.

Novelty contends that rather than copy, it merely made a similar doll based on the same comic archetype, that of "a typical man wearing jeans and a T-shirt in a chair doing the 'pull my finger' joke." That, Novelty argues, is the idea, not the expression, and the reason that the two dolls are similar is they are both based on that idea. The district court found that Novelty tried to shoehorn too much into the "idea" and that the only idea here is that of a "plush doll that makes a farting sound and articulates jokes when its finger is activated." As the district court put it:

> Fred—a smiling, black-haired balding Caucasian male, wearing a white tank top and blue pants, reclining in a green armchair, who makes a farting sound, vibrates and utters phrases such as "Did somebody step on a duck?" and "Silent but deadly" after the protruding finger on his right hand is pinched—is plaintiff's expression of that idea.

It is, of course, a fundamental tenet of copyright law that the idea is not protected, but the original expression of the idea is. Although it is not always easy to distinguish idea from expression, by the same token the task is not always hard. Novelty urges that the similarity of the two dolls reflects the fact that Fred himself is only minimally creative, representing a combination of elements that were in the public domain or were *scenes a faire.* The problem with this argument is that the very combination of these elements as well as the expression that is Fred himself are creative.

Novelty wants us to take the entity that is Fred, subtract each element that it contends is common, and then consider whether Novelty copied whatever leftover components are creative. But this ignores the fact that the details–such as the appearance of Fred's face or even his chair–represent creative expression. It is not the idea of a farting, crude man that is protected, but this particular embodiment of that concept. Novelty could have created another plush doll of a middle-aged farting man that would seem nothing like Fred. He could, for example, have a blond mullet and wear flannel, have a nose that is drawn on rather than protruding substantially from the rest of the head, be standing rather than ensconced in an armchair, and be wearing shorts rather than blue pants. To see how easy this could be, one need look no further than Tekky's Frankie doll, which is also a plush doll, but differs in numerous details: he is not sitting, and he has blond hair, a tattoo, and a red-and-white striped tank. Frankie is not a copy of Fred. Fartman is. We have no trouble concluding that the district court properly granted partial summary judgment to Tekky on the issue of liability for copyright infringement.

* * *

We AFFIRM the judgment of the district court.

QUESTIONS FOR DISCUSSION FOR CASE 2.4

1. Why is a plush doll copyrightable subject matter?

2. What is the "idea" behind Fred? What is the "expression" of that idea? How are these concepts relevant to the inquiry into whether Novelty infringed on Tekky's copyright in Fred?

3. Was it necessary for Tekky to prove that Novelty had access to Fred? Why or why not? Was it necessary for Tekky to prove substantial similarity between Fartman and Fred? Why or why not?

4. What is the "corporate receipt" doctrine? How does it apply in this case?

2.5 Copyright—Fair Use

A.V. v. iParadigms, LLC, 562 F.3d 630 (4th Cir. 2009)

Plaintiffs brought this copyright infringement action against defendant iParadigms, LC, based on its use of essays and other papers written by plaintiffs for submission to their high school teachers through an online plagiarism detection service operated by iParadigms. * * * The district court granted summary judgment in favor of iParadigms on plaintiffs' copyright infringement claim based on the doctrine of fair use. * * *

* * * We affirm the grant of summary judgment on the plaintiffs' copyright infringement claim ....

I.

Defendant iParadigms owns and operates "Turnitin Plagiarism Detection Service," an online technology system designed to "evaluate[ ] the originality of written works in order to prevent plagiarism." According to iParadigms, Turnitin offers high school and college educators an automated means of verifying that written works submitted by students are originals and not the products of plagiarism. When a school subscribes to iParadigms' service, it typically requires its students to submit their written assignments "via a web-based system available at *www.turnitin.com* or via an integration between Turnitin and a school's course management system." * * *

After a student submits a writing assignment, Turnitin performs a digital comparison of the student's work with content available on the Internet, including "student papers previously submitted to Turnitin, and commercial databases of journal articles and periodicals." For each work submitted, Turnitin creates an "Originality Report" suggesting a percentage of the work, if any, that appears not to be original. The

assigning professor may, based on the results of the Originality Report, further explore any potential issues.

The Turnitin system gives participating schools the option of "archiving" the student works. When this option is selected, Turnitin digitally stores the written works submitted by students "so that the work becomes part of the database used by Turnitin to evaluate the originality of other student's works in the future." The archived student works are stored as digital code, and employees of iParadigms do not read or review the archived works.

* * *

When they initiated the lawsuit, the four plaintiffs were minor high school students [enrolled at two different schools] .... According to the complaint, both schools required students to submit their written assignments via Turnitin.com to receive credit; failure to do so would result in a grade of "zero" for the assignment under the policy of both schools.

* * *

Plaintiffs filed a complaint alleging that iParadigms infringed their copyright interests in their works by archiving them in the Turnitin database without their permission. The district court granted summary judgment to iParadigms .... * * *

[T]he court determined that iParadigms' use of each of the plaintiffs' written submissions qualified as a "fair use" under 17 U.S.C. § 107 and, therefore, did not constitute infringement. In particular, the court found that the use was transformative because its purpose was to prevent plagiarism by comparative use, and that iParadigms' use of the student works did not impair the market value for high school term papers and other such student works.

* * *

II. Plaintiffs' Appeal

* * * The owner of a copyright enjoys "a bundle of exclusive rights" under section 106 of the Copyright Act, including the right to copy, the right to publish and the right to distribute an author's work. These rights "vest in the author of an original work from the time of its creation." "'Anyone who violates any of the exclusive rights of the copyright owner,' that is, anyone who trespasses into his exclusive domain by using or authorizing the use of the copyrighted work … 'is an infringer of the copyright.'"

The ownership rights created by the Copyright Act, however, are not absolute; these rights, while exclusive, are "limited in that a copyright does not secure an exclusive right to the use of facts, ideas, or other knowledge." Rather, copyright protection extends only to the author's manner of expression.

Moreover, the copyright owner's rights are subject to several exceptions enumerated by the Copyright Act. * * *

One of these statutory exceptions codifies the common-law "fair use" doctrine, which "allows the public to use not only facts and ideas contained in a copyrighted work, but also expression itself in certain circumstances." "From the infancy of copyright protection, some opportunity for fair use of copyrighted materials has been thought necessary to fulfill copyright's very purpose, '[t]o promote the Progress of Science and useful Arts ….'" Courts have traditionally regarded "fair use" of a copyrighted work as "a privilege in others than the owner of the copyright to use the copyrighted material in a reasonable manner without his consent."

* * *

Section 107 provides that "the fair use of a copyrighted work … for purposes such as criticism, comment, news reporting, teaching (including multiple copies for classroom use), scholarship, or research, is not an infringement of copyright." Congress provided four nonexclusive factors for courts to consider in making a "fair use" determination:

(1) the purpose and character of the use, including whether such use is of a commercial nature or is for nonprofit educational purposes;

(2) the nature of the copyrighted work;
(3) the amount and substantiality of the portion used in relation to the copyrighted work as a whole; and
(4) the effect of the use upon the potential market for or value of the copyrighted work.

Section 107 contemplates that the question of whether a given use of copyrighted material is "fair" requires a case-by-case analysis in which the statutory factors are not "treated in isolation" but are "weighed together, in light of the purposes of copyright."

With these general principles in mind, we consider each of the statutory factors.

First Factor

The first fair use factor requires us to consider "the purpose and character of the use, including whether such use is of a commercial nature or is for nonprofit educational purposes." A use of the copyrighted material that has a commercial purpose "tends to weigh against a finding of fair use." "The crux of the profit/nonprofit distinction is not whether the sole motive of the use is monetary gain but whether the user stands to profit from exploitation of the copyrighted material without paying the customary price."

In assessing the "character" of the use, we should consider the specific examples set forth in section 107's preamble, "looking to whether the use is for criticism, or comment, or news reporting, and the like," with the goal of determining whether the use at issue "merely supersedes the objects of the original creation, or instead adds something new, with a further purpose or different character." Courts, therefore, must examine "whether and to what extent the new work is transformative …. [T]he more transformative the new work, the less will be the significance of other factors, like commercialism, that may weigh against a finding of fair use. A "transformative" use is one that "employ[s] the quoted matter in a different manner or a different purpose from the original," thus transforming it.

In considering the character and purpose of iParadigms' use of the student works, the district court focused on the question of whether the use was transformative in nature. The court concluded that "iParadigms, through Turnitin, uses the papers for an entirely different purpose, namely, to prevent plagiarism and protect the students' written works from plagiarism … by archiving the students' works as digital code." Although the district court recognized that iParadigms intends to profit from its use of the student works, the court found that iParadigms' use of plaintiffs' works was "highly transformative," and "provides a substantial public benefit through the network of educational institutions using Turnitin." Accordingly, the court concluded that the first factor weighed in favor of a finding of fair use.

Plaintiffs argue the district court's analysis contained several flaws. First, they suggest that the district court ignored the commercial nature of iParadigms' use of their materials, highlighting the fact that iParadigms is a for-profit company that enjoys millions of revenue dollars based on its ever-increasing database of student works. * * *

* * * [T]he fact that the disputed use of copyrighted material is commercial is not determinative in and of itself. * * * [A]lthough a commercial use finding generally weighs against a finding of fair use, it must "be weighed along with [the] other factors in fair use decisions."

In this case, the district court determined that the commercial aspect was not significant in light of the transformative nature of iParadigms' use. The district court simply weighed the commercial nature of iParadigms' use along with other fair use factors, as is appropriate under Supreme Court precedent.

Plaintiffs also argue that iParadigms' use of their works cannot be transformative because the archiving process does not *add* anything to the work—Turnitin merely stores the work unaltered and in its entirety. This argument is clearly misguided. The use of a copyrighted work need not alter or augment the work to be transformative in nature. Rather, it can be transformative in function or purpose without altering or actually adding to the original work. iParadigms' use of plaintiffs' works had an entirely different function and purpose than the original works; the fact that there was no substantive alteration to the works does not preclude the use from being transformative in nature.

* * *

The district court, in our view, correctly determined that the archiving of plaintiffs' papers was transformative and favored a finding of "fair use." iParadigms' use of these works was completely unrelated to expressive content and was instead aimed at detecting and discouraging plagiarism.

Second Factor

In considering the nature of the copyrighted work, the Supreme Court has instructed that "fair use is more likely to be found in factual works than in fictional works," whereas "a use is less likely to be deemed fair when the copyrighted work is a creative product." This postulate recognizes the notion that a work is entitled to greater copyright protection as it comes closer to "the core of creative expression." However, if the disputed use of the copyrighted work "is not related to its mode of expression but rather to its historical facts," then the creative nature of the work is mitigated. And, in fact, the district court concluded that iParadigms' use of the plaintiffs' works "relate[d] solely to the comparative value of the works" and did not "diminish[ ] the incentive for creativity on the part of students." The district court noted that, if anything, iParadigms' use of the students' works fostered the development of original and creative works "by detecting any efforts at plagiarism by other students."

* * *

Plaintiffs contend that the district court's consideration of the "nature of the copyrighted works" factor was flawed for a second reason: the district court ignored the fact that the works in question were works of fiction and poetry, which are considered "highly creative" in nature and deserving of the strongest protection. * * * Rather than ignore it, however, the district court simply concluded that even if the plaintiffs' works were highly creative in nature, iParadigms' use of the plaintiffs' works was not related to the creative core of the works. * * * iParadigms' use of the works in the case—as part of a digitized database from which to compare the similarity of typewritten characters used in other student works—is likewise unrelated to any creative component. Thus, we find no fault in the district court's application of the second fair use factor.

Third Factor

The third fair use factor requires us to consider "the amount and substantiality of the portion used in relation to the copyrighted work as a whole." Generally speaking, "as the amount of the copyrighted material that is used increases, the likelihood that the use will constitute a 'fair use' decreases." But this statutory factor also requires courts to consider, in addition to quantity, the "quality and importance" of the copyrighted materials used, that is, whether the portion of the copyrighted material was "the heart of the copyrighted work." Although "[c]opying an entire work weighs against finding a fair use, ... it does not *preclude* a finding of fair use"; therefore, "[t]he extent of permissible copying varies with the purpose and character of the use."

The district court found that this factor, like the second factor, did not favor either party. The court concluded that although iParadigms uses substantially the whole of plaintiffs' works, iParadigms' "use of the original works is limited in purpose and scope" as a digitized record for electronic "comparison purposes only." * * *

* * *

* * * We find no error in the district court's analysis.

Fourth Factor

Finally, § 107 directs us to examine the market of the copyrighted work to determine "the effect of the use upon the potential market for or value of the copyrighted work." The Supreme Court described this factor as the "single most important element of fair use," considering that a primary goal of copyright is to ensure that "authors [have] the opportunity to realize rewards in order to encourage them to create." By contrast, "a use that has no demonstrable effect upon the potential market for, or the value of, the copyrighted work need not be prohibited in order to protect the author's incentive to create."

Our task is to determine whether the defendants' use of plaintiffs' works "would materially impair the marketability of the work[s] and whether it would act as a market substitute" for them. We focus here not upon "whether the secondary use suppresses or even destroys the market for the original work or its potential derivatives, but [upon] whether the secondary use *usurps the market of the original work.*" An adverse market effect, in and of itself, does not preclude application of the fair use defense. "The fair use doctrine protects against a republication which offers the copyrighted work in a secondary packaging, where potential customers, having read the secondary work, will no longer be inclined to purchase again something they have already read."

The analysis of whether the disputed use offers a market substitute for the original work overlaps to some extent with the question of whether the use was transformative. To the extent this issue arises in fair use cases, it often does so when the secondary use at issue involves a scholarly critique or parody of the original work.

But regardless of whether the defendant used the original work to critique or parody it, the transformative nature of the use is relevant to the market effect factor.

* * *

* * * The district court considered the potential market effects suggested by plaintiffs but concluded that plaintiffs' arguments were theoretical and speculative. Plaintiffs' most plausible theory was that iParadigms' archiving of their papers impaired the sale of the papers to high school students in the market for unpublished term papers, essays and the like. Undoubtedly, there is a market for students who wish to purchase such works and submit them as their own for academic credit. And, iParadigms' archiving of such papers on the Turnitin website might well impair the marketability of such works to student buyers intending to submit works they did not author without being identified as plagiarists.

As noted by the district court, however, the plaintiffs testified that they would not sell the works at issue here to any dealer in such a market because such a transaction would make them party to cheating and would encourage plagiarism. Furthermore, to the extent that iParadigms' use would adversely affect plaintiffs' works in this particular market, we must consider the transformative nature of the use. Clearly no market substitute was created by iParadigms, whose archived student works do not supplant the plaintiffs' works in the "paper mill" market so much as merely suppress demand for them, by keeping record of the fact that such works had been previously submitted. In our view, then, any harm here is not of the kind protected against by copyright law.

In sum, we conclude, viewing the evidence in the light most favorable to the plaintiffs, that iParadigms' use of the student works was "fair use" under the Copyright Act and that iParadigms was therefore entitled to summary judgment on the copyright infringement claim.

* * *

QUESTIONS FOR DISCUSSION FOR CASE 2.5

1. What is the test for evaluating whether a defendant's actions constitute "fair use" under copyright law? Is that test found in the Copyright Act or in case law?
2. Why does the court state in the last paragraph that it "view[s] the evidence in the light most favorable to the plaintiffs"?
3. The court seems to say that turnitin.com affects only the market for unethical uses of the papers submitted (e.g., resale to other students or a "paper mill"). Can you think of any legitimate uses of student papers that would be impeded by this service?

DISCUSSION QUESTIONS

1. Which of the following would receive patent or copyright law protection?
   a. A method of manufacturing cereal that enables the product to remain fresh longer after the box has been opened.
   b. Nike's slogan: "Just do it."
   c. A new theory involving market segmentation strategies.
   d. Common seaweed when manipulated in particular ways that render it an effective drug for several types of illnesses.
   e. A new, nonfunctional shape for a flashlight.
   f. A new, functional shape for a flashlight.
2. Seiko Epson Corp. sued Nu-Kote International, alleging that Nu-Kote had infringed on its design patent for ink cartridges for printers. The district court held that Seiko Epson's design patent was invalid because: (1) the cartridge is not visible after its installation and during use and thus its design was "not a matter of concern to consumers," and (2) the design is not aesthetically pleasing. Is the district court's reasoning correct? What are the requirements for a valid design patent?
3. Rotec Industries is the assignee of the '291 patent for a crane conveyor belt system used to carry concrete over long distances for construction projects such as river dams. The defendants, a group of corporations including Mitsubishi Corp., signed an agreement with the Chinese government to provide a crane conveyor belt system for its Three Gorges Dam project. Rotec alleged that the defendants were offering to sell a conveyor system that infringed upon its '291 patent.

   Rotec sued for patent infringement. The evidence at trial showed: (1) the agreement among the defendants called for all of the conveyor components to be made in Japan and China; (2) no components were made in the United States; (3) the bid proposal, including the description of the product and the proposed price, was finalized in Hong Kong and presented in China; (4) all negotiations with the Chinese government prior to signing the agreement took place in China; and (5) the agreement was signed in China. How should the court rule on Rotec's claim and why?
4. Chung filed for a design patent for a cigarette packet that allowed the cigarettes to be pulled out of the packet lengthwise rather than by their ends. In explaining the reason for his design, Chung stated: "I was motivated … to design a new cigarette package … when I … happened to see … workers pull out cigarettes from the packages holding their filter-tip top with dirty fingers during work to smoke them. Some even used their teeth to pull them out so as not to contaminate the filter-tip end with dirty fingers, and some others tore open the bottom part of the package to take out cigarettes from the bottom."

   Does Chung's invention satisfy the requirements for a design patent? Why or why not?
5. Konrad invented a system that allowed a computer user to access and search a database residing on a remote computer. He filed for a patent on January 8, 1993, which ultimately issued.

   In 2000, Konrad filed a patent infringement suit against 39 entities, arguing that they had infringed his patent. The defendants moved for summary judgment, arguing that prototypes of the invention were in public use or on sale prior to January 8, 1992.

   Konrad had demonstrated his system to University of California computing personnel in 1991. During these demonstrations, Konrad would turn on his system and let people try it out. These individuals were not told to keep the information confidential nor were they required to sign a confidentiality requirement. Konrad did not keep records of these demonstrations, nor did he solicit feedback from the users.

   Konrad contended that the 1991 demonstrations were experimental uses for the purposes of obtaining technical information for upgrades and refining the invention. Konrad testified that the purpose of the demonstrations was to convince the University of California computing services people that there was a "viable project." He also testified that he hoped the demonstrations would make the university personnel more supportive of his project; ultimately, he was seeking outside endorsements of his invention.

Is Konrad's patent invalid under Section 102(b)?

6. Jeffrey Mendler, a professional photographer, signed a licensing agreement with Winterland Production, Ltd., a manufacturer of screen-printed apparel, that allowed Winterland to use several photographs that Mendler had taken of the America's Cup yacht race as "guides, models, and examples, for illustrations to be used on screenprinted T-shirts or other sportswear." Several years later, Mendler discovered that Winterland had put out a line of T-shirts that displayed a digitally altered version of the image from one of Mendler's photographs. Winterland had scanned Mendler's photograph and had flipped the image horizontally, had reconstructed the missing tip of a sail that had been cut off in the original photograph, and had altered the colors of the sky somewhat.

Mendler complained that the licensing agreement did not authorize such a use and that Winterland had infringed upon his copyright. Winterland argued that the changes that it had made had altered the image on the T-shirt from a photograph to an illustration based on a photograph. The parties agree that the license did not authorize Winterland to use photographic reproductions of Mendler's work but only to use the photographs as a "guide, model, or example" to achieve an end result that was an "illustration" and not a photographic reproduction. What must a plaintiff show to establish copyright infringement? Has infringement occurred here?

7. Fashion Victim, Inc., sells a T-shirt called Skeleton Woopee with a fanciful design depicting skeletons engaging in sexual activity in seven different positions. Skeleton Woopee is Fashion's best-selling product. Fashion sold 55,000 shirts since the shirts' introduction in 1990. In 1992, Sunrise Turquoise, Inc., featured a shirt in its catalogue that was very similar to the Skeleton Woopee T-shirt. Fashion Victim sued Sunrise for copyright infringement. At trial, the evidence indicated that Sunrise had heard of the idea of a T-shirt depicting skeletons in sexual positions from a potential customer but had not seen or directly copied the Skeleton Woopee shirt. Should Sunrise be held liable for copyright infringement? Why or why not?

8. When Universal City Studios, Inc., and Amblin' Entertainment, Inc., were producing the movie *How to Make an American Quilt,* they contracted with Barbara Brown, a well-known professional quilter. Brown agreed to design patterns for 15 quilt blocks for $50 per block. One of these designs was known as the Wedding Block. Under the contract, Brown was to retain the copyright to the designs, but Universal was authorized to use the design to create two copies of a prop quilt (known as the "The Life Before" quilt) for the movie.

In designing a second quilt for the movie, Universal's technical consultant, Patricia McCormick, created a block design known as the Marriage Block. Both McCormick's Marriage Block and Brown's Wedding Block depict a scene with a black bird flying over a man and a woman holding hands. In the Marriage Block, however, the crow points downward, while the crow in the Wedding Block points upward. In addition, the Marriage Block includes a figure of the sun, but the Wedding Block does not. McCormick later wrote a book in which she stated: "I made [the Marriage Block] by using the pattern Barbara Brown had designed for … The Life Before quilt …. The block in this quilt is a duplication of the … block in The Life Before quilt."

Brown sued for copyright infringement. Does McCormick's Marriage Block design infringe Brown's Wedding Block design? Why or why not?

9. Cory Van Rijn, Inc., (CVR) copyrighted various humanized raisin characters that it had developed. The California Raisin Advisory Board then developed Claymatic raisin characters for use in an advertising campaign. While both sets of characters had raisin bodies, the Board's characters had detailed eyes with eyebrows and upper and lower lids; detailed mouths with upper and lower lips; detailed noses with nostrils; long and wire-like arms and legs; four-fingered, gloved hands; high-top basketball sneakers; and blue, red, and yellow sunglasses. CVR's raisin characters had exaggerated, cartoon-like eyes; lipless mouths or no mouths at all; short and pudgy arms; no legs; three-fingered, gloveless hands; various types of shoes (none of which were high-top sneakers); and black, mirrored sunglasses. CVR conceded that the characters were not identical but

argued that the characters were similar enough that an ordinary reasonable person would perceive the two groups as being "cousins in an extended raisin family."

CVR sued the Board for copyright infringement. How should the court rule on CVR's claim and why?

10. Iowa Pedigree (IP) wanted to develop software for use in its business of assisting dog breeders and brokers in complying with American Kennel Club licensing and registration requirements. In May 1989, IP asked Gary Harter to develop this program for it. For the next six years, Harter worked on a variety of projects for IP. He developed several computer programs, maintained IP's computers, and serviced the software of IP's clients.

Throughout Harter's employment with IP, IP reported his pay to the IRS on form 1099 as payment to an independent contractor. Harter reported the pay as self-employed income. IP did not withhold for income or social security taxes. Harter received payment on an irregular basis, sometimes being paid as often as three times within one month and sometimes going as long as seven months without payment. Harter did not punch a time clock or submit the hours worked to IP except in the form of an invoice. IP directed the hours and days that he would work. Harter did some work at home but primarily worked at IP's offices, using its equipment.

Harter also continued to consult for other companies during his employment with IP. In 1992, Harter hired an assistant to work on a particular project and paid the assistant himself. Harter received no medical, retirement, or vacation benefits from IP. Harter traveled extensively with the owner of IP throughout the six-month period to service clients. Harter attended several trade shows for IP as well, in which he wore an IP "uniform" and worked at the IP booth answering questions regarding IP's services. IP paid for his expenses on these trips. IP directed the projects that Harter worked on, ensuring that the programs would meet licensing and compliance requirements.

In 1996, several IP clients terminated their business relationship with IP and began receiving services directly from Harter. IP then sued Harter for copyright infringement, claiming that IP was the sole owner of the copyrights in the programs that Harter had developed for it. Who owns the copyrights in these programs—Harter or IP? What test do the courts apply in resolving issues of this type?

11. Maclean Hunter Market Reports, Inc. ("Maclean") publishes the "Automobile Red Book-Official Used Car Valuations" (the "Red Book"). The Red Book is published eight times a year, in three different regional versions, and lists the editors' projections of "average" valuations of used cars up to seven years old sold in that region, broken down by automobile make, model, body style, engine type, options, and mileage. The valuation figures are predictions made by the editors, based on a variety of data and their own professional judgment, and are not based on either historical market prices or quotations, or upon mathematical formulae.

CCC Information Services provides information to customers as to the valuation of used vehicles via a computer database. CCC has been loading Red Book data onto its computer network and has been republishing various forms of Red Book information to its customers. As a result, CCC earned significant revenue, while Maclean has had a significant reduction in its number of subscriptions.

How should the court rule on Maclean's infringement claim against CCC?

12. Bell South Advertising & Publishing Corp. ("BAPCO") publishes a classified "yellow pages" advertising directory for the Greater Miami area. The directory is organized into an alphabetical list of business classifications and each business subscriber is listed under one heading at no charge. Subscribers may pay for listings under additional headings or for a display ad.

Donnelley Information Publishing, Inc. began proposing and selling classified advertisements for a competitive directory. Donnelley generated its sales lead sheets for soliciting advertisers for its competitive directory by creating a database of subscriber contact information and business classification from information copied from the BAPCO directory. Donnelley did not copy the text or graphic material from advertisements in BAPCO's directory, or the layout or typeface of the material.

BAPCO alleged it had engaged in several "acts of selection" in compiling its listings. For example, BAPCO determined the geographic scope of its directory, and the closing date after which no changes would be accepted, it "selected" its listings by requiring subscribers to have a business telephone number, and it relied on several marketing techniques, such as determining the number of free listings offered to each subscriber, selecting which customers to make an on-site sales call to, selecting the date when the sales campaign would begin, or selecting the procedure for recommending the purchase of multiple listings.

How should the court rule on BAPCO's claim of infringement?

13. Rzeppa was an engineer for a company that had a patent for an improvement in a constant velocity universal joint. The company had difficulties adapting the invention for commercial use. Rzeppa worked for more than a year in an effort to perfect and develop the universal joint so that it could be produced commercially for a profit. He requested that the company provide him with an assistant, so the company assigned Stuber, an experienced draftsman in its engineering department, to work with Rzeppa full-time. Stuber's job was to make drawings of the various sizes of the universal joint that Rzeppa was working on so that it could be properly manufactured. The company had required Rzeppa to sign an invention assignment agreement, but did not ask Stuber to do so.

While on his lunch hour one day, Stuber conceived of the idea of a self-piloting, constant velocity, universal joint with eccentric surfaces that eliminated the problems associated with the universal joint that Rzeppa was working on. Stuber immediately made a drawing of his idea. During his lunch hour the next day, he made another, more detailed, drawing, which he showed to Rzeppa and company officials. Rzeppa stated that the idea was of no value, and the company officials stated that they did not understand it. Stuber continued to make detailed drawings during his lunch hour and while at home. Eventually, after a period of several months, the company made models of the joint invented by Stuber, and they proved successful. Stuber informed the company he had applied for a patent on his invention, and demanded that the company pay a royalty for use of the invention. The company contends that the invention belongs to it. Who is right, and why?

14. Salvino Figurine Manufacturing, Inc. entered into a licensing agreement with the Major League Baseball Players Association to produce stuffed animal toys, known as Bamm Bears, bearing the names of individual players. Ty, Inc., who produced Beanie Babies stuffed toys, sued for copyright infringement, claiming that Salvino's bears were substantially similar to its Beanie Babies bears. What legal test should the court apply in determining whether Salvino infringed Ty's copyright?

15. Invitrogen Corp. held a process patent on the introduction of recombinant DNA molecules into receptive *E. coli* cells. Invitrogen sued Stratagene for infringement of the patent. Strategene defended by arguing that the Invitrogen's patent was invalid due to public use under Section 102(b).

The parties both agreed that Invitrogen used the process protected by the patent in its own laboratories more than one year prior to filing for a patent. Invitrogen did not sell the process or any products made with it. Rather, it kept the use of the process confidential and the process was known only within the company, Invitrogen did use the process in its own laboratories to grow cells to be used in other research within the company.

The district trial ruled that this use of the invention in Invitrogen's general business of widespread research was for commercial advantage and generated commercial benefits. The court determined that this was "public use" that had occurred more than one year prior to the filing for the patent application, and that the patent was thus invalid.

Invitrogen appealed this decision. How should the appellate court rule, and why?

16. Clock Spring, L.P., and Wrapmaster, Inc., are high-pressure gas pipeline repair companies. Clock Spring is the exclusive licensee of the '307 patent, which covers a method for repairing damaged high-pressure gas pipes. Clock Spring sued Wrapmaster for infringement; Wrapmaster defended by claiming that the '307 patent was invalid. Specifically, Wrapmaster claimed that a 1989 demonstration of the method by the named inventor was an invalidating public use because it occurred almost three years before the patent application was filed. In the demonstration, the repair method was performed in front of representatives of several gas transmission companies. These representatives were not told to keep the method confidential. In addition, the inventor did not control either the circumstances of or the personnel involved in the demonstration and did not use the findings from the demonstration to refine and perfect the invention.

Clock Spring argued that the demonstration was an experimental use, not a public use. How should the court rule on Clock Spring's claim? What effect will this ruling have on the validity of the '307 patent?

17. Situation Management Services (SMS) provides consulting services to domestic and international clients. In providing these services, SMS developed copyrighted training materials consisting of several hundred pages of instruction regarding techniques for effective communication and negotiation within the workplace. SMS sued ASP Consulting, Inc., a competitor that had been formed by former SMS employees, alleging that ASP had infringed its copyright by copying and using its training materials.

    The trial court found that the training materials were not copyrightable material because, in its view, the materials were "filled with generalizations, platitudes, and observations of the obvious," that they contain "not-so-stunning revelations," and teach "at their creative zenith, ... common-sense communication skills." The trial court concluded that SMS works were "dominated by unprotectable material. These works exemplify the sorts of training programs that serve as fodder for sardonic workplace humor that has given rise to the popular television show *The Office* and the movie *Office Space*. They are aggressively vapid ...."

    Did the trial court apply the correct standard in evaluating the originality of SMS's material? If SMS challenges this outcome on appeal, how should the appellate court rule, and why?

Protection of Intellectual Property Assets through Trade Secret Law, Contractual Agreements and Business Strategies

In this chapter, we consider the third category of intellectual property law protection, trade secret law, as well as the law relating to protection of unsolicited ideas. The chapter also discusses strategies that businesses can follow to best protect their intellectual property assets, including the use of contractual agreements such as covenants not to compete and nondisclosure agreements (NDAs).

Trade Secret Law

Trade secret protection is a critical issue for businesses in two respects. First, businesses need to know what to do to protect their trade secrets from being misappropriated. Misappropriation most commonly involves illegal disclosures by former employees or raids by competitors and, somewhat less frequently, misappropriation by foreign enterprises. Misappropriation is a particular risk in high-tech industries in which employee mobility and turnover are high. Second, businesses need to understand the consequences of deliberately or inadvertently misappropriating another's trade secrets. What civil and/or criminal penalties might apply?

Definition of "Trade Secret"

While patent and copyright laws arise under federal law, trade secret law is primarily state law, although, as we will see, the federal Economic Espionage Act addresses theft of trade secret information in certain circumstances.

Originally, trade secret law was developed through the common law. A few states, including Massachusetts, New Jersey, New York, and Texas, continue to protect trade secrets under the common law. These states generally follow the definition of a *trade secret* found in the Restatement of Torts Section 757, comment b:

> A trade secret may consist of any formula, pattern, device or compilation of information which is used in one's business, and which gives him an opportunity to obtain an advantage over competitors who do not know or use it.

The majority of the states and the District of Columbia have codified the common law of trade secrets by adopting some version of the Uniform Trade Secrets Act (UTSA). The UTSA defines a *trade secret* as:

information, including a formula, pattern, compilation, program, device, method, technique, or process, that:

(i)   derives independent economic value, actual or potential, from not being generally known to, and not being readily ascertainable by proper means by, other persons who can obtain economic value from its disclosure or use, and

(ii) is the subject of efforts that are reasonable under the circumstances to maintain its secrecy.[1]

The definitions of trade secret under the UTSA and the Restatement are quite similar.[2] In general, trade secrets include business and commercial information that: (1) has commercial value, (2) is not in the public domain, and (3) is subject to reasonable steps to maintain secrecy. Trade secrets include any information that can be of value to a company and its competitors, such as formulas, processes, computer programs, customer and supplier lists, strategic business data, financial projections, research results, marketing strategies, customer needs and profiles, business or product plans, and negative know-how (i.e., knowledge of what does or does not work), provided the information meets the requirements for secrecy. Thus, trade secret law protects assets that are not patentable as well as those that are. The requirement that trade secrets have "commercial value" does not mean that the business must currently have competitors who might value the information. Rather, it means only that there must be actual or potential value from the information being held secret; potential rather than actual competition is sufficient.

In addition, trade secret information need not be kept absolutely secret, just "reasonably" secret. What is "reasonable" will vary with the circumstances. Generally, companies should limit the information to those employees who have a need to know and should take precautions to ensure confidentiality. Obviously, the firm must share trade secret information with necessary employees and even with outsiders, such as consultants, in certain circumstances. As one court noted: "The secrecy need not be absolute; the owner of a trade secret may, without losing protection, disclose it to a licensee, an employee, or a stranger, if the disclosure is made in confidence, express or implied."[3] To maintain the trade secret status of the information, however, the company must ensure that only a few, authorized outsiders know of the information and that those persons make an effort to keep it secret (see Case Illustration 3.1).

Public or readily available or ascertainable information is not entitled to trade secret protection. For example, trade secret information that can be quickly and easily reverse-engineered is entitled to little or no protection. (*Reverse-engineering* refers to the process of starting with a product and working backward to identify the process that led to its development or manufacture.) However, publicly-known information that is compiled or combined in a way that provides a competitive advantage that is not generally known in the industry may be protected as a trade secret.

---

[1] The UTSA can be viewed at the website of the National Conference of Commissioners on Uniform State Laws at www.nccusl.org

[2] The most recent attempt to organize the law of trade secrets occurred in the Restatement (Third) of Competition Section 39 (1995), which provided a similar definition of trade secret: "A trade secret is any information that can be used in the operation of a business or other enterprise and that is sufficiently valuable and secret to afford an actual or potential economic advantage over others."

[3] *Tao of Sys. Integration, Inc. v. Analytical Servs. & Materials, Inc.,* 299 F. Supp. 2d 565, 574 (E.D. Va. 2004).

CASE ILLUSTRATION 3.1

INCASE, INC. v. TIMEX CORP.,
488 F.3D 46 (1ST CIR. 2007)

FACTS Incase designs and manufactures injection-molded plastic packaging products. It does not normally charge directly for design services, but provides those in conjunction with manufacturing.

Incase designed and developed two unique watch cases for Timex. Incase produced more than 2 million units of the first design. However, despite numerous exchanges and communications regarding the second design, Timex never placed an order or entered into a contract with Incase for the second type of watch case. Eventually, an Incase executive was in a large retail store and noticed Timex watches being sold in watch cases virtually identical to the Incase design. It turned out that Timex had contracted with a Philippine manufacturing company for the production of the second type of case.

Incase argued that its design was proprietary and confidential, and it sued Timex for misappropriation of a trade secret. Although Incase won a jury verdict of $131,191, the trial judge overturned the verdict as a matter of law. Incase appealed.

DECISION The appellate court affirmed the trial court, stating:

To prevail on a claim of misappropriation of trade secrets, a plaintiff must show: 1) the information is a trade secret; 2) the plaintiff took reasonable steps to preserve the secrecy of the information; and 3) the defendant used improper means, in breach of a confidential relationship, to acquire and use the trade secret. In issuing its judgment as a matter of law, the
*court held that Incase had not presented any evidence that the information was secret or that it had taken reasonable steps to preserve the secrecy of the information. * * **

The appeal on this claim turns on the second element of the misappropriation cause of action: whether Incase took reasonable steps to preserve the secrecy of the ... design. The district court noted that no documents were marked "confidential" or "secret"; there were no security precautions or confidentiality agreements; Incase had not told Timex the design was a secret; and Incase's principal designer on the project, Bob Shelton, did not think the design was a secret. Timex adds that Frank Zanghi, Incase's vice president, did not tell anyone at Timex that the design was confidential.

The appellate court went on to note: "The fact that Incase kept its work for Timex private from the world is not sufficient; discretion is a normal feature of a business relationship. Instead, there must be affirmative steps to preserve the secrecy of the information as against the party against whom the misappropriation claim is made. Here, there is no evidence that any such steps were taken." The court concluded: "Protecting a trade secret 'calls for constant warnings to all persons to whom the trade secret has become known and obtaining from each an agreement, preferably in writing, acknowledging its secrecy and promising to respect it.'"

Thus, the appellate court affirmed the district court's judgment as a matter of law on the misappropriation of trade secrets claim.

◆ *See Discussion Cases 3.1, 3.2, 3.3.*

Trade secret protection lasts only as long as the secret is maintained. Once the trade secret information enters the public domain, whether through careless security measures by the trade secret owner or through misappropriation or independent creation by another, the trade secret is lost.

Patent Protection versus Trade Secret Protection

In many instances, an invention may qualify for either patent or trade secret protection. In these cases, the inventor must choose which form of protection to pursue, as these are mutually exclusive options. A single invention cannot be protected through both patent and trade secret. For example, if the inventor makes secret commercial use of the invention for more than one year, the inventor loses the right to seek patent protection under the Patent Act and must protect the invention, if at all, as a trade secret. Conversely, once a patent is issued or after the patent application is laid open, the information becomes public and trade secret protection is no longer possible.

United States law provides inventors with more flexibility in choosing between patent and trade secret protection than do the laws of most other countries, although that flexibility has been considerably reduced in light of the 1999 amendments to the Patent Act (discussed in Chapter 2). If the inventor does not file for foreign patents and his application for a U.S. patent is denied, the inventor can request that the application not be released to the public. The inventor can then treat the invention as a trade secret.

Most other countries do not offer inventors even this limited choice. Rather, they treat patent applications as public information and typically "lay open" the application within 18 months of its filing. Filing for a patent application in these countries thus automatically takes the information into the public domain and makes trade secret protection unavailable even if the patent ultimately does not issue. Similarly, if a U.S. inventor files for foreign patents, her U.S. patent application is also automatically laid open and her opportunity to seek trade secret protection lost. U.S. inventors should keep this limitation in mind in evaluating whether to pursue foreign patents on their inventions.

In deciding which form of protection—patent or trade secret—to pursue, the inventor must consider several factors:

- *Duration of protection.* Patents are limited to a term of 20 years, while trade secret protection lasts as long as the information remains secret. Theoretically, a trade secret can last forever. In practical terms, however, the life of a trade secret varies greatly depending upon the type of invention and the industry involved. The formula for Coca-Cola, which is a trade secret, is over 100 years old; a trade secret in the rapidly changing computer industry, on the other hand, may last only a year, or even less.
- *Scope of protection.* Patent protection is stronger than trade secret protection because it prevents even someone who independently invented the invention from making, using, selling, offering to sell, or importing the invention during the patent period. Trade secret protection, on the other hand, prohibits persons from using or disclosing the information only if they learned of it improperly. It does nothing to prevent persons who acquired the information independently or through legitimate means, such as reverse-engineering, from using the information.
- *Cost.* While it can be expensive and time-consuming to acquire a patent, trade secrets arise automatically under the law. There are no application procedures, no filing fees, and no formalities that must be followed. It can be expensive to maintain a trade secret, however, as discussed below.

Ownership of Trade Secrets Created by Employees

Ownership issues arise when the trade secret involved is not a preexisting one revealed to the employee in the scope of her employment but, rather, is a trade secret created by the employee. If the parties had the foresight to sign an express agreement assigning ownership of such trade secrets to one party or the other, that agreement controls. In the absence of such an agreement, the question becomes whether the trade secret is the property of the employer or the employee.

Generally, the trade secret belongs to the employer if: (1) the employee was hired specially to do research of the type that led to the trade secret, and (2) the employer has put substantial time and resources at the disposal of the employee to develop the trade secret. Thus, a research scientist who develops a new substance while in his research lab at work has created a trade secret that belongs to the employer. In such instances, the employee is under a duty not to use or disclose the trade secret, even in the absence of an express employment contract so stating. If these two conditions are not met, however, the trade secret belongs to the employee. For example, if Employer, a manufacturer of treadmills, hires Employee as a salesperson assigned to its wholesale clients and Employee, in her garage and on or her own time, invents an improved treadmill, the trade secret belongs to Employee.

If the employee was not hired to do research and development but nonetheless created a trade secret related to the employer's business during working hours or using the employer's equipment or materials, the employee owns the trade secret. The employer, however, has *shop rights* in the trade secret. Shop rights are an irrevocable, nontransferable, royalty-free right or license to use the trade secret in the employer's business.

Generally, employers are not satisfied with obtaining shop rights in such trade secrets and want to own the trade secret outright. An *invention assignment agreement* (discussed below) is critical in such instances.

Misappropriation of a Trade Secret

Generally, *misappropriation* of a trade secret can occur in one of two ways: (1) an employee or other person with a duty of confidentiality toward the trade secret owner may wrongfully disclose or use the information, or (2) a competitor may wrongfully obtain the information.

Violation of a Duty of Confidentiality If the defendant has a *duty of confidentiality* toward the trade secret owner, the defendant's disclosure or use of the trade secret is misappropriation. The duty of confidentiality most commonly arises as a result of a special relationship between the parties, such as an employer-employee, partner, or attorney-client relationship. This duty arises automatically under the law and does not depend upon the existence of any type of contract. An employee, for example, has a legal duty not to use or disclose his employer's trade secrets without permission if the employee learned of those secrets within the scope of his employment even if the employee has not signed an employment agreement or other contract expressly addressing this topic. This duty of confidentiality binds the employee even after he leaves the employer's employ. Thus, an employee cannot take the employer's trade secrets to a new job.

Although not legally required, from the employer's perspective it is always better to have an express, written *nondisclosure agreement* (NDA). The NDA usually requires the employee to expressly agree not to use or disclose any trade secrets belonging to the employer and often requires the employee to assign in advance to the employer all trade secrets he might create. (This topic is discussed further below.) The courts generally enforce such agreements provided that they are not unconscionable.

Another type of express agreement that is often used is a *covenant not to compete*, also known as a *noncompete agreement*. These agreements generally require the employee not to compete or to work for a competitor for a specified time period in a specified geographic region after leaving the employer's employ. The advantage, from the employer's perspective, of using such an agreement is that the agreement can cover confidential proprietary information that might not rise to the level of a trade secret. The disadvantage is that the courts dislike noncompete agreements as a matter of public policy and carefully scrutinize them to make certain that they do not infringe upon an employee's ability to make a living. Noncompete agreements are invalid in a few states, such as California. (Noncompete agreements are discussed in more detail below.)

A number of courts have adopted the *inevitable disclosure rule*, which permits an employer to obtain an injunction prohibiting an employee from working for a direct competitor, even in the absence of a noncompete agreement, when it would be difficult for the employee to perform his new job without disclosing or relying upon the former employer's trade secrets. This rule recognizes that people cannot easily segregate general information or knowledge from the trade secrets and confidential information of former employers.

The courts hesitate to issue injunctions under the inevitable disclosure rule, however, because of their concern that individuals not be deprived of their livelihoods. The Pennsylvania Supreme Court described the policy conflicts that nondisclosure rules generally raise, noting that trade secret law:

> brings to the fore a problem of accommodating competing policies in our law: the right of a businessman to be protected against unfair competition stemming from the usurpation of his trade secrets and the right of an individual to the unhampered pursuit of the occupations and livelihoods for which he is best suited …. Society as a whole greatly benefits from technological improvements. Without some means of post-employment protection to assure that valuable developments or improvements are exclusively those of the employer, the businessman could not afford to subsidize research or improve current methods. * * *

> On the other hand, any form of post-employment restraint reduces the economic mobility of employees and limits their personal freedom to pursue a preferred course of livelihood. The employee's bargaining position is weakened because he is potentially shackled by the acquisition of alleged trade secrets; and thus, paradoxically, he is restrained, because of his increased expertise, from advancing further in the industry in which he is most productive.[4]

To avoid liability for misappropriation of a competitor's trade secrets, a company should take care when recruiting new employees. In some instances, it may be best not to recruit particular individuals. The recruit should be informed at the beginning of the interview process that the interviewing company does not want information about or access to any competitor's trade secrets. If the recruit is hired, she should be informed again (in writing) of this policy. The recruit should not bring confidential documents or materials to the new job and should not be placed into jobs in which she might be tempted to use such information, even inadvertently, including jobs that involve reverse-engineering or independent creation of products similar to those of the previous employer. If the recruit has entered into a noncompete agreement or NDA with the former employer, the new employer should review the contracts carefully to ensure that the new employment does not violate any of the valid provisions of the agreements. The new employer should document in writing all efforts undertaken to avoid trade secret misappropriation in the event that the previous employer alleges misappropriation at some point in the future.

Unlawful Acquisition of a Competitor's Trade Secret Information   Certain types of behavior are regarded as unlawful means of obtaining trade secret information. *Illegal conduct*, such as theft, trespass, fraud, misrepresentation, wiretapping, and bribery, is not permitted. Acquisition of a competitor's trade secrets through *industrial espionage*, such as electronic surveillance or spying, is also not permitted. Moreover, a competitor who purchases trade secret information, knowing that it was improperly obtained, is liable for misappropriation just as though the competitor had engaged in the misappropriation directly.

Lawful Acquisition of a Competitor's Trade Secret Information   There are a number of legitimate means by which a competitor can gain access to trade secret information. If the owner (or its employee) puts the information into the public domain, e.g., by publishing it in brochures or other materials or by talking about it in public places, competitors may legally use that information. In addition, competitors are permitted to reverse-engineer trade secret information through inspection of a product or

---

[4]*Wexler v. Greenberg,* 160 A.2d 430, 434-35 (Pa. 1960).

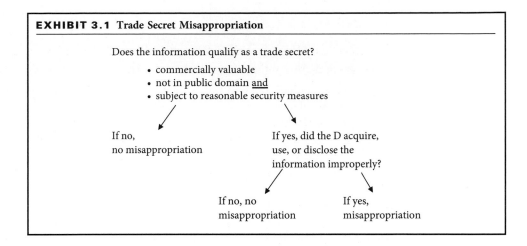

EXHIBIT 3.1 Trade Secret Misappropriation

Does the information qualify as a trade secret?

- commercially valuable
- not in public domain <u>and</u>
- subject to reasonable security measures

If no,
no misappropriation

If yes, did the D acquire,
use, or disclose the
information improperly?

If no, no
misappropriation

If yes,
misappropriation

examination of published literature. Competitors may also independently create the information without incurring liability for misappropriation.

It is also legal for a company to obtain public information about its competitor's trade secrets through *competitive intelligence* activities. These activities include the gathering of either primary data (i.e., information gathered from direct sources such as telephone or in-person interviews) or secondary data (i.e., information gathered from indirect sources, such as consultants, published documents, or patents). For example, competitive intelligence information can be obtained through Internet searches, attendance at trade shows, interviews with securities analysts and suppliers, examinations of UCC filings, visits to competitors' facilities, or discussions with competitors' customers.[5]

While a firm can use competitive intelligence techniques proactively to enhance its own market position, the firm also needs to be aware that it may be the target of such actions by its competitors as well. Although a firm cannot block all such activities by its competitors, simple steps such as shredding sensitive documents before placing them in the trash, monitoring factory visits from outsiders, and controlling access to sensitive data can minimize the risks (see Exhibit 3.2).

Remedies for Trade Secret Misappropriation

Two general types of remedies are available for trade secret misappropriation: (1) injunctions and (2) monetary damages. In addition, the federal Economic Espionage Act provides for criminal penalties for certain types of trade secret misappropriation.

Injunctions   Generally, it is relatively easy to get an injunction against trade secret misappropriation. The more difficult question typically is how long the injunction should last. The majority of courts limit the injunction to the life of the trade secret. This can be measured up front by how long the court estimates the trade secret will endure. Alternatively, the court can issue an injunction of indefinite length that allows the defendant to petition the court to have the injunction lifted if and when the trade secret enters the public domain (e.g., through reverse-engineering or independent creation by others).

A minority of courts will issue a perpetual injunction on the theory that the defendant's breach of confidence or improper conduct warrants such punishment. This prevents the

---

[5]For general information on the competitive intelligence industry, see the webpage of the Society of Competitive Intelligence Professionals at www.scip.org

EXHIBIT 3.2

LAWFUL ACQUISITION OF A COMPETITOR'S TRADE SECRETS	UNLAWFUL ACQUISITION OF A COMPETITOR'S TRADE SECRETS

• accessing information in public domain
• competitive intelligence
• reverse-engineering
• independent creation
	• violation of duty of confidentiality
	  • duty implied by law as result of special relationship
	  • duty created by express contract
	• illegal conduct
	• industrial espionage
	• knowingly obtaining information misappropriated by another

defendant from using the trade secret information even once it is generally known within the industry and is available to other competitors. It thus puts the defendant at a considerable disadvantage compared both to the plaintiff and to other competitors.

Monetary Damages   Depending upon the circumstances, the court may select from a variety of types of monetary damages:

1. the *lost profits* that the trade secret owner has incurred as a result of the defendant's misappropriation of the trade secret;
2. *unjust enrichment damages*, often measured as the amount of profits that the defendant made as a result of the misappropriation; or
3. a *reasonable royalty* for the defendant's use of the trade secret during the time at issue (measured by the amount that reasonable parties would have agreed to if they had willingly negotiated for a license to use the trade secret during an arm's-length transaction).

Double Damages and Attorneys' Fees   Under the UTSA, the court can award up to *double damages* for willful and malicious trade secret misappropriation. In addition, the court can award *attorneys fees* to the prevailing party in cases of willful and malicious misappropriation by the defendant or bad faith by the trade secret owner. As noted in Chapter 2, enhanced damages and awards of attorneys' fees are rare in the U.S. legal system and are available only where specifically authorized by statute.

Criminal Prosecution   Both civil and criminal proceedings can be brought against an individual alleged to have engaged in misappropriation. As of 1996, only about one-half of the states had statutes imposing criminal sanctions for theft of a trade secret. To address this gap in enforcement, Congress enacted the Economic Espionage Act,[6] which took effect January 1, 1997. This federal statute provides that individuals convicted of trade secret theft can be fined up to $250,000 and corporations up to $5 million. In both instances, the fines can be doubled if the defendant acted in concert with a foreign instrumentality. In addition to the fines, the court may impose jail terms of up to 10 years (15 years if the defendant acted in concert with a foreign instrumentality) and subject the defendant to forfeiture of property.

---

[6]18 U.S.C. §§ 1831-1839.

Congress's main purpose in enacting the Economic Espionage Act was to provide redress for illegal activities of foreign governments, although the Act applies to purely domestic trade secret misappropriation as well. The Department of Justice, which enforces the Act, has stated that it will exercise restraint in bringing federal charges under the Act, noting that civil remedies for trade secret misappropriation are generally available under state law. In determining whether federal criminal prosecution is also appropriate in any particular circumstance, the Department of Justice considers factors such as: "(a) the scope of the criminal activity, including evidence of involvement by a foreign government, foreign agent or foreign instrumentality; (b) the degree of economic injury to the trade secret owner; (c) the type of trade secret misappropriated; (d) the effectiveness of available civil remedies; and (e) the potential deterrent value of the prosecution."[7]

In 2008, for example, a Chinese national residing in California, Xiaodong Sheldon Meng, a software engineer, was sentenced under the EEA to 24 months in prison, three years of supervised release following his prison term, a fine of $10,000, and a forfeiture of computer equipment used in the violation. Meng misappropriated trade secrets involving products used to simulate real-world motion for military-training purposes, with an intent to benefit a foreign government (the People's Republic of China Navy Research Center).[8]

Protection of Trade Secrets

Businesses must have reasonable security precautions in place in order to claim protection for their trade secrets. A proactive policy is best. The company should start by conducting a trade secret audit to gain an understanding of what trade secrets it owns and how well its current company policy protects those secrets. The audit should be repeated periodically to ensure that appropriate measures are taken to protect new trade secrets as well.

Employees are the largest source of leaks of trade secrets, so careful management of the employer-employee relationship is needed. All employees should be informed about the company's trade secret policies and the consequences of violating those policies. The company should develop written policies regarding trade secret protection and should communicate those policies clearly and emphatically to all employees who might have access to such secrets. Access to trade secrets should be limited to those employees who have a need to know specific information, and the employees should be explicitly instructed that the information is a trade secret. The company should clearly label confidential documents as such but should avoid labeling every piece of information "confidential." In addition to making it difficult for employees to distinguish between truly secret information and routine information, incorrect or excessive designation of information as confidential may weaken the company's ability to assert trade secret protection in the event of misappropriation or litigation.

The company should destroy written information once it is no longer needed. The company should instruct employees to use passwords and security codes on sensitive computer files and to lock desks, filing cabinets, and offices when not in use. It should caution employees not to discuss confidential information in the presence of outsiders, over unsecure phone lines (particularly over cell phones), or in public. The company should also monitor and restrict access by plant visitors, including repair or service personnel.

The most important element of a proactive trade secret program, however, is the use of express contractual agreements, especially NDAs. This is a contractual promise by an employee not to make unauthorized use or disclosure of trade secrets. Senior managers

---

[7]See www.usdoj.gov/usao/eousa/foia_reading_room/usam/title9/59mcrm.htm

[8]See www.usdoj.gov/opa/pr/2008/June/08-nsd-545.html

and technical staff should also be required to sign noncompete agreements. NDAs and noncompete agreements are discussed in more detail below.

Finally, the company should conduct exit interviews to remind departing employees of their obligation to maintain the employer's trade secrets even after they have ceased working for the employer.

International Aspects of Trade Secret Protection

As with patent law, the ability of the United States to regulate trade secrets abroad is constrained by its territorial boundaries. When a U.S. court is unable to obtain jurisdiction over the parties or when the infringing goods are not imported into the United States, U.S. courts and government agencies are generally powerless to restrict a foreign party's exploitation of a competitor's trade secrets abroad, even if the exploitation would be illegal under U.S. law.

As a result, businesses need to be very careful when they license or transfer trade secrets abroad. Whenever a business establishes foreign operations, enters into ventures with foreign partners, or shares information or personnel with foreign sources, the business needs to carefully investigate the host country's trade secret laws, as those laws will likely govern in the event of a dispute or problem.

Laws regarding trade secret protection vary greatly around the world, but generally we are seeing a movement toward greater protection of trade secrets and greater harmonization of national laws. Japan, Korea, and Mexico enacted their first trade secret protection statutes in 1991; China followed in 1993. In addition, the Trade-Related Aspects of Intellectual Property Rights (TRIPS) Agreement of the Uruguay Round of GATT requires member countries to protect against the acquisition, disclosure, or use of a party's trade secrets "in a manner contrary to honest commercial practices." This agreement should ultimately lead to stronger and more harmonized trade secret protection laws among member countries.

The Law of Unsolicited Ideas

Very often, individuals develop ideas for new products or services that they are unable or unwilling to pursue on their own. The inventor will offer the idea to an established company, hoping that the company will compensate the inventor in exchange for the right to commercialize the invention. Both inventors who approach companies and the companies who are approached need to be careful about the manner in which the relationship develops, lest they find themselves in an undesirable legal position.

From the Inventor's Perspective

Before disclosing his invention to the company, the inventor must make certain that the company recognizes either that it must pay for the idea or, if it chooses not to purchase the invention, that it must keep the idea confidential. If the inventor simply reveals the details of his invention without first obtaining this understanding, the inventor could inadvertently lose his rights in the invention.

Thus, before revealing the invention, the inventor should contact the company to make certain that the company understands that the inventor is seeking to sell or license the invention. As a practical matter, the inventor should get the company to sign an agreement stating that the company will review the invention but will keep the invention confidential and will pay a reasonable purchase price or royalties if it pursues the idea. Often, such agreements state that the company is not obligated to pay if it was already familiar with the invention or if the invention was already publicly known. Even if the parties do not enter into an express contract, the courts may well "imply" the existence

CASE ILLUSTRATION 3.2

REEVES v. ALYESKA PIPELINE SERVICE, 56 P.3D 660 (ALASKA 2002)

FACTS John Reeves, the owner of a tourist attraction in Fairbanks, conceived of and developed an idea to build a visitor center at a turnout overlooking the Trans-Alaska Pipeline near Fairbanks. After receiving an assurance from Alyeska's Fairbanks manager, Keith Burke, that the idea was "between us," Reeves orally described his idea. Burke indicated it "looked good," and asked Reeves to submit a written proposal, which he did. Alyeska subsequently ceased dealing with Reeves and built the visitor center on its own. Reeves sued Alyeska, arguing that in return for Reeves disclosing his idea to Burke, Alyeska had promised not to implement or disclose Reeves's idea without allowing him to participate in the implementation. A jury awarded Reeves damages under various alternative contract and tort theories.

Alyeska argued on appeal that the disclosure agreement was unenforceable, pointing to Reeves' testimony at trial that Alyeska had not promised to pay him a specified amount for disclosure of his idea "or even an unspecified reasonable value." It thus argued that the disclosure agreement was unenforceable because it lacked essential contract terms and was overly vague.

DECISION The Alaska Supreme Court had already rejected a similar argument by Alyeska in an earlier proceeding involving these parties. The court noted that it had held in its earlier opinion that:

contract and contract-like theories may protect individuals who spend their time and energy developing unoriginal or non-novel ideas that others find useful, because "it would be inequitable to prevent these individuals from obtaining legally enforceable compensation from those who voluntarily choose to benefit from the services of the 'idea-person.'" We further explained that "if parties voluntarily choose to bargain for an individual's services in disclosing or developing a non novel or unoriginal idea, they have the power to do so." [A] disclosure contract is not a typical agreement for the sale of goods or services at an agreed-upon price; rather, it is an agreement for disclosure of an idea in exchange for a promise not to use the idea without including the disclosing party in its implementation.

The court found that "the record contains sufficient evidence to support a finding that, in return for Reeves's agreement to disclose his idea, Alyeska promised him either confidentiality or participation in implementing the visitor center project. This promise is sufficiently definite as a matter of law to establish an enforceable disclosure agreement. Similarly, there can be no question that Reeves produced sufficient evidence to support the jury's finding that Alyeska breached this agreement by unilaterally exploiting Reeves's idea."

of a contract that protects the interests of the inventor provided the inventor has made his position clear prior to revealing his ideas (see Case Illustration 3.2).

From the Company's Perspective

Companies who may be approached by inventors with unsolicited ideas face a different set of problems. Many companies are inundated by calls and letters from inventors regarding unsolicited ideas and inventions. The companies may well already be aware of similar inventions or may be working on similar inventions themselves. The companies are legitimately concerned that rejected inventors will conclude that a company who later comes out with a similar invention stole the unsolicited idea from the inventor and will sue.

Most companies have standard procedures for dealing with the submission of unsolicited ideas.[9] Many simply do not consider unsolicited ideas under any circumstances and return the letter of inquiry to the sender without reviewing the ideas contained in it.

---

[9]For an example, see the Hershey Company website, at www.thehersheycompany.com/legal_info.asp

Some companies review unsolicited ideas but require the inventor to first sign a written waiver (generally supplied by the company) that relieves the company of any liability for disclosing confidential information and that explicitly states that no relationship is formed between the parties as a result of the company's review of the inventor's materials. Many of these companies review the invention only if it is already covered by a patent. This policy ensures that the ownership rights in the invention are both clear and assignable in the event the company wishes to pursue the invention.

◆ *See Discussion Case 3.5.*

Business Strategies for Protecting Intellectual Property Assets

Companies can take a number of actions to protect their intellectual property assets. Specifically, in many (but not all) instances, firms may be able to use contractual agreements, such as covenants not to compete and NDAs, to protect these assets. More generally, companies should conduct periodic intellectual property audits to determine the nature and scope of their assets and to evaluate protection measures in place. In addition, several specialized software programs are now on the market to assist companies in managing their intellectual property assets.

Contractual Agreements

There are several different types of contractual agreements that employers should consider using to protect their interests in intellectual property assets, including covenants not to compete, NDAs, and invention assignment agreements. Each of these agreements is governed by state law.

Covenants Not to Compete   *Covenants not to compete* are agreements in which the employee agrees not to compete with the employer in certain specified manners after leaving its employ. Noncompete covenants are also commonly used when a business is sold (to prevent the former owner from competing with the new owner) or when a partnership is dissolved (to prevent one partner from competing with another). Typically, these agreements restrict the ability of the former employee to work for competitors, conduct or solicit business from the former employer's customers, or use the former employer's confidential business information. Covenants not to compete are governed by the common law regarding restraints of trade (discussed further in Chapter 4).

As a matter of public policy, courts dislike noncompete covenants. The courts are concerned that such agreements may prevent an employee from making a livelihood in his profession. In addition, the courts favor the free flow of labor and fear that widespread use of noncompete covenants could impede a competitive marketplace for labor. As a result, some states do not permit such agreements. Many other states place significant restrictions upon the use of such agreements, permitting them, for example, in the sale of a business but not in the employment context.

In general, covenants not to compete must meet several legal requirements. First, they must be ancillary (or subordinate) to another contractual agreement. In an employee-employer relationship, this generally means that the parties must have entered into a formal, written employment contract. In the absence of such an employment contract, many courts regard the covenant not to compete as an illegal restraint on trade.

Second, the covenant not to compete must be narrowly drawn so as to protect only the legitimate interests of the employer. Mere protection of the employer from competition is insufficient. Rather, the covenant must be designed to protect business assets such as trade secrets of the employer, a customer base, confidential business information, or business goodwill.

Third, the covenant not to compete must be restricted in terms of both: (1) duration and (2) geographic scope. These determinations are highly fact-specific and are made on a case-by-case basis. Covenants with a duration of one year or less are generally considered valid; covenants of several years are generally considered overbroad. As a general rule, the covenant should not exceed the period of any employment contract given to the employee. Thus, if the employee has a two-year employment contract, the covenant not to compete should not extend more than two years after termination of that employment.

The advent of the Internet and the increasingly rapid pace at which technology is changing are having profound impacts on the way in which courts evaluate the reasonable duration of covenants not to compete. Even one-year noncompete agreements that historically would have been found valid in virtually every instance have been held invalid in the fast-paced high-technology world. Employers may need to revise their standard boilerplate noncompete agreements and tailor them to the specifics of the industry in which they operate.

Permissible geographic scope is determined by the scope of the company's activities. As a general rule, the geographic area covered by the covenant cannot exceed the area in which the employer currently does business. As commerce continues to become more national and international in scope, however, and as business activity on the Internet continues to develop, this rule is likely to erode (see Case Illustration 3.3).

The most common remedy granted for breach of a valid covenant not to compete is an *injunction* that requires the employee to adhere to the terms of the covenant and to cease any impermissible competition. *Monetary damages* are also available in some instances.

◆ *See Discussion Cases 3.3, 3.4.*

Nondisclosure Agreements   A *nondisclosure agreement* (also known as a *proprietary information agreement*) is a contractual agreement that prohibits an employee from revealing or using trade secrets or proprietary information. Although the common law of unfair competition generally prohibits employees from using or disclosing trade secrets or other confidential information even in the absence of an explicit contractual agreement, it is still wise for employers to use an NDA.

Use of such agreements not only strengthens the employer's legal position in the event of a breach by showing that the employer has taken reasonable measures to protect its trade secrets but also serves to emphasize to the employee the importance of trade secret protection. In addition, the NDA may protect confidential information that does not rise to the level of a trade secret and thus is not protected under common law. Courts do not like NDAs as a matter of public policy, however, and often impose significant limitations on them.

An NDA can be a stand-alone document or can be part of a larger employment contract. *Every* employee with potential access to trade secrets, including clerical and custodial staffs, should be required to sign an NDA. In addition, consultants, independent contractors, potential investors, and others with access to trade secrets should be required to sign a confidentiality agreement before any confidential information is released to them.

CASE ILLUSTRATION 3.3

MARKET ACCESS INTERNATIONAL, INC. v. KMD MEDIA, LLC, 72 VA. CIR. 355 (2006)

FACTS Plaintiff produces and distributes trade publications on homeland security and information technology security. Plaintiff contracted with Defendant to sell advertising space in its publication *Homeland Defense Journal.* Under this agreement, Defendant agreed not to compete with Plaintiff by selling or promoting publications that competed with Plaintiff's publication for a period of one year following termination of the agreement.

Plaintiff alleged that Defendant conspired to create a competing publication and sued for enforcement of its noncompete agreement. Defendant argued that the lack of a geographic limitation rendered the noncompetition agreement unenforceable as a matter of law.

DECISION The court enforced the agreement. The court stated:

> Under Virginia law, a non-competition agreement may be enforced if the agreement is (1) narrowly drawn to protect an employer's business interest, (2) is not unduly burdensome on an employee's ability to earn a living, and (3) is not against public policy. Central to the analysis considering the reasonableness of these agreements is whether there are reasonable limits on duration, geographic area and whether the scope of the restrictions is narrowly tailored to protect the employer's interest.
>
> In this analysis Virginia courts do not consider geographic limitations alone; instead Virginia courts must consider together the intended function of the agreement and its duration as well as whether it contains a geographic limitation.

The court noted that many noncompete agreements contain geographical provisions limiting the area where the employee is not permitted to seek competing work to the area the business can expect to operate. While it is relatively easy to define this scope when a business operates in a regional market:

> with the advent of the Internet and the nationalization of everything from products to ideas, this has become substantially more difficult. Homeland Defense Journal *holds itself out as a national publication, and indeed homeland security itself is an issue that often lends itself to discussion on the national level.*

While the agreement at issue lacked a geographic limitation, the agreement had a duration of only one year and limited the prohibited activities to those in direct competition with one journal. Moreover, the agreement explicitly recognized Defendant's continuing relationship with other military publications it represented. Thus, the terms of the noncompete agreement were narrowly tailored to protect Plaintiff's legitimate business interests while not prohibiting Defendant from competing in its chosen field, and so the noncompete agreement was enforceable.

Even states that do not allow covenants not to compete typically allow NDAs. Although a few states impose the same restrictions upon NDAs as they do upon noncompete agreements (i.e., restrictions on duration, geographic area, and scope), most states do not hold NDAs to the same level of scrutiny as they do noncompete agreements.

A properly drawn NDA does several things. First, the NDA provides clear notice to the employee of the confidential nature of the information at issue. Generally, the law does not impose a duty upon an employee to maintain the confidentiality of information when the employee has not been notified that the information is secret. Second, the NDA informs the employee as to her responsibilities regarding such information (particularly required efforts to maintain its confidentiality). Finally, an NDA should contain a promise (covenant) from the employee prohibiting the employee from disclosing or using such information after termination of employment (see Exhibit 3.3).

EXHIBIT 3.3

PROPRIETARY INFORMATION AGREEMENT

This Agreement between XYZ, Inc. including its direct and indirect subsidiaries and affiliates (hereinafter "XYZ, Inc.") and _____ (herein after "Employee") shall govern the responsibilities of Employees with respect to proprietary information. Entering into this agreement is a condition of Employee's employment by XYZ, Inc. but the agreement does not purport to set forth the terms of said employment.

WITNESSETH:

WHEREAS, Employee is or desires to be employed by XYZ, Inc. or one of its direct or indirect subsidiaries or affiliates in a capacity in which Employee may receive or contribute to proprietary information which may or may not be patentable;

WHEREAS, XYZ, Inc. and its direct and indirect subsidiaries and affiliates develop and use valuable technical and non-technical proprietary information which XYZ, Inc. may wish to protect either by patents or by keeping material secret and proprietary;

NOW THEREFORE, in consideration of Employee's employment by XYZ, Inc. or the relevant direct or indirect subsidiary or affiliate, it is agreed as follows:

1. Employee shall not disclose or use for Employee or others at any time either during or subsequent to said only employment proprietary information of XYZ, Inc. of which Employee becomes informed during said employment, whether or not developed by Employee, without first obtaining the written consent of XYZ, Inc. over the signature of a company officer. Employee understands that the term "proprietary information" means any information not generally known or previously published by XYZ, Inc. which gives or is intended to give XYZ, Inc. an advantage over its competitors who do not have the information. Such proprietary information includes but is not limited to, secret information relating to marketing plans, products, formulas, processes, manufacturing techniques, personnel information, financial data, production information, software, and the like.

2. Misuse or unauthorized disclosure of proprietary information may result in legal and/or disciplinary action up to and including termination.

3. The obligations of Employee under this agreement shall continue beyond the termination of employment with respect to proprietary information received by Employee during the period of employment and shall be binding upon Employee's assigns, executors, administrators, and legal representatives.

4. This agreement supersedes and replaces any existing agreement, written or otherwise, entered into by Employee and XYZ, Inc. relating generally to the same subject matter. It is expressly understood, however, that nothing contained herein shall in any way alter the terms of any agreement between XYZ, Inc. and Employee, or any representative of Employee, with respect to collective bargaining agreements, termination, or any other aspects of employment which may be present and form part of an employment agreement between XYZ, Inc. and Employee.

Employee is to be employed at _____, a direct or indirect subsidiary of XYZ, Inc.

XYZ, Inc.   **Employee**

By_____   By_____

Date_____   Date_____

Invention Assignment Agreements   An *invention assignment agreement* is one in which the employee agrees to assign to the employer any inventions that he or she may conceive of or create during her term of employment. The courts will enforce such agreements but will scrutinize them to make certain that they are fair. Thus, both the duration of the agreement and the scope of the rights granted must be reasonable under the circumstances.

The agreement should require the employee to disclose any preexisting inventions to which the employee claims ownership, as well as require the employee to disclose all inventions made during the course of employment as they occur. The agreement should also require the employee to cooperate in the pursuit of patents or copyrights on the inventions (see Exhibit 3.4).

Intellectual Property Audits

Every business should periodically conduct an *intellectual property audit*—a systematic review of the patent, copyright, trade secret, and trademark assets of the firm and an analysis of the company's procedures for protecting those assets. A thorough intellectual property audit not only discloses the nature and extent of the intellectual property assets owned by the company but also reveals gaps in existing company policy by uncovering information, ideas, or inventions that should be protected by intellectual property laws but are not. The ultimate outcomes of the audit should be an inventory of the intellectual property assets held by the company and the creation of processes and procedures that will ensure that these assets are identified and protected in the future.

Because intellectual property assets implicate legal, technological, and business concerns, audits should be conducted by a team of persons from the marketing, research, manufacturing, information technology, and legal functions. The actual performance of the audit will vary according to the extent and nature of the company's intellectual property activities.

In general, the audit team should inventory all inventions made by the company and should determine whether appropriate patents are in place. In particular, the company should evaluate its business processes to determine whether it should pursue business method patents on any of those processes. The audit team should determine whether third parties are infringing upon patents belonging to the company or whether the company is, even inadvertently, infringing upon the patents of others.

The audit team should identify all confidential or proprietary information held by the company and should review and assess the company's trade secret efforts. If necessary, the company should implement additional measures to ensure that confidential information retains its secret status. In particular, the company should institute explicit email and Internet-use policies regarding the distribution of sensitive or confidential information and should employ state-of-the-art computer security and encryption technology.

The audit team should inventory all copyrighted works owned by the company. The audit team should review all agreements entered into with third parties who have created "works for hire" to ensure that proper assignments of the copyright to the company have been made. The company should also review the actions of its employees, as the company may incur copyright infringement liability for employee activities such as the loading of unlicensed software onto the company's network or the unauthorized photocopying of materials. The company should clarify employee policies prohibiting such practices, if necessary.

EXHIBIT 3.4 Invention and Work Product Agreement

This Agreement between XYZ, Inc. including its direct and indirect subsidiaries and affiliates (hereinafter "XYZ, Inc.") and _____ (herein after "Employee") shall govern the responsibilities of Employee with respect to inventions. Entering into this agreement is a condition of Employee's employment by XYZ, Inc. but the agreement does not purport to set forth the terms of said employment.

WHEREAS, Employee is or desires to be employed by XYZ, Inc. or one of its direct or indirect subsidiaries or affiliates in a capacity in which Employee may contribute to and/or make inventions which may or may not be patentable;

WHEREAS, XYZ, Inc. and its direct and indirect subsidiaries and affiliates develop and use valuable technical and non-technical proprietary information and inventions which XYZ, Inc. and/or its direct and indirect subsidiaries and affiliates may wish to prevent others from using either by patents or by keeping this material secret and proprietary;

NOW, THEREFORE, in consideration of Employee's employment or continued employment by XYZ, Inc. or the relevant direct or indirect subsidiary or affiliate, it is agreed as follows:

1. Employee agrees to make a prompt and complete disclosure of every invention (as hereafter defined) which Employee conceives of or reduces to practice, and any patent application which Employee files, during the term of Employee's employment and further agrees that every said invention and patent application is the property of XYZ, Inc. Employee understands that the term "invention" means any discoveries, developments, concepts, and ideas whether patentable or not, which relate to any present or prospective activities of XYZ, Inc. with which activities Employee is acquainted as a result or consequence of Employee's employment with XYZ, Inc. Such inventions would include, but not be limited to processes, methods, products, software, apparatus, trade mark, trade names, advertising, and promotional material, as well as improvements therein and know-how related thereto. Employee further agrees that upon XYZ, Inc.'s request, but without expense to Employee, Employee will execute any so-called applications, assignments, and other instruments which XYZ, Inc. shall deem necessary or convenient for the protection of its said property in the United States and/or foreign countries and to render aid and assistance in any litigation or other proceeding pertaining to said property.

2. XYZ, Inc. agrees that any invention made by Employee in which XYZ, Inc. states in writing over the signature of its President & Vice President that it has no interest, may be freely-exploited by Employee.

3. Employee agrees that all writings, illustrations, models, and other such materials produced by Employee or put into Employee's possession by XYZ, Inc. during the term of and relating to Employee's employment are at all times XYZ, Inc.'s property and Employee will deliver the same over to XYZ, Inc. upon request or upon termination of Employee's employment and shall be work made for hire under U.S. Copyright Laws. To the extent that such works are not works made for hire as defined by U.S. Copyright Law, Employee hereby assigns, transfers, and grants to XYZ, Inc. any and all rights (including but not limited to copyrights) in and to all works provided hereunder. Any and all copyright ownership claims which Employee may raise as a result of work undertaken pursuant to this agreement are hereby assigned, transferred, and granted to XYZ, Inc.

4. This Agreement does not apply to an invention for which no equipment, supplies, facility, or trade secret information of employer was used and which was developed entirely on the Employee's own time, and (1) which does not relate (a) directly to the business of the employer or (b) to the employer's actual or demonstrably anticipated research or development or (2) which does not result from any work performed by the Employee for the employer.

5. The obligations of Employee under this agreement shall continue beyond the termination of employment with respect to inventions conceived or made by Employee during the period of employment, and shall be binding upon Employee's assigns, executors, administrators, and other legal representatives.

6. This Agreement supersedes and replaces any existing agreement, written or otherwise, entered into by Employee and XYZ, Inc. relating generally to the same subject matter. It is expressly understood, however, that nothing contained herein shall in any way alter the terms of any agreement between XYZ, Inc. and Employee, or any representative of Employee, with respect to collective bargaining agreements, termination, or any other aspects of employment which may be present and form part of an employment agreement between XYZ, Inc. and Employee.

Employee is to be employed at (insert XYZ, Inc. company) a direct or indirect subsidiary of XYZ, Inc.

XYZ, Inc.   **Employee**

By _____   By _____

Date _____   Date _____

This document is reprinted with the permission of the American Corporate Counsel Association (ACCA) as it originally appeared in the ACCA's Intellectual Property InfoPAK[SM] Copyright 1997, the American Corporate Counsel Association, all rights reserved.

The audit team should identify all trademarks being used by the company. It should evaluate unregistered marks to determine whether the company should register those marks. The audit team should determine whether third parties are infringing upon the company's trademarks or whether the company is infringing, even inadvertently, upon the marks of others.

Finally, the audit team should scrutinize employment agreements to make certain that the company is using and enforcing appropriate invention assignment agreements, noncompete covenants, and NDAs.

EXHIBIT 3.5 Summary of U.S. Intellectual Property Law

	ASSET PROTECTED	SOURCE OF PROTECTION	HOW ASSET CREATED	LENGTH OF PROTECTION	STANDARDS	WHAT CONSTITUTES INFRINGEMENT
Patent—Utility	Machines, industrial processes, compositions of matter, and articles of manufacture	Patent Act (federal statute)	By U.S. PTO upon application of inventor	Application filed after 6/8/95: 20 years from date of application Earlier applications: 17 years from date of issuance	Must be novel, nonobvious, and useful	Manufacture, use, offer for sale, or sale in U.S.; or use and sale in U.S. if invention made outside U.S. by patented process
Patent—Design	Ornamental designs for manufactured articles	Patent Act (federal statute)	By U.S. PTO upon application of inventor	14 years from date of issuance	Must be novel, nonobvious, and ornamental	Designs appear same to ordinary observer
Copyright	Expressions of ideas fixed in tangible form	Copyright Act (federal statute)	Automatically upon creation of a work of authorship	For post-1978 works: life of author plus 70 yrs.; works for hire: at least 95 yrs. after publication or 120 yrs. after creation	Must be original work of authorship fixed in tangible medium	Copying
Trade Secret	Business and commercial information	State statute or common law; Federal Economic Espionage Act	Automatically upon investment of time and money, provided security measures are taken	As long as information remains confidential	Must be confidential and commercially valuable information	Misappropriation
Trademark	Identifying words, names, symbols, or devices	Lanham Act (federal statute); common law	(1) Through adoption and use or (2) Through intent to use plus registration	As long as mark is used commercially	Must identify and distinguish goods or services	Confusion, mistake, or deception likely

DISCUSSION CASES

3.1 Trade Secrets—Definition

Al Minor & Associates, Inc. v. Martin, 881 N.E.2d 850 (Ohio 2008)

Robert E. Martin, a former employee of Al Minor & Associates, Inc. ("AMA") appeals from a decision of the Franklin County Court of Appeals that affirmed a trial court judgment that ... entered a $25,973 verdict in favor of AMA for fees not generated from former clients Martin had solicited using information he had memorized while working for AMA. * * *

[T]he issue here concerns whether the use of a memorized client list can be the basis of a trade secret violation pursuant to Ohio's Uniform Trade Secrets Act ("UTSA"). After review, we have concluded that the client information at issue in this case did not lose its status as a trade secret, or the protection of the UTSA, because it had been memorized by a former employee.

AMA is an actuarial firm that designs and administers retirement plans and that employs several "pension analysts" who work with approximately 500 clients. Al Minor Jr., who founded AMA in 1983 and serves as its president and sole shareholder, developed AMA's clientele, for which the firm maintains a confidential list.

In 1998, AMA hired Martin as a pension analyst but did not require him to sign either an employment contract or noncompete agreement. In 2002, while still employed by AMA, Martin organized his own company, Martin Consultants, L.L.C., with the purpose of providing the same type of services as AMA. In 2003, he resigned from AMA and, without taking any documents containing confidential client information, successfully solicited 15 AMA clients with information from his memory.

After learning of Martin's competing business, AMA filed the instant action against him ... claiming that he had violated Ohio's Trade Secrets Act by using confidential client information to solicit those clients. [The trial court found for AMA and awarded AMA a judgment of $25,973 against Martin.] * * *

Martin appealed ... , arguing that a memorized client list does not satisfy the definition of a trade secret, a contention disputed by AMA. The court of appeals affirmed the trial court .... * * *

In this court, Martin asserts that a client list memorized by a former employee cannot be the basis of a trade secret violation and that the appellate court's decision in this case overly restricts his right to compete in business against AMA. He also argues that AMA should not have the right to control the use of his memory and that AMA had the opportunity to protect its confidential information by way of an employment contract, which it did not do.

AMA counters that public policy in Ohio favors the protection of trade secrets, whether written or memorized; that the definition of a trade secret should focus on the nature of the information and potential harm that its use would cause the former employer; and that no meaningful difference exists between a written and memorized client list.

* * *

Ohio's protection of trade secrets arose at common law. In one of the earliest appellate decisions concerning trade secrets, *Natl. Tube Co. v. Eastern Tube Co.* (1902), an Ohio circuit court defined a trade secret as "a plan or process, tool, mechanism, or compound, known only to its owner and those of his employees to whom it is necessary to confide it, in order to apply it to the uses for which it is intended." In 1937, the court acknowledged that "[t]he authorities are quite uniform that disclosures of trade secrets by an employee secured by him in the course of confidential employment will be restrained by the process of injunction, and in numerous instances attempts to use for himself or for a new employer information relative to the trade or business in which he had been engaged, such as lists of customers regarded as confidential, have been restrained."

* * *

In 1994, the General Assembly enacted the UTSA, R.C. 1333.61 through 1333.69, which defines a "trade secret" as:

"[I]nformation, including the whole or any portion or phase of any scientific or technical information, design, process, procedure, formula, pattern, compilation, program, device, method, technique, or improvement, or any business information or plans, financial information, or listing of names, addresses, or telephone numbers, that satisfies both of the following:

(1) "It derives independent economic value, actual or potential, from not being generally known to, and not being readily ascertainable by proper means by, other persons who can obtain economic value from its disclosure or use."

(2) "It is the subject of efforts that are reasonable under the circumstances to maintain its secrecy." R.C. 1333.61(D)."

Furthermore, in [*State ex rel The Plain Dealer v. Ohio Dept. of Ins.*, 687 N.E.2d 661 (Ohio 1997)], we established a six-factor test for determining whether information constitutes a trade secret pursuant to R.C. 1333.61(D): "(1) The extent to which the information is known outside the business; (2) the extent to which it is known to those inside the business, *i.e.*, by the employees; (3) the precautions taken by the holder of the trade secret to guard the secrecy of the information; (4) the savings effected and the value to the holder in having the information as against competitors; (5) the amount of effort or money expended in obtaining and developing the information; and (6) the amount of time and expense it would take for others to acquire and duplicate the information."

Neither R.C. 1333.61(D) nor any provision of the UTSA suggests that, for purposes of trade secret protection, the General Assembly intended to distinguish between information that has been reduced to some tangible form and information that has been memorized. R.C. 1333.61(D) refers only to "information," including "any business information or plans, financial information, or listing of names, addresses, or telephone numbers," and the statute makes no mention of writings or other physical forms that such information might take. Furthermore, nothing in our six-factor test adopted in *Plain Dealer* indicates that the determination of whether a client list constitutes a trade secret depends on whether it was capable of being memorized or had been memorized.

The legislature, when enacting R.C. 1333.61(D), could have excluded memorized information from the definition of a trade secret or added a requirement that such information be reproduced in physical form in order to constitute a trade secret. But it did not, and we are not in a position to read such language into the statute. * * *

In addition, more than 40 other states have adopted the Uniform Trade Secrets Act in substantially similar form, and the majority position is that memorized information can be the basis for a trade secret violation. We acknowledge, however, that some courts adhere to the contrary position.

The majority position among our sister states is relevant with respect to the legislature's intent, because … "[t]he purpose of the enactment of the Uniform Trade Secrets Act was … 'to make uniform the law with respect to their subject among states enacting them.'"

Treatises on the subject of trade secrets also support the majority position that the determination of whether a client list is a protected trade secret does not depend on whether a former employee has memorized it. For example, in 2 Louis Altman, Callmann on Unfair Competition, Trademarks and Monopolies (5th Ed. 2005) 14-192–14-195, Section 14.25, the text states that, "[a]s to customer lists, the older rule in some jurisdictions permits taking by memorization. In principle, however, the distinction between written and memorized information should not be encouraged. The form of the information and the manner in which it is obtained are unimportant; the nature of the relationship and the defendant's conduct should be the determinative factors. The distinction places a premium upon good memory and a penalty upon forgetfulness, and it cannot be justified either from a logical or pragmatic point of view."

Citing more recent cases, the Callmann treatise explains, "The modern trend is to discard the written-memorized distinction; and the Uniform Trade Secrets Act has abrogated the common law rule which permitted misappropriation of customer lists by memorization." * * *

* * *

Based on the foregoing, we conclude that the determination of whether a client list constitutes a trade secret pursuant to R.C. 1333.61(D) does not depend on whether it has been memorized by a former employee. Information that constitutes a trade secret pursuant to R.C. 1333.61(D) does not lose its character as a trade secret if it has been memorized. It is the information that is protected by the UTSA, regardless of the manner, mode, or form in which it is stored—whether on paper, in a computer, in one's memory, or in any other medium.

Every employee will of course have memories casually retained from the ordinary course of employment. The Uniform Trade Secrets Act does not apply to the use of memorized information that is not a trade secret pursuant to R.C. 1333.61(D).

* * *

In this case, AMA's client list constituted a trade secret pursuant to R.C. 1333.61(D), and the fact that Martin had memorized that client list before leaving AMA does not change its status as a trade secret or remove it from the protection of the UTSA. For these reasons, we therefore affirm the judgment of the court of appeals.

Judgment accordingly.

___

QUESTIONS FOR DISCUSSION FOR CASE 3.1

1. Was the definition of a test for trade secrets in Ohio developed by the legislature, the courts, or both?
2. Are the decisions of courts in other states on the issue presented in this case binding on the Ohio Supreme Court? If not, why does this court consider those decisions?
3. AMA failed to have Martin sign an employment contract protecting its confidential information. Why is that failure irrelevant to the outcome of this case?

___

3.2 Trade Secrets—Required Elements
Strategic Directions Group, Inc. v. Bristol-Myers Squibb Co., 293 F.3d 1062 (8th Cir. 2002)

Strategic Directions Group, Inc. (SDG) appeals from a judgment of the district court granting summary judgment in favor of Bristol-Myers Squibb Company (Bristol-Myers) in this trade secrets … case. We affirm.

Background
SDG is a marketing research company owned and operated by Carol and Doran Levy. Bristol-Myers is a pharmaceutical company which manufactures Pravachol, a drug designed to reduce cholesterol. In 1996, a Bristol-Myers' marketing manager read the Levys' 1993 book, *Segmenting the Mature Market*, which dealt with marketing strategies for targeting consumers over 50 years old. One chapter of the book dealt with health issues. Based on survey responses to 50 classification questions, the book divided the market into four different kinds of customers, or segments. The classifications questions were statements to which the respondents were asked to agree or disagree, such as "I am careful to eat a balanced diet" and "I believe in getting a yearly physical from my doctor."

In May 1997 Bristol-Myers agreed to pay SDG $275,000 for "a copy of a reduced battery of classification questions for use in connection with the collection of data from persons calling a [Bristol-Myers'

toll-free] telephone number" published in Pravachol advertisements. The agreement further provided that the questions were only to be used "in connection with the database collected for Pravachol and only in connection with the [toll-free] telephone number." In June 1997, SDG submitted nine questions relating to diet, medication, medical check-ups, and insurance. Bristol-Myers used some of them in a set of questions posed to callers to the toll-free telephone number. For example, callers to the telephone number were asked to agree or disagree to varying degrees to statements, including "I maintain a regular schedule of medical check-ups with my doctor" and "I am careful to eat a balanced diet." Bristol-Myers also used three of the classification questions in a follow-up survey of persons who had called the toll-free number.

In 1999, SDG filed a complaint against Bristol-Myers, alleging … a misappropriation of trade secrets claim in violation of Minn. Stat. § 325C.01. The district court granted Bristol-Myers's motion for summary judgment as to the trade secret claim …. As to the trade secret claim, the district court held that the nine questions SDG had provided Bristol-Myers were not trade secrets, because they were not secret. Among other things, the district court noted the questions were readily ascertainable in public sources, such as the Levys' 1993 book, SDG annual surveys, and a copyright filing. Indeed, the district court noted that the nine questions SDG claimed were trade secrets were specifically designed for public consumption on the toll-free telephone number. * * *

* * *

Discussion

* * *

The district court did not err in granting summary judgment in favor of Bristol-Myers on SDG's trade secrets claim. To qualify as a trade secret under Minn. Stat. § 325C.01, "(1) the information must not be generally known nor readily ascertainable; (2) the information must derive independent economic value from secrecy; [and] (3) the plaintiff must make reasonable efforts to maintain secrecy." *Widmark v. Northrup King Co.*, 530 N.W.2d 588, 592 (Minn. Ct. App. 1995). SDG does not, and could not, dispute that the individual questions were readily ascertainable and that it made no attempt to keep them secret. To the contrary, SDG concedes that the nine questions were in *Segmenting the Mature Market* and presented in its annual surveys, public seminars, and a copyright filing. Thus, not only did SDG fail to make a reasonable effort to keep the questions secret, it repeatedly placed them in the public domain. Indeed, as the district court noted, the "questions were specifically designed for public consumption." Anyone calling the toll-free telephone number had access to the questions.

SDG argues that even if the individual questions were not trade secrets, their combination was statutorily protected. We disagree. In some cases, a novel or unique combination of elements may constitute a trade secret. However, as here, "mere variations on widely used [information] cannot be trade secrets." For example, in *Jostens, Inc. v. Nat'l Computer Sys., Inc.*, 318 N.W.2d 691, 699 (Minn. 1982) the Minnesota Supreme Court held that a computer system was not a trade secret because it was merely a combination of known sub-systems, explaining the combination did not "achieve the degree of novelty or 'unknownness' needed for a trade secret." Such is also the case here. "Simply to assert a trade secret resides in some combination of otherwise known data, is not sufficient …." *Id.* Although Bristol-Myers paid SDG for selecting a reduced number of questions from its battery of questions, "the law of trade secrets will not protect talent or expertise, only secret information." Here, the questions, individually or in combination, were not secret.

* * *

Accordingly, we affirm the judgment of the district court.

QUESTIONS FOR DISCUSSION FOR CASE 3.2

1. Why did the court find that SDG did not have a protectable trade secret?
2. Why did the court find that Bristol-Myers had not engaged in misappropriation?
3. If SDG did not have a valid trade secret here, why did Bristol-Myers enter into a contract to pay SDG $275,000 for these questions?

3.3 Noncompete Covenant, Trade Secrets—Required Elements
Del Monte Fresh Produce, N.A., Inc. v. Chiquita Brands Int'l, Inc., 616 F. Supp. 2d 805 (E.D. Ill. 2009)

Del Monte Fresh Produce N.A., Inc., alleges its former employee Kim Kinnavy breached her confidentiality and non-compete agreement when she left Del Monte to work for Chiquita Brands International. * * * Kinnavy den[ies] the allegations and move[s] for summary judgment …. * * *

I. Factual Background

For such a complex case, the facts are quite simple. Kim Kinnavy worked in the Illinois office of Del Monte as

district sales manager from 1999 until she resigned in 2007. As a sales manager, Kinnavy worked with customers who had banana supply contracts. Del Monte gave its sales managers—including Kinnavy—laptop computers and access to Del Monte's customer database. Two weeks before Kinnavy resigned, she used her laptop to e-mail herself files with the following titles: (a) Fuel surcharge: (b) Revised royal; (c) Contract renewals; (d) Pineapple update; (e) Phone list; (f) North American Customer Database 2005; (g) Fax List—Old Machine; (h) Fax List—III-6-06; and (i) CUSTMAST.xls. Kinnavy also e-mailed a copy of the "Fax List" and the "Phone List" to Mike Elsen, a broker working in Phoenix Arizona. Kinnavy denies she used the files for commercial purposes or that the files contained confidential information. After resigning, Kinnavy went to work for one of Del Monte's chief competitors: Chiquita Brands International.

Upon learning of Kinnavy's new employment, Del Monte sued Kinnavy in the Circuit Court of Cook County. Next, Del Monte removed the case to this Court on the basis of diversity jurisdiction .... The essence of Del Monte's complaint is that Kinnavy violated federal law, and breached her employment agreements by working for a competitor and e-mailing confidential information to a third party. * * * Kinnavy move[s] for summary judgment on all claims.

* * *

III. Analysis

* * *

D. The Non-Compete Agreement is Unenforceable

Counts VI and VII of Del Monte's Amended Complaint alleges Kinnavy breached Del Monte's "Policy of Trade Secret and Non-Competition." ("Non-Compete Agreement") The Non-Compete agreement states:

> For a period of 12 months from the date of Employee's separation from the employment with the Company, the Employee shall not be employed by ... or connected in any manner with, any business which represents, distributes, sells or brokers fresh vegetables, fresh fruit, and other fresh produce products: (a) to any person who or entity which is a customer of the Company on the date of termination of the Employee's employment ... or during the 12 month period prior thereto ... or (b) on behalf of or supplied by any person who or entity which is a supplier of the Company at the date of termination ...

* * *

As a general rule, Illinois courts are reluctant to enforce restrictive covenants. Post-employment restrictive covenants "operate as partial restrictions on trade" and must be carefully scrutinized by the reviewing court. Nevertheless, a restrictive covenant may be enforceable if its terms are "reasonable and necessary to protect a legitimate business interest of the employer." A "restrictive covenant's reasonableness is measured by its hardship to the employee, its effect upon the general public, and the reasonableness of the time, territory, and activity restrictions."

The Non-Compete agreement signed by Kinnavy is too broad and far-reaching to be enforceable. First, the Non-Compete contains no geographic restrictions. Thus, even if Kinnavy were to move to Lagos, Nigeria, she would still be bound by the restrictive covenant; this is unreasonable. In response, Del Monte argues extra restrictions are necessary because it is a multinational firm that competes globally. This argument misses the mark. For example, in *Roberge v. Qualitek Int'l, Inc.*, [2002 U.S. Dist. LEXIS 1217, at *12 (N.D. Ill. Jan. 28, 2002)], the court analyzed a similar contention by an employer seeking to enforce a non-compete:

> Qualitek asserts that because it has customers globally and has competitors throughout the United States ... inserting an arbitrary boundary such as prohibiting Roberge from competing with Qualitek in the State of Illinois ... would not protect Qualitek's legitimate interests. While this is perhaps the most logical argument [Qualitek] could make ... *it is a position that has been rejected countless times by both state and federal courts in Illinois* [citing cases] Given this compelling authority we reject Qualitek's argument ...

2002 U.S. Dist. LEXIS 1217, at *16-17 (emphasis added).

The Non-Compete agreement also contains blanket prohibitions on the *types* of employment Kinnavy can pursue. In Illinois, "an individual has a fundamental right to use his general knowledge and skills to purse the occupation for which he is best suited." But here, the Non-Compete prohibits Kinnavy from "being connected in *any manner* with" an entity that bought fruit, vegetables, or other produce from Del Monte. Under these terms, Kinnavy could not work as a cashier at a Piggly-Wiggly that bought produce from Del Monte. These restrictions are simply too broad to be enforceable. * * * Similarly, in *Telxon Corp. v. Hoffman*, the court refused to enforce a non-compete agreement where the scope of the prohibited activities [was] so broad that "the agreement would preclude Hoffman from working as a competitor's janitor." 720 F. Supp. 657, 665 (N.D. Ill. 1989). Because agreements "which restrict the signor's ability to work for a competitor without regard to capacity have repeatedly been declared contrary to law" the Court finds Del Monte's Non-Compete agreement is unenforceable.

Finally, Del Monte asks the Court—in the event the Non-Compete is found to be invalid—to re-write the contract so it is in compliance with Illinois law. The Court declines Del Monte's invitation. The Non-Compete agreement is simply too broad and far-reaching to be salvageable. Kinnavy's motion for summary judgment as to Counts VI is granted.

E. The Court Declines to Sever the Invalid Portion of the Contract

The Court finds the restrictive covenant contained in the "Policy of Trade Secret and Non-Competition" is invalid as a matter of law. Therefore, the Court must decide whether the valid portions of the contract can be severed from the document. In general, "courts which will enforce a contract with a portion severed generally do so when the severed portion does not go to the contract's essence." Here, the non-competition clause was an essential feature of the contract at issue. The plain language of the contract states:

> *each of the above provisions is essential to* the Company and the Company would not furnish the Employee the consideration set forth in this Policy absent the Employee's agreement to abide by and be bound by each of the above provisions.

This language alone dooms Del Monte's severability argument.

It is clear Del Monte intended this contract to be an all or nothing, take it or leave it proposition. In other words, the contract is not divisible. Again, the language of the contract is instructive: "The Company would not furnish the Employee the consideration set forth in this Policy absent the Employee's agreement to abide by and be bound by *each of the above provisions.*" The Court will not sever the Non-Compete clause from the rest of the contract. Accordingly, the "Policy of Trade Secret and Non-Competition" is invalid and unenforceable. The Court grants Kinnavy's motion for summary judgment as to Count VII.

F. Del Monte's Illinois Trade Secret Act Claim is Deficient

Del Monte argues Kinnavy misappropriated certain confidential Del Monte data, and in doing so, she violated the Illinois Trade Secret Act. Specifically, Del Monte contends Kinnavy misappropriated: "prices, customer requirements, customer names, and contact information." In response, Kinnavy contends the type of information she allegedly misappropriated is not protected under the [Illinois Trade Secret Act]. The Court agrees.

Under the Illinois Trade Secrets Act [ITSA], a plaintiff may recover for damages incurred as a result of the misappropriation of a trade secret. In order "to state a claim for trade secret misappropriation under the ITSA, a plaintiff must establish that it had: (1) a trade secret, (2) that the defendant misappropriated and (3) used for business purposes." At issue here is whether Del Monte satisfied the first element. The ITSA defines "trade secret" as:

> information, including but not limited to, technical or non-technical data, a formula, pattern, compilation, program, device, method, technique, drawing, process, financial data, or list of actual or potential customers or suppliers, that:
>
> (1) is sufficiently secret to derive economic value, actual or potential, from not being generally known to other persons who can obtain economic value from its disclosure or use; and
> (2) is the subject of efforts that are reasonable under the circumstances to maintain its secrecy or confidentiality.

Del Monte argues its price information qualifies as a trade secret. But, the "Illinois appellate courts which have addressed the issue have consistently held that price information which is disclosed by a business to any of its customers ... does not constitute trade secret information protected by the Act." For example, in *Trailer Leasing*, the court declined to find that pricing information was a trade secret:

> It is also unclear as to why general rate information constitutes a trade secret. By all accounts, this is a highly competitive business, and it is unlikely that rate information is ever secret, and if so, that it remains secret for very long. If competitor "A" gives a customer an advantageous rate, it will not be long before the customer shops that rate around and tries to get competitor "B" to go even lower; that is the nature of a competitive market.

Trailer Leasing Co. v. Associates Commer Corp., 1996 U.S. Dist. LEXIS 11366, at *3 (N.D. Ill. Aug. 8 1996). There is no indication Del Monte's customers were prohibited from divulging the prices they paid for bananas. There is no indication Kinnavy misappropriated a pricing formula. As such, the Court finds that price information alone cannot constitute a trade secret.

Del Monte also asserts the identity of its customers is entitled to protection under the ITSA. This is incorrect. Rick Cooper—Vice President of Sales and Kinnavy's supervisor—gave the following testimony during his deposition:

Q: Are you contending that Chiquita does not know who your customers are?

A: No. No, I'm not.

Q: Do you know who Chiquita's customers are?

A: Yes, we do.

Q: Is there anything confidential about that?

A: No.

To be sure, Del Monte and Chiquita are fierce competitors. But, there seems to be little doubt about which customers are buying bananas from which company. Indeed, all one needs to do is go to the grocery store and look at the sticker on the bananas to see whether Del Monte or Chiquita is supplying the fruit. There is no protectable interest where a business' customers are known throughout the industry. For example, one of the clients Del Monte claims it lost because of Kinnavy—The Horton Fruit Company—prominently displays on its website that it is "a licensed Dole re-packer." During Cooper's deposition, he admitted there would be nothing confidential or improper about someone walking into a grocery store and asking who supplied their bananas. The ITSA requires the protected information to be "sufficiently secret to derive economic value." Here, the identity of customers buying fruit from Del Monte was not sufficiently secret to warrant protection under the ITSA.

Customer contact information that takes little effort to compile is not protectable under the ITSA. Cooper acknowledged Del Monte and Chiquita are well aware of each other's customers. Thus, an individual would only need to look in the yellow pages to obtain the contact information of Del Monte customers. During his deposition Cooper was asked why the "phone list" Kinnavy e-mailed to Mike Elsen would be valuable to a competitor, he replied that it would "save somebody the time of looking Albertson's Denver location up in the phonebook." A list of grocery stores' phone numbers is not "sufficiently secret" to confer trade secret status on Del Monte's contact list.

Finally, Del Monte contends information about its customers' needs and requirements is entitled to protection as a trade secret. The Seventh Circuit addressed a similar situation in *Curtis 1000 v. Suess*, where a stationary [sic] company sued an ex-employee who left to work for a competitor. The Curtis 1000 company claimed the knowledge of its customers' requirements was entitled to trade secret protection. The court began by noting that an employee can gain valuable insight into the behavior of long-term customers: "Customers often conceal their real needs, preferences, and above all, reservation prices in order to induce better terms from sellers. Suess presumably had sniffed out those true needs, preferences, and reservation prices." The operative question, however, is whether the employee is selling a service or whether the employee is selling goods where there is no qualitative differentiation across the marketplace, in other words, a mere commodity:

Illinois cases distinguish between sellers of services, especially professional services such as accounting and consulting, and sellers of ordinary goods. In the former class, where the quality of the seller's service is difficult to determine by simple inspection, customers come to repose trust in a particular seller, and that trust is a valuable business asset, created by years of careful management, that the employee is not allowed to take away with him.

In the latter class, involving the sale of goods, the element of trust is attenuated, particularly where as in this case the good is a simple and common one sold under competitive conditions. In these cases, Illinois law does not permit the seller to claim a protectable interest in his relations with his customers ... For here current price and quality, rather than a past investment in meeting customers' needs, are the decisive factors in the continued success of the firm, and they of course are not appropriated by the departing employee.

Curtis 1000 v. Suess, 24 F.3d 941, 948 (7th Cir. 1994).

Kinnavy handled banana supply contracts for Del Monte. Bananas are simple, non-unique goods. The Court concludes Kinnavy and Del Monte were selling a commodity, rather than providing a service. In other words, the "decisive factors" in customers choosing Del Monte are pricing and quality. These are things that cannot be appropriated by Kinnavy. For example, Sean Walsh—the director of produce for Spartan Grocery Stores, Inc.—testified Spartan switched its contract from Del Monte to Chiquita in large part because Chiquita's bananas were cheaper. This would make sense given that Spartan was buying a commodity. Simply put, if Del Monte provides delicious bananas to its customers at prices below Chiquita its business will succeed. The record does not support Del Monte's claim that knowledge of its customers' requirements is a trade secret. The Court grants Kinnavy's motion for summary judgment as to Count VIII.

＊ ＊ ＊

QUESTIONS FOR DISCUSSION FOR CASE 3.3

1. Why is this state law claim being heard in federal court?
2. Why does the court conclude that this noncompete agreement is unenforceable? What terms in the agreement would need to be redrafted in order to make the agreement enforceable?
3. Why does court decline to exercise the "blue pencil rule" to salvage this agreement?
4. What information did Del Monte claim were trade secrets? Why did the court conclude there were no protectable trade secrets here?
5. Do you believe that Kinnavy's actions were ethical? Why, or why not?

3.4 Covenants Not to Compete

Ticor Title Insurance Co. v. Cohen, 173 F.3d 63 (2d Cir 1999)

Defendant Kenneth C. Cohen (defendant or appellant) appeals from a judgment entered July 1, 1998 in the United States District Court for the Southern District of New York (Martin, J.) that issued a permanent injunction against him and in favor of plaintiffs Ticor Title Insurance Co. and Chicago Title Insurance Co. ＊ ＊ ＊

A principal question to be resolved is whether appellant's services as an employee were so unique to his employer as to provide a basis for injunctive relief. In analyzing whether an employee's services are unique, the focus today is less on the uniqueness of the individual person of the employee, testing whether such person is extraordinary in the sense, for example, of Beethoven as a composer, Einstein as a physicist, or Michelangelo as an artist, where one can fairly say that nature made them and then broke the mold. Instead, now the inquiry is more focused on the employee's relationship to the employer's business to ascertain whether his or her services and value to that operation may be said to be unique, special or extraordinary; that inquiry, because individual circumstances differ so widely, must of necessity be on a case-by-case basis.

Background
Facts Relating to Employment
A. The Parties
Plaintiffs are affiliated companies that sell title insurance nationwide. Title insurance insures the buyer of real property, or a lender secured by real property, against defects in the legal title to the property, and guarantees that, in the event a defect in title surfaces, the insurer will reimburse the insured for losses associated with the defect, or will take steps necessary to correct it. This kind of insurance is almost always purchased when real estate is conveyed. Ticor has been, and remains today, the leading title insurance company in New York State. It focuses primarily on multi-million dollar transactions that are handled by real estate lawyers. On large transactions more than one title insurance company is often employed in order to spread the risk.

Defendant Cohen was employed by Ticor as a title insurance salesman. Title insurance salespeople contact real estate attorneys, handle title searches for them, and sell them policies; those salespeople from different title insurance companies compete to insure the same real estate transaction, seeking their business from the same group of widely-known attorneys. Due to the nature of the business, those attorneys commonly have relationships with more than one title insurance company.

Cohen began working for Ticor in 1981, shortly after graduating from college, as a sales account manager and within six years was a senior vice president in charge of several major accounts. Thus, he has been a title insurance salesman for Ticor for nearly all of his professional career. His clients have consisted almost exclusively of real estate attorneys in large New York law firms. As his supervisor testified, Cohen obtains his business due to his knowledge of the business, his professionalism, his ability to work through problems, and his ability to get things done.

B. Employment Contract

Ticor and Cohen, both represented by counsel, entered into an Employment Contract on October 1, 1995. There were extensive negotiations over its terms, including the covenant not to compete, which is at issue on this appeal. The contract's stated term is until December 31, 1999, although Cohen—but not Ticor-could terminate it without cause on 30 days' notice.

The non-compete provision ... stated that during his employment with Ticor and "for a period ending on the earlier of ... June 30, 2000 or ... 180 days following [his] termination of employment," Cohen would not:

> for himself, or on behalf of any other person, or in conjunction with any other person, firm, partnership, corporation or other entity, engage in the business of Title Insurance ... in the State of New York.

* * *

It also contains the following express representation regarding the material nature of the covenant not to compete:

> [Ticor] is willing to enter into this contract only on condition that [Cohen] accept certain post-employment restrictions with respect to subsequent reemployment set forth herein and [Cohen] is prepared to accept such condition.

Negotiation of the post-employment non-competition provision of the Employment Contract culminated in a fax from Cohen's counsel to Ticor's counsel dated October 27, 1995 in which Cohen's counsel provided a proposed final version that included some additional modifications. Ticor accepted this proposed final version, and it was embodied, *verbatim*, in the final executed agreement. Thus, the non-compete provision defendant now asserts is unenforceable was drafted (in its final form) by his own lawyer.

Cohen enjoyed exclusive responsibility for key Ticor accounts throughout the entire term of his employment. A number of the accounts for which defendant had exclusive responsibility predated his 17-year employment, and no other Ticor sales representative was permitted to service them during the term of the Employment Contract.

In consideration for Cohen's agreeing to the recited post-employment restrictions, he was made one of the highest paid Ticor sales representatives, being guaranteed during the term of the Employment Contract annual compensation of $600,000, consisting of a base salary of $200,000 plus commissions. His total compensation in 1997 exceeded $1.1 million.

In addition to compensation, defendant received expense account reimbursements that by 1997 exceeded $150,000 per year, and which included fully paid memberships in exclusive clubs, as well as tickets to New York's professional sporting events and Broadway shows. His fringe benefits went far beyond those provided other Ticor sales representatives whose expense reimbursements are generally limited to $30,000 per year. Cohen also had his own six person staff at Ticor, all of whom reported directly to him. No other Ticor representative had such staff support.

C. Breach of Contract

On April 20, 1998 TitleServ, a direct competitor of Ticor, offered to employ Cohen. As part of that offer, TitleServ agreed to indemnify Cohen by paying him a salary during the six-month period (*i.e.*, the 180 days hiatus from employment) in the event that the covenant not to compete was enforced. Defendant sent plaintiff a letter on April 21, 1998 notifying it of his resignation effective May 21, 1998 and agreed to begin working for TitleServ on May 27, 1998.

Appellant commenced employment with his new employer on that date. His employment contract there guarantees him a minimum salary of $750,000 and a signing bonus of $2 million dollars, regardless of the outcome of this litigation. Cohen has received this signing bonus and has begun receiving salary payments, as scheduled. He admits to speaking with 20 Ticor customers about TitleServ before submitting his letter of resignation, and telling each of them that he was considering leaving Ticor and joining a competitor firm. Cohen maintains that this was an effort on his part to learn more information about TitleServ, including its ability to service the New York market and the opportunity he was being offered.

During the course of this due diligence, Cohen insists he never discussed transferring any business from Ticor to TitleServ, nor did he discuss any specific deals. However, this assertion is undermined by defendant's deposition testimony concerning conversations with Martin Polevoy of the Bachner Tally law firm, in which he admits he directly solicited Polevoy's business for TitleServ and, after initial resistance from Polevoy, eventually secured a promise that Polevoy follow him by taking his firm's insurance business to TitleServ.

Prior Proceedings

Ticor commenced this action on June 5, 1998 and applied that day for a temporary restraining order and preliminary injunction. [T]he district court entered a temporary restraining order. * * * On June 19, 1998 the district court heard further argument and extended the temporary restraining order for an additional ten days. * * *

On July 1, 1998 the district court issued its opinion and order permanently enjoining Cohen from working in the title insurance business and from appropriating Ticor's corporate opportunities with its current or prospective customers for a period of six months. * * *

* * * From the grant of a permanent injunction, Cohen appeals. We affirm.

Discussion

* * *

I Injunctive Relief

A. Irreparable Harm

An award of an injunction is not something a plaintiff is entitled to as a matter of right, but rather it is an equitable remedy issued by a trial court, within the broad bounds of its discretion, after it weighs the potential benefits and harm to be incurred by the parties from the granting or denying of such relief. An order involving injunctive relief will not be reversed unless it is contrary to some rule of equity or results from a discretion improvidently exercised. In other words, such an order is subject to reversal only for an abuse of discretion or for a clear error of law.

An injunction should be granted when the intervention of a court of equity is essential to protect a party's property rights against injuries that would otherwise be irremediable. The basic requirements to obtain injunctive relief have always been a showing of irreparable injury and the inadequacy of legal remedies. * * *

[W]e think for several reasons irreparable harm has shown to be present in this case. Initially, it would be very difficult to calculate monetary damages that would successfully redress the loss of a relationship with a client that would produce an indeterminate amount of business in years to come. In fact, the employment contract sought to be enforced concedes that in the event of Cohen's breach of the post-employment competition provision, Ticor shall be entitled to injunctive relief, because it would cause irreparable injury. * * * We agree with the district court that irreparable injury exists in this case.

II Covenant Not to Compete

A. In General

We turn to the merits. To gain some insight into the subject of non-competition contracts, we look to an early common law case in England where much of the law in this area was set forth. That case is *Mitchell v. Reynolds*, 1 P. Wins. 181, 24 Eng. Rep. 347 (Q.B. 1711), which has, through the ensuing 290 years, been frequently cited and followed. There, plaintiff alleged defendant had for good consideration assigned him his bakehouse in Liquorpond Street for five years, and defendant had agreed not to engage in trade as a baker in that neighborhood for that time, and if he did he had to play plaintiff 50 pounds. When defendant began baking again, seeking the local trade, plaintiff sued. Defendant declared that because he was a baker by trade, the bond not to engage in that trade was void as a restraint on a person's ability to earn his livelihood. [The court] disagreed and held that this particular restraint of trade was not void, because a "man may, upon a valuable consideration, by his own consent and for his own profit, give over his trade; and part with it to another in a particular place." The English court added that all contracts containing only a bare restraint of trade and more must be void, but where circumstances are shown that make it a "reasonable and useful contract," the contract will be ruled good and enforced by the courts.

The issue of whether a restrictive covenant not to compete is enforceable by way of an injunction depends in the first place upon whether the covenant is reasonable in time and geographic area. In this equation, courts must weigh the need to protect the employer's legitimate business interests against the employee's concern regarding the possible loss of livelihood, a result strongly disfavored by public policy in New York.

A scholarly commentator described the tension between these competing concerns, which we face in the case at hand, in this fashion: An employer will sometimes believe its clientele is a form of property that belongs to it and any new business a salesperson drums up is for its benefit because this is what the salesperson was hired and paid to do. The employee believes, to the contrary, the duty to preserve customer relationships ceases when employment ends and the employee's freedom to use contacts he or she developed may not be impaired by restraints that inhibit competition and an employee's ability to earn a living. The always present potential problem is whether a customer will come to value the salesperson more than the employer's product. When the product is not that much different from those available from competitors, such a customer is ripe to abandon the employer and follow the employee should he go to work for a competitor.

That scenario fits the circumstances revealed by the present record. The way to deal with these conflicting interests is by contract, which is what the parties before us purported to do, only now appellant insists ... that the non-compete provision is void as a contract in restraint of trade and therefore violates public policy.

The law points in a different direction. Over a hundred years ago New York's highest court observed ... that contracts in partial restraint of trade, if reasonable, are permitted. Because of strong public policy militating against the sanctioning of a person's loss of the ability to earn a livelihood, New York law subjects a non-compete covenant by an employee to "an overriding limitation of reasonableness" which hinges on the facts of each case. Assuming a covenant by an employee not to compete surmounts its first hurdle, that is, that it is reasonable in time and geographic scope, enforcement will be granted to the extent necessary (1) to prevent an employee's solicitation or disclosure of trade secrets, (2) to prevent an employee's release of confidential information regarding the employer's customers, or (3) in those cases where the employee's services to the employer are deemed special or unique. In the case at hand we are satisfied that the reasonableness test was met because the duration of the covenant was relatively short (six months) and the scope was not geographically overbroad. In any event, appellant does not argue that the covenant is unreasonable in time and scope. Rather, he argues that the services he provided to Ticor were not sufficiently unique to justify injunctive relief.

B. Unique Services

New York, following English law, recognizes the availability of injunctive relief where the non-compete covenant is found to be reasonable and the employee's services are unique. Services that are not simply of value to the employer, but that may also truly be said to be special, unique or extraordinary may entitle an employer to injunctive relief. An injunction may be used to bar such person from working elsewhere. If the unique services of such employee are available to a competitor, the employer obviously suffers irreparable harm.

Unique services have been found in various categories of employment where the services are dependent on an employee's special talents, such categories include musicians, professional athletes, actors and the like. In those

kinds of cases injunctive relief has been available to prevent the breach of an employment contract where the individual performer has such ability and reputation that his or her place may not easily be filled. We recognized this category of uniqueness in the case of the services of an acrobat who, in his performance, with one hand lifted his co-performer, a grown man, from a full-length position on the floor, an act described as "the most marvelous thing that has ever been [done] before." * * *

It has always been the rule, however, that to fall within this category of employees against whom equity will enforce a negative covenant, it is not necessary that the employee should be the only "star" of his employer, or that the business will grind to a halt if the employee leaves. Hence, as noted earlier, in determining uniqueness the inquiry now focuses more on the employee's relationship to the employer's business than on the individual person of the employee.

The "unique services" category has not often been the basis upon which a New York court has granted an injunction, and thus its full ambit there is unclear. However, in *Maltby v. Harlow Meyer Savage, Inc.,* 166 Misc. 2d 481, 486, 633 N.Y.S.2d 926 (Sup. Ct. N.Y. County 1995), aff'd, 223 A.D.2d 516, 637 N.Y.S.2d 110 (1st Dep't 1996), the Supreme Court in New York County found that several currency traders were unique employees because they had "unique relationships with the customers with whom they have been dealing," which were developed while they were employed and, partially at the employer's expense. The district court found the facts in *Maltby* so similar to those in the case at hand that it felt compelled in applying New York law to grant an injunction. Like *Maltby*, all of Cohen's clients came to him during his time at Ticor, and were developed, in part, at Ticor's expense. For example, about half of Cohen's clients he had attracted himself, but the other half were inherited from other departing Ticor salesmen. Cohen maintained these relationships, at least in part, by the use of the substantial entertainment expense account provided by Ticor. For instance, in 1997 Cohen spent $170,000 entertaining clients, and in the first five months of 1998 he spent about $138,000.

The trial court found Cohen's relationship with clients were "special" and qualified as unique services. It deemed these relationships unique for several reasons. First, since the costs and terms of title insurance in New York are fixed by law, competition for business relies more heavily on personal relationships. Second, since potential clients—New York law firms with real estate practices—are limited and well known through the industry, maintaining current clients from this established group is crucial. Third, the trial court noted that, as in *Maltby*, Cohen had negotiated his employment contract and the non-compete clause with the assistance of counsel and not from an inferior bargaining position.

Maltby found a trader's absence from the market for six months did not make him unemployable or affect his ability to earn a living in the industry. Here, the non-compete period is also six months, and quite plainly Cohen is not disabled from reviving his relationships with clients after the six months' absence, which would allow a new Ticor salesman sufficient opportunity to establish a fledgling relationship with Cohen's clients at Ticor.

Appellant maintains that *Maltby* can be distinguished, because in that case the employees were paid their base salary during the restricted period, while Cohen will receive nothing during his six-month hiatus. The significance of the salary paid in *Maltby* was that it helped alleviate the policy concern that non-compete provisions prevent a person from earning a livelihood. Here, by the same token, part of Cohen's $600,000 per year salary was in exchange for his promise not to compete for six months after termination, and since the employer had given Cohen sufficient funds to sustain him for six months, the public policy concern regarding impairment of earning a livelihood was assuaged. * * *

* * *

As stated in *Service Sys. Corp. v. Harris*, 41 A.D.2d 20, 23–24, 341 N.Y.S.2d 702 (4th Dep't 1973), "an employer has sufficient interest in retaining present customers to support an employee covenant where the employee's relationship with the customers is such that there is a substantial risk that the employee may be able to divert all or part of the business." In the present case this risk is clearly evidenced by the fact that in 1997 another employee, Neil Clarke, left for TitleServ and took 75 percent of his clients with him. And, this is further demonstrated by appellant's successful solicitation of a law firm to follow him to TitleServ.* * *

* * *

Conclusion

For the reasons stated, therefore, the judgment entered in district court enjoining defendant under the noncompetition contract is affirmed.

QUESTIONS FOR DISCUSSION FOR CASE 3.4

1. What role does precedent play in this decision?
2. What factors led this court to conclude that the noncompete agreement was enforceable?
3. How does the court balance the interests of the employee and employer in deciding whether to issue an injunction?

3.5 Protection of Unsolicited Ideas

Vent v. Mars Snackfood U.S., LLC, 611 F. Supp. 2d 333 (S.D. N.Y. 2009)

Bonnie Vent, a citizen of California, filed this action against Mars Snackfood US, LLC, and Mars, Inc. (collectively, "Mars"), corporations that are considered for purposes of diversity jurisdiction citizens of New Jersey and Virginia. * * *

* * * Mars filed a motion to dismiss …. In her opposition to Mars's motion to dismiss, Ms. Vent … agrees with Mars's assertion that New Jersey law controls the … misappropriation of idea claim.

* * *

For the following reasons, the Court grants Mars's motion to dismiss.

I

Background

Ms. Vent is a freelance entertainment broker, focusing particularly on actors and actresses from classic television programs. As relevant here, Ms. Vent represented various individuals who starred in the 1960s television program "The Addams Family," including the actors and actress who played Cousin It (Felix Silla), Pugsley (Ken Weatherwax), and Wednesday (Lisa Loring).

In August 2006, Ms. Vent was preparing to help launch the release of the Addams Family DVD Volume 1. She called Claire O'Donnell, a senior marketing buyer for Mars based in New Jersey. During this telephone call, Ms. Vent claims that she "pitched a specific, novel, and concrete idea for a cross-promotion between Addams Family characters and M&M's candies [sic] for Halloween." According to the Amended Complaint, "[t]he idea conveyed by [Ms. Vent] to Ms. O'Donnell specifically mentioned the use of animated M&M's characters [sic] with Addams Family characters for a cross-promotion of the two products (M&M's candies and Addams Family DVD)." In this conversation, Ms. Vent also told O'Donnell that her clients—Loring, Weatherwax, and Silla—were available to appear in the advertisement. * * *

The Amended Complaint alleges that the idea was shared in confidence, although it does not describe any particular statements or actions substantiating this assertion. It also alleges that "a confidential or fiduciary relationship existed between" Ms. Vent and O'Donnell because "the parties did not deal on equal terms." Further, the Amended Complaint alleges that Ms. Vent "trusted and relied on Ms. O'Donnell ... to protect her interests" in the marketing idea.

The Amended Complaint states that Ms. Vent's idea was "novel and concrete." The idea allegedly was not in use in the entertainment or advertising industries at the time; "showed genuine novelty and invention [] and was not merely a clever or useful adaptation of existing knowledge; was "definite and well-developed (i.e., the specific use of M&M's animated characters with Addams Family characters)"; was "taken [from] existing material [and] common sources and combined and arranged them into a new form"; and was given "a unique application in a different manner and for a different purpose than what previously existed." The Amended Complaint concedes, however, that, prior to Ms. Vent's telephone conversation with O'Donnell, Mars had promoted its M&M's products with movie releases and, particularly, with DVDs.

Shortly after this initial telephone conversation, O'Donnell informed Ms. Vent that Mars had declined to use her idea for a cross-promotion between Addams Family characters and M&M's candies. About eight months after Mars's refusal, however, Ms. Vent claims that Mars produced several advertisements featuring her idea of cross-promoting Addams Family characters with M&M's candies. These advertisements consisted of M&M's chocolate candy animated characters transmogrified to resemble the cast of television program and the Addams Family theme song (including the finger snaps).

* * *

II

Discussion

* * *

B. New Jersey Law Governing Misappropriation of Idea

Under New Jersey law, a party may incur liability for the misappropriation of an idea if "'(1) the idea was novel; (2) it was made in confidence [to the defendant]; and (3) it was adopted and made use of [by the defendant in connection with his own activities].'"

Although novelty has not been clearly defined under New Jersey law, courts have set forth some general guidelines that are helpful in analyzing this fluid concept. An idea is not novel, for example, if "it was merely 'a different application of a long-established principle []' or if 'a competitive product similar to [the plaintiff's] was [already] on the market.'" "[I]nnovation, originality, or invention" are probative of an idea's novelty. An idea that is an "adaptation of an existing idea or [that] embodies elements long in use" may be novel if "the adaptation or combination would lead to a significantly new and useful result." Nevertheless, "[a]n idea lacks novelty if it is merely a clever or useful adaptation of existing knowledge, or it is no more than a variation on a basic theme." Given these general principles, ... the following factors are relevant to the novelty inquiry:

> (1) the idea's specificity or generality (is it a generic concept or one of specific application?), (2) the idea's commonality (how many people know of this idea?), (3) the idea's originality (how different is this idea from generally known ideas?), (4) the idea's commercial viability (how widespread is the idea's use in the industry?), (5) the idea's obviousness (was the idea an obvious adaptation or application of an idea already in the domain of public knowledge?), and (6) the idea's secrecy (did an otherwise novel idea lose its novelty status because of inadequate steps taken to maintain the idea's secrecy?).

* * *

In addition to the novelty requirement, a plaintiff asserting a misappropriation of idea claim must show that he or she shared the idea in confidence. "An idea … is accorded no protection in the law," New Jersey courts have held, "unless it is acquired and used in such circumstances that the law will imply a contractual or fiduciary relationship between the parties." New Jersey law defines a fiduciary relationship as one in which "one party places trust and confidence in another who is in a dominant or superior position."

1.

Ms. Vent's misappropriation of idea claim must be dismissed on the ground that her idea lacks novelty. Even accepting as true the factual allegations contained in Ms. Vent's Amended Complaint and drawing all inferences in her favor, Ms. Vent's idea was merely "a variation on a basic theme."

As a preliminary matter, the Court notes Ms. Vent's idea was general and undeveloped. She did not draft any examples or sketches of the advertisement, did not specify the medium that the advertisement would take, and did not write a script. This lack of development assumes particular relevance given the prior cross-promotion advertisements produced by Mars. Although Ms. Vent's specified using animated M&M's candies and members of the Addams Family cast in cross-promoting the Addams Family DVD and Mars's products, her Amended Complaint *concedes* that, prior to Ms. Vent's telephone call to O'Donnell, Mars had promoted its M&M's products with movie releases and, particularly, with DVDs. Indeed, in 2004, Mars produced and televised a cross-promotion of Shrek 2 and M&M's, featuring animated M&M's candies and members of the Shrek 2 cast. Accordingly, Ms. Vent's idea also was not "different … from generally known ideas," but rather "an obvious adaptation … of an idea already in the domain of public knowledge." Thus, Ms. Vent's general and undeveloped idea, as pitched to Mars, does not contain any novel aspects—unique visual presentation or particularly witty dialogue, for example—that would set it apart from already extant cross-promotion ideas. Ms. Vent's idea involved minimum creativity—she merely took an existing basic theme (cross-promoting DVDs and M&M's) and substituted her own product without adding any unique or creative details or elements.

Ms. Vent submits that she has stated a plausible claim of novelty because the DVD that she was seeking to promote—the Addams Family—was a classic television program, whereas Mars's previous cross-promotion was a relatively recent animated movie. This is insufficient. Under New Jersey law, "[a]n idea will not satisfy the novelty requirement if it is not *significantly* different from, or is an obvious adaptation or combination of ideas in the public domain."

* * * Ms. Vent's idea was generic, commonly known, commercially available, and obvious.

* * *

Consequently, Ms. Vent's misappropriation claim must be dismissed on the issue of novelty.

2.

Independently, Ms. Vent's claim also must be dismissed because her Amended Complaint contains *no* allegations that raise a plausible claim that her idea was shared in confidence. The Amended Complaint appears to assert two bases for establishing the confidence element. First, it states—summarily and without any substantiating factual allegations—that Ms. Vent "presented her idea to Defendants in confidence." Second, the Amended Complaint asserts that "a confidential or fiduciary relationship existed between" Ms. Vent and O'Donnell because "the parties did not deal on equal terms."

Neither of these assertions is sufficient to survive Mars's motion to dismiss. Although Ms. Vent claims that she presented her idea to O'Donnell in confidence, the Amended Complaint does not assert that she told O'Donnell that the idea was being shared in confidence or that she otherwise indicated to Mars the confidential nature of her idea. Ms. Vent does not allege that she requested a confidentiality agreement or even that she limited the dissemination of her idea. * * *

Furthermore, Ms. Vent's claim that she and O'Donnell had a fiduciary relationship is unmeritorious. Ms. Vent, an entertainment broker and a business person, cold-called O'Donnell to pitch an arms-length advertisement transaction. This was not a "special relationship based on trust and confidence." Ms. Vent and O'Donnell did not have a long-standing business relationship, O'Donnell did not agree to serve as a fiduciary, nor did O'Donnell have any special knowledge or skills or occupy a superior position.

Accordingly, Ms. Vent's Amended Complaint fails to plead a plausible claim that she divulged her idea to O'Donnell in confidence. Therefore, Mars's motion to dismiss is granted on this basis as well.

Conclusion

For the foregoing reasons, the Court grants Mars's motion to dismiss. * * *

QUESTIONS FOR DISCUSSION FOR CASE 3.5

1. Why is this state law claim being heard in federal court?

2. Under New Jersey law, misappropriation of an idea requires the plaintiff to show three elements. Which element or elements were at issue here? Why?

3. What steps could Vent have taken to protect her idea initially?

DISCUSSION QUESTIONS

1. Stutz Motor Car of America, Inc., an automotive manufacturer, received a patent in 1986 for a "shock absorbing air bladder" for use in footwear. However, Stutz never manufactured a shoe with this innovation. In 1989, Reebok began producing the PUMP, a very successful line of athletic shoes with an air bladder different in design but similar in concept to Stutz's invention. Because Reebok's design was not sufficiently similar to Stutz's to constitute patent infringement, Stutz sued instead for trade secret misappropriation. Should Stutz prevail on its misappropriation claim? Why, or why not?

2. Palm Beach Blood Bank, a nonprofit organization, hired several employees who used to work for American Red Cross, another nonprofit organization. One of the employees took Red Cross's blood donor list to Palm Beach, and Palm Beach used the list to recruit donors. Many of the Red Cross donors advertised that they were Red Cross donors, and the Red Cross posted the donor list on a computer bulletin board. How should the court rule on Red Cross's claim of trade secret misappropriation? Are there any policy arguments against enjoining the use of the donor list by Palm Beach Blood Bank?

3. Christopher M. developed a secret recipe for fudge. His fudge was very popular, and he closely guarded his secret by keeping only one copy of his recipe and storing it at a location outside his factory. Additionally, he divided up the manufacturing process and allowed his employees to see only the part of the manufacturing process in which they were engaged. However, one employee, Hennon, gained Christopher M.'s confidence and through the course of his year-long employment was able to see most of the manufacturing process. Hennon also learned the ingredients of the fudge recipe because he had the sensitive task of typing the ingredients into a computer system. Hennon left Christopher M.'s factory, taking several confidential computer disks and documents. He then produced his own line of fudge with similar, if not identical, properties. Hennon had not signed a confidentiality agreement. Christopher M. sued for trade secret misappropriation. Should he win? Why, or why not?

4. Northeast Coating Technologies, Inc., (NCT) is a start-up corporation in the business of "vacuum coating" metals. To lure potential investors, NCT created a prospectus that included its business plan, including its orders from suppliers. This prospectus was widely distributed and contained a disclaimer that the information in the prospectus was confidential. Several copies of the prospectus ended up in the hands of potential competitors of NCT. The competitors used the business plan in NCT's prospectus to plan strategies to prevent NCT from successfully competing with them. If NCT sues for misappropriation of the "trade secret" material in the prospectus, should it win? Why, or why not?

5. I Can't Believe It's Yogurt (ICBIY), a frozen yogurt company, required potential franchise owners to attend "Yogurt University"—a training program designed to teach owners how to run an ICBIY store. In addition to teaching potential owners how to mix and freeze yogurt, Yogurt University also teaches potential owners how to structure the store. ICBIY claimed that particular floor tile patterns move customers through the store more efficiently. In addition, ICBIY used certain paint color schemes, logos, menu boards, windows, and common business marketing practices to distinguish an ICBIY store and improve business results. ICBIY considered these store designs and practices to be trade secrets. However, ICBIY did not require potential owners to sign a confidentiality agreement until the individual signed a franchise agreement. Gunn attended Yogurt University, became a franchisee, and set up his store. Irregular yogurt

shipments from ICBIY and late payments of franchise royalties by Gunn created a rocky relationship between the parties, however. Eventually, ICBIY canceled Gunn's franchise. Gunn continued to use ICBIY's logo and trade secret information in his business. ICBIY sued Gunn for trade secret misappropriation. Should ICBIY win? Why, or why not?

6. Carolina Chemical Equipment Company (CCEC), a company involved in sales of chemical and cleaning supplies, required its employees to sign a covenant not to divulge trade secrets. The covenant provided in part:

> [Employee] agrees not to divulge any trade secrets of the Corporation. Trade secrets means any knowledge or information concerning any aspect of the business of the Corporation which could, if divulged to a direct or indirect competitor, adversely affect the business of the Corporation, its prospects or competitive position. Seller shall not use for his own benefit any trade secret of the Corporation in any manner whatsoever.

Muckenfuss signed the agreement when he was hired. He also signed a covenant not to compete for one year after leaving the company. After several years of employment, Muckenfuss left CCEC. He did not work in the chemical industry for over one year, but eventually he went to work for one of CCEC's direct competitors, where he sold products to some of CCEC's customers that were essentially the same products that CCEC sells. CCEC sued Muckenfuss for trade secret misappropriation. Should CCEC win? Why, or why not?

7. Cybex, a division of Lumex, is the largest manufacturer of exercise and weight-training equipment. Pursuant to its normal business practices, Cybex required its worldwide head of marketing, Greg Highsmith, to sign a noncompete agreement. The agreement provided that Highsmith was not to work for a competitor for six months after leaving Cybex. However, the agreement allowed Highsmith to work for a competitor whose business was "diversified," provided Highsmith worked on product lines that were not in direct competition with Cybex products. The agreement also provided for six months of compensation and employee benefits in the event that Highsmith left Cybex and the terms of the restrictive covenant prevented him from obtaining another job during the noncompete period.

Highsmith left Cybex and went to work for Life Fitness, a competitor, within a matter of days. Although Life Fitness sent several letters to Cybex, assuring Cybex that it had not and would not induce Highsmith to violate his duty of confidentiality, Cybex filed suit for a preliminary injunction prohibiting Highsmith from working for Cybex for a period of six months. Should the court grant the injunction? Why, or why not?

8. Phillips manufactures "single-pole" tree stands—a device that allows hunters to sit perched in a tree to await deer or other game. A group of investors expressed interest in buying the venture, and purchase negotiations began. In the course of the process, Phillips sent the investors information about his company, including prospectuses and videotapes. Phillips also gave the investors a tour of the plant and showed them firsthand the manufacturing process. Although Phillips had never patented his tree stand, he knew that without knowledge of the manufacturing process, building the stand would be cost-prohibitive. During the course of the negotiations, the investors bought several samples of the stand. Although Phillips wanted to sell the company and tried to make several concessions in the purchase price, the investors were unable to obtain financing, and the deal fell through. Sometime later, a company founded by the investors began to manufacture nearly identical "single-pole" tree stands. Phillips sued for trade secret misappropriation, but the investors claimed that they had lawfully reverse-engineered the tree stand. Which party should win and why? What type of remedy, if any, should the court award?

9. In 1983, J & K Ventures, Inc., signed a 10-year franchise agreement with American Speedy Printing Centers with plans to establish a printing center in Tampa, Florida. In addition, J & K Ventures signed a nondisclosure agreement that also contained a covenant not to compete within a 10-mile radius of the franchise. J & K Ventures operated the Tampa printing center until July 1993, as agreed in the franchise agreement. Toward the end of the 10 years, however, the relationship between the two companies deteriorated, so J & K Ventures decided to allow the franchise agreement to expire without renewal. No other Speedy franchises operated within the 10-mile radius agreed to under the franchise agreement. Following the expiration of the agreement, J & K Ventures maintained a printing center at the same location and telephone number under the name Express Printing Center. Express Printing Center

expanded its basis of operations and offered more expanded services under the new name.

Speedy brought suit for violation of the noncompetition covenants. J & K Ventures asserted that Florida Statute Section 542.33(2)(b) makes the noncompete agreement void. Section 542.33(2)(b) states: "[Licensee] may agree with the licensor to refrain from carrying on or engaging in a similar business and from soliciting old customers within a reasonable limited time and area, so long as the licensor … continues to carry on a like business therein." How should the court rule on Speedy's claim, and why?

10. Communication Technical Systems, Inc., (CTS) began providing computer programming services for Gateway 2000, Inc., (Gateway), in July 1994. Rickey Densmore, a programmer for CTS, worked on the Gateway account in Chicago for two weeks before transferring to Gateway's South Dakota production site. In September, Gateway entered into an agreement with CTS called the "Agreement Not to Recruit," in which Gateway promised not to hire, solicit, or recruit any CTS employee while CTS was working on the Gateway account, nor for a one-year period after CTS ceased working on the account.

In December, Densmore expressed his dissatisfaction with CTS to a Gateway employee, who suggested that Densmore talk to Gateway's legal counsel about possibly being hired by Gateway. Densmore talked to Gateway counsel, but they refused to discuss the possibility, citing the "Agreement Not to Recruit." On December 15, Gateway gave CTS proper 30-day notice of its intent to terminate CTS's services. On January 20, 1995, Densmore resigned from CTS to begin his own consulting firm, Corinium Consulting, Inc. Densmore contacted Gateway, stating that he was now free to program for Gateway and was free of any restrictions imposed by the "Agreement Not to Recruit." Three days later, Gateway hired Densmore's firm for a five-month programming job.

Section 53-9-8 of the South Dakota statutes states: "Every contract restraining exercise of a lawful profession, trade, or business is void to that extent …." Section 53-9-11 provides an important exception, however, that allows noncompete covenants. CTS brought this suit against Densmore for breach of the "Agreement Not to Recruit." How should the court rule on CTS's claim, and why?

11. Donald Ray Dawson was an initial 49 percent investor and promoter in Temps Plus, Inc., a Blytheville, Arkansas, temporary-employment agency. In May 1996, Temps Plus bought all of Dawson's 49 percent interest in the corporation for $95,000. As part of the transaction, Dawson agreed "that for a period of five (5) years from the execution of this Agreement, he will not directly or indirectly, whether as an owner, partner, or employee, compete with Temps Plus, Inc., within a radius of seventy (70) miles from Blytheville, Arkansas." Dawson later did not recall reading that portion of the agreement.

Approximately one year later, Dawson, along with his brother, hired two employees away from Temps Plus in anticipation of creating the Dawson Employment Agency. Two weeks later, Dawson and his brother formed their own employment agency corporation, Steve Dawson Employment Services, Inc. (SDES), in Blytheville. In April, Temps Plus sued SDES for breach of the noncompete agreement. How should the court rule, and why?

12. In the mid-1980s, Deere & Co. became interested in installing a draft sensor device on its tractors, which would regulate the depth and mechanical forces on the plow. In June 1986, Deere entered an agreement with Revere Transducers to install the "Gozinta" strain gauge on Deere tractors to serve as draft sensor devices. Revere and Deere worked jointly on the project, taking four years to develop the product. Revere specially hired two men, engineer Francis Delfino and product manager Greg Eckart, in late summer 1986 to work on the "Gozinta" project. Both signed nondisclosure agreements, in which they agreed not to disclose any inventions or discoveries either during their employment or for a one-year period after their employment. No other formal agreements existed between Revere and the two men who, in all other respects, were at-will employees.

The "Gozinta" turned out to be a failure. Deere believed the defect resulted from Revere's decision to use poor-quality knurls without consulting Deere. Due to significant downsizing, Delfino and Eckart were told that they would be released in 1989. At about the same time, Eckart was independently studying the viability of a sensor that could be welded to the plow instead of pressed—an idea previously rejected by Revere. Delfino and Eckart spoke with Deere about the possibility of starting a new company to supply Deere with the welded sensors, and Deere stressed that, if they proceeded, it was vital that they took no documents, models, or engineering drawings from Revere.

In March 1989, Delfino and Eckart started their own company—D & E Sensor Manufacturing, Inc. D & E formally proposed its idea for the new sensor—the "weldzinta"—to Deere and received a purchase order from Deere for $172,900. Revere sued Deere for tortious interference of contract. Deere argued that the suit should be dismissed on the grounds that the nondisclosure contract was not enforceable. Under Iowa law, restrictive covenants are evaluated under a three-pronged test: (1) is the restriction reasonably necessary for the protection of the employer's business?; (2) is the restriction unreasonably restrictive of the employee's rights?; and (3) is the restriction prejudicial to the public interest? Is the NDA enforceable? Why, or why not?

13. Mark Brown, Deborah Christopher, and David Graben (the "defendants") were employees of Allied Supply Company, Inc., an industrial supply company. All three held managerial positions; Brown and Christopher were also corporate officers. On January 19, 1988, the three individuals resigned and formed their own industrial supply company.

Allied filed suit against them, alleging that the defendants had misappropriated customer and vendor lists before they left. Allied contended that those lists were trade secrets, and that, by misappropriating the lists, the defendants had violated both the common law and the Alabama Trade Secrets Act.

Evidence at trial showed "at least 10 Allied employees had free access to the lists. In addition, the lists were not marked 'confidential'; the lists were taken home by employees; multiple copies of each list existed; and the information on the lists was contained in the receptionist's Rolodex file." How should the court rule on this claim?

14. RKR Dance Studios hired Jessica Makowski as an at-will employee. At that time, Makowski signed a noncompete agreement. In 2006, Makowski signed a new noncompete, allegedly in consideration for new training programs provided by RKR. The 2006 agreement provided that Makowski would not, for a period of two years after leaving RKR's employ, work as a dance instructor or provide dance lessons in the employ of a competitor within 15 miles or within 10 miles of certain dance studios. As a result,

the covenant appeared to include all dance studios nationally. In 2007, Makowski left the employ of RKR and went to work for a competitor. When RKR attempted to enforce the noncompete clause, Makowski argued that it was unenforceable. How should the court rule on this claim?

15. Podiatrist Kenneth Krueger was employed by Central Indiana Podiatry, PC (CIP) from 1996 to 2005, under a series of employment agreements that were renewed every year or two. Each agreement restricted Krueger, for a period of two years after leaving CIP's employ, from revealing the names of patients, contacting patients, or soliciting CIP employees. The agreements also prohibited Krueger from practicing podiatry for two years within fourteen listed central Indiana counties, and "any other county where CIP maintained an office" during the time of the agreements, or any county adjacent thereto. CIP had offices in two unlisted counties, and another 27 counties were adjacent to these sixteen, making a total of 43 counties in which Krueger's activities were restricted. (Essentially the agreement covered the central half of Indiana.) In the last two years of his employ with CIP, Krueger practiced in three counties–Marion, Tippecanoe, and Howard.

Krueger was terminated by CIP in 2005, and went to work for Meridian Health Group, PC two months later. Meridian was located in Hamilton county, which was one of the counties listed in Krueger's noncompete agreement and which was immediately north of Marion County. Krueger provided a copy of the CIP patient list to Meridian and mailed a letter to CIP patients announcing his new employment with Meridian in a location "approximately 10 minutes" from Krueger's previous office. When Meridian sought an injunction against Krueger, Krueger argued that the noncompete agreement was not reasonable in its terms.

Was the noncompete agreement reasonable in its time limits? Was it reasonable in its geographic scope? If the court finds that any of the terms were unreasonable, what remedies can the court offer?

PART 3

Legal Issues Relating to Product Distribution

Chapter 4
Antitrust Law

Chapter 5
The Franchisor-Franchisee Relationship

CHAPTER 4

Antitrust Law

"Antitrust laws ... are the Magna Carta of free enterprise. They are as important to the preservation of economic freedom and our free-enterprise system as the Bill of Rights is to the protection of our fundamental personal freedoms."[1]

Overview

The purpose of the federal antitrust laws is to control private economic power by promoting and encouraging competition. Competition is valued highly within our legal and economic system for a variety of reasons. Competition is believed to: (1) keep costs and prices lower and quality higher; (2) encourage product and service innovation and efficient allocation of resources; and (3) give consumers broader choices in the marketplace. In short, competition maximizes consumer welfare. In a truly competitive market, firms try to attract consumers by cutting prices and increasing the quality of the products or services they offer.

At the same time, however, antitrust law recognizes that efficiency concerns also come into play. While we want to foster competition, we do not want to inhibit innovation, nor do we want to restrict economies of scale or economies of scope. We also want to promote lower transaction costs and improved quality. Thus, antitrust law must balance a number of competing concerns.

Federal antitrust law is founded on four statutes: the Sherman Act, the Clayton Act, the Robinson-Patman Act, and the Federal Trade Commission (FTC) Act. Each of these federal statutes is designed to reach certain types of anticompetitive behavior. The language of these statutes is often extremely broad and general. As a result, much of antitrust law has been formed through the court opinions that interpret and apply these statutes. As you can imagine, the courts' analyses of the antitrust statutes are heavily influenced by economic concepts such as supply and demand curves, cost, revenue, and market structure.

Antitrust litigation is usually lengthy and complex and the outcomes highly fact-specific. While monopolization that results from unfair business practices is illegal, monopolization that results from business skill is not. Identical pricing that results from collusion among competitors is illegal, but identical pricing that results from intense marketplace competition is not. Cooperation among competitors that results in reduced competition that harms consumers is illegal, but cooperation that increases competition and benefits consumers (such as industry standardization for component parts) is not.

---

[1] *United States v. Topco Assoc., Inc.,* 405 U.S. 596, 610 (1972).

In addition, as the U.S. Supreme Court has emphasized, antitrust laws are designed for the "protection of competition, not competitors."[2] Harm to an individual firm by a competitor, even if motivated by pure malice, does not lead to an antitrust violation unless the competitive process itself is harmed (e.g., through an increase in market prices or decrease in market production).

It is important that management and marketing personnel alike understand the basics of antitrust law and the parameters of legal and illegal competitive behaviors. Managers are often surprised to discover that actions that they regard as sound business strategies not only are illegal but subject the firm to substantial fines and/or civil damages. In addition, the individual managers involved in antitrust violations may personally face similar fines and/or damages and may even be imprisoned in certain instances. Thus, knowledge of the antitrust laws is important not only to the firm but also to the manager personally.[3]

Companies should work closely with their corporate or outside legal counsel to develop a compliance program that informs officers, managers, salespersons, and other employees about their responsibilities under the antitrust laws. A well-designed compliance program outlines proper policies and procedures to minimize the likelihood of antitrust violations and provides for periodic monitoring of firm activities and individual actions to ensure that the firm is meeting its compliance goals.

Common Law Contracts in Restraint of Trade

Although antitrust law is primarily statutory today, it is important to realize that the common law also prohibits contracts in restraint of trade and monopolistic combinations, at least in some instances. Because the common law rules arise under state law, they can vary from state to state.

The Restatement (Second) of Contracts states that a contract is in "restraint of trade" if "its performance would limit competition in any business or restrict a promisor in the exercise of a gainful occupation."[4] Contracts in restraint of trade are not automatically illegal; rather, *unreasonable* contracts in restraint of trade are unenforceable on public policy grounds. A contract is considered unreasonable if: (1) "the restraint is greater than is needed to protect the promisee's legitimate interest," or (2) the restraint poses an undue hardship on the promisor or excessive likely injury to the public.[5]

Generally, the types of enforceable restraints include covenants not to compete by the seller of a business, by a partner in a business, or by an employee. Covenants not to compete in the context of employment agreements are discussed in greater detail in Chapter 3.

The enforceability of a covenant not to compete that relates to the activities of a business depends upon the factual circumstances in which the covenant was used. "Naked" covenants (e.g., covenants that are not incidental to the sale of a business) are generally considered unreasonable. Thus, an agreement between Company A and Company B in which A pays B not to compete with A's business would generally be unenforceable. Similarly, if Company A and Company B were already competitors, an agreement between A and B that B would cease competing with A would also be unenforceable.

---

[2]*Brown Shoe Co. v. United States*, 370 U.S. 294, 320 (1962).

[3]For general information on antitrust law, including a list of links to other antitrust-related websites, see www.antitrustinstitute.org

[4]Restatement (Second) of Contracts § 186.

[5]*Id.* § 188.

If Company A were to purchase Company B's business, on the other hand, A and B could legally enter into a covenant prohibiting B from competing with A.

Covenants not to compete that are ancillary to the sale of a business are typically limited to a reasonable geographic location and to a reasonable time duration. A reasonable geographic location is usually defined as the territory in which the business was previously conducted plus the area in which it may be conducted in the reasonably foreseeable future. Where the covenant is broader in geographic scope or time duration than is necessary and legal, many courts use the "blue pencil rule" to rewrite the covenant to limit it to whatever geographic or time restraint the court deems is appropriate under the circumstances. Other courts simply hold that the covenant is invalid and refuse to enforce it at all.

The usual remedy given for the violation of a valid covenant is *injunctive relief* that prevents the promisor from violating the covenant. *Monetary damages* may be available in certain instances, though this remedy often does not fully compensate the promisee for the injury it suffered as a result of the violation.

The federal antitrust statutes are by far the most important source of law regarding illegal restraints of trade and monopolistic combinations today. The remainder of this chapter focuses on these statutes.

The Federal Antitrust Statutes

The federal antitrust statutes arose out of dissatisfaction with the common law's treatment of contracts in restraint of trade. In particular, the common law was seen as providing inadequate protection to injured parties. While the common law protects the parties to the covenants at issue, it does not generally provide relief or remedies to the public or to third parties harmed by such restraints of trade. In addition, the common law is not uniform but, rather, varies from state to state, making it difficult for interstate businesses to monitor their behavior.

As the United States moved from an agrarian economy to an industrialized one in the late nineteenth century, there were increasing abuses within the economy by large industrial interests, such as railroads and manufacturers. Many of these large businesses engaged in predatory practices, driving out small competitors and then restricting output and increasing prices. In particular, there was great societal concern about "trusts" (i.e., combinations of companies that were able to control entire industries so as to increase monopoly power). The Standard Oil Trust created by John D. Rockefeller was one of the first such trusts, but trusts were created in other industries as well, such as the whiskey, sugar, and lead industries. Ultimately, Congress responded to these concerns by passing a series of antitrust acts. The major statutes are described here briefly, followed by a discussion of specific types of illegal anticompetitive behaviors.

The Sherman Act

The first federal legislation passed to address the economic abuses by large trusts was the Sherman Act of 1890.[6] This Act created a new, federal cause of action to reach two types of anticompetitive behavior: (1) restraints of trade and (2) illegal monopolization or attempts to monopolize. As the Supreme Court explained:

> The Sherman Act was designed to be a comprehensive charter of economic liberty aimed at preserving free trade and unfettered competition as the rule of trade. It rests on the premise that the unrestrained interaction of competitive forces will yield the

---

[6]15 U.S.C § 1 *et seq.*

best allocation of our economic resources, the lowest prices, the highest quality and the greatest material progress, while at the same time providing an environment conducive to the preservation of our democratic political and social institutions.[7]

Section 1 of the Sherman Act prohibits contracts, combinations, and conspiracies that restrain trade; Section 2 prohibits certain monopolies and attempts to monopolize. The language of these two provisions is surprisingly brief:

Section 1: Every contract, combination in the form of trust or otherwise, or conspiracy, in restraint of trade or commerce among the several States, or with foreign nations, is hereby declared to be illegal ….

Section 2: Every person who shall monopolize, or attempt to monopolize, or combine or conspire with any other person or persons, to monopolize any part of the trade or commerce among the several States, or with foreign nations, shall be deemed guilty of a felony ….

The courts have provided many layers of interpretation to this short and seemingly simple language. For example, Section 1 of the Sherman Act prohibits "every contract, combination … or conspiracy in restraint of trade." Taken literally, the language of Section 1 would make illegal virtually all business contracts, even those that benefit society and the economy. Every contract between a buyer and a seller, no matter how simple in content or short in duration, limits the market activity of those two parties in the subject matter of that contract and for the duration of the transaction. Thus, in 1911, the Supreme Court determined that only agreements that *unreasonably* restrain trade are unlawful.[8]

As discussed below, certain restraints of trade are deemed automatically unreasonable and so are illegal *per se*, while others are adjudged on a case-by-case basis under the "rule of reason." In addition, it is not necessarily illegal for a company to have or to try to obtain a monopoly position; rather, Section 2 only prohibits maintenance or acquisition of a monopoly position through unfair or abusive methods.

Note as well that Section 1 requires the actions of two or more persons acting together, as it is impossible for an individual to contract, combine, or conspire alone. Much antitrust litigation centers on whether concerted action has occurred. While the Supreme Court has ruled that an agreement between a parent corporation and its wholly-owned subsidiary does not violate Section 1 (because the two entities are viewed as a single firm),[9] it is unclear whether agreements between a parent and a less-than-wholly-owned subsidiary may potentially violate Section 1.

Section 2 of the Sherman Act applies both to persons acting in concert and to those acting alone. In practice, Section 2 is generally applied to firms acting alone to illegally gain monopoly power, while combinations and conspiracies to monopolize are usually prosecuted under Section 1.

The Clayton Act

In 1914, Congress enacted the Clayton Act[10] in response to perceived shortcomings in the Sherman Act. Unlike the Sherman Act, which is essentially remedial in nature (in that it reaches actual anticompetitive behavior), the Clayton Act is preventative in

---

[7]*Northern Pacific Railway Co. v. United States*, 356 U.S. 1, 4 (1958).

[8]See *Standard Oil Co. of New Jersey v. United States*, 221 U.S. 1 (1911).

[9]*Copperweld Corp. v. Independence Tube Corp.*, 467 U.S. 752 (1984).

[10]15 U.S.C. §§ 12-27; 44.

nature, as it is directed toward trying to prevent anticompetitive behavior "in its incipiency" and before it harms the public.[11]

The Clayton Act addresses behavior such as certain exclusionary practices, mergers, and interlocking directorates. In particular, Section 3 of the Clayton Act provides:

> Section 3: [I]t shall be unlawful for any person in commerce … to lease or make a sale or contract for the sale of goods for use, consumption, or resale within the United States … on the condition, agreement or understanding that the lessee or purchaser thereof shall not use or deal in the goods … of a competitor … of the lessor or seller, where the effect of such lease, sale … or such condition, agreement, or understanding may be to substantially lessen competition or tend to create a monopoly in any line of commerce.

Section 3 thus prohibits activities such as tie-in sales, exclusive dealing arrangements, and requirements contracts in which the effect of such arrangements "may be to substantially lessen competition or tend to create a monopoly." Note, however, that this section applies only to the sale of goods, not to the sale of services.

Among its other provisions, Section 4 of the Clayton Act allows private parties injured by violations of the Sherman or Clayton Act to sue for treble damages. This provision thus encourages private parties to bring actions to enforce these antitrust statutes. Section 7 prohibits mergers or acquisitions in which the effect "may be substantially to lessen competition, or tend to create a monopoly" in "any line of commerce or in any activity affecting commerce in any section of the country." Section 8 prohibits certain interlocking directorates but has not been vigorously enforced. These latter two provisions are less important to the marketing function and so are not discussed further.

The Federal Trade Commission Act

The Federal Trade Commission (FTC) Act[12] was also enacted in 1914. The FTC Act created the Federal Trade Commission, a consumer protection agency, and gave that agency broad powers to enforce certain antitrust acts.[13] Under a 1938 amendment to the FTC Act, the FTC has two mandates: (1) to protect the marketplace from unfair methods of competition and (2) to prevent unfair or deceptive practices that harm consumers. Specifically, Section 5(a)(1) of the FTC Act provides:

> Section 5(a)(1): Unfair methods of competition in or affecting competition and unfair or deceptive acts or practices in or affecting commerce, are hereby declared unlawful.

Section 5 authorizes the FTC to take preemptive action against potential violations of the Sherman or Clayton Acts—"to stop in their incipiency acts and practices which, when full blown, would violate" those statutes.[14] Section 5 also reaches unfair or deceptive conduct that is outside the provisions of the antitrust statutes.

Only the FTC may sue to enforce Section 5; private individuals have no cause of action under this statute. The FTC also has authority, concurrent with the Department of Justice (DOJ)[15] and private parties, to enforce the Clayton Act and the Robinson-Patman Act. In addition, while the FTC does not have express authority to enforce the Sherman

---

[11]*FTC v. Motion Picture Advertising Service Co.*, 344 U.S. 392, 394 (1953).

[12]15 U.S.C. §§ 41-57a.

[13]The FTC's home page, which contains information about its antitrust enforcement activities, is found at www.ftc.gov

[14]*FTC v. Motion Picture Advertising Service Co.*, 344 U.S. 392, 394 (1953).

[15]The Department of Justice's home page, which contains information about its antitrust enforcement activities, is found at www.usdoj.gov

Act, the courts have read Section 5 of the FTC Act broadly enough that violation of Section 1 or Section 2 of the Sherman Act generally is also a violation of Section 5; thus, the FTC may issue cease-and-desist orders against violations of the Sherman Act.

This chapter focuses on the provisions of the FTC Act directed toward anticompetitive behavior. The "unfair or deceptive acts or practices" provisions of the FTC Act and the consumer protection role of the FTC are discussed further in Chapter 7 and Chapter 8.

The Robinson-Patman Act

The Robinson-Patman Act of 1936[16] is actually an amendment of Section 2 of the Clayton Act. The Robinson-Patman Act was designed to address very specific types of pricing behaviors, particularly those behaviors that favored chain stores, which were in their infancy at the time of the statute's enactment, over traditional small independent retailers. Thus, this federal statute makes it illegal to give, induce, or receive discriminatory prices or supplementary services, except under certain specified circumstances, where the effect of the discrimination would be to substantially lessen competition or tend to create a monopoly.

There are three main sections to the Robinson-Patman Act. Section 2 (there is no Section 1) addresses price discrimination. In particular, Section 2(a) provides:

> Section 2(a) Price Discrimination. [I]t shall be unlawful for any person engaged in commerce, in the course of such commerce, either directly or indirectly, to discriminate in price between different purchasers of commodities of like grade and quality, where either or any of the purchases involved in such discrimination are in commerce, where such commodities are sold for use, consumption, or resale, within the United States ... and where the effect of such discrimination may be substantially to lessen competition or tend to create a monopoly in any line of commerce, or to injure, destroy, or prevent competition with any person who either grants or knowingly receives the benefit of such discrimination, or with customers of either of them ....

Section 3 establishes criminal liability for certain types of discriminatory pricing. (This provision is seldom enforced.) Section 4 exempts cooperative associations and nonprofit institutions from the Act.

Thus, Section 2 of the Robinson-Patman Act would prohibit a lumber supplier from offering a discount (including allowances for advertisements, counter displays, and samples) to a large home improvement chain unless a "proportional discount" is given to independent lumber supply stores as well. (What is "proportional" is a question of fact to be decided on a case-by-case basis.) Similarly, a firm cannot offer a *wholesaler's* or *broker's discount* to a customer who is not a true wholesaler, even if that customer is a large retail chain that purchases more than the average wholesaler. Cooperative advertising and other promotional assistance are permitted, provided such assistance is offered to all customers on proportionally equal terms.

The Antitrust Statutes Generally

The antitrust statutes apply to most parties involved in business transactions, including corporations, partnerships, sole proprietorships, individuals, trade associations, professionals (such as doctors and lawyers), and certain activities of nonprofit organizations. Labor unions and agricultural organizations are essentially exempt from the provisions

---

[16]15 U.S.C. § 13.

of the Sherman and Clayton Acts, and certain other industries, such as export trade associations, the insurance industry, stock exchanges, utilities, railroads, and shipping, may be exempt from specific provisions as well, at least in certain instances.

The antitrust laws are complex, and it can be difficult for a company to know whether a particular contemplated action is legal. Thus, both the DOJ and the FTC have a procedure by which a company can seek an advisory opinion on the legality of a proposed action before undertaking it. Each has also published guidelines on how the antitrust implications of specific actions or issues, such as the licensing of intellectual property, international operations, collaborations among competitors, and health care industry practices, are analyzed.[17]

While the federal antitrust statutes reach only activities that affect interstate or foreign commerce, this encompasses most U.S. business activities. The courts have interpreted the interstate commerce requirement as requiring only that the business or activity, even if otherwise purely intrastate, have a substantial economic effect on interstate commerce. As the Supreme Court stated, "If it is interstate commerce that feels the pinch, it does not matter how local the operation that applies the squeeze."[18]

The Rule of Reason Versus *Per Se* Violations

Alleged antitrust practices are judged under one of two standards. Certain practices, such as horizontal agreements among competitors to fix prices or divide markets, are regarded as so inherently harmful to competition and consumers that they are deemed *per se* violations and are automatically illegal. In such instances, the plaintiff need only demonstrate that the prohibited practice occurred; the plaintiff need not show that the practice had an anticompetitive effect, nor may the defendant argue that the practice was in fact procompetitive. The Supreme Court described the illegal *per se* category as follows:

> [T]here are certain agreements or practices which because of their pernicious effect on competition and lack of any redeeming virtue are conclusively presumed to be unreasonable and therefore illegal without elaborate inquiry as to the precise harm they have caused or the business excuse for their use. This principle of *per se* unreasonableness not only makes the type of restraints which are proscribed by the Sherman Act more certain to the benefit of everyone concerned, but it also avoids the necessity for an incredibly complicated and prolonged economic investigation into the entire history of the industry involved, as well as related industries, in an effort to determine at large whether a particular restraint has been unreasonable—an inquiry so often wholly fruitless when undertaken.[19]

According to a recent Supreme Court decision:

> Resort to *per se* rules is confined to restraints ... "that would always or almost always tend to restrict competition and decrease output." To justify a *per se* prohibition a restraint must have "manifestly anticompetitive" effects, and "lack ... any redeeming virtue."
>
> As a consequence, the *per se* rule is appropriate only after courts have had considerable experience with the type of restraint at issue, and only if courts can predict

---

[17]These guidelines generally can be located on the websites of the FTC, www.ftc.gov, and the DOJ, www.usdoj.gov

[18]*United States v. Women's Sportswear Manufacturers Assoc.*, 336 U.S. 460, 464 (1949).

[19]*Northern Pacific Railway Co. v. United States*, 356 U.S. 1, 5 (1958).

with confidence that it would be invalidated in all or almost all instances under the rule of reason.[20]

In recent years, in particular, the courts have been reluctant to label conduct as *per se* illegal and the number of activities that qualify as *per se* violations has declined. Instead, most alleged antitrust violations are examined under the *rule of reason* and are deemed illegal if the practice significantly restricts competition and has no overriding business justification. This flexible standard mandates a case-by-case determination that takes into consideration a number of factors, "including specific information about the relevant business, its condition before and after the restraint was imposed, and the restraint's history, nature, and effect,"[21] and whether the business involved has market power.[22] In short, it requires the court to balance the anticompetitive effects of the restraint against its procompetitive effects. The sole focus under the rule of reason is the effects of the challenged action on competition; the social or political effects of the challenged action are irrelevant, no matter how beneficial they may be.

The Supreme Court has also enunciated a third—intermediate—standard, known as the "quick look" analysis. Under this analysis, certain types of activities are presumed to be anticompetitive unless the defendant shows that the activity has a procompetitive effect. If the defendant can make such a showing, the activity is judged under the rule of reason; if the defendant cannot, the conduct is illegal *per se.*

Remedies for Antitrust Violations

The federal antitrust laws provide for civil or criminal actions against violators. (In some instances, both civil and criminal actions can be filed for the same conduct.) Depending upon the nature of the violation, remedies may include fines, imprisonment, money damages, injunctive relief, court-ordered restructuring of a firm, or some combination of these.

The federal antitrust laws are enforced through a variety of mechanisms. The Antitrust Division of the DOJ can bring criminal and civil enforcement actions. The Bureau of Competition of the FTC can bring civil enforcement actions (but not criminal actions). The state attorneys general can bring civil suits under the Clayton Act on behalf of injured consumers in their states. Finally, private parties can bring antitrust actions to redress injuries.

Both the government and private plaintiffs can sue for *equitable relief* for antitrust violations. Most antitrust violations result in equitable relief. The relief can take many forms, including a restraint on particular acts or conduct, compelled licensing of a patent or other intellectual property asset on a reasonable royalty basis, or the cancellation of contracts. *Preliminary injunctions* are also available to both the government and private parties against conduct that would irreparably injure the plaintiff, provided the plaintiff can show a likelihood of success on the merits and a public interest in the injunction.

Damages are also available in antitrust cases. In fact, in an effort to encourage private enforcement of the antitrust laws, Section 4 of the Clayton Act authorizes "any person … injured in his business or property by reason of anything in the antitrust laws" to recover treble damages, plus costs and attorneys fees.

---

[20]*Leegin Creative Leather Products v. PSKS, Inc.,* 551 U.S. 877, 886 (2007).

[21]*State Oil Co. v. Khan,* 522 U.S. 3, 10 (1997).

[22]*Copperweld Corp. v. Independence Tube Corp.,* 467 U.S. 752, 768 (1984).

The Clayton and the FTC Acts do not provide for *criminal sanctions*. Violations of Sections 1 and 2 of the Sherman Act, on the other hand, can be prosecuted as felonies. The current maximum fine under the Sherman Act is $1 million for individuals and $100 million for corporations. Individuals may also be imprisoned for up to 10 years.[23]

These criminal sanctions have real teeth. In April 2009, for example, two subsidiaries of the Swedish company Trelleborg AB agreed to plead guilty and pay $11 million in fines for participation in separate conspiracies affecting the sale of marine products in the U.S. and elsewhere. The conspiracies violated the Sherman Act. Five former executives of the subsidiaries also pled guilty to participating in the conspiracies. Each was sentenced to a prison term (which ranged from 6 months to 24 months) and to pay a criminal fine (which ranged from $60,000 to $300,000).[24]

The annual amount of criminal fines obtained by the Antitrust Division has skyrocketed over the last decade. In addition, the federal Amended Sentencing Guidelines, which became effective in 1991, make it substantially more likely than in the past that individuals convicted for antitrust violations will serve a prison sentence[25] (see Exhibit 4.1).

EXHIBIT 4.1 Antitrust Division, Workload Statistics, FY 1999–2008

FINES IMPOSED	1999	2000	2001	2002	2003	2004	2005	2006	2007	2008
Individual: Total Individual Fines ($000)	12,273	5,180	2,019	8,685	470	644	4,483	3,650	15,109	1,485
Number of Individuals Fined	50	43	20	19	16	15	22	17	25	23
Corporate: Total Corporate Fines ($000)	959,866	303,241	270,778	93,826	63,752	140,586	595,966	469,805	615,671	695,042
Number of Corporations Fined	25	26	14	17	17	13	18	18	12	12
Total Fines Imposed ($000)	972,138	308,421	272,797	102,511	64,222	141,230	600,449	473,455	630,780	696,527

INCARCERATION	1999	2000	2001	2002	2003	2004	2005	2006	2007	2008
Number of Individuals Sentenced	54	47	24	36	30	28	27	27	39	31
Number of Individuals Sentenced to Incarceration Time	28	18	11	19	15	20	18	18	34	19
Total Number of Actual Days of Incarceration Imposed by the Court	6,662	5,584	4,480	10,501	9,341	7,334	13,157	13,157	31,391	14,331

Source: www.usdoj.gov/atr/public/workstats.pdf

[23] 15 U.S.C. §§ 1, 2.

[24] U.S. Department of Justice Press Release, April 20, 2009 (available at www.usdoj.gov/opa/pr/2009/April/09-at-369.html).

[25] Trade Reg. Rep. (CCH) Para. 13,250, U.S. Sentencing Guidelines Part R. The guidelines are also available online at www.ussc.gov/guidelin.htm

As a practical matter, the DOJ generally seeks criminal sanctions under the Sherman Act only for *per se* violations of the statutes (discussed below) or for egregious predatory conduct. In recent years, the DOJ has particularly focused on the prosecution of international cartels that victimize American businesses and consumers. The DOJ may prosecute actions that constitute antitrust violations under other statutes as well, such as statutes that prohibit perjury, obstruction of justice, conspiracies to defraud the United States, and mail and wire fraud.

The federal Amended Sentencing Guidelines provide real incentives for companies to establish compliance programs. Under the Guidelines, if a company has an effective compliance program "to prevent and detect violations of law" but an antitrust violation nonetheless occurs, the fines assessed against the company may be substantially reduced. In addition, if a company's compliance program reveals the existence of an antitrust violation, the company and its management and employees who admit involvement may avoid criminal prosecution if they report the illegal activity to the DOJ at an early stage and if they meet certain other requirements.[26] A separate leniency program applies to individuals who report illegal antitrust activity to the DOJ in the absence of a company admission of culpability.[27]

The following discussion focuses on those antitrust actions most relevant to marketing practices: (1) horizontal restraints among competitors; (2) vertical restraints between buyers and sellers; (3) maintenance or creation of a monopoly; and (4) price discrimination.

Horizontal Restraints Among Competitors

Trade restraints can be either horizontal or vertical. *Horizontal restraints* occur among competitors at the same level in the chain of distribution, such as among manufacturers or among wholesalers (see Exhibit 4.2). *Vertical restraints* occur among parties at different levels in the chain of distribution, such as between a manufacturer and a wholesaler (see Exhibit 4.4).

To compete horizontally, firms must be at the *same level of distribution* and compete in the same *product* and *geographic* markets. For example, if Firm A and Firm B both sell potato chips in the southeast Michigan region, they compete horizontally. If Firm A sells in southeast Michigan and Firm B in the Northern California region, however, they would be operating in different geographic markets and would not be competing horizontally. If both operate in southeast Michigan, but Firm A sells potato chips and Firm B sells processed cheese, they would be operating in different product markets and again would not compete horizontally.

EXHIBIT 4.2 Horizontal Restraints

Competitor A ←→ Competitor B ←→ Competitor C

[26]U.S. Department of Justice, Antitrust Division, Corporate Leniency Program, Trade Reg. Rep. (CCH) Para. 13,113 (Aug. 10, 1993). This program can be found online at www.usdoj.gov

[27]U.S. Department of Justice, Antitrust Division, Leniency Policy for Individuals, Trade Reg. Rep. (CCH) Para. 13,114 (Aug. 10, 1994). This policy can be found online at www.usdoj.gov

These determinations are very fact-specific in most instances. If Firm A sells potato chips, for example, and Firm B sells pretzels, the court would need to determine whether the relevant product market should be defined as potato chips or whether it would include some broader definition of snack foods, such as salty, hand-held snacks. Not surprisingly, when an illegal horizontal restraint is alleged, the issue of the correct definition of the relevant market is usually hotly litigated.

Certain agreements among competitors may be legal because they have the effect of benefiting consumers (for example, by promoting standardization within an industry that facilitates interchangeability of products, such as component parts). Similarly, competitors can safely lobby together for legislative or regulatory change and can participate in trade association activities that do not stray into the realm of competitive decision making, such as pricing decisions or market allocations.

Other agreements among competitors may have the effect of reducing competition, however, and so are illegal. Certain horizontal restraints, such as price-fixing, are presumed to always be anticompetitive in effect and so are deemed illegal *per se.* Other horizontal restraints are viewed as being potentially procompetitive and so are evaluated under the rule of reason (see Exhibit 4.3).

Horizontal restraint cases raise difficult issues of proof. To succeed in an action under Section 1 of the Sherman Act, the plaintiff must show the existence of an agreement among the defendants. (Recall that Section 1 does not reach unilateral conduct but only agreements among two or more parties.) *Direct evidence*, such as written documentation of the agreement, minutes of a meeting in which agreement was reached, or testimony by a person with personal knowledge of the agreement, while most probative, can be difficult to obtain, if indeed it exists at all.

Because direct evidence of an antitrust violation generally is so difficult to obtain, many cases turn on *circumstantial evidence.* As the Supreme Court put it, "[C]ircumstantial evidence is the lifeblood of antitrust law."[28] Thus, agreements can be shown by inference—i.e., by a combination of circumstantial evidence, such as the existence of a meeting among the competitors before they implemented certain practices (even if the plaintiff has no evidence of the actual agenda of the meeting), records of telephone calls, or signaling behavior. *Signaling behavior* occurs when one company indirectly tells a competitor that it intends to raise prices by a specified amount. Competitors often disseminate information regarding things such as prices, costs, or inventories through mechanisms such as trade associations or the popular press. The courts usually (but not always) regard the exchange of price information as a violation of Section 1 of the

---

EXHIBIT 4.3 **Potential Illegal Horizontal Restraints Among Competitors**

- price-fixing and bid-rigging
- group boycotts and concerted refusals to deal
- horizontal market allocations
- agreements to restrict advertising
- joint ventures

---

[28]*United States v. Falstaff Brewing Co.*, 410 U.S. 526, 532 n.13 (1973).

Sherman Act. Most antitrust lawyers advise their clients not to share price information with competitors as a result. Courts generally are less concerned about the exchange of nonprice information, such as joint market surveys or joint advertising, unless such sharing lessens competition.

Circumstantial evidence of a Section 1 violation may be demonstrated through parallel behavior (known as *conscious parallelism*) by independent firms, such as persistent setting of prices at the same level or simultaneous changing of prices. Parallel behavior might just as easily result from intense competition, however, as from anticompetitive behavior, making it an ambiguous indicator of an antitrust violation. Where the parallel business behavior can be explained in terms of the independent business judgment of each defendant, no antitrust violation would occur. (Such acts may violate the prohibition in Section 5 of the FTC Act against "unfair methods of competition," however.) The courts thus usually require additional evidence of illegal behavior (known as *plus factors*), such as complex actions that would benefit each competitor only if all competitors acted in a prescribed manner (see Case Illustration 4.1).

CASE ILLUSTRATION 4.1

IN RE BABY FOOD ANTITRUST LITIGATION, 166 F.3D 112 (3D CIR. 1999)

FACTS Plaintiffs, who were direct purchasers of baby food from the defendant manufacturers, including wholesalers and supermarket chains, sued the major manufacturers of baby food: Gerber Products Company, H. J. Heinz Co., and Beech-Nut (which was owned at first by Nestlé Food Company and later by Ralston Purina Company). Collectively, the three defendants accounted for over 98 percent of all baby food products manufactured and sold in the United States. Gerber, in particular, accounted for 70 percent of the total U.S. market.

Gerber had positioned itself as the "premium" brand. Heinz had carved out a market niche as the "value" brand. Beech-Nut was originally positioned as a "value" brand but repositioned itself as a "premium" brand with a strong regional presence in the northeast United States.

The plaintiffs alleged that from 1975 to 1993, the defendants engaged in an unlawful conspiracy in violation of Section 1 of the Sherman Act "to fix, raise, and maintain wholesale prices and price levels of baby food in the United States." In particular, the plaintiffs alleged that the defendants exchanged information with each other regarding future price increases before they announced those increases to the public. The plaintiffs argued that the defendants had no legitimate business reason for informing each other before

informing the public. The plaintiffs alleged that if Gerber, the dominant company in the industry and the price leader, decided to raise its prices, the other competitors had to follow the price increase immediately or the time gap between Gerber's increases and the other companies' increases would disturb their respective market shares. Giving advance notice solved this problem. The plaintiffs argued that advance notice did occur, showing that an agreement to conspire existed among the defendants.

DECISION The trial court granted summary judgment to the defendants, and the appellate court affirmed.

Although plaintiffs lacked direct evidence of price-fixing, the appellate court noted that they could support their claim with circumstantial evidence of conscious parallelism. "The theory of conscious parallelism is that uniform conduct of pricing by competitors permits a court to infer the existence of a conspiracy between those competitors. The theory is generally applied to highly concentrated markets where few sellers exist and where they establish their prices, not by express agreement, but rather in a consciously parallel fashion. Thus, when two or more competitors in such a market act separately but in parallel fashion in their pricing decisions, this may provide probative evidence of an understanding by the competitors to fix prices."

(Continued)

The court explained:

In an oligopolistic market, meaning a market where there are few sellers, interdependent parallelism can be a necessary fact of life but be the result of independent pricing decisions.

In a market served by three large companies, each firm must know that if it reduces its price and increases its sales at the expense of its rivals, they will notice the sales loss, identify the cause, and probably respond. In short, each firm is aware of its impact upon the others. Though each may independently decide upon its own course of action, any rational decision must take into account the anticipated reaction of the other two firms. Whenever rational decision-making requires an estimate of the impact of any decision on the remaining firms and an estimate of their response, decisions are said to be "interdependent." Because of their mutual awareness, oligopolists' decisions may be interdependent although arrived at independently.

Because the evidence of conscious parallelism is circumstantial in nature, courts are concerned that they do not punish unilateral, independent conduct of competitors. They therefore require that evidence of a defendant's parallel pricing be supplemented with "plus factors." The simple term "plus factors" refers to "the additional facts or factors required to

be proved as a prerequisite to finding that parallel action amounts to a conspiracy." They are necessary conditions for the conspiracy inference. They show that the allegedly wrongful conduct of the defense was conscious and not the result of independent business decisions of the competitors. The plus factors may include, and often do, evidence demonstrating that the defendants: (1) acted contrary to their economic interests, and (2) were motivated to enter into a price fixing conspiracy. Once the plaintiffs have presented evidence of the defendants' consciously parallel pricing and supplemented this evidence with plus factors, a rebuttable presumption of conspiracy arises.

The court found that the evidence was insufficient to prove conscious parallelism on the part of the defendants. Because Gerber controlled 70 percent of the baby food market and was the acknowledged industry leader, Gerber's pricing most likely did influence its competitors' pricing. However, the court stated, "Conscious parallelism ... will not be inferred merely because the evidence tends to show that a defendant may have followed a competitor's price increase."

In the absence of "probative proof of concerted action" by the defendants, the appellate court affirmed the district court's grant of summary judgment to the defendants.

Price-Fixing

Horizontal price-fixing occurs when competitors agree on price or price-related issues (such as credit terms). According to the Supreme Court, "Under the Sherman Act, a combination formed for the purpose and with the effect of raising, depressing, fixing, pegging, or stabilizing the price of a commodity in interstate or foreign commerce is illegal *per se.*"[29] The list of behaviors that are defined as "price-fixing" is extensive, including the setting of minimum prices, the setting of maximum prices, the setting of "list prices" (even where the list price is simply the starting point for customer negotiations, such as in automobile sales), production limits (even where no actual price is fixed), agreements regarding the availability of short-term credit, and agreements not to advertise prices. Regulated industries, such as railroads and public utilities, may fix prices or rates without violating the antitrust laws, however, provided they act within the limits established by their regulatory agencies.

◆ *See Discussion Case 4.1.*

Although we most commonly think of price-fixing as occurring among sellers of goods or services, agreements among buyers to set the price that they will pay for goods or services or the quantities that they will purchase is also price-fixing.

The plaintiff bears the burden of proving price-fixing. This can be a difficult burden to meet. Price similarities or simultaneous changes in prices may result from normal

---

[29]*United States v. Socony-Vacuum Oil Co.*, 310 U.S. 150, 223 (1940).

economic conditions rather than from illegal firm behavior. If the price of raw timber increases as a result of changing conditions in the international timber markets, for example, the net effect may be a change in the wholesale price of lumber that causes competing lumber yards in a particular area to raise their retail prices by the same amount at the same time. In the absence of an agreement among the lumber yards to set the price, there would be no antitrust violation.

Price-fixing and its parallel behavior, *bid-rigging* (i.e., when two or more firms agree not to bid against each other to supply products or services to governmental units, or when they agree on the level of their individual bids), are considered by the DOJ to be the worst type of antitrust violation because such behavior invariably harms consumers by raising prices. The DOJ has made criminal prosecution of such behavior a top antitrust enforcement priority, and many corporate officers and managers have been imprisoned for such violations.

Group Boycotts and Concerted Refusals to Deal

As the Supreme Court has stated, a firm has the "right to deal, or refuse to deal, with whomever it likes, as long as it does so independently."[30] Thus, a unilateral refusal to deal does not violate Section 1 of the Sherman Act, although it may violate Section 2 as an illegal monopolization or attempt to monopolize, as discussed below.

Section 1 of the Sherman Act prohibits group boycotts or concerted refusals to deal. These are agreements among competitors not to deal with another person or business, to deal only on certain terms, or to coerce suppliers or customers not to deal with that person or business. Such an agreement violates the antitrust laws if it forces that party to pay higher prices, prevents a firm from entering a market, or disadvantages a competitor.

Although group boycotts or concerted refusals to deal historically were treated as per se violations, the law is unclear on this issue, and most such actions are analyzed under the rule of reason today (see Case Illustration 4.2).

CASE ILLUSTRATION 4.2

GREGORY v. FORT BRIDGER RENDEZVOUS ASS'N, 448 F.3D 1195 (10TH CIR. 2006)

FACTS The Fort Bridger Rendezvous Association (FBRA) hosts an annual event (the "Rendezvous") at which participants reenact an annual gathering held by local fur traders from 1825 to 1840. Activities include shooting, archery and knife-throwing competitions, and "traders" who sell accurate replicas of pre-1840s merchandise. The event is the largest of this type in the region, and attracts up to 50,000 visitors. The FBRA has about 90 members, about half of whom are traders at the Rendezvous. A trader does not have to be a member of the FBRA to participate. The FBRA monitors

traders' goods for authenticity and has a system for issuing permits to traders. Space for traders is limited and there are more applicants than permits available.

The Gregorys are traders, but not FBRA members. The Gregorys had exhibited at the Rendezvous for several years, but relations between the Gregorys and the FBRA deteriorated and became contentious. In 2002, the Gregorys were denied a permit to participate. The Gregorys filed suit, alleging, among other things, that the FBRA engaged in a horizontal group boycott by refusing to permit them to sell their goods at the Rendezvous.

(Continued)

---

[30]*Monsanto Co. v. Spray-Rite Service Corp.*, 465 U.S. 752, 761 (1984).

The trial court granted summary judgment to FBRA on both claims, and the Gregorys appealed.

DECISION The appellate court affirmed the trial court's decision. The Gregorys had argued that by excluding them from the 2002 Rendezvous, the FBRA had engaged in a horizontal "group boycott," which they contended was *per se* illegal under Section 1 of the Sherman Act.

The appellate court found that there is a presumption in favor of applying the rule of reason to boycott cases. The *per se* rule is appropriately applied only to a boycott that "facially appears to be one that would always or almost always tend to restrict competition and decrease output...." Although the *per se* rule has been applied to a few group boycotts, those cases generally have involved firms with market power who boycotted suppliers or customers in order to deter them from doing business with a competitor.

The court noted that traders other than the Gregorys had also been denied space at the 2002 Rendezvous, for a variety of reasons. Mere denial of a space does not therefore necessarily imply anticompetitive animus. Moreover, denial of space to one trader opens up space for another trader and so overall does not have a predominantly anticompetitive effect.

The court went on to note that although the FBRA's behavior was not *per se* illegal, it should also be evaluated under the rule of reason. Because the purpose of the antitrust laws is to protect the public, the FBRA's conduct had to be judged in terms of its effect upon consumers, not upon competitors. The Gregorys had not argued that the denial of a permit for the 2002 Rendezvous violated the rule of reason test, and in fact, the denial of a permit to the Gregorys allowed a different trader to receive a permit and participate, which would indicate no detrimental effect on consumers. A plaintiff does not meet its burden under the rule of reason test when the challenged behavior by the defendant merely results in "a reshuffling of competitors with no detrimental effect on competition."

Thus, the appellate court affirmed the trial court's grant of summary judgment to the defendants.

Horizontal Market Allocations

Agreements among competitors to divide markets (defined by geographic territories, customer types, or product classes) are illegal *per se* as such agreements effectively give each firm a monopoly within its assigned territory.

➡ *See Discussion Case 4.1.*

Agreements to Restrict Advertising

Agreements among competitors to restrict price advertising may be illegal if the restrictions deprive customers of valuable information. Similarly, restrictions on nonprice advertising may also be illegal if the restrictions have anticompetitive effects and no reasonable business justification.

Joint Ventures

A *joint venture* is a business association between two or more firms organized to carry out a specific business endeavor, such as joint research or a joint sales agency. If the purpose of the joint venture is to engage in behavior that is illegal *per se*, such as price-fixing or horizontal market allocation, the joint venture itself is illegal *per se*. Otherwise, the joint venture is evaluated under the rule of reason.

In 1984, Congress enacted the National Cooperative Research Act to alleviate concerns among businesses that joint research and development ventures might somehow violate the antitrust statutes. Joint ventures covered by the Act are evaluated under the rule of reason, are liable only for single (not treble) damages, and may qualify for "safe harbor" protection if they have less than a 20 percent market share. In 1993, the Act was extended to protect joint production ventures as well.

In April 2000, the FTC and the DOJ jointly issued *Antitrust Guidelines for Collaborations Among Competitors.*[31] These guidelines address the various types of horizontal agreements that competitors may form, such as joint ventures and strategic alliances, and provide an analysis that firms and their lawyers may apply in evaluating whether a proposed collaboration is likely to run afoul of the antitrust laws.

Vertical Restraints Against Competition

While relationships among competitors are described as being "horizontal," the relationships created between suppliers, manufacturers, wholesalers, retailers, and consumers of a product are described as "vertical" (see Exhibit 4.4). Certain agreements between such parties are illegal under Sections 1 and 2 of the Sherman Act and Section 3 of the Clayton Act. Some such agreements are illegal *per se*, while others are evaluated under the rule of reason (see Exhibit 4.5).

◆ *See Discussion Case 4.2.*

Resale Price Maintenance Agreements

Manufacturers often want to establish the prices at which their distributors sell to customers. A manufacturer who has established a marketing program that positions its product as a high-prestige item will not want its distributors to dilute that product image by selling at a discount. The manufacturer would thus want to set a *minimum* price at which its distributors may sell. On the other hand, a manufacturer who is seeking high-volume sales, perhaps in an effort to establish economies of scale in production or to gain a prominent

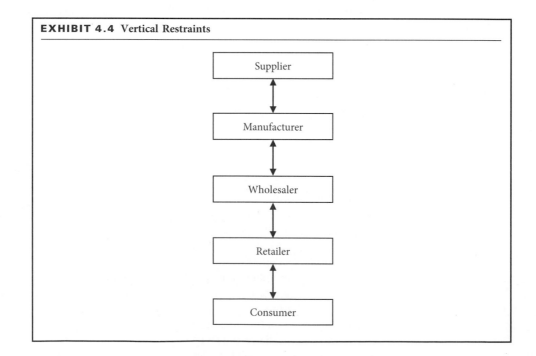

EXHIBIT 4.4 Vertical Restraints

Supplier

Manufacturer

Wholesaler

Retailer

Consumer

---

[31]The guidelines are available on the DOJ's website. See www.usdoj.gov

---

EXHIBIT 4.5 Potential Illegal Vertical Restraints Against Competition

---

- resale price maintenance agreements
- nonprice agreements between manufacturer and dealer
- tying arrangements

---

market share, will not want its distributors to reduce those sales by overpricing. The manufacturer would thus want to set a *maximum* price at which its distributors may sell.

In either event, the manufacturer's and the distributors' interests may well diverge. The distributors' total profits, for example, may be higher if sales are lower but prices are higher than those sought by the manufacturer.

In a 5–4 decision in 2007, *Leegin Creative Leather Products v. PSKS, Inc.*,[32] the Supreme Court overruled almost a century of precedent by holding that all vertical price restraints are to be evaluated under the rule of reason. The Court found that there can be "precompetitive justifications" for a manufacturer's use of vertical resale price maintenance, including encouraging retailers to invest in services or promotional efforts that better serve consumers and stimulating interbrand competition by reducing intrabrand competition. The Court also noted that vertical resale price maintenance can have anticompetitive effects, such as facilitating manufacturer cartels, assisting collusion among retailers to fix prices to consumers, or permitting a powerful manufacturer or retailer to abuse that power by limiting sales of products of rivals or new entrants, or to limit distribution to competitor retailers.

See Discussion Cases 4.2, 4.3.

Manufacturers are free to announce "suggested retail prices" as long as the prices are merely suggested and the action is unilateral. In *United States v. Colgate & Co.*, the Supreme Court stated:

> In the absence of a purpose to create or maintain a monopoly the [Sherman] act does not restrict the long recognized right of a trader or manufacturer engaged in an entirely private business, freely to exercise his own independent discretion as to parties with whom he will deal; and, of course, he may announce in advance the circumstances under which he will refuse to sell.[33]

In addition, the manufacturer may even announce that it will terminate its dealings with any retailer who fails to adhere to the suggested pricing. As long as the manufacturer adheres strictly to its policy, it will likely avoid any antitrust problems. A manufacturer who announces such a policy and then engages in a pattern of suspending and reinstating retailers who first fail to adhere but then agree to do so, however, or who engages in other mechanisms to obtain adherence to its retail prices may well find that it is liable for unlawful resale price maintenance.

An unlawful vertical price-fixing agreement can be either express, as evidenced by written or oral agreements, or inferred from the course of conduct between the parties, such as withholding dealer allowances or increasing wholesale prices to dealers who do not comply with suggested prices.

---

[32]551 U.S. 877 (2007).

[33]250 U.S. 300, 307 (1919).

Most cases in this area are brought by private parties—usually dealers who claim that they were unlawfully terminated because they failed to adhere to the manufacturer's prices (see Case Illustration 4.3).

CASE ILLUSTRATION 4.3

MONSANTO CO. v. SPRAY-RITE SERVICE CORP., 465 U.S. 752 (1984)

FACTS Spray-Rite Service Corp., an agricultural herbicide distributor, sued Monsanto Co., a chemical manufacturer, under Section 1 of the Sherman Act, alleging that Monsanto and some of its distributors had conspired to fix the resale prices of Monsanto's herbicides and that Monsanto had terminated Spray-Rite's distributorship in furtherance of this policy and had encouraged distributors to boycott Spray-Rite.

From 1957 to 1968, Spray-Rite had sold agricultural herbicides manufactured by Monsanto. Spray-Rite was a family-owned discount operation, which bought in large quantities and sold at a low margin. In 1968, Monsanto refused to renew Spray-Rite's one-year distributorship term. At the time, Spray-Rite was Monsanto's tenth-largest distributor (out of approximately 100 distributors) and 16 percent of its sales were Monsanto products. Although Spray-Rite was subsequently able to purchase some Monsanto products from other distributors, it was unable to purchase as much of Monsanto's products as it wanted or as early in the growing season as it wanted,

Monsanto argued that it had terminated Spray-Rite's distributorship because of Spray-Rite's failure to hire trained salesmen and to promote sales to dealers.

DECISION At trial, the jury found that Spray-Rite's termination was the result of a conspiracy between Monsanto and its distributors to set resale prices and awarded $3.5 million in damages, which the District Court trebled to $10.5 million. The U.S. Court of Appeals for the Seventh Circuit affirmed on the grounds that there was sufficient evidence to show that there was a conspiracy to set resale prices because proof of termination following competitor complaints is sufficient to support an inference of concerted action. The evidence at trial had shown numerous complaints from distributors to Monsanto about Spray-Rite's price-cutting practices.

The U.S. Supreme Court also affirmed but found that the Court of Appeals had applied an incorrect standard to the evidence in the case. The Supreme Court stated:

[T]he fact that a manufacturer and its distributors are in constant communication about prices and marketing strategy does not alone show that the distributors are not making independent pricing decisions. A manufacturer and its distributors have legitimate reasons to exchange information about the prices and the reception of their products in the market.

Inferring a price-fixing agreement from the existence of complaints from other distributors, or even from the fact that termination resulted in response to complaints, could deter or penalize legitimate conduct. Something more than mere complaints is necessary.

Thus, the Supreme Court held, to support a finding of an unlawful contract, combination, or conspiracy, "the antitrust plaintiff should present direct or circumstantial evidence that reasonably tends to prove that the manufacturer and others 'had a conscious commitment to a common scheme designed to achieve an unlawful objective.'"

The Supreme Court found that there was sufficient evidence for the jury to have concluded that Monsanto and its distributors had conspired to maintain resale prices and to terminate price cutters. The evidence included: (1) threats that Monsanto would not ship adequate supplies of Monsanto products to price-cutting distributors; (2) after Monsanto complained to a parent company about its subsidiary's price-cutting, the parent instructed the subsidiary to comply, and the subsidiary assured Monsanto that it would; and (3) a Monsanto distributors' newsletter, sent to its dealer-customers, which could reasonably have been interpreted as referring to agreements that distributors and dealers would maintain prices, that Monsanto's company-operated distributors would not undercut those prices, and that discounters would be terminated.

Moreover, there was circumstantial evidence showing that Spray-Rite's termination was made pursuant to a conspiracy between Monsanto and its competitors. Spray-Rite's president had testified that Monsanto made explicit threats to terminate Spray-Rite unless it raised its prices. In a post-termination meeting between Spray-Rite and Monsanto, Monsanto mentioned the many complaints it had received about Spray-Rite's prices as a factor in its termination decision.

Nonprice Agreements Between a Manufacturer and a Dealer

Arrangements in which the manufacturer imposes limitations on how or where a dealer may sell a product (i.e., such things as location restrictions, service obligations, or customer or territorial limitations) are judged under the rule of reason and are generally upheld.

These types of agreements may reduce *intrabrand competition* between local dealers selling a particular manufacturer's products but may well enhance *interbrand* competition between dealers selling competing manufacturers' products. Generally, courts are more concerned with protecting interbrand rather than intrabrand competition. If there is no interbrand competition for the product, however (i.e., the manufacturer has no competitors), the courts may view intrabrand competition as more critical and may thus restrict the manufacturer's right to pick and choose among its prospective dealers or distributors.

Similarly, *exclusive dealing* agreements, in which a supplier prohibits its distributors from selling the products of competing suppliers, are evaluated under the rule of reason and are generally legal if the supplier can show that that there is a legitimate business reason for the arrangement, such as a franchisor's need to protect its mark and goodwill. If the effect is to restrict competition, however, courts will likely find the agreement illegal.

As a practical matter, the vast majority of nonprice vertical restraint cases are decided in favor of the defendant. It is very difficult for a plaintiff to show an illegal nonprice vertical restraint.

Tying Arrangements

Tying arrangements or *tie-in sales* involve the sale of a desired product or service (the *tying product*) upon the condition that the buyer purchase a second product or service (the *tied product*) that the customer may not want or may be able to purchase elsewhere at lower cost. To get the desired product, the purchaser must accept the undesired product as well. For example, a PC manufacturer who requires a purchaser to buy an expensive printer in order to get access to a new and desirable computer would be tying the purchase of the computer (the tying product) to the purchase of the printer (the tied product).

Tying arrangements are governed by several of the antitrust acts. Section 3 of the Clayton Act prohibits tying arrangements involving goods but not those involving services, intangibles, or real property. Section 1 of the Sherman Act also applies to tying arrangements, including the services, intangibles, and real property instances not covered by the Clayton Act. Section 5 of the FTC Act covers tying arrangements that would be illegal under either the Clayton or the Sherman Acts. The analysis is the same under all of the acts.

A tying arrangement is illegal *per se* if:

1. the tying and tied products or services are two separate products or services;
2. the seller possesses sufficient economic power in the tying market to be able to restrain appreciably competition in the tied market; and
3. the arrangement involves a "not insubstantial" amount of interstate commerce.

The concern is that a seller in such a position can force out existing producers of tied products and can block new entrants by forcing them to enter both the tied and tying markets in order to compete.

Tying arrangements that do not meet these three standards are evaluated under the rule of reason and may be legal, though the courts generally view such arrangements with disfavor because of their potential anticompetitive effects. The courts often uphold tying arrangements in the franchisor-franchisee context, however, because of business justifications supporting such arrangements. Franchising law is discussed further in Chapter 5.

For the *per se* test to apply, the seller must have market power in the tying product market, usually defined by courts as at least a 30 percent share of an appropriately defined economic market. Until recently, case law had held that where the defendant holds a patent on the tying product, market power is presumed. This meant that the defendant had the burden of proving that market power did not exist, rather than the plaintiff having the burden of proving that it did.

In 2006, however, the Supreme Court ruled in *Illinois Tool Works, Inc. v. Independent Ink* that this presumption of market power is incorrect. The Court stated: "Congress, the antitrust enforcement agencies, and most economists have reached the conclusion that a patent does not necessarily confer market power upon the patentee."[34] Thus the plaintiff must now prove that the defendant has economic power in the tying market in order for the *per se* rule to apply.

Firms may attempt to use tying arrangements for a variety of reasons. If the firm has monopoly power in the tying product market, it may be able to use the tying arrangement to obtain monopoly power in the tied product market as well. Firms may also use this arrangement in an attempt to avoid price controls or to engage in price discrimination. Firms may engage in such behavior for legitimate reasons as well. For example, the firm may be attempting to take advantage of efficiencies or economies of scale. Similarly, the firm may attempt to protect its goodwill by refusing to provide replacement parts to nonauthorized service providers. The courts view such actions with a skeptical eye, however. As the Supreme Court stated, "The only situation ... in which the protection of goodwill may necessitate the use of tying clauses is where specifications for a substitute would be so detailed that they could not practicably be supplied."[35]

Monopolization and Attempts to Monopolize
Monopolization by a Single Firm

Antitrust law is concerned that firms with *monopoly power* will exclude competitors from the market, reduce output, and thus raise prices for goods and services. In a truly competitive market, a firm has no power to control the prices at which it sells its products as those prices are dictated by market conditions beyond its control. In an imperfect market, firms with monopoly or oligopoly power can raise their prices without losing all of their customers. Their *market power* (i.e., their power to profitably reduce output and raise prices above marginal costs) is limited only by the availability of other products that customers would find suitable substitutes or by the lack of barriers to entry by other firms.

It is not illegal for a firm to have a monopoly position in a market if that power results from a superior product or service, business acumen, or historical accident. As the U.S. Court of Appeals for the Second Circuit once noted: "The successful competitor, having been urged to compete, must not be turned upon when he wins."[36] However, Section 2 of the Sherman Act makes it illegal for a firm to maintain or to attempt to create a monopoly through actions that unreasonably exclude firms from the market or that significantly impair their ability to compete. Such antitrust violations may involve a single firm acting unilaterally or a group of firms acting together to monopolize a market. Conspiracies to monopolize are usually prosecuted under Section 1 of the Sherman Act and are discussed below. Section 2 of the Sherman Act applies to *monopsony* power (i.e., monopoly buying power), as well as to monopoly power.

[34]547 U.S. 28, 45 (2006).

[35]*Standard Oil Co. of California v. United States*, 337 U.S. 293 (1949).

[36]*United States v. Aluminum Co. of America*, 148 F.2d 416, 430 (2d Cir. 1945).

According to the U.S. Supreme Court, *monopolization* consists of two elements:

1. the possession of monopoly power in the relevant market; and
2. unfair attainment or maintenance of that power, "as opposed to growth or development as a consequence of a superior product, business acumen, or historic accident."[37]

Monopoly Power in the Relevant Market Firms that possess a large amount of market power in their relevant market are said to have "monopoly power." For purposes of the antitrust statutes, a firm does not have to have 100 percent of the market in order to have a monopoly position. Rather, a firm with a market share in excess of 70 percent is likely to be deemed to have monopoly power. A firm with a market share of less than 40 percent is unlikely to be found to have monopoly power. If the firm has between 40 percent and 70 percent market share, the court has to make a case-by-case determination as to whether the firm possesses monopoly power. Even where a firm has a high market share, it is not deemed to have monopoly power if the barriers to entry are so slight that other competitors could easily enter the market.

In determining whether a company has monopoly power, the relevant market must be defined. To answer this, the court must determine: (1) the relevant geographic market and (2) the relevant product market.

The defendant, of course, will try to define both of these markets broadly, which will reduce the defendant's relevant market share and make it less likely that the defendant will be found to have monopoly power. The plaintiff, on the other hand, will try to define each of these markets narrowly, which will increase the defendant's relevant market share and increase the likelihood that the court will find the defendant to be a monopolist. Thus, the definitions of the relevant geographic and product markets tend to be litigated vigorously.

The relevant *geographic market* can be international, national, regional, or local, depending upon the type of product or service at issue. It is usually defined as the area in which the defendant and competing sellers sell the product at issue, considering factors such as transportation costs, delivery limitations, customer convenience and preferences, and the locations and facilities of other producers and distributors. According to the U.S. Court of Appeals for the 11th Circuit: "A geographic market is only relevant for monopoly purposes where these factors show that consumers within the geographic area cannot realistically turn to outside sellers should prices rise within the defined area."[38]

The relevant *product market* is determined primarily by customer preferences and the extent to which customers view products as being reasonably interchangeable. Obviously, this determination is subject to a large amount of interpretation and is the subject of much litigation. While two brands of potato chips are logically viewed as being in the same product market, are potato chips and tortilla chips? Potato chips and pretzels? Potato chips and other salty snack foods, such as peanuts? Potato chips and all snack foods, including cookies, candy, and ice cream?

◆ *See Discussion Cases 4.4, 4.5.*

Most products or services fall into the *multiple brand product market* in which several products or services are viewed as interchangeable substitutes and thus compete. However, in a 1992 case, *Eastman Kodak Co. v. Image Technical Services, Inc.*, the Supreme Court held that a single brand of a product or service could constitute a

---

[37]*United States v. Grinnell Corp.*, 384 U.S. 563, 570 (1966).

[38]*T. Harris Young & Associates, Inc. v. Marquette Electronics, Inc.*, 931 F.2d 816, 823 (11th Cir. 1991).

separate market under certain circumstances. Kodak controlled nearly all of the parts market and 80 percent to 95 percent of the service market on its equipment. The Supreme Court found that: "Because service and parts for Kodak equipment are not interchangeable with other manufacturers' service and parts, the relevant market from the Kodak equipment owner's perspective is composed only of those companies that service Kodak machines."[39]

Unfair Attainment or Maintenance of Monopoly Power   The second required element of illegal monopolization is that the firm has engaged in some form of prohibited market behavior. As already noted, the possession of monopoly power itself is not illegal; rather, it is the possession of monopoly power through predatory or coercive behavior that is prohibited. Judge Learned Hand, in a famous case known as *The Alcoa Case*,[40] stated that illegal monopoly power exists where the firm purposefully and intentionally acquired, maintained, or exercised that power, unless it is shown that the monopoly power was either: (1) attained by "superior skill, foresight, or industry" or (2) "thrust upon" the firm as a result of a thin market or economies of scale. This latter category encompasses "innocently acquired" or "natural" monopolies, such as those enjoyed by a small-town newspaper where the market will support only one such paper,[41] by a professional football team in a city in which there are insufficient fans to support more than one such team,[42] or when large economies of scale exist, such as those enjoyed by oil pipeline distribution networks or electricity suppliers.

The types of acts that constitute predatory or coercive behavior include conduct that excludes or bars competitors from the marketplace (such as increasing production capacity to supply all demand before a competitor can enter the field[43]), predatory pricing, and certain refusals to deal.

Predatory pricing is usually defined as pricing below average variable cost. The concern is that a firm attempting to create a monopoly will set prices low to eliminate competition and then raise prices once it has driven all of the other firms from the market. It can be difficult and expensive for a plaintiff to show that predatory pricing has occurred. According to the Supreme Court, for predatory pricing to occur under Section 2 of the Sherman Act: (1) the plaintiff must prove below-cost pricing by the defendant (measured by average variable cost) and (2) the defendant must have a dangerous probability of recouping the money that it lost on below-cost pricing (i.e., by increasing the market price after it has driven its competitors from the marketplace).[44] If the defendant is not in a position to recoup its losses, consumer welfare (and competition) is actually enhanced because consumers face lower aggregate prices in the marketplace. Individual competitors may be harmed by such a strategy but, as stated earlier, the antitrust laws are designed to protect consumers and competition as a whole, not individual competitive firms.

In 2007, the Supreme Court considered the related issue of *predatory bidding* in *Weyerhaeuser Co. v. Ross-Simmons Hardwood Lumber Co.*[45] Predatory bidding occurs when a buyer purchases its inputs at such unreasonably high prices that competitors are unable to purchase the inputs and still sell their end products at a profit. Thus, the buyer can drive weaker competitors out of the market and establish a buyer's monopoly

---

[39]504 U.S. 451, 482 (1992).

[40]*United States v. Aluminum Co. of America*, 148 F.2d 416 (2d Cir. 1945).

[41]*Union Leader Corp. v. Newspapers of New England, Inc.*, 284 F.2d 582 (1st Cir. 1960).

[42]*American Football League v. National Football League*, 323 F.2d 124 (4th Cir. 1963).

[43]*United States v. Aluminum Co. of America*, 148 F.2d 416 (2d Cir. 1945).

[44]*Brooke Group, Ltd. v. Brown & Williamson Tobacco Corp.*, 509 U.S. 209 (1993).

[45]549 U.S. 312 (2007).

(*monopsony*). The *Weyerhaueser* Court ruled that a plaintiff in a predatory bidding case must meet the same two-pronged test by showing that: (1) the increased bids "caused the cost of the relevant output to rise above the revenues generated in the sale of those outputs" and (2) the defendant has "a dangerous probability of recouping the losses incurred in bidding up input prices through the exercise of monopsony power."[46]

Generally, as already discussed, firms may unilaterally *refuse to deal* with particular competitors or purchasers without violating the antitrust laws. There is an exception to this general rule, however, known as the *essential facilities doctrine*. If a firm has exclusive access to a facility that is "essential" to competition, the courts may require the firm to provide access to that facility to its competitors on a reasonable, nondiscriminatory basis. To prove monopolization of an "essential facility," the plaintiff generally must show: "(1) control of the essential facility by a monopolist; (2) a competitor's inability practically or reasonably to duplicate the essential facility; (3) the denial of the use of the facility to a competitor; and (4) the feasibility of providing the facility."[47] Because of the difficulties of meeting this standard of proof, this doctrine is seldom used.

◆ *See Discussion Case 4.5.*

Attempted Monopolization

Section 2 of the Sherman Act also prohibits "attempts to monopolize." *Attempted monopolization* generally requires a showing that: (1) the defendant has engaged in predatory or anticompetitive conduct (2) with a specific intent to monopolize and (3) that there is a dangerous probability of the defendant's success.

The required specific intent can be proved by direct evidence (such as internal memos outlining the firm's plans to illegally obtain a monopoly) or by inference from unfair conduct on the part of the defendant, such as inducing other firms to boycott the defendant's competitors or discriminatory pricing. The same types of predatory or anticompetitive behavior that are condemned in monopolization cases are condemned in attempt-to-monopolize cases.

◆ *See Discussion Cases 4.4, 4.5.*

Conspiracy to Monopolize

Section 2 of the Sherman Act states that it is illegal for any person "to conspire with any other person or persons to monopolize …." Any such violation is also a violation of Section 1's prohibition against conspiracies in restraint of trade. Such actions are almost always prosecuted under Section 1's broader language.

Price Discrimination

The Robinson-Patman Act prohibits discrimination in the prices charged or supplementary services offered to competing purchasers where such discrimination harms competition unless there is a legitimate business justification for the difference. It is intended primarily to protect small, independent businesses from injury caused by discriminatory pricing. *Price discrimination* is defined as identical or similar products being sold at prices that have different ratios to the marginal costs of producing the products.

Price discrimination can enhance profits for the seller who charges a higher price to those customers willing to pay more for the product or service and lower prices to those unwilling to pay. Price discrimination can exist only in markets with a few sellers or with

---

[46]*Id.* at 325.

[47]*MCI Communications Corp. v. American Tel. & Tel. Co.*, 708 F.2d 1081, 1132-33 (7th Cir. 1983).

differentiated products or services. In competitive markets with homogenous products, firms do not have the ability to charge different prices to different buyers. Moreover, price discrimination is more common with services than with goods. If a buyer is able to resell the goods, for example, there is an opportunity for an arbitrageur to buy the good at the lower price and resell it at the higher price. Services, on the other hand, are more difficult to resell. However, the Robinson-Patman Act does not reach sales of services, only sales of goods.

As a practical matter, the DOJ and the FTC seldom take enforcement actions under the Robinson-Patman Act today. Private plaintiffs, on the other hand (particularly resellers charged the higher price), bring frequent suits. Private plaintiffs face a difficult burden of proof in Robinson-Patman Act suits. Even if the plaintiff wins at trial, it is likely to find its victory overturned by the appellate court.

Many states also have laws prohibiting price discrimination. Often, these laws are modeled on the Robinson-Patman Act, but they typically apply only to intrastate activities. Several state acts regulate price discrimination involving services as well as commodities.

Elements of Price Discrimination

The requirements of the Robinson-Patman Act are set forth in Section 2(a) of the Clayton Act. This section makes it unlawful for any person (1) engaged in commerce (2) to discriminate in price between different purchasers (3) of commodities of like grade and quality (4) where the effect may be to substantially lessen competition in any line of commerce, or tend to create a monopoly, or (5) to injure, destroy, or prevent competition with any person who either grants or knowingly receives the benefits of such discrimination, or with the customers of either of them. Thus, even if all other elements of a Robinson-Patman Act case are satisfied, there is no violation if there is no reasonable likelihood of injurious effects on competition.

There are some key points to recognize from this statutory language. First, both the seller who offers and the buyer who knowingly receives discriminatory prices or supplementary services are guilty of violating the Act. In addition, a buyer who knowingly induces an unlawful discriminatory price or supplementary service is in violation of the Act. Thus, a buyer cannot use its superior purchasing power to force sellers into granting discriminatory prices or supplementary services.

Second, the Robinson-Patman Act applies only to "commodities," which includes only tangible goods. Services and intangibles, such as brokerage services, newspaper advertising, cable television, cellular telephone services, mutual fund shares, patent licenses, leases, and real property, are excluded. Electricity, however, is considered a commodity for purposes of the Act.

Third, for a violation to occur, there must be at least two sales (leases, consignments, and license agreements do not count) to two different purchasers, at least one of which must be across a state line. The purchases must occur at fairly contemporaneous times, as determined by market conditions (see Case Illustration 4.4).

Fourth, the Robinson-Patman Act reaches indirect, as well as direct, price discrimination. Thus, discrimination that results from preferential credit terms, quantity discounts, or supplementary services, such as promotional assistance, is illegal. The Act also prohibits certain other types of discounts, rebates, and allowances and prohibits the selling of goods at unreasonably low prices for the purpose of destroying competition or eliminating a competitor.

Fifth, to be of "like grade or quality," the two products need not be identical but must be viewed by buyers as being interchangeable and substitutable.

Sixth, the Act permits recovery for three categories of price discrimination. *Primary-line price discrimination* occurs when a seller's price discrimination harms competition with its direct competitors and usually takes the form of predatory pricing. (Recall that

CASE ILLUSTRATION 4.4

CROSSROADS COGENERATION CORP. v. ORANGE & ROCKLAND UTILITIES, INC., 159 F.3D 129 (3D CIR. 1998)

FACTS An electric cogenerator brought several antitrust allegations against a utility that had refused to purchase energy from it. One of the allegations involved price discrimination. Specifically, the cogenerator alleged that the utility had offered to sell electricity to the cogenerator's customers at a lower price than that offered by the cogenerator, that the reduced price was not offered to all customers, and that such an action violates the Robinson-Patman Act.

DECISION In affirming the trial court's dismissal of the claim, the appellate court stated:

The Robinson-Patman Act, which amended the Clayton Act, prohibits price discrimination "where the effect of such discrimination may be substantially to lessen competition or tend to create a monopoly." In order to state a claim under the Robinson-Patman

Act, a plaintiff must allege facts to demonstrate that (1) the defendant made at least two contemporary sales of the same commodity at different prices to different purchasers; and (2) the effect of such discrimination was to injure competition.

The appellate court found that the plaintiff had not satisfied the first element because it had alleged only that the defendant had "offered" to sell electricity at a rate lower than that charged by the plaintiff, rather than actually engaging in a sale. As the court noted, "Merely offering lower prices to a customer does not state a price discrimination claim."

Moreover, the plaintiff had not satisfied the second element either, as it had made no allegation of predatory conduct or other injury to competition, such as below-market prices. Merely approaching the plaintiff's customer does not constitute an antitrust violation.

predatory pricing may also violate the Sherman Act.) *Secondary-line price discrimination* occurs when a seller's price discrimination impacts competition among the seller's purchasers (i.e., there are purchasers who compete with each other, some of whom receive the favored price and some of whom do not). *Tertiary-line price discrimination* occurs when a seller's price discrimination harms competition between customers of the favored and disfavored purchasers, even though the favored and disfavored purchasers do not compete directly against one another. This occurs when the recipient of a favored price passes that lower price along to purchasers in the next level of distribution. Purchasers from other secondary-line sellers are injured because they do not receive the lower price. These purchasers may sue and recover damages from the discriminating secondary-line seller (see Case Illustration 4.5).

Finally, the Robinson-Patman Act does not apply to sales to federal, state, or local governments, nonprofit institutions, or cooperative associations, or to export sales.

Price discrimination in goods and services may also violate the Sherman Act if it constitutes a restraint of trade or an attempt to monopolize, or may violate Section 5 of the FTC Act if it is an unfair method of competition.

Defenses

There are three statutory *defenses* that sellers can raise in response to allegations of illegal price discrimination: (1) cost justification; (2) response to market conditions; and (3) meeting competition.

Section 2(a) of the Robinson-Patman Act states that "nothing herein contained shall prevent differentials which make only due allowance for differences in the cost of manufacture, sale, or delivery resulting from the differing methods or quantities in which such commodities are sold or delivered." If the defendant can prove a *valid cost justification*

CASE ILLUSTRATION 4.5

VOLVO TRUCKS NORTH AM., INC v. REEDER-SIMCO GMC, INC., 546 U.S. 164 (2006)

FACTS Reeder-Simco GMC, Inc. (Reeder), was a franchised regional dealer of Volvo heavy-duty trucks. It sold those trucks to retail customers. Generally, customers would solicit bids from dealers of various truck manufacturers; more rarely, a customer would solicit bids from two or more dealers franchised by the same manufacturer. The dealer would then request a discount off the wholesale price from the manufacturer.

Volvo Trucks North America, Inc. decided on a case-by-case basis whether to offer dealers a discount off the wholesale price, and if so, how much of a discount. Volvo's stated policy in the rare cases in which a retail customer solicited a bid from more than one franchised dealer was to offer the same discount to each dealer. The dealers would use the price offered by Volvo in preparing their bids to potential customers. The dealer would then place an order only for those trucks for which it had successfully obtained a buyer, and the trucks would be specially-built to the customer's specifications by Volvo.

Reeder filed a suit under the Robinson-Patman Act, alleging that its sales and profits had declined because Volvo offered other dealers more favorable price discounts. Reeder's claims were apparently fueled, at least in part, by its suspicion that it was one of several dealers that Volvo had targeted for termination as part of a cost-saving measure.

The trial court entered judgment for Reeder; the Court of Appeals for the Eighth Circuit affirmed. Volvo appealed to the U.S. Supreme Court.

DECISION The U.S. Supreme Court reversed, finding that Volvo was not liable for secondary-line price discrimination under the Robinson-Patman Act because there was no showing of discrimination between dealers competing to sell to the same retail customers.

The Court explained the purposes of the Robinson-Patman Act as follows:

> [The] Robinson-Patman [Act] does not "ban all price differences charged to different purchasers of commodities of like grade and quality"; rather, the Act proscribes "price discrimination only to the extent that it threatens to injure competition."

To show price discrimination that injures competition among Volvo's dealerships, Reeder had to show, among other things, that (1) Volvo "discriminate[d] in price between" Reeder and another purchaser of Volvo trucks; and (2) "'the effect of such discrimination may be … to injure, destroy, or prevent competition' to the advantage of a favored purchaser." Volvo argued that Reeder had not identified any differentially-priced transaction in which it was both a "purchaser" under the Act and "in actual competition" with a favored purchaser for the same customer.

The Court agreed, concluding that Reeder had failed to bring in evidence to show that it had suffered an injury under the Robinson-Patman Act. The Court noted:

> Reeder did offer evidence of two instances in which it competed head to head with another Volvo dealer. When multiple dealers bid for the business of the same customer, only one dealer will win the business and thereafter purchase the supplier's product to fulfill its contractual commitment ….

However, the Court went on to note that Reeder did not show that Volvo had discriminated against it in these head-to-head transactions:

> Reeder's evidence showed loss of only one sale to another Volvo dealer, a sale of 12 trucks that would have generated $30,000 in gross profits for Reeder. Per its policy, Volvo initially offered Reeder and the other dealer the same concession. Volvo ultimately granted a larger concession to the other dealer, but only after it had won the bid. In the only other instance of head-to-head competition Reeder identified, Volvo increased Reeder's initial 17% discount to 18.9%, to match the discount offered to the other competing Volvo dealer; neither dealer won the bid. In short, if price discrimination between two purchasers existed at all, it was not of such magnitude as to affect substantially competition between Reeder and the "favored" Volvo dealer.

The Court ultimately concluded that Reeder was asking it to expand the reach of the Robinson-Patman Act to cases of a type the Act was never intended to reach. Such an extension, the Court found, would be inconsistent with "broader policies of the antitrust laws."

for the price discrimination, it has an absolute defense to allegations of violation of the Act. This requires the defendant to make a detailed showing of *actual* cost savings attributable to the quantity sold, such as showing that the lower price simply represents the passing on of cost savings achieved through producing and shipping in large quantities. As a practical matter, it is difficult for defendants to calculate and prove such actual cost savings; thus, this defense is rarely used.

Section 2(a) also allows price variations designed to meet fluid product or market conditions, such as the deterioration of perishable goods, obsolescence of seasonal goods, a distress sale under court order, or a legitimate going-out-of-business sale. This defense, which is seldom used, is known as the *market conditions* defense.

Section 2(b) provides that a seller can defend by showing that its lower price was "made in good faith to meet an equally low price of a competitor"—the so-called "*meeting competition in good faith defense.*" To use this defense, the seller must show that: (1) at the time the price concession was made, the facts before it "would lead a reasonable and prudent person to believe that the granting of a lower price would in fact meet the equally low price of a competitor"[48] and (2) the price concession met but did not beat the competitive price for a similar product.

Antitrust and the Internet

The rapid growth of information technology and the Internet have raised new types of antitrust issues. Some commentators have argued that antitrust enforcement is less important in such an environment as new entrants can easily enter markets and supplant dominant market participants who try to assert market power or otherwise abuse their market position. The Antitrust Division of the DOJ, however, has taken the position that first-mover advantages associated with information technology systems raise special risks that dominant market participants will be able to capture markets and engage in anticompetitive behaviors. The Division believes that antitrust enforcement may well be even more important in such an environment.

State Antitrust Enforcement

Although the discussion in this chapter has focused primarily on federal antitrust laws, states are also active in antitrust enforcement. Most states have antitrust statutes, which are often patterned after the federal statutes. These statutes are enforced through the offices of the state attorneys general and, in many states, by private plaintiffs as well. These statutes address intrastate anticompetitive behavior rather than the interstate behavior targeted by the federal statutes. Over 40 states provide for criminal enforcement of state antitrust laws, with 25 of those states making antitrust violations felonies. Like the federal statutes, state antitrust law generally provides for recovery of treble damages, costs, and reasonable attorneys fees.

State antitrust laws can vary from federal law in some instances. For example, the State of Maryland has enacted a statute, effective October 1, 2009, that prohibits manufacturers from requiring retailers to charge minimum prices for their goods. The Maryland legislation was a direct response to the 2007 decision of the U.S. Supreme Court in *Leegin Creative Leather Products v. PSKS, Inc.* (discussed *supra*), in which the Court ruled that such agreements were no longer *per se* illegal under federal antitrust law.

In addition, state attorneys general may well use state antitrust laws to address the behavior of firms that might escape the attention of federal antitrust enforcement

[48]*FTC v. A. E. Staley Mfg. Co.*, 324 U.S. 746, 760 (1945).

agencies. In January, 2009, for example, a Texas hospital agreed to pay $700,000 to settle claims of the Texas attorney general alleging that it had orchestrated agreements among several health plans not to do business with a new competitor hospital. In January 2008, an insurance firm entered into a consent decree with nine states and the District of Columbia, agreeing to pay $6 million to settle claims relating to a nationwide bid-rigging and price-fixing scheme for commercial insurance.

◆ *See Discussion Case 4.5.*

International Implications of Antitrust Laws

The United States enforces its antitrust laws abroad, both civilly and criminally, and, in fact, is more aggressive than other countries in extending the extraterritorial reach of such laws. Under U.S. Supreme Court doctrine, conduct that would violate U.S. law if it occurred in the United States is also a violation if it occurred abroad but affected imports into the U.S.[49] The DOJ's *Antitrust Guidelines for International Operations*[50] state two purposes behind the extraterritorial application of U.S. antitrust law: (1) to protect U.S. consumers from conduct that raises prices or limits choices and (2) "to protect American export and investment opportunities against privately imposed restrictions."

The DOJ has specifically targeted international price-fixing and market-allocation cartels in its enforcement efforts, stating that it will focus its enforcement efforts primarily on boycotts and cartels that injure American exports or affect American consumers.[51] Not only have the cartel fines collected by the Antitrust Division risen dramatically in recent years, but top executives of cartels (including foreign nationals) have been sentenced to imprisonment and cartels have been subjected to civil treble-damage liability.[52] Many foreign nations have followed the United States' lead and are also focusing their antitrust enforcement efforts more intensely on international cartels. Over 100 jurisdictions have anti-cartel legislation. In addition, the United States has entered into cooperation agreements with several nations, including Australia, Brazil, Canada, the European Union, Germany, Israel, and Japan. These agreements are designed to enhance the abilities of governmental authorities to investigate and prosecute international cartel activities.

Cartel violations are treated seriously by most antitrust regulators. In November, 2008, the European Commission imposed a record fine of over €1.3 billion against car glass producers involved in a market-sharing cartel. At about the same time, three foreign electronics manufacturers pled guilty to violating U.S. antitrust law for engaging in price-fixing in the sale of LCD panels. One of the companies, LG Display Co., Ltd., a South Korean firm, agreed to pay a $400 million fine, the second-highest fine imposed to date by the DOJ's antitrust division. Both cases signal the importance that antitrust enforcement agencies around the world are placing on addressing cartel behavior.

As you can imagine, the extension of U.S. antitrust law to foreign firms has created some serious policy conflicts with foreign governments. Under the *sovereign immunity doctrine*, the United States does not apply its laws to foreign governments. Thus, if a foreign firm's activities are mandated (as opposed to merely tolerated) by its government, the U.S. antitrust laws do not apply to it.

---

[49]*United States v. Aluminum Co. of America*, 148 F.2d 416 (2d Cir. 1945).

[50]See www.usdoj.gov/atr/public/guidelines/guidelin.htm

[51]Department of Justice, Antitrust Division, 1999 Annual Report, at p. 5.

[52]See Gerald F. Masoudi, *Cartel Enforcement in the United States (and Beyond)*, at www.usdoj.gov/atr/public/speeches/221868.htm

Over 80 foreign nations also have antitrust legislation. Most Southeast Asian and Latin American countries have or are drafting antitrust laws. The European Union's competition policy is found within Articles 85 and 86 of the Treaty of Rome and is similar to Sections 1 and 2 of the Sherman Act. Most foreign antitrust laws, like the U.S. laws, provide for extraterritorial jurisdiction if the defendant's conduct affects markets in those nations. Thus, a company cannot assume that just because it has no assets in a particular foreign nation, it is not subject to that nation's antitrust provisions.

DISCUSSION CASES

4.1 Horizontal Price-Fixing, Horizontal Market Allocation
Palmer v. BRG of Georgia, Inc., 498 U.S. 46 (1990)

OPINION: PER CURIAM. In preparation for the 1985 Georgia Bar Examination, petitioners contracted to take a bar review course offered by respondent BRG of Georgia, Inc. (BRG). [T]hey contend that the price of BRG's course was enhanced by reason of an unlawful agreement between BRG and respondent Harcourt Brace Jovanovich Legal and Professional Publications (HBJ), the Nation's largest provider of bar review materials and lecture services. The central issue is whether the 1980 agreement between respondents violated § 1 of the Sherman Act.

HBJ began offering a Georgia bar review course on a limited basis in 1976, and was in direct, and often intense, competition with BRG during the period from 1977 to 1979. * * * In early 1980, they entered into an agreement that gave BRG an exclusive license to market HBJ's material in Georgia and to use its trade name "Bar/Bri." The parties agreed that HBJ would not compete with BRG in Georgia and that BRG would not compete with HBJ outside of Georgia. Under the agreement, HBJ received $100 per student enrolled by BRG and 40% of all revenues over $350. Immediately after the 1980 agreement, the price of BRG's course was increased from $150 to over $400.

[T]he District Court held that the agreement was lawful. The United States Court of Appeals for the Eleventh Circuit, with one judge dissenting, agreed with the District Court that *per se* unlawful horizontal price fixing required an explicit agreement on prices to be charged or that one party have the right to be consulted about the other's prices. The Court of Appeals also agreed with the District Court that to prove a *per se* violation under a geographic market allocation theory, petitioners had to show that respondents had subdivided some relevant market in which they had previously competed. * * *

In *United States v. Socony-Vacuum Oil Co.,* 310 U.S. 150 (1940), we held that an agreement among competitors to engage in a program of buying surplus gasoline on the spot market in order to prevent prices from falling sharply was unlawful, even though there was no direct agreement on the actual prices to be maintained. We explained that "under the Sherman Act a combination formed for the purpose and with the effect of raising, depressing, fixing, pegging, or stabilizing the price of a commodity in interstate or foreign commerce is illegal *per se.*"

The revenue-sharing formula in the 1980 agreement between BRG and HBJ, coupled with the price increase that took place immediately after the parties agreed to cease competing with each other in 1980, indicates that this agreement was "formed for the purpose and with the effect of raising" the price of the bar review course. It was, therefore, plainly incorrect for the District Court to enter summary judgment in respondents' favor. Moreover, it is equally clear that the District Court and the Court of Appeals erred when they assumed that an allocation of markets or submarkets by competitors is not unlawful unless the market in which the two previously competed is divided between them.

In *United States v. Topco Associates, Inc.,* 405 U.S. 596 (1972), we held that agreements between competitors to allocate territories to minimize competition are illegal:

One of the classic examples of a *per se* violation of § 1 is an agreement between competitors at the same level of the market structure to allocate territories in order to minimize competition …. This Court has reiterated time and time again that "[h]orizontal territorial limitations … are naked restraints of trade with no purpose except stifling of competition." Such limitations are *per se* violations of the Sherman Act.

The defendants in *Topco* had never competed in the same market, but had simply agreed to allocate markets. Here, HBJ and BRG had previously competed in the Georgia market; under their allocation agreement, BRG received that market, while HBJ received the remainder of the United States. Each agreed not to compete in the other's territories. Such agreements are anticompetitive regardless of whether the parties split a market within which both do business or whether they merely reserve one market for one and another for the other. Thus, the 1980 agreement between HBJ and BRG was unlawful on its face.

The petition for a writ of certiorari is granted, the judgment of the Court of Appeals is reversed, and the case is remanded for further proceedings consistent with this opinion.

It is so ordered.

JUSTICE SOUTER took no part in the consideration or decision of this case.

QUESTIONS FOR DISCUSSION FOR CASE 4.1

1. What is the relevant market?
2. What do you think the purpose of the agreement between these two firms was? Do you think that the managers of these companies could have legitimately thought that their contract was not against the public interest?
3. Do you think that the result would have been the same if the companies had decided to form a joint venture in Georgia? What standard would the court use to review a joint venture?
4. Recall from the chapter discussion that a joint venture is illegal *per se* where its purpose is to engage in behavior that is illegal *per se*. Do you think that it is harder to prove that a joint venture has an illegal purpose or to prove the existence of a horizontal market allocation?
5. Does your answer to Question 4 suggest greater leeway for joint ventures? Can you think of reasons why courts might allow joint ventures greater freedom than two independent companies?

4.2 Vertical Price Restraints, Rule of Reason
Leegin Creative Leather Products v. PSKS, Inc., 551 U.S. 877 (2007)

OPINION BY: Justice Kennedy delivered the opinion of the Court.

In *Dr. Miles Medical Co. v. John D. Park & Sons Co.*, 220 U.S. 373 (1911), the Court established the rule that it is *per se* illegal under § 1 of the Sherman Act for a manufacturer to agree with its distributor to set the minimum price the distributor can charge for the manufacturer's goods. * * * The Court has abandoned the rule of *per se* illegality for other vertical restraints a manufacturer imposes on its distributors. Respected economic analysts, furthermore, conclude that vertical price restraints can have procompetitive effects. We now hold that *Dr. Miles* should be overruled and that vertical price restraints are to be judged by the rule of reason.

I

Petitioner, Leegin Creative Leather Products, Inc. (Leegin), designs, manufactures, and distributes leather goods and accessories. In 1991, Leegin began to sell belts under the brand name "Brighton." The Brighton brand has now expanded into a variety of women's fashion

accessories. It is sold across the United States in over 5,000 retail establishments, for the most part independent, small boutiques and specialty stores. * * * Leegin asserts that, at least for its products, small retailers treat customers better, provide customers more services, and make their shopping experience more satisfactory than do larger, often impersonal retailers. * * *

Respondent, PSKS, Inc. (PSKS), operates Kay's Kloset, a women's apparel store in Lewisville, Texas. Kay's Kloset buys from about 75 different manufacturers and at one time sold the Brighton brand. * * * Kay's Kloset became the destination retailer in the area to buy Brighton products. Brighton was the store's most important brand and once accounted for 40 to 50 percent of its profits.

In 1997, Leegin instituted the "Brighton Retail Pricing and Promotion Policy." Following the policy, Leegin refused to sell to retailers that discounted Brighton goods below suggested prices. The policy contained an exception for products not selling well that the retailer did not plan on reordering. * * *

Leegin adopted the policy to give its retailers sufficient margins to provide customers the service central to its distribution strategy. It also expressed concern that discounting harmed Brighton's brand image and reputation.

* * *

In December 2002, Leegin discovered Kay's Kloset had been marking down Brighton's entire line by 20 percent. Kay's Kloset contended it placed Brighton products on sale to compete with nearby retailers who also were undercutting Leegin's suggested prices. Leegin, nonetheless, requested that Kay's Kloset cease discounting. Its request refused, Leegin stopped selling to the store. The loss of the Brighton brand had a considerable negative impact on the store's revenue from sales.

PSKS sued Leegin in the United States District Court for the Eastern District of Texas. It alleged, among other claims, that Leegin had violated the antitrust laws by "enter[ing] into agreements with retailers to charge only those prices fixed by Leegin." Leegin planned to introduce expert testimony describing the procompetitive effects of its pricing policy. The District Court excluded the testimony, relying on the *per se* rule established by *Dr. Miles.* * * * The jury agreed with PSKS and awarded it $1.2 million. Pursuant to [federal statute], the District Court trebled the damages and reimbursed PSKS for its attorney's fees and costs. It entered judgment against Leegin in the amount of $3,975,000.80.

The Court of Appeals for the Fifth Circuit affirmed. * * * We granted certiorari to determine whether vertical minimum resale price maintenance agreements should continue to be treated as *per se* unlawful.

II

Section 1 of the Sherman Act prohibits "[e]very contract, combination in the form of trust or otherwise, or conspiracy, in restraint of trade or commerce among the several States." While § 1 could be interpreted to proscribe all contracts, the Court has never "taken a literal approach to [its] language." Rather, the Court has repeated time and again that § 1 "outlaw[s] only unreasonable restraints."

The rule of reason is the accepted standard for testing whether a practice restrains trade in violation of § 1. "Under this rule, the factfinder weighs all of the circumstances of a case in deciding whether a restrictive practice should be prohibited as imposing an unreasonable restraint on competition." Appropriate factors to take into account include "specific information about the relevant business" and "the restraint's history,

nature, and effect." Whether the businesses involved have market power is a further, significant consideration. In its design and function the rule distinguishes between restraints with anticompetitive effect that are harmful to the consumer and restraints stimulating competition that are in the consumer's best interest.

The rule of reason does not govern all restraints. Some types "are deemed unlawful *per se.*" The *per se* rule, treating categories of restraints as necessarily illegal, eliminates the need to study the reasonableness of an individual restraint in light of the real market forces at work, and, it must be acknowledged, the *per se* rule can give clear guidance for certain conduct. Restraints that are *per se* unlawful include horizontal agreements among competitors to fix prices, or to divide markets.

Resort to *per se* rules is confined to restraints, like those mentioned, "that would always or almost always tend to restrict competition and decrease output." To justify a *per se* prohibition a restraint must have "manifestly anticompetitive" effects.

As a consequence, the *per se* rule is appropriate only after courts have had considerable experience with the type of restraint at issue, and only if courts can predict with confidence that it would be invalidated in all or almost all instances under the rule of reason. It should come as no surprise, then, that "we have expressed reluctance to adopt *per se* rules with regard to restraints imposed in the context of business relationships where the economic impact of certain practices is not immediately obvious." * * *

III

The Court has interpreted *Dr. Miles* as establishing a *per se* rule against a vertical agreement between a manufacturer and its distributor to set minimum resale prices. * * *

* * *

Dr. Miles ... treated vertical agreements a manufacturer makes with its distributors as analogous to a horizontal combination among competing distributors. * * * Our recent cases formulate antitrust principles in accordance with the appreciated differences in economic effect between vertical and horizontal agreements, differences the *Dr. Miles* Court failed to consider.

The reasons upon which *Dr. Miles* relied do not justify a *per se* rule. As a consequence, it is necessary to examine, in the first instance, the economic effects of vertical agreements to fix minimum resale prices, and to determine whether the *per se* rule is nonetheless appropriate.

A

Though each side of the debate can find sources to support its position, it suffices to say here that economics literature is replete with procompetitive justifications for a manufacturer's use of resale price maintenance. Even those more skeptical of resale price maintenance acknowledge it can have procompetitive effects.

* * *

The justifications for vertical price restraints are similar to those for other vertical restraints. Minimum resale price maintenance can stimulate interbrand competition—the competition among manufacturers selling different brands of the same type of product—by reducing intrabrand competition—the competition among retailers selling the same brand. The promotion of interbrand competition is important because "the primary purpose of the antitrust laws is to protect [this type of] competition." A single manufacturer's use of vertical price restraints tends to eliminate intrabrand price competition; this in turn encourages retailers to invest in tangible or intangible services or promotional efforts that aid the manufacturer's position as against rival manufacturers. Resale price maintenance also has the potential to give consumers more options so that they can choose among low-price, low-service brands; high-price, high-service brands; and brands that fall in between.

Absent vertical price restraints, the retail services that enhance interbrand competition might be underprovided. This is because discounting retailers can free ride on retailers who furnish services and then capture some of the increased demand those services generate. Consumers might learn, for example, about the benefits of a manufacturer's product from a retailer that invests in fine showrooms, offers product demonstrations, or hires and trains knowledgeable employees. Or consumers might decide to buy the product because they see it in a retail establishment that has a reputation for selling high-quality merchandise. If the consumer can then buy the product from a retailer that discounts because it has not spent capital providing services or developing a quality reputation, the high-service retailer will lose sales to the discounter, forcing it to cut back its services to a level lower than consumers would otherwise prefer. Minimum resale price maintenance alleviates the problem because it prevents the

discounter from undercutting the service provider. With price competition decreased, the manufacturer's retailers compete among themselves over services.

Resale price maintenance, in addition, can increase interbrand competition by facilitating market entry for new firms and brands. "[N]ew manufacturers and manufacturers entering new markets can use the restrictions in order to induce competent and aggressive retailers to make the kind of investment of capital and labor that is often required in the distribution of products unknown to the consumer." New products and new brands are essential to a dynamic economy, and if markets can be penetrated by using resale price maintenance there is a procompetitive effect.

Resale price maintenance can also increase interbrand competition by encouraging retailer services that would not be provided even absent free riding. It may be difficult and inefficient for a manufacturer to make and enforce a contract with a retailer specifying the different services the retailer must perform. Offering the retailer a guaranteed margin and threatening termination if it does not live up to expectations may be the most efficient way to expand the manufacturer's market share by inducing the retailer's performance and allowing it to use its own initiative and experience in providing valuable services.

B

While vertical agreements setting minimum resale prices can have procompetitive justifications, they may have anticompetitive effects in other cases; and unlawful price fixing, designed solely to obtain monopoly profits, is an ever present temptation. Resale price maintenance may, for example, facilitate a manufacturer cartel. An unlawful cartel will seek to discover if some manufacturers are undercutting the cartel's fixed prices. Resale price maintenance could assist the cartel in identifying price-cutting manufacturers who benefit from the lower prices they offer. Resale price maintenance, furthermore, could discourage a manufacturer from cutting prices to retailers with the concomitant benefit of cheaper prices to consumers.

Vertical price restraints also "might be used to organize cartels at the retailer level." A group of retailers might collude to fix prices to consumers and then compel a manufacturer to aid the unlawful arrangement with resale price maintenance. In that instance the manufacturer does not establish the practice to stimulate services or to promote its brand but to give inefficient retailers higher profits. Retailers with better distribution systems and lower cost structures would be prevented from charging lower prices by the agreement. Historical examples suggest this possibility is a legitimate concern.

A horizontal cartel among competing manufacturers or competing retailers that decreases output or reduces competition in order to increase price is, and ought to be, *per se* unlawful. To the extent a vertical agreement setting minimum resale prices is entered upon to facilitate either type of cartel, it, too, would need to be held unlawful under the rule of reason. This type of agreement may also be useful evidence for a plaintiff attempting to prove the existence of a horizontal cartel.

Resale price maintenance, furthermore, can be abused by a powerful manufacturer or retailer. A dominant retailer, for example, might request resale price maintenance to forestall innovation in distribution that decreases costs. A manufacturer might consider it has little choice but to accommodate the retailer's demands for vertical price restraints if the manufacturer believes it needs access to the retailer's distribution network. A manufacturer with market power, by comparison, might use resale price maintenance to give retailers an incentive not to sell the products of smaller rivals or new entrants. As should be evident, the potential anticompetitive consequences of vertical price restraints must not be ignored or underestimated.

C

Notwithstanding the risks of unlawful conduct, it cannot be stated with any degree of confidence that resale price maintenance "always or almost always tend[s] to restrict competition and decrease output." Vertical agreements establishing minimum resale prices can have either procompetitive or anticompetitive effects, depending upon the circumstances in which they are formed. * * *

* * *

Resale price maintenance, it is true, does have economic dangers. If the rule of reason were to apply to vertical price restraints, courts would have to be diligent in eliminating their anticompetitive uses from the market. This is a realistic objective, and certain factors are relevant to the inquiry. For example, the number of manufacturers that make use of the practice in a given industry can provide important instruction. When only a few manufacturers lacking market power adopt the practice, there is little likelihood it is facilitating a manufacturer cartel, for a cartel then can be undercut by rival manufacturers. Likewise, a retailer cartel is

unlikely when only a single manufacturer in a competitive market uses resale price maintenance. Interbrand competition would divert consumers to lower priced substitutes and eliminate any gains to retailers from their price-fixing agreement over a single brand. Resale price maintenance should be subject to more careful scrutiny, by contrast, if many competing manufacturers adopt the practice.

The source of the restraint may also be an important consideration. If there is evidence retailers were the impetus for a vertical price restraint, there is a greater likelihood that the restraint facilitates a retailer cartel or supports a dominant, inefficient retailer. If, by contrast, a manufacturer adopted the policy independent of retailer pressure, the restraint is less likely to promote anticompetitive conduct. A manufacturer also has an incentive to protest inefficient retailer-induced price restraints because they can harm its competitive position.

As a final matter, that a dominant manufacturer or retailer can abuse resale price maintenance for anticompetitive purposes may not be a serious concern unless the relevant entity has market power. If a retailer lacks market power, manufacturers likely can sell their goods through rival retailers. And if a manufacturer lacks market power, there is less likelihood it can use the practice to keep competitors away from distribution outlets.

* * *

For all of the foregoing reasons, we think that were the Court considering the issue as an original matter, the rule of reason, not a *per se* rule of unlawfulness, would be the appropriate standard to judge vertical price restraints.

IV

* * *

A

Stare decisis, we conclude, does not compel our continued adherence to the *per se* rule against vertical price restraints. As discussed earlier, respected authorities in the economics literature suggest the *per se* rule is inappropriate, and there is now widespread agreement that resale price maintenance can have procompetitive effects. It is also significant that both the Department of Justice and the Federal Trade Commission—the antitrust enforcement agencies with the ability to assess the long-term impacts of resale price maintenance—have recommended that this Court replace the *per se* rule with the traditional rule of reason. * * *

Other considerations reinforce the conclusion that *Dr. Miles* should be overturned. Of most relevance, "we have overruled our precedents when subsequent cases have undermined their doctrinal underpinnings." The Court's treatment of vertical restraints has progressed away from *Dr. Miles*' strict approach. We have distanced ourselves from the opinion's rationales. This is unsurprising, for the case was decided not long after enactment of the Sherman Act when the Court had little experience with antitrust analysis. * * *

* * *

B

* * *

For these reasons the Court's decision in *Dr. Miles Medical Co.* is now overruled. Vertical price restraints are to be judged according to the rule of reason.

V

* * *

The judgment of the Court of Appeals is reversed, and the case is remanded for proceedings consistent with this opinion.

It is so ordered.

QUESTIONS FOR DISCUSSION FOR CASE 4.2

1. What is the difference between the rule of reason and *per se* illegality in antitrust cases? Are these standards created by Congress or the courts?
2. What is the difference between interbrand and intrabrand competition? Which type of competition is antitrust law primarily designed to promote?
3. Vertical price restraints may lead to higher prices for the manufacturer's goods, but the Court does not find this particularly troubling. Why might higher prices not necessarily indicate anticompetitive conduct?
4. What types of activities might send a signal that resale price maintenance is being used for anticompetitive purposes?

4.3 Rule of Reason, Vertical Maximum Resale Price Maintenance
State Oil Co. v. Khan, 522 U.S. 3 (1997)

OPINION: JUSTICE O'CONNOR delivered the opinion of the Court.

Under § 1 of the Sherman Act, "[e]very contract, combination …, or conspiracy, in restraint of trade" is illegal. *In Albrecht v. Herald Co.,* 390 U.S. 145 (1968), this Court held that vertical maximum price fixing is a *per se* violation of that statute. In this case, we are asked to reconsider that decision in light of subsequent decisions of this Court. We conclude that *Albrecht* should be overruled.

I

Respondents, Barkat U. Khan and his corporation, entered into an agreement with petitioner, State Oil Company, to lease and operate a gas station and convenience store owned by State Oil. The agreement provided that respondents would obtain the station's gasoline supply from State Oil at a price equal to a suggested retail price set by State Oil, less a margin of 3.25 cents per gallon. Under the agreement, respondents could charge any amount for gasoline sold to the station's customers, but if the price charged was higher than State Oil's suggested retail price, the excess was to be rebated to State Oil. Respondents could sell gasoline for less than State Oil's suggested retail price, but any such decrease would reduce their 3.25 cents-per-gallon margin.

* * *

Respondents sued State Oil …, alleging in part that State Oil had engaged in price-fixing in violation of § 1 of the Sherman Act by preventing respondents from raising or lowering retail gas prices. According to the complaint, but for the agreement with State Oil, respondents could have charged different prices based on the grades of gasoline, … thereby achieving increased sales and profits. * * *

* * * [T]he District Court entered summary judgment for State Oil on respondents' Sherman Act claim.

The Court of Appeals for the Seventh Circuit reversed. * * *

We granted certiorari to consider … whether State Oil's conduct constitutes a *per se* violation of the Sherman Act. * * *

II

A

Although the Sherman Act, by its terms, prohibits every agreement "in restraint of trade," this Court has long recognized that Congress intended to outlaw only unreasonable restraints. As a consequence, most antitrust claims are analyzed under a "rule of reason," according to which the finder of fact must decide whether the questioned practice imposes an unreasonable restraint on competition, taking into account a variety of factors, including specific information about the relevant business, its condition before and after the restraint was imposed, and the restraint's history, nature, and effect.

Some types of restraints, however, have such predictable and pernicious anticompetitive effect, and such limited potential for procompetitive benefit, that they are deemed unlawful *per se*. *Per se* treatment is appropriate "[o]nce experience with a particular kind of restraint enables the Court to predict with confidence that the rule of reason will condemn it." * * *

A review of this Court's decisions leading up to and beyond *Albrecht* is relevant to our assessment of the continuing validity of the *per se* rule established in *Albrecht*. Beginning with *Dr. Miles Medical Co. v. John D. Park & Sons Co.,* 220 U.S. 373 (1911), the Court recognized the illegality of agreements under which manufacturers or suppliers set the minimum resale prices to be charged by their distributors. By 1940, the Court broadly declared all business combinations "formed for the purpose and with the effect of raising, depressing, fixing, pegging, or stabilizing the price of a commodity in interstate or foreign commerce" illegal *per se*. *United States v. Socony-Vacuum Oil Co.,* 310 U.S. 150 (1940). Accordingly, the Court condemned an agreement between two affiliated liquor distillers to limit the maximum price charged by retailers in *Kiefer-Stewart Co. v. Joseph E. Seagram & Sons, Inc.,* 340 U.S. 211 (1951), noting that agreements to fix maximum prices, "no less than those to fix minimum prices, cripple the freedom of traders and thereby restrain their ability to sell in accordance with their own judgment."

In subsequent cases, the Court's attention turned to arrangements through which suppliers imposed restrictions on dealers with respect to matters other than resale price. In *White Motor Co. v. United States,* 372 U.S. 253 (1963), the Court considered the validity of a manufacturer's assignment of exclusive territories to its distributors and dealers. The Court determined that too little was known about the competitive impact of such vertical limitations to warrant treating them as *per se* unlawful. Four years later, in *United States v. Arnold, Schwinn & Co.,* 388 U.S. 365 (1967), the Court reconsidered the status of exclusive dealer territories and held that, upon the transfer of title to goods to a distributor, a supplier's imposition of territorial restrictions on the distributor was "so obviously destructive of competition" as to constitute a *per se* violation of the Sherman Act. * * *

Albrecht, decided the following Term, involved a newspaper publisher who had granted exclusive territories to independent carriers subject to their adherence to a maximum price on resale of the newspapers to the public. Influenced by its decisions in *Socony-Vacuum, Kiefer-Stewart,* and *Schwinn,* the Court concluded that it was *per se* unlawful for the publisher to fix the maximum resale price of its newspapers. * * *

Albrecht was animated in part by the fear that vertical maximum price-fixing could allow suppliers to discriminate against certain dealers, restrict the services that dealers could afford to offer customers, or disguise minimum price fixing schemes. * * *

* * *

Nine years later, in *Continental T.V., Inc. v. GTE Sylvania Inc.,* 433 U.S. 36 (1977), the Court overruled *Schwinn,* thereby rejecting application of a *per se* rule in the context of vertical nonprice restrictions. The Court acknowledged the principle of *stare decisis,* but explained that the need for clarification in the law justified reconsideration of *Schwinn:*

Since its announcement, *Schwinn* has been the subject of continuing controversy and confusion, both in the scholarly journals and in the federal courts. The great weight of scholarly opinion has been critical of the decision, and a number of the federal courts confronted with analogous vertical restrictions have sought to limit its reach. In our view, the experience of the past 10 years should be brought to bear on this subject of considerable commercial importance.

* * *

Subsequent decisions of the Court ... have hinted that the analytical underpinnings of *Albrecht* were substantially weakened by *GTE Sylvania*. * * *

* * *

B

Thus, our reconsideration of *Albrecht's* continuing validity is informed by several of our decisions, as well as a considerable body of scholarship discussing the effects of vertical restraints. Our analysis is also guided by our general view that the primary purpose of the antitrust laws is to protect interbrand competition. "Low prices," we have explained, "benefit consumers regardless of how those prices are set, and so long as they are above predatory levels, they do not threaten competition." * * *

So informed, we find it difficult to maintain that vertically-imposed maximum prices could harm consumers or competition to the extent necessary to justify their *per se* invalidation. * * *

* * *

After reconsidering *Albrecht's* rationale and the substantial criticism the decision has received, ... we conclude that there is insufficient economic justification for *per se* invalidation of vertical maximum price-fixing.

* * *

C

Despite what Chief Judge Posner aptly described as *Albrecht's* "infirmities, [and] its increasingly wobbly, moth-eaten foundations," there remains the question whether *Albrecht* deserves continuing respect under the doctrine of *stare decisis*. The Court of Appeals was correct in applying that principle despite disagreement with *Albrecht*, for it is this Court's prerogative alone to overrule one of its precedents.

We approach the reconsideration of decisions of this Court with the utmost caution. *Stare decisis* reflects "a policy judgment that 'in most matters it is more important that the applicable rule of law be settled than that

it be settled right.'" It "is the preferred course because it promotes the evenhanded, predictable, and consistent development of legal principles, fosters reliance on judicial decisions, and contributes to the actual and perceived integrity of the judicial process." This Court has expressed its reluctance to overrule decisions involving statutory interpretation, and has acknowledged that *stare decisis* concerns are at their acme in cases involving property and contract rights. Both of those concerns are arguably relevant in this case.

But "[s]tare decisis is not an inexorable command." In the area of antitrust law, there is a competing interest, well-represented in this Court's decisions, in recognizing and adapting to changed circumstances and the lessons of accumulated experience. Thus, the general presumption that legislative changes should be left to Congress has less force with respect to the Sherman Act in light of the accepted view that Congress "expected the courts to give shape to the statute's broad mandate by drawing on common-law tradition." * * * Accordingly, this Court has reconsidered its decisions construing the Sherman Act when the theoretical underpinnings of those decisions are called into serious question.

* * *

* * * In overruling *Albrecht*, we of course do not hold that all vertical maximum price-fixing is *per se* lawful. Instead, vertical maximum price-fixing, like the majority of commercial arrangements subject to the antitrust laws, should be evaluated under the rule of reason. * * *

* * * We therefore vacate the judgment of the Court of Appeals and remand the case for further proceedings consistent with this opinion.

It is so ordered.

QUESTIONS FOR DISCUSSION FOR CASE 4.3

1. What is the doctrine of *stare decisis*? Under what circumstances will the Supreme Court reverse its own precedents?
2. How could vertical maximum price-fixing benefit consumers?
3. Why would a company want to set a maximum price for its goods?
4. Do you think it would be legal for a company to set a maximum price for its distributors but not for itself?

4.4 Monopolization, Attempted Monopolization
Christy Sports, LLC v. Deer Valley Resort Co., Ltd.,
555 F.3d 1188 (10th Cir. 2009)

When the Deer Valley Resort Company ("DVRC") was developing its world-renowned ski resort in the Wasatch Mountains, it sold parcels of land within the resort village to third parties, while reserving the right of approval over the conduct of certain ancillary businesses on the property, including ski rentals. For about fifteen years, DVRC granted permission to Cole Sports and plaintiff-appellant Christy Sports to rent skis in competition with its own ski rental outlet. More recently, however, DVRC revoked that permission, presumably in order to gain more business for its own newly-opened mid-mountain ski rental store. The question is whether this revocation violated the antitrust laws. We conclude that it did not.

I. Background

Deer Valley is one of three resorts in the vicinity of Park City, Utah. Many—indeed, "the vast majority," according to the Complaint—of Deer Valley's patrons are destination skiers who fly into Salt Lake City and then take a forty-five minute bus or shuttle ride to the resort. The resort itself is divided into two areas: the base area, located at the bottom of the mountain, and the ritzier mid-mountain village, located halfway up the slope. * * *

Originally, DVRC owned all the property at the mid-mountain village, but over the years it has sold parcels to third parties. In 1990, DVRC sold one such parcel to S.Y. and Betty Kimball, subject to a restrictive covenant that prohibited use of the property for either ski rental or real estate sales office purposes without DVRC's express written consent. The Kimballs built a commercial building and leased space in it to Christy's corporate predecessor, Bulrich Corporation. The lease expressly prohibited both the rental of skis and the operation of a real estate office. The next year, though, DVRC gave Bulrich permission to rent skis in return for 15% of the rental revenue. When Bulrich merged with another company in 1994 and formed Christy Sports, LLC, Christy continued to operate the rental business. According to the complaint, Christy stopped paying DVRC 15% of its rental revenue in 1995, though the reason for this change is unknown. Christy rented skis at the Deer Valley mid-mountain village with no objection from DVRC until 2005. During that time, DVRC was the sole purveyor of rental skis at the base area but did not have a ski rental operation at mid-mountain.

DVRC opened a mid-mountain ski rental outlet in 2005. In August of that year, the resort notified Christy that, beginning the following year's ski season, the restrictive covenant would be enforced and Christy would no longer be allowed to rent skis. * * * This leaves that majority of skiers who fly into Salt Lake City and then shuttle to Deer Valley with few choices: they can carry unwieldy ski equipment onto the plane, take a shuttle into Park City and hunt for cheaper ski rentals in town, or rent from the more conveniently located DVRC location. Christy predicts, not improbably, that most consumers will choose the third option.

Christy argues that DVRC's decision to begin enforcing its restrictive covenant is an attempt to monopolize the market of ski rentals available to destination skiers in Deer Valley, or, alternatively, to the destination skiers in the mid-mountain village itself. It alleges that by eliminating its competitors, DVRC will be able to increase prices and reduce output, thus harming consumers. The complaint states that the number of skis available for rental mid-mountain will decline by 620 pairs, and the price will increase by at least twenty-two to thirty-two percent.

* * *

II. Analysis

* * *

Christy has alleged that DVRC violated § 2 of the Sherman Act by either actual or attempted monopolization. "The offense of monopoly under § 2 of the Sherman Act has two elements: (1) the possession of monopoly power in the relevant market and (2) the willful acquisition or maintenance of that power." Similarly, an attempt claim must show "(1) that the defendant has engaged in predatory or anticompetitive conduct with (2) a specific intent to monopolize and (3) a dangerous probability of achieving monopoly power," with the third element requiring "consider[ation] [of] the relevant market and the defendant's ability to lessen or destroy competition in that market." Under both types of § 2 claims Christy must therefore plead both power in a relevant market and anticompetitive conduct. The relevant market, according to Christy's complaint, is the market for ski rentals to destination skiers in Deer Valley in general or, even more narrowly, the market for ski rentals in the mid-mountain village. The alleged anticompetitive conduct is the enforcement of the restrictive covenant.

* * *

We begin our analysis with DVRC's original decision to impose the restrictive covenant.

A. Imposition of the Restrictive Covenant

We agree with the defendant that the creator of a resort has no obligation under the antitrust laws to allow competitive suppliers of ancillary services on its property. A theme park, for example, does not have to permit third parties to open restaurants, hotels, gift shops, or other facilities within the park; it can reserve to itself the right to conduct such businesses and receive revenues from them. Accordingly, if it sells land within the resort to third parties, the antitrust laws do not bar the resort owner from imposing a covenant against use of the property for competitive businesses. This is so even if food, rooms, gifts, or other ancillary goods and services would be cheaper and more plentiful if the resort owner allowed competition in these businesses.

This conclusion can be reached either by reference to the proper definition of a market or by reference to the absence of anticompetitive conduct. Some courts, faced with cases of this sort, have found the market definition implausible. The Seventh Circuit took this approach in Elliott v. United Center, 126 F.3d 1003 (7th Cir. 1997), when a peanut vendor challenged a sports arena's decision to ban outside food and thereby monopolize the market for food concessions within the arena. The court rejected that market definition as implausible, saying:

> The logic of [the] argument would mean that exclusive restaurants could no longer require customers to purchase their wines only at the establishment, because the restaurant would be "monopolizing" the sale of wine within its interior. Movie theaters, which traditionally (and notoriously) earn a substantial portion of their revenue from the sale of candies, popcorn, and soda, would be required by the antitrust laws to allow patrons to bring their own food.

Other courts agree. Hospitals alleged to have monopolized the market for medical services within that

single hospital and a cemetery alleged to have monopolized the market for tombstones within that cemetery, were all declared too narrow to constitute a relevant market. Perhaps even closer to this case is Hack v. President & Fellows of Yale College, 237 F.3d 81, 85 (2d Cir. 2000), in which Yale University was alleged to have monopolized the market for on-campus housing within its sprawling complex of facilities. The Second Circuit rejected the idea that it is impermissible for an institution to monopolize one particular product within an establishment that provides a variety of interrelated services, the most important one of which is education. The alleged market was too narrow.

Although discussion of sports arenas and universities seems to suggest that Christy's shortcomings lie with its alleged geographic market, the actual problem lies with its product market. In these cases the two are difficult to disentangle because the product (rental skis, as here, or housing, as in *Hack*) is intimately related to the location. Consumers do not travel to Deer Valley for rental skis, just as they do not attend Yale to live in an Eero Saarinen-designed dormitory. The true product in these cases is the overall experience. Deer Valley offers a cluster of products that combine to create a destination ski experience; rental skis are only one small component. The complaint alleges nothing to suggest that destination skiers are choosing their ski resort based on the price of rental skis, separate and apart from the cluster of services associated with the destination-ski experience. To define one small component of the overall product as the relevant product market is simply implausible.

Alternatively, one could say that the monopolization claim would fail because the alleged conduct is not anticompetitive. Even if a firm has monopoly power in a relevant market, a plaintiff must also show "the willful acquisition or maintenance of that power as distinguished from growth or development as a consequence of a superior product, business acumen, or historic accident." Deer Valley is not required to invite competitors onto its property to rent skis to its patrons, even if a failure to do so would mean it is the sole supplier of rental skis at the ski area.

* * *

Having invested time and money in developing a premier ski resort that attracts skiers from across the nation, DVRC could recoup its investment in a number of ways. It could increase the price of lift tickets, raise room rates, serve only high-priced food, or, as it seems to have chosen, delve more deeply into the rental ski market. This does not mean consumers have no protection. The ski resort industry is competitive (and Christy does not allege otherwise). Families contemplating ski vacations have many options, and they presumably compare quality and price. If they are rational, the price they are concerned about is the sum of all of their prospective vacation costs, including not just lift ticket prices and resort lodging, but air fare, food and drink, apres-ski entertainment, ski rentals, and the like. A resort that facilitates lower ski rental prices by allowing competition is able to price other aspects of the ski vacation experience more aggressively. The competitive discipline comes not from introducing competition with respect to each component of the experience, but from competition with other ski resorts with respect to the entire package. Christy has not alleged, and it would not likely be plausible to allege, that DVRC's decision to foreclose competition in the ski rental business at the mid-mountain village will have any effect on the market for ski resort vacations as a whole.

Indeed, allowing resorts to decide for themselves what blend of vertical integration and third party competition will produce the highest return may well increase competition in the ski resort business as a whole, and thus benefit consumers. This flexibility about business strategies induces entrants into the ski resort business by allowing them to reserve the benefits of their investments to themselves. * * *

* * *

[H]aving created a resort destination, antitrust will not force a resort developer to share its internal profit-making opportunities with competitors. The relevant market requirement reaches this result by finding implausible a market definition that singles out a small component of the cluster of services that constitutes the actual product; the anticompetitive conduct requirement reaches it by saying that it is not anticompetitive to refuse to grant access to competitors.

B. Revocation of Consent to Operate a Ski Rental Facility

* * *

[T]he plaintiff argues primarily that, having allowed third parties to engage in the ski rental business for almost fifteen years, DVRC violated § 2 of the Sherman Act when it revoked that permission and took over the ski rental business for itself.

We do not see the logic in this argument. If antitrust law permits a resort operator to organize its business in either of two ways, by providing ancillary services itself or by allowing third parties to provide the service on a competitive basis, we do not see why an initial decision to adopt one business model would lock the resort into that approach and preclude adoption of the other at a later time. * * *

* * *

DVRC should not be forever locked into a business decision made in 1990, especially when it took an affirmative step to preserve its future flexibility by bargaining for a restrictive covenant. This is so even if Christy is correct that by enforcing the restrictive covenant DVRC could increase the price and decrease the output of ski rentals at Deer Valley. It had the right to do so from the beginning, and the fact that it chose to do otherwise for some time does not eliminate that right. The antitrust laws should not be allowed to stifle a business's ability to experiment in how it operates, nor forbid it to change course upon discovering a preferable path.

* * *

III. Conclusion

Because Christy Sports has failed to plead a plausible claim for either attempted or actual monopolization under § 2 of the Sherman Act, we **AFFIRM** the district court's dismissal for failure to state a claim.

QUESTIONS FOR DISCUSSION FOR CASE 4.4

1. What are the required elements of a monopolization claim? Attempted monopolization?
2. To show a violation of Section 2 of the Sherman Act, the plaintiff must show both that the defendant has market power in a relevant market and that it has engaged in anticompetitive conduct. What arguments did Christy Sports put forth on these two elements? What conclusions did the court reach about these two elements?
3. Why does the court conclude that competition is not harmed if DVRC enforces its covenant and becomes the sole ski rental operator in this geographic area?
4. Do you think that this outcome is fair to Christy Sports? Could Christy Sports have planned its own business activities so as to avoid or minimize the financial ramifications of DVRC acting in this manner?

4.5 Monopolization, Attempted Monopolization, Definition of Market, Essential Facility, State Antitrust Law

Green County Food Market, Inc. v. Bottling Group, LLC, 371 F.3d 1275 (10th Cir. 2004)

Plaintiffs, retail grocery stores operating in the Tulsa, Oklahoma area, brought this diversity action under the Oklahoma Antitrust Reform Act against their local distributor of Pepsi and affiliated beverage products and its holding company ("Bottling Group" and "Holdings"). Plaintiffs alleged that Bottling Group unlawfully discontinued sales to Plaintiffs in response to a price discrimination lawsuit Plaintiffs had previously brought against Bottling Group's predecessor-in-interest. The district court granted summary judgment in favor of Bottling Group and Holdings. On appeal, Plaintiffs primarily challenge the district court's definition of the relevant product market. We … AFFIRM.

Background

Plaintiffs are corporations that operate grocery stores, each owned in whole or in part by either Steven Davis or Brian Honel. Plaintiff Brissa, Inc. (operated by Mr. Honel) and Plaintiff Plaza Redbud Inc. (operated by Mr. Davis) had purchased Pepsi and affiliated beverage products from Beverage Products Corporation ("BPC"), the exclusive distributor of these products in the Tulsa area. By 1997, Mr. Honel and Mr. Davis had recognized that they were often unable to sell their Pepsi products at prices competitive with other area grocery stores. Mr. Honel and Mr. Davis compared their invoices from BPC and discovered that BPC had been charging them different wholesale prices for the beverage products it distributed. On January 5, 1999, Plaintiffs Brissa and Plaza Redbud sued BPC for price discrimination under Oklahoma antitrust laws.

On February 8, BPC transferred all assets, liabilities, and stock to Bottling Group Holdings, Inc. ("Holdings"), which the same day transferred the same assets, liabilities, and stock to Bottling Group, LLC ("Bottling Group"). Bottling Group is majority owned by Holdings, and Holdings is indirectly wholly owned by The Pepsi Bottling Group, Inc.

On February 11, Bottling Group discontinued sales to Plaintiffs Brissa and Plaza Redbud because of a "distinct decrease in the level of trust" between Bottling Group and each grocery store stemming from the pending price discrimination lawsuit. Bottling Group has also refused to distribute its products to other Plaintiff grocery stores that Mr. Honel and Mr. Davis have acquired. Plaintiffs therefore have no access, other than retail purchase, to the 155 Pepsi and affiliated beverage products distributed by Bottling Group.

Plaintiffs filed this lawsuit against both Bottling Group and Holdings under §§ 203[2] and 205 of the Oklahoma Antitrust Reform Act. The complaint alleged monopolization, attempt to monopolize, and conspiracy to monopolize under § 203(B) and denial of access to an essential facility under § 203(C), and requested injunctive relief and monetary damages under § 205. All allegations were predicated on Bottling Group's refusal to deal with Plaintiffs following Plaintiffs' initiation of the price discrimination lawsuit against BPC.

The district court denied Plaintiffs' request for a preliminary injunction and granted summary judgment in favor of Bottling Group and Holdings. * * *

Plaintiffs timely filed this appeal. * * *

Discussion

Plaintiffs' allegations focused exclusively on alleged monopolization under § 203(B) and denial of access to an essential facility under § 203(C).

* * *

B. The Relevant Product Market

The Oklahoma Antitrust Reform Act is construed in accordance with federal antitrust law. Sections 203(B) and 203(C) of the Oklahoma Antitrust Reform Act both require that the plaintiff prove a relevant market.

---

[2]Section 203 of the Oklahoma Antitrust Reform Act provides in relevant part:

A. Every act, agreement, contract, or combination in the form of a trust, or otherwise, or conspiracy in restraint of trade or commerce within this state is hereby declared to be against public policy and illegal.

B. It is unlawful for any person to monopolize, attempt to monopolize, or conspire to monopolize any part of trade or commerce in a relevant market within this state.

C. [I]t is unlawful for any person in control of an essential facility to unreasonably refuse to give a competitor or customer of an entity controlling an essential facility access to it upon reasonable terms if the effect of such denial is to injure competition.

Under § 203(B), "it is unlawful for any person to monopolize, attempt to monopolize, or conspire to monopolize any part of trade or commerce in a relevant market within this state." Accordingly, to establish liability under § 203(B), a plaintiff must first define the relevant market.

Under § 203(C), "it is unlawful for any person in control of an essential facility to unreasonably refuse to give a competitor or customer of an entity controlling an essential facility access to it upon reasonable terms if the effect of such denial is to injure competition." Pursuant to the statute, an "essential facility" is a facility which, inter alia, "is controlled by an entity that possesses monopoly power." "Monopoly power" is "the power to control market prices or exclude competition." To prove monopoly power, the plaintiff must first define the relevant market.

Accordingly, both § 203(B) and § 203(C) require proof of a relevant market. The relevant market inquiry has two components: geographic market and product market. Only the latter is an issue in this appeal.

The Supreme Court articulated the standard for defining the relevant product market …. A relevant product market consists of "products that have reasonable interchangeability for the purposes for which they are produced—price, use and qualities considered." The interchangeability of products is measured by, and is substantially synonymous with, cross-elasticity. A market is "cross-elastic" if rising prices for one product causes consumers to switch to the other product.

The Supreme Court has also recognized the existence of submarkets within a larger product market. The boundaries of such a submarket are defined by such factors as industry or public recognition of the submarket as a separate economic entity, the product's peculiar characteristics and uses, unique production facilities, distinct customers, distinct prices, and sensitivity to price changes and specialized vendors. "The same proof which establishes the existence of a relevant product market also shows (or … fails to show) the existence of a product submarket." * * *

1. Products of a single manufacturer or brand

In general, a manufacturer's own products do not themselves comprise a relevant product market.

As the Supreme Court stated …:

Where there are market alternatives that buyers may readily use for their purposes, illegal monopoly does not exist merely because the product said to be monopolized differs from others. If it were not so, only physically identical products would be a part of the market.

Similarly, we have said that "a company does not violate the Sherman Act by virtue of the natural monopoly it holds over its own product." Even where brand loyalty is intense, courts reject the argument that a single branded product constitutes a relevant market.

Nonetheless, products of a single manufacturer may in rare circumstances constitute a relevant product market. In Eastman Kodak Co. v. Image Technical Services, Inc., [504 U.S. 451 (1992)], the Supreme Court held that the relevant product market must be defined in terms of the choices of products and services available to Kodak equipment owners. Because Kodak equipment owners were locked into Kodak parts and services, Kodak parts and services were not interchangeable with the parts and services of other manufacturers. Accordingly, only those companies that serviced Kodak machines comprised the relevant product market.

The Supreme Court has acknowledged in dicta that the soft drink industry is a prototypical example of an industry in which products are so interchangeable that control over one brand cannot be an illegal monopoly. The Court said that "this power that … soft-drink manufacturers have over their trademarked products is not the power that makes an illegal monopoly." "There are certain differences in the formulae for soft drinks but one can hardly say that each one is an illegal monopoly."

Accordingly, Pepsi branded beverage products cannot alone comprise a relevant product market. Plaintiffs attempt to avoid this conclusion by offering evidence that consumers are "brand loyal" to Pepsi branded products. Mr. Davis, one of the grocery store owners in this case, testified that in his experience, people are brand loyal to Pepsi because instead of substituting Coke if they do not find Pepsi on the grocery store shelves they look elsewhere for Pepsi. Brand loyalty of consumers to particular soft drinks is an insufficient basis for concluding that Pepsi constitutes a relevant product market. Plaintiffs have offered no other evidence to show that Pepsi products are not reasonably interchangeable with Coke products or other branded soft drinks.

Nor have Plaintiffs offered any evidence pertaining to the specific factors listed by the Supreme Court in Brown Shoe, such as evidence that Pepsi prices are insensitive to price changes in other branded soft drinks. In short, Plaintiffs have offered no evidence other than their own testimony pertaining to brand loyalty to prove that Pepsi branded products constitutes a market distinct from other soft drink products.

* * *

Conclusion

We hold that Plaintiffs['] … claims under §§ 203(B) and 203(C) of the Act require proof of a relevant product market. We further hold that Plaintiffs have failed to establish a genuine dispute that the products distributed by Bottling Group alone constitute a relevant product market. Accordingly, the district court's grant of summary judgment in favor of Bottling Group and Holdings is AFFIRMED.

QUESTIONS FOR DISCUSSION FOR CASE 4.5

1. This case arose under the Oklahoma antitrust statute. How similar or dissimilar is the language of that statute to the corresponding federal statute?
2. The court discusses the "essential facilities" doctrine. What do you suppose the plaintiffs were alleging the "essential facility" at issue here was? Why did their argument fail?
3. Do you agree that Pepsi and Coca Cola products are interchangeable? Do you agree with the court's determination that Pepsi products are not their own relevant product market for purposes of the antitrust laws? Is there a way to reconcile consumer behavior with regard to this product with the rules of antitrust law?

DISCUSSION QUESTIONS

1. Russell Stover Candies, Inc., sells and ships its box chocolates and candies to more than 18,000 retailers throughout the country. Most of the retailers are department, drug, card, and gift stores. Russell Stover designates resale prices for all of its products and communicates those prices to retailers by price lists, invoices, order forms, and preticketing of all of its products. Russell Stover also announces to each prospective retailer the circumstances under which it will refuse to sell; i.e., whenever Russell Stover reasonably believes that a prospective retailer will resell Stover products at less than designated prices and whenever an existing retailer has actually sold Stover products at less than designated prices. Russell Stover does not request or accept express assurances from existing or prospective retailers regarding resale prices, however. Russell Stover has, in the past, refused to sell to prospective retailers or has terminated existing retailers based on these policies. As a result, 97.4 percent of Stover products are sold at or above the designated resale price.

   The FTC determined that Russell Stover had violated Section 1 of the Sherman Act by illegally combining with the retail dealers to fix retail prices.

   Russell Stover has appealed the FTC's decision to the Court of Appeals. How should the appellate court rule on this issue?

2. Anti-Monopoly, Inc., developed and marketed a family board game called Anti-Monopoly. It possessed less than 1 percent of the market for family board games. Hasbro, Inc., the leading manufacturer of family board games, has more than 80 percent of the market. Toys "R" Us is the largest retailer of family board games, with about 35 percent to 40 percent of the retail market. K-Mart is the second-largest such retailer, with about 15 percent of the retail market. Anti-Monopoly and Hasbro compete directly for space in retail stores such as these. Anti-Monopoly brought suit against Hasbro, alleging that Hasbro exercised control over Toys "R" Us and K-Mart by conditioning the sale of its family board games to such retailers on the retailers not purchasing family board games from Anti-Monopoly and other small competitors. Anti-Monopoly alleged that Hasbro's control of Toys "R" Us and K-Mart constituted monopolization of an essential facility in violation of Section 2 of the Sherman Act. How should the court rule on this claim?

3. Jimi Rose owned a business, first known as Hollywood Nights and then as Goodfellas, which he wanted to advertise in the *Morning Call*, a local newspaper. He alleged that space and layout restrictions were placed on his ads and that on several occasions, his ads were not run at all, while white competitors in similar businesses faced no such restrictions. He alleged that he was told by the *Morning Call* that his ads were prurient and inferior to those of his white competitors, yet the *Morning Call* accepted prurient and sexually suggestive ads

from those competitors. He further alleged that the *Morning Call* refused to accept his ads for over a year and that the ban extended to the classified want ads, which prevented him from seeking new employees. Finally, Rose alleged that the ban on his advertising cost him valuable business, as hotel guests and convention participants did not know that his business existed. Rose contended that the *Morning Call's* behavior toward him was racially motivated.

Rose sued the *Morning Call*, alleging that the *Morning Call* enjoyed monopoly power over an essential facility, newspaper advertising, and that its use of that power to exclude Rose from advertising his business and from placing classified ads had an anticompetitive effect. Rose described the relevant geographic market as the Lehigh Valley in Pennsylvania and the relevant product market as advertising in the *Morning Call*. He alleged that the *Morning Call's* actions diminished his ability to compete in the marketplace and caused "serious and permanent damage" to him and his business.

Is the *Morning Call* an essential facility? Has Rose defined the relevant markets correctly? If you were the judge, how would you rule on this claim, and why?

4. Cancall Communications, Inc., a distributor of prepaid wireless telephone services, acquired airtime on Omnipoint Corp.'s network that it then resold to its customers. In the prepaid wireless telecommunications industry, each consumer must use a telephone handset that is specifically programmed to access a specific network. The service providers supply Subscriber Identification Module Cards (SIM Cards) to each of their customers. The SIM cards contain specific information about each consumer and enable that consumer to access the network. Omnipoint refused to sell Cancall SIM cards alone, but instead required that Cancall's customers purchase new handsets, which were manufactured by three handset manufacturers (the Equipment Manufacturers) and supplied to Omnipoint for use with its network. While direct Omnipoint customers could purchase the handsets from Omnipoint for $49, Omnipoint charged Cancall $189 for the same handsets. The Equipment Manufacturers refused to sell the handsets directly to Cancall. Cancall has alleged that the Equipment Manufacturers have violated the Robinson-Patman Act. Have they? Why, or why not?

5. Digital Equipment Corp. (DEC) manufactures computer hardware. In April 1994, DEC introduced its Alpha line of mid-range servers. It offered a three-year warranty on the servers, even though the industry standard at the time was to offer a one-year warranty. DEC offered the longer warranty as part of its strategy to compete with its industry rivals, such as IBM, Sun Microsystems, and Hewlett-Packard.

SMS Systems Maintenance Services, Inc., an independent service organization (ISO) that operates nationally and specializes in servicing DEC equipment, accused DEC of violating Section 2 of the Sherman Act, alleging that longer warranties unfairly constrained consumers' ability to choose their preferred service providers and thus paved the way for a monopoly in the services aftermarket for DEC computers. There is a strong aftermarket for servicing computers, and many ISOs compete vigorously with manufacturers for this business. SMS argued that a purchaser with a warranty will not use an ISO because the purchaser will not want to pay twice for the same service. In framing its argument, SMS alleged that the relevant market was the aftermarket for repair services for DEC computers. Has SMS defined the relevant market correctly? How should the court rule on its claim?

6. Full Draw Productions, an archery trade show promoter, held its first Bowhunting Trade Show (BTS) in 1990. At the time, it was the only merchandise mart devoted solely to archery equipment. Archery manufacturers and distributors purchased exhibition space, and dealers paid a fee to attend. The same year, Full Draw entered into a five-year agreement with AMMO, a trade association, in which Full Draw paid AMMO 10 percent of its BTS gross revenues in exchange for AMMO's endorsement of the show. In 1994, AMMO tried to increase this fee to 30 percent. AMMO also discussed buying the BTS from Full Draw and threatened to boycott the BTS unless Full Draw sold the show to AMMO on the terms offered by AMMO. AMMO and Full Draw did not reach an agreement.

In 1995, AMMO decided that it would present its own archery trade show, to be held one week after the 1997 BTS. Several archery manufacturers and distributors, a publishing company, and a representative for archery manufacturers (the defendants) had supported and participated in AMMO's actions against Full Draw to date. The defendants decided to boycott the BTS to eliminate it as a competitor to AMMO's new trade show. The defendants allegedly: (1) advertised that they would attend only the AMMO trade show in 1997; (2) informed others at the 1996 BTS that they would attend only the AMMO show the following year; (3) persuaded others to boycott the BTS and attend only the AMMO show by repeatedly stating that key manufacturers and distributors would not attend the 1997 BTS and that the BTS would be a failure and probably not even occur; (4) created a "climate of fear of retribution and loss of business" for attending the BTS and retaliated against businesses that did attend the 1997 BTS; (5) agreed among themselves and caused other AMMO members to agree not to attend the 1997 BTS; and (6) actually boycotted the 1997 BTS.

The 1997 BTS failed financially and was eliminated as a competitor to future AMMO shows, leaving AMMO as the only supplier in the market of archery trade shows in the United States.

Full Draw sued the defendants, claiming a violation of the Sherman Act. The district court dismissed Full Draw's antitrust claims, noting that Full Draw had alleged that the defendants' actions had driven it out of business, but had not alleged that those acts caused harm to consumers or competition:

> and this is unsurprising where Defendants are many of the relevant consumers and their acts increased, albeit temporarily, competition. By definition, it would seem that where a majority of consumers believe that a monopoly producer is not performing adequately and decide to provide an alternative for themselves and other consumers, there can be no antitrust injury, particularly where, as here, there have been no allegations that harm was caused to any other consumers (e.g., the other exhibitors or the attendees of the shows) by reduced output or increased prices.

Full Draw has appealed. How should the appellate court rule? Is the trial court's analysis correct and persuasive? Why, or why not?

7. Plaintiffs operate lodges and provide lodging referral services in the Big Bear Valley recreational area. For years, the two ski resorts in the area, Snow Summit, Inc., and Bear Mountain, Inc., offered bulk discounts on lift tickets to lodges and tourist businesses, including Plaintiffs. Plaintiffs would then offer "ski packages" of lodging and lift tickets at attractive prices to consumers.

Plaintiffs alleged as follows: In 1994, the president of Snow Summit helped form a local association to promote the Big Bear Valley. Plaintiffs were told that unless they joined the association (and paid up to 2.5 percent of their incomes as dues), neither Snow Summit nor Bear Mountain would sell them discount lift tickets nor honor any tickets purchased by them. Association members were also prohibited from selling, trading, or conveying discount lift tickets to Plaintiffs. The Association then adopted rules prohibiting members from belonging to other local referral services in which nonmembers participated and from referring business to nonmembers. Association members also agreed on uniform rates and charges for lodge accommodations, ski packages, and resort services and published advertising materials reflecting these rates. Plaintiffs alleged both price-fixing and group boycott violations on the part of the Association, Snow Summit and Bear Mountain, and certain other members of the Association.

The district court dismissed Plaintiffs' complaint, stating: "This is not an antitrust case, period." Plaintiffs have appealed. How should the appellate court rule, and why?

8. National Parcel Service is a "zone shipper," a shipping company that receives packages from mail order and retail catalog merchants and delivers them in bulk to U.S. Postal Service (USPS) bulk mail distribution centers. This enables National to charge lower prices than United Parcel Service (UPS), because UPS charges a premium for residential deliveries, and to offer faster service than USPS.

J. B. Hunt is an interstate trucking company. In mid-1994, a J. B. Hunt subsidiary entered the zone shipping market, targeting the customers of National and another zone shipper, GTC, with low prices. J. B. Hunt's initial strategy was to make "whatever price concessions you need to give or whatever, get us in the business quickly." J. B. Hunt's revenues grew quickly even though it lost money, while National lost business. National brought a suit, seeking damages for predatory pricing under Section 2 of the Sherman Act. Has J. B. Hunt engaged in predatory pricing? Why, or why not?

9. From 1992 to 1996, Generac Corp. served as a dealer of certain generators that it manufactured under license from Caterpillar, Inc. The license agreement gave Generac the right to develop and manufacture a line of generators that were

marketed under Caterpillar's Olympian trademark and that were distributed by Caterpillar dealers in specified territories. Generac was assigned North, Central, and South America, as well as 17 countries in the Far East. Caterpillar agreed not to license anyone else to sell generator sets within Generac's territory under the Olympian trademark but could sell or license others to sell generators in the Generac territory under a different trademark. In the United States and Canada, Generac was permitted to sell Olympian products only to Caterpillar dealers who had been designated by Caterpillar as a Power Systems Distributor (PSD). Generac also promised not to appoint any new distribution outlets for its own branded sets in a Caterpillar dealer's territory as long as the dealer was adequately covering its sales territory for Olympian sets. The agreement was for an indefinite duration and could be terminated by either party upon 24 months' written notice or with cause upon 120 days' notice.

Through June, 1996, Generac spent $10.5 million on sales, service, and warranties to promote and support the Olympian line and invested more than $660,000 in the engineering and development of the line. It constructed a new manufacturing facility at a cost of $5.24 million. It paid Caterpillar more than $5.6 million in fees and generated sales of Olympian products of more than $124.4 million. Ultimately, Olympian products represented about 58 percent of Generac's total industrial sales.

In May, 1996, Caterpillar informed Generac that it was terminating the agreement effective June 30, 1998, so that it could form a new business relationship with Emerson Electric Company. Generac felt that it was the victim of a "classic free ride"—that it had invested millions to develop the market for the Olympian line, only to be deprived of the opportunity to reap the long-term benefits.

Generac sued for antitrust violations, claiming that the restrictions placed on it violated Section 1 of the Sherman Act as a *per se* unlawful horizontal market division. Is Generac right? Why, or why not?

10. InvaCare Corp. is a competitor of Respironics, Inc., a manufacturer of positive airway pressure devices ("PAPs") and masks used to treat obstructive sleep apnea ("OSA"). Respironics is one of three major competitors in the OSA field; there are other, smaller competitors as well. Invacare alleged that Respironics had entered into agreements with sleep labs under which Respironics would sell its products to the labs at predatorily low prices; in exchange, the labs allegedly would agree to prescribe only Respironics' products. Although Invacare had no direct evidence of such exclusive agreements between Respironics and sleep labs, it pointed out that Respironics gave sleep labs almost 600,000 free masks over a four-year period, at a cost of $1.5 million. Respironics' sales training materials stated that the purpose of distributing free masks to sleep labs was to encourage the labs to prescribe its masks and PAPs and to discourage customers from buying competitive products. Some sleep labs received free masks from several companies and Invacare itself provided free or below-cost masks to sleep labs. Should Invacare succeed on its motion for summary judgment?

11. Richard Campfield owns an auto-glass repair shop and holds fourteen patents for processes to repair or prevent windshield cracks. Although industry practice is to replace, not repair, windshields with cracks longer than 6 inches, Campfield believes that it is not only feasible, but safer, to repair cracks between 6 and 18 inches, rather than to replace the windshield. After failing to convince auto insurance companies to alter their repair policies to allow repair instead of replacement, Campfield sued State Farm Insurance Company and its agent, Lynx Services, Inc., alleging that they had engaged in illegal cooperation that resulted in a group boycott that was sufficient to show a *per se* violation of the Sherman Act.

State Farm is one of the largest automobile insurers in the United States. Its insureds make approximately 1.7 million claims for glass-related damage, such as windshield cracks and broken headlights, each year. State Farm contracts with glass shops to perform the needed services. State Farm outsourced management of the provision of these services to Lynx Services, Inc., a company that provides insurance claim processing services.

How should the court rule on Campfield's allegation that State Farm and Lynx had engaged in a group boycott constituting a *per se* violation of the Sherman Act?

12. R.J. Reynolds sells cigarettes, including such well-known brands as Camel, Winston, Salem, and Doral. Cigarettes Cheaper! is a discounter and operates a chain of retail outlets. Cigarettes Cheaper! argued that Reynolds had violated the Robinson-Patman Act by charging different prices to different retail dealers, and in particular by refusing to sell cigarettes to Cigarettes Cheaper! at its greatest level of discounts.

Because cigarette manufacturers are unable to advertise through many normal promotional channels, such as television, radio, billboards, and many magazines, they rely heavily upon point-of-sale promotional efforts, such as signs, placards, product positioning, and shelf space commitments, and other devices. Typically, manufacturers will offer discounts to retailers who promote their products; the greater the promotion efforts, the greater the discounts in the wholesale price.

Reynolds admitted that it sold to other retailers for less than it sold to Cigarettes Cheaper! It justified this action however, by arguing that Cigarettes Cheaper! could have received these same discounts had it engaged in the same promotional efforts as did the other retailers, and that the discounts it offered were necessary to meet competition from its major competitor, Philip Morris. Cigarettes Cheaper! had entered in a marketing agreement with Philip Morris and did not engage in the level of marketing support needed to receive Reynolds' greatest level of discounts.

Is Reynolds permitted to vary the discounts its offers to competing retailers based upon considerations such as the promotional efforts made by the retailers?

CHAPTER 5

The Franchisor-Franchisee Relationship

Since World War II, franchising has become a growth industry, both in the United States and internationally. As of 2005, there were over 900,000 franchised locations in the United States, providing 11 million direct jobs and generating $880 billion in direct economic output.[1] Many types of businesses use franchise systems, including automobile dealerships, gasoline stations, convenience stores, soft drink bottlers, travel agencies, restaurants, car rental agencies, pet stores, cleaning services, hair salons, tax preparation services, tutoring services, and day care centers. Although no definitive recent statistics exist, analysts generally agree that 35 percent to 40 percent of retail sales occurs through franchised businesses.[2] This chapter addresses legal issues that are specific to the franchisor-franchisee relationship.

Overview

The term *franchise* refers to a contractual relationship where one party (the *franchisor*) licenses another party (the *franchisee*) to use the franchisor's trade name, trademarks, copyrights, and other property in the distribution and sale of goods or services in accordance with established practices and standards. "Franchise" is used to refer both to the contractual agreement between the franchisor and the franchisee and to the franchise outlet itself.

Both the franchisor and the franchisee can obtain significant benefits from a well-conducted franchise relationship. The franchisee receives the opportunity to start and own a business, even though the franchisee may have limited capital and/or experience. The franchisee also obtains access to the franchisor's goodwill, training, and supervision, as well as access to product supplies and marketing expertise generally available only to larger business concerns. The franchisor receives the influx of the franchisee's capital (which facilitates expansion), a larger asset base, enhanced goodwill generated by the franchisee's business efforts, and access to a known distribution network.

The franchise system poses risks for both parties as well, however. The franchisor must work to ensure consistent quality and operational standards throughout the franchise system, which can be both costly and difficult. The franchisee, on the other hand,

---

[1]See *Economic Impact of Franchised Business*, vol. 2, available on the Web site of the International Franchise Association, a franchising advocacy group, at www.franchise.org. For general information franchise industry trends and statistics, see Goizueta Business School's site at http://business.library.emory.edu/info/franchising/trends.html#stats

[2]See Francine Lafontaine, "Myths and Strengths of Franchising," *Financial Times*, Mastering Strategies Series, November 22, 1999, reprinted in *Mastering Strategy: The Complete MBA Companion in Strategy* (London: FT Prentice Hall, 2000), 140–45.

must guard against abuses by the franchisor of its generally superior knowledge of the business and market power.

As discussed later in this chapter, the federal government, acting through the Federal Trade Commission (FTC), regulates only limited aspects of the franchise relationship—primarily issues relating to disclosure.[3] Most regulation of the franchise relationship occurs at the state level.

Some municipalities have, in recent years, sought to restrict or limit the location of franchised businesses through local ordinances, fearing that such "formula" businesses may detract from the local character or may damage local businesses. Ordinances that attempt to block franchises from entering local markets may well be unconstitutional under the Commerce Clause of the U.S. Constitution.

◆ *See Discussion Case 5.1.*

Types of Franchises

There are two primary categories of franchises: *product and trade name franchises* and *business format franchises*. In a *product and trade name franchise*, the franchisor licenses a franchisee to sell its product, either exclusively or with other products. The franchisee often has the exclusive right to sell the product in a designated area or territory. These franchises essentially function as a distribution system for the franchisor's goods. Automobile dealerships and beer distributorships, for example, fall within this category.

In a *business format franchise*, the franchisee operates a business under the franchisor's trade name and is identified as a member of a select group of persons who deal in this particular good or service. The franchisor sells a "way of doing business" to the franchisee in exchange for royalties and fixed fees. Generally, the franchisee must follow a standardized or prescribed format as to methods of operation, including things such as use of trade or service marks, site selection, design of the facility, hours of business, and qualifications and training of employees. Fast-food restaurants, hotels, and rental services are generally set up as business format franchises.

Definition of a "Franchise"

It is often difficult to distinguish between a franchise and other forms of branded distribution. The label that the parties attach to their relationship does not necessarily control. In many states, "franchise" is defined statutorily. The Illinois Franchise Disclosure Act is typical:

(1) "Franchise" means a contract or agreement, either expressed or implied, whether oral or written, between two or more persons by which:
   (a) a franchisee is granted the right to engage in the business of offering, selling, or distributing goods or services, under a marketing plan or system prescribed or suggested in substantial part by a franchisor; and
   (b) the operation of the franchisee's business pursuant to such plan or system is substantially associated with the franchisor's trademark, service mark, trade name, logotype, advertising, or other commercial symbol designating the franchisor or its affiliate; and

---

[3]For information on the FTC's role in franchise regulation, see www.ftc.gov/bcp/menus/business/franchise.shtm

(c) the person granted the right to engage in such business is required to pay, directly or indirectly, a franchise fee of $500 or more ....[4]

Most state statutes and the federal amended Franchise Disclosure Rule (discussed below) provide that, in order for a franchise relationship to exist, there must be a contract or agreement, either express or implied, oral or written, that meets three requirements:

1. *Use of mark.* The franchisee must receive a license to use the franchisor's trade or service mark, trade name, logotype, advertising, or other commercial symbol in connection with the sale or distribution of goods or services.
2. *Assistance to or control over franchisee's operations.* The franchisor must somehow assist or control the franchisee's operations, usually through the provision of a marketing plan or system prescribed in total or substantial part by the franchisor. Under the amended Franchise Disclosure Rule, significant types of *control* can take many forms:
   - site approval for unestablished businesses;
   - site design or appearance requirements;
   - hours of operations;
   - production techniques;
   - accounting practices;
   - personnel policies;
   - promotional campaigns requiring franchisee participation or financial contribution;
   - restrictions on customers; and
   - locale or area of operation.[5]

   Under the amended Rule, significant types of *assistance* include:
   - providing formal sales, repair, or business training programs;
   - establishing accounting systems;
   - furnishing management, marketing, or personnel advice;
   - selecting site locations;
   - furnishing systemwide networks and websites; and
   - furnishing a detailed operating manual.[6]
3. *Franchise fee.* Under most (though not all) state franchise statutes, a franchise relationship does not exist in the absence of a payment of a "franchise fee." This requirement is easily met, however, as most state statutes define a franchise fee as any payment above a minimal amount (usually $500) required for the right to enter into the franchise business (excluding purchases or leases of real property and purchases of goods at bona fide wholesale prices). It does not matter whether the parties have labeled the payment a "franchise fee" or not.

Thus, business arrangements such as licenses, joint ventures, strategic alliances, distribution agreements, dealer or sales agent agreements, and subcontractor agreements may potentially be regulated as franchises, even if the parties did not contemplate a franchise relationship (see Case Illustration 5.1).

To avoid the inadvertent creation of a franchise, a supplier or manufacturer should be careful about licensing others to use its marks, should exercise restraint in providing assistance to or control over a distributor's business, and should not require any payment from its dealers above a bona fide wholesale price. A more extensive (but often impractical) strategy is for the supplier or manufacturer to use its own sales force and retail outlets and avoid the use of dealers altogether.

---

[4]815 Ill. Comp. Stat. 705/3 (2007).

[5]See www.ftc.gov/bcp/edu/pubs/business/franchise/bus70.pdf

[6]*Id.*

CASE ILLUSTRATION 5.1

JEROME-DUNCAN, INC. v. AUTO-BY-TEL, LLC, 989 F. SUPP. 838 (E.D. MICH. 1997), *AFF'D,* 176 F.3D 904 (6TH CIR. 1999)

FACTS Jerome-Duncan, Inc. (JDI), a Ford dealership, entered into a five-year contract with Auto-by-Tel (ABT), which operated an Internet site, through which it referred potential customers to car dealers. Under the contract, JDI was to be the exclusive dealer to which ABT would refer potential Ford customers in a four-county area. Either party could terminate the contract on 30 days' notice. After JDI refused ABT's request to renegotiate the contractual terms, ABT gave notice that it was terminating the contract. JDI sued, claiming that the contract was a "franchise agreement" under the Michigan Franchise Investment Law (MFIL) and therefore could not be terminated without good cause, despite the express termination provision.

DECISION The trial court noted that the policy behind the MFIL was to remedy perceived abuses by large franchisors against unsophisticated investor franchisees. JDI, which was the largest Ford dealership in the metro Detroit area and which had annual sales in excess of $130 million, was not the type of franchisee that the MFIL was intended to protect.

Moreover, the MFIL defines a "franchise agreement" as one in which: (1) the franchisee is subject to a marketing plan or system prescribed in substantial part by the franchisor; (2) the franchisee is allowed to use the mark, trade name, or other commercial symbol of the franchisor; and (3) the franchisee is required to pay a franchise fee.

The trial court found that neither of the first two requirements had been met. First, JDI attempted to classify ABT's website as a "virtual dealership" and argued that JDI thus operated an ABT "virtual dealership" franchise. JDI pointed to the specific guidelines given by ABT regarding customer contacts, the training provided by ABT to a JDI executive who was to serve as the "ABT representative," and the limited territory that it received from ABT. The trial court rejected this argument, finding that because JDI was

selling Ford products, not ABT goods or services, it was not operating under a "marketing plan prescribed by a franchisor."

Second, JDI was not engaged in distributing goods or services substantially associated with the mark of ABT. Although ABT required JDI to place the ABT logo on certain print advertisements, place an "authorized Auto-by-Tel dealer" sign in its showroom, use the ABT logo on business cards, and assign titles such as "Auto-by-Tel manager" to its employees, the court found that JDI's sales were still primarily associated with the Ford mark borne by the cars it sold. Thus, the second requirement of the MFIL was also not met.

The court listed several other factors that courts consider in determining whether a relationship is a "franchise": "(1) franchisor control over hours and days of operation: (2) placing of signs advertising the franchisor; (3) loans by franchisor of equipment; (4) franchisor auditing of franchisee's books; (5) franchisor inspection of franchisee's premises; (6) franchisor control over lighting at franchisee's place of business; (7) franchisor requiring the franchisee to wear uniforms; (8) franchisor control over the setting of prices; (9) franchisor licensing of sales quotas; (11) [*sic*] franchisor training of employees; and (12) offer by franchisor of financial support." The majority of these factors were not present in this case.

The trial court did note that JDI had paid a start-up fee of $3,500 and was required to pay a monthly fee of $500. These payments would likely constitute a "franchise fee" under the MFIL had the other two elements of a franchise been satisfied.

Because the contractual agreement between JDI and ABT did not meet the definition of a franchise agreement, the MFIL did not apply. Thus, the termination provisions of the agreement controlled and ABT had not violated any state law by terminating the relationship. The trial court awarded summary judgment to ABT.

◆ *See Discussion Cases 5.2, 5.3.*

Creation of a Franchise

Franchisors usually recruit franchisees by advertising their particular business. Interested parties then contact the franchisor, who sends out a "franchise kit." The kits tend to describe the franchise business in very positive terms, which can be misleading to unsophisticated potential franchisees. The federal and state disclosure rules discussed later in this chapter are intended to alleviate this problem.

Once the parties agree to the franchise relationship, they typically sign a detailed contractual agreement. The agreement is almost always drafted by the franchisor and, not surprisingly, often tends to favor that party substantially. These agreements are usually long (often 30 to 50 pages) and are often very complicated. Because of the disparity in bargaining power between the parties, in the event of litigation, the courts generally scrutinize the agreements to make sure that the stronger party (the franchisor) has not taken unfair advantage of the weaker party (the franchisee) (see Case Illustration 5.2).

Generally, the franchise agreement imposes a limited variety of obligations upon the franchisor. The franchisor typically gives the franchisee the right to use its trademark and/or standardized product or service in exchange for a franchise fee. The franchisor generally advertises the product or service in exchange for an advertising fee (often calculated as a percentage of gross sales). The franchisor also provides training programs and manuals and sets out detailed guidelines for the day-to-day operation of the business. Established

---

CASE ILLUSTRATION 5.2

NAGRAMPA v. MAILCOUPS, INC., 469 F.3D 1257 (9TH CIR. 2006) (EN BANC)

FACTS The franchisee and franchisor had entered into an agreement for a direct-mail advertising franchise. The agreement had a provision stating that disputes were to be arbitrated. After two unprofitable years of operation, the franchisee unilaterally terminated the relationship. The franchisor then started an arbitration proceeding, claiming that the franchisee owed it over $80,000 in fees. The franchisee challenged the validity of the arbitration clause in court.

DECISION The appellate court ruled that the arbitration clause was both procedurally and substantively unconscionable and thus unenforceable. Under California law (which governed the agreement), "[p]rocedural unconscionability analysis focuses on 'oppression' or 'surprise.'" Furthermore, "[o]ppression arises from an inequality of bargaining power that results in no real negotiation and an absence of meaningful choice," while "[s]urprise involves the extent to which the supposedly agreed-upon terms are hidden in a prolix printed form drafted by the party seeking to enforce them." By contrast, "[a]n arbitration provision is substantively unconscionable if it is '"overly harsh"' or generates '"one-sided" results.'" The court explained that "the paramount consideration in assessing [substantive] conscionability is mutuality."

Here, the franchise agreement was procedurally unconscionable because the franchisee was in a "substantially weaker bargaining position" than the franchisor, the franchisor had drafted the franchise agreement, and the franchisor had presented the agreement to the franchisee on a "take-it-or-leave-it" basis. In fact, the franchisee's efforts to negotiate certain of the terms had been rebuffed by the franchisor.

The franchise agreement was also substantively unconscionable because it lacked mutuality (in that it allowed the franchisor to bring certain actions in court while restricting the franchisee's causes of action against the franchisor to arbitration proceedings) and the forum designated for arbitration (the franchisor's home of Boston, Massachusetts) was oppressive to the franchisee, who was located in California.

franchisors often designate a particular location for the franchise outlet, design and arrange for standardized construction of the facility, and install fixtures and equipment.

The franchisee, on the other hand, is generally required to follow the procedures specified by the franchisor or risk termination. The franchise agreement usually mandates strict accounting procedures and authorizes the franchisor to inspect the books and records at any time. The franchisee is required to pay a number of types of fees as well, such as:

- an initial license fee (i.e., a lump-sum payment for receiving the franchise);
- a royalty fee (i.e., a payment for the use of the franchisor's trade name, property, and assistance, usually calculated as a percentage of gross sales and payable on a monthly basis);
- an assessment fee (which covers things such as advertising, promotional, and administrative costs and which is usually calculated as either a flat monthly or annual fee or as a percentage of gross sales);
- lease fees (i.e., payments for any equipment or land leased from the franchisor); and
- costs of supplies (i.e., payments for any supplies purchased from franchisor).

The franchise agreement also typically requires the franchisee to obtain liability insurance to protect both the franchisor and the franchisee against casualty losses and tort suits and requires the franchisee to comply with state law workers' compensation requirements.

The franchise agreement usually sets forth the duration of the franchise (typically 10 to 20 years) and usually provides for renewals of the term. Typically, the agreement contains a covenant not to compete, which prohibits the franchisee from competing with the franchisor for a stated period after termination of the franchise relationship. (Covenants not to compete are discussed in more detail in Chapter 3.)

Finally, the agreement usually requires the franchisor to give the franchisee a certain time period (e.g., 10 days) to cure any default under the agreement. The franchisor typically must then give notice of termination. In states that regulate termination and nonrenewal of franchises, the franchisor must generally wait a set time period after giving notice (often 90 days) before the termination is actually effective. Most states do not regulate termination and nonrenewal, however. In those states, the franchisee receives only those protections provided by the franchise agreement.

Regulation of the Franchise Relationship

On the one hand, franchise relationships can promote competitive markets, which, as we have noted before, the law favors. On the other hand, the disparity in the bargaining relationship between the franchisor and the franchisee can lead to abuses. Franchise law thus generally attempts to facilitate the franchise relationship while putting in place safeguards to prevent overreaching behavior by the franchisor (who typically is the dominant party in the relationship).

Prior to the 1970s, there was little regulation of franchise relationships at either the state or the federal levels. With the exception of disclosure requirements (discussed below), there are only two areas of significant federal regulation of the franchise relationship today. First, the federal Automobile Dealers' Franchise Act[7] prevents automobile company franchisors from terminating their dealers without just cause. (Many state legislatures have also passed statutes protecting automobile dealerships from the disproportionately greater power of car manufacturers.) Second, the federal Petroleum Marketing Practices Act[8] protects motor fuel distributors and dealers from arbitrary terminations.

---

[7]15 U.S.C. § 1221 *et seq.*
[8]15 U.S.C. §§ 2801-2806, 2821-2824, 2841.

Today, regulation of the offer and sale of franchises or of the franchisor-franchisee relationship can be regulated under one of three sets of laws: (1) federal or state registration and disclosure laws and regulations; (2) state franchise "relationship" laws; and (3) "business opportunities" laws. Most regulation occurs at the state level, which means, of course, that regulation can vary from state to state. State law generally applies to a franchise relationship if: (1) the offer or sale of a franchise is made in or from a state; (2) the franchise will be located within the state; or (3) the intended franchisee is a resident of the state. Franchisors thus must plan their business activities carefully to avoid inadvertently incurring legal liability.

Disclosure

Federal Disclosure Rules   Existing federal law primarily addresses *disclosure* issues. (The FTC has declined to regulate the ongoing franchise relationship, although it has the power to do so.) In 1979, the FTC issued its FTC Franchise Disclosure Rule.[9] The FTC recently amended the Franchise Rule; these amendments took full effect on July 1, 2008. The amended Rule requires each regulated franchisor to prepare an extensive document, the Franchise Disclosure Document (FDD), for each potential franchise purchaser.

Under the amended Rule, the franchisor's disclosure must include a number of types of information, including: (1) the history of the franchisor; (2) required fees and investment costs; (3) information about the franchisor; (4) financial statements of the franchisor; (5) the litigation and bankruptcy history of the franchisor; and (6) a copy of the franchisor's standard franchise agreement. The written disclosures must be provided to the potential franchisee at least 14 calendar days before the prospective franchisee signs any binding agreement or makes any payments to the franchisor. The Rule mandates that certain cautionary statements be explicitly and conspicuously made in the document. The amended Rule also provides for a sophisticated franchisee exemption, which means the Rule will not apply to franchisees whose initial investment is at least $1 million (excluding franchisor financing and unimproved real estate). Also exempted are "large" franchisees, which are entities with at least five years in business and with a net worth at least $5 million and "insider" franchise purchases involving owners or officers of the franchisor or individuals with at least two years' management experience within the franchise system.

The FTC's Franchise Disclosure Rule does not require that the franchisor file its disclosure with the FTC, and no federal agency reviews or approves the contents of the disclosure. Nonetheless, the Rule is a federal trade regulation with the full force and effect of federal law, and failure to make proper disclosure is an unfair or deceptive trade practice under Section 5 of the FTC Act. Thus, if the FTC discovers that the franchisor made an inaccurate disclosure, the FTC may seek injunctions, civil penalties (including fines of up to $11,000 for each violation), and consumer redress as remedies. These penalties can be severe. The courts have imposed civil penalties of up to $870,000 in a single case and have ordered consumer redress of up to $4.9 million. The Rule does not provide a cause of action to private parties (such as a potential franchisee misled by an incorrect disclosure), however.

The original FTC Franchise Rule applied to both traditional franchises and certain business opportunities, such as vending machines and display rack business opportunity ventures. The amended Rule applies only to franchises. The FTC has expressed an intent

---

[9]16 C.F.R. Part 436. The FTC's Web site, www.ftc.gov, contains various types of information on franchises, including a Guide to the FTC Franchise Rule.

to deal with amendments to existing business opportunity disclosure requirements through separate rule making in the future.

State Disclosure Rules   Fifteen states have franchise investment laws that require franchisors to provide disclosures to potential purchasers as well.[10] State disclosures are made on the same FDD used for federal disclosures. Unlike the federal Disclosure Rule, the state disclosure laws will permit private parties to sue for violations. Thus, the state statutes can provide a more direct remedy for aggrieved investors.

Thirteen of these states require registration as well as disclosure.[11] In effect, these states treat the sale of a franchise like the sale of a security. These states generally require the franchisor to file a registration document with state regulators and to obtain their approval before offering franchises to potential buyers. Some states also require franchisors to submit advertisements for franchises for review or approval prior to publication.

Business Opportunity Statutes   Twenty-six states have *business opportunity statutes*, which regulate the offer and sale of distribution arrangements directed at unsophisticated "consumer" dealers or distributors.[12] Unlike "franchises," "business opportunities" do not require the use of the seller's trademark. (This is the key distinction between the two categories in most states.)

The definition of a business opportunity is quite broad in most states, encompassing virtually any type of business activity that might be offered for sale. Under Texas law, for example, the existence of a marketing program and a payment exceeding $500 suffices. These state statutes generally require registration and disclosure similar to those required by franchise laws. These state statutes also usually regulate the ongoing business relationship between the seller and the buyer. In addition to providing for a private cause of action for damages and rescission, the business opportunity statutes often give the buyer the right to rescind the agreement within one year of execution and to receive a refund in the event the seller violates the statute. In many instances, a single transaction may be subject to both the business opportunity statute and the state franchise laws.

Legal Issues Arising from the Franchise Relationship

Many types of legal issues can arise in the franchisor-franchisee relationship. These are generally state law issues. About one-half of the states have "franchise relationship" statutes that may regulate items such as: (1) termination of a franchise; (2) transfer or sale of a franchise; and (3) discrimination among franchisees on things such as royalties or other fees. Even in states without such laws, various types of issues may arise in the franchisor-franchisee relationship, and may be addressed under other statutes or under common law.

---

[10]These states are California, Hawaii, Illinois, Indiana, Maryland, Michigan, Minnesota, New York, North Dakota, Oregon, Rhode Island, South Dakota, Virginia, Washington, and Wisconsin. See www.ftc.gov/bcp/franchise/netdiscl.shtm

[11]These states are California, Hawaii, Illinois, Indiana, Maryland, Minnesota, New York, North Dakota, Rhode Island, South Dakota, Virginia, Washington, and Wisconsin. *Id.*

[12]These states are Alaska, California, Connecticut, Florida, Georgia, Illinois, Indiana, Iowa, Kentucky, Louisiana, Maine, Maryland, Michigan, Minnesota, Nebraska, New Hampshire, North Carolina, Ohio, Oklahoma, South Carolina, South Dakota, Texas, Utah, Virginia, Washington, and Wisconsin. See www.ftc.gov/bcp/franchise/netbusop.shtm

Existence of a Franchise Relationship

It is sometimes difficult to tell whether the relationship between the parties is truly a franchisor-franchisee relationship or whether it involves an employer-employee or principal-agent relationship. It is important from the franchisor's perspective that this relationship be clear, as franchisors are generally not liable for the torts or contractual breaches of their franchisees, but employers or principals may be liable for the torts or breaches of their employees or agents.

It is also important from the franchisee's perspective that the franchisor-franchisee relationship be clear. In some instances, franchisees get certain rights under state law that employees, agents, or other parties do not. For example, many state laws prohibit termination of a franchise without good cause but permit termination of other types of dealers without cause if the underlying contract so permits. On the other hand, if the purported franchisee is found to be an employee, she may be protected by laws regarding unemployment insurance, wages, civil rights, and other employment-related regulation that would not apply to franchisees (see Case Illustration 5.3).

Vicarious Liability of a Franchisor

Although a franchise relationship ordinarily shields a franchisor from liability for the torts or contractual breaches of its franchisee, customers, patrons, or other injured parties may nonetheless succeed in holding the franchisor vicariously liable for the wrongful acts of its franchisees under certain circumstances. There are three theories under which a franchisor might potentially be held liable: (1) the franchisor was *negligent;* (2) the franchisee was an *actual agent* of the franchisor; or (3) the franchisee was an *apparent agent* of the franchisor. All three theories are based to some extent upon the franchisor's exertion of "control" over some aspect of the franchisee's activities. For example, if the franchisor exercises control over the terms and conditions of employment of the franchisee's employees, it may find itself liable for the franchisee's violations of labor or employment laws or for acts of the employees that violate antidiscrimination laws.

CASE ILLUSTRATION 5.3

IN RE FRANCIS, 668 N.Y.S.2D 55 (N.Y. APP. DIV. 3D DEP'T 1998)

FACTS West Sanitation Services, Inc., provides restroom sanitizing services to commercial customers. Glenroy Francis was hired in 1986 as a serviceperson for specified routes. In 1987, West began a franchise program. Francis signed a 23-page franchise agreement. As a franchisee, he performed the same functions that he had as an employee. In 1992, West terminated Francis' franchise for cause. Francis then applied for unemployment insurance benefits. Employees are entitled to such benefits, but franchisees are not.

DECISION The New York Unemployment Insurance Appeal Board determined that West "exercised a sufficient degree of direction and control over [Francis] … to establish an employment relationship." Among the factors cited by the Board were West's assignment of a territory and/or customers to Francis; retention of active client control, including billing; establishing weekly schedules for customer service; "paying" Francis; specification of products that could be used; provision of new customer accounts; inspection and evaluation of Francis' performance; requirement that Francis use West's logo; requirement that Francis submit reports; and restrictions on Francis' right to transfer his interest in the customer accounts.

Thus, the Board ruled that West was liable for unemployment insurance contributions for Francis and other similarly-situated individuals. The Appellate Division of the New York Supreme Court upheld the Board upon appeal.

Negligence claims against a franchisor usually arise in the context of premises liability claims. To recover for negligence, the plaintiff must prove: (1) that the franchisor owed a duty of care to the plaintiff; (2) that the duty of care was breached; (3) that the breach caused the plaintiff's injury; and (4) that the plaintiff suffered actual injury.

Thus, if a person is assaulted in a franchise outlet, the franchisor typically is not liable for any resulting injuries because the franchisor does not generally owe a legal duty of care to persons who enter the franchisee's premises. (The franchisee, on the other hand, depending upon the circumstances, might incur liability for failing to provide a secure setting.) The franchisor might assume such a duty of care, however, by exercising control over things such as lighting, security, and general layout of the building. The issue raised in most such cases, then, is whether the franchisor indeed assumed such a duty of care. This is a highly fact-specific inquiry that the court must undertake on a case-by-case basis (see Case Illustration 5.4).

CASE ILLUSTRATION 5.4

WU v. DUNKIN' DONUTS, INC., 105 F. SUPP. 2D 83 (E.D. N.Y. 2000), *AFF'D*, 4 FED. APPX. 82 (2D CIR. 2001)

FACTS Wendy Hong Wu was an employee of a 24-hour donut store owned by Turnway Donuts, Inc., under a franchise agreement with Dunkin' Donuts, Inc. Early one morning, when Wu was working alone at the store, two teenagers entered the store, gained access to the employee area behind the counter, and brutally attacked and raped Wu. Wu filed suit against Dunkin' Donuts, arguing that the attack resulted in part from the vicarious negligence of Dunkin' Donuts. In particular, she argued that Dunkin' Donuts was vicariously liable for the franchisee's negligent provision of security.

DECISION According to the trial court, the issue presented was whether a franchisor's making of recommendations regarding security matters to its franchisees renders the franchisor legally responsible for ensuring the safety of its franchisees' employees.

The court identified the applicable legal rule as follows: "In deciding whether a franchisor may be held vicariously liable for acts of its franchisees, courts determine whether the franchisor controls the day-to-day operations of the franchisee, and more specifically, whether the franchisor exercises a considerable degree of control over the instrumentality at issue in a given case." The cases from this and other jurisdictions indicate that the franchisor must exercise very specific control over the franchisee and its operations before vicarious liability will attach. For example, a franchisor who retains the right to terminate the relationship for failure to meet standards or to reenter premises and inspect generally does not exercise sufficient control

over the franchisee's security practices so as to give rise to a legal duty on the part of the franchisor.

The trial court concluded that "absent a showing of actual control over the security measures employed by the franchisee, franchisors have no legal duty in such cases." Wu pointed to three particular practices that she argued showed that Dunkin' Donuts retained actual control over security measures. She argued that Dunkin' Donuts: (1) required that the franchisee remain open 24 hours a day; (2) controlled the purchase of security equipment and required a functioning alarm system; and (3) required a site plan that revealed to passersby that Wu was alone.

The court quickly dismissed the first argument, stating that while the requirement that the franchisee stay open 24 hours a day may have heightened the need for adequate security, Dunkin' Donuts did not mandate specific security measures or otherwise control or limit the franchisee's response to this increased risk. Thus, Dunkin' Donuts could not be held vicariously liable on these grounds.

Nor did the evidence support Wu's second argument. While Dunkin' Donuts made security equipment available for purchase and suggested that alarms and other burglary prevention techniques were important, Dunkin' Donuts did not mandate or otherwise exercise control over the purchase of security equipment. Indeed, the franchisee here had unilaterally hired a security consultant and had installed its own security system, including a clear partition, alarm system, and video camera.

Finally, the evidence also did not support Wu's claim that Dunkin' Donuts had required a site plan that revealed to persons outside the store that Wu was working alone. While Dunkin' Donuts *did* provide a standard site plan to its franchisees, the franchise agreement did not require franchisees to conform to this standard plan and, in fact, the franchisee in this instance had made significant interior alterations to the store without seeking or receiving Dunkin' Donuts' prior approval.

The court concluded by noting a public policy concern raised by Wu's arguments: "The possibility … that the recommended security measures might have helped protect Wu highlights a public policy concern that the court also believes counsels against imposing liability on Dunkin' Donuts under the circumstances of this case. Dunkin' Donuts expressed a laudable desire to assist its franchisees in protecting their employees and customers, Imposing liability on the basis of such advice could discourage franchisors such as Dunkin' Donuts from taking steps to promote an awareness of security issues among franchisees."

Because "there [was] no evidence that Dunkin' Donuts actually mandated specific security equipment, or otherwise controlled the steps taken by its franchisees in general, and [this franchisee] in particular, to protect employees," the court held that Dunkin' Donuts was not vicariously liable for Wu's injuries. The court granted summary judgment to Dunkin' Donuts.

If the franchisor is too closely involved with the operation of the franchisee, the franchisee may be treated as being the *actual agent* of the franchisor. Under agency law, the principal (the franchisor) may be held liable for the wrongful acts of the agent (the franchisee). If individuals arc lcd to believe that they are dealing with the franchisor directly, rather than with a franchisee operation or with an authorized agent of the franchisor, the franchisor can be held liable under an *apparent agency* theory.

◆ *See Discussion Case 5.4.*

Franchisors should be careful about the degree of control that they exercise over their franchisees' activities lest they find themselves liable in unexpected situations. Franchisors should take care not to involve themselves in issues such as employment-related decisions or the day-to-day operations of their franchisees (see Case Illustration 5.5).

Franchisors generally are permitted to exercise control to the extent necessary to ensure that the franchisees conform to specified quality or operational standards. In many franchise industries, such as fast-food restaurants, this may well be a very extensive amount of control. The franchise agreement should specify, however, that the franchisor's control is based solely on the need to ensure compliance with stated quality standards and that any comments made by the franchisor regarding other issues are merely suggestions and not commands. Many franchise agreements also contain *indemnification clauses*, which provide that if a third party (including an employee) brings a claim against the franchisor, the franchisee will bear all costs related to the suit and any resulting liability. Franchisors may also require franchisees to carry insurance policies covering employment-related or premises liability claims. Finally, all franchise operations should be required to prominently display signs indicating local ownership. This simple measure can help the franchisor avoid an apparent agency relationship, although it may not completely insulate the franchisor from liability.

Franchise Antitrust Issues

Tying Arrangements Much of the antitrust tie-in litigation (discussed earlier in Chapter 4) over the past 20 years has dealt with franchise contracts, particularly fast-food franchises. Most franchise antitrust claims involve allegations of illegal *tying* by the franchisor. A tying arrangement occurs when a seller conditions the sale of a desired (*tying*) item on the purchase of a second (*tied*) item. The U.S. Supreme Court has established that a tie is unlawful *per se* if the seller possesses economic power in the market

CASE ILLUSTRATION 5.5

HAMLIN v. MOTEL 6, 2000 OHIO APP. LEXIS 2439 (JUNE 9, 2000)

FACTS Plaintiffs Abby Fogt and Mary Carter worked at a Motel 6 franchise located in Troy, Ohio. The franchise was owed by BVP, Inc., and the motel was managed by Lisa Serafini. Plaintiffs alleged that they were sexually harassed, assaulted, and abused by Serafini during their employment. Plaintiffs informed Motel 6, the franchisor, of their allegations. Both testified at trial that they were told to "keep it quiet" and that Motel 6 would conduct an on-site investigation. The Director of Franchise Operations for Motel 6 admitted in a deposition that he had received a call from someone complaining of sexual harassment at the Troy Motel 6, that he had told the caller that he would speak to the franchise owner about the matter, that he did refer the complaint to the franchise owner, and that he did not follow up on the complaint.

Plaintiffs filed suit against the franchisor, Motel 6, alleging that: (1) an actual or apparent agency relationship existed between Motel 6 and BVP such that Motel 6 should be held liable for the actions of its franchisee; and (2) that Motel 6 had voluntarily assumed a duty of care to investigate sexual harassment complaints made by employees of its franchisees.

The trial court granted summary judgment to Motel 6. Plaintiffs appealed.

DECISION The appellate court rejected plaintiffs' argument that an actual agency relationship existed between Motel 6 and BVP, stating: "The key factor in determining the existence of an agency relationship is the right of control vested in the principal."

The court noted that the franchise agreement at issue here, at first glance, appeared to give Motel 6 the right to control employment decisions for its franchisees. The franchise agreement provided that Motel 6 had the authority to approve any manager with authority over the "day-to-day" operations of its franchisees and that Motel 6 could terminate the franchise of any franchisee who did not "comply promptly" with the standards contained in its confidential manuals. The manuals specifically stated that Motel 6 "will not tolerate discrimination or the appearance of discrimination of any kind" with regard to either employment practices or room availability. The manuals also stated that employees "may" be dismissed for "offending, disrupting,

or harassing guests or fellow employees" at the franchisee's discretion.

However, the franchise agreement also specifically stated that the franchisee is "solely responsible" for all employment decisions, including firing, hiring, training, wages, and discipline. BVP did not ask Motel 6 for assistance in making employment decisions and Motel 6 did not involve itself with such issues. The appellate court concluded that Motel 6 did not have the right to control employment decisions of the franchisee. The court thus rejected plaintiffs' claim that Motel 6 was liable under an actual agency theory.

Even when actual agency does not exist, "apparent agency may be conferred if the principal holds its agent out to the public as possessing sufficient authority to act on its behalf and the person dealing with the agent knew these facts and, acting in good faith, had reason to believe that the agent possessed the necessary authority." Here, however, plaintiffs had both testified that they knew that Motel 6 did not own the motel, that BVP was their employer, that Motel 6 was not involved with employee discipline, and that Serafini made the hiring and firing decisions at the Troy franchise. Thus, no apparent agency relationship existed here either.

The appellate court concluded, however, that the statements made by the Director of Franchise Operations for Motel 6 raised a genuine issue of material fact with regard to plaintiffs' claim that Motel 6 voluntarily assumed the duty of investigating and rectifying the alleged harassment. The court also found that there was a genuine issue of fact as to whether Motel 6 exercised ordinary care in carrying out this duty (assuming such a duty existed). While a jury might find that Motel 6 did exercise ordinary care by referring the complaint to the franchisee, the jury might instead find that the Motel 6 was obligated to do something more.

The appellate court thus reversed the trial court's grant of summary judgment to Motel 6 and remanded the case for further proceedings on the issue of whether Motel 6, a franchisor, voluntarily assumed a duty to investigate sexual harassment complaints made by employees of its franchisee. The court affirmed the lower court's rulings on the agency arguments.

for the tying item and if the arrangement involves a "not insubstantial" amount of interstate commerce.[13] Tying arrangements that do not meet this standard are evaluated under the rule of reason and may be legal, although courts generally view them with disfavor because of their potential anticompetitive effects.

Tie-in arrangements are common in the franchise setting. A franchisor invariably wants to impose quality control standards on its franchisees, so the standard franchise agreement contains quality control restrictions. Very often the agreement requires the franchisee to purchase supplies and products from the franchisor at set prices or from suppliers who can meet the exact specifications and standards of the franchisor. Usually, the franchisor designates "approved" suppliers from which the franchisees may purchase.

In most franchise tie-in litigation, the plaintiff is a franchisee (or class of franchisees) and the defendant is the franchisor. The complaint is usually that the franchisee was able to obtain a franchise only on the condition that it purchase some additional item or items from the franchisor or a franchisor-approved vendor as well. Thus, the tying item is the franchise itself and the tied item is essential food ingredients or the primary product sold by the franchisor or its approved vendor.

Originally, franchisees won many of these cases. In recent years, however, franchisors have tended to prevail. *Queen City Pizza, Inc. v. Domino's Pizza, Inc.*,[14] decided by the U.S. Court of Appeals for the Third Circuit in 1997, is an example of this trend. Under the rationale of the *Domino's Pizza* court, if a product that is substitutable for the tied product is available in the marketplace, it will be difficult for a franchisee to plead a relevant antitrust market in the tied product, even if the franchise agreement prohibits the franchisee from purchasing that product.

Other courts have rejected the *Domino's Pizza* approach, stating that the validity of a tying claim by a franchisee must be determined by the amount of information possessed by the franchisee at the time it signed the franchise agreement and by the cost barriers to franchisees' switching franchises, not by whether the tied product has substitutes in the marketplace.[15]

◆ *See Discussion Case 5.5.*

Vertical Price Restraints   Many franchisors would like to be able to control the price at which their franchisees sell their products or services. Vertical price restraints have long been suspect under the antitrust law. Originally, these restraints were deemed illegal *per se*, but over the past decade the U.S. Supreme Court has rejected that standard and has adopted the rule of reason standard instead.

First, in 1997, the U.S. Supreme Court decided *State Oil Co. v. Khan*,[16] in which the Court determined vertical *maximum* price-fixing was no longer illegal *per se* but, rather, must be judged by a rule of reason. The Court ruled that a supplier's imposition of maximum resale prices upon its distributors may have procompetitive effects and actually result in lower prices for consumers. In such an instance, the price-fixing ought not to be barred. The court must make a fact-specific inquiry into the specific challenged conduct, the industry and market involved, the purported justification for the conduct, and intended and actual effects of the conduct on interbrand competition. If the conduct is found to have anticompetitive effects, it is illegal.

---

[13]*Northern Pacific Railroad Co. v. United States,* 356 U.S. 1, 6 (1958).

[14]124 F.3d 430 (3d Cir. 1997).

[15]See *Collins v. International Dairy Queen,* 980 F. Supp. 1252 (M.D. Ga. 1997); *Wilson v. Mobil Oil Corp.,* 940 F. Supp. 944 (E.D. La. 1996).

[16]522 U.S. 3 (1997). This case is reproduced in Discussion Case 4.3.

Second, in 2007, the Supreme Court held in *Leegin Creative Leather Products, Inc. v. PSKS, Inc.*[17] that vertical *minimum* price restraints must also be evaluated under a rule of reason and that such a restraint is illegal only if its anticompetitive affects outweigh its precompetitive effects.

Franchisors should be aware, however, that even if a vertical price-fixing scheme is allowed under the federal antitrust laws, it might still be illegal under state laws relating to consumer protection, unfair trade practices, or franchises. Thus, a franchisor considering vertical price restraints, either maximum or minimum, should always seek legal counsel before implementing such a price scheme. Antitrust law is discussed in greater detail in Chapter 4. Consumer protection and unfair trade practice laws are discussed in Chapter 8.

Co-Branding

Co-branding involves the operation of two or more types of franchises or nonfranchised businesses under a single roof. Many fast-food franchises have entered into co-branding relationships, such as Taco Bell and KFC, and Burger King and TCBY. Co-branding allows franchisors to expand into nontraditional locations, opens up access to desirable sites, allows for cost savings and operating efficiencies, and promotes competitive positioning of the brands. Co-branding works best when it provides synergy between the offerings, such as offering a dessert (frozen yogurt) at a burger chain.

Co-branding results in a complex legal relationship. Suppose, for example, a donut chain and a Mexican fast-food chain decide to co-brand on the theory that the relationship will increase each party's sales in its weaker daily sales time slots. Typically, one party will be the "host franchisor," who already has in place an existing franchise system, has control over the physical sites on which the co-branded business will operate, and who will exercise some control over how the franchisees operate the "guest" brand. The host and guest franchisors will have to decide upon a structure, which can be as complex as a *subfranchise* (in which the guest franchisor grants a "master franchise" to the host franchisor, who then subfranchises the co-brand to its franchisees) or a *cofranchise* (in which the guest franchisor offers the co-brand directly to the host's franchisees with the consent of the host franchisor), or as simple as a *lease* or a *license*. Whatever the structure agreed upon, the parties will probably need to alter their standard franchise agreements to cover topics such as protection of trade secrets and proprietary information, noncompete covenants, royalty arrangements, and termination provisions.[18] Co-branding can also raise issues of "encroachment," discussed below.

Encroachment

Encroachment has been defined as expansion by the franchisor beyond the point that the franchisor would have expanded had it owned all its own outlets.[19] It occurs when a franchisor sells a franchisee an outlet in a particular location, then sells another outlet in close vicinity to a different franchisee. The original franchisee is harmed because the new outlet draws customers and revenue from the original outlet. The franchisor, on the other hand, benefits because royalties from two stores, even though they may cannibalize each other, are greater than royalties from a single store.

Particularly as a result of the growth in co-branding, encroachment issues have been very prominent and prevalent in recent years. Generally, the contractual language of the franchise agreement determines whether impermissible encroachment has occurred.

---

[17]551 U.S. 877 (2007).

[18]See generally Kenneth R. Costello, "Baskin Donuts: Hidden Pitfalls in Co-Branding," *Franchising Business & Law Alert* 3, no. 11 (July 1997), 11.

[19]Warren S. Grimes, "When Do Franchisors Have Market Power? Antitrust Remedies for Franchisor Opportunism," 65 *Antitrust L.J.* 105, 138 (1996).

AAA ABACHMAN ENTERPRISES, INC. v. STANLEY STEEMER INTERNATIONAL, INC., 268 FED. APPX. 864 (11TH CIR. 2008)

FACTS AAA Abachman Enterprises, Inc. (Abachman), is a Stanley Steemer International, Inc., franchisee, with a perpetual and exclusive license to "own and operate a Stanley Steemer carpet and upholstery cleaning business" in the upper half of Palm Beach County, Florida. The franchise agreement gave Abachman the sole right to use Stanley Steemer's "trademarks, service marks, patents, [and] trade secrets … solely in a Stanley Steemer Business in that area and in no other manner."

In February 2006, the franchisor, Stanley Steemer, granted two businesses owned by Thomas Scalera an "exclusive license to own and operate a Stanley Steemer Duct Cleaning Business" for a five year term, and "to use the Stanley Steemer Duct Cleaning Marks, proprietary equipment and products … in a Stanley Steemer Duct Cleaning Business" in a territory that included the upper half of Palm Beach County and so overlapped with Abachman's territory.

Abachman sued Stanley Steemer, alleging that Stanley Steemer had breached its franchise agreement by contracting with Scalera's companies.

DECISION The district court granted summary judgment to Stanley Steemer International, Inc., and the court of appeals affirmed. The appellate court stated: "'Where the terms in a contract are not ambiguous, courts are constrained to apply the plain language of the contract.' The terms of Abachman's franchise agreement with Stanley Steemer are not ambiguous; they give Abachman the exclusive right to use the mark in its carpet and upholstery business 'and in no other manner.'" Thus, the court concluded, "Stanley Steemer retain[ed] the right to license its trademark to Scalera's businesses to use in connection with duct cleaning."

If, under the terms of the agreement, the franchisee received an exclusive territory, the franchisor is clearly prohibited from locating other units within that territory. (The franchisor may try to avoid such restrictions by offering a similar, but not identical, product, such as a different brand of hotel franchise, within the territory.) Similarly, if the franchise agreement explicitly states that the franchisor has an unrestricted right to locate additional units or that the franchisee does not have an exclusive territory, that language will control as well (see Case Illustration 5.6).

Many encroachment cases involve a middle ground, however, in which the franchise agreement grants a small, protected territory to the franchisee. The franchisor then locates a new unit outside that protected territory but close enough to have a negative impact on the revenues or profitability of the original franchisee. These cases generally implicate the *implied covenant of good faith*. Under the Restatement (Second) of Contracts, "[e]very contract imposes upon each party a duty of good faith and fair dealing …."[20] This implied covenant is overridden by express language, such as a contractual provision stating that the franchisor has complete discretion to establish new franchises at any location outside the protected territory even if the new units harm the existing franchisee. Where such explicit contractual provisions are missing, however, the courts have to determine whether the franchisor's actions violated its duty of good faith and fair dealing. In general, the franchisors have tended to win these disputes.

As a practical matter, franchisors should state their encroachment policies explicitly within their franchise agreements so as to avoid litigation with disappointed franchisees.

---

[20]Restatement (Second) of Contracts § 205.

Other mechanisms, such as granting franchisees the right of first refusal on new units, can be used to address these problems as well.

The amended Franchise Disclosure Rule also addresses encroachment by requiring the franchisor to disclose whether it or an affiliate has used or has the right to use other distribution channels, including the Internet, catalog sales, telemarketing, or other direct sales, to make sales within the franchisee's territory.

Termination Issues

Generally, franchise agreements provide that the franchisor can terminate the franchise if certain events occur. Most provide for termination "for cause," which includes situations such as the franchisee failing to meet quality control standards or failing to pay required fees. Some state laws restrict the franchisor's ability to terminate or refuse to renew a franchise without cause. A minority of states require that the franchisor provide notice—often 90 or 180 days in advance—before terminating or refusing to renew a franchise.

The courts are concerned that terminations will leave a franchisee with little or nothing to show for what might have been a very large investment of time and money. Thus, the courts often try to protect the franchisee in termination cases. They do not, however, prevent a franchisor from terminating franchisees that fail to meet the obligations of their franchise agreements. In addition, even in states that require "good cause" for termination, the courts recognize that the franchisor's own economic circumstances are relevant to the determination of whether termination was justified. Thus, the courts generally do not second-guess the franchisor's decision to terminate when it is supported by evidence of losses, flat or declining profits or sales, or cancellation of an entire product line.

Multi-Level Marketing

Multi-level marketing, also known as *network* or *matrix marketing*, involves sales of goods or services through distributors, where distributors are typically promised commissions both on their own sales and on sales their recruits have made. It often involves sales of consumer products by independent distributors, often in consumers' homes. Amway, Mary Kay, and Tupperware are well-known multi-level marketing businesses.

Pyramid or *Ponzi schemes*, which are a form of multi-level marketing that involves paying commissions to distributors for recruiting new distributors, are illegal in most states and can violate the federal Postal Lottery Statute.[21] Pyramid schemes inevitably collapse once no new distributors can be recruited, causing most people involved (except those at the very top) to lose their money.

To avoid prohibitions against pyramid schemes, multi-level marketing plans should pay commissions only on sales and not for recruitment of new participants. If the multi-level marketing plan involves the sale of business opportunities or franchising, it must comply with the requirements of applicable disclosure and/or registration laws.

Franchising and the Internet

Franchisors have been quick to take advantage of the opportunities that the Internet provides. In many respects, however, franchising law has not kept up with the technological advances of the Internet. The rules governing the use of the Internet in this setting are uncertain. In addition, many established franchisors had not anticipated the opportunities that the Internet would create and so had not planned properly in their franchise agreements to address the host of issues that this new communication medium raises.

---

[21]18 U.S.C. § 1302.

Franchisors face several issues with regard to Internet activities, including: (1) what disclosure obligations apply to a franchisor's advertising of franchises on the Internet? (2) what control does a franchisor have over its franchisee's Internet activities? and (3) when do Internet activities rise to the level of "encroachment"?

"Offering" Franchises on the Internet

Many franchisors maintain Internet sites that contain general information about their franchise system that could be construed as an "offer" of a franchise, thus triggering state disclosure and registration requirements. In addition, the franchise laws in several states require that all franchise advertisements proposed for use within the state be submitted to (and often approved by) state officials prior to use. Definitions of advertisements are broad enough to include website content. California, for example, defines an "advertisement" as "any written or printed communication or any communication by means of recorded telephone messages or spoken on radio, television, or similar communications media, published in connection with an offer or sale of a franchise."[22]

Thus, franchisors with websites must be concerned with two issues: (1) must they register in all of the states requiring franchise registration? and (2) must they submit the content of their websites to those states that require franchise advertisements to be approved by state authorities before use?

Currently, the marketing of franchises online is not directly regulated in most states; thus, it not yet clear how most state franchise laws apply to activities on the Internet. Websites reach individuals in every state, and the owner of the site cannot control its dissemination. It initially would appear, therefore, that if a franchisor's website contains information that would cause the site to be a "franchise offer," the site must be registered in all states requiring registration.

States have taken action to lessen this burden on franchisors. In Indiana, for example, the Indiana Securities Administrator issued an order stating that an Internet offer of a franchise will be exempt from Indiana registration requirements if: (1) the offer indicates that franchises will not be sold to persons in Indiana; (2) an offer is not otherwise addressed to any person in Indiana; and (3) no sales of franchises are made in Indiana as a result of the Internet offer.[23] Thus, to avoid registration in Indiana, the franchisor must post a statement on its website stating that franchises are not available within the state and are not sold within the state. Similar rules apply in the other states that regulate franchise advertising.

As already noted, some states require submission or approval of advertisements for franchises. It is not yet clear whether franchisors must submit their website content for approval in states requiring submissions or approvals of advertisements, but it would appear that they should not. Most states exempt advertisements appearing in publications with at least two-thirds of their circulation outside the state from these regulations. Although the states have not yet provided their formal positions on this issue, websites would seem to fall squarely within this exemption.

Franchisor Control Over Franchise Internet Activities

Cybersquatting—the use of an Internet domain name by a company or individual who does not hold the trademark or trade name in that name—is a common problem. Domain names such as "mcdonalds.com," "mtv.com," "panavision.com," and "coke.com" were all originally held by persons other than the registered trademark owners. Cybersquatting issues are discussed in more detail in Chapter 6.

---

[22]Cal. Corp. Code § 31003 (2007).

[23]Admin. Order 97-0378AO (Dec. 24, 1997).

The franchise relationship adds another dimension to the cybersquatting problem: a franchisee may register and use a domain name belonging to its franchisor. For example, California Closets Co., a franchisor of closet organization system stores, obtained a temporary restraining order preventing its franchisee from using the domain name "californiacloset.com."[24]

Many existing franchise agreements were drafted before the explosion in Internet activity and do not explicitly address Internet issues. Existing language in these documents addressing the franchisor's intellectual property rights in its marks and trade names may prove insufficient to protect the franchisor's interests. New franchise agreements should explicitly address these issues, of course, including topics such as the franchisee's right to establish an Internet site and restrictions upon its content (generally, prior approval of the franchisor of all content is required), permissible domain names, and required "links" between the franchisee's site and the franchisor's site.

Internet "Encroachment" Issues

In addition, the Internet poses a special type of encroachment issue for franchisees. While a franchisee might have been granted an exclusive territorial area under its franchise contract, an Internet "virtual store" operated by the franchisor can easily interfere with the franchisee's sales, placing the franchisor in direct competition with its franchisees. While properly drawn new franchise agreements should explicitly address this issue, older agreements that predate the growth of the Internet do not. Franchisees and franchisors thus have found themselves in litigation as they struggle to determine how existing contract language should be applied to a situation neither party could have anticipated at the time of contracting.

International Issues in Franchising

U.S. franchisors often wish to expand their operations abroad. Federal and state franchising laws generally do not govern such transactions; rather, the franchisor must adhere to the laws of the country or countries in which it wishes to offer franchises. At least 20 countries currently regulate franchising, and more countries are expected to adopt such laws.

Three basic forms of franchising are found at the international level. The most common form is the use of a *master franchise agreement*. Under this arrangement, the franchisor enters into a master franchise agreement with a subfranchisor (usually a foreign national), which authorizes the subfranchisor to (1) develop and operate franchises and (2) grant subfranchises to others. *Direct franchising*, in which the franchisor contracts directly with franchisees in the host country, works best when the laws and customs of the host country are similar to those of the United States. Finally, the franchisor may enter into a *joint venture* with an overseas partner. There are, of course, many variations on these basic categories. The choice of method used depends upon cultural differences between the home and host countries; legal constraints imposed by the host country; and business factors, such as financial and personnel constraints, difficulty of managing relationships over long distances, and differences in commercial practices between the two countries involved.

Offering franchises in foreign countries raises a number of legal issues that are different from those found in domestic franchising relationships. Intellectual property issues become particularly critical in foreign franchising activities. The franchisor faces two separate tasks with regard to intellectual property issues in foreign franchising activities. First, it must determine whether existing marks, trade names, and logos will function in

---

[24]*California Closet Co. v. Space Organization Systems, Inc.,* CCH Bus. Franchise Guide ¶ 11,150 (E.D. Wis. 1997).

the new country, both in terms of being culturally and linguistically acceptable and in terms of whether the mark is sufficiently distinct from other marks already in use. Second, the franchisor must be concerned with protection of intellectual property assets. Will the host country's laws adequately protect marks, trade secrets, and copyrights? Should the franchisor apply for additional patents? (Intellectual property law issues are discussed in more detail in Chapter 2, Chapter 3, and Chapter 6.)

In addition, the franchisor must be concerned with the franchise laws, specifically, and business laws, generally, of the host country. Most countries do not regulate franchises, but the franchisor must determine whether disclosure and/or registration laws apply; what securities or antitrust restrictions might be imposed; whether foreign investments and technology transfers are regulated; what contract, commercial, taxation, and labor laws apply; whether import or export controls are in place; what packaging, labeling, or food and drug regulations apply; and what impact the immigration laws might have on staffing and personnel decisions.

DISCUSSION CASES

5.1 Constitutionality of Local Ordinances Restricting Franchise Location
Island Silver & Spice, Inc. v. Islamorada, 542 F.3d 844 (11th Cir. 2008)

Defendant-Appellant Islamorada, Village of Islands ("Islamorada") appeals from a judgment of the United States District Court for the Southern District of Florida granting injunctive and monetary relief in favor of Plaintiffs-Appellees Island Silver & Spice, Inc., Glenn S. Saiger, and Virginia Saiger (collectively "Island Silver") and invalidating an Islamorada zoning ordinance's "formula retail" restrictions as violations of the Dormant Commerce Clause. We affirm the judgment of the district court.

Background

In January 2002, Islamorada enacted Ordinance 02-02, which prohibited "formula restaurant[s]" and restricted "formula retail" establishments to limited street level frontage and total square footage. The ordinance defines formula retail as:

[a] type of retail sales activity of retail sales establishment ... that is required by contractual or other arrangement to maintain any of the following: standardized array of services or merchandise, trademark, logo, service mark, symbol, decor, architecture, layout, uniform, or similar standardized feature.

Island Silver owns and operates an independent retail store in Islamorada. In June 2002, Island Silver

entered into a contract to sell its property to a developer seeking to establish a Walgreens drug store in the same footprint of Island Silver's existing mixed-retail store. After unsuccessfully protesting the ordinance's restrictions on formula retail stores through the local administrative process, the developer withdrew from the purchase. Island Silver brought a complaint against Islamorada in district court, seeking damages, injunctive relief, and a writ of mandamus on the grounds that the ordinance's formula retail provisions violated its rights [under various provisions of the U.S. and Florida Constitutions].

On February 28, 2007, the district court granted injunctive and monetary relief in favor of Island Silver and invalidated the ordinance's formula retail provisions. The district court found that the provisions violated the Dormant Commerce Clause because they had a discriminatory impact on interstate commerce unsupported by a legitimate state purpose and the putative local benefits were outweighed by the burden imposed on interstate commerce. Islamorada appeals.

* * *

Discussion

The Dormant Commerce Clause prohibits "regulatory measures designed to benefit in-state economic interests by burdening out-of-state competitors." To determine whether a regulation violates the Dormant Commerce Clause, we apply one of two levels of analysis. If a regulation "directly regulates or discriminates against interstate commerce," or has the effect of favoring "in-state economic interests," the regulation must be shown to "advance[ ] a legitimate local purpose that cannot be adequately served by reasonable nondiscriminatory alternatives." If a regulation has "only indirect effects on interstate commerce," we "examine[ ] whether the State's interest is legitimate and whether the burden on interstate commerce clearly exceeds the local benefits."

The district court correctly determined that the formula retail provision does not facially discriminate against interstate commerce. With respect to the provision's effects, however, the parties stipulated that the ordinance "effectively prevents the establishment of new formula retail stores," and "[a] facility limited to no more than 2,000 square feet or 50' of frontage [as required by the ordinance] can not accommodate the minimum requirements of nationally and regionally branded formula retail stores." Although the fact that the burden of a regulation falls onto a subset of out-of-state retailers "does not, by itself, establish a claim of discrimination against interstate commerce," the ordinance's effective elimination of all new interstate chain retailers has the "practical effect of ... discriminating against" interstate commerce. The formula retail provision is therefore subject to elevated scrutiny.

Under the elevated scrutiny test, a regulation must be supported by "a legitimate local purpose that cannot be adequately served by reasonable nondiscriminatory alternatives." The burden is on Islamorada to justify the ordinance's discriminatory effects.

The ordinance's stated local purposes include the preservation of "unique and natural" "small town" community characteristics, encouragement of "small scale uses, water-oriented uses, [and] a nationally significant natural environment," and avoidance of increased "traffic congestion ... [and] litter, garbage and rubbish offsite." The parties stipulated, however, that "Islamorada has a number of [pre-existing] 'formula retail' businesses," Islamorada "has no Historic District, and there are no historic buildings in the vicinity of [Island Silver's] property," and "[t]he Ordinance is not necessary for preservation of the historic characteristics of any buildings in the Village." In addition, because the ordinance "does not address small formula retail stores, which are permitted under the ordinance,

but would presumably affect the Village's small town character as well," or large non-chain businesses, the district court found that "[r]estricting formula retail stores, while allowing other large [and] non-unique structures, does not preserve a small town character." The district court properly determined that, although "[i]n general, preserving a small town community is a legitimate purpose ..., in this instance, [Islamorada] has not demonstrated that it has any small town character to preserve."

With respect to the stated purpose of encouraging small-scale and natural uses, the parties also stipulated that Islamorada's existing "zoning allows the use of the property as a retail pharmacy ... and other retail uses," and that Island Silver operated as "a street level business comprising over twelve thousand square feet of floor area," which "greatly exceeds the [ordinance's] dimensional limitations" for formula retail businesses. The district court correctly found that Islamorada "[did] not explain why the ordinance singles out retail stores and restaurants with standardized features," and that the record did not indicate that Islamorada is "uniquely relaxed or natural," or that there is "a predominance of natural conditions and characteristics over human intrusions."

Similarly, the stated purposes of reducing traffic and garbage are undermined by the parties' stipulations that Islamorada has existing "land development regulations, other than the Ordinance, that govern and control traffic generation of retail uses," and "that limit the dimensions, location, and use of buildings and signs." The district court therefore properly concluded that Islamorada failed to provide a legitimate local purpose to justify the ordinance's discriminatory effects, and that even if such purpose had been shown, "the ordinance does not serve this interest."

Islamorada's failure to indicate a legitimate local purpose to justify the ordinance's discriminatory effects is sufficient to support the district court's determination that the formula retail provision is invalid under the Dormant Commerce Clause. It should be noted, however, that Islamorada does not assert that the stated purposes of the ordinance cannot be furthered by reasonable nondiscriminatory alternatives, such as Islamorada's existing land development regulations. Even under the balancing approach advocated by Islamorada, the stipulated facts indicate that the formula retail provision's disproportionate burden on interstate commerce, such as the effective exclusion of interstate formula retailers, clearly outweighs any legitimate local benefits.

Accordingly, the district court did not err in concluding that the ordinance's formula retail provision violated the Dormant Commerce Clause.

Conclusion

We therefore AFFIRM the judgment of the district court.

QUESTIONS FOR DISCUSSION FOR CASE 5.1

1. Why did the Village of Islamorado pass this ordinance restricting the location of certain businesses within the village limits? What governmental purpose was this ordinance intended to promote?

Is that a legitimate purpose for a local government to pursue?

2. The Commerce Clause of the U.S. Constitution gives Congress the right to regulate commerce among the states. This case deals with the "Dormant Commerce Clause." How does the court define the "Dormant Commerce Clause"?

3. The court describes a two-part test for evaluating whether ordinances violate the Dormant Commerce Clause. What is that test? Which part of the test did the Village's ordinance violate? What would the Village need to show in order for its ordinance to be valid?

5.2 Existence of Franchise Relationship
To-Am Equipment Co., Inc. v. Mitsubishi Caterpillar Forklift America, Inc., 152 F.3d 658 (7th Cir. 1998)

Legal terms often have specialized meanings that can surprise even a sophisticated party. The term "franchise," or its derivative "franchisee," is one of those words. The question in this case is whether the district court correctly ruled that certain payments that To-Am Equipment Company made to Mitsubishi Caterpillar Forklift America (MCFA), in connection with To-Am's distributorship for certain Mitsubishi products, could constitute franchise fees within the meaning of the Illinois Franchise Disclosure Act of 1987. That ruling in turn set the stage for a jury verdict in To-Am's favor awarding it $1.525 million in damages for MCFA's termination of its distribution agreement. MCFA challenges the lower court's legal ruling on appeal. * * * We affirm.

I.

The Mitsubishi keiretsu (the traditional Japanese form of conglomerate) is a well known manufacturer of heavy equipment, including forklift trucks. In June 1985, To-Am entered into a dealership agreement for these forklifts with [MCFA]. * * * To-Am had been doing business in south Chicago since 1973, servicing, renting, and repairing fork-lifts. Over the years it also sold a number of different brands of forklifts ..., though prior to its contract with MCFA it sold only used forklifts. Before allowing To-Am to become a Mitsubishi dealer MCFA required To-Am to relocate to a larger showroom. To-Am complied and moved to Frankfort, Illinois. During the years it served as a

Mitsubishi dealer To-Am continued to handle used forklifts manufactured by Mitsubishi's competitors—in other words, the dealership did not require exclusivity on To-Am's part. On the other hand, the agreement conferred on To-Am an exclusive Area of Primary Responsibility (APR), consisting of four Illinois counties and one county in Indiana, in which MCFA did not have and agreed not to create a competing dealership.

Under the 1985 contract ..., To-Am was required to participate in Mitsubishi's warranty program. This meant, among other things, that To-Am had to maintain trained personnel and provide prompt warranty and non-warranty service on all Mitsubishi products within its APR. To comply with these requirements, To-Am participated in all of MCFA's training programs, apparently for the most part at its own expense. Article III para. 14 of the agreement expressly required To-Am to "maintain an adequate supply of current [MCFA] sales and service publications." To-Am did so by keeping a master set of manuals in its parts department, a second set in its service department, and additional manuals in its mobile service vehicles.... MCFA provided one set of these manuals in 1985 when To-Am became a distributor, but thereafter To-Am had to order additional manuals for the other locations where it kept manuals, for updating, and when manuals wore out. MCFA invoiced To-Am for these additional manuals, and over the years To-Am paid over $1,600 for them. * * *

In February 1994, MCFA notified To-Am that it was terminating the dealership agreement effective

April 2, 1994, in accordance with Article XI para. 1 of the agreement, which permitted either party to terminate upon 60 days' written notice "or as required by law." This step was a blow to To-Am's business …. The reason was simple: Mitsubishi fork-lifts were the only new vehicles that To-Am had been selling. Even though new truck sales are themselves relatively low profit generators for dealers, they can create substantial downstream business, ranging from trade-ins that could be resold as used equipment or carried as rental equipment, to service and parts sales. Testimony at trial indicated that, while dealer profit margins on new equipment sales might be as low as 3%, the margins on these downstream business opportunities ranged from 30% to 50%. Thus, the loss of To-Am's line of new trucks had ripple effects on its business going far beyond the immediate lost sales.

To-Am therefore brought this suit against MCFA …. To-Am alleged violations of the Illinois Franchise Disclosure Act for the wrongful termination of its franchise without good cause ….

* * * Prior to trial MCFA conceded that To-Am met the requirement under the Franchise Disclosure Act that the franchisee's business be substantially associated with the franchisor's trademark. MCFA also conceded that the termination was without good cause, as the Act uses the term. * * *

II

* * *

A. Franchise Fees

The Franchise Disclosure Act defines a franchise fee as follows:

[A]ny fee or charge that a franchisee is required to pay directly or indirectly for the right to enter into a business or sell, resell, or distribute goods, services or franchises under an agreement, including, but not limited to, any such payments for goods or services, provided that the Administrator may by rule define what constitutes an indirect franchise fee, and provided further that the following shall not be considered the payment of a franchise fee [setting forth six exceptions, none of which MCFA argues apply here].

As this section specifically contemplates, the Illinois Attorney General, as the Administrator of the statute, has issued a number of pertinent implementing regulations. First, he has elaborated on the definition of the term "franchise fee":

A franchise fee within the meaning of Section 3(14) of the Act may be present regardless of the designation given to or the form of the fee, whether payable in lump sum or installments, definite or indefinite in amount, or partly or wholly contingent on future sales, profits or purchases of the franchise business.

14 Ill. Admin. Code § 200.104. In addition, § 200.105 explains:

(a) Any payment(s) in excess of $500 that is required to be paid by a franchisee to the franchisor or an affiliate of the franchisor constitutes a franchise fee unless specifically excluded by Section 3(14) of the Act.

…

(c) A payment made to a franchisor or affiliate for equipment, materials, real estate services, or other items shall not constitute a franchise fee if the purchase of the items is not required by the franchisor or the franchisee is permitted to purchase the items from sources other than the franchisor or its affiliates and the item is available from such other sources.

These definitions are obviously sweeping in their scope. The sum of $500, all that has to be paid over the entire life of a franchise, is less than small change for most businesses of any size. Furthermore, the regulations explicitly allow this small amount to be paid either in a lump sum or in installments, to be "definite or indefinite" in amount, and to be "partly or wholly contingent" on different, possibly quite unpredictable, variables. In short, the Illinois legislature and the designated Administrator, the Attorney General, could not have been more clear. They wanted to protect a wide class of dealers, distributors, and other "franchisees" from specified acts, such as terminations of their distributorships (franchises) for anything less than "good cause." * * *

MCFA begins with the factual assertion that To-Am was not required to pay it anything under the terms of the agreement, and certainly no form of franchise fee. It is true that the agreement has no article entitled "Periodic Franchise Payments," but the Illinois statute and administrative regulations we have just quoted make it clear that no such precision is required. Article III para. 14 says that the dealer was required to "maintain an adequate supply of current [MCFA] sales and service publications." The jury was entitled to view this as an indirect fee or charge for the right to enter into the business of distributing MCFA lift trucks, which was payable over time, and which exceeded the statutory floor of $500 by a factor of more than three. Given MCFA's control of the supply of these manuals, it easily could have built a franchise fee into their price. * * *

* * *

Like many manufacturers, MCFA simply did not appreciate how vigorously Illinois law protects "franchisees." This does not mean that terminations are impossible, but it does mean that they usually must be the subject of negotiation unless the manufacturer is able to show "good cause." MCFA has conceded that it cannot meet that standard .... While we understand MCFA's concern that dealerships in Illinois are too easily categorized as statutory franchisees, that is a concern appropriately raised to either the Illinois legislature or Illinois Attorney General, not to this court. We therefore AFFIRM the judgment of the district court.

QUESTIONS FOR DISCUSSION FOR CASE 5.2

1. How does the Illinois Franchise Disclosure Act define a "franchise"? What elements of that definition were at issue here?
2. Do you think that either To-Am or MCFA thought it was creating a franchise relationship when the parties first entered into this relationship?
3. Do you think that the outcome of this case is fair? What public policy considerations might support this outcome?
4. Where should franchisors such as MCFA go to seek redress from this statute and its broad definition of franchises?

5.3 Existence of Franchise Relationship
Mary Kay, Inc. v. Isbell, 999 S.W.2d 669 (Ark. 1999)

This case requires our interpretation of the Arkansas Franchise Practices Act and whether the Act applies to the business relationship established between appellee Janet Isbell and appellant Mary Kay, Inc. This court's jurisdiction is also invoked because the case presents issues of first impression and of substantial public interest and issues involving the need for clarification and development of the law.

Isbell's relationship with Mary Kay commenced in 1980 when she signed an agreement to be a beauty consultant for Mary Kay. As a consultant, Isbell was denominated an independent contractor, and, as such, she agreed to promote and sell Mary Kay products to customers at home demonstration parties; she was prohibited by the agreement from selling or displaying those products in retail sales or service establishments. Instead, a Mary Kay consultant's locations for selling products are her home or those of her potential customers. After serving a short period as a beauty consultant and recruiting a sufficient number of her customers to be Mary Kay consultants, Isbell became entitled to be a unit sales director. Isbell signed her first sales director agreement on September 1, 1981, and a second one on July 1, 1991. As a director, Isbell continued to recruit beauty consultants and to help and motivate members of her unit in the sale of Mary Kay cosmetics. She also continued to serve as a beauty consultant. Isbell earned compensation in the form of a commission on sales she made directly to customers as a consultant; as sales director, she additionally received override commissions based on sales made by the consultants she recruited.

In 1994, Isbell leased storefront space in a Little Rock mall and used the space as a training center. It was about this time when Mary Kay began receiving complaints about Isbell's operation. By letter dated April 11, 1994, Mary Kay's legal coordinator, Sherry Gragg, referred Isbell to the parties' Sales Director Agreement and the company's Director's Guide which was made a part of that agreement. Gragg related that Isbell's office or training center was to be used only as a teaching center and to hold unit meetings. Gragg further instructed that Isbell's office or center should not give the appearance of a cosmetic studio, facial salon, or retail establishment, or be used to display or store Mary Kay products. Gragg reiterated that, under the parties' agreement, a sales director's office could not appear to be a Mary Kay store or be used to make direct sales to customers. Finally, Gragg admonished Isbell to discontinue all photo sessions of potential customers at such location and to remove any window sign advertising "glamour tips" or face makeover programs taking place at the center. Mary Kay also received complaints of Isbell's (1) overly aggressive recruiting, (2) listing of fictitious recruits as consultants, and (3) check kiting practices.

Eventually, in September of 1995, Mary Kay's vice president of sales development, Gary Jinks, notified Isbell by letter that, under the terms of their agreement, the company was terminating its beauty consultant and sales director agreements, and the termination was effective thirty days from the date of the letter. Isbell filed suit against Mary Kay …, alleging that she was a franchisee under Arkansas's Franchise Practices Act and that Mary Kay failed to comply with the provisions of the Act when terminating Isbell. Isbell asserted, among other things, that Mary Kay's letter of termination failed to comply with § 4-72-204 of the Act because the letter did not give her ninety days' notice or set forth the reasons for her termination. * * *

[The trial court ruled as a matter of law that Mary Kay's termination of Isbell had violated the Act and the jury returned a verdict in Isbell's favor in the amount of $110,583.33. Both sides appealed.]

* * *

The threshold issue to be decided is whether the Arkansas Franchise Practices Act applies, because if it does, Isbell would be entitled to the designation of franchisee and permitted to invoke the protections and benefits of that Act. The other five issues raised by the respective parties come into play only if the Act is ruled applicable to this case. * * *

To determine whether the Arkansas Franchise Practices Act applies to this case depends upon our interpretation and construction of the pertinent provisions of the Act. In this view, we turn first to Ark. Code Ann. § 4-72-202 (1), which in relevant part defines "franchise" to mean the following:

[A] written or oral agreement for a definite or indefinite period, in which a person grants to another a license to use a trade name, trademark, service mark, or related characteristic within an exclusive or nonexclusive territory, or to sell or distribute goods or services within an exclusive or nonexclusive territory, at wholesale, retail, by lease agreement, or otherwise.

Clearly, Mary Kay entered into a written agreement with Isbell so that Isbell, as an independent contractor, could use Mary Kay's trademark and name to sell its products as provided by their agreement. * * *

While the Act's definition of franchise is helpful, that definition alone is not dispositive of the issue as to whether Isbell, under the parties' agreement, is or is not a franchisee. * * * Section 4-72-203 clearly provides the Act applies only to a franchise that contemplates or

requires the franchise to establish or maintain a place of business in the state. Next, § 4-72-202 (6) defines "place of business" under the Act as meaning "a fixed geographical location at which the franchisee [1] displays for sale and sells the franchisor's goods or [2] offers for sale and sells the franchisor's services." * * * In sum, citing these two statutes, Mary Kay submits that no fixed geographical location for selling products or services was ever contemplated, much less required, by the parties' agreement, and this reason is sufficient alone to preclude Isbell's reliance on the Act. We agree.

We first should note that Isbell concedes that, as a sales director, her agreements with Mary Kay provided that she could not display for sale or sell Mary Kay products from an office, whether that office was located in her home or her training center. * * *

While conceding that the parties' agreements never contemplated that Isbell would or could sell the franchisor's *goods* from a fixed location, she argues no such prohibition prevented her from selling Mary Kay *services* from her home or training center. Specifically, Isbell suggests the facial makeovers and "Glamour Shots" photo sessions that were a part of Mary Kay's demonstration and training program constituted services that the parties contemplated could be sold by Isbell from her center. * * *

* * * [Mary Kay's] Director's Guide, which was made a part of the parties' agreements, very clearly provided that a sales director's office, albeit it her home or training center, could only be used to interview potential recruits and hold unit meetings and other training events. The Guide further provided that the office or center should not give the appearance of a cosmetic studio, facial salon or retail establishment, or give the appearance of being a "Mary Kay" store. * * * Thus, nowhere in the parties' Guide or agreements can it be fairly said that the parties ever contemplated that Isbell could use her office or center as a fixed location to display or sell Mary Kay products or services.

* * *

Finally, Isbell argues that her home constituted a place of business under the Act because as a consultant she occasionally displayed and sold products there. This argument, however, is not supported by the parties' agreement, since it never contemplated a fixed location for the display and sale of products. As previously stated, a Mary Kay consultant's locations for selling products are her home or those of her potential customers. * * * It is thus clear that the requirement of a fixed location is not satisfied by occasional sales from either Isbell's home or the homes of her potential customers.

In sum, we conclude that the agreements between Janet Isbell and Mary Kay did not contemplate the establishment of a fixed place of business as that term is defined in Ark. Code Ann. § 4-72-202 (6). As such, the business relationship entered into by Isbell and Mary Kay was not a franchise within the protection of the Arkansas Franchise Practices Act, and the court below erred in so holding. We therefore reverse and dismiss.

QUESTIONS FOR DISCUSSION FOR CASE 5.3

1. Why has the Arkansas Supreme Court agreed to hear this case?
2. Why is it important from each party's perspective whether Isbell had a fixed place of business?

5.4 Vicarious Liability of Franchisor
Miller v. McDonald's Corp., 945 P.2d 1107 (Or. App. 1997)

Plaintiff seeks damages from defendant McDonald's Corporation for injuries that she suffered when she bit into a heart-shaped sapphire stone while eating a Big Mac sandwich that she had purchased at a McDonald's restaurant in Tigard. The trial court granted summary judgment to defendant on the ground that it did not own or operate the restaurant; rather, the owner and operator was a non-party, 3K Restaurants (3K), that held a franchise from defendant. Plaintiff appeals, and we reverse.

Most of the relevant facts are not in dispute …. 3K owned and operated the restaurant under a License Agreement (the Agreement) with defendant that required it to operate in a manner consistent with the "McDonald's System." The Agreement described that system as including proprietary rights in trade names, service marks and trademarks, as well as

> designs and color schemes for restaurant buildings, signs, equipment layouts, formulas and specifications for certain food products, methods of inventory and operation control, bookkeeping and accounting, and manuals covering business practices and policies.

The manuals contain "detailed information relating to operation of the Restaurant," including food formulas and specifications, methods of inventory control, bookkeeping procedures, business practices, and other management, advertising, and personnel policies. 3K, as the licensee, agreed to adopt and exclusively use the formulas, methods, and policies contained in the manuals, including any subsequent modifications, and to use only advertising and promotional materials that defendant either provided or approved in advance in writing.

The Agreement described the way in which 3K was to operate the restaurant in considerable detail. It expressly required 3K to operate in compliance with defendant's prescribed standards, policies, practices, and procedures, including serving only food and beverage products that defendant designated. 3K had to follow defendant's specifications and blueprints for the equipment and layout of the restaurant, including adopting subsequent reasonable changes that defendant made, and to maintain the restaurant building in compliance with defendant's standards. 3K could not make any changes in the basic design of the building without defendant's approval.

The Agreement required 3K to keep the restaurant open during the hours that defendant prescribed, including maintaining adequate supplies and employing adequate personnel to operate at maximum capacity and efficiency during those hours. 3K also had to keep the restaurant similar in appearance to all other McDonald's restaurants. 3K's employees had to wear McDonald's uniforms, to have a neat and clean appearance, and to provide competent and courteous service. 3K could use only containers and other packaging that bore McDonald's trademarks. The ingredients for the foods and beverages had to meet defendant's standards, and 3K had to use "only those methods of food handling and preparation that [defendant] may designate from time to time." * * * The manuals gave further details that expanded on many of these requirements.

In order to ensure conformity with the standards described in the Agreement, defendant periodically sent field consultants to the restaurant to inspect its operations. 3K trained its employees in accordance with defendant's materials and recommendations and sent some of them to training programs that defendant administered. Failure to comply with the agreed standards could result in loss of the franchise.

Despite these detailed instructions, the Agreement provided that 3K was not an agent of defendant for any purpose. Rather, it was an independent contractor and was responsible for all obligations and liabilities, including claims based on injury, illness, or death, directly or indirectly resulting from the operation of the restaurant.

Plaintiff went to the restaurant under the assumption that defendant owned, controlled, and managed it. So far as she could tell, the restaurant's appearance was similar to that of other McDonald's restaurants that she had patronized. Nothing disclosed to her that any entity other than defendant was involved in its operation. The only signs that were visible and obvious to the public had the name "McDonald's," the employees wore uniforms with McDonald's insignia, and the menu was the same that plaintiff had seen in other McDonald's restaurants. The general appearance of the restaurant and the food products that it sold were similar to the restaurants and products that plaintiff had seen in national print and television advertising that defendant had run. To the best of plaintiff's knowledge, only McDonald's sells Big Mac hamburgers.

In short, plaintiff testified, she went to the Tigard McDonald's because she relied on defendant's reputation and because she wanted to obtain the same quality of service, standard of care in food preparation, and general attention to detail that she had previously enjoyed at other McDonald's restaurants.

Under these facts, 3K would be directly liable for any injuries that plaintiff suffered as a result of the restaurant's negligence. The issue … is whether there is evidence that would permit a jury to find defendant vicariously liable for those injuries because of its relationship with 3K. Plaintiff asserts two theories of vicarious liability, actual agency and apparent agency. We hold that there is sufficient evidence to raise a jury issue under both theories. * * *

The kind of actual agency relationship that would make defendant vicariously liable for 3K's negligence requires that defendant have the right to control the *method* by which 3K performed its obligations under the Agreement. * * *

* * *

* * * The Delaware Supreme Court stated the [right to control] test as it applies to [a franchise relationship]:

> If, in practical effect, the franchise agreement goes beyond the stage of setting standards, and allocates to the franchisor the right to exercise control over

the daily operations of the franchise, an agency relationship exists.

* * *

[W]e believe that a jury could find that defendant retained sufficient control over 3K's daily operations that an actual agency relationship existed. The Agreement did not simply set standards that 3K had to meet. Rather, it required 3K to use the precise methods that defendant established, both in the Agreement and in the detailed manuals that the Agreement incorporated. Those methods included the ways in which 3K was to handle and prepare food. Defendant enforced the use of those methods by regularly sending inspectors and by its retained power to cancel the Agreement. That evidence would support a finding that defendant had the right to control the way in which 3K performed at least food handling and preparation. In her complaint, plaintiff alleges that 3K's deficiencies in those functions resulted in the sapphire being in the Big Mac and thereby caused her injuries. Thus, * * * there is evidence that defendant had the right to control 3K in the precise part of its business that allegedly resulted in plaintiff's injuries. That is sufficient to raise an issue of actual agency.

Plaintiff next asserts that defendant is vicariously liable for 3K's alleged negligence because 3K was defendant's apparent agent.[4] The relevant standard is in *Restatement (Second) of Agency*, § 267, which we adopted in *Themins v. Emanuel Lutheran*, 637 P.2d 155 (Or. App. 1981):

> One who represents that another is his servant or other agent and thereby causes a third person justifiably to rely upon the care or skill of such apparent agent is subject to liability to the third person for harm caused by the lack of care or skill of the one appearing to be a servant or other agent as if he were such.

We have not applied § 267 to a franchisor/franchisee situation, but courts in a number of other jurisdictions have done so in ways that we find instructive. In most cases the courts have found that there was a jury issue of apparent agency. The crucial issues are whether the putative principal held the third party out as an agent and whether the plaintiff relied on that holding out.

---

[4]Apparent agency is a distinct concept from apparent authority. Apparent agency creates an agency relationship that does not otherwise exist, while apparent authority expands the authority of an actual agent.

We look first at what may constitute a franchisor's holding a franchisee out as its agent. In the leading case of *Gizzi v. Texaco, Inc.*, 437 F.2d 308 (5th Cir. 1971), the plaintiff purchased a used Volkswagen van from a Texaco service station. He was injured when the brakes failed shortly thereafter. The franchisee had worked on the brakes before selling the car. The station prominently displayed Texaco insignia, including the slogan "Trust your car to the man who wears the star." Texaco engaged in considerable national advertising to convey the impression that its dealers were skilled in automotive servicing. About 30 percent of Texaco dealers sold used cars. There was a Texaco regional office across the street from the station, and those working in that office knew that the franchisee was selling cars from the station. Based on this evidence, the court concluded, under New Jersey law, that the question of apparent agency was for the jury.

* * *

In *Crinkley v. Holiday Inns, Inc.*, 844 F.2d 156 (4th Cir. 1988), the defendant required the use of the Holiday Inn trade name and trademarks, was the original builder of the hotel, and engaged in national advertising that promoted its system of hotels without distinguishing between those that it owned and those that it franchised. The only indication that the defendant did not own this particular Holiday Inn was a sign in the restaurant that stated that the franchisee operated it. Based on this evidence, the court concluded, under North Carolina law, that apparent agency was a question for the jury.

In each of these cases, the franchise agreement required the franchisee to act in ways that identified it with the franchisor. The franchisor imposed those requirements as part of maintaining an image of uniformity of operations and appearance for the franchisor's entire system. Its purpose was to attract the patronage of the public to that entire system. The centrally imposed uniformity is the fundamental basis for the courts' conclusion that there was an issue of fact whether the franchisors held the franchisees out as the franchisors' agents.

In this case, for similar reasons, there is an issue of fact about whether defendant held 3K out as its agent. Everything about the appearance and operation of the Tigard McDonald's identified it with defendant and with the common image for all McDonald's restaurants that defendant has worked to create through national

advertising, common signs and uniforms, common menus, common appearance, and common standards. The possible existence of a sign identifying 3K as the operator does not alter the conclusion that there is an issue of apparent agency for the jury. There are issues of fact of whether that sign was sufficiently visible to the public, in light of plaintiff's apparent failure to see it, and of whether one sign by itself is sufficient to remove the impression that defendant created through all of the other indicia of its control that it, and 3K under the requirements that defendant imposed, presented to the public.

Defendant does not seriously dispute that a jury could find that it held 3K out as its agent. Rather, it argues that there is insufficient evidence that plaintiff justifiably relied on that holding out. It argues that it is not sufficient for her to prove that she went to the Tigard McDonald's because it was a McDonald's restaurant. Rather, she also had to prove that she went to it because she believed that *McDonald's Corporation* operated both it and the other McDonald's restaurants that she had previously patronized. * * *

Defendant's argument both demands a higher level of sophistication about the nature of franchising than the general public can be expected to have and ignores the effect of its own efforts to lead the public to believe that McDonald's restaurants are part of a uniform national system of restaurants with common products and common standards of quality. * * *

Plaintiff testified in her affidavit that her reliance on defendant for the quality of service and food at the Tigard McDonald's came in part from her experience at other McDonald's restaurants. * * * A jury could find that it was defendant's very insistence on uniformity of appearance and standards, designed to cause the public to think of every McDonald's, franchised or unfranchised, as part of the same system, that makes it difficult or impossible for plaintiff to tell whether her previous experiences were at restaurants that defendant owned or franchised.

* * *

[P]laintiff testified that she relied on the general reputation of McDonald's in patronizing the Tigard restaurant and in her expectation of the quality of the food and service that she would receive. Especially in light of defendant's efforts to create a public perception of a common McDonald's system at all McDonald's restaurants, whoever operated them, a jury could find that plaintiff's reliance was objectively reasonable. The trial court erred in granting summary judgment on the apparent agency theory.

Reversed and remanded.

QUESTIONS FOR DISCUSSION FOR CASE 5.4

1. What is the difference between actual and apparent agency? What tests are used to evaluate whether each is present in a given case?
2. How visible and obvious do you think signs should be telling customers that a franchisee owns and operates a business? On your last trip to a fast-food restaurant, did you notice who owned the restaurant?
3. Is it fair to hold McDonald's Corporation liable when its franchisee cooks the food and is most likely in the best position to control whether foreign objects enter the food?
4. What public policy considerations come into play when you make this determination?
5. What can a franchisor do to protect itself against liability arising out of the acts of its franchisee?
6. Procedurally, what will happen next in this case?

5.5 Franchise Antitrust Issues

Sheridan v. Marathon Petroleum Co., LLC, 530 F.3d 590 (7th Cir. 2008)

The plaintiffs, a Marathon dealer in Indiana and a company owned by him to whom he assigned his dealership contract, filed suit against Marathon under section 1 of the Sherman Act, 15 U.S.C. § 1, charging it with tying the processing of credit card sales to the Marathon franchise …. The tying arrangement is challenged under section 1 of the Sherman Act rather than section 3 of the Clayton Act because the things alleged to be tied—the franchise and the processing service—are services rather than commodities. [T]he standards for adjudicating tying under the two statutes are now recognized to be the same.

＊ ＊ ＊

The complaint alleges that as a condition of granting a dealer franchise Marathon requires the dealer to agree to process credit card "purchases of petroleum and other products, services provided and merchandise sold at or from the [dealer's] Premises" through a processing service designated by Marathon. The terms of the dealership (set forth in a dealers' handbook cited in the complaint) impose the requirement only with regard to sales paid for with Marathon's proprietary credit card, which however the dealer is required to accept in payment. A dealer who wanted to process sales paid for with other credit cards by means of a different processing system would be contractually free to do so, but he would have to duplicate the processing equipment supplied by Marathon. We'll assume that this would be so costly as to compel dealers to process all their credit card sales by means of Marathon's designated system, since that system can process credit card sales whether or not they are made with Marathon's credit card, thereby enabling the dealer to handle all such sales with one set of equipment. So Marathon *might* be said to have tied the processing of *all* credit card sales by its dealers to the Marathon franchise, and so we'll assume—for the moment. The plaintiffs contend that such a tie-in is a per se violation of the Sherman Act.

In a tying agreement, a seller conditions the sale of a product or service on the buyer's buying another product or service from or (as in this case) by direction of the seller. The traditional antitrust concern with such an agreement is that if the seller of the tying product is a monopolist, the tie-in will force anyone who wants the monopolized product to buy the tied product from him as well, and the result will be a second monopoly. This will happen, however, only if the tied product is used mainly with the trying product; if it has many other uses, the tie-in will not create a monopoly of the tied product. Suppose the tying product is a mimeograph machine and the tied product is the ink used with the machine, as in the old case of *Henry v. A.B. Dick Co.*, 224 U.S. 1 (1912). Since only a small percentage of the total ink supply was used with mimeograph machines, A.B. Dick's monopoly would not have enabled it to monopolize the ink market. If, moreover, A.B. Dick did obtain a monopoly of that market and used it to jack up the price of ink, customers for its machines would not be willing to pay as much for them because their cost of using them would be higher. In economic terms, the machine and the ink used with it are complementary products, and raising the price of a product reduces the demand for its complements. (If the price of nails rises, the demand for hammers will fall.)

Only if all or most ink were used in conjunction with mimeograph machines might the manufacturer use the tie-in to repel competition. For then someone who wanted to challenge the mimeograph monopoly might have difficulty arranging for a supply of ink for his customers unless he entered the ink business. That might be hard for him to do. Entering two markets having unrelated production characteristics might both entail delay and increase the risk and hence cost of the new entrant.

Tying agreements can also be a method of price discrimination—the more ink the buyer of a mimeograph machine uses, and hence the more he uses the machine, the more valuable in all likelihood the machine is to him. In that event, by charging a high price for the ink and a low price for the machine, the manufacturer can extract more revenue from the higher-value (less elastic) users without losing too many of the low-value users, since they don't use much ink and hence are not much affected by the high price of the ink but benefit from the low price of the machine. However, price discrimination does not violate the Sherman Act unless it has an exclusionary effect. And a monopolist doesn't have to actually take over the market for the tied product in order to discriminate in price. He just has to interpose himself between the sellers of the tied product and his own customers so that he can reprice that product to his customers.

The Supreme Court used to deem tying agreements illegal provided only that, as the language of section 3 of the Clayton Act seemed to require, the tying arrangement embraced a nontrivial amount of interstate commerce. Beginning in the 1970s, however, the Court began to reexamine and in some instances discard antitrust doctrines that (like tying agreements) place limitations on distributors or dealers. The Court has not discarded the tying rule, and we have no authority to do so. But it has modified the rule by requiring proof that the seller has "market power" in the market for the tying product ….

So "market power" is key, but its meaning requires elucidation. *Monopoly* power we know is a seller's ability to charge a price above the competitive level (roughly speaking, above cost, including the cost of capital) without losing so many sales to existing competitors or new entrants as to make the price increase unprofitable. The word "monopoly" in the expression "monopoly power" was never understood literally, to mean a market with only one seller; a seller who has a large market share may be able to charge a price persistently above the competitive level despite the existence of competitors. Although the price increase will reduce the seller's output (because quantity demanded falls as price rises), his competitors, if they are small, may not be able to take up enough of the slack by expanding their own output to bring price back down to the competitive level; their costs of doing so would be too high—that is doubtless *why* they are small.

As one moves from a market of one very large seller plus a fringe of small firms to a market of several large firms, monopoly power wanes. Now if one firm tries to charge a price above the competitive level, its competitors may have the productive capacity to be able to replace its reduction in output with an increase in their own output at no higher cost, and price will fall back to the competitive level. Eventually a point is reached at which there is no threat to competition unless sellers are able to agree, tacitly or explicitly, to limit output in order to drive price above the competitive level. The mere possibility of collusion cannot establish monopoly power, even in an attenuated sense to which the term "market power" might attach, because then *every* firm, no matter how small, would be deemed to have it, since successful collusion is always a possibility.

The plaintiffs in drafting their complaint were at least dimly aware that they would have to plead and prove that Marathon had significant unilateral power over the market price of gasoline and so could charge a supra-competitive price (folded into the price for gasoline that it charges its dealers) for credit card processing. But all that the complaint states on this score is that Marathon is "the fourth-largest United States-based integrated oil and gas company and the fifth-largest petroleum refiner in the United States" and sells "petroleum products to approximately 5,600 Marathon and Speedway branded direct-served retail outlets and approximately 3,700 jobber-served retail outlets." Marathon and Speedway's alleged annual sales of six billion gallons of gasoline (improperly swollen by inclusion of Speedway's sales) is only 4.3 percent of total U.S. gasoline sales per year …. That is no one's idea of market power.

Marathon does of course have a "monopoly" of Marathon franchises. But "Marathon" is not a market; it is a trademark; and a trademark does not confer a monopoly; all it does is prevent a competitor from attaching the same name to his product. "Not even the most zealous antitrust hawk has ever argued that Amoco gasoline, Mobil gasoline, and Shell gasoline"— or, we interject, Marathon gasoline—"are three [with

Marathon, four] separate product markets." The complaint does not allege that there are any local gasoline markets in which Marathon has monopoly (or market) power. No market share statistics for Marathon either locally or nationally are given, and there is no information in the complaint that would enable local shares to be calculated.

What is true is that a firm selling under conditions of "monopolistic competition"—the situation in which minor product differences (or the kind of locational advantage that a local store, such as a barber shop, might enjoy in competing for some customers) limit the substitutability of otherwise very similar products—will want to trademark its brand in order to distinguish it from its competitors' brands. But the exploitation of the slight monopoly power thereby enabled does not do enough harm to the economy to warrant trundling out the heavy artillery of federal antitrust law. And anyway in this case monopolistic competition is not alleged either. So we are given no reason to doubt that if Marathon raises the price of using the Marathon name above the competitive level by raising the price of the credit card processing service that it offers, competing oil companies will nullify its price increase simply by keeping their own wholesale gasoline prices at the existing level. The complaint does not allege that Marathon is colluding with the other oil companies to raise the price of credit card processing ....

There is more that is wrong with the plaintiffs' charge of illegal tying. Earlier we assumed that Marathon had indeed tied credit card processing to the franchise, but that assumption will not withstand scrutiny. All it has done is require its franchisees to honor Marathon credit cards and to process sales with them through the system designated by Marathon so that customers of Marathon who use its card have the same purchasing experience no matter which Marathon gas station they buy from. The combination of card and card processing enables Marathon to offset

in an economical and expeditious manner revenues from credit card sales against costs of gasoline sold to the dealers. When a dealer makes a sale with a credit card, the Marathon processing system credits his Marathon account with the price of the sale and thus reduces the amount of money that the dealer owes Marathon for the gasoline that he buys from it.

The plaintiffs do not challenge Marathon's right to offer this service. But once it is in place the dealer has a powerful incentive to route *all* his credit card transactions through the Marathon system, as otherwise he would have to duplicate the processing equipment that Marathon supplies and lose the benefit of being able to use his retail sales revenue to offset what he owes Marathon. The additional cost of using multiple card processing systems is not a penalty imposed by Marathon to force the use of its system, but an economy that flows directly from Marathon's offering its own credit card and credit card processing service. To call this tying would be like saying that a manufacturer of automobiles who sells tires with his cars is engaged in tying because, although the buyer is free to buy tires from someone else, he is unlikely to do so, having paid for the tires supplied by the car's manufacturer.

* * *

AFFIRMED.

QUESTIONS FOR DISCUSSION FOR CASE 5.5

1. What does the plaintiff allege are the tied and tying products or services?
2. How does the court determine what the relevant market is in this case? Why is the relevant market not defined as Marathon franchisees, as they are the ones subject to this credit card processing requirement?
3. Why does the court conclude that there is not illegal tying going on here? Is it likely that the plaintiff has other economically viable choices available to it?

DISCUSSION QUESTIONS

1. Several plaintiffs brought actions against Conoco, Inc., claiming that they had been discriminated against on the basis of their race when they attempted to make purchases at three gas stations in Texas operated under the Conoco brand. Conoco directly owned and operated one of the stations, and independent contractors licensed to use the

Conoco trademark operated the other two stations. Evidence, including videotapes, indicated that the clerks had refused to serve the customers and had used racial epithets during some of the incidents. What factors should the court consider and what tests should it apply in determining whether Conoco should be held liable?

2. Lockard worked as a waitress for a Pizza Hut franchise owned by A & M Food Services. The national Pizza Hut franchisor produces several training documents for employees, including a booklet on how to bring sexual harassment complaints to the manager or district representative. The Pizza Hut franchisees actually operated and controlled the restaurants' day-to-day business. Lockard claimed that the restaurant that she worked at maintained a hostile environment because the manager played songs on the jukebox with sexually explicit lyrics. Furthermore, the manager made her serve two specific customers who had a history of making sexual advances to her at the restaurant. She complained that she did not want to serve the customers, but the manager demanded that she do so. When she went back to their table, the customers grabbed and groped her as she tried to take their orders. Lockard quit and sued the franchisor and the franchisee. Should Lockard recover against the franchisor? The franchisee?

3. University Motors, a West Virginia business, entered into a franchise agreement with General Motors Corp. (GMC). The agreement specified that University Motors would require approval from GMC if it wanted to sell another line of vehicles. University Motors began selling a Nissan line of vehicles without first obtaining GMC approval. GMC sought to terminate the franchise and hand-delivered a letter to University Motors stating that the franchise would end 90 days from receipt of the letter. GMC stated that the reason for the termination was the new vehicle line and various deficiencies in University Motor's sales. University Motors filed suit to prevent termination of the franchise, claiming that GMC had violated a West Virginia statute that required a franchisor to deliver a termination letter by certified mail and to give the franchisee 180 days to cure the problem. The statute also required that the franchisor have a good faith reason for terminating because of poor sales or service performance. Should GMC be permitted to terminate University Motors? Why, or why not?

4. Shell Oil Co. owned a gas station and property in Deerfield Beach, Florida. In 1995, Shell entered into a "Motor Fuel Station Lease" with A. Z. Services, Inc., which provided that A. Z. would lease the gas station and property for five years. The parties also entered into a "Dealer Agreement," which established a franchise agreement between the two parties. Under the Dealer Agreement, A. Z. had the right to operate the gas station under Shell's trademarks, brand name, service marks, and other Shell identifications in connection with the sale of motor fuel and other petroleum products. A year later, without notice to or consent by Shell, A. Z. removed all Shell trademarks and identification, stopped selling Shell products, and began selling the products of a Shell competitor, Skipper's Choice. Shell terminated the franchise agreement and filed suit seeking an injunction to prohibit A. Z. from selling Skipper's Choice products and to vacate the property. A. Z. defended by claiming that Shell had unlawfully tied the lease of the property to the sale of Shell fuel. How should the court rule on this antitrust claim?

5. In 1995, Golf U.S.A. entered into a franchise agreement granting Express Golf the right to operate a retail store using Golf U.S.A.'s methods, name, designs, systems, and service marks. The franchise agreement also stated that "[a]ny and all disputes, claims and controversies arising out of or relating to this Agreement … shall be resolved by arbitration conducted in Oklahoma County, State of Oklahoma." Golf U.S.A. is an Oklahoma corporation. The golf retail store failed within nine months, and Charles Barker, the sole shareholder of Express Golf, brought this action against Golf U.S.A. for fraudulent misrepresentation. He alleged that Golf U.S.A. misrepresented the success of its retail operations, thereby leading him to sign the franchise agreement. Golf U.S.A. moved to dismiss the case, arguing that the dispute should be decided by arbitration and not by the judiciary. Barker claimed that the arbitration clause was unconscionable and therefore unenforceable. No statute prohibits the inclusion of arbitration clauses in franchise agreements. Should Barker be permitted to litigate in court or should the arbitration clause of the franchise agreement control?

6. Weaver operated two Burger King restaurants under two separate franchise agreements. Restaurant 1 was located in Great Falls, Montana, and Weaver leased the facility from Burger King. Restaurant 2 was also located in Great Falls, but Weaver owned the facility. Both franchise agreements required Weaver to make monthly royalty payments and advertising contributions to Burger King Corp. and provided that Florida law would control in the event of a dispute. The agreement for Restaurant 1 contained no provisions regarding geographic scope, but the agreement for Restaurant 2 stipulated that "this franchise is for the specified location only and does not in any

way grant or imply any area, market, or territorial rights proprietary to FRANCHISEE." Neither agreement contained any limitations on the locations of future Burger King restaurants.

In 1989, another Burger King franchise opened in Great Falls. Weaver was upset by the competition, felt that Burger King had breached its obligations under the franchise agreements, and stopped making rent, royalty, and advertising payments, though he continued to use Burger King's marks and system. Burger King sued for breach of contract. Weaver counterclaimed, arguing that Burger King had breached the implied covenant of good faith and fair dealing, which, under Florida law, is part of every contract. Florida law does not recognize actions for breach of an implied covenant of good faith and fair dealing when: (a) the party breaching the implied covenant has performed all of the express contractual provisions in good faith and (b) the implied duty that was breached would vary the express terms of the contract. Which party should prevail here, and why?

7. In 1993, Airborne Freight Corp. (Airborne), a package delivery service, and East Wind Express, Inc. (East Wind) entered into a contract under which East Wind agreed to provide services to Airborne, such as pickup, transport, and delivery of shipments between Airborne's customers and facilities in northern Oregon. Customers would call Airborne and ask to have a package delivered to another area. Airborne would radio an East Wind driver, who would then pick up the customer's package. Airborne billed the customer and assumed all liability for the package from the time of arrival at its pickup to the package's final destination. Under the contract, Airborne paid East Wind based on the average number of packages carried per day, and East Wind was "not entitled to receive any portion of any charges made by Airborne to its shippers." The contract also stated that East Wind's use of Airborne's trademarks on its uniforms and trucks was an advertising service and was to be compensated according to advertising fees. Airborne specified the standards that applied to the use of its trademarks by East Wind.

Eventually, the relationship between the two companies disintegrated, and Airborne terminated the contract. East Wind brought this action against Airborne, asserting that at-will terminations violated the Washington Franchise Investment Protection Act. Airborne argued that East Wind was an independent contractor, who could be terminated at will, and not a franchisee. What are the requirements for a franchise relationship? Under these standards, is Airborne a franchisee or an independent contractor?

8. As of June 1995, Little Caesar Enterprises, Inc. (LCE) had 536 franchises nationwide operating 2,867 carryout-type restaurants. LCE also owned and operated 1,000 carryout restaurants and 500 restaurants located in Kmart stores. Blue Line Distributing, Inc., purchased the necessary supplies for the restaurants, bundled them into single units, and sold them to the franchisees. In June 1989, LCE and Blue Line entered into a licensing agreement granting Blue Line the exclusive right to distribute products containing the Little Caesar logo. Franchise agreements used to give franchisees the right to use LCE-approved alternative suppliers, but the 1990 Franchise Agreement excluded logoed products from the list of products that could be obtained from alternative suppliers. Logoed products, such as paper products, condiments, and packaging, are necessary to the operation of a franchise.

Plaintiffs bought Little Caesar franchises between 1990 and 1995 and are operating under the 1990 Franchise Agreement. They argue that Blue Line charges supracompetitive prices for the logoed products and that the exclusive license granted to Blue Line precludes them from obtaining cheaper products from alternative suppliers. They have brought this class action, alleging that LCE has unlawfully tied Blue Line's products to the purchase of a Little Caesar franchise. LCE argues that plaintiffs knew about the Blue Line distributorship, agreed to the terms when signing the 1990 Agreement, and that LCE lacks sufficient market power to force a tying arrangement on plaintiffs. How should the court resolve this antitrust claim, and why?

9. Tosco Corporation is an independent refiner and marketer of petroleum products. In 1994, Tosco purchased from BP Exploration & Oil, Inc. ("BP") all service stations owned by BP in Northern California, along with a license to use the "BP" trademark in California. The license for the trademark expires on August 1, 2006, and Tosco pays BP royalties for the use of the marks. In accordance with the sale, BP terminated all franchises, and Tosco subsequently offered the terminated franchisees a new franchise agreement to sell petroleum products under the "BP" trademark. The new franchise agreements were scheduled to expire on April 15, 1998.

On March 31, 1997, Tosco purchased the 76 Products Company from Union Oil Company of

California, which included approximately 900 service stations in California and the right to use the "Union 76" and "76" trademarks in perpetuity.

In 1997, Tosco decided that it would be most effective to sell products at the service stations under only one brand and chose to sell under the "Union 76" trademark because use of that mark required no royalty payments. In December 1997, Tosco offered all of its BP franchisees renewal of the franchise agreement on condition that they sell fuel under the "Union 76" mark.

Plaintiffs are service station dealers who refused to agree to the change in marks, preferring to retain the "BP" mark. Tosco notified plaintiffs that their franchises would not be renewed for failure to agree to a change in a provision of the franchise agreement. Plaintiffs brought this action, contending that under the Petroleum Marketing Practices Act (PMPA) Tosco could not condition renewal of a franchise agreement on the franchisee's consent to "rebrand" the product. The relevant portion of the PMPA states that such conditional agreements are lawful, as long as the "changes or additions are the result of determinations made by the franchisor in good faith and in the normal course of business" and not for the purpose of preventing renewal of the franchise.

What factors should the court consider in resolving this dispute?

10. Dana Hoffnagle was an employee at a McDonald's restaurant owned by a franchisee, Rapid-Mac, Inc. At 10:00 one evening, two men entered the restaurant, grabbed Hoffnagle, and took her out to the parking lot where they attempted to force her into their car. Tammy Geiger, a managerial employee, came to Hoffnagle's assistance and helped her escape from the men and return to the restaurant. Geiger noticed the two men driving their car around the parking lot, but did not lock the doors or telephone the police. Later, one of the men reentered the restaurant and again attempted to force Hoffnagle outside. Geiger intervened again, and the men left the restaurant premises. Geiger then telephoned the police department.

Hoffnagle filed for workers' compensation benefits from her employer, Rapid-Mac, which she received. She then filed suit against McDonald's Corp., which was Rapid-Mac's franchisor, arguing that McDonald's Corp. had the ability to control the operations of the franchisee and was liable for negligence for failing to exercise such control.

The contractual agreements between McDonald's and Rapid-Mac required the franchisee to adhere to the franchisor's standards and policies "for providing for the uniform operation of all McDonald's restaurants within the McDonald's system including, but not limited to, serving only designated food and beverage products, the use of only prescribed equipment and building layout and designs, strict adherence to designated food and beverage specifications and to prescribed standards of quality, service and cleanliness in [the] restaurant operation." The agreements also required Rapid-Mac to adopt and use business manuals prepared by McDonald's and for McDonald's to make training available at "Hamburger University" for the franchisee and its managerial employees. McDonald's had the right to inspect the restaurant at all reasonable times to ensure compliance with the standards and policies and had the right to terminate the franchisee if the standards and policies were not met.

Hoffnagle argued that these agreements gave McDonald's the right to control the restaurant and property upon which she was assaulted and that McDonald's was liable for negligence in failing to exercise that control, particularly in failing to provide adequate security or in failing to direct the franchisee to provide adequate security. Specifically, she argued that the franchisee's managerial employee, Geiger, was not appropriately trained because she failed to lock the doors or telephone the police after the first assault. Should McDonald's, as the franchisor, be liable for Hoffnagle's injuries? What factors would you consider in making this determination?

11. Martinez was injured when he was struck by a bicycle being ridden by Pardo. At the time of the accident, Pardo was making deliveries for his employer, Higher Powered Pizza, which was a franchisee of Papa John's International, Inc. Martinez sued Papa John's, arguing that it was vicariously liable for the acts of its franchisee.

The franchisee agreement between Higher Powered Pizza and Papa John's stated that the franchisee "shall have full responsibility for the conduct and terms of employment for [its] employees and the day-to-day operation of [its] business"; the only control the agreement reserved to Papa John's involved enforcement of standards in areas such as food quality and preparation, hours of operation, menu items, employee uniform guidelines, and packaging requirements. This included the right to perform inspections (limited to review of sales and order forms), audits to ensure compliance with company standards, and observation of interaction with customers.

Should Papa John's be held liable for the injuries caused to Pardo?

12. Defendant manufactures a line of upscale sodas marketed under the name "Stewart's." Plaintiffs are several beverage distributors who distributed Defendant's sodas in Minnesota. Plaintiffs were distributors of beer before Defendant approached them. Thus, Plaintiffs already owned the facilities (e.g., warehouses and refrigerators) and equipment (e.g., trucks and handcarts), and already employed the personnel (e.g., drivers, warehouse workers, and bookkeepers) necessary for the distribution of beverages at the time they began distributing Stewart's sodas.

After several years of using Plaintiffs as its distributors, Defendant decided to distribute its products directly, and terminated Plaintiffs' distribution agreements.

The Minnesota Franchise Act (MFA) protects franchisees from being terminated without good cause by franchisors. Defendant argues that it did not need "good cause" to terminate the Plaintiffs, however, because it was not a franchisor and Plaintiffs were not franchisees within the meaning of the MFA.

Plaintiffs argued that they were franchisees under the "business opportunity" provision of the MFA, which defines a "franchise" as: "the sale or lease of any products ... to the purchaser ... for the purpose of enabling the purchaser to start a business and in which the seller: ... (iii) guarantees that the purchaser will derive income from the business which exceeds the price paid to the seller."

How should the court rule on the Plaintiffs' claim? What policy considerations support that outcome?

PART 4

Legal Issues Relating to Product Promotion

Chapter 6
Trademark Law

Chapter 7
Commercial Speech and Regulation of Advertising

Chapter 8
Consumer Protection Law

CHAPTER 6
Trademark Law

This chapter discusses the fourth major category of intellectual property law: trademark law. (Patent and copyright law are discussed in Chapter 2 and trade secret law in Chapter 3.)

Trademarks are the words or symbols used by companies or individuals to distinguish or identify their goods or services, to indicate consistent source and quality, and to facilitate advertising and sales. Because trademarks are so effective in fulfilling these critical roles, they are extremely valuable to their owners. Businesses spend a great deal of time and money both creating and protecting their marks.

Companies need to consider trademarks at two important junctures. First, companies need to devote significant attention and resources to selection of the proper trademark during the development stage of their product or service. A carefully and wisely chosen mark can increase the likelihood that the product or service will prove marketable, generate valuable goodwill, and enhance the firm's bottom line. A poorly chosen mark can detract from the desirability or marketability of the product or service and even embroil the firm in expensive litigation.

Second, once the company has chosen the mark and has begun using it to promote the product or service, the company must guard against unauthorized use of the mark by others. Failure to do so can result in the loss of a valuable intellectual property asset. Both of these issues are discussed in this chapter.

Overview

A *trademark* is a word, symbol, name, device, or combination thereof used by a manufacturer or merchant to identify and distinguish its goods from those manufactured or sold by others and to indicate the source of goods. Although we tend to think of trademarks as being words (such as *Rubbermaid* or *Rocsports*), many trademarks are actually symbols—the "Golden Arches" used by McDonald's, for example, or the "bitten apple" used by Apple computer products.

Trademarks serve four purposes:

1. they provide an identification symbol for a particular merchant's goods or services;
2. they indicate that the goods or services to which the trademark has been attached are from a single source;
3. they guarantee that all goods or services to which the trademark has been attached are of a consistent quality; and
4. they advertise the goods or services.

Essentially, the trademark tells the consumer what a product or service is called, where it comes from, and who is responsible for its creation. However, the trademark does not necessarily identify the manufacturer or provider of goods or services. *Yoplait* identifies a brand of yogurt, for example, but it does not necessarily indicate that the yogurt is manufactured by a company called Yoplait. The yogurt may be produced by a different company licensed to use the *Yoplait* mark.

Both consumers and businesses benefit from the use of trademarks. Consumers rely upon trademarks to identify the source of goods or services. The mark helps the consumer repeat purchases that were satisfactory and avoid repeating purchases that were not. Businesses use marks to help create and protect business goodwill. *Goodwill* refers to a business's image, good reputation, and expectation of repeat patronage and is a valuable asset in most industries.

While the primary function of trademarks themselves is to promote the interests of the mark owner, the primary focus of trademark *law* is to protect the consumer from deception, not to protect the value of the trademark to its owner. Protection of the trademark owner's rights is secondary.

Nonetheless, although trademark law is primarily concerned with consumer protection, confused or misled consumers may not sue for relief under trademark law. Rather, only the owners or users of marks have a cause of action. In addition, trademark law is self-policing. Trademark owners must sue to enforce their rights; no government agency will enforce those rights on their behalf.

Origins of Trademark Law

As discussed in earlier chapters, patent and copyright law are federal law, while trade secret law is primarily state law. By contrast, trademark law arises under both state and federal law.

Trademark law originally started out as one of several related doctrines arising under the state law of unfair competition. (Unfair competition law is discussed in Chapter 7.) The federal Lanham Act,[1] which was enacted in 1946 and which addresses trademarks, codified and expanded these state common law notions. The most significant innovation under this act was the creation of a federal register (the *Principal Register*) for trademarks.

The federal Lanham Act did not preempt state law. Thus, today trademark owners can sue for violation of their rights in their trademarks under:

1. the state common law of unfair competition;
2. state trademark statutes; and/or
3. the federal Lanham Act.

State and federal claims can be brought in the same suit. (This is an example of concurrent jurisdiction, discussed in Chapter 1.)

Types of Marks

There are four different categories of marks, only one of which is actually properly referred to as a "trademark." For most purposes, the law regarding all four is the same, both under the Lanham Act and under state law. We tend to refer to all four categories as "marks" or—more commonly but imprecisely—as "trademarks."

A *trademark* is a word, name, symbol, device, or any combination thereof that is used to distinguish the goods of one person from goods manufactured or sold by others. Examples include Volvo automobiles, General Mills cereals, and Sony camcorders.

A *service mark* is much the same as a trademark but is used to identify services rather than goods. Examples include Red Lobster for restaurants and State Farm for insurance services.

---

[1]15 U.S.C. §§ 1051-1128.

A *certification mark* is used to certify that goods or services of others have certain characteristics, such as adhering to certain standards regarding quality or accuracy, regional origin, or method of manufacture. Well-known examples include Underwriters' Laboratories and the Good Housekeeping Seal of Approval. Because consumers tend to rely upon these certifications, the Lanham Act restricts their use in a number of ways. In particular, companies are not permitted to certify their own goods or services, and certifying entities must be objective and cannot discriminate in certifying the goods and services of others.

A *collective mark* can take one of two forms. A *collective membership mark* is used to indicate membership within an organization, such as a union or professional society. The mark "ILGWU" on clothing, for example, indicates that it was made by members of the International Ladies Garment Workers Union (as opposed to a nonunion shop). A *collective trademark* or *collective service mark* is adopted by a collective organization (such as a cooperative) for use by members in selling individual goods or services. The organization itself does not sell goods or services, although it may advertise or promote the goods or services sold under the mark by others. In many instances, the collective mark serves the same purpose as a certification mark.

Creating and Protecting a Mark
Distinctiveness of the Mark

A company faces a number of business considerations when it selects a mark. The mark should be easy to pronounce, easy to remember, and unique. It should convey a positive image about the product and company and should communicate product concepts and qualities. In this environment of global business activity, it should also work well around the world and should not invoke any negative connotations in other languages.

A company's primary legal consideration in choosing a mark should be its *distinctiveness* (see Exhibit 6.1). The more distinctive the mark is, the greater the legal protection that it receives.

Inherently distinctive marks receive the most protection. These include *fanciful marks*, which are marks that consist of made-up words or combinations of letters and numbers with no meaning other than their trademark meaning (such as Exxon, Clorox, or Kodak), and *arbitrary marks*, which are marks that have no real connection to the product or service being sold (such as Penguin books, Beefeater gin, or Blue Diamond nuts). Arbitrary

---

EXHIBIT 6.1 Distinctiveness of Marks

CLASSIFICATION OF MARK	PROTECTION
Inherently Distinctive • Fanciful Marks • Arbitrary Marks • Suggestive Marks	Protected immediately upon use
Not Inherently Distinctive • Descriptive Marks • Geographic Terms • Personal Names	Protected once secondary meaning arises
Nondistinctive • Generic Terms	None

and fanciful marks are considered inherently distinctive because a consumer would immediately connect them with their product or service, as there is no other meaning to attach to them.

Suggestive marks are also considered inherently distinctive. These are marks that do not immediately create an association with the product but indirectly describe the product or service that they identify. The consumer must expend some mental effort to associate them with a description of the product. Examples include Greyhound for a bus service, Intuit for software, and Chicken of the Sea for tuna.

Marks that are not inherently distinctive are protected only once they acquire a *secondary meaning*. This means that over time and with sufficient exposure consumers cease to recognize just the primary, descriptive meaning of the mark and, instead, develop a mental association between the mark and the source of the product. A mark owner can show the existence of a secondary meaning either through proof of long and extensive use of the mark, through long and extensive advertising, or through scientifically conducted consumer surveys.

Several types of marks fall within this category, including *descriptive marks, geographic terms*, and *personal names*. Examples include Sears department stores, Chap-Stick lip balm, Tender Vittles cat food, and McDonald's restaurants. The limitation on the use of personal names reflects the fact that people traditionally like to use their own surnames for their businesses. The law does not want to place too many barriers in their way in doing so. Once the first user has established a secondary meaning in the mark, however, later users may be barred from using the mark, even if it is indeed the later user's own name.

Generic terms receive no trademark protection. Mark users are not permitted to monopolize a term to which all producers or providers need access. It does not matter that the term may acquire a secondary meaning over time. Thus, a producer could not use the mark "cider" to identify the product coming from a particular mill (see Case Illustration 6.1). Many terms that were once enforceable trademarks have become generic over time and are no longer protected by trademark law. For example, aspirin, escalator, yo yo, kerosene, mimeograph, and linoleum all were once protected trademarks that have become genericized over time. Trademark owners must constantly police the use of their marks to prevent them from becoming generic terms (see Exhibit 6.2).

What May Constitute a Mark?

Marks may consist of words, drawings, abstract designs, slogans (e.g., "Just Do It"), distinctive packaging features, sounds (e.g., NBC's three-note chime, the roar of the MGM lion), smells (e.g., plumeria blossoms for sewing thread, floral scents for fuel additives), or virtually anything else that can be used to identify the good or service involved.[2] Most marks consist of words or numbers. These can be real or coined words, a combination of words and numbers, or numbers alone.

Drawings and other art forms may be used for marks. Realistic drawings of the product or service are generally considered descriptive and are protected only if they have obtained a secondary meaning. Nonrealistic drawings—such as the Mr. Peanut mark of a humanized peanut with a monocle, walking cane, and top hat—may be considered suggestive, arbitrary, or fanciful and so inherently distinctive.

Trade dress can also be registered and protected. Trade dress refers to things like a distinctive shape (the Coca-Cola bottle) or packaging (Kodak's yellow film box) or decor (Banana Republic clothing stores). Trade dress may be protected as a mark if it makes a separate commercial impression and if its impact on the consumer is primarily to identify or distinguish the product or service, not merely to serve as ornamentation.

---

[2]To listen to some trademarked sounds, go to www.uspto.gov/go/kids/kidsound.html

CASE ILLUSTRATION 6.1

BOSTON DUCK TOURS, LP v. SUPER DUCK TOURS, LLC, 531 F.3D 1 (1ST CIR. 2008)

FACTS Boston Duck Tours, LP, and Super Duck Tours, LLC, offered sightseeing tours in Boston using amphibious vehicles known as "ducks." (The vehicles are named after World War II army amphibious vehicles called "DUKWs.") Similar types of tours are offered in several U.S. and foreign cities.

Boston Duck has offered tours since 1994. Its service is well-known and popular, and over 585,000 people took a Boston Duck tour in 2006. It holds several state and federal trademark registrations for the word mark "Boston Duck Tours." Super Duck began offering its tours in 2001 in Maine. It began operating in the Boston area in May, 2007. Super Duck has a federal registration on the word mark "Super Duck Tours."

Boston Duck sued Super Duck for trademark infringement, and was awarded a preliminary injunction preventing Super Duck from using the term "duck tour." Super Duck appealed, arguing that the phrase "duck tour" was generic.

DECISION The appellate court reversed the award of a preliminary injunction in favor of Boston Duck.

The court stated, "[A] generic term, such as 'car' or 'pizza,' … does not have capacity as a source-identifier because it designates the class, or 'genus' of goods. Rather than answering the question 'where do you come from?', a generic term merely explains 'what are you?'" The court went on to explain:

> Because they serve primarily to describe products rather than identify their sources, generic terms are incapable of becoming trademarks, at least in connection with the products that they designate. Awarding trademark rights to any user of the term, especially the first user, would harm competitors and consumers alike. Competitors unable to use a common term that describes or designates their product are at a significant disadvantage communicating to

potential customers the nature and characteristics of the product. Likewise, consumers will be forced either to pay a higher price to purchase the desired goods from the seller who owns the generic term as a trademark or expend additional time investigating the alternative products available. Therefore, in accord with the primary justifications for protecting trademarks—to aid competition and lower consumers' search costs—the law does not grant any party exclusive rights to use generic terms as trademarks.

In evaluating a genericism claim, the court should consider several sources to determine what the "primary significance" of the phrase is: "(1) consumer surveys; (2) the use of the term in media publications; (3) use of the term by competitors in the industry; (4) purchaser testimony concerning the term; and (5) the plaintiff's use of the term." Here, the evidence showed that "duck tours" is widely used in the media in a generic sense to refer to amphibious, sightseeing tours. In addition, of the at least 36 companies providing such tour services around the world, 32 use the term "duck" in their company or trade name, and more than 10 use both the words "duck" and "tour."

The appellate court concluded that when consumers hear the term "duck tour," they associate it primarily with a service, not a source. Thus:

> To grant Boston Duck exclusive rights to use the phrase in the Boston area would be to erect a barrier of entry into the marketplace, thereby preventing other entities, such as Super Duck, from calling their product by its name. Super Duck, as well as other potential competitors, would be placed at a significant market disadvantage.

The appellate court thus found that the phrase "duck tour" was generic in connection with the services (amphibious boat tours) offered by both parties.

Trade dress originally referred to the complete package or container in which a product was sold and that was typically discarded after purchase. Over the past two decades, however, the definition of trade dress has been expanded to include the appearance of the product itself. This expansion led to uncertainty in the legal rules that apply to protected trade dress. In the past few years, the U.S. Supreme Court has decided three cases

EXHIBIT 6.2 Once a trademark, not always a trademark

XEROX

Once a trademark, not always a trademark.

They were once proud trademarks, now they're just names. They failed to take precautions that would have helped them have a long and prosperous life.

We need your help to stay out of there. Whenever you use our name, please use it as a proper adjective in conjunction with our products and services: e.g., Xerox copiers or Xerox financial services. And never as a verb: "to Xerox" in place of "to copy," or as a noun: "Xeroxes" in place of "copies."

With your help and a precaution or two on our part, it's "Once the Xerox trademark, always the Xerox trademark."

Team Xerox. We document the world.

XEROX® is a registered trademark of XEROX CORPORATION.

Reprinted with the permission of the XEROX CORPORATION.

that delineate the parameters of trade dress protection. The cases illustrate the iterative process that the courts go through as they try to develop common law principles that fit a variety of circumstances.

In *Two Pesos, Inc. v. Taco Cabana, Inc.*,[3] a 1992 decision, the Supreme Court determined that the trade dress of a restaurant could be protected without a showing of secondary meaning if it were inherently distinctive and not merely descriptive. In a 1995 decision, *Qualitex Co. v. Jacobson Products Co.*,[4] the Supreme Court held that *color* could be protected trade dress, provided it had obtained a secondary meaning (e.g., pink for NutraSweet packages). Finally, in a 2000 decision, *Wal-Mart Stores, Inc. v. Samara Brothers, Inc.*,[5] the Supreme Court determined that trade dress that consists of the *appearance of the product* requires a showing of secondary meaning because appearance is usually not considered a means of identifying the source of a product. The Court reconciled these three cases by stating that the analysis of trade dress protection depends upon whether the asserted trade dress is considered a *package* or a *product design*—a distinction the Court acknowledged is not always easily made. Package trade dress (which apparently encompasses restaurant design of the type found in *Two Pesos*) does not require a showing of secondary meaning, but product design does.

Physical features of the product itself or its container may also be protected as a mark as long as those features are distinctive and nonfunctional. Functional features, however, must be protected, if at all, under utility patents. Companies may not use trademark law as a means of avoiding the restrictions of patent law or to obtain a monopoly on functional features (see Case Illustration 6.2).

➡️ *See Discussion Cases 6.1, 6.2.*

A single design can be protected by both trademark and design patent laws, however, provided the design meets the statutory requirements for each. Black and Decker's Dustbuster vacuum cleaner, for example, was the subject of both trademark protection and a design patent.

Some types of things cannot be registered as marks. *Scandalous or immoral marks*, which are marks that offend the conscience or moral feeling or which are shocking to the sense of decency or propriety, receive no protection. For example, the Patent and Trademark Office (PTO) denied registration of a depiction of a defecating dog for shirts.[6]

Deceptive marks also receive no protection. These are marks that either falsely indicate that the good or service has a particular characteristic or is associated with a particular person or institution or mislead consumers by incorrectly describing the good or service in a way that would be material to the average consumer (see Case Illustration 6.3).

Trademark Searches

Before a new mark is used, the proposed user should do a *trademark search* to ensure that the mark is not identical or substantially similar to a mark already in use. Trademark searches usually involve a review of the state and federal trademark registers and a review of telephone directories, magazines, and trade journals to see if the mark is in

---

[3] 505 U.S. 763 (1992).

[4] 514 U.S. 159 (1995).

[5] 529 U.S. 205 (2000).

[6] *The Greyhound Corp. v. Both Worlds, Inc.*, 6 U.S.P.Q.2d 1635 (T.T.A.B. 1988).

CASE ILLUSTRATION 6.2

THE ANTIOCH CO. v. WESTERN TRIMMING CORP., 347 F.3D 150 (6TH CIR. 2003)

FACTS The Antioch Company markets scrapbook albums under the mark "CREATIVE MEMORIES." Antioch's albums have several distinctive characteristics, including: (1) a dual strap-hinge that enables the album to lie flat when open and that facilitates the insertion of additional pages; (2) a spine cover that disguises the hinge; and (3) ribbed edges on the album pages that reinforce the page, keep them separated, and cover the staples.

A competitor, Western Trimming Corporation (Westrim), sold "knock-off" copies of Antioch's album. Westrim had begun making its copies after it had determined that Antioch's patents that potentially covered these features had expired. Antioch sued for trade dress infringement, claiming it had protected trade dress in these three features. The trial court granted summary judgment to Westrim, and Antioch appealed.

DECISION The appellate court affirmed the decision of the trial court, noting that trade dress protection does not extend to functional products: "Otherwise, 'trademark law, which seeks to promote competition by protecting a firm's reputation,' would 'instead inhibit[] legitimate competition by allowing a producer to control a useful product feature.'" Moreover, that control would exist "in perpetuity" as a form of monopoly.

To establish trade dress infringement, the plaintiff "must 'show that the allegedly infringing feature is not "functional" … and is likely to cause confusion with the product for which protection is sought.'" The appellate court agreed with the trial court's determination that the three features specified were functional, stating: "The dual strap-hinge design, spine cover, padded album cover, and reinforced pages are all components

that are essential to the use of Antioch's album and affect its quality."

Moreover, the court noted, "where the claimed trade dress is actually a *type* of product, one supplier may not monopolize the configuration to the exclusion of others." Although Antioch argued that Westrim could make other types of albums, such as a post-bound album, which would have much of the same functionality as Antioch's dual strap-hinge album, the court found that "irrelevant." As the U.S. Supreme Court has stated, "[I]f a particular design is functional, other producers do not have 'to adopt a different design simply to avoid copying it.'" Antioch's design features allowed the album to "function optimally" and met the "functional demands of scrapbook enthusiasts." In addition, by using its own distinctive logo, stickers, face sheet, etc., Westrim sufficiently signaled consumers that its albums were not made by Antioch, despite the functional similarity of the two products.

The court also rejected Antioch's argument that Westrim's admitted copying of Antioch's product was somehow wrongful:

What Antioch fails to appreciate is that "copying is not always discouraged or disfavored" and can have "salutary effects." "Copying preserves competition, which keeps downward pressure on prices and encourages innovation." As the Supreme Court has advised, "trade dress protection must subsist with the recognition that in many instances there is no prohibition against copying goods and products." Unless an intellectual property right protects a product, "competitors are free to copy at will."

Thus, the appellate court affirmed the trial court's grant of summary judgment to Westrim.

use. In addition, the PTO maintains an online database of every trademark that is pending or that has been issued.[7] Many private firms specialize in conducting trademark searches, and several private companies offer subscription access to online databases, such as Trademarkscan, that list international, federal, and/or state trademarks and/or domain names.

---

[7]See www.uspto.gov

IN RE SOUTH PARK CIGAR, INC., 82 U.S.P.Q.2D (BNA) 1507 (TTAB 2007)

FACTS South Park Cigar, Inc., located in Cincinnati, Ohio, sought to register the mark YBOR GOLD for cigars and other tobacco products. The PTO refused to register the mark on the grounds that the mark was "primarily geographically deceptively misdescriptive." To show that a mark is geographically misdescriptive, the PTO must show: "(1) the primary significance of the mark is a generally known geographic location, (2) the consuming public is likely to believe the place identified by the mark indicates the origin of the goods bearing the mark, when in fact the goods do not come from that place, and (3) the misrepresentation would be a material factor in the consumer's decision to purchase the goods." South Park Cigar, Inc., appealed the denial to the Trademark Trial and Appeal Board (TTAB).

DECISION The TTAB upheld the denial of registration, finding that all three elements had been met.

First, Ybor City is a "generally known geographic location." Ybor City is a well-known, historically Latin, neighborhood in Tampa, Florida. It is listed in major travel guides, and is found on a number of Internet sites and maps as well. The neighborhood is named after a Spanish cigar maker who arrived in 1886 via Cuba and Key West. At one time, 140 Ybor City cigar factories were producing over 250 million cigars each year. Though the cigar-making industry has declined dramatically, 10 cigar retail stores, 12 mail order cigar retailers, and 4 cigar manufacturers are still located in Ybor City, and the neighborhood is a popular entertainment district.

Second, the TTAB found that the consuming public would be likely to believe that the cigars at issue came from Ybor City, when in fact they did not. The TTAB found that "the relevant purchasing public, i.e., cigar aficionados who visit or read about Ybor City, as well as other visitors or potential visitors to Tampa and to the Ybor City area of Tampa," were likely to draw an association between Ybor City and cigars. South Park Cigars, Inc., however, is located in Ohio, and has no connection to Ybor City. South Park Cigar, Inc., argued that it intended to move its operations to Tampa and to produce its cigars in Ybor City. The TTAB rejected this argument, noting that there was no evidence in the record indicating that South Park Cigar had actually done so.

Finally, the TTAB concluded that "the association between Ybor City and applicant's cigars which is evoked (falsely) by applicant's YBOR GOLD mark would materially affect the relevant public's decision to purchase applicant's goods." Although Ybor City is now primarily known as an entertainment destination for tourists and locals, cigars remain a "principal product" of Ybor City, "in view of the dense concentration of cigar retailers and manufacturers located within its confines." Although the TTAB recognized that Ybor City was no longer "the cigar capital of the world," the area's "emphasis on and celebration of its cigar culture, both present and historical, remains a significant and indeed prominent feature of the area's appeal." Thus, the TTAB concluded that purchasers were likely to mistakenly assume that cigars sold under the YBOR GOLD mark had some connection to Ybor City, and that assumption would be material to the consumer's decision to purchase cigars.

Thus, South Park Cigar, Inc., was denied registration of the mark "YBOR GOLD" for its cigars.

If the proposed user has a particular domain name in mind to go along with the mark, it would be wise to search the websites of the domain name registration companies to determine if the domain name is available. If not, the proposed user may wish to select a different mark and corresponding domain name.

Creation and Ownership of the Mark

Creation of the Mark To create a mark, the user must be the first to use it in trade and must continue to use it thereafter. This requires that the mark be physically attached to the goods, their labels or containers, and advertising and that the goods then be sold or distributed. For services, the mark must be used or displayed in the course of selling or advertising the services.

What happens if two persons use the same mark? For marks that are inherently distinctive, the first to use the mark (the *senior user*) will have priority in the mark. The exception is where the second to use the mark (the *junior user*) in good faith establishes a strong consumer identification with the mark in a separate geographic area. The junior user will have priority in that (but no other) geographic area. If the senior user has federally registered the mark, however, the senior user will have nationwide rights to the mark in every area in which it is not already in use at the time the senior user began using it.

Registration of the Mark   A mark user is permitted (but not required) to place its mark on the federal trademark register (the Principal Register) provided: (1) the mark is distinctive, and (2) the mark is in use in commerce across state, territorial, or international lines. If the mark is used only on a local service business, such as a dance studio, it probably will not qualify for federal registration unless the user can show that the business has a significant number of interstate or international customers.

Placement on the Principal Register provides many legal advantages:

1. it provides constructive notice nationwide of the user's claim to the mark (thus preventing later users from claiming that they were using the mark in good faith);
2. it establishes evidence of the registrant's ownership of the mark;
3. it allows the owner to sue in federal (rather than state) court in the event of infringement or dilution;
4. it makes the registrant's right to the mark virtually (though not absolutely) incontestable after five years of continuous use;
5. it enables the registrant to seek assistance from the U.S. Customs Service in preventing importation into the United States of articles bearing an infringing mark;
6. it can provide a basis for obtaining registration in foreign countries; and
7. it allows the registrant to obtain rights in the mark in a larger geographic area than that allowed under common law (i.e., exclusive nationwide ownership except in areas where the mark is already in use by prior owners who did not register).

Application for Registration   The Lanham Act provides for two different types of registration on the Principal Register.[8] If the mark has already been used in trade, the user may file a *use* application with the PTO. One application can cover goods and services in several product and/or service categories. The applicant must select the classes to be included in the application and must pay a separate fee for each class so specified. Although the fees for obtaining a trademark are relatively modest (the current fee for an electronic application for registration is $325[9]), the fees can add up rapidly if the applicant files for several product and/or service categories. As a practical matter, however, the applicant should file as broad an application as possible so as to protect its mark from infringement by use in an unclaimed class.

The application is reviewed by an examiner. If the examiner approves the application, the mark is published in the *Official Gazette*. People who feel that they may be injured by the registration (for example, because the mark is confusingly similar to their own) may file an opposition challenging the registration. If the PTO decides that registration is appropriate, it issues a certificate of registration.

---

[8]Application forms are available on the Web and can be filed electronically or can be downloaded, filled out, and mailed in. See www.uspto.gov

[9]For a complete and current fee schedule, see www.uspto.gov

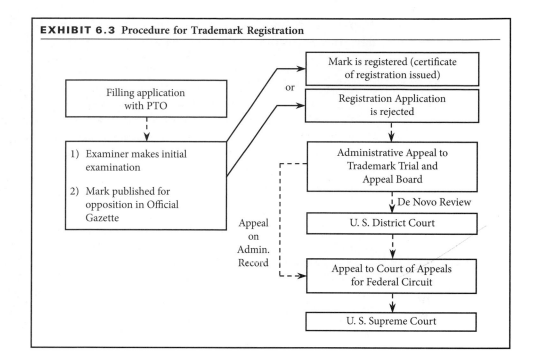

EXHIBIT 6.3 Procedure for Trademark Registration

A registration is good for 10 years, although the mark owner must file an affidavit in the sixth year showing that the mark is still in use. The registration may be renewed for additional 10-year periods as long as the mark remains in commercial use. Realize that *registration* of the mark is separate from *ownership* of the mark. The mark owner owns the mark as long as the mark remains in commercial use. While registration is a wise idea because of the many benefits it confers, it is not legally required.

If the PTO examiner rejects the registration application, the applicant may appeal to the Trademark Trial and Appeal Board. If the applicant loses before the Board, the applicant may appeal on the administrative record to the U.S. Court of Appeals for the Federal Circuit (CAFC) or *de novo* to the U.S. District Court (see Exhibit 6.3).

If the applicant has not yet used the mark in trade, but has a bona fide intent to do so in the near future, the applicant may file an *intent to use* application. The PTO makes an initial examination of the application and publishes it for opposition in the *Official Gazette*. The applicant then has six months to begin actual use of the mark. (This time period can be extended up to two and one-half years upon a showing of good cause.) When the applicant makes the first use of the mark in trade, the applicant must file a statement of use with the PTO. The PTO then conducts a second examination. If the mark is deemed acceptable, it is then placed on the Principal Register.

Cancellation of a Mark During the first five years of registration, a person who believes herself to be injured by a registration may petition the PTO to cancel it. After five years, the mark can be challenged on only very limited grounds, such as the mark has become generic or has been abandoned or the mark was obtained through fraud. The mark *cannot* be challenged at this point on the grounds that it is not inherently distinctive and lacks secondary meaning, that it is confusingly similar to a more senior mark, or that it is functional.

Notice   Under the Lanham Act, registrants must provide notice of the registration by displaying the mark with the following words or symbol:

"Registered in U.S. Patent and Trademark Office" *or*
"Reg. U.S. Pat. & Tm. Off." *or*
®

What, then, does the familiar ™ or ℠ symbol mean? It indicates that the user is using the word, phrase, symbol, or design as a trade or service mark but has not federally registered it. Such marks may still receive some protection under state or federal trademark law, but they do not receive the heightened protection given to federally registered marks.

If the registrant fails to provide proper notice of the registration, the registrant will be able to recover profits and damages in the event of infringement only if the registrant can prove that the defendant had *actual* notice of the registration. This can be very difficult to prove in many instances, so providing proper registration notice is an important preventative measure for mark owners to take.

Supplemental and State Registers   In addition to the Principal Register, the Lanham Act creates a *Supplemental Register*, which is used for marks that are not distinctive enough to be placed on the Principal Register. Most marks used to distinguish goods or services can be placed on the Supplemental Register, including descriptive and geographical terms and surnames. Generic marks may not be placed on the Supplemental Register, however, nor may immoral, deceptive, or scandalous marks.

Generally, the applicant should apply to the Principal Register first and apply to the Supplemental Register only if that application is denied. Although placement on the Supplemental Register confers few legal benefits, it often deters others from making use of an identical or substantially similar mark. In particular, marks that appear on the Supplemental Register may display the ® symbol or "Reg. U.S. Pat. Off." abbreviation, which is likely to discourage potential infringers. In addition, the PTO will not register a junior mark that is identical to a mark found on the Supplemental Register and used on closely related goods or services. Placement on the Supplemental Register for five years helps establish secondary meaning for the mark, which qualifies the mark for the Principal Register and all of the greater legal benefits that go along with such placement. Thus, marks can move from the Supplemental Register to the Principal Register as they gain distinctiveness over time.

In addition, every state has its own registration system. States do not provide for intent-to-use registration; thus, the mark must be in use before it can be registered with any state. State registration is particularly important to those mark users whose marks are not in interstate or international use and thus cannot be placed on the federal register.

What are the benefits of state registration to a mark owner whose mark already appears on the Principal Register? State registration provides additional notice to junior users or potential infringers and, in a few states, provides some benefits in the event of successful litigation (e.g., recovery of attorneys fees or punitive damages). In addition, mark owners who register at both the state and federal levels have a choice of remedies and courts in which to sue. Thus, many mark owners opt to place their marks on both the federal and state registers.

U.S. Customs Service Assistance

Under the U.S. Customs Act, a mark owner who has registered its mark on the Principal Register or a copyright owner who has registered its work with the Copyright Office may record that mark or copyright with the U.S. Customs Service, listing any authorized importers or sources of the goods. This record is placed on a national database that is available to all customs offices in every U.S. port of entry.

The customs inspectors are authorized to seize imported products that infringe on U.S. marks or copyrights. To get full benefit of these provisions, however, mark owners (or copyright owners) must monitor the importation of goods carefully themselves. Because of the sheer volume of imports entering the United States on a daily basis, the Customs Service responds most often to tips from owners rather than conducting its own independent investigations. Infringing products are destroyed at the importer's expense. If the counterfeit mark can be removed or obliterated without destroying the goods or if the mark owner agrees, the goods may be donated to a charitable organization. The mark owner can also waive its right to object to the infringing goods and allow the goods to be released to the importer.

If the Customs Service is not certain whether the goods involved infringe on U.S. marks or copyrights, it can detain the shipment. The U.S. mark or copyright owner has 30 days in which to file a Petition for Exclusion and a bond in an amount determined by the U.S. Customs Office. The U.S. Customs Headquarters then determines whether the goods are infringing. If so, the bond is returned to the mark or copyright owner and the goods are destroyed. If not, the goods are released for import and the importer receives the full amount of the bond to compensate it for its losses.

In FY 2008, the Customs Service seized almost 15,000 shipments with intellectual property rights violations with a value in excess of $272 million. Eighty-one percent of total domestic value seized originated in China.[10]

Trademark Infringement and Dilution

Generally, mark owners are concerned with two types of potential injury. First, if the plaintiff and the defendant are direct competitors, the defendant's use of an identical or substantially similar mark may confuse consumers such that consumers purchase the defendant's goods or services when, in fact, they actually intended to buy the plaintiff's. This is *trademark infringement*. Second, even if the plaintiff and defendant are not in direct competition and even if customers are not confused by the use of identical or substantially similar marks, the defendant's use of the identical or similar mark may diminish the strength of the plaintiff's mark by tarnishing the reputation of the plaintiff's mark or by blurring the distinctiveness of the plaintiff's mark. This is *trademark dilution*.

Infringement

Trademark infringement occurs when one party (the junior user) uses a trademark (the junior mark) that is identical or substantially similar to the existing mark (the senior mark) of another user (the senior user) on competing goods or services, such that prospective purchasers are likely to be confused, mistaken, or deceived as to the identity or source of the goods or services involved. Both the federal Lanham Act and the state law of every state provide a cause of action for trademark infringement. In order to establish trademark infringement, the plaintiff must show:

1. that the mark is valid (federally registered marks are presumed valid);
2. that the plaintiff is the senior user of the mark; and
3. that the junior user's use of the mark creates a *likelihood of confusion* in the minds of the purchasers of the product or service in question.

This last factor examines whether the defendant's use of its mark is likely to cause an appreciable number of consumers to be confused about the source, affiliation, or sponsorship of goods or services.

---

[10]See www.cbp.gov for additional information and statistics.

In determining whether a likelihood of confusion exists, the courts generally examine several factors, such as:

1. the strength of the plaintiff's mark;
2. the similarity between the two marks (e.g., appearance, sound, meaning);
3. the similarity of the products involved;
4. the likelihood that the plaintiff will enter the defendant's market (even if the plaintiff is not currently in the defendant's market, the court will consider how likely it is that the plaintiff may want to enter that market in the future);
5. the extent of actual consumer confusion;
6. the defendant's lack of good faith in adopting the mark;
7. the quality of the defendant's product; and
8. the sophistication of the buyers (the more sophisticated the consumers or the more expensive the goods or services, the less likely it is that consumers will be misled).[11]

No factor is considered determinative, and the courts may weigh the factors differently depending upon the facts of the case before them.

Inherent within the notion of a likelihood of confusion is the requirement that the goods or services involved be similar. Trademark infringement is unlikely, for example, where the mark "Mayflower" is used by both a sailboat company and a moving company, because the typical consumer would not confuse the two companies and their products or services.[12]

A defendant can be held liable for *contributory infringement* if he intentionally suggests that another person infringe upon a mark and the other person actually does so. For example, suppose that the defendant manufactures goods that are identical to the plaintiff's goods and sells them to retailers, suggesting to the retailers that they sell these as the plaintiff's goods to customers who ask for the plaintiff's goods by name. If a retailer actually does so, the retailer is liable for trademark infringement and the defendant is liable for contributory infringement. A defendant can also be held liable for contributory infringement if the defendant sells the goods to a buyer knowing that the buyer will use the goods in direct infringement of the plaintiff's mark (see Case Illustration 6.4).

◆ *See Discussion Case 6.4.*

Defenses to an Infringement Action   A defendant can raise *fair use* as a defense to an allegation of mark infringement. For example, if the plaintiff uses her surname as a mark for her product, the plaintiff is not permitted to assert a monopoly in that mark (unless the mark has acquired secondary meaning). The defendant is permitted to make "fair use" of the surname in selling his own goods. Fair use also encompasses comparative advertising, parodies involving the mark, journalistic uses of the mark, and use of the mark to describe comparability of aftermarket goods (see Case Illustration 6.5).

To determine whether a particular use is "fair," the courts consider: (1) the manner in which the defendant used the mark; (2) whether the defendant is acting in good faith; and (3) whether the defendant's use is likely to confuse consumers. The last factor is the most important. While the courts may tolerate a small degree of consumer confusion if the other elements of fair use are present, if substantial confusion exists, there can be no fair use.

---

[11]These factors were articulated by the U.S. Court of Appeals for the Second Circuit in *Polaroid Corp. v. Polarad Electronics Corp.*, 287 F.2d 492, 495 (2d Cir. 1961). Other courts of appeals use similar tests.

[12]See *Aero Mayflower Transit Co. v. Snark Prods., Inc.*, 190 U.S.P.Q. 100, 106 (T.T.A.B. 1976).

CASE ILLUSTRATION 6.4

TIFFANY (NJ) INC. v. EBAY, INC.,
576 F. SUPP. 2D 463 (S.D. N.Y. 2008)

FACTS Tiffany, "the famous jeweler with the coveted blue boxes," sued eBay, alleging that hundreds of thousands of counterfeit Tiffany silver jewelry items were offered for sale on eBay from 2003 to 2006. Tiffany sought to hold eBay liable for direct and contributory trademark infringement, unfair competition, false advertising, and direct and contributory trademark dilution, on the grounds that eBay facilitated and allowed these counterfeit items to be sold on its website.

DECISION After holding a bench trial, the court determined that Tiffany had failed to carry its burden of proof on all of these claims, and entered judgment for eBay. The court summarized the positions of the parties as follows:

> Tiffany acknowledges that individual sellers, rather than eBay, are responsible for listing and selling counterfeit Tiffany items. Nevertheless, Tiffany argues that eBay was on notice that a problem existed and accordingly, that eBay had the obligation to investigate and control the illegal activities of these sellers—specifically, by preemptively refusing to post any listing offering five or more Tiffany items and by immediately suspending sellers upon learning of Tiffany's belief that the seller had engaged in potentially infringing activity. In response, eBay contends that it is Tiffany's burden, not eBay's, to monitor the eBay website for counterfeits and to bring counterfeits to eBay's attention. eBay claims that in practice, when potentially infringing listings were reported to eBay, eBay immediately removed the offending listings. It is clear that Tiffany and eBay alike have an interest in eliminating counterfeit Tiffany merchandise from eBay—Tiffany to protect its famous brand name, and eBay to preserve the reputation of its website as a safe place to do business. Accordingly, the heart of this dispute is not whether counterfeit Tiffany jewelry should flourish on eBay, but rather, who should bear the burden of policing Tiffany's valuable trademarks in Internet commerce.

With regard to the contributory infringement claim, specifically, the court found that the burden of policing the trademarks at issue should fall on Tiffany, the trademark holder:

> [T]he Court finds that eBay is not liable for contributory trademark infringement. In determining whether eBay is liable, the standard is not whether eBay could reasonably anticipate possible infringement, but rather whether eBay continued to supply its services to sellers when it knew or had reason to know of infringement by those sellers .... Here, when Tiffany put eBay on notice of specific items that Tiffany believed to be infringing, eBay immediately removed those listings. eBay refused, however, to monitor its website and preemptively remove listings of Tiffany jewelry before the listings became public. The law does not impose liability for contributory trademark infringement on eBay for its refusal to take such preemptive steps in light of eBay's "reasonable anticipation" or generalized knowledge that counterfeit goods might be sold on its website. Quite simply, the law demands more specific knowledge as to which items are infringing and which seller is listing those items before requiring eBay to take action.

> The result of the application of this legal standard is that Tiffany must ultimately bear the burden of protecting its trademark. Policymakers may yet decide that the law as it stands is inadequate to protect rights owners in light of the increasing scope of Internet commerce and the concomitant rise in potential trademark infringement. Nevertheless, under the law as it currently stands, it does not matter whether eBay or Tiffany could more efficiently bear the burden of policing the eBay website for Tiffany counterfeits—an open question left unresolved by this trial. Instead, the issue is whether eBay continued to provide its website to sellers when eBay knew or had reason to know that those sellers were using the website to traffic in counterfeit Tiffany jewelry. The Court finds that when eBay possessed the requisite knowledge, it took appropriate steps to remove listings and suspend service. Under these circumstances, the Court declines to impose liability for contributory trademark infringement.

CASE ILLUSTRATION 6.5

JORDACHE ENTERPRISES, INC. v. HOGG WYLD, LTD., 625 F. SUPP. 48 (D. N.M. 1985), AFF'D, 828 F.2D 1482 (10TH CIR. 1987)

FACTS Jordache Enterprises, Inc., manufactured and licensed the manufacture of a line of apparel, including designer blue jeans, under the mark *Jordache*. In 1984, Jordache sold 20 million pairs of Jordache jeans, with gross sales of $500 million and advertising expenses of $30 million. Hogg Wyld, Ltd. marketed large-size designer blue jeans under the mark Lardashe. In 1984 (its first year of operation), Hogg Wyld sold approximately 1,300 pairs of jeans and did not advertise.

The Jordache mark consisted of the word "Jordache" in block letters superimposed over a drawing of a horse's head. The Lardashe mark consisted of the name "Lardashe" stitched in script lettering on the rear pocket of the jeans, an inverted-heart-shaped embroidered design on the pocket, and an embroidered appliqué of a pig's head and feet sewn onto the fabric so that the pig appeared to be peering out of the top of the pocket.

Jordache sued Hogg Wyld for trademark infringement.

DECISION Hogg Wyld argued that it had chosen the "Lardashe" name as a more polite variant of a childhood nickname used by one of its founders, and that it had not intended any similarity with the Jordache mark. The court did not believe Hogg Wyld's testimony on this issue, noting that other names considered and rejected by Hogg Wyld included "Calvin Swine," "Sow-soon," and "Horse's ashe."

However, the court also found that Hogg Wyld's "intent was to employ a name that, to some extent parodied or played upon the established trademark Jordache." Parodies are permitted under trademark law where the junior mark is used only for humorous purposes and not to mislead or confuse the consumer. "That the defendant's joke mark calls the plaintiff's mark to mind is necessary for there to be a humorous parody at all .... But the requirement of trademark law is that a likely source of confusion of source, sponsorship or affiliation be proven, which is not the same things as a 'right' not to be made fun of."

Thus, the court found, because the Lardashe mark was an obvious parody of the Jordache mark, and because the two marks created "a very different concept image, and 'feel'," the Lardashe mark did not confuse consumers as to source, affiliation, or sponsorship, and so did not infringe.

◆ *See Discussion Case 6.3.*

A defendant can also raise *abandonment* of a mark as a defense. Under the Lanham Act, abandonment occurs when the registrant discontinues its use throughout the United States and has no intent to resume the use within the reasonably foreseeable future. Nonuse of a mark for three consecutive years is evidence of abandonment. Abandonment also occurs when the registrant engages in acts that cause the mark to lose its significance, such as licensing others to use the mark without adequately supervising such use or failing to protest the unauthorized use of the mark by other parties.

Remedies for Infringement   There are two basic types of remedies for trademark infringement: (1) injunctions and (2) damages. Courts routinely grant *injunctions* in the trademark area. Both *preliminary* and *permanent injunctions* are available.

In addition, a prevailing plaintiff may recover *actual damages*. A plaintiff may suffer lost sales and injury to its reputation and goodwill as a result of the defendant's infringement. The plaintiff may recover these losses, but they can be difficult to prove and quantify. Therefore, the Lanham Act provides that courts can award up to *treble damages*, if necessary, to adequately compensate the plaintiff. As a practical matter, however, courts are reluctant to do so in the absence of willful behavior by the defendant.

The plaintiff may also recover the *profits* the defendant made from the infringing activity. In addition, the Lanham Act allows the court to award reasonable *attorneys fees* to the prevailing party in "exceptional" cases. Generally, this means that the infringement must have been malicious, fraudulent, deliberate, or willful.

◆ *See Discussion Case 6.4.*

Gray Markets/Parallel Importation *Gray markets* (also called *parallel importation*) involve goods that are produced and sold for overseas markets but which are then imported (or reimported) into the United States. The result is a multibillion-dollar-a-year industry that angers and frustrates U.S. manufacturers and diminishes their profits.

The gray market exists because U.S. manufacturers routinely sell consumer goods at deep discounts (often through distributors) in foreign markets. The discounts may reflect the fact that the foreign distributor, rather than the U.S. manufacturer, is incurring the foreign marketing and advertising costs or may simply reflect the U.S. manufacturer's business strategy in attempting to expand its foreign markets. The price difference may also be an unintended consequence of currency fluctuations. The price differential is often large enough that a distributor can then reimport the goods to the United States at a price that undercuts the domestic market.

The existence of gray markets raises a number of competing policy concerns. Gray marketeers argue that their activities are legal because the goods they sell are genuine and bear lawful trademarks. Thus, they contend, consumers are not confused as to the source or origin of their goods. Consumer advocates argue that the gray market is a good thing because it allows consumers to purchase goods at a lower cost, thus preventing price gouging by manufacturers. Manufacturers' groups, on the other hand, complain that gray marketeers are able to reap the benefits of the manufacturers' expensive marketing and advertising campaigns without incurring any of the accompanying costs. Companies that hold exclusive rights to distribute and sell products in the United States are also upset at facing unanticipated competition from importers and sellers of gray market goods.

Generally, the importation and sale of gray market goods is not considered infringement of a U.S. mark if the imported goods are identical to the goods sold by the U.S. registrant (e.g., are of the same grade and quality, contain the same ingredients or components, and carry the same warranties and service commitments). Under the "material differences" test, however, if the imported goods are materially different in even one respect from goods produced for the domestic market, the importation and sale of the goods will infringe the U.S. mark. This test was originally articulated in *Original Appalachian Artworks, Inc. v. Granada Electronics, Inc.*[13] The defendant had imported gray market Cabbage Patch Kids dolls that had been intended for sale in Spain. Although the dolls bore the plaintiff's trademark, their "birth certificates" and "adoption papers" were in Spanish and could not be processed by the plaintiff's fulfillment houses in the United States. Thus, the buyers of the dolls could not participate in the "adoption process" that was critical to the dolls' commercial success. The Second Circuit found that this material difference created customer confusion over the source of the goods and diminished the plaintiff's goodwill. The dolls thus infringed on the plaintiff's U.S. trademark.

The material differences test recognizes that when the imported goods are identical to the U.S. goods and bear the same mark, customers will not be confused as to the source or origin of the goods.[14] However, where there is even one "material" difference (defined as a difference that consumers would likely consider in making their purchasing decision), customer confusion is likely and the U.S. trademark holder's goodwill is diminished. Because manufacturers often alter products to satisfy specific preferences in different national markets, such differences are likely to exist in many, though not all, instances.

---

[13]816 F.2d 68 (2d Cir. 1987).

[14]Courts have thus rejected trademark infringement claims where the gray market goods were identical to the domestic goods. See *NEC Electronics v. CAL Circuit Abco*, 810 F.2d 1506 (9th Cir. 1987); *Weil Ceramics & Glass, Inc. v. Dash*, 878 F.2d 659 (3d Cir. 1989).

Under the U.S. Customs Service's so-called *Lever* Rule, the U.S. trademark owner can restrict the importation of certain gray market goods that bear genuine trademarks if the goods are identical or substantially indistinguishable from those appearing on authorized goods so as to cause customer confusion.[15] To restrict the importation of the gray market goods, however, the U.S. mark holder must submit an application to Customs that describes the physical and material differences between the gray market goods and the domestic goods.

If the importer of the goods can show that the imported goods are identical to the domestic goods, the Customs Service cannot detain the imported goods. In addition, the importer can exempt the goods from *Lever* Rule protection by attaching a tag or label that states: "This product is not a product authorized by the United States trademark owner for importation and is physically and materially different from the authorized product." The importer must place the label in close proximity to the trademark in its most prominent location on the article itself or its retail package.

In recent years, plaintiffs have also turned to copyright law for protection from gray marketeers. Many gray market items, such as books, videos, and CDs, are both copyrighted and trademarked. Even where the product itself is not copyrighted, its label, manual, or instructions may be. Analysts originally thought that copyright law would provide more protection to the U.S. registrants. In 1998, however, the U.S. Supreme Court issued a decision that cast doubt upon the amount of copyright protection available in this area, *Quality King Distributors, Inc. v. L'Anza Research Int'l, Inc.* (see Case Illustration 6.6). In effect, the *L'Anza Research* Court indicated that gray market issues should be dealt with in the political and legislative arenas, not in the courts.

CASE ILLUSTRATION 6.6

QUALITY KING DISTRIBUTORS, INC. v. L'ANZA RESEARCH INT'L, INC., 523 U.S. 135 (1998)

FACTS L'Anza Research International, a U.S. manufacturer of hair products, limited its domestic sales to distributors who agreed to sell only to authorized retailers within limited geographic areas. L'Anza promoted its domestic sales with extensive advertising and special retailer training. L'Anza Research sold its shampoo to foreign distributors for 35 percent to 40 percent less than in the United States, but did not engage in comparable advertising or promotion.

L'Anza sold the shampoo at issue to a distributor in the United Kingdom, who sold it to a distributor in Malta, who sold it to Quality King Distributors, Inc. Quality King imported the shampoo for resale in the United States without L'Anza's permission and sold it at a discount to unauthorized retailers.

L'Anza held a copyright on the labels placed on the packaging. L'Anza did not argue that anyone had made unauthorized copies of the label but rather argued that the domestic resales of the containers containing the labels violated its exclusive right to distribute copies of its labels. The Copyright Act makes unauthorized importation of copyrighted works illegal.

L'Anza sued Quality King for violation of its exclusive right to distribute its copyrighted materials. The trial court entered summary judgment for L'Anza. The Ninth Circuit affirmed. Quality King appealed to the Supreme Court.

DECISION The Supreme Court reversed. It found that under the "first sale" doctrine, the copyright owner's exclusive right to sell a work stops with the first sale of that work. The Court stated: "Once the copyright owner places a copyrighted item in the stream of commerce by selling it, he has exhausted his statutory right to control its distribution." Thus, once L'Anza sold the shampoo bottles to the first distributor, L'Anza lost the right to control further distribution of the labels.

---

[15]19 C.F.R. § 133.23. The Rule implements the decision in *Lever Bros. Co. v. United States,* 981 F.2d 1330 (Fed. Cir. 1993).

So what can a manufacturer do to avoid the gray market problem? Unfortunately, options are limited. The manufacturer could simply not export its goods. That option is obviously unappealing to most businesses because it generally results in smaller markets and reduced profits. Companies can prohibit reimportation in their sales contracts (although such clauses can be hard to enforce). They can also label their products in the foreign language (thus making them harder to reimport and sell in the U.S. market) or can incorporate some other form of "material difference" in products manufactured for export.

Counterfeiting   Counterfeiting involves the intentional, knowing use of a false mark that is identical or substantially similar to a registered mark on goods or services of the same type.[16] A 2007 study by the Organization for Economic Co-operation and Development (OECD) estimated that the annual value of international physical trade in counterfeited consumer goods was $200 billion.[17] Counterfeiting is considered to be a particularly egregious form of trademark infringement, and the courts are quick to sanction behavior they find inappropriate. For example, in *Rolex Watch, U.S.A. v. Michel Co.*,[18] the Ninth Circuit ruled that a jeweler who had sold used Rolex watches that had been repaired or customized with non-Rolex parts without removing the original Rolex marks had engaged in counterfeiting.

Federal law provides special remedies for counterfeiting, including recovery of attorney fees, treble damages, and seizure of the offending goods. In addition, the federal statutes provide for both civil and criminal penalties for counterfeiting, including fines of up to $15 million, and prison terms of up to 20 years.[19] The Prioritizing Resources and Organization for Intellectual Property Act of 2008 (the PRO-IP Act) enhanced statutory damages for counterfeiting. Under the PRO-IP Act, treble damages are now available against not only violators who intentionally use a counterfeit mark, but also those who supply goods or services necessary for commission of a counterfeiting violation, if the provider intended that the goods or services be put to such a use. It also raises the cap on statutory damages in trademark infringement cases to a minimum of $1,000 or a maximum of $200,000 per mark; the maximum statutory damage award for willful violations is now $2 million per mark. In addition, the PRO-IP Act provides for not only forfeiture of the infringing articles, but also forfeiture of any property used to facilitate the counterfeiting and any property derived from such counterfeiting.

The line between traditional trademark infringement and counterfeiting is often blurry. If a manufacturer puts a false "Rolex" mark on a watch and markets it as a real "Rolex," the manufacturer has engaged in counterfeiting. If the manufacturer puts a "Polex" mark on the watch, the manufacturer has engaged in infringement (or possibly dilution).

Dilution

Dilution occurs when a company uses a mark that is identical or substantially similar to a "famous" mark. The concern here is *not* that the consumer might be misled (that is an infringement notion) but that the value of the mark to the owner might be diminished because consumers will no longer associate the mark exclusively with the original user.

---

[16]For general information on counterfeiting, see the website of the International AntiCounterfeiting Coalition, at www.iacc.org

[17]See OECD, *The Economic Impact of Counterfeiting and Piracy*, 2007, at p. 15, *available at* www.oecd.org/dataoecd/13/12/38707619.pdf. This figure excludes both domestic and digital counterfeited or pirated goods.

[18]179 F.3d 704 (9th Cir. 1999).

[19]18 U.S.C. § 2320.

Thus, unlike trademark infringement law, dilution law's primary focus is not the consumer but the value of the trademark to the mark owner.

Suppose, for example, that an unauthorized Kodak piano is sold in the marketplace. If consumers saw the piano and began thinking that Eastman Kodak Co. now sells musical instruments (or licenses another to do so under its mark), Eastman Kodak could sue for trademark infringement. If consumers recognized that Eastman Kodak was not in the piano business, but the presence of the Kodak piano led consumers to no longer exclusively associate the mark with Eastman Kodak and its photographic supplies (even though the consumers recognized the independent existence of the two separate entities using the mark), Eastman Kodak could sue for dilution.[20]

Until 1996, dilution was only a state law action. Although over one-half of the states have dilution statutes, these state laws historically provided little relief to injured mark owners. Congress determined that a federal cause of action was necessary to provide protection to distinctive or well-known marks, which are generally used nationwide.

The Federal Trademark Dilution Act of 1995[21] created a federal cause of action for trademark dilution. We have seen a rapid increase in the number of dilution actions brought since this statute was passed. The federal Act did not preempt state law, so plaintiffs today may sue both under the Dilution Act and under any applicable state statute as well. This Act was amended by the Trademark Dilution Revision Act (TDRA) in 2006.

The Dilution Act defines "dilution by blurring" as an "association arising from the similarity between a mark or trade name and a famous mark that impairs the distinctiveness of the famous mark."[22] "Dilution by tarnishment" is defined as "association arising from the similarity between a mark or trade name and a famous mark that harms the reputation of the famous mark."[23]

Under the 2006 TDRA, "the owner of a famous mark that is distinctive, inherently or through acquired distinctiveness" may obtain an injunction against a junior user who uses a mark likely to cause blurring or tarnishment of that famous mark, "regardless of the presence or absence of actual or likely confusion, of competition, or of actual economic injury."[24] A junior user is one who uses a mark similar or identical to the mark that has already become famous. Unlike trademark infringement, dilution law does not require that the goods or services be similar or competing, nor does it require the plaintiff to show that customers may be confused or deceived by the use of the junior mark.

To recover for dilution, the plaintiff must first show that its mark is "famous." The key purpose of dilution statutes, whether state or federal, is to protect a mark's "selling power." Weak or new marks have no such selling power to be protected and therefore cannot be diluted. Although there is no list of "famous marks" that one can turn to, the Act defines a mark as famous "if it is widely recognized by the general consuming public of the United States as a designation of source of the goods or services of the mark's owner." In making this determination, the court can consider "all relevant factors," including:

1. the duration, extent and geographic reach of advertising and publicity of the mark, whether advertised or publicized by the owner or third parties;

[20]See H.R. Rep No. 104-374 at 3 (1995).
[21]15 U.S.C. § 1125 (c).
[22]15 U.S.C § 1125(c)(2)(B).
[23]15 U.S.C. § 1125(c)(2)(C).
[24]15 U.S.C. § 1125(c)(1).

2. the amount, volume, and geographic extent of sales of goods or services offered under the mark;
3. the extent of actual recognition of the mark; and
4. whether the mark [was registered under federal law].[25]

As noted above, there are two forms of dilution actions: (1) tarnishment and (2) blurring. Although blurring is the more common type of dilution action brought, plaintiffs are generally more likely to win in tarnishment cases than they are in blurring cases.

◆ *See Discussion Case 6.3.*

Tarnishment   *Tarnishment* occurs when a junior user uses the senior user's mark or a similar mark in a manner that could hurt the reputation of the senior user's mark. Tarnishment typically involves the use of a famous mark on products of shoddy quality or the use of the mark in an unwholesome or unsavory context (usually involving sexual, obscene, or illegal activity). Examples of cases where the courts have issued preliminary injunctions prohibiting uses that tarnish a senior mark include the use of "Candyland" to identify a sexually explicit Internet site,[26] the use of "Buttwiser" on T-shirts,[27] and the use of "Adultsrus.com" for an Internet site on which sexual devices were sold.[28]

Blurring   *Blurring* occurs when a famous mark (or one very similar to it) is used in connection with the noncompeting goods or services of another, resulting in a "whittling away" of the senior mark's value over time as it is used in connection with the goods or services of another. Although consumers are not confused by the different uses of the mark, the concern is that over time they will cease to associate the mark exclusively with the mark owner's goods or services.

The TDRA instructs a court to consider "all relevant factors" in evaluating whether dilution by blurring has occurred, including the following six specific factors:

1. the degree of similarity between the mark or trade name and the famous mark;
2. the degree of inherent or acquired distinctiveness of the famous mark;
3. the extent to which the owner of the famous mark is engaging in substantially exclusive use of the mark;
4. the degree of recognition of the famous mark;
5. whether the user of the mark or trade name intended to create an association with the famous mark; and
6. any actual association between the mark or trade name and the famous mark.[29]

Defenses to Dilution Actions   Certain types of uses are permitted under the federal Dilution Act, including fair use of the mark in comparative advertising, noncommercial use of the mark, parody, and all forms of news reporting and commentary.

◆ *See Discussion Case 6.3.*

Remedies Under the Dilution Act   The remedies provided by the act are extensive. A plaintiff whose famous mark has been diluted is entitled to a *preliminary* and/or

---

[25]15 U.S.C. § 1125(c)(2)(A).

[26]*Hasbro, Inc. v. Internet Entertainment Group, Ltd.,* 40 U.S.P.Q.2d 1479 (W.D. Wash. 1996). "CANDY LAND" is a registered mark for children's toys.

[27]*Anheuser-Busch, Inc. v. Andy's Sportswear, Inc.,* 40 U.S.P.Q.2d 1542 (N.D. Cal. 1996).

[28]*Toys "R" Us, Inc. v. Akkaoui,* 40 U.S.P.Q.2d 1836 (N.D. Cal. 1996).

[29]15 U.S.C. § 1125 (c)(2)(B).

permanent injunction against the junior user's commercial use of the mark. If the plaintiff can show that the offending party acted willfully, it may be entitled to additional remedies, including an *accounting of profits, actual damages, attorneys fees*, and an order requiring *destruction* of the offending items.

International Trademark Law Issues

When a company is considering expansion abroad, it is essential that the company consider its trademark strategy *before* it actually enters the foreign market. The company's ability to protect and use its chosen mark depends upon the laws of the countries in which it is operating. Thus, local legal counsel is almost always needed.

The company's first step should be to conduct a trademark search to see if the mark is available in other countries. If the mark is not available or not viable in the foreign market, the company needs to choose a different mark. In some countries, for example, letters and/or numbers may not be registered as marks.

Moreover, while in the United States the first to *use* the mark generally obtains the rights to it, in most other countries, the first to *register* receives the mark. As a result, many companies take the defensive maneuver of filing for marks even in countries where they have no immediate intention of operating, in order to stop trademark piracy. The applicant typically must use the mark within that country within a certain time period (usually three to five years) or lose the mark. As markets continue to globalize, however, countries are becoming more sympathetic to the owners of well-known marks. For example, Kmart won the right to protect its mark in Jamaica, even though Kmart, which had registered its marks in Jamaica, was not actually doing business there. The court recognized that with the advent of international commercial technology and travel, greater protection of marks is required.[30]

Generally, the company must file for separate trademark protection in each country in which it wants to claim the mark. There are a few exceptions to the general rule that mark registrations must be filed on a country-by-country basis. For example, a single Benelux registration may be obtained for Belgium, the Netherlands, and Luxembourg. The European Union allows a single application to be made to the Office of Harmonization of the Internal Market for a trademark that is good in all EU member countries. To qualify for a Community trademark, the trademark must be acceptable to all member countries. If the mark does not qualify for Community trademark status, the applicant can still file separate national registration applications in the various member countries.

Finally, the Protocol Relating to the Madrid Agreement Concerning the International Registration of Trademarks allows an applicant to file an international application automatically in any of the member countries upon registration of the mark in the home country. Each country has the right to refuse registration of the mark, however. As of 2009, there were 78 parties to the Protocol, including the United States.[31] International registration of trademarks under the Madrid Protocol usually results in lower filing fees and a streamlined process that offers significant savings over country-by-country filings.

Trademark registrations are potentially renewable forever in most countries. The initial term of the registration is generally 10 years in most countries, as it is in the United States. In most countries, the registration will be canceled if it is shown that the registrant has not used the mark commercially for a specified time period (usually three to five years).

---

[30]Dyann L. Kostello, "When Goodwill Is Established, Rights May Follow," *The National Law Journal*, May 18, 1998, p. C8.

[31]A list of member countries can be found at www.wipo.org

Trademarks on the Internet

The Internet and e-commerce activities have led to a number of specialized trademark issues. The law is still evolving in this area.

Cybersquatting

Domain names are the names given to groups of computers on the Internet; essentially, it is an address that tells users where to find a website. In the United States, domain names are managed by the Internet Corporation for Assigned Names and Numbers (ICANN), a private, nonprofit organization created at the request of the government.[32]

Businesses often want to use their trademarks as domain names. Trademarks historically were limited in reach and operated only nationally. The law recognized that it would be inappropriate to allow one user to register or claim a mark in one country and then prevent everyone else in the world, even in a distant country and with a different product line, from using that same mark. Trademark law even today is territorially based, and rights obtained in one jurisdiction are good only in that particular jurisdiction. Use of a mark within the United States, for example, does not confer rights abroad, nor does use of a mark abroad confer rights in the United States. It is very possible, therefore, for separate firms or individuals to possess and use identical marks in different countries.

Domain names, on the other hand, are inherently global in reach and must be unique in order for the system to operate. Thus, only one user may possess any given domain name. Conflicts develop when multiple people want to use a particular name. The law has not yet developed adequately to fully resolve these conflicts. As a result, we see a number of legal issues involving trademarks and the Internet.

Cybersquatting occurs when a user registers a well-known mark as a domain name and then attempts to sell the domain name back to the mark holder. Some mark holders sue (usually under theories of trademark infringement, trademark dilution, and/or unfair competition) to obtain the domain name from the cybersquatter; others pay the cybersquatter's price if they determine that paying would be cheaper than the costs of litigation. Generally, U.S. courts have proven more sympathetic to the mark holders than to the cybersquatters when these cases have made it to court.

In addition, the *Anticybersquatting Consumer Protection Act*[33] (ACPA) took effect in 1999. This federal statute is intended to combat the growing problem of trademark infringement and unfair competition on the Internet. The ACPA permits the owner of a registered or common law mark to sue anyone who, with a bad faith intent to profit, registers, traffics in, or uses a domain name that, among other provisions: (1) is identical or confusingly similar to a mark that is distinctive at the time when the domain name is registered or (2) is identical or confusingly similar to or dilutive of a mark that is famous at the time the domain name is registered.

The ACPA provides a long, nonexclusive list of factors that the court may consider in determining whether bad faith exists. These factors include: (1) intention to divert customers in a way that could harm the goodwill of a mark; (2) intention to sell the domain name for financial gain without having shown any intent to use the domain name in the bona fide offering of goods or services; and (3) registration of multiple marks that the registrant knows are identical or confusingly similar to a protected mark.

With certain exceptions, the ACPA also prohibits registration of a domain name that is identical or confusingly similar to another living person's name "with the specific intent to profit from such name by selling the domain name" to that person or a third

---

[32]For general information on ICANN, see www.icann.org

[33]15 U.S.C. § 1125(d).

party. This provision is directed primarily at protecting famous people, such as celebrities or athletes, who would have a specific interest in obtaining the domain names associated with their own names.

Generally, the remedies provided under the ACPA are the same as those provided for other Lanham Act violations: (1) return of the defendant's *profits;* (2) *actual damages,* which may be increased up to three times, in the court's discretion; and (3) *costs* of litigation. The Act also provides for *statutory damages* of $1,000 to $100,000 in the court's discretion, per domain name, in lieu of actual damages and profits. Finally, the Act allows for *injunctions* ordering cancellation or transfer of domain names that violate the ACPA. The only remedy available for registration of a domain name consisting of the name of a famous person is injunctive relief, however, as well as costs and attorneys fees, which may be awarded in the court's discretion.

Finally, the ACPA also allows *in rem* jurisdiction, which allows a mark owner to file an action against the domain name itself rather than against the cyberpirate. This allows the mark owner to sue even where the cyberpirate is unknown or personal jurisdiction over the cyberpirate cannot be established. The remedies for such an action are limited to an injunction ordering the forfeiture or cancellation of the domain name or the transfer of the domain name to the mark owner.

ICANN provides the Uniform Domain Name Dispute Resolution Policy (UDRP) as an alternative to federal litigation. The policy sets forth an arbitration-type procedure for resolving some (though not all) domain name disputes. While the ACPA makes bad faith registration alone actionable, the UDRP requires registration coupled with use of the domain name. Remedies under the UDRP are limited to requiring the cancellation or transfer of an infringing domain name.

Typopiracy

Typopiracy or *typosquatting* is also a problem with Internet domain names. Websites try to take advantage of common typographical errors that users might make in typing in a Web address to direct users to a different website. The typopirate then sells advertising space on the site to businesses who want their banners seen by the accidental traffic generated. A number of large and legitimate Web businesses have placed banner ads on typopirates' sites.

In April 1999, a federal district court issued a preliminary injunction in what is believed to be the first typopiracy decision.[34] Paine Webber, Inc., maintained a website at www.painewebber.com. It filed suit for trademark infringement and dilution against Rafael Fortuny after it discovered that users who mistakenly omitted the "period" after "www" ended up at Fortuny's pornographic website. The company found the "typo" site after a customer complained about reaching the pornographic site while trying to access Paine Webber's webpage. A Paine Webber employee had incorrectly typed a "hot link" to Paine Webber's page, omitting the period after "www." The court ruled that Paine Webber was likely to succeed on the merits of its dilution claim because its mark is famous and would be tarnished by association with a pornographic site. The court also found an injunction was necessary to prevent irreparable harm to Paine Webber and ordered Network Solutions, Inc., the domain name registrar, to place the disputed name on hold pending the outcome of the litigation.

Portals, Banner Advertising, and Metatags

Trademark infringement issues can also arise through the use of *portals* or *banner advertising.* Businesses may register their websites through Internet *portals*, or directories. The

[34]*Paine Webber, Inc. v. wwwpainewebber.com,* 1999 U.S. Dist. Lexis 6552 (E.D. Va. April 9, 1999).

business can often then select keywords that consumers may use to search the directory. When a business selects a competitor's trademark as a portal keyword, trademark infringement issues may arise.[35]

Banner advertising is prominently displayed at the top of a screen when the user enters a keyword into the portal website. In addition to a list of search "hits," a large advertisement appears on the screen. Because most of the Internet sites that actually generate revenue do so through the sale of advertising space on the site, banner advertising is a very common practice. Several lawsuits have been filed by companies as a result of advertisers using others' trademarks as keywords to trigger banner advertising for competitors' products or services.

A *metatag* is an HTML code embedded on a webpage and used to identify site content. Some website owners have used metatags to manipulate search engines to find and display their webpages. Many search engines have diminished or eliminated their reliance on metatags in their search algorithms as a result of this manipulation. When a website owner inserts a metatag that is the trademark of a competitor so as to lure consumers to its site, its actions may constitute trademark infringement.[36]

◆ *See Discussion Case 6.4.*

Linking Issues

Other Internet practices can also raise legal issues. *Hyperlinking* to a competitor's site without permission may also constitute trademark infringement, particularly where a logo, as opposed to a word mark, is used to designate the link. In *framing*, the linked site is retrieved as a "window" within the linking site. The linking site's URL is displayed on the user's browser, and the linking site may continue to display its own content, including paid advertising, as the frame or border of the linked site. Linking is thus analogous to picture-in-picture television. Because the URL does not change but continues to display the address of the linking rather than the linked site, framing can create false associations between the linking site and its advertisers, on the one hand, and the linked site on the other. (It can also raise copyright infringement concerns.[37])

Deep linking occurs when the link takes the user to a page within the linked site, bypassing the linked site's home page and, very likely, its marks and paid advertising. Ticketmaster, for example, sued Microsoft, because Microsoft used a deep link to Ticketmaster's ticket-buying service. Ticketmaster alleged that this created a false impression of a business relationship between the two parties and enabled Microsoft customers to bypass Ticketmaster's advertisers, thus depriving it of revenue. The dispute was settled, with Microsoft agreeing to link directly to Ticketmaster's home page, rather than deep linking within its site.[38]

Internet Strategies for Business

How should marketers manage these complex and often unresolved Internet trademark law issues? First, become aware of the Internet environment in which your trademark may be used. Look for typopiracy around your website. Run searches with your

---

[35]See *Nettis Environment, Ltd. v. IWI, Inc.,* 46 F. Supp. 2d 722 (N.D. Ohio 1999); *Playboy Enterprises v. Netscape Communications Corp.,* 55 F. Supp. 2d 1070 (S.D. Cal. 1999), *aff'd,* 202 F.3d 278 (9th Cir. 1999).

[36]See *Deltek, Inc. v. Iuvo Systems, Inc.,* 2009 U.S. Dist. LEXIS 33555 (E.D. Va. 2009).

[37]See *Futuredontics, Inc. v. Applied Anagramics, Inc.,* 1998 U.S. Dist. Lexis 2265 (CD. Cal. Jan. 30, 1998).

[38]"Techweek; A Quick Look at the Latest Technology News; Lawsuits Challenge Net Advertising Policies," *The Atlanta Journal and Constitution,* Feb. 21, 1999, p. O1H; Bob Tedeschi, "Ticketmaster and Microsoft Settle Suit on Internet Linking," *New York Times,* Feb. 15, 1999, at C6.

trademarks to determine whether your competitors may be using them in portals or banner advertising. Second, evaluate your own activities for potential liability. Review your portal and banner advertising practices to make certain that you are not infringing upon the trademark rights of your competitors and thus exposing your company to legal liability. Use of another's trademark for comparative advertising purposes is generally permissible, but other uses may not be. Avoid framing or deep linking, and use caution when linking to the sites of others. In many instances, it may be wise to enter into a specific linking agreement. Finally, post disclaimers for linked materials.

DISCUSSION CASES

6.1 Trademark Protection—Color as a Mark

Qualitex Co. v. Jacobson Products Co., U.S. 159 (1995)

OPINION: JUSTICE BREYER The question in this case is whether the Trademark Act of 1946 (Lanham Act) permits the registration of a trademark that consists, purely and simply, of a color. We conclude that, sometimes, a color will meet ordinary legal trademark requirements. And, when it does so, no special legal rule prevents color alone from serving as a trademark.

I

The case before us grows out of petitioner Qualitex Company's use (since the 1950's) of a special shade of green-gold color on the pads that it makes and sells to dry cleaning firms for use on dry cleaning presses. In 1989, respondent Jacobson Products (a Qualitex rival) began to sell its own press pads to dry cleaning firms; and it colored those pads a similar green-gold. In 1991, Qualitex registered the special green-gold color on press pads with the Patent and Trademark Office as a trademark. Qualitex subsequently added a trademark infringement count to an unfair competition claim in a lawsuit it had already filed challenging Jacobson's use of the green-gold color.

Qualitex won the lawsuit in the District Court. But, the Court of Appeals for the Ninth Circuit set aside the judgment in Qualitex's favor on the trademark infringement claim because, in that Circuit's view, the Lanham Act does not permit Qualitex, or anyone else, to register "color alone" as a trademark.

The Courts of Appeals have differed as to whether or not the law recognizes the use of color alone as a trademark. Therefore, this Court granted certiorari. We now hold that there is no rule absolutely barring the use of color alone, and we reverse the judgment of the Ninth Circuit.

II

* * * Both the language of the [Lanham] Act and the basic underlying principles of trademark law would seem to include color within the universe of things that can qualify as a trademark. The language of the Lanham Act describes that universe in the broadest of terms. It says that trademarks "includ[e] any word, name, symbol, or device, or any combination thereof." Since human beings might use as a "symbol" or "device" almost anything at all that is capable of carrying meaning, this language, read literally, is not restrictive. The courts and the Patent and Trademark Office have authorized for use as a mark a particular shape (of a Coca-Cola bottle), a particular sound (of NBC's three chimes), and even a particular scent (of plumeria blossoms on sewing thread). If a shape, a sound, and a fragrance can act as symbols why, one might ask, can a color not do the same?

A color is also capable of satisfying the more important part of the statutory definition of a trademark, which requires that a person "us[e]" or "inten[d] to use" the mark

> to identify and distinguish his or her goods, including a unique product, from those manufactured or sold by others and to indicate the source of the goods, even if that source is unknown.

15 U.S.C. § 1127. True, a product's color is unlike "fanciful," "arbitrary," or "suggestive" words or designs, which almost *automatically* tell a customer that they

refer to a brand. The imaginary word "Suntost," or the words "Suntost Marmalade," on a jar of orange jam immediately would signal a brand or a product "source"; the jam's orange color does not do so. But, over time, customers may come to treat a particular color on a product or its packaging (say, a color that in context seems unusual, such as pink on a firm's insulating material or red on the head of a large industrial bolt) as signifying a brand. And, if so, that color would have come to identify and distinguish the goods—i.e., "to indicate" their "source"—much in the way that descriptive words on a product (say, "Trim" on nail clippers or "Car-Freshner" on deodorizer) can come to indicate a product's origin. In this circumstance, trademark law says that the word (e.g., "Trim"), although not inherently distinctive, has developed "secondary meaning." ("[S]econdary meaning" is acquired when "in the minds of the public, the primary significance of a product feature … is to identify the source of the product rather than the product itself."). * * *

We cannot find in the basic objectives of trademark law any obvious theoretical objection to the use of color alone as a trademark, where that color has attained "secondary meaning" and therefore identifies and distinguishes a particular brand (and thus indicates its "source"). * * *

Neither can we find a principled objection to the use of color as a mark in the important "functionality" doctrine of trademark law. The functionality doctrine prevents trademark law, which seeks to promote competition by protecting a firm's reputation, from instead inhibiting legitimate competition by allowing a producer to control a useful product feature. It is the province of patent law, not trademark law, to encourage invention by granting inventors a monopoly over new product designs or functions for a limited time, after which competitors are free to use the innovation. If a product's functional features could be used as trademarks, however, a monopoly over such features could be obtained without regard to whether they qualify as patents and could be extended forever (because trademarks may be renewed in perpetuity). * * * This Court consequently has explained that, "[i]n general

terms, a product feature is functional," and cannot serve as a trademark, "if it is essential to the use or purpose of the article or if it affects the cost or quality of the article," that is, if exclusive use of the feature would put competitors at a significant non-reputation-related disadvantage. Although sometimes color plays an important role (unrelated to source identification) in making a product more desirable, sometimes it does not. And, this latter fact—the fact that sometimes color is not essential to a product's use or purpose and does not affect cost or quality—indicates that the doctrine of "functionality" does not create an absolute bar to the use of color alone as a mark.

It would seem, then, that color alone, at least sometimes, can meet the basic legal requirements for use as a trademark. It can act as a symbol that distinguishes a firm's goods and identifies their source, without serving any other significant function. * * * [Qualitex's] green-gold color acts as a symbol. Having developed secondary meaning (for customers identified the green-gold color as Qualitex's), it identifies the press pads' source. And, the green-gold color serves no other function. * * * Accordingly, unless there is some special reason that convincingly militates against the use of color alone as a trademark, trademark law would protect Qualitex's use of the green-gold color on its press pads.

* * *

IV

* * * For these reasons, the judgment of the Ninth Circuit is reversed.

QUESTIONS FOR DISCUSSION FOR CASE 6.1

1. Why did the Supreme Court choose to hear this case?
2. Can color be an inherently distinctive mark? When can color be protected as a mark?
3. Can color be protected as a trademark if it enhances the performance of the product? Why or why not?

6.2 Trade Dress Protection—Functionality

TrafFix Devices, Inc. v. Marketing Displays, Inc., U.S. 23 (2001)

KENNEDY, J., delivered the opinion for a unanimous Court.

Temporary road signs with warnings like "Road Work Ahead" or "Left Shoulder Closed" must withstand strong gusts of wind. An inventor named Robert Sarkisian obtained two utility patents for a mechanism built upon two springs (the dual-spring design) to keep these and other outdoor signs upright despite adverse wind conditions. The holder of the now-expired Sarkisian patents, respondent Marketing Displays, Inc. (MDI), established a successful business in the manufacture and sale of sign stands incorporating the patented feature. MDI's stands for road signs were recognizable to buyers and users (it says) because the dual-spring design was visible near the base of the sign.

This litigation followed after the patents expired and a competitor, TrafFix Devices, Inc., sold sign stands with a visible spring mechanism that looked like MDI's. MDI and TrafFix products looked alike because they were. When TrafFix started in business, it sent an MDI product abroad to have it reverse engineered, that is to say copied. Complicating matters, TrafFix marketed its sign stands under a name similar to MDI's. MDI used the name "WindMaster," while TrafFix, its new competitor, used "WindBuster."

MDI brought suit under the Trademark Act of 1964 (Lanham Act), against TrafFix for trademark infringement (based on the similar names), trade dress infringement (based on the copied dual-spring design) and unfair competition. * * *

I

We are concerned with the trade dress question. The District Court ruled against MDI on its trade dress claim. After determining that the one element of MDI's trade dress at issue was the dual-spring design, it held that "no reasonable trier of fact could determine that MDI has established secondary meaning" in its alleged trade dress. In other words, consumers did not associate the look of the dual-spring design with MDI. As a second, independent reason to grant summary judgment in favor of TrafFix, the District Court determined the dual-spring design was functional. On this rationale secondary meaning is irrelevant because there can be no trade dress protection in any event. * * * Summary judgment was entered against MDI on its trade dress claims.

The Court of Appeals for the Sixth Circuit reversed the trade dress ruling. The Court of Appeals held the District Court had erred in ruling MDI failed to show a genuine issue of material fact regarding whether it had secondary meaning in its alleged trade dress, and had erred further in determining that MDI could not prevail in any event because the alleged trade dress was in fact a functional product configuration. The Court of Appeals suggested the District Court committed legal error by looking only to the dual-spring design when evaluating MDI's trade dress. Basic to its reasoning was the Court of Appeals' observation that it took "little imagination to conceive of a hidden dual-spring mechanism or a tri or quad-spring mechanism that might avoid infringing [MDI's] trade dress." The Court of Appeals explained that "if TrafFix or another competitor chooses to use [MDI's] dual-spring design, then it will have to find *some other way* to set its sign apart to avoid infringing [MDI's] trade dress." It was not sufficient, according to the Court of Appeals, that allowing exclusive use of a particular feature such as the dual-spring design in the guise of trade dress would "hinder competition somewhat." Rather, "exclusive use of a feature must 'put competitors at a *significant* non-reputation-related disadvantage' before trade dress protection is denied on functionality grounds." In its criticism of the District Court's ruling on the trade dress question, the Court of Appeals took note of a split among Courts of Appeals in various other Circuits on the issue whether the existence of an expired utility patent forecloses the possibility of the patentee's claiming trade dress protection in the product's design. To resolve the conflict, we granted certiorari.

II

It is well established that trade dress can be protected under federal law. The design or packaging of a product may acquire a distinctiveness which serves to identify the product with its manufacturer or source; and a design or package which acquires this secondary meaning, assuming other requisites are met, is a trade dress which may not be used in a manner likely to cause confusion as to the origin, sponsorship, or approval of the goods. In these respects protection for trade dress exists to promote competition. As we explained just last Term, various Courts of Appeals have allowed claims of trade dress infringement relying on the general provision of the Lanham Act which provides a cause of action to one who is injured when a person uses "any word, term name, symbol, or device, or any combination thereof … which is likely to cause confusion … as to the origin, sponsorship, or approval of his or her goods." Congress confirmed this statutory protection for trade dress by amending the Lanham Act to recognize the concept. Title 15 U.S.C. § 1125(a)(3) provides: "In a civil action for trade dress infringement under this chapter for trade dress not registered on the principal register, the person who asserts trade dress protection has the burden of proving that the matter sought to be protected is not functional." This burden of proof gives force to the well-established rule that trade dress protection may not be claimed for product features that are functional. * * *

Trade dress protection must subsist with the recognition that in many instances there is no prohibition against copying goods and products. In general, unless an intellectual property right such as a patent or copyright protects an item, it will be subject to copying. As the Court has explained, copying is not always discouraged or disfavored by the laws which preserve our competitive economy. Allowing competitors to copy will have salutary effects in many instances. "Reverse engineering of chemical and mechanical articles in the public domain often leads to significant advances in technology."

The principal question in this case is the effect of an expired patent on a claim of trade dress infringement. A prior patent, we conclude, has vital significance in resolving the trade dress claim. A utility patent is strong evidence that the features therein claimed are functional. If trade dress protection is sought for those features the strong evidence of functionality based on the previous patent adds great weight to the statutory presumption that features are deemed functional until proved otherwise by the party seeking trade dress protection. Where the expired patent claimed the features in question, one who seeks to establish trade dress protection must carry the heavy burden of showing that the feature is not functional, for instance by showing that it is merely an ornamental, incidental, or arbitrary aspect of the device.

In the case before us, the central advance claimed in the expired utility patents (the Sarkisian patents) is the dual-spring design; and the dual-spring design is the essential feature of the trade dress MDI now seeks to

establish and to protect. The rule we have explained bars the trade dress claim, for MDI did not, and cannot, carry the burden of overcoming the strong evidentiary inference of functionality based on the disclosure of the dual-spring design in the claims of the expired patents.

The dual springs shown in the Sarkisian patents were well apart (at either end of a frame for holding a rectangular sign when one full side is the base) while the dual springs at issue here are close together (in a frame designed to hold a sign by one of its corners). As the District Court recognized, this makes little difference. The point is that the springs are necessary to the operation of the device. * * *

The rationale for the rule that the disclosure of a feature in the claims of a utility patent constitutes strong evidence of functionality is well illustrated in this case. The dual-spring design serves the important purpose of keeping the sign upright even in heavy wind conditions; and, as confirmed by the statements in the expired patents, it does so in a unique and useful manner. As the specification of one of the patents recites, prior art "devices, in practice, will topple under the force of a strong wind." The dual-spring design allows sign stands to resist toppling in strong winds. Using a dual-spring design rather than a single spring achieves important operational advantages. For example, the specifications of the patents note that the "use of a pair of springs … as opposed to the use of a single spring to support the frame structure prevents canting or twisting of the sign around a vertical axis," and that, if not prevented, twisting "may cause damage to the spring structure and may result in tipping of the device." In the course of patent prosecution, it was said that "the use of a pair of spring connections as opposed to a single spring connection … forms an important part of this combination" because it "forces the sign frame to tip along the longitudinal axis of the elongated ground-engaging members." The dual-spring design affects the cost of the device as well; it was acknowledged that the device "could use three springs but this would unnecessarily increase the cost of the device." These statements made in the patent applications and in the course of procuring the patents demonstrate the functionality of the design. MDI does not assert that any of these representations are mistaken or inaccurate, and this is further strong evidence of the functionality of the dual-spring design.

III

In finding for MDI on the trade dress issue the Court of Appeals gave insufficient recognition to the importance of the expired utility patents, and their evidentiary significance, in establishing the functionality of the device. * * * Discussing trademarks, we have said "'in general terms, a product feature is functional,' and cannot serve as a trademark, 'if it is essential to the use or purpose of the article or if it affects the cost or quality of the article.'" Expanding upon the meaning of this phrase, we have observed that a functional feature is one the "exclusive use of [which] would put competitors at a significant non-reputation-related disadvantage." The Court of Appeals in the instant case seemed to interpret this language to mean that a necessary test for functionality is "whether the particular product configuration is a competitive necessity." This was incorrect as a comprehensive definition. As explained in [earlier Supreme Court decisions], a feature is also functional when it is essential to the use or purpose of the device or when it affects the cost or quality of the device. * * *

* * * In the instant case, beyond serving the purpose of informing consumers that the sign stands are made by MDI (assuming it does so), the dual-spring design provides a unique and useful mechanism to resist the force of the wind. Functionality having been established, whether MDI's dual-spring design has acquired secondary meaning need not be considered.

There is no need, furthermore, to engage, as did the Court of Appeals, in speculation about other design possibilities, such as using three or four springs which might serve the same purpose. Here, the functionality of the spring design means that competitors need not explore whether other spring juxtapositions might be used. The dual-spring design is not an arbitrary flourish in the configuration of MDI's product; it is the reason the device works. Other designs need not be attempted.

Because the dual-spring design is functional, it is unnecessary for competitors to explore designs to hide the springs, say by using a box or framework to cover them, as suggested by the Court of Appeals. The dual-spring design assures the user the device will work. If buyers are assured the product serves its purpose by seeing the operative mechanism that in itself serves an important market need. It would be at cross-purposes to those objectives, and something of a paradox, were we to require the manufacturer to conceal the very item the user seeks.

In a case where a manufacturer seeks to protect arbitrary, incidental, or ornamental aspects of features of a product found in the patent claims, such as arbitrary curves in the legs or an ornamental pattern painted on the springs, a different result might obtain. There the manufacturer could perhaps prove that those aspects do not serve a purpose within the terms of the utility patent. The inquiry into whether such features, asserted to be trade dress, are functional by reason of their inclusion in the claims of an expired utility patent could be aided by going beyond the claims and examining the patent and its prosecution history to see if the feature in question is shown as a useful part of the invention. No such claim is made here, however. MDI in essence seeks protection for the dual-spring design alone. The asserted trade dress consists simply of the dual-spring design, four legs, a base, an upright, and a sign. MDI has pointed to nothing arbitrary about the components of its device or the way they are assembled. The Lanham Act does not exist to reward manufacturers for their innovation in creating a particular device; that is the purpose of the patent law and its period of exclusivity. The Lanham Act, furthermore, does not protect trade dress in a functional design simply because an investment has been made to encourage the public to associate a particular functional feature with a single manufacturer or seller. * * * Whether a utility patent has expired or there has been no utility patent at all, a product design which has a particular appearance may be functional because it is "essential to the use or purpose of the article" or "affects the cost or quality of the article."

* * * The judgment of the Court of Appeals is reversed, and the case is remanded for further proceedings consistent with this opinion.

QUESTIONS FOR DISCUSSION FOR CASE 6.2

1. Under what circumstances is copying of products and services legally permitted?
2. What is the relationship between utility patents, trade dress protection, and functionality?
3. Procedurally, what will happen next in this case?

6.3 Trademark Infringement, Dilution, Defenses, First Amendment
Mattel, Inc. v. MCA Records, Inc., F.3d 894 (9th Cir. 2002)

If this were a sci-fi melodrama, it might be called Speech-Zilla meets Trademark Kong.

I

Barbie was born in Germany in the 1950s as an adult collector's item. Over the years, Mattel transformed her from a doll that resembled a "German street walker," as she originally appeared, into a glamorous, long-legged blonde. Barbie has been labeled both the ideal American woman and a bimbo. She has survived attacks both psychic (from feminists critical of her fictitious figure) and physical (more than 500 professional makeovers). She remains a symbol of American girlhood, a public figure who graces the aisles of toy stores throughout the country and beyond. With Barbie, Mattel created not just a toy but a cultural icon.

With fame often comes unwanted attention. Aqua is a Danish band that has, as yet, only dreamed of attaining Barbie-like status. In 1997, Aqua produced the song Barbie Girl on the album *Aquarium*. In the song, one bandmember impersonates Barbie, singing in a high-pitched, doll-like voice; another bandmember, calling himself Ken, entices Barbie to "go party." * * * Barbie Girl singles sold well and, to Mattel's dismay, the song made it onto Top 40 music charts.

Mattel brought this lawsuit against the music companies who produced, marketed and sold Barbie Girl. * * * The district court … granted MCA's motion for summary judgment on Mattel's federal and state-law claims for trademark infringement and dilution. * * *

Mattel appeals the district court's ruling that Barbie Girl is a parody of Barbie … ; that MCA's use of the term Barbie is not likely to confuse consumers as to Mattel's affiliation with Barbie Girl or dilute the Barbie mark …. * * *

* * *

III

A. A trademark is a word, phrase or symbol that is used to identify a manufacturer or sponsor of a good or the provider of a service. It's the owner's way of preventing others from duping consumers into buying a product they mistakenly believe is sponsored by the trademark owner. A trademark "informs people that trademarked products come from the same source." * * *

The problem arises when trademarks transcend their identifying purpose. Some trademarks enter our public discourse and become an integral part of our vocabulary. How else do you say that something's "the Rolls Royce of its class?" What else is a quick fix, but a Band-Aid? Does the average consumer know to ask for aspirin as "acetyl salicylic acid?" Trademarks often fill in gaps in our vocabulary and add a contemporary flavor to our expressions. Once imbued with such expressive value, the trademark becomes a word in our language and assumes a role outside the bounds of trademark law.

Our likelihood-of-confusion test generally strikes a comfortable balance between the trademark owner's property rights and the public's expressive interests. But when a trademark owner asserts a right to control how we express ourselves—when we'd find it difficult to describe the product any other way (as in the case of aspirin), or when the mark (like Rolls Royce) has taken on an expressive meaning apart from its source-identifying function—applying the traditional test fails to account for the full weight of the public's interest in free expression.

The First Amendment may offer little protection for a competitor who labels its commercial good with a confusingly similar mark, but "trademark rights do not entitle the owner to quash an unauthorized use of the mark by another who is communicating ideas or expressing points of view." Were we to ignore the expressive value that some marks assume, trademark rights would grow to encroach upon the zone protected by the First Amendment. Simply put, the trademark owner does not have the right to control public discourse whenever the public imbues his mark with a meaning beyond its source-identifying function.

B. There is no doubt that MCA uses Mattel's mark: Barbie is one half of Barbie Girl. But Barbie Girl is the title of a song about Barbie and Ken, a reference that—at least today—can only be to Mattel's famous couple. We expect a title to describe the underlying work, not to identify the producer, and Barbie Girl does just that.

The Barbie Girl title presages a song about Barbie, or at least a girl like Barbie. The title conveys a message to consumers about what they can expect to discover in the song itself; it's a quick glimpse of Aqua's take on their own song. The lyrics confirm this: The female singer, who calls herself Barbie, is "a Barbie girl, in [her] Barbie world." She tells her male counterpart (named Ken), "Life in plastic, it's fantastic. You can brush my hair, undress me everywhere/Imagination, life is your creation." And off they go to "party." The song pokes fun at Barbie and the values that Aqua contends she represents. The female singer explains, "I'm a blond bimbo girl, in a fantasy world/Dress me up, make it tight, I'm your dolly."

The song does not rely on the Barbie mark to poke fun at another subject but targets Barbie herself. * * * [W]here an artistic work targets the original and does not merely borrow another's property to get attention, First Amendment interests weigh more heavily in the balance.

The Second Circuit has held that "in general the [Lanham] Act should be construed to apply to artistic works only where the public interest in avoiding consumer confusion outweighs the public interest in free expression." * * *

* * *

A title is designed to catch the eye and to promote the value of the underlying work. Consumers expect a title to communicate a message about the book or movie, but they do not expect it to identify the publisher or producer. If we see a painting titled "Campbell's Chicken Noodle Soup," we're unlikely to believe that Campbell's has branched into the art business. Nor, upon hearing Janis Joplin croon "Oh Lord, won't you buy me a Mercedes-Benz?," would we suspect that she and the carmaker had entered into a joint venture. A title tells us something about the underlying work but seldom speaks to its origin:

> Though consumers frequently look to the title of a work to determine what it is about, they do not regard titles of artistic works in the same way as the names of ordinary commercial products. Since consumers expect an ordinary product to be what the name says it is, we apply the Lanham Act with some rigor to prohibit names that misdescribe such goods. But most consumers are well aware that they cannot judge a book solely by its title any more than by its cover.

[L]iterary titles do not violate the Lanham Act "unless the title has no artistic relevance to the underlying work whatsoever, or, if it has some artistic relevance, unless the title explicitly misleads as to the source or the content of the work." * * *

[W]e conclude that MCA's use of Barbie is not an infringement of Mattel's trademark. [T]he use of Barbie in the song title clearly is relevant to the underlying work, namely, the song itself. As noted, the song is about Barbie and the values Aqua claims she represents. The song title does not explicitly mislead as to the source of the work; it does not, explicitly or otherwise, suggest that it was produced by Mattel. The *only* indication that Mattel might be associated with the song is the use of Barbie in the title .... We therefore agree with the district court that MCA was entitled to summary judgment on this ground. * * *

IV

Mattel separately argues that, under the Federal Trademark Dilution Act ("FTDA"), MCA's song dilutes the Barbie mark in two ways: It diminishes the mark's capacity to identify and distinguish Mattel products, and tarnishes the mark because the song is inappropriate for young girls.

"Dilution" refers to the "whittling away of the value of a trademark" when it's used to identify different products. For example, Tylenol snowboards, Netscape sex shops and Harry Potter dry cleaners would all weaken the "commercial magnetism" of these marks and diminish their ability to evoke their original associations. These uses dilute the selling power of these trademarks by blurring their "uniqueness and singularity," and/or by tarnishing them with negative associations.

By contrast to trademark infringement, the injury from dilution usually occurs when consumers *aren't* confused about the source of a product: Even if no one suspects that the maker of analgesics has entered into the snowboard business, the Tylenol mark will now bring to mind two products, not one. Whereas trademark law targets "interference with the source signaling function" of trademarks, dilution protects owners "from an appropriation of or free riding on" the substantial investment that they have made in their marks.

Originally a creature of state law, dilution received nationwide recognition in 1996 when Congress amended the Lanham Act by enacting the FTDA. The statute protects "the owner of a famous mark ... against another person's commercial use in commerce of a mark or trade name, if such use begins after the mark has become famous and causes dilution of the distinctive quality of the mark." Dilutive uses are prohibited unless they fall within one of the three statutory exemptions discussed below. * * * Barbie easily qualifies under the FTDA as a famous and distinctive mark, and reached this status long before MCA began to market the Barbie Girl song. The commercial success of Barbie Girl establishes beyond dispute that the Barbie mark satisfies each of these elements.

We are also satisfied that the song amounts to a "commercial use in commerce." Although this statutory language is ungainly, its meaning seems clear: It refers to a use of a famous and distinctive mark to sell goods other than those produced or authorized by the mark's owner. That is precisely what MCA did with the Barbie mark: It created and sold to consumers in the marketplace commercial products (the Barbie Girl single and the *Aquarium* album) that bear the Barbie mark.

MCA's use of the mark is dilutive. MCA does not dispute that, while a reference to Barbie would previously have brought to mind only Mattel's doll, after the song's popular success, some consumers hearing Barbie's name will think of both the doll and the song, or perhaps of the song only. This is a classic blurring injury and is in no way diminished by the fact that the song itself refers back to Barbie the doll. To be dilutive, use of the mark need not bring to mind the junior user alone. The distinctiveness of the mark is diminished if the mark no longer brings to mind the senior user alone.[4]

We consider next the applicability of the FTDA's three statutory exemptions. These are uses that, though potentially dilutive, are nevertheless permitted: comparative advertising; news reporting and commentary; and noncommercial use. The first two exemptions clearly do not apply; only the exemption for noncommercial use need detain us.

A "noncommercial use" exemption, on its face, presents a bit of a conundrum because it seems at odds with the earlier requirement that the junior use be a "commercial use in commerce." If a use has to be commercial in order to be dilutive, how then can it also be noncommercial … ? If the term "commercial use" had the same meaning in both provisions, this would eliminate one of the three statutory exemptions defined by this subsection, because any use found to be dilutive would, of necessity, not be noncommercial.

Such a reading of the statute would also create a constitutional problem, because it would leave the FTDA with no First Amendment protection for dilutive speech other than comparative advertising and news reporting. This would be a serious problem because the primary (usually exclusive) remedy for

dilution is an injunction. As noted above, tension with the First Amendment also exists in the trademark context, especially where the mark has assumed an expressive function beyond mere identification of a product or service. These concerns apply with greater force in the dilution context because dilution lacks two very significant limitations that reduce the tension between trademark law and the First Amendment.

First, depending on the strength and distinctiveness of the mark, trademark law grants relief only against uses that are likely to confuse. A trademark injunction is usually limited to uses within one industry or several related industries. Dilution law is the antithesis of trademark law in this respect, because it seeks to protect the mark from association in the public's mind with wholly unrelated goods and services. The more remote the good or service associated with the junior use, the more likely it is to cause dilution rather than trademark infringement. A dilution injunction, by contrast to a trademark injunction, will generally sweep across broad vistas of the economy.

Second, a trademark injunction, even a very broad one, is premised on the need to prevent consumer confusion. This consumer protection rationale—averting what is essentially a fraud on the consuming public—is wholly consistent with the theory of the First Amendment, which does not protect commercial fraud. Moreover, avoiding harm to consumers is an important interest that is independent of the senior user's interest in protecting its business.

Dilution, by contrast, does not require a showing of consumer confusion, and dilution injunctions therefore lack the built-in First Amendment compass of trademark injunctions. In addition, dilution law protects only the distinctiveness of the mark, which is inherently less weighty than the dual interest of protecting trademark owners and avoiding harm to consumers that is at the heart of every trademark claim.

Fortunately, the legislative history of the FTDA suggests an interpretation of the "noncommercial use" exemption that both solves our interpretive dilemma and diminishes some First Amendment concerns: "Noncommercial use" refers to a use that consists entirely of noncommercial, or fully constitutionally protected, speech. Where, as here, a statute's plain meaning "produces an absurd, and perhaps unconstitutional, result[, it is] entirely appropriate to consult all public materials, including the background of [the statute] and the legislative history of its adoption."

The legislative history bearing on this issue is particularly persuasive. First, the FTDA's sponsors in both the

---

[4]Because we find blurring, we need not consider whether the song also tarnished the Barbie mark.

House and the Senate were aware of the potential collision with the First Amendment if the statute authorized injunctions against protected speech. Upon introducing the counterpart bills, sponsors in each house explained that the proposed law "will not prohibit or threaten noncommercial expression, such as parody, satire, editorial and other forms of expression that are not a part of a commercial transaction." The House Judiciary Committee agreed in its report on the FTDA.

The FTDA's section-by-section analysis presented in the House and Senate suggests that the bill's sponsors relied on the "noncommercial use" exemption to allay First Amendment concerns. At the request of one of the bill's sponsors, the section-by-section analysis was printed in the Congressional Record. Thus, we know that this interpretation of the exemption was before the Senate when the FTDA was passed, and that no senator rose to dispute it.

To determine whether Barbie Girl falls within this exemption, we look to our definition of commercial speech under our First Amendment caselaw. "Although the boundary between commercial and noncommercial speech has yet to be clearly delineated, the 'core notion of commercial speech' is that it 'does no more than propose a commercial transaction.'" If speech is not "purely commercial"—that is, if it does more than propose a commercial transaction—then it is entitled to full First Amendment protection.

In [*Hoffman v. Capital Cities/ABC, Inc.*, 255 F.3d 1180 (9th Cir. 2001)], a magazine published an article featuring digitally altered images from famous films. Computer artists modified shots of Dustin Hoffman, Cary Grant, Marilyn Monroe and others to put the actors in famous designers' spring fashions; a still of Hoffman from the movie "Tootsie" was altered so that he appeared to be wearing a Richard Tyler evening gown and Ralph Lauren heels. Hoffman, who had not given permission, sued under the Lanham Act and for violation of his right to publicity.

The article featuring the altered image clearly served a commercial purpose: "to draw attention to the for-profit magazine in which it appeared" and to sell more copies. Nevertheless, we held that the article was fully protected under the First Amendment because it included protected expression: "humor" and "visual and verbal editorial comment on classic films and famous actors." Because its commercial purpose was "inextricably entwined with [these] expressive elements," the article and accompanying photographs enjoyed full First Amendment protection.

Hoffman controls: Barbie Girl is not purely commercial speech, and is therefore fully protected. To be sure, MCA used Barbie's name to sell copies of the song. However, as we've already observed, the song also lampoons the Barbie image and comments humorously on the cultural values Aqua claims she represents. Use of the Barbie mark in the song Barbie Girl therefore falls within the noncommercial use exemption to the FTDA. For precisely the same reasons, use of the mark in the song's title is also exempted.

* * *

AFFIRMED.

QUESTIONS FOR DISCUSSION FOR CASE 6.3

1. How does the court explain the relationship between First Amendment rights to free speech and trademark infringement law? Between free speech and trademark dilution law? Between trademark infringement law and trademark dilution law?
2. Why does the court conclude there is no trademark infringement?
3. Why does the court conclude there is no trademark dilution?

6.4 Trademarks—Infringement, Metatags, Remedies
Venture Tape Corp. v. McGills Glass Warehouse, F.3d 56 (1st Cir. 2008)

McGills Glass Warehouse ("McGills"), an internet-based retailer of stained-glass supplies, and its owner Donald Gallagher, appeal from a district court judgment finding them liable for infringement of the registered trademarks "Venture Tape" and "Venture Foil," and awarding the marks' owner, Venture Tape Corporation ("Venture"), an equitable share of McGills' profits, as well as costs and attorney's fees. We affirm.

I.

In 1990, Venture, a manufacturer of specialty adhesive tapes and foils used in the stained-glass industry, procured two federal trademark registrations for products called "Venture Tape" and "Venture Foil," respectively. Over the next fifteen years, Venture expended hundreds of thousands of dollars to promote the two marks in both print and internet advertising. Consequently, its products gained considerable popularity, prestige, and good will in the world-wide stained glass market.

Through its internet website, McGills also sells adhesive tapes and foils which directly compete with "Venture Tape" and "Venture Foil." Beginning in 2000, and without obtaining Venture's permission or paying it any compensation, McGills' owner Donald Gallagher intentionally "embedded" the Venture marks in the McGills website, both by including the marks in the website's metatags—a component of a webpage's programming that contains descriptive information about the webpage which is typically not observed when the webpage is displayed in a web browser—and in white lettering on a white background screen, similarly invisible to persons viewing the webpage. Gallagher, fully aware that the McGills website did not sell these two Venture products, admittedly took these actions because he had heard that Venture's marks would attract people using internet search engines to the McGills website.

Because the marks were hidden from view, Venture did not discover McGills' unauthorized use of its marks until 2003. It then promptly filed suit against McGills and Gallagher in federal district court, alleging federal trademark infringement, unfair competition, false designation of origin, and trademark dilution [under Massachusetts law]. The district court ... granted summary judgment for Venture on all counts, and requested that Venture submit a motion itemizing any damages, costs, and attorney's fees attributable to McGills' trademark infringement, all of which are potentially recoverable under the Lanham Act.

Although Venture adduced evidence that McGills generated almost $1.9 million in gross sales during the period of its infringement from 2000-2003, Venture eventually requested only $230,339.17, the amount that it estimated to be McGills' net profits. Citing McGills' willful infringement and alleging McGills engaged in obstructionist discovery tactics, Venture sought $188,583.06 in attorney's fees and $7,564.75 in costs. After a hearing on Venture's motion, the district court granted Venture's requested recovery. McGills and Gallagher now appeal from the district court's grant of summary judgment to Venture on Lanham Act liability, and from the district court's award of profits and attorney's fees.

II.

A. Lanham Act Liability

McGills first contends that the district court improvidently granted summary judgment for Venture on appellees' liability under the Lanham Act.[4] * * *

"The purpose of a trademark is to identify and distinguish the goods of one party from those of another. To the purchasing public, a trademark 'signi[fies] that all goods bearing the trademark' originated from the same source and that 'all goods bearing the trademark are of an equal level of quality.'" To establish trademark infringement under the Lanham Act, Venture was required to prove that: (1) it owns and uses the "Venture Tape" and "Venture Foil" marks; (2) McGills used the same or similar marks without Venture's permission; and (3) McGills' use of the Venture marks likely confused internet consumers, thereby causing Venture harm (e.g., lost sales). The parties agree that no genuine factual dispute exists concerning the first two elements of proof.[5]

Our focus then becomes the "likelihood of confusion" among internet consumers. This inquiry requires us to assess eight criteria: (1) the similarity of Venture's and McGills' marks; (2) the similarity of their goods; (3) the relationship between their channels of trade (*e.g.,* internet-based commerce); (4) the relationship between their advertising; (5) the classes of their prospective purchasers; (6) any evidence of actual confusion of internet consumers; (7) McGills' subjective intent in using Venture's marks; and (8) the overall strength of Venture's marks [hereinafter "*Pignons* factors" or "*Pignons* analysis"].[6] No single criterion is necessarily dispositive in this circumstantial inquiry.

By the conduct of its case below, McGills effectively admitted seven of the eight elements of the *Pignons* analysis. The record contains numerous admissions that metatags and invisible background text on McGills' website incorporated Venture's exact marks. In his deposition, Gallagher admitted that the parties are direct

---

[4] * * * On appeal, McGills does not address the grant of summary judgment to Venture on Count 4, the state trademark dilution claim. Hence we do not address it either.

[5] Venture's registration of the two marks, when coupled with its continuous use of them from 1990 to 1995, is incontestible evidence of Venture's exclusive right to use the marks. Further, McGills concedes that, without Venture's permission, Gallagher embedded the marks *verbatim* on the McGills website.

[6] Venture's unfair competition claim (Count 2) and false designation claim (Count 3) are subject to the same legal standard—namely, "likelihood of confusion"—as its Count 1 infringement claim.

competitors in the stained glass industry and that both companies use websites to promote and market their products. Gallagher even admitted that he intentionally used Venture Tape's marks on McGills' website for the express purpose of attracting customers to McGills' website and that he chose "Venture Tape" because of its strong reputation in the stained glass industry. These admissions illustrate the similarity (indeed, identity) of the marks used, the similarity of the goods, the close relationship between the channels of trade and advertising, and the similarity in the classes of prospective purchasers. They also support the conclusions that McGills acted with a subjective intent to trade on Venture's reputation and that Venture's mark is strong. Accordingly, only the sixth factor— evidence of actual consumer confusion—is potentially in dispute.

On appeal, McGills argues that Gallagher had no way of knowing whether or not his use of the Venture marks on the McGills website had been successful, i.e., whether the marks actually lured any internet consumer to the website. Thus, the company contends that summary judgment in Venture's favor was improper because there was no evidence of actual confusion. However, McGills' various protestations below and on appeal that there is no direct evidence of actual consumer confusion, even if accepted as true, are ultimately beside the point.

Although Venture might have attempted to adduce evidence of actual consumer confusion (e.g., internet user market surveys) in support of a favorable *Pignons* determination, the absence of such proof is not dispositive of the *Pignons* analysis. "[A] trademark holder's burden is to show likelihood of confusion, not actual confusion. While evidence of actual confusion is 'often deemed the best evidence of possible future confusion, proof of actual confusion is not essential to finding likelihood of confusion.'"

McGills' admissions regarding the other seven *Pignons* factors, particularly Gallagher's admission that his *purpose* in using the Venture marks was to lure customers to his site, permit us to conclude that no genuine dispute exists regarding the likelihood of confusion. As a result, Venture was entitled to summary judgment on the liability issue.

B. Award of Profits under the Lanham Act

Because Venture established its entitlement to summary judgment on Lanham Act liability, it was potentially entitled—subject to applicable principles of equity—to

recover, *inter alia*, McGills' profits during the period that McGills infringed the Venture marks. McGills argues on appeal that the district court erred in awarding Venture $230,339.17, McGills' net profits for the three-and-a-half-year period of infringement. * * *

* * *

McGills raises two substantive objections to the award of profits. First, the company challenges the district court's finding that the infringement here was "willful," asserting that such a finding is a prerequisite to an award of profits under the Lanham Act. We have previously declined to reach the question of whether "willfulness" is required as a foundation for such an award, and we need not decide the issue here. Even assuming that "willfulness" is required, McGills has not demonstrated that the district court's finding of "willfulness" was clearly erroneous. McGills asserts that Gallagher's admittedly intentional use of the Venture marks to lure customers to his site was not "willful" because Gallagher was unaware that such use of the marks was illegal. However, the district court specifically noted that McGills had programmed its website so that Venture's marks were displayed in the same color as the webpage background, concealing them from view. We can find no clear error in the district court's conclusion that such intentional concealment provides strong circumstantial evidence of "willfulness."

Second, McGills attacks the award by claiming that it overstates the actual harm to Venture. McGills first complains that Venture did not even attempt to show actual harm, and suggests that this failure means that there was no actual harm. Our case law does not support that inference. When a mark owner cannot prove actual damages attributable to the infringer's misconduct (e.g., specific instances of lost sales), its recovery of an equitable share of the infringer's profits serves, *inter alia*, as a "rough measure" of the likely harm that the mark owner incurred because of the infringement, while also preventing the infringer's unjust enrichment and deterring further infringement. The district court explicitly concluded that the profits award here was "sufficiently substantial to serve these purposes without being unduly large or burdensome." We find no fault with this conclusion.

McGills' alternative theory is that the award of profits is overstated because the "only possible enrichment" to McGills from the use of the Venture marks would have arisen from its sales of foils and tapes. McGills argues, without marshaling any competent evidence, that its sales of those products amounted to less than one percent of its total sales. McGills complains that Venture should have known this and provided more detailed breakdowns to the court. McGills asserts that Venture "copied over 5000 records," but "carefully chose to show none of it to the Court."

This argument entirely misplaces the burden of proof for a profit award under the Lanham Act. We have held that "once the plaintiff has shown direct competition and infringement, the statute places the burden on the infringer to show the limits of the direct competition." This allocation of burdens arises from the language of the Lanham Act itself: "In assessing profits the plaintiff shall be required to prove defendant's sales only; defendant must prove all elements of cost or deduction claimed." Here, Venture met its burden by introducing tax returns showing Venture's gross sales over the relevant time period. McGills then had the burden of producing evidentiary documentation that some of those sales were unrelated to and unaided by McGills' illicit use of Venture's marks. The company produced no such evidence. As a result, there was no clear error in the district court's determination that $230,339.17 represented an equitable share of McGills' $1.9 million in gross sales during the three-and-a-half year infringement period.

C. Attorney's Fee Award

Finally, McGills challenges the district court's award of $188,583.06 in attorney's fees. The Lanham Act permits the court to award reasonable attorney's fees to the prevailing party in "exceptional cases." * * * The district court has discretion to consider an infringement case "exceptional" if, after reviewing the totality of the circumstances, it finds that the infringer's actions were "malicious, fraudulent, deliberate, or willful." As we noted above, the district court did not err in concluding that McGills' infringement was "willful." Accordingly, it did not abuse its discretion in determining that this is an "exceptional case" where an award of attorney's fees is appropriate.

Affirmed.

QUESTIONS FOR DISCUSSION FOR CASE 6.4

1. Did the plaintiff have to show actual consumer confusion or a likelihood of consumer confusion to support its claim? Did the plaintiff succeed in meeting its burden of proof on trademark infringement?
2. How did the trial court calculate damages? Was its calculation correct? Which party has the burden of proof on determination of damages?
3. Under what circumstances may a court award attorneys' fees to a prevailing party under the Lanham Act?

DISCUSSION QUESTIONS

1. Steinway & Sons, the makers of high-quality pianos, sued a company that produced clip-on beverage can handles under the mark "STEIN-WAY." Under what theory would Steinway & Sons sue? Should Steinway & Sons prevail?
2. Identify each of the following marks as arbitrary or fanciful, suggestive, descriptive, or generic:
   a. "Hard Rock Cafe" for a restaurant/bar
   b. "Raisin Bran" for breakfast cereal
   c. "Coppertone" for sun lotion
   d. "Nyquil" for cold medicine
   e. "Pioneer" for sugar
   f. "Brim" for coffee
   g. "Lite Cola" for a reduced-calorie soft drink
3. L'Oreal wanted to introduce a "hair cosmetic" product that gave hair a blue, green, or other vivid-color tint. L'Oreal wanted to market the product under the name "Zazu" and began to investigate the availability of this trademark. L'Oreal found out that the mark was in use by a clothing manufacturer and a hair salon, Zazu Hair Design (ZHD). L'Oreal contacted both companies to inquire about their intended use of the mark. L'Oreal paid $125,000 to the clothing manufacturer, which was producing clothing with the mark, for the right to use the mark for its hair cosmetic. However, when L'Oreal asked ZHD if it were producing products with the mark, ZHD informed L'Oreal that it had not yet produced products but was "working on it."

Satisfied that the ZHD state trade name did not prevent its use of the mark, L'Oreal applied for federal registration of the Zazu mark on June 12, 1986, and began advertising and shipping large quantities of product in August 1986. However, in the meantime, ZHD began to develop a line of hair care products under the Zazu name in 1985. During November 1985 and February 1986, ZHD sold two bottles of its new formula to friends and one carton of bottles to another hair salon. These sales were informal, and the product was sold in plain bottles with a ZHD business card taped to the product. ZHD was confident of its line's success and placed a large manufacturing order in late 1985. Additionally, ZHD began selling small quantities of hand-filled and -labeled bottles of the products from its salon in September 1986. ZHD sued to enjoin L'Oreal from using the trademark Zazu and for damages. What result?

4. Jim Henson's popular characters, the Muppets, starred in the movie *Muppet Treasure Island*, in which Henson's production company introduced a new character—a wild boar named Spa'am. Hormel Foods, which manufactures Spam luncheon meat, took offense at its mark being associated with this character. Hormel sued Henson's production company to enjoin the use of the mark. Should the court prohibit the production company from using the mark? Why, or why not?

5. Shark Products began the manufacture and sale of a hair care product under the name "Miracle Gro." Stern's, which has been producing the Miracle-Gro line of plant foods since 1951 and had federally registered the mark, objected to Shark's use of the mark. In prelitigation negotiations, Shark assured Stern's that it would modify its packaging of the Miracle Gro hair products. Although Shark did modify the packing of its hair care products, it did not remove the words "Miracle Gro" from the product. Stern's sued for trademark infringement and dilution. What result?

6. Tour 18 is a golf course that replicates distinctive holes from some of the world's most famous golf courses. The course offers replicas from 16 different golf courses including Pinehurst, Pebble Beach, and Sea Pines' Harbour Town course. Tour 18's promotional material, tee markers, course signs, and dining room menus all make reference to the more well-known courses. For example, Tour 18 refers to the replica of Harbour Town's famous 18th hole as the "Lighthouse Hole," which is also what golfers call Harbour Town's hole. In addition, Tour 18's dining room offers "Pebble Beach" French toast and

"Pinehurst" tuna salad. Tour 18 does use a disclaimer that notes that none of the replicas are sponsored or endorsed by the more famous golf courses. Nevertheless, Pebble Beach, along with several other courses, objects to the copying of its hole designs and the use of its registered service marks. It sues for trademark and trade dress infringement as well as trademark dilution. What result?

7. When the New Kids on the Block were a popular musical group, several newspapers and magazines ran polls in which fans were asked to vote for their favorite member of the group. The ads for the polls contained copy such as "Who is the most popular New Kid?". Fans called 900 numbers to vote, and the companies running the polls charged a fee per vote. The New Kids on the Block took exception to the use of their name in such a moneymaking enterprise and sued for trademark infringement. What result?

8. Harley-Davidson motorcycles are often called "hogs." Indeed, some dictionaries even define "hog" as a motorcycle, especially a large one. While Harley-Davidson had mixed feelings about its products being referred to as a "hog," with the unsavory Hell's Angels image that the term conjures, it also recognized the marketing potential of the term. As a result, Harley-Davidson finally registered the term "hog" as trademark for its motorcycles in 1990.

Ronald Grottanelli, like many motorcycle enthusiasts, had used the term "hog" when referring to Harley-Davidson motorcycles for many years. In fact, he had been operating a motorcycle repair shop since 1969 under the name "The Hog Farm." In addition, Grottanelli offered products such as Hog Wash, an engine degreaser, and a "Hog Trivia" board game. Harley-Davidson sued for trademark infringement and dilution. What result?

9. Mana Products and Columbia Cosmetics both sell cosmetic products to beauty salons and other retailers. The retailers then label the products with their own names and resell them to the public. One of Mana's products is an unusually-shaped black makeup compact; Columbia sells an identical item. Mana claimed that the shape and black color of its compact case are protectable trade dress, and it sued Columbia for infringement. Can the color of a compact case be a protectable trade dress? What are the possible consequences if it is?

10. Disc Golf Association (DGA) manufactures equipment for the game of "disc golf." Disc golf is played like normal golf, but with flying discs like Frisbees.

The object of the game is to throw the disc into the "hole" in as few attempts as possible. DGA manufactures disc golf "holes," which consist of a target of suspended loose chains that are designed to deflect a thrown disc into a basket below. DGA's patent on this device expired in 1994. Champion Discs, a competitor, subsequently began to make similar disc golf targets. DGA sued for trademark and trade dress infringement. What result?

11. Leatherman Tool Group, Inc., was the first to market a multifunction pocket tool, which it sold under the name "Pocket Survival Tool" (PST). Cooper Industries, Inc., became aware of the PST and its market success. It admittedly copied the PST "almost exactly" and came out with a multipurpose tool, called the Toolzall that differed in appearance from the PST in only three respects: (1) it was marked with a different name than the PST; (2) it had different fasteners than those used on the PST; and (3) it had a serrated blade, which the PST did not.

    Leatherman filed suit and obtained a preliminary injunction prohibiting Cooper from marketing the Toolzall on the grounds that the overall appearance of the PST was protected trade dress. At trial, the jury found that Cooper had infringed on Leatherman's protected trade dress, and the court issued a permanent injunction prohibiting Cooper from marketing the original Toolzall. Cooper appealed. What legal rules should the court apply in evaluating this appeal?

12. The well-known publication, *The Economist*, brought a UDRP action to gain control of the domain name www.theeconomist.com. The registrant of the domain name had registered the name 11 years earlier. For over five years, the registrant did not use the name. The registrant then created a single-page site, which had a photograph of prominent economist Alan Greenspan with a legend underneath reading "Alan Greenspan, Chairman Federal Reserve Board is The Economist of the century," and links to websites concerning Greenspan and the Federal Reserve System. Under the UDRP, to succeed, *The Economist* had to show: (1) the disputed domain name was identical or confusingly similar to a trademark or service mark in which *The Economist*

had rights; (2) the registrant had no rights or legitimate interests in the disputed domain name; and (3) the disputed domain name had been registered and was being used in bad faith by the registrant. How should the Panel decide this case?

13. Louisiana State University, Ohio State University, the University of Oklahoma, and the University of Southern California have each adopted a two-color scheme to represent their schools. These color combinations have been in use over 100 years and are easily recognized by those familiar with the schools. The schools sell tens of millions of dollars of merchandise each year using these color schemes, the color schemes are frequently referenced in media accounts, and the universities advertise their color schemes in a multitude of ways.

    Smack Apparel Co. manufacturers T-shirts aimed at college sports fans. It uses school colors and various printed messages associated with the schools on its shirts.

    The universities sued Smack for trademark infringement, arguing that the color combinations acted as a source identifier, especially when used with other indicia identifying the school. The schools had not registered these color combinations as marks, however. How should the court rule on the universities' claims?

14. Louis Vuitton Malletier S.A., a French corporation located in Paris that manufactures luxury luggage, handbags, and accessories, sued Haute Diggity Dog, LLC, a Nevada corporation that manufactures and sells pet products nationally, alleging trademark infringement and trademark dilution. Haute Diggity Dog manufactures plush dog chew toys parodying famous trademarks on luxury products. Louis Vuitton Malletier's complaint involved chew toys in the shape of small handbags mimicking a $1,190 Louis Vuitton handbag and labeled "Chewy Vuitton." (Other toys marketed by Haute Diggity Dog were named "Chewnel No. 5," "Furcedes," "Sniffany & Co.," and "Dogior.")

    What legal rules should the court apply in evaluating Louis Vuitton Malletier's allegations of trademark infringement and dilution? How should the court rule on these claims?

CHAPTER 7

Commercial Speech and the Regulation of Advertising

Marketers who wish to advertise their goods or services—and few marketers do not–find themselves faced with an extensive and often bewildering array of state and federal laws regulating their activities. Most of the regulation is designed to protect consumers from false or deceptive advertising, but it does so in widely divergent ways. Some of the laws arise under state common law; some under state or federal statutory law; and some under federal or state agency regulation. Some give the injured consumer the right to sue and recover redress; some give aggrieved competitors the right to sue; and others permit only the government to sue, with redress sometimes going to the government and sometimes to the consumer.

All such laws are constrained by the First Amendment to the U.S. Constitution, however, which protects free speech, including commercial speech. Thus, regulations affecting advertising practices reflect a tension between protecting the advertiser's right to free speech, on the one hand, and the consumer's right to not be misled or deceived, on the other. This chapter first discusses commercial free speech, then examines various forms of state and federal regulation of advertising practices.

Commercial Free Speech

Commercial speech is expression that is related to the economic interests of the speaker and its audience. It is protected under the First Amendment to the U.S. Constitution, which provides in relevant part: "Congress shall make no law ... abridging the freedom of speech ...." The most common form of commercial speech, not surprisingly, is advertising. As Justice Stevens stated in one commercial speech case:

> Advertising has been a part of our culture throughout our history. Even in colonial days, the public relied on "commercial speech" for vital information about the market. Early newspapers displayed advertisements for goods and services on their front pages, and town criers called out prices in public squares. Indeed, commercial messages played such a central role in public life prior to the Founding that Benjamin Franklin authored his early defense of a free press in support of his decision to print, of all things, an advertisement for voyages to Barbados.[1]

Not all speech is protected under the First Amendment, however, nor does all protected speech receive the same degree of protection. Some speech, such as obscenity, receives no protection at all. At the other end of the spectrum, political speech, which is considered essential to the functioning of a democracy, receives the greatest degree of First Amendment protection from government intrusion.

---

[1] *44 Liquormart, Inc. v. Rhode Island,* 517 U.S. 484, 495 (1996).

Until the 1970s, the Supreme Court had ruled that commercial speech was not entitled to protection under the First Amendment. The Court then recognized that such speech is important for the functioning of a free market. In 1976, in *Virginia State Board of Pharmacy v. Virginia Citizens Consumer Council, Inc.*,[2] the Supreme Court reversed its former stance. The Court explained: "[P]eople will perceive their own best interests if only they are well enough informed, and the best means to that end is to open the channels of communication to them rather than close them."[3]

Today, commercial speech is afforded an intermediate level of First Amendment protection. The Supreme Court has determined that commercial speech is entitled to "'a limited measure of protection commensurate with its subordinate position in the scale of First Amendment values,' and is subject to 'modes of regulation that might be impermissible in the realm of noncommercial expression.'"[4] Commercial free speech claims are typically evaluated under a four-part analysis articulated by the Supreme Court in *Central Hudson Gas & Electric Corp. v. Public Service Commission of New York*[5] in 1980. The *Central Hudson* test asks:

1. Is the speech protected by the First Amendment (i.e., does it concern lawful activity and is it not misleading)?
2. Is the asserted governmental interest in the regulation substantial?
3. Does the regulation directly advance the governmental interest asserted to a material degree?
4. Is the regulation no more extensive than necessary to serve that interest?

In subsequent cases, the Supreme Court has refined the *Central Hudson* test, establishing, for example, that to satisfy the third factor, the government bears the burden of showing that its regulation will advance its governmental interest "to a material degree."[6] In addition, the Court has clarified that under the fourth factor, the government is not required to employ the least restrictive regulation possible to accomplish its goal, but that it must show a "reasonable 'fit' between the legislature's ends and the means chosen to accomplish those ends."[7]

The Supreme Court's current commercial speech doctrine is not completely settled. Several years ago, the Supreme Court seemed to be stepping back from First Amendment protection of commercial speech. The Supreme Court's 1996 decision in *44 Liquormart, Inc. v. Rhode Island*,[8] however, revived the commercial speech doctrine. The *44 Liquormart* Court reversed a decision of the First Circuit, which had upheld a Rhode Island statute banning the advertising of retail liquor prices. The statute was challenged by in-state and out-of-state liquor vendors who wanted to advertise their prices in Rhode Island. The statute was defended by the State of Rhode Island and by local Rhode Island liquor stores who wished to maintain their prices. They argued that advertising liquor prices would lead to price wars and the lowering of prices, which would then lead to more sales and excessive drinking.

The Supreme Court held that the ban on price advertising was a violation of commercial free speech because it did not directly advance the state's interest in the promotion

---

[2]425 U.S. 748 (1976). This case involved the constitutionality of a Virginia statute that defined the advertising of prescription drug prices by licensed pharmacists as a form of unprofessional conduct.

[3]*Id.* at 770.

[4]*Board of Trustees of State University of New York v. Fox*, 492 U.S. 469, 477 (1989) (citations omitted).

[5]447 U.S. 557 (1980).

[6]See *Edenfield v. Fane*, 507 U.S. 761, 771 (1993).

[7]See *Board of Trustees of State University of New York v. Fox*, 492 U.S. 469, 480 (1989).

[8]517 U.S. 484 (1996).

of temperance and because it was more extensive than necessary to serve that interest. (In short, the state statute failed the third and fourth prongs of the *Central Hudson* test.) Although the Court was unanimous in agreeing that the statute was unconstitutional, the Court could not agree on the reasoning supporting that decision. Ultimately, the Justices issued four separate opinions. Despite the Justices' inability to agree on the proper rationale for striking down the regulation at issue, *44 Liquormart* seems to indicate that the Court will examine the third prong of the *Central Hudson* test carefully and will likely strike down any absolute prohibition on commercial speech that is not closely tailored to protect consumers from false or deceptive information.

On the flip side of the coin, the Supreme Court has also held that regulations designed to compel parties to engage in commercial speech, such as regulations mandating financial contributions to industry advertising campaigns, also will be scrutinized carefully. Generally, the Court has upheld such schemes when the compelled speech is ancillary to a larger regulatory scheme, but not when it is the primary purpose of the scheme (see Case Illustration 7.1).

CASE ILLUSTRATION 7.1

VIDEO SOFTWARE DEALERS ASS'N v. SCHWARZENEGGER, 556 F.3D 950 (9TH CIR. 2009)

FACTS The state of California passed a statute imposing restrictions and a labeling requirement on the sale or rental of "violent video games," such as *Grand Theft Auto: Vice City, Postal 2,* and *Duke Nukem 3D,* to minors. The state legislature stated that it had a compelling interest in passing the statute: "preventing psychological or neurological harm to minors who play violent video games."

The Video Software Dealers Association and the Entertainment Software Association challenged the statute, arguing that it violated their First Amendment rights. The trial court granted summary judgment to the Associations, and the state appealed.

DECISION On appeal, the Ninth Circuit held that: (1) the Act's ban on sales or rentals was an invalid content-based restriction on speech and (2) the Act's labeling requirement was invalid as it compelled false speech.

First, the court noted: "Existing case law indicates that minors are entitled to a significant measure of First Amendment protections, that content-based regulations are presumptively invalid and subject to strict scrutiny, and that if less restrictive means for achieving a state's compelling interest are available, they must be used." Only in "relatively narrow and well-defined circumstances may government bar public dissemination of protected materials to" minors.

Although the U.S. Supreme Court has recognized that "there is a compelling interest in protecting the physical and psychological well-being of minors," the state failed to prove that the harm it was concerned with was real and that the Act would alleviate that harm in a direct and material manner. The evidence presented by the state on this issue did not "establish[ ] or suggest[ ] a causal link between minors playing violent video games and actual psychological or neurological harm, and inferences to that effect would not be reasonable."

Moreover, the state failed to show that less restrictive means of achieving its goal were not available. The state seemed more focused on the "most-effective" means of achieving its objective, rather than the "least-restrictive" means. Parental controls available on modern gaming systems could further the government's purpose in protecting minors, as would an enhanced educational program aimed at retailers and parents regarding the industry's own rating system. Thus, the statute was not "narrowly tailored."

Second, the court found that the Act's labeling provision, which required that the front of the package of a "violent video game" be labeled with a four-square-inch label reading "18" was unconstitutional. Compelled speech is permissible if the "disclosure requirements are reasonably related to the State's interest in preventing deception of customers." Here, though, the statute was compelling video game manufacturers to display the state's subjective opinion, not

(Continued)

to disclose purely factual information. Because the court had already determined that the statute's provisions barring rental or purchase of games by minors was unconstitutional and because there is no state-mandated age threshold for purchasing or renting video games, the state-mandated label conveyed a false statement that certain conduct (purchase or rental of the video by a minor) is illegal when it is not. As the court noted, "[T]he State has no legitimate reason to force retailers to affix false information on their products." Thus, the statute's labeling requirement was unconstitutional.

◆ *See Discussion Cases 7.1, 7.2.*

Because misleading speech is not protected by the First Amendment, the government may regulate and prohibit advertising that is false, deceptive, or misleading. The government may also prohibit the advertising of illegal activities and may impose time, manner, or place restrictions on advertising. As the following discussion indicates, both the federal and state governments are very active in the regulation of advertising.

Common Law Causes of Action

Theoretically, a consumer who has been injured by false or deceptive advertising could rely upon common law contract or tort causes of action for relief. Realistically, the common law causes of action are less efficacious and thus less used than the statutory and regulatory causes of action. For example, a consumer who has been misled by false advertising could sue for *breach of contract.* The consumer might encounter difficulty in proving the existence of a contract, however, for, as discussed in Chapter 9, the courts generally view advertisements merely as invitations to negotiate, not as offers to enter into a contract on the terms stated in the advertisement.

Similarly, a consumer could sue for the tort of *fraudulent misrepresentation* (also known as *deceit* or *fraud*). To prove fraud, the plaintiff must show that the defendant intentionally misled the plaintiff by making a material misrepresentation upon which the plaintiff relied and that the plaintiff suffered injury as a result of that misrepresentation. The plaintiff must demonstrate that the defendant knew the misrepresentation was false, which can create difficult questions of proof. Furthermore, the misrepresentation must involve a statement of fact, not opinion, which can be a murky distinction in the advertising area.

In addition, the laws of *unfair competition* prevent false, deceptive, and unauthorized business practices, particularly in the areas of sales and advertising. Unfair competition law is an evolving and expanding field that encompasses a number of different theories used to control improper conduct in the marketplace. The most common of causes of action in this area are: (1) the right of publicity; (2) palming off (or passing off); (3) false advertising; and (4) disparagement. All of these causes of action originally started out as state common law torts. Today, the last three (but not the right of publicity) now have federal causes of action arising under the Lanham Act. Although a plaintiff is likely to state a claim under both state and federal law for these actions, federal law is generally regarded as the more important source of protection and relief in most instances.

The right of publicity is discussed next. The remaining three causes of action are discussed below in the context of the federal Lanham Act.

Right of Publicity

The *right of publicity* "signifies the right of an individual, especially a public figure or celebrity, to control the commercial value and exploitation of his name and picture or likeness and to prevent others from unfairly appropriating this value for commercial benefit."[9] "Commercial," in this context, is generally defined narrowly as being undertaken in the course of advertising or of promoting or selling a product or service, not simply of being part of a business venture or profit-motivated endeavor. Thus, the right of publicity generally does not prohibit the use of an individual's name, picture, or likeness "in news reporting, commentary, entertainment, works of fiction or nonfiction, or in advertising that is incidental to such uses."[10]

The right of publicity is somewhat akin to copyright law, but it differs from copyright law in a very key respect. To be copyrighted, works must exist in a tangible form; the right of publicity, on the other hand, protects the identity and/or persona of an individual and thus protects "intangible" as well as tangible forms of expression, such as a voice or live performance. Where copyright law and the right of publicity overlap, federal copyright law preempts state publicity right law. (Copyright law is discussed in Chapter 2.)

The right of publicity arises under state law and is relatively new, having been first articulated about 60 years ago.[11] About one-half of the states recognize the right of publicity as either a common law or statutory right.[12] In a few states, it arises under both common and statutory law (see Case Illustration 7.2).

CASE ILLUSTRATION 7.2

BURCK v. M MARS, INC., 571 F. SUPP. 2D 446 (S.D. N.Y. 2008)

FACTS Plaintiff Robert Burck had performed as a "street entertainer" in New York City's Times Square as The Naked Cowboy for over a decade. Burck performed wearing only a white cowboy hat, cowboy boots, and underwear, and carried a guitar strategically placed to give the illusion of nudity. He became a popular tourist attraction.

In April, 2007, defendants Mars, Incorporated ("Mars"), the maker of M&M candies, and Chute Gerdeman, Inc. ("Chute"), an advertising and design agency, began running an animated cartoon advertisement on two huge video billboards in Times Square. The ad starred a blue M&M dressed "exactly like The Naked Cowboy," wearing only a white cowboy hat, cowboy boots, and underwear, and carrying a guitar.

Burck sued, alleging that Defendants had violated his "right to publicity" under New York law. New York does not have a common law right to publicity. However, Sections 50 and 51 of the state Civil Rights Act protect against use "for advertising purposes, or for the purposes of trade, the name, portrait or picture of any living person without having first obtained the written consent of such person."

DECISION The court noted that Defendants had not used Burck's "portrait" or "picture." They "did not use an actual photograph or picture of Burck himself, nor did they use a recognizable likeness or representation of him." Moreover:

The plain language of the Civil Rights Law makes it clear that the statutory right to privacy does not extend to fictitious characters adopted or created by celebrities .... The Naked Cowboy is not a living person, but a character Burck takes on when performing. The privacy statutes were not intended to protect a trademarked, costumed character publicly performed by a person.

The court concluded: "[T]here was no attempt to create a portrait or picture of Burck himself. Rather, the purportedly infringing images were M&M characters wearing Burck's signature outfit. The images were not portraits or pictures of Burck as The Naked Cowboy, but of M&Ms dressed as The Naked Cowboy." Thus, the court dismissed Burck's right of publicity claim.

---

[9]*Estate of Presley v. Russen,* 513 F. Supp. 1339 (D.N.J. 1981).

[10]Restatement (Third) of Unfair Competition § 47.

[11]See *Haelan Labs., Inc. v. Topps Chewing Gum, Inc.,* 202 F.2d 866 (2d Cir. 1953).

[12]J. T. McCarthy, *The Rights of Publicity and Privacy,* § 6.6 (2000).

How might a plaintiff's identity be appropriated? First, an unauthorized use of a name, likeness, or nickname for commercial purposes is not permitted. "Crazylegs Hirsh," for example, a famous football player and team manager, recovered against a cosmetics company that used the name "Crazylegs" to market and promote a shaving cream for women's legs.[13] Similarly, eight actors from the TV show *The Sopranos* settled a lawsuit with electronics retailer Best Buy for $1.5 million. Best Buy ran a newspaper ad in 2002 featuring a publicity photograph from the show with text that read: "They got all the shows a guy wants, plus *The Sopranos*. What, you got a problem with that?" In 2009, actor and director Woody Allen settled a dispute with clothing retailer American Apparel for $5 million for the unauthorized use of his image. The company had used a still photo of Allen, dressed as an Orthodox Jew, from the movie *Annie Hall*, on two billboards, displayed for one week in Los Angeles and New York.[14]

Second, the unauthorized use of phrases associated with the plaintiff is prohibited. Johnny Carson, for example, recovered against a defendant who rented out "Here's Johnny!" portable toilets and advertised itself as "The World's Foremost Comodian."[15]

Third, the unauthorized use of impersonators is prohibited. Bette Midler recovered against Ford Motor Co., who had hired a singer to imitate Midler's famous rendition of "Do You Want to Dance" after Midler had refused to perform in the commercial herself.[16] Tom Waits won a similar suit against Frito-Lay, Inc., and its ad agency for imitating Waits in a radio ad for Salsa Doritos.[17]

In about one-half of the states recognizing this legal right, the right of publicity ceases at death. In 2007, for example, a court ruled that under New York law, Marilyn Monroe's publicity rights in photographer Sam Shaw's iconic images of her with her skirt blowing up in the film *The Seven Year Itch* ceased at her death in 1962. Thus, the photographer's estate was not liable for permitting the images to be used on a T-shirt sold by the discount retailer Target in 2005.[18] In the remaining states, the right is considered an economic interest that passes to the heirs at the individual's death. In the states in which it does survive death, it lasts for either the same time as copyright protection extends (typically, the life of the author plus 70 years) or for a specific time period set by the state. In Indiana, for example, that time period is 100 years after death.[19] The typical remedies for violation of the right of publicity include *preliminary* and/or *permanent injunctions, monetary damages*, and, in extreme cases, *punitive damages*.

Statutory and Regulatory Causes of Action

State Statutes

Aggrieved consumers may sue under state statutory law for injury resulting from deceptive advertising. For example, if the advertising can be construed as creating an express warranty, an injured consumer may sue for breach of express warranty under the Uniform Commercial Code (UCC). (Warranty issues are discussed in Chapter 10.) In addition, several states have private attorney general laws that permit consumers to bring suits for deceptive trade practices. For example, a class action suit was brought under California law against Kenner Corporation. Kenner had claimed that its Easy Bake

---

[13]*Hirsch v. S. C. Johnson & Son, Inc.*, 280 N.W.2d 129 (Wis. 1979).

[14]Palmeri, "American Apparel Settles with Woody Allen," *Business Week* (May 18, 2009).

[15]*Carson v. Here's Johnny Portable Toilets, Inc.*, 810 F.2d 104 (6th Cir. 1987).

[16]*Midler v. Ford Motor Co.*, 849 F.2d 460 (9th Cir. 1988).

[17]*Waits v. Frito-Lay, Inc.*, 978 F.2d 1093 (9th Cir. 1992).

[18]*Shaw Family Archives Ltd. v. CMG Worldwide, Inc.*, 486 F.Supp.2d 309 (S.D.N.Y. 2007).

[19]Ind. Code § 32-36-1-8.

Oven allowed children to bake treats in under 10 minutes. The plaintiffs claimed that the toy ovens actually took 29 to 34 minutes to bake the treats. The case was ultimately settled under a confidentiality agreement.[20]

Generally, however, the state statutes are seldom used. Instead, most false or deceptive advertising cases are brought under the federal Lanham Act or under regulation arising under the Federal Trade Commission (FTC) Act. The rest of this chapter focuses primarily on these federal causes of action.

The Lanham Act

In addition to providing for the registration and protection of trademarks (discussed in Chapter 6), the federal Lanham Act[21] forbids false designations of origin and false or misleading descriptions or representations of fact.

The Lanham Act provides a cause of action to competitors (but not consumers) who are injured by false advertising. The purpose of the Lanham Act is to ensure truthfulness in advertising and to prohibit misrepresentations of quality regarding either the advertiser's products or the products of its competitor. Thus, the Act prohibits the use of any false "description or representation" in connection with any goods or services. Many of the causes of action provided by the Lanham Act are also actionable under state law, so often a plaintiff may sue under either or both.

Passing Off   *Passing off*, also known as *palming off*, occurs when the defendant makes some sort of false representation that misleads consumers into thinking that the defendant's goods or services originate from, are sponsored by, or are affiliated with the plaintiff. Essentially, it is an attempt by the defendant to fool customers into thinking that the defendant's own goods or services are those of a competitor. *Reverse passing off* occurs when the defendant sells the plaintiff's product or service as the defendant's own (see Case Illustration 7.3).

Passing off can take a number of different forms. The defendant may make a direct false representation, such as telling customers that goods come from the plaintiff when they do not. Passing off can also involve an indirect false representation, such as the defendant showing the customer "samples" that are actually the plaintiff's goods and not its own. Passing off often involves the use of a trademark, trade name, or trade dress that is identical or confusingly similar to a mark, name, or trade dress of a competitor. A single act of the defendant can often be challenged both as passing off and as trademark infringement (discussed in Chapter 6).

Passing off is actionable under both common law and the federal Lanham Act. Remedies available under the common law for passing off include *injunctions* against further passing off and *damages* (measured by plaintiff's loss and/or defendant's profits). *Punitive damages* may also be available in egregious cases. Remedies for passing off under the Lanham Act are the same as the remedies for trademark infringement (discussed in Chapter 6): *preliminary* and/or *permanent injunctions* and *damages*, as well as the possible recovery of *treble damages* and *attorneys' fees*.

False Advertising   State and federal laws provide several causes of action for *false advertising*. A plaintiff may sue under state common law for false advertising when a competitor misrepresents the nature or characteristics of her own goods to consumers by making untrue, unsupported, or deceptive claims. The plaintiff must be able to demonstrate, however, that the defendant's false advertising resulted in an actual loss of

---

[20]See Jeff Barge, *Advertising Legal Wars Heating Up: Lawsuits Filed Over Pitches for Long-lasting Antacid, Quick-Baking Toy Ovens*, 82 A.B.A. J. 32 (Apr. 1996).

[21]15 U.S.C. §§ 1051-1129.

CASE ILLUSTRATION 7.3

BY RITE DISTRIBUTING, INC. v. THE COCA-COLA CO., 577 F. SUPP. 530 (D. UTAH 1983)

FACTS By-Rite Distributing, Inc., operated and sold self-service soft drink dispensing systems under the name "Carb-A-Drink." By-Rite used the system in some of its own convenience stores and marketed the system to others. The Carb-A-Drink system consisted of a large unit of fountain dispensing equipment, equipped with 10–20 heads dispensing up to 40 flavors of soft drinks. The fountain heads bore the trademarks of the products being dispensed. A customer would obtain an empty two-liter bottle bearing the trademark "CARB-A-DRINK" and would fill the bottle at the dispensing station. The customer was encouraged to return to the store and refill the bottle or other package of his own at the fountain. Thus, customers could and did fill empty bottles containing the trademarks of one soft drink manufacturer with products manufactured by another company. By-Rite also marketed a six-pack carrying case so that customers could fill and take home a number of bottles at one time. The bottles (and their contents) could remain in the customers' possession for three or more weeks and were often consumed by individuals other than those who purchased the products.

Several major soft drink producers, including The Coca-Cola Company, PepsiCo, Inc., Sunkist Soft Drinks, Inc., and Seven-Up USA, Inc., filed for a preliminary injunction, contending that By-Rite's activities constituted reverse passing off in violation of the Lanham Act.

DECISION The federal trial court agreed, stating: "Although purchasers at a Carb-A-Drink fountain will believe that they are buying the … defendants' products because they can see the trademarks on the fountain heads, other users who later drink these beverages at home, at picnics or elsewhere, will see only the CARB-A-DRINK trademark on the bottle, and they may be led to believe that it is a CARB-A-DRINK product. To the extent that they are satisfied with the product, only CARB-A-DRINK will benefit."

The court thus issued a preliminary injunction preventing By-Rite from selling in bottles soft drinks mixed from the defendant's fountain syrups. By-Rite was permitted to sell the products in cups, however.

customers for the plaintiff, which is a difficult burden of proof to meet. If the plaintiff and the defendant are the only competitors in the market, the plaintiff may be able to meet this burden. If there are several competitors, however, the plaintiff may well find it impossible to prove that, in the absence of the defendant's false advertising, customers would have bought from the plaintiff (as opposed to one of the other competitors).

To counter this difficult burden of proof, many states now have statutes prohibiting false advertising. The statutes vary considerably from state to state. Some allow state agencies to sue, some allow consumers to sue, and others allow competitors to sue. The 12 or so states that have adopted the Uniform Deceptive Trade Practices Act (UDTPA) allow any person "likely to be damaged" by the false advertising to sue for injunctive relief.

The federal Lanham Act provides a cause of action for false advertising that is considerably broader than the common law action for false advertising. Section 43(a) of the Act provides:

> Any person who, on or in connection with any goods or services, or any container for goods, uses in commerce any … false or misleading description of fact, or false or misleading representation of fact, which … in commercial advertising or promotion, misrepresents the nature, characteristics, qualities, or geographic origin of his or her or another person's goods, services, or commercial activities, shall be liable in a civil action by any person who believes that he or she is likely to be damaged by such act.[22]

---

[22]15 U.S.C. § 1125(a)(1)(B).

To receive *injunctive relief under* Section 43(a), the plaintiff must show: (1) the defendant made a false or misleading statement of fact in advertising about its own product; (2) the statement actually deceived or had the capacity to deceive a substantial segment of the audience; (3) the deception was material (i.e., it was likely to influence consumers' purchasing decisions); (4) the defendant caused its goods to enter interstate commerce; and (5) the plaintiff was or is likely to be injured as a result. Note that to receive an injunction the plaintiff need not show actual injury—the potential for injury is sufficient (see Case Illustration 7.4).

To receive *monetary damages*, the plaintiff must prove that the advertisement was false, that consumers actually relied upon the false advertisement, and that the plaintiff's business incurred economic injury.

CASE ILLUSTRATION 7.4

THE PROCTER & GAMBLE CO. v. ULTREO, INC., 574 F. SUPP. 2D 339 (S.D. N.Y. 2008)

FACTS The Procter and Gamble Company ("P&G"), the manufacturer of Oral B toothbrushes and dental care products, sued Ultreo, Inc., creator and manufacturer of the Ultreo toothbrush, alleging that Ultreo made false and misleading advertising claims in violation of federal and state law with respect to the ultrasound component of the Ultreo toothbrush. P&G sought a preliminary injunction enjoining Ultreo from disseminating any "advertising, marketing, or promotional statements, whether made expressly or by implication, that the ultrasound feature of its toothbrush has any effect upon plaque removal or teeth cleaning, or that its ultrasound feature is magic or in any way falsely describing the nature of ultrasound cycles."

DECISION The court denied P&G's motion for preliminary injunction because it had failed to show a likelihood of irreparable harm if the preliminary injunction were not granted.

The court stated the general rule: "A party seeking preliminary injunctive relief must establish: (1) either (a) a likelihood of success on the merits of its case or (b) sufficiently serious questions going to the merits to make them a fair ground for litigation and a balance of hardships tipping decidedly in its favor, and (2) a likelihood of irreparable harm if the requested relief is denied." Moreover, "[a] preliminary injunction is an 'extraordinary remedy' that should not be routinely granted."

There are limited instances in which irreparable harm is presumed: (1) when comparative advertising is literally false and mentions the plaintiff's product by name; (2) when comparative advertising is literally false and makes it obvious to the viewing public that the

advertisement is targeted at the plaintiff even though the plaintiff is not mentioned by name; and (3) when the defendant's false or misleading advertising claims create a danger to public health. None of these instances were present in this dispute, so P&G was not entitled to a presumption of irreparable harm.

Thus, P&G had to demonstrate that it would be irreparably harmed by Ultreo's allegedly false and misleading advertising. The court stated:

> Because "[i]t is virtually impossible to prove that so much of one's sales will be lost or that one's goodwill will be damaged as a direct result of a competitor's advertisement," a plaintiff "need not … point to an actual loss or diversion of sales" to satisfy this requirement. At the same time, "something more than a plaintiff's mere subjective belief that [it] is injured or likely to be damaged is required before [it] will be entitled even to injunctive relief." In general, "[t]he likelihood of injury and causation will not be presumed, but must be demonstrated in some manner." Finally, "injunctive relief is not barred just because the possibility that the total pecuniary harm might be relatively slight."

P&G argued that introduction of the Ultreo toothbrush would cause P&G to lose sales. However, the court found that P&G had failed to draw a logical causal connection between Ultreo's allegedly false advertising and P&G's sales position. P&G failed to differentiate between sales lost to allegedly false advertising and sales lost "due to healthy market competition." P&G could not complain of sales lost as a result of Ultreo's lawful market entry.

(Continued)

P&G also argued that the evidence indicated that a substantial percentage of consumers were being misled by the advertising, which provided P&G with a reasonable basis to believe that the false advertising would cause it injury. The court found that the consumer surveys that P&G relied upon were "deeply flawed." For example, one survey failed to employ a control group, used "filter" questions that were actually leading questions, and improperly conflated survey responses. Thus, the court found the surveys failed to demonstrate irreparable harm to P&G resulting from Ultreo's advertising.

Finally, the court also noted that although P&G first complained about Ultreo's advertising in March, 2007, it waited six months to file for a preliminary injunction. The court stated: "[T]he failure to act sooner undercuts the sense of urgency that ordinarily accompanies a motion for preliminary relief and suggests that there is, in fact, no irreparable injury." By contrast, "a short delay does not weigh against irreparable harm 'where there is good reason for it, as when a plaintiff is not certain of the infringing activity or has taken additional time to examine the infringing product.'" While the six-month delay was not dispositive of P&G's claims, the court noted that "P&G failed adequately to explain the reason for the delay…." Thus, P&G's motion for preliminary injunction was denied.

Under the Lanham Act, the defendant's statements need not be literally false. Rather, to establish a false advertising claim under the Lanham Act, the plaintiff must show either that (1) the advertisement is literally false as a factual matter, or (2) although literally true, the advertisement actually deceives or confuses consumers. Thus, representations that are literally true but because of innuendo, omission, or ambiguity may be deemed "implicitly false" subject the defendant to liability. Where representations are implicitly, rather than literally, false, the plaintiff is required to demonstrate that consumers were in fact misled by the representations. This is usually accomplished through consumer surveys or market studies (see Case Illustration 7.5).

➡ *See Discussion Case 7.3.*

CASE ILLUSTRATION 7.5

S.C. JOHNSON & SON v. CLOROX CO., 2000 U.S. DIST. LEXIS 3621 (S.D.N.Y. JAN. 7, 2000); *S.C. JOHNSON & SON v. CLOROX CO.,* 2000 U.S. DIST. LEXIS 4977 (S.D. N.Y. APRIL 6, 2000)

FACTS Clorox Co. ran 15- and 30-second television advertisements showing a water-filled Slide-Loc food storage bag manufactured by its competitor, S.C. Johnson & Sons, Inc., turned upside-down. The advertisements showed water leaking out of the bag at a rapid rate, with air bubbles forming in the bag. As stated by the trial court, "[T]he overall impression, that is, the overall depiction in the commercial itself is of a rapid and substantial leakage and flow of water out of the Slide-Loc bag. This is rendered even more graphic because there is a goldfish depicted in the bag which is shown to be in jeopardy because the water is running out at such a rate." S.C. Johnson & Co, filed suit, claiming that the advertisement was literally false and requesting an injunction prohibiting further airing of the advertisements.

DECISION The court found that when the Slide-Loc bags and Clorox's own Glad bags were subjected to the same quality control tests, two-thirds of both types of the bags showed some leakage. However, the "'great majority" of the leaks were small and very slow and occurred only when the bags were held upside-down. Because normal consumers do not use the bags to hold water, particularly upside-down, and because the commercial greatly exaggerated the leakage of Slide-Loc bags, the court found that aspect of the advertisements to be literally false. It enjoined Clorox Co. from running the advertisements.

Three months later, the parties were back before the same court. Clorox Co. had revised its advertisement and was airing a new 15-second commercial as well as

(Continued)

running a print ad in a popular women's magazine. The new commercial, like the original one, displayed a bag filled with water, containing a goldfish, and held upside-down. It did not, however, display a rate of leakage as fast as that shown in the original ad. The print ad had a single image of a Slide-Loc bag with a large drop of water about to fall away and the goldfish in danger of suffocating.

The court again found that both advertisements were literally false because they did not indicate that leakage occurs in only a certain percentage of such bags rather than all of them, and because nothing indicated the degree of risk of such leakage.

Thus, the court issued an injunction against both the new commercial and the print advertisement.

Commercial Disparagement   *Commercial disparagement*, also known as *product disparagement*, is closely related to false advertising. It arises when the defendant makes false or deceptive representations about the quality of *plaintiff's* goods or services (as opposed to false or deceptive representations about the quality of *defendant's* own goods or services, which would be false advertising).

Commercial disparagement, like false advertising, can arise under state common law. The requirements vary from state to state, but, generally, the plaintiff is required to show (1) a false representation and (2) a specific economic loss (also known as "special damages"). General statements of comparison ("Product X is better than Product Y") or *puffing* (i.e., obviously exaggerated claims about a product or service or vague generalizations, such as "Product X is the best") do not constitute commercial disparagement. The special damages element requires the plaintiff to show that it suffered actual, specific harm as a result of the defendant's disparagement, such as lost business and revenue. Some jurisdictions also add a third element by requiring the plaintiff to show that the defendant intended to harm the plaintiff or at least acted with a reckless disregard for the effect of the disparagement on the plaintiff.

The UDTPA allows injunctive relief against false or misleading statements of fact that disparage the goods, services, or business of another, if the plaintiff shows that it is "likely to be damaged" by the statements.

Section 43(a) of the federal Lanham Act prohibits disparaging statements about a plaintiff's goods or services as well as false statements about the defendant's own goods or services. It is similar to the common law's cause of action for commercial disparagement. Section 43(a) does not require a showing of intent to harm, however, nor does it require proof of specific economic loss to support injunctive relief (though proof of actual economic harm is required for recovery of monetary damages).

The Federal Trade Commission Act

The Federal Trade Commission (FTC) is responsible for enforcement of the FTC Act,[23] which is designed to promote competition and to protect the public from unfair and deceptive acts and practices in the marketing of goods and services. The FTC was created by Congress in 1914 to bolster the country's then weak antitrust laws. (The antitrust role of the FTC is discussed in Chapter 4.)

Section 5 of the FTC Act provides that one of the FTC's tasks is to prevent "unfair or deceptive acts or practices [and] unfair methods of competition"; this is where the FTC's ability to regulate advertising is found. Today, the FTC has primary responsibility for regulating deceptive advertising in the United States. Although the discussion in this chapter focuses primarily on advertising issues, it is important to note that the FTC's jurisdiction extends to all kinds of deceptive or unfair acts, including marketing and

---

[23]15 U.S.C. §§ 41-58.

promotional activities and sales practices in general, not just to advertising violations. These issues are discussed further in Chapter 8.

The FTC is an independent federal administrative agency. As such, it is not subject to political control as are executive branch agencies. The FTC is headed by five commissioners who are appointed by the President and confirmed by the Senate for staggered seven-year terms. The President also appoints one of the commissioners as chair of the FTC.

Much of the FTC's regulation of deceptive or unfair acts or practices focuses on deceptive advertising, including deceptive price and quality claims, false testimonials, and the use of mock-ups. The FTC has issued a number of guides and policy statements that clarify these rules for industry and the public,[24] such as a guide on the use of endorsements and testimonials. The FTC also promulgates policy statements on topics such as comparative advertising claims and substantiation for product claims. These guides and policy statements do not have the force of law, but they are very useful tools in helping businesses to understand what activities or practices are legal or illegal.

Although the FTC's authority to regulate extends only to advertising that promotes goods and services involved in interstate commerce, the courts define interstate commerce so broadly that the majority of goods or services fall within this category. Truly local advertising is regulated, if at all, at the state level. Most states do have laws, known as "Little FTC Acts," that regulate state advertising activities.

The FTC has jurisdiction over most ads for most products and services. Certain other government agencies can investigate advertising by certain specialized industries, such as airlines, banks, insurance companies, telephone and cable companies, and companies that sell securities and commodities. Additional special laws apply to ads for certain products or services, such as consumer leases, credit, 900 telephone numbers, and products sold through mail order or telephone sales. These issues are discussed further in Chapter 8.

The FTC Act does not give consumers or competitors the right to sue; rather, only the FTC may bring suit under the Act. FTC action can originate from an FTC-initiated investigation of business behavior or from an informal complaint made by a competitor or consumer. The FTC generally does not release the name of the complainant unless required to do so by law.

Because the FTC lacks the resources to respond to all complaints made, it investigates those that most directly implicate its mission of protecting consumers and fostering free competition. In particular, in making its enforcement decisions, the FTC tends to focus on national (as opposed to local) advertising, advertising that represents a pattern of deception (as opposed to an isolated dispute between a consumer and business or between two competitors), and cases that could affect consumer health or safety or result in widespread economic injury. The FTC's mandate is to act when it appears both that a company's advertising is deceptive *and* that FTC action is in the public interest. Thus, the FTC does not become involved in purely private disputes. While FTC investigations of an advertiser are confidential, FTC formal actions against an advertiser (such as filing a lawsuit or reaching settlement with the advertiser) are made public.

After investigating, the FTC staff submits a recommendation to the commission recommending that the case be closed, that the commission settle the case, or that the FTC issue a formal complaint against the respondent. If the case is settled, the parties enter into a *consent order* in which the FTC agrees not to pursue the case further in return for the business agreeing to refrain from engaging in specified acts. The business does not necessarily admit to having engaged in any illegal activities, however. Violation of a consent order is a civil infraction punishable by fines of up to $11,000 per day.

---

[24]These are available online at www.ftc.gov

If a formal complaint is issued (and the FTC and the business do not agree on a settlement), the case is heard by an administrative law judge (ALJ) in an administrative hearing. The ALJ listens to evidence and arguments made by legal counsel for both the business and the FTC and issues an initial decision.

The decision of the ALJ becomes the decision of the full commission after 30 days unless the commission determines on its own to review it, or unless either party appeals to the commission. When the full commission reviews an ALJ decision, it may affirm the decision, modify it, or reverse it. If the commission affirms or modifies the decision, it issues an order against the business. Once the order is issued, the business has 60 days to appeal to the U.S. Court of Appeals. From there, either party may file for a writ of certiorari from the Supreme Court.

The penalties available under the FTC Act vary with the nature of the violation. The FTC or the courts can issue a *cease-and-desist order*, which requires the advertiser to stop running the deceptive or unfair ad or to stop engaging in the deceptive or unfair practice, to obtain substantiation for claims made in future ads, to report periodically to the FTC about that substantiation, and to pay a fine of $11,000 per day per ad if the advertiser violates the law in the future.

Violations can also result in *civil penalties* that can range up to millions of dollars depending upon the nature of the violation. In some cases, advertisers have been required to provide *consumer redress* in the form of full or partial refunds to all consumers who bought the product.

The FTC can also require an advertiser to engage in *corrective advertising*. This usually takes the form of requiring the advertiser to air a new ad to correct the misinformation contained in the original ad, to notify purchasers about deceptive claims in ads, or to provide other information to consumers. The FTC has required corrective advertising in a number of consent orders[25] but has seldom ordered this remedy in litigated cases. (However, competitors do routinely seek, and often receive, corrective advertising in a number of other contexts, including under Section 43(a) of the Lanham Act.[26])

In the 1970s, the FTC challenged Warner-Lambert Company's 40-year advertising campaign touting Listerine mouthwash as a cure for colds. The commission ordered the company to undertake $10 million of corrective advertising (its average annual advertising budget at the time), stating that corrective advertising is appropriate when: (1) the advertisement is deceptive; (2) the advertisement played a substantial role in creating or reinforcing in the public's mind a false and material belief; and (3) the belief survives even once the deceptive advertisement ceases[27] (see Case Illustration 7.6).

Finally, in extreme instances, the FTC has actually *banned* individuals from future participation within an industry or has required individuals to post a *bond* before continuing business.

General Principles of FTC Regulation of Business Acts and Practices

Generally, the law requires that advertising be: (1) truthful and not misleading; (2) substantiated (i.e., backed up by evidence); and (3) fair. In particular, the FTC can regulate

---

[25]See, e.g., *Eggland's Best, Inc.*, Docket No. C-3520 (Aug. 15, 1994); *Unocal Corp.*, 117 F.T.C. 500 (1994); *AHC Pharmaceuticals, Inc.*, 95 F.T.C. 528 (1980).

[26]See *Alpo PetFoods, Inc. v. Ralston Purina Co.*, 720 F. Supp. 194 (D.D.C. 1989), *aff'd in pertinent part and vacated in part*, 913 F.2d 958 (D.C. Cir. 1990); *John Wright, Inc. v. Casper Corp.*, 419 F. Supp. 292 (E.D. Pa. 1976), *aff'd in pertinent part sub nom., Donsco, Inc. v. Casper Corp.*, 587 F.2d 602 (3d Cir. 1978); *Ames Publishing Co. v. Walker-Davis Publications, Inc.*, 372 F. Supp. 1 (E.D. Pa. 1974).

[27]*Warner-Lambert Co. v. F.T.C.*, 86 F.T.C. 1398, 1499-1500 (1975), *aff'd*, 562 F.2d 749 (D.C. Cir. 1977).

CASE ILLUSTRATION 7.6

NOVARTIS CORP. v. FTC, 223 F.3D 783 (D.C. CIR. 2000)

FACTS Ciba-Geigy Corporation purchased the Doan's analgesic pain reliever brand in 1987. Ciba's consumer perception research indicated that its target market—back pain sufferers likely to use over-the-counter pain relievers—rated Doan's below its competitors in relieving back pain. From 1988 to 1996, first Ciba and then Novartis Corporation, its successor, engaged in a $55 million ad campaign that stressed that Doan's had a special efficacy in relieving back pain. Ciba/Novartis had no substantiation for claiming the product was superior to other over-the-counter analgesics in relieving back pain.

DECISION After the FTC took action, the advertising agency entered into a consent order with the FTC regarding its role in the ad campaign, agreeing to have scientific evidence to support claims regarding the efficacy, safety, benefits, or performance of any over-the-counter analgesic it advertised. The charges against Novartis were heard in an administrative hearing before an ALJ, who found the company liable for deceptive advertising. However, the ALJ declined to order corrective advertising, finding that the third element of the *Warner-Lambert* test (i.e., that the belief survives even once the deceptive advertising ceases) had not been met. In reaching this determination, the ALJ relied upon Novartis' evidence showing low 24- and 72-hour recall regarding the superiority claim and the fact that the ad campaign had been much shorter than the multi-decade Listerine campaign.

On appeal, the FTC ordered the company to carry the statement "Although Doan's is an effective pain reliever, there is no evidence that Doan's is more effective than other pain relievers for back pain" on all packaging and advertising materials for one year, excluding radio and television ads of less than 15 seconds, until it had expended on corrective advertising an amount equal to the average spent annually during the eight years of the advertising campaign.

Novartis Corp. then appealed to the U.S. Court of Appeals, arguing that the advertisements were not "deceptive" because the claim made was not material. Novartis also argued that there was no evidence that consumers had actually relied upon the claims and that the FTC's action infringed on its First Amendment right to commercial speech. The Court of Appeals rejected all of Novartis' claims and upheld the FTC's findings.

business acts or practices that are either (1) unfair or (2) deceptive. A marketing practice can be unfair without being deceptive, and vice versa. Thus, separate rules apply to each of these areas.

Unfairness　The FTC Act does not list unfair trade practices, as Congress was aware that such a list would necessarily be incomplete and would quickly become outdated. Instead, the Commission was given the task of identifying unfair trade practices, with the understanding that criteria for defining these would evolve and develop gradually.

The FTC's *Policy Statement on Unfairness*[28] explains the factors that the FTC now looks at in evaluating whether a business action is unfair. According to the *Policy Statement*, an advertisement or business practice is unfair: (1) if it causes or is likely to cause substantial consumer injury; (2) that a consumer could not reasonably avoid; and (3) the injury is not outweighed by any countervailing benefits to consumers or competition.

"Substantial injury" generally refers to monetary harm or unwarranted health and safety risks. Trivial, speculative, or merely emotional harms generally do not suffice to render an advertisement unfair. The *Policy Statement* specifically notes that certain practices may cause some consumer injury but that the injury may be offset by benefits to consumers. For example, an advertiser's failure to present technical data on the product may hamper a consumer's ability to choose but may also result in a reduced price. Such

---

[28]www.ftc.gov/bcp/policystmt/ad-unfair.htm

trade-offs are permissible provided that the net effect upon consumers is not injurious. Moreover, the FTC generally regards consumers as having free choice and expects that the marketplace will correct many unfair practices (i.e., consumers will simply refuse to buy from companies engaging in unfair practices). However, the FTC also recognizes that certain selling practices, such as withholding critical price or performance data, overt coercion, or undue influence over susceptible classes of purchasers (such as children or the terminally ill), may prevent the market from operating fairly and so may require agency intervention.

Deception   Advertising is more likely to run afoul of the ban against deceptive practices than it is the rules addressing unfair business practices. Deceptive practices involve acts such as false oral or written representations, misleading price claims, sales of dangerous or systematically defective products or services without adequate disclosures, bait-and-switch tactics, and failure to meet warranty obligations.

Under the FTC's *Policy Statement on Deception*,[29] an advertisement or other type of business practice is *deceptive:* (1) if it contains a representation, omission, or practice that (2) is likely to mislead consumers acting reasonably under the circumstances and (3) is "material" (i.e., is important to a consumer's decision to buy or use the product, such as representations about a product's performance, price, features, or effectiveness). Although this standard does not refer explicitly to an injury, the *Policy Statement* provides:

> Injury to consumers can take many forms. Injury exists if consumers would have chosen differently but for the deception. If different choices are likely, the claim is material, and injury is likely as well. Thus, injury and materiality are different names for the same concept.

The FTC can show that an advertisement is deceptive either by (1) proving its falsity or (2) showing that its proponent lacked a reasonable basis for asserting its truth. An advertiser can be liable even if it did not intend or did not know that its advertisement was deceptive.

To determine whether an advertisement is deceptive, the FTC begins by evaluating the ad from the perspective of the "reasonable consumer." As the FTC noted in an early case:

> An advertiser cannot be charged with liability in respect of every conceivable misconception, however outlandish, to which his representations might be subject among the foolish or feeble-minded. Some people, because of ignorance or incomprehension, may be misled by even a scrupulously honest claim. Perhaps a few misguided souls believe, for example, that all "Danish pastry" is made in Denmark. Is it "therefore" an actionable deception to advertise "Danish pastry" when it is made in this country? Of course not. A representation does not become "false and deceptive" merely because it will be unreasonably misunderstood by an insignificant and unrepresentative segment of the class of persons to whom the representation is addressed.[30]

If the representation or sales practice is targeted toward a specific audience, such as children, the elderly, or doctors, the FTC considers the effect of the representation or practice upon a reasonable member of that group. Note, however, that the standard is whether the practice is *likely* to mislead consumers; actual deception is not required. However, the FTC does not pursue advertising claims based upon subjective claims (e.g., taste, feel, appearance, or smell) or upon cases involving puffing.

---

[29]www.ftc.gov/bcp/policystmt/ad-decept.htm

[30]*In re Heinz W. Kirchner*, 63 F.T.C. 1282, 1290 (1963).

The FTC evaluates the entire ad—words, phrases, and pictures—to determine what message it conveys to consumers. The FTC also examines whether the ad omits information in such a way as to deceive or mislead the consumer. The makers of Campbell soup, for example, advertised that "most" Campbell soups were low in fat and cholesterol (a truthful statement) and were thus useful in fighting heart disease. However, the advertisements failed to point out that the soups were high in sodium and that high-sodium diets may increase the risk of heart disease. The FTC ruled that the company's failure to disclose the sodium content of the soups was deceptive. Campbell Soup Co. entered into a consent agreement in which it agreed to disclose the sodium content of any soup containing more than 500 milligrams of sodium per eight-ounce serving in any ad that directly or by implication mentioned heart disease in connection with the soup. Campbell also agreed not to make any direct or implied representation regarding soup and the reduction of the risk of heart disease unless it possessed, at the time of the representation, "competent and reliable scientific or medical evidence" to that effect.[31]

The FTC evaluates both "express" and "implied" claims, and the advertisers must have proof to substantiate both types of claims made in an ad. An *express* claim is a statement literally made within the ad. An *implied* claim is made indirectly or through inference. Thus, a claim that "XYZ Sunscreen prevents skin cancer" is an express claim that the sunscreen does indeed prevent skin cancer. A claim that "XYZ Sunscreen blocks the harmful sun rays that cause skin cancer" is an implied claim. A reasonable consumer could conclude from the latter statement that XYZ Sunscreen prevents skin cancer.

The advertiser must disclose whatever qualifying information is necessary to ensure that the express or implied claims are not misleading to the consumer. All such disclosures must be clear, conspicuous, and in the same language as that used principally in the advertisement. A *disclosure* or *disclaimer* does not rectify a false or deceptive claim.

The FTC considers certain types of representations presumptively "material," including express claims, implied claims intentionally made by the seller, and claims or omissions involving health, safety, or other areas with which a reasonable consumer would be concerned, such as the efficacy or cost of the product or service, durability, performance, quality, or warranties. Thus, in scrutinizing advertising, the FTC pays the most attention to ads that make claims about health or safety (e.g., "XYZ Antibacterial Soap kills germs") and ads that make claims that consumers would have difficulty evaluating for themselves (e.g., "XYZ Laundry Detergent is safe for septic systems"). The FTC is less concerned with ads that make subjective claims or claims that consumers can easily judge for themselves (e.g., "Everybody loves XYZ cereal").

The FTC also scrutinizes carefully advertising that is aimed at children, because children are less-sophisticated consumers and are often more susceptible to deception. Advertising aimed at children is evaluated from a child's, not an adult's, perspective. The FTC works with the Children's Advertising Review Unit (CARU) of the Council of Better Business Bureaus (CBBB)[32] on children's advertising issues. CARU, created in 1974, is a private, self-regulatory group that promotes truthful, accurate, and socially responsible advertising that is sensitive to the needs of children. CARU monitors advertisements directed to children age 12 and under in broadcast and cable television, radio, children's magazines, comic books, and online services.

The FTC Act also requires *substantiation* of advertising. A firm's failure to possess and rely upon a reasonable basis for objective claims made in advertisements is itself an unfair or deceptive trade practice. The advertiser bears the burden of demonstrating an ad is true. (Contrast this to the Lanham Act where the consumer or competitor bears the

---

[31]*In re Campbell Soup Co.*, 1991 F.T.C. LEXIS 303 (Apr. 17, 1991).

[32]CARU's website is www.caru.org

burden of demonstrating that the ad is false.) The FTC regards advertising substantiation as very important and has issued a *Policy Statement Regarding Advertising Substantiation*.[33] The advertiser and its ad agency must have evidence to support any claims made *before* the advertisement is run. The amount of evidence required depends upon the claim or claims made, but, at a minimum, the advertiser must have the level of evidence that it says that it has. Thus, if a toothpaste ad states that "three out of four dentists recommend" a particular brand, the advertiser must have competent and reliable *scientific* evidence to support that claim.

◆ *See Discussion Case 7.4.*

Advertising agencies, website designers, and catalog marketers, as well as advertisers themselves, may be held liable for deceptive ads. In considering whether a third party, such as an ad agency, should be held liable, the FTC looks at that party's participation in the preparation of the deceptive ad and whether it knew or should have known that the ad included false or deceptive claims. Ad agencies and website designers have a legal duty to independently verify the information used to substantiate claims and may not rely upon the advertiser's representation or assurance regarding claim substantiation.

Specific Advertising Practices

The FTC has issued guidances on several types of advertising practices to assist advertisers in determining what is or is not permissible.

Deceptive Pricing   The FTC has issued a *Guides Against Deceptive Pricing*.[34] The FTC defines *deceptive pricing* as any practice that tends to mislead or deceive consumers about the price that they are paying for goods or services. Deceptive pricing includes, for example, statements regarding the former or regular price of the merchandise that are false or two-for-one deals or offers of free merchandise coupled with a purchase where the advertiser has simply inflated the regular price of the merchandise bought to cover the costs of the supposedly "free" goods.

The *Deceptive Pricing Guides* provide some very specific rules regarding pricing strategies. For example, retail price comparisons ("Brand Y Printers, Price Elsewhere $329, Our Price $299") are permissible provided that a number of the principal retail outlets in the area regularly sell Brand Y Printers for $329. Where only a few outlets sell the printer for that price, however, and the majority sell the printer for less, the advertisement would contain deceptive pricing information. Similarly, it is permissible to advertise a discount from the manufacturer's list or suggested retail price only if a substantial number of sales are made in the area at the list or suggested retail prices. If most goods are sold in the area at a lower price, the consumer would be likely to be misled by the advertisement promising a reduction.

Bait-and-switch advertising is also regulated by the FTC. According to the FTC *Guides Against Bait Advertising*,[35] bait-and-switch advertising occurs when the seller: (1) refuses to show, demonstrate, or sell the advertised item; (2) disparages the advertised product; (3) fails to have reasonable quantities of it on hand (unless the advertisement indicates the quantities are limited); (4) fails to take orders to deliver the item within a reasonable time; (5) shows a product that is defective or impractical for the use implied or stated in the advertisement; or (6) discourages salespersons from selling the item. In effect, the

---

[33]www.ftc.gov/bcp/guides/ad3subst.htm

[34]www.ftc.gov/bcp/guides/decptprc.htm

[35]www.ftc.gov/bcp/guides/baitads-gd.htm

company has advertised a product but has no intention of actually selling the consumer that item. Rather, the company intends to sell the consumer a different product, usually at a higher price. The product advertised at the lower price serves as the "bait"; once the consumer is in the store, he or she is encouraged to "switch" to the higher-priced product. The FTC considers bait-and-switch advertising to be deceptive.

Endorsements and Testimonials   The FTC has issued a document entitled *FTC Guides Concerning Use of Endorsements and Testimonials in Advertising*.[36] Advertisers commonly use actors, sports stars, and other prominent public figures to endorse or provide testimonials about their products. Such *endorsements* or *testimonials* are considered deceptive if the person involved does not in fact use or prefer the product. The advertiser can use the endorsement only as long as the endorser continues to use and prefer the product.

To give an "expert" opinion regarding a product or service, the endorser must indeed be sufficiently qualified to be regarded as an expert in the field. In addition, the expert must evaluate, examine, or test the product in the same manner that other experts in the field would normally use to substantiate the claims made in the advertisement.

If the advertisement contains an endorsement by what is represented to be an individual or group of "actual" consumers, actual consumers must be used or the advertisement must clearly and conspicuously disclose that the individuals depicted are actors, not actual consumers. In addition, the endorsement must reflect the *typical* experience of consumers who use the product, not the idiosyncratic experiences of one or a few consumers. The advertiser must disclose any payments made to the consumer for making the endorsement and generally must disclose any relationship between any endorser and the advertiser (such as an employee or family relationship) that might affect the weight or credibility of the endorsement.

Mock-ups   It is deceptive to show an advertisement that purports to be an actual product demonstration but is in fact a *mock-up* or *simulation*. Any use of a mock-up should be revealed, unless the mock-up or prop is necessary because of the difficulty of showing the actual product in the advertisements. This is why advertisers can use props, such as substituting mashed potatoes for ice cream (which would otherwise quickly melt under photographic lights), provided that the prop is not being used as actual proof of a product claim (such as the rich texture of the ice cream).

Volvo Corporation learned the dangers of not revealing mock-ups the hard way. It showed a television ad that depicted an oversized "monster" pickup truck driving over a row of cars. All of the cars except the Volvo were crushed. Volvo did not disclose that the Volvo automobile used in the ad had been structurally strengthened with steel and wood, while the other cars had been structurally weakened. Volvo and its advertising agency each paid a $150,000 fine to the FTC, though neither admitted to any wrongdoing. The consent order also prohibited further misrepresentations of the strength, structural integrity, or crashworthiness of any vehicle or of the safety of any occupant in a collision.[37]

The FTC also scrutinizes *product demonstrations* to make certain that they are truthful and not misleading. Advertisers should make certain that their product demonstrations accurately depict the product's qualities and capabilities and do not exaggerate or misrepresent the product or a competing product in any manner. In particular, advertisers should be certain that photographic techniques do not misrepresent or distort the

[36] www.ftc.gov/bcp/guides/endorse.htm

[37] "F.T.C. Accords on Volvo Ads," *The New York Times*, Aug. 22, 1991, at D19.

product's characteristics or qualities. Campbell Soup Co., for example, was held liable when its advertisement depicted bowls of soup filled with chunky ingredients. Marbles had actually been placed at the bottoms of the bowls in order to raise the ingredients to the surface.[38]

Comparative Advertising   The FTC has issued a *Statement of Policy Regarding Comparative Advertising*.[39] The FTC encourages the naming of or reference to competitors in advertising, even where the references are negative, provided that the statements are clear, truthful, and nondeceptive. Truthful and nondeceptive comparative advertising provides important information to consumers and can assist them in making informed, rational purchase choices. It can also lead to product innovation and improvement and to lower prices in the marketplace. For these reasons, the FTC generally opposes industry codes or standards that restrain comparative advertising or that require higher standards of substantiation for such advertising.

Sweepstakes and Contests   Sweepstakes-type promotions that require the participants to make a purchase are illegal. Each state also regulates sweepstakes and contests. It is imperative, therefore, that promoters examine the laws of each state in which they intend to advertise such activities.

EXHIBIT 7.1 Lanham Act v. FTC Act

	PURPOSE	WHO CAN BE A PLAINTIFF	WHO BEARS BURDEN OF PROOF	PRIMARY REMEDIES

Lanham Act	• Forbids false designation of origin and false or misleading descriptions or representations of fact
	• Includes:
	  ▪ passing off
	  ▪ false advertising
	  ▪ commercial disparagement
		Competitors	Plaintiff must prove that ads are *literally* false *or* that there is an actual deception	• Injunctive Relief
				• Monetary Damages
				• Costs and Attorneys' Fees in Exceptional Cases

FTC Act	• Prevents trade practices and acts that are:
	  ▪ unfair *or*
	  ▪ deceptive
	• Includes:
	  ▪ deceptive pricing
	  ▪ deceptive endorsements and testimonials
	  ▪ deceptive mock-ups
	  ▪ deceptive comparative advertising
		FTC	FTC must show ad has *capacity* to deceive or mislead the public	• Cease-and-Desist Order
				• Civil Penalties
				• Consumer Redress
				• Corrective Advertising

---

[38]*In re Campbell Soup Co.*, 77 F.T.C. 664 (1970). See also *In re Mattel, Inc.*, 79 F.T.C. 667 (1971), *modified*, 104 F.T.C. 555 (1984) (toy car's speed exaggerated).

[39]www.ftc.gov/bcp/policystmt/ad-compare.htm

State attorneys general have been particularly vigilant about sweepstakes abuses. For example, 39 states and the District of Columbia reached multimillion-dollar settlements with American Family Publishers (AFP). The states had alleged that AFP, in an effort to sell magazine subscriptions, had conducted misleading sweepstakes campaigns that had tricked many people into believing that they had won $11 million. The states also alleged that dozens of elderly people had traveled to Tampa, Florida (the return address listed on the entry) to collect a prize that they had not in fact won. While AFP admitted to no wrongdoing, it AFP agreed to stop telling people that they were "winners" or "finalists" unless in fact they actually were. In addition, future language stating that the individual "may already be a winner" must include in type not less than half that size the disclaimer "if you have the winning ticket." Several of the settlements also created funds for consumer redress.[40]

The National Advertising Division

The National Advertising Division (NAD)[41] of the CBBB offers a private court that both consumers and companies can use to resolve disputes. The advantages of using this private court rather than normal litigation are that the process can be kept private (whereas litigation is necessarily public); it often is much cheaper; and disputes can be resolved quickly (often within 60 days).

The NAD was created by the advertising community in 1971 as part of its effort to foster voluntary self-regulation, minimize government regulation, and increase public confidence in the credibility of advertising. It responds to complaints about national advertising brought by a variety of parties, including individual consumers, advertisers, the Better Business Bureau, and trade associations. The NAD also monitors national broadcast and cable television and print advertising and initiates its own complaints.

The NAD provides attorneys who review and evaluate claims substantiation and who investigate complaints about truth and accuracy in national advertising. The NAD may recommend that an advertiser voluntarily modify or discontinue false or inaccurate claims, but it does not impose penalties. NAD decisions are published on-line at its website. Unresolved controversies are referred to the National Advertising Review Board (NARB), a peer-review group composed of 70 advertising professionals and public interest members. The dispute is heard by a five-person panel of NARB members at a round-table review. The panel either overturns or upholds the NAD's decision. If the advertiser fails to comply with a NAD or NARB panel decision, the NAD may refer the file to the appropriate government agency and release information regarding the referral to the public and the press.

Advertising on the Internet

Advertising on the Internet raises a number of special legal issues. Some of these, such as deep linking and banner advertisements, are discussed in Chapter 6 in the context of trademark law. The discussion in this chapter focuses on the FTC's online advertising

---

[40]See "American Family Publishers, Spokesmen Settle Sweepstakes Lawsuit," *The Entertainment Litigation Reporter* (July 31, 1999); Lisa Renze-Rhodes, "Attorney General Declares State a Winner," *The Indiana Lawyer* (June 9, 1999), at p. 12; "NY Reaches $800,000 Settlement with American Family Publishers," *Gaming Industry Litigation Reporter* (Sept. 1998), p. 10.

[41]NAD's website can be found at www.nadreview.org

guidelines and on privacy issues. Unsolicited commercial e-mail, or spam, is addressed in Chapter 8.

On-line Advertising

The FTC has issued two documents addressing online advertising activities—*Dot Com Disclosures: Information about Online Advertising*[42] and *Advertising and Marketing on the Internet: Rules of the Road.*[43] Generally, online advertising is subject to the same rules that apply to advertising in other media. The FTC takes its role in regulating Internet advertising seriously and has brought numerous enforcement actions to stop advertising abuses online.

The same *disclosure* requirements that apply to traditional advertising media apply to online advertising. To ensure that disclosures are clear and conspicuous in online ads, however, the FTC's *Dot Com Disclosures* document tells advertisers to consider:

- the *placement* of the disclosure in the ad,
- the *proximity* of the disclosure to the relevant claim,
- the *prominence* of the disclosure,
- whether other parts of the ad *distract attention* from the disclosure,
- whether the ad is so long the disclosure should be *repeated*,
- whether audio disclosures are presented in *adequate volume and cadence*,
- whether visual disclosures appear for sufficient *duration*, and
- whether the language of the disclosure is *understandable* to the intended audience.

The online version of the *Dot Com Disclosures* document contains examples of mock ads illustrating these factors.

Privacy Issues

The growth in electronic commerce has lead to many concerns about *privacy* issues. Online marketers can gather large amounts of information about actual or possible customers through the Web and the Internet. Website owners can use "cookies"[44] to store user information for future retrieval on the individual hard drives of users visiting their sites. Internet service providers (ISPs) can track a user's navigation through the Web by capturing "click stream data" (i.e., electronic records of the user's activities).

Currently, there is no single federal law directly governing consumer privacy issues in the United States, although there is a patchwork of federal and state statutes and case law that provide protections in specific circumstances. So, for example, the FTC can use the FTC Act to respond to unfair or deceptive acts by enforcing companies' promises about how they collect, use, and protect personal information of consumers.

In addition to the FTC Act, other federal statutes address specific privacy issues. Concerns about the online privacy of children led Congress to adopt the *Children's Online Privacy Protection Act* (COPPA).[45] COPPA regulates the operators of websites directed to children under the age of 13. It limits the use of personal information gathered online

---

[42]This guide can be found at www.ftc.gov/bcp/edu/pubs/business/ecommerce/bus41.pdf

[43]This guide can be found at www.ftc.gov/bcp/edu/pubs/business/ecommerce/bus28.htm

[44]A "cookie" is "a small data text file that is transferred from a Web server computer and sent back to the server computer whenever an HTML file request is made." Michael D. Scott, *Internet Technology Law Desk Reference* 111 (1999).

[45]15 U.S.C. §§ 6501-6508.

from such children and requires "verifiable parental consent" before such personal information can be collected. The FTC enforces the provisions of COPPA. The FTC issued its *Financial Privacy Rule* to address privacy concerns arising out of consumers' transactions with financial institutions.[46] The *Fair Credit Reporting Act* protects the privacy of information in consumer reports.[47]

The FTC promotes industry self-regulation in the privacy arena. Several trade associations have established privacy principles and guidelines for their members to follow in doing business on the Internet, including The Online Privacy Alliance,[48] The Direct Marketing Association,[49] and TRUSTe.[50] In addition, businesses can obtain "privacy seals" from various organizations, such as BBBOnLine, a subsidiary of the CBBB. These seals give customers assurance that a website is abiding by its posted privacy protection policy.

Generally, all businesses that collect data online should post a prominent privacy policy on their website addressing issues such as the identity of the data gatherer, the purposes of the data, how long and in what manner the data will be kept, and how individuals may access their data or correct inaccuracies in it.

The European Union and countries in the Pacific Rim (including Hong Kong and New Zealand) have been much more proactive than the United States in protecting personal information on the Internet. The *European Union Personal Data Directive*,[51] for example, became effective in October 1998. The Directive places limitations on the type of data that can be collected, the manner in which it can be collected, and the manner in which it may be used. It also grants certain rights, including access, to the provider of the information. The Directive also provides that the data can be transferred to another country only if the other country provides an "adequate level of protection" to the data. Because the United States does not currently meet this standard, the directive would have put U.S. businesses at a disadvantage. Thus, the U.S. Department of Commerce and the European Commission developed a "safe harbor" framework in 2000 that enables U.S. companies adhering to the framework to be certain that they provide "adequate" privacy protection.[52]

International Advertising Law

Regulation of advertising, whether online or conventional, varies greatly from country to country. Comparative advertising, for example, is prohibited in Germany, and several Scandinavian countries prohibit advertising directed at children. It is essential that marketers consult with attorneys of the country or countries in which they plan to advertise before beginning any advertising efforts overseas. Internet advertisers, in particular, need to be sensitive to the different regulatory regimes to which their sites may be subject. Information on international advertising law often can be found online. For example, the European Commission's Consumer Affairs website contains valuable information on EC advertising law.[53]

---

[46]www.ftc.gov/privacy/privacyiniatives/financial_rule.html

[47]www.ftc.gov/privacy/privacyinitiatives/credit.html

[48]www.privacyalliance.org

[49]www.the-dma.org/index.php

[50]www.truste.org

[51]Council Directive 95/46, 1995 O.J. (L 281) 31.

[52]See http://www.export.gov/safeharbor/index.asp

[53]http://ec.europa.eu/consumers/index_en.htm

DISCUSSION CASES

7.1 Commercial Speech
Rubin v. Coors Brewing Co., 514 U.S. 476 (1995)

OPINION: JUSTICE THOMAS Section 5(e)(2) of the Federal Alcohol Administration Act prohibits beer labels from displaying alcohol content. We granted certiorari in this case to review the Tenth Circuit's holding that the labeling ban violates the First Amendment because it fails to advance a governmental interest in a direct and material way. Because § 5(e)(2) is inconsistent with the protections granted to commercial speech by the First Amendment, we affirm.

I

Respondent brews beer. In 1987, respondent applied to the Bureau of Alcohol, Tobacco and Firearms (BATF), an agency of the Department of the Treasury, for approval of proposed labels and advertisements that disclosed the alcohol content of its beer. BATF rejected the application on the ground that the Federal Alcohol Administration Act (FAAA or Act) prohibited disclosure of the alcohol content of beer on labels or in advertising. Respondent then filed suit in the District Court … seeking a declaratory judgment that the relevant provisions of the Act violated the First Amendment; respondent also sought injunctive relief barring enforcement of these provisions. The Government took the position that the ban was necessary to suppress the threat of "strength wars" among brewers, who, without the regulation, would seek to compete in the marketplace based on the potency of their beer.

The District Court granted the relief sought, but a panel of the Court of Appeals for the Tenth Circuit reversed and remanded. Applying the framework set out in *Central Hudson Gas & Elec. Corp. v. Public Serv. Comm'n of N.Y.,* 447 U.S. 557 (1980), the Court of Appeals found that the Government's interest in suppressing alcoholic "strength wars" was "substantial." * * * The court remanded for further proceedings to ascertain whether a "reasonable fit" existed between the ban and the goal of avoiding strength wars.

After further factfinding, the District Court upheld the ban on the disclosure of alcohol content in advertising but invalidated the ban as it applied to labels. * * * On the case's second appeal, the Court of Appeals affirmed the District Court. After reviewing the record, the Court of Appeals concluded that the Government had failed to demonstrate that the prohibition in any way prevented strength wars. The court found that there was no evidence of any relationship between the publication of factual information regarding alcohol content and competition on the basis of such content.

We granted certiorari to review the Tenth Circuit's decision that § 205(e)(2) violates the First Amendment. We conclude that the ban infringes respondent's freedom of speech, and we therefore affirm.

II

A

* * * The [FAAA] establishes national rules governing the distribution, production, and importation of alcohol and established a Federal Alcohol Administration to implement these rules. Section 5(e)(2) of the Act prohibits any producer, importer, wholesaler, or bottler of alcoholic beverages from selling, shipping, or delivering in interstate or foreign commerce any malt beverages, distilled spirits, or wines in bottles

> unless such products are bottled, packaged, and labeled in conformity with such regulations, to be prescribed by the Secretary of the Treasury, with respect to packaging, marking, branding, and labeling and size and fill of container … as will provide the consumer with adequate information as to the identity and quality of the products, the alcoholic content thereof *(except that statements of, or statements likely to be considered as statements of, alcoholic content of malt beverages are prohibited unless required by State law and except that, in case of wines, statements of alcoholic content shall be required only for wines containing more than 14 per centum of alcohol by volume,) the net contents of the package, and the manufacturer or bottler or importer of the product.*

27 U.S.C. § 205(e)(2) (emphasis added). The Act defines "malt beverage [s]" in such a way as to include all beers and ales.

Implementing regulations promulgated by BATF … prohibit the disclosure of alcohol content on beer labels. In addition to prohibiting numerical indications of alcohol content, the labeling regulations proscribe descriptive terms that suggest high content, such as "strong," "full strength," "extra strength," "high test," "high proof," "pre-war strength," and "full oldtime alcoholic strength." The prohibitions do not preclude labels from identifying a beer as "low alcohol," "reduced alcohol," "non-alcoholic," or "alcohol-free." By statute and by regulation, the labeling ban must give way if state law requires disclosure of alcohol content.

B

Both parties agree that the information on beer labels constitutes commercial speech. Though we once took the position that the First Amendment does not protect commercial speech, we repudiated that position in *Virginia Bd. of Pharmacy v. Virginia Citizens Consumer Council, Inc.*, 425 U.S. 748 (1976). There we noted that the free flow of commercial information is "indispensable to the proper allocation of resources in a free enterprise system" because it informs the numerous private decisions that drive the system. Indeed, we observed that a "particular consumer's interest in the free flow of commercial information … may be as keen, if not keener by far, than his interest in the day's most urgent political debate."

Still, *Virginia Board of Pharmacy* suggested that certain types of restrictions might be tolerated in the commercial speech area because of the nature of such speech. In later decisions we gradually articulated a test based on "the 'commonsense' distinction between speech proposing a commercial transaction, which occurs in an area traditionally subject to government regulation, and other varieties of speech." *Central Hudson* identified several factors that courts should consider in determining whether a regulation of commercial speech survives First Amendment scrutiny:

> For commercial speech to come within [the First Amendment], it at least must concern lawful activity and not be misleading. Next, we ask whether the asserted governmental interest is substantial. If both inquiries yield positive answers, we must determine whether the regulation directly advances the governmental interest asserted, and whether it is not more extensive than is necessary to serve that interest.

We now apply *Central Hudson's* test to § 205(e)(2).

III

Both the lower courts and the parties agree that respondent seeks to disclose only truthful, verifiable, and nonmisleading factual information about alcohol content on its beer labels. Thus, our analysis focuses on the substantiality of the interest behind § 205(e)(2) and on whether the labeling ban bears an acceptable fit with the Government's goal. A careful consideration of these factors indicates that § 205(e)(2) violates the First Amendment's protection of commercial speech.

A

* * * [T]he Government contends that § 205(e)(2) advances Congress' goal of curbing "strength wars" by beer brewers who might seek to compete for customers on the basis of alcohol content. * * *

* * *

Rather than suppressing the free flow of factual information in the wine and spirits markets, the Government seeks to control competition on the basis of strength by monitoring distillers' promotions and marketing. * * * [T]he Government here has a significant interest in protecting the health, safety, and welfare of its citizens by preventing brewers from competing on the basis of alcohol strength, which could lead to greater alcoholism and its attendant social costs. * * * Both panels of The Court of Appeals that heard this case concluded that the goal of suppressing strength wars constituted a substantial interest, and we cannot say that their conclusion is erroneous.

* * *

B

The remaining *Central Hudson* factors require that a valid restriction on commercial speech directly advance the governmental interest and be no more extensive than necessary to serve that interest. * * * The Tenth Circuit found that § 205(e)(2) failed to advance the interest in suppressing strength wars sufficiently to justify the ban. We agree.

Just two Terms ago, in *Edenfield v. Fane*, 507 U.S. 761 (1993), we had occasion to explain the *Central Hudson* factor concerning whether the regulation of commercial speech "directly advances the governmental interest asserted." In *Edenfield*, we decided that the Government carries the burden of showing that the challenged regulation advances the Government's interest "in a direct and material way." That burden "is not satisfied by mere speculation or conjecture; rather, a governmental body seeking to sustain a restriction on commercial speech must demonstrate that the harms it recites are real and that its restriction will in fact alleviate them to a material degree." * * *

The Government attempts to meet its burden by pointing to current developments in the consumer market. It claims that beer producers are already competing and advertising on the basis of alcohol strength in the "malt liquor" segment of the beer market. The Government attempts to show that this competition threatens to spread to the rest of the market by directing our attention to respondent's motives in bringing this litigation. Respondent allegedly suffers from consumer misperceptions that its beers contain less alcohol than other brands. According to the Government, once respondent gains relief from § 205(e)(2), it will use its labels to overcome this handicap.

Under the Government's theory, § 205(e)(2) suppresses the threat of such competition by preventing consumers from choosing beers on the basis of alcohol content. It is assuredly a matter of "common sense" that a restriction on the advertising of a product characteristic will decrease the extent to which consumers select a product on the basis of that trait. * * *

We conclude that § 205(e)(2) cannot directly and materially advance its asserted interest because of the overall irrationality of the Government's regulatory scheme. While the laws governing labeling prohibit the disclosure of alcohol content unless required by state law, federal regulations apply a contrary policy to beer advertising. Like § 205(e)(2), these restrictions prohibit statements of alcohol content in advertising, but, unlike § 205(e)(2), they apply only in States that affirmatively prohibit such advertisements. As only 18 States at best prohibit disclosure of content in advertisements, brewers remain free to disclose alcohol content in advertisements, but not on labels, in much of the country. The failure to prohibit the disclosure of alcohol content in advertising, which would seem to constitute a more influential weapon in any strength war than labels, makes no rational sense if the Government's true aim is to suppress strength wars.

Other provisions of the FAAA and its regulations similarly undermine § 205(e)(2)'s efforts to prevent strength wars. While § 205(e)(2) bans the disclosure of alcohol content on beer labels, it allows the exact opposite in the case of wines and spirits. Thus, distilled spirits may contain statements of alcohol content, and such disclosures are required for wines with more than 14 percent alcohol. If combating strength wars were the goal, we would assume that Congress would regulate disclosure of alcohol content for the strongest beverages as

well as for the weakest ones. Further, the Government permits brewers to signal high alcohol content through use of the term "malt liquor." Although the Secretary has proscribed the use of various colorful terms suggesting high alcohol levels, manufacturers still can distinguish a class of stronger malt beverages by identifying them as malt liquors. One would think that if the Government sought to suppress strength wars by prohibiting numerical disclosures of alcohol content, it also would preclude brewers from indicating higher alcohol beverages by using descriptive terms.

* * *

Even if § 205(e)(2) did meet the *Edenfield* standard, it would still not survive First Amendment scrutiny because the Government's regulation of speech is not sufficiently tailored to its goal. The Government argues that a sufficient "fit" exists here because the labeling ban applies to only one product characteristic and because the ban does not prohibit all disclosures of alcohol content—it applies only to those involving labeling and advertising. In response, respondent suggests several alternatives, such as directly limiting the alcohol content of beers, prohibiting marketing efforts emphasizing high alcohol strength (which is apparently the policy in some other western nations), or limiting the labeling ban only to malt liquors, which is the segment of the market that allegedly is threatened with a strength war. We agree that the availability of these options, all of which could advance the Government's asserted interest in a manner less intrusive to respondent's First Amendment rights, indicates that § 205(e)(2) is more extensive than necessary.

IV

In sum, although the Government may have a substantial interest in suppressing strength wars in the beer market, the FAAA's countervailing provisions prevent § 205(e)(2) from furthering that purpose in a direct and material fashion. The FAAA's defects are further highlighted by the availability of alternatives that would prove less intrusive to the First Amendment's protections for commercial speech. Because we find that § 205(e)(2) fails the *Central Hudson* test, we affirm the decision of the court below.

QUESTIONS FOR DISCUSSION FOR CASE 7.1

1. Which prongs of the *Central Hudson* test were at issue in this case?

2. Why do you think that Coors wanted to put the alcohol content on its beer labels? The Court noted that Coors was concerned with the public's opinion that its beer had a low alcohol content. Does this turn alcohol content into a marketing point? Would this run counter to the government's significant interest in avoiding a "strength war"?

3. What other ways could the government have advanced its interest in preventing strength wars? Does Section 205(e)(2) fail on its own merits or because it was part of an inconsistent scheme of government regulation?

7.2 Commercial Speech
United States v. United Foods, Inc., 533 U.S. 405 (2001)

JUSTICE KENNEDY delivered the opinion of the Court.

Four Terms ago, in *Glickman v. Wileman Brothers & Elliott, Inc.*, 521 U.S. 457 (1997), the Court rejected a First Amendment challenge to the constitutionality of a series of agricultural marketing orders that, as part of a larger regulatory marketing scheme, required producers of certain California tree fruit to pay assessments for product advertising. In this case a federal statute mandates assessments on handlers of fresh mushrooms to fund advertising for the product. * * *

The statute in question, enacted by Congress in 1990, is the Mushroom Promotion, Research, and Consumer Information Act, 7 U.S.C. § 6101 *et seq*. The Act authorizes the Secretary of Agriculture to establish a Mushroom Council to pursue the statute's goals. Mushroom producers and importers, as defined by the statute, submit nominations from among their group to the Secretary, who then designates the Council membership. To fund its programs, the Act allows the Council to impose mandatory assessments upon handlers of fresh mushrooms in an amount not to exceed one cent per pound of mushrooms produced or imported. The assessments can be used for "projects of mushroom promotion, research, consumer information, and industry information." It is undisputed, though, that most monies raised by the assessments are spent for generic advertising to promote mushroom sales.

Respondent United Foods, Inc., is a large agricultural enterprise based in Tennessee. It grows and distributes many crops and products, including fresh mushrooms. In 1996 respondent refused to pay its mandatory assessments under the Act. The forced subsidy for generic advertising, it contended, is a violation of the First Amendment. * * *

* * * The District Court, holding *Glickman* dispositive of the First Amendment challenge, granted the Government's motion for summary judgment.

The Court of Appeals for the Sixth Circuit held this case is not controlled by *Glickman* and reversed the District Court. We agree with the Court of Appeals and now affirm.

A quarter of a century ago, the Court held that commercial speech, usually defined as speech that does no more than propose a commercial transaction, is protected by the First Amendment. "The commercial marketplace, like other spheres of our social and cultural life, provides a forum where ideas and information flourish."

We have used standards for determining the validity of speech regulations which accord less protection to commercial speech than to other expression. That approach, in turn, has been subject to some criticism. We need not enter into the controversy, for even viewing commercial speech as entitled to lesser protection, we find no basis under either *Glickman* or our other precedents to sustain the compelled assessments sought in this case. It should be noted, moreover, that the Government itself does not rely upon *Central Hudson* to challenge the Court of Appeals' decision, and we therefore do not consider whether the Government's interest could be considered substantial for purposes of the *Central Hudson* test. The question is whether the government may underwrite and sponsor speech with a certain viewpoint using special subsidies exacted from a designated class of persons, some of whom object to the idea being advanced.

Just as the First Amendment may prevent the government from prohibiting speech, the Amendment may prevent the government from compelling individuals to express certain views, or from compelling certain individuals to pay subsidies for speech to which they object. Our precedents concerning compelled contributions to speech provide the beginning point for our analysis. The fact that the speech is in aid of a commercial purpose does not deprive respondent of all First Amendment protection …. The subject matter of the speech may be of interest to but a small segment of the population; yet those whose business and livelihood depend in some way upon the product involved no doubt deem First Amendment protection to be just as important for them as it is for other discrete, little noticed groups in a society which values the freedom resulting from speech in all its diverse parts. First Amendment concerns apply here because of the requirement that producers subsidize speech with which they disagree.

"The general rule is that the speaker and the audience, not the government, assess the value of the information presented." There are some instances in which compelled subsidies for speech contradict that constitutional principle. Here the disagreement could be seen as minor: Respondent wants to convey the message that its brand of mushrooms is superior to those grown by other producers. It objects to being charged for a message which seems to be favored by a majority of producers. The message is that mushrooms are worth consuming whether or not they are branded. First Amendment values are at serious risk if the government can compel a particular citizen, or a discrete group of citizens, to pay special subsidies for speech on the side that it favors; and there is no apparent principle which distinguishes out of hand minor debates about whether a branded mushroom is better than just any mushroom. As a consequence, the compelled funding for the advertising must pass First Amendment scrutiny.

In the Government's view the assessment in this case is permitted by *Glickman* because it is similar in important respects. It imposes no restraint on the freedom of an objecting party to communicate its own message; the program does not compel an objecting party (here a corporate entity) itself to express views it disfavors; and the mandated scheme does not compel the expression of political or ideological views. These points were noted in *Glickman* in the context of a different type of regulatory scheme and are not controlling of the outcome. The program sustained in *Glickman* differs from the one under review in a most fundamental respect. In *Glickman* the mandated assessments for speech were ancillary to a more comprehensive program restricting marketing autonomy. Here, for all practical purposes, the advertising itself, far from being ancillary, is the principal object of the regulatory scheme.

In *Glickman* we stressed from the very outset that the entire regulatory program must be considered in resolving the case. In deciding that case we emphasized "the importance of the statutory context in which it arises." The California tree fruits were marketed "pursuant to detailed marketing orders that had displaced many aspects of independent business activity." Indeed, the marketing orders "displaced competition" to such an extent that they were "expressly exempted from the antitrust laws." The market for the tree fruit regulated by the program was characterized by "collective action, rather than the aggregate consequences of independent competitive choices." The producers of tree fruit who were compelled to contribute funds for use in cooperative advertising "did so as a part of a broader collective enterprise in which their freedom to act independently was already constrained by the regulatory scheme." The opinion and the analysis of the Court proceeded upon the premise that the producers were bound together and required by the statute to market their products according to cooperative rules. To that extent, their mandated participation in an advertising program with a particular message was the logical concomitant of a valid scheme of economic regulation.

The features of the marketing scheme found important in *Glickman* are not present in the case now before us. As respondent notes, and as the Government does not contest, almost all of the funds collected under the mandatory assessments are for one purpose: generic advertising. Beyond the collection and disbursement of advertising funds, there are no marketing orders that regulate how mushrooms may be produced and sold, no exemption from the antitrust laws, and nothing preventing individual producers from making their own marketing decisions. As the Court of Appeals recognized, there is no "heavy regulation through marketing orders" in the mushroom market. Mushroom producers are not forced to associate as a group which makes cooperative decisions. "The mushroom growing business … is unregulated, except for the enforcement of a regional mushroom advertising program," and "the mushroom market has not been collectivized, exempted from antitrust laws, subjected to a uniform price, or otherwise subsidized through price supports or restrictions on supply."

It is true that the party who protests the assessment here is required simply to support speech by others, not to utter the speech itself. We conclude, however, that the mandated support is contrary to the First Amendment principles set forth in cases involving expression by groups which include persons who object to the speech, but who, nevertheless, must remain members of the group by law or necessity.

The Government claims that, despite the lack of cooperative marketing, the *Abood* rule [*Abood v. Detroit Bd. of Ed.,* 431 U.S. 209 (1977)], protecting against compelled assessments for some speech is inapplicable. We did say in *Glickman* that *Abood* "recognized a First Amendment interest in not being compelled to contribute to an organization whose expressive activities conflict with one's 'freedom of belief.'" We take further instruction, however, from *Abood's* statement that speech need not be characterized as political before it receives First Amendment protection. A proper application of the rule in *Abood* requires us to invalidate the instant statutory scheme. Before addressing whether a conflict with freedom of belief exists, a threshold inquiry must be whether there is some state imposed obligation which makes group membership less than voluntary; for it is only the overriding associational purpose which allows any compelled subsidy for speech in the first place. In *Abood*, the infringement upon First Amendment associational rights worked by a union shop arrangement was "constitutionally justified by the legislative assessment of the important contribution of the union shop to the system of labor relations established by Congress." To attain the desired benefit of collective bargaining, union members and nonmembers were required to associate with one another, and the legitimate purposes of the group were furthered by the mandated association.

A similar situation obtained in *Keller v. State Bar of Cal.,* [496 U.S. 1 (1990)]. A state-mandated, integrated bar sought to ensure that "all of the lawyers who derive benefit from the unique status of being among those admitted to practice before the courts [were] called upon to pay a fair share of the cost." Lawyers could be required to pay monies in support of activities that were germane to the reason justifying the compelled association in the first place, for example expenditures (including expenditures for speech) that related to "activities connected with disciplining members of the Bar or proposing ethical codes for the profession." Those who were required to pay a subsidy for the speech of the association already were required to associate for other purposes, making the compelled contribution of monies to pay for expressive activities a necessary incident of a larger expenditure for an otherwise proper goal requiring the cooperative activity. The central holding in *Keller*, moreover, was that the objecting members were not required to give speech subsidies for matters not germane to the larger regulatory purpose which justified the required association.

The situation was much the same in *Glickman*. As noted above, the market for tree fruit was cooperative. To proceed, the statutory scheme used marketing orders that to a large extent deprived producers of their ability to compete and replaced competition with a regime of cooperation. The mandated cooperation was judged by Congress to be necessary to maintain a stable market. Given that producers were bound together in the common venture, the imposition upon their First Amendment rights caused by using compelled contributions for germane advertising was, as in *Abood* and *Keller*, in furtherance of an otherwise legitimate program. [T]he majority of the Court in *Glickman* found the compelled contributions were nothing more than additional economic regulation, which did not raise First Amendment concerns.

The statutory mechanism as it relates to handlers of mushrooms is concededly different from the scheme in *Glickman*; here the statute does not require group action, save to generate the very speech to which some handlers object. In contrast to the program upheld in *Glickman*, where the Government argued the compelled contributions for advertising were "part of a far broader regulatory system that does not principally concern speech," there is no broader regulatory system in place here. We have not upheld compelled subsidies for speech in the context of a program where the principal object is speech itself. * * * The only program the Government contends the compelled contributions serve is the very advertising scheme in question. * * * The cooperative marketing structure relied upon by a majority of the Court in *Glickman* to sustain an ancillary assessment finds no corollary here; the expression respondent is required to support is not germane to a purpose related to an association independent from the speech itself; and the rationale of *Abood* extends to the party who objects to the compelled support for this speech. For these and other reasons we have set forth, the assessments are not permitted under the First Amendment.

* * *

For the reasons we have discussed, the judgment of the Court of Appeals is
Affirmed.

QUESTIONS FOR DISCUSSION FOR CASE 7.2

1. The Court states that *Glickman* is not controlling precedent for this case. How does the Court distinguish

Glickman from this case? What was different about the regulatory schemes that were involved in these two cases?

2. How could the government rewrite the regulatory scheme involving mushroom growers to make this forced subsidy constitutional?

7.3 Lanham Act—False Advertising

Time Warner Cable, Inc. v. DirecTV, Inc., 497 F.3d 144 (2d Cir. 2007)

Defendant-Appellant DIRECTV, Inc. ("DIRECTV") appeals from the … opinion and order of the United States District Court for the Southern District of New York …, preliminarily enjoining it from disseminating, in any market in which Plaintiff-Appellee Time Warner Cable, Inc. ("TWC") provides cable service, certain television commercials and Internet advertisements found likely to violate the Lanham Act on literal falsity grounds.

This appeal requires us to clarify certain aspects of our false advertising doctrine. We make three clarifications in particular. First, we hold that an advertisement can be literally false even though it does not explicitly make a false assertion, if the words or images, considered in context, necessarily and unambiguously imply a false message. Second, we decide that the category of non-actionable "puffery" encompasses visual depictions that, while factually inaccurate, are so grossly exaggerated that no reasonable consumer would rely on them in navigating the marketplace. Third, we conclude that the likelihood of irreparable harm may be presumed where the plaintiff demonstrates a likelihood of success in showing that the defendant's comparative advertisement is literally false and that given the nature of the market, it would be obvious to the viewing audience that the advertisement is targeted at the plaintiff, even though the plaintiff is not identified by name. * * *

Factual Background

A. The Parties

TWC and DIRECTV are major players in the multichannel video service industry. TWC is the second-largest cable company in the United States, serving more than 13.4 million subscribers. Like all cable providers, TWC must operate through franchises let by local government entities; it is currently the franchisee in the greater part of New York City. DIRECTV is one of the country's largest satellite service providers, with more than 15.6 million customers nationwide. Because DIRECTV broadcasts directly via satellite, it is not subject to the same franchise limitations as cable companies. As a result, in the markets where TWC is the franchisee, DIRECTV and other satellite providers pose the greatest threat to its market share. * * *

TWC offers both analog and digital television services to its customers. DIRECTV, on the other hand, delivers 100% of its programming digitally. Both companies, however, offer high-definition ("HD") service on a limited number of their respective channels. Transmitted at a higher resolution than analog or traditional digital programming, HD provides the home viewer with theater-like picture quality on a wider screen. * * * To view programming in HD format, customers of either provider must have an HD television set.

There is no dispute, at least on the present record, that the HD programming provided by TWC and DIRECTV is equivalent in picture quality. In terms of non-HD programming, digital service generally yields better picture quality than analog service, because a digital signal is more resistant to interference. That said, TWC's analog cable service satisfies the technical specifications, *e.g.* signal level requirements and signal leakage limits, set by the Federal Communications Commission ("FCC"). * * *

B. Directv's "Source Matters" Campaign

In the fall of 2006, DIRECTV launched a multimedia advertising campaign based on the theme of "SOURCE MATTERS." The concept of the campaign was to educate consumers that to obtain HD-standard picture quality, it is not enough to buy an HD television set; consumers must also receive HD programming from the "source," *i.e.*, the television service provider.

1. Jessica Simpson Commercial

As part of its new campaign, DIRECTV began running a television commercial in October 2006 featuring celebrity Jessica Simpson. In the commercial, Simpson, portraying her character of Daisy Duke from the movie *The Dukes of Hazzard*, says to some of her customers at the local diner:

Simpson: Y'all ready to order?

　　Hey, 253 straight days at the gym to get this body and you're not gonna watch me on DIRECTV HD?

　　You're just not gonna get the best picture out of some fancy big screen TV without DIRECTV.

　　It's broadcast in 1080i. I totally don't know what that means, but I want it.

* * *

　　* * * The Revised Simpson Commercial … ends with [the] tag line: "For an HD picture that can't be beat, get DIRECTV."

2. William Shatner Commercial

DIRECTV debuted another commercial in October 2006, featuring actor William Shatner as Captain James T. Kirk, his character from the popular *Star Trek* television show and film series. The following conversation takes place on the Starship Enterprise:

Mr. Chekov: Should we raise our shields, Captain?

Captain Kirk: At ease, Mr. Chekov.

　　Again with the shields. I wish he'd just relax and enjoy the amazing picture clarity of the DIRECTV HD we just hooked up.

　　With what Starfleet just ponied up for this big screen TV, settling for cable would be illogical.

Mr. Spock: [Clearing throat.]

Captain Kirk: What, I can't use that line?

* * *

　　[The] Revised Shatner Commercial [ends] with the … tag line, "For an HD picture that can't be beat, get DIRECTV."

3. Internet Advertisements

DIRECTV also waged its campaign in cyberspace, placing banner advertisements on various websites to promote the message that when it comes to picture quality, "source matters." The banner ads have the same basic structure. They open by showing an image that is so highly pixelated that it is impossible to discern what is being depicted. On top of this indistinct image is superimposed the slogan, "SOURCE MATTERS." After about a second, a vertical line splits the screen into two parts, one labeled "OTHER TV" and the other "DIRECTV." On the OTHER TV side of the line, the picture is extremely pixelated and distorted, like the opening image. By contrast, the picture on the DIRECTV side is exceptionally sharp and clear. The DIRECTV screen reveals that what we have been looking at all along is an image of New York Giants quarterback Eli Manning; in another ad, it is a picture of two women snorkeling in tropical waters. The advertisements then invite browsers to "FIND OUT WHY DIRECTV'S picture beats cable" and to "LEARN MORE" about a special offer. In the original design, users who clicked on the "LEARN MORE" icon were automatically directed to the HDTV section of DIRECTV's website.

　　In addition to the banner advertisements, DIRECTV created a demonstrative advertisement that it featured on its own website. Like the banner ads, the website demonstrative uses the split-screen technique to compare the picture quality of "DIRECTV" to that of "OTHER TV," which the ad later identifies as representing "basic cable," *i.e.*, analog cable. The DIRECTV side of the screen depicts, in high resolution, an image of football player Kevin Dyson making a touchdown at the Super Bowl. The portion of the image on the OTHER TV side is noticeably pixelated and blurry. This visual display is accompanied by the following text: "If you're hooking up your high-definition TV to basic cable, you're not getting the best picture on every channel. For unparalleled clarity, you need DIRECTV HD. You'll enjoy 100% digital picture and sound on every channel and also get the most sports in HD-including all your favorite football games in high definition with NFL SUNDAY TICKET."

Procedural History

* * *

B. Preliminary Injunction Motion

[TWC filed motions for a preliminary injunction, challenging the Revised Simpson and Revised Shatner Commercials, and the Internet Advertisements.]

C. The District Court's February 5, 2007 Opinion and Order

On February 5, 2007, the District Court issued a decision granting TWC's motion. The District Court determined that TWC had met its burden of showing that each of the challenged advertisements was likely to be proven literally false. * * *

Discussion

A party seeking preliminary injunctive relief must establish: (1) either (a) a likelihood of success on the merits of its case or (b) sufficiently serious questions going to the merits to make them a fair ground for litigation and a balance of hardships tipping decidedly in its favor, *and* (2) a likelihood of irreparable harm if the requested relief is denied. * * *

A. Likelihood of Success on the Merits
1. Television Commercials

* * *

Two different theories of recovery are available to a plaintiff who brings a false advertising action under § 43(a) of the Lanham Act. First, the plaintiff can demonstrate that the challenged advertisement is literally false, *i.e.*, false on its face. When an advertisement is shown to be literally or facially false, consumer deception is presumed and "the court may grant relief without reference to the advertisement's [actual] impact on the buying public." "This is because plaintiffs alleging a literal falsehood are claiming that a statement, on its face, conflicts with reality, a claim that is best supported by comparing the statement itself with the reality it purports to describe."

Alternatively, a plaintiff can show that the advertisement, while not literally false, is nevertheless likely to mislead or confuse consumers. "[P]laintiffs alleging an implied falsehood are claiming that a statement, whatever its literal truth, has left an impression on the listener [or viewer] that conflicts with reality"—a claim that "invites a comparison of the impression, rather than the statement, with the truth." Therefore, whereas "plaintiffs seeking to establish a literal falsehood must generally show the substance of what is conveyed, … a district court *must* rely on extrinsic evidence [of

consumer deception or confusion] to support a finding of an implicitly false message."[3]

Here, TWC chose to pursue only the first path of literal falsity, and the District Court granted the preliminary injunction against the television commercials on that basis. In this appeal, DIRECTV does not dispute that it would be a misrepresentation to claim that the picture quality of DIRECTV HD is superior to that of cable HD. Rather, it argues that neither commercial explicitly makes such a claim, and therefore cannot be literally false.

a. Revised Simpson Commercial

DIRECTV's argument is easily dismissed with respect to the Revised Simpson Commercial. In the critical lines, Simpson tells audiences, "You're just not gonna get the best picture out of some fancy big screen TV without DIRECTV. It's broadcast in 1080i." These statements make the explicit assertion that it is impossible to obtain "the best picture"—*i.e.*, a "1080i"-resolution picture—from any source other than DIRECTV. This claim is flatly untrue; the uncontroverted factual record establishes that viewers can, in fact, get the same "best picture" by ordering HD programming from their cable service provider. We therefore affirm the District Court's determination that the Revised Simpson Commercial's contention "that a viewer cannot 'get the best picture' without DIRECTV is … likely to be proven literally false."

b. Revised Shatner Commercial

The issue of whether the Revised Shatner Commercial is likely to be proven literally false requires more analysis. When interpreting the controversial statement, "With what Starfleet just ponied up for this big screen TV, settling for cable would be illogical," the District Court looked not only at that particular text, but also at the surrounding context. In light of Shatner's opening comment extolling the "amazing picture quality of [] DIRECTV HD" and the announcer's closing remark highlighting the unbeatable "HD picture" provided by DIRECTV, the District Court found that the line in the middle—"settling for cable would be illogical"—clearly referred to cable's HD picture quality. Since it would only be "illogical" to "settle" for cable's HD picture if

---

[3]Under either theory, the plaintiff must also demonstrate that the false or misleading representation involved an inherent or material quality of the product. TWC has met this requirement, as it is undisputed that picture quality is an inherent and material characteristic of multichannel video service.

it was materially inferior to DIRECTV's HD picture, the District Court concluded that TWC was likely to establish that the statement was literally false.

* * *

[We] now formally adopt what is known in other circuits as the "false by necessary implication" doctrine. Under this doctrine, a district court evaluating whether an advertisement is literally false "must analyze the message conveyed in full context," *i.e.*, it "must consider the advertisement in its entirety and not … engage in disputatious dissection." If the words or images, considered in context, necessarily imply a false message, the advertisement is literally false and no extrinsic evidence of consumer confusion is required. However, "only an *unambiguous* message can be literally false." Therefore, if the language or graphic is susceptible to more than one reasonable interpretation, the advertisement cannot be literally false. There may still be a "basis for a claim that the advertisement is misleading," but to resolve such a claim, the district court must look to consumer data to determine what "the person to whom the advertisement is addressed find[s] to be the message." In short, where the advertisement does not unambiguously make a claim, "the court's reaction is at best not determinative and at worst irrelevant."

Here, the District Court found that Shatner's assertion that "settling for cable would be illogical," considered in light of the advertisement as a whole, unambiguously made the false claim that cable's HD picture quality is inferior to that of DIRECTV's. We cannot say that this finding was clearly erroneous, especially given that in the immediately preceding line, Shatner praises the "amazing picture clarity of DIRECTV HD." We accordingly affirm the District Court's conclusion that TWC established a likelihood of success on its claim that the Revised Shatner Commercial is literally false.

2. Internet Advertisements

We have made clear that a district court must examine not only the words, but also the "visual images … to assess whether [the advertisement] is literally false." It is uncontroverted that the images used in the Internet Advertisements to represent cable are inaccurate depictions of the picture quality provided by cable's digital or analog service. The Internet Advertisements are therefore explicitly and literally false.

DIRECTV does not contest this point. Rather, it asserts that the images are so grossly distorted and exaggerated that no reasonable buyer would take them to be accurate depictions "of how a consumer's television picture would look when connected to cable." Consequently, DIRECTV argues, the images are obviously just puffery, which cannot form the basis of a Lanham Act violation. * * *

This Court has had little occasion to explore the concept of puffery in the false advertising context. In *Lipton v. Nature Co.*, 71 F.3d 464 (2d Cir. 1995), the one case where we discussed the subject in some depth, we characterized puffery as "[s]ubjective claims about products, which cannot be proven either true or false." We also cited to the Third Circuit's description of puffery …: "Puffery is an exaggeration or overstatement expressed in broad, vague, and commendatory language. 'Such sales talk, or puffing, as it is commonly called, is considered to be offered and understood as an expression of the seller's opinion only, which is to be discounted as such by the buyer …. The 'puffing' rule amounts to a seller's privilege to lie his head off, so long as he says nothing specific.'" Applying this definition, we concluded that the defendant's contention that he had conducted "thorough" research was just puffery, which was not actionable under the Lanham Act.

* * * Unlike words, images cannot be vague or broad. To the contrary, visual depictions of a product are generally "specific and measurable," and can therefore "be proven either true or false," as this case demonstrates. Yet, if a visual representation is so grossly exaggerated that no reasonable buyer would take it at face value, there is no danger of consumer deception and hence, no basis for a false advertising claim.

Other circuits have recognized that puffery can come in at least two different forms. The first form we identified in *Lipton*—"a general claim of superiority over comparable products that is so vague that it can be understood as nothing more than a mere expression of opinion." The second form of puffery, which we did not address in *Lipton*, is "an exaggerated, blustering, and boasting statement upon which no reasonable buyer would be justified in relying." We believe that this second conception of puffery is a better fit where, as here, the "statement" at issue is expressed not in words, but through images.

* * *

Our review of the record persuades us that the District Court clearly erred in rejecting DIRECTV's puffery defense. The "OTHER TV" images in the Internet Advertisements are—to borrow the words of Ronald Boyer, TWC's Senior Network Engineer—"unwatchably blurry, distorted, and pixelated, and … nothing like the images a customer would ordinarily see using Time Warner Cable's cable service." Boyer further explained that

> the types of gross distortions shown in DIRECTV's Website Demonstrative and Banner Ads are not the type of disruptions that could naturally happen to an analog or non-HD digital cable picture. These advertisements depict the picture quality of cable television as a series of large colored square blocks, laid out in a grid like graph paper, which nearly entirely obscure the image. This is not the type of wavy or "snowy" picture that might occur from degradation of an unconverted analog cable picture, or the type of macro-blocking or "pixelization" that might occur from degradation of a digital cable picture. Rather, the patchwork of colored blocks that DIRECTV depicts in its advertisement appears to be the type of distortion that would result if someone took a low-resolution photograph and enlarged it too much or zoomed in too close. If DIRECTV intended the advertisement to depict a pixelization problem, this is a gross exaggeration of one.

As Boyer's declaration establishes, the Internet Advertisements' depictions of cable are not just inaccurate; they are not even remotely realistic. It is difficult to imagine that any consumer, whatever the level of sophistication, would actually be fooled by the Internet Advertisements into thinking that cable's picture quality is so poor that the image is "nearly entirely obscure[d]." As DIRECTV states in its brief, "even a person not acquainted with cable would realize TWC could not realistically supply an unwatchably blurry image and survive in the marketplace."

* * *

For these reasons, we conclude that the District Court exceeded its permissible discretion in preliminarily enjoining DIRECTV from disseminating the Internet Advertisements.

B. Irreparable Harm

A plaintiff seeking a preliminary injunction under the Lanham Act must persuade a court not only that it is likely to succeed on the merits, but also that it is likely to suffer irreparable harm in the absence of immediate relief. Because "[i]t is virtually impossible to prove that so much of one's sales will be lost or that one's goodwill will be damaged as a direct result of a competitor's advertisement," we have resolved that a plaintiff "need not … point to an actual loss or diversion of sales" to satisfy this requirement. At the same time, "something more than a plaintiff's mere subjective belief that [it] is injured or likely to be damaged is required before [it] will be entitled even to injunctive relief." The rule in this Circuit, therefore, is that a plaintiff "must submit proof which provides a reasonable basis" for believing that the false advertising will likely cause it injury.

In general, "[t]he likelihood of injury and causation will not be presumed, but must be demonstrated in some manner." We have held, however, that these elements may be presumed "where [the] plaintiff demonstrates a likelihood of success in showing literally false [the] defendant's comparative advertisement which mentions [the] plaintiff's product by name." We explained the reason for the presumption in *McNeilab, Inc. v. American Home Products Corp.*, 848 F.2d 34 (2d Cir. 1988). There, we observed that in the case of a "misleading, non-comparative commercial[] which tout[s] the benefits of the product advertised but ma[kes] no direct reference to any competitor's product," the injury "accrues equally to all competitors; none is more likely to suffer from the offending broadcasts than any other." Thus, "some indication of actual injury and causation" is necessary "to satisfy Lanham Act standing requirements and to ensure [the] plaintiff's injury [is] not speculative." By contrast, where the case presents a false comparative advertising claim, "the concerns … regarding speculative injury do not arise." This is because a false "comparison to a specific competing product necessarily diminishes that product's value in the minds of the consumer." Accordingly, no proof of likely injury is necessary.

Although neither of the television commercials identifies TWC by name, the rationale for a presumption of irreparable harm applies with equal force to this case. The Revised Shatner Commercial explicitly disparages the picture quality of "cable." As the District Court found, TWC *is* "cable" in the areas where it is the franchisee. Thus, even though Shatner does not identify TWC by name, consumers in the markets covered by the preliminary injunction would undoubtedly understand his derogatory statement, "settling for cable would be illogical," as referring to TWC. Because the Revised Shatner Commercial "necessarily diminishes" TWC's value "in the minds of the consumer," the

District Court properly accorded TWC a presumption of irreparable harm.

The Revised Simpson Commercial … does not explicitly refer to "cable." However, the fact that the commercial does not name plaintiff's product is not necessarily dispositive. [T]he application of the presumption is disfavored "where the products are not obviously in competition *or* where the defendant's advertisements make no direct reference to any competitor's products." According to a survey in the record, approximately 90% of households have either cable or satellite service. Given the nearly binary structure of the television services market, it would be obvious to consumers that DIRECTV's claims of superiority are aimed at diminishing the value of cable—which, as discussed above, is synonymous with TWC in the areas covered by the preliminary injunction. Therefore, although the Revised Simpson Commercial does not explicitly mention TWC or cable, it "necessarily diminishes" the value of TWC's product. The District Court thus did not err in presuming that TWC has "a reasonable basis" for believing that the advertisement will likely cause it injury.

In sum, we conclude that the District Court did not exceed its allowable discretion in preliminarily enjoining the further dissemination of the Revised Simpson and Revised Shatner Commercials in any market where TWC is the franchisee. * * *

Conclusion

For the foregoing reasons, we AFFIRM the preliminary injunction in part [and] VACATE it in part ….

QUESTIONS FOR DISCUSSION FOR CASE 7.3

1. If you think a competitor has issued a false or misleading advertisement, what types of information do you need to gather to persuade a court to issue a preliminary injunction?
2. Practically speaking, why would a competitor want to argue that an advertisement is literally false rather than implicitly false?
3. What is the difference between puffery and misrepresentation?
4. Could the FTC have brought an action against DIRECTV? If so, on what basis?

7.4 Commercial Speech, FTC Act—Deceptive Advertising
Kraft, Inc. v. FTC, 970 F.2d 311 (7th Cir. 1992)

Kraft, Inc. ("Kraft") asks us to review an order of the Federal Trade Commission ("FTC" or "Commission") finding that it violated §§ 5 and 12 of the Federal Trade Commission Act ("Act"). The FTC determined that Kraft, in an advertising campaign, had misrepresented information regarding the amount of calcium contained in Kraft Singles American Pasteurized Process Cheese Food ("Singles") relative to the calcium content in five ounces of milk and in imitation cheese slices. The FTC ordered Kraft to cease and desist from making these misrepresentations and Kraft filed this petition for review. We enforce the Commission's order.

I

Three categories of cheese compete in the individually wrapped process slice market: process cheese food slices, imitation slices, and substitute slices. Process cheese food slices, also known as "dairy slices," must contain at least 51% natural cheese by federal regulation. Imitation cheese slices, by contrast, contain little

or no natural cheese and consist primarily of water, vegetable oil, flavoring agents, and fortifying agents. * * * Substitute slices fit somewhere in between; they fall short of the natural cheese content of process cheese food slices yet are nutritionally superior to imitation slices. Consistent with FTC usage, we refer to both imitation and substitute slices as "imitation" slices.

Kraft Singles are process cheese food slices. In the early 1980s, Kraft began losing market share to an increasing number of imitation slices that were advertised as both less expensive and equally nutritious as dairy slices like Singles. Kraft responded with a series of advertisements, collectively known as the "Five Ounces of Milk" campaign, designed to inform consumers that Kraft Singles cost more than imitation slices because they are made from five ounces of milk rather than less expensive ingredients. The ads also focused on the calcium content of Kraft Singles in an effort to capitalize on growing consumer interest in adequate calcium consumption.

The FTC filed a complaint against Kraft charging that this advertising campaign materially misrepresented the calcium content and relative calcium benefit of Kraft Singles. The FTC Act makes it unlawful to engage in unfair or deceptive commercial practices, or to induce consumers to purchase certain products through advertising that is misleading in a material respect. Thus, an advertisement is deceptive under the Act if it is likely to mislead consumers, acting reasonably under the circumstances, in a material respect. * * * In implementing this standard, the Commission examines the overall net impression of an ad and engages in a three-part inquiry: (1) what claims are conveyed in the ad; (2) are those claims false or misleading; and (3) are those claims material to prospective consumers.

Two facts are critical to understanding the allegations against Kraft. First, although Kraft does use five ounces of milk in making each Kraft Single, roughly 30% of the calcium contained in the milk is lost during processing. Second, the vast majority of imitation slices sold in the United States contain 15% of the U.S. Recommended Daily Allowance (RDA) of calcium per ounce, roughly the same amount contained in Kraft Singles. Specifically then, the FTC complaint alleged that the challenged advertisements made two implied claims, neither of which was true: (1) that a slice of Kraft Singles contains the same amount of calcium as five ounces of milk (the "milk equivalency" claim); and (2) that Kraft Singles contain more calcium than do most imitation cheese slices (the "imitation superiority" claim).

The two sets of ads at issue in this case, referred to as the "Skimp" ads and the "Class Picture" ads, ran nationally in print and broadcast media between 1985 and 1987. The Skimp ads were designed to communicate the nutritional benefit of Kraft Singles by referring expressly to their milk and calcium content. The broadcast version of this ad on which the FTC focused contained the following audio copy:

Lady (voice over): I admit it. I thought of skimping. Could you look into those big blue eyes and skimp on her? So I buy Kraft Singles. Imitation slices use hardly any milk. But Kraft has five ounces per slice. Five ounces. So her little bones get calcium they need to grow. No, she doesn't know what that big Kraft means. Good thing I do.

Singers: Kraft Singles. More milk makes 'em ... more milk makes 'em good.

Lady (voice over): Skimp on her? No way.

The visual image corresponding to this copy shows, among other things, milk pouring into a glass until it reaches a mark on the glass denoted "five ounces." The commercial also shows milk pouring into a glass which bears the phrase "5 oz. milk slice" and which gradually becomes part of the label on a package of Singles. In January 1986, Kraft revised this ad, changing "Kraft *has* five ounces per slice" to "Kraft is *made from* five ounces per slice," and in March 1987, Kraft added the disclosure, "one 3/4 ounce slice has 70% of the calcium of five ounces of milk" as a subscript in the television commercial and as a footnote in the print ads.

The Class Picture ads also emphasized the milk and calcium content of Kraft Singles but, unlike the Skimp ads, did not make an express comparison to imitation slices. The version of this ad examined by the FTC depicts a group of school children having their class picture taken, and contains the following audio copy:

Announcer (voice over): Can you see what's missing in this picture?

Well, a government study says that half the school kids in America don't get all the calcium recommended for growing kids. That's why Kraft Singles are important. Kraft is made from five ounces of milk per slice. So they're concentrated with calcium. Calcium the government recommends for strong bones and healthy teeth!

Photographer: Say Cheese!

Kids: Cheese!

Announcer (voice over): Say Kraft Singles. 'Cause kids love Kraft Singles, right down to their bones.

The Class Picture ads also included the subscript disclaimer mentioned above.

After a lengthy trial, the Administrative Law Judge (ALJ) concluded that both the Skimp and Class Picture ads made the milk equivalency claim. * * * Further, the ALJ concluded that both sets of ads falsely conveyed the imitation superiority claim .... According to the ALJ, both claims were material because they implicated important health concerns. He therefore ordered Kraft to cease and desist from making these claims about any of its individually wrapped slices of process cheese food, imitation cheese, or substitute cheese.

The FTC affirmed the ALJ's decision, with some modifications. As to the Skimp ads, the Commission found that four elements conveyed the milk equivalency claim: (1) the use of the word "has" in the phrase "Kraft has five ounces per slice"; (2) repetition of the precise amount of milk in a Kraft Single (five ounces); (3) the use of the word "so" to link the reference to milk with the reference to calcium; and (4) the visual image of milk being poured into a glass up to a five-ounce mark, and the superimposition of that image onto a package of Singles. It also found two additional elements that conveyed the imitation superiority claim: (1) the express reference to imitation slices combined with the use of comparative language ("hardly any," "but"); and (2) the image of a glass containing very little milk during the reference to imitation slices, followed by the image of a glass being filled to the five-ounce mark during the reference to Kraft Singles. The Commission based all of these findings on its own impression of the advertisements and found it unnecessary to resort to extrinsic evidence; it did note, however, that the available extrinsic evidence was consistent with its determinations.

The Commission then examined the Class Picture ads—once again, without resorting to extrinsic evidence—and found that they contained copy substantially similar to the copy in the Skimp ads that conveyed the impression of milk equivalency. It rejected, however, the ALJ's finding that the Class Picture ads made an imitation superiority claim, determining that the ads neither expressly compared Singles to imitation slices, nor contained any visual images to prompt such a comparison, and that available extrinsic evidence did not support the ALJ's finding.

The FTC next found that the claims were material to consumers. It concluded that the milk equivalency claim is a health-related claim that reasonable consumers would find important and that Kraft believed that the claim induced consumers to purchase Singles. The FTC presumed that the imitation superiority claim was material because it found that Kraft intended to make that claim. It also found that the materiality of that claim was demonstrated by evidence that the challenged ads led to increased sales despite a substantially higher price for Singles than for imitation slices.

Finally, the FTC modified the ALJ's cease and desist order by extending its coverage from "individually wrapped slices of cheese, imitation cheese, and substitute cheese" to "any product that is a cheese, related cheese product, imitation cheese, or substitute cheese." The Commission found that the serious, deliberate nature of the violation, combined with the transferability of the violations to other cheese products, justified a broader order. Kraft filed this petition to set-aside the Commission's order or, alternatively, to modify its scope.

* * *

III.

Kraft['s] … principal claim is that the FTC erred as a matter of law in not requiring extrinsic evidence of consumer deception. Without such evidence, Kraft claims (1) that the FTC had no objective basis for determining if its ads actually contained the implied claims alleged, and (2) that the FTC's order chills constitutionally protected commercial speech. Alternatively, Kraft contends that substantial evidence does not support the FTC's finding that the Class Picture ads contain the milk equivalency claim. Finally, Kraft maintains that even if it did make the alleged milk equivalency and imitation superiority claims, substantial evidence does not support the FTC's finding that these claims were material to consumers. We address each contention in turn.

A.

1.

In determining what claims are conveyed by a challenged advertisement, the Commission relies on two sources of information: its own viewing of the ad and extrinsic evidence. Its practice is to view the ad first and, if it is unable on its own to determine with confidence what claims are conveyed in a challenged ad, to turn to extrinsic evidence. The most convincing extrinsic evidence is a survey "of what consumers thought upon reading the advertisement in question," but the Commission also relies on other forms of extrinsic evidence including consumer testimony, expert opinion, and copy tests of ads.

Kraft has no quarrel with this approach when it comes to determining whether an ad conveys *express* claims, but contends that the FTC should be required, as a matter of law, to rely on extrinsic evidence rather than its own subjective analysis in all cases involving allegedly *implied* claims.[4] The basis for this argument is

---

[4]Express claims directly represent the fact at issue while implied claims do so in an oblique or indirect way. To illustrate, consider the following. Suppose a certain automobile gets poor gas mileage, say, 10 miles per gallon. One advertisement boasts that it gets 30 miles per gallon while another identifies the car as the "Miser," depicts it rolling through the countryside past one gas station after another, and proclaims that the car is inexpensive to operate. Both ads make deceptive claims: the first does so expressly, the second does so impliedly.

that implied claims, by definition, are not self-evident from the face of an ad. This, combined with the fact that consumer perceptions are shaped by a host of external variables—including their social and educational backgrounds, the environment in which they view the ad, and prior experiences with the product advertised—makes review of implied claims by a five-member commission inherently unreliable. The Commissioners, Kraft argues, are simply incapable of determining what implicit messages consumers are likely to perceive in an ad. Making matters worse, Kraft asserts that the Commissioners are predisposed to find implied claims because the claims have been identified in the complaint, rendering it virtually impossible for them to reflect the perceptions of unbiased consumers.

Kraft buttresses its argument by pointing to the use of extrinsic evidence in an analogous context: cases brought under § 43(a) of the Lanham Act. Courts hearing deceptive advertising claims under that Act, which provides a private right of action for deceptive advertising, generally require extrinsic proof that an advertisement conveys an implied claim. Were this a Lanham Act case, a reviewing court in all likelihood would have relied on extrinsic evidence of consumer perceptions. While this disparity is sometimes justified on grounds of advertising "expertise"—the FTC presumably possesses more of it than courts—Kraft maintains this justification is an illusory one in that the FTC has no special expertise in discerning consumer perceptions. Indeed, proof of the FTC's inexpertise abounds: false advertising cases make up a small part of the Commission's workload, most commissioners have little prior experience in advertising, and the average tenure of commissioners is very brief. That evidence aside, no amount of expertise in Kraft's view can replace the myriad of external variables affecting consumer perceptions. Here, the Commission found implied claims based solely on its own intuitive reading of the ads (although it did reinforce that conclusion by examining the proffered extrinsic evidence). Had the Commission fully and properly relied on available extrinsic evidence, Kraft argues it would have conclusively found that consumers do not perceive the milk equivalency and imitation superiority claims in the ads.

While Kraft's arguments may have some force as a matter of policy, they are unavailing as a matter of law. Courts, including the Supreme Court, have uniformly rejected imposing such a requirement on the FTC, and we decline to do so as well. We hold that the Commission may rely on its own reasoned analysis to determine what claims, including implied ones, are

conveyed in a challenged advertisement, so long as those claims are reasonably clear from the face of the advertisement.

* * *

2.

The crux of Kraft's first amendment argument is that the FTC's current subjective approach chills some truthful commercial speech. * * * Society has a strong interest "in the free flow of commercial information" critical to a free market economy, and it is this interest the first amendment vindicates in protecting commercial speech. However, "[f]alse, deceptive, or misleading advertising" does not serve that interest and thus this category of commercial speech "remains subject to restraint."

Kraft contends that by relying on its own subjective judgment that an ad, while literally true, implies a false message, the FTC chills nonmisleading, protected speech because advertisers are unable to predict whether the FTC will find a particular ad misleading. Advertisers can run sophisticated pre-dissemination consumer surveys and find no implied claims present, only to have the Commission determine in its own subjective view that consumers would perceive an implied claim. Indeed, Kraft maintains that is precisely what happened here. Even more troubling, Kraft maintains that the ads most vulnerable to this chilling effect are factual, comparative ads, like the Five Ounces of Milk campaign, of greatest benefit to consumers. The net result of the Commission's subjective approach will be an influx of soft "feel good" ads designed to avoid unpredictable FTC decisions. The way to avoid this chilling effect, according to Kraft, is to require the Commission to rely on objective indicia of consumer perceptions in finding implied claims.

Kraft's first amendment challenge is doomed by the Supreme Court's holding in *Zauderer v. Office of Disciplinary Counsel*, 471 U.S. 626 (1985) ....

[Z]auderer teaches that consumer surveys are not compelled by the first amendment when the alleged deception although implied, is conspicuous. In both *Zauderer* and here, an omitted piece of information—the definition of a key contractual term in *Zauderer*, the effect of processing on nutrient content here—led to potential consumer deception, and in both cases the ads were literally true, yet impliedly misleading. Kraft's implied claims were reasonably clear from the face of the ads and not unpredictable to Kraft. * * * Because we conclude that the Commission was not required to rely

on extrinsic evidence, we need not examine the extrinsic evidence proffered by Kraft that it says contravenes the Commission's findings. We note, however, that the Commission did thoroughly examine this evidence, albeit after the fact, and found that it did not refute the implied claim findings and that some of the evidence was based on unsound consumer testing methodologies.

Our holding does not diminish the force of Kraft's argument as a policy matter, and, indeed, the extensive body of commentary on the subject makes a compelling argument that reliance on extrinsic evidence should be the rule rather than the exception. Along those lines, the Commission would be well-advised to adopt a consistent position on consumer survey methodology—advertisers and the FTC, it appears, go round and round on this issue—so that any uncertainty is reduced to an absolute minimum.

B.

Alternatively, Kraft argues that substantial evidence does not support the FTC's finding that the Class Picture ads convey a milk equivalency claim. * * *

We find substantial evidence in the record to support the FTC's finding. Although Kraft downplays the nexus in the ads between milk and calcium, the ads emphasize visually and verbally that five ounces of milk go into a slice of Kraft Singles; this image is linked to calcium content, strongly implying that the consumer gets the calcium found in five ounces of milk. * * *

Kraft asserts that the literal truth of the Class Picture ads—they *are* made from five ounces of milk and they *do* have a high concentration of calcium—makes it illogical to render a finding of consumer deception. The difficulty with this argument is that even literally true statements can have misleading implications. Here, the average consumer is not likely to know that much of the calcium in five ounces of milk (30%) is lost in processing, which leaves consumers with a misleading impression about calcium content. The critical fact is not that reasonable consumers might believe that a 3/4 ounce slice of cheese actually contains five ounces of *milk*, but that reasonable consumers might believe that a 3/4 ounce slice actually contains the *calcium* in five ounces of milk.

C.

Kraft next asserts that the milk equivalency and imitation superiority claims, even if made, are not material

to consumers. A claim is considered material if it "involves information that is important to consumers and, hence, likely to affect their choice of, or conduct regarding a product." The Commission is entitled to apply, within reason, a presumption of materiality, and it does so with three types of claims: (1) express claims; (2) implied claims where there is evidence that the seller intended to make the claim; and (3) claims that significantly involve health, safety, or other areas with which reasonable consumers would be concerned. Absent one of these situations, the Commission examines the record and makes a finding of materiality or immateriality.

Here, the ALJ concluded that both claims were presumptively material because calcium is a significant health concern to consumers. The Commission upheld this conclusion, although it applied a presumption of materiality only to the imitation superiority claim. Kraft asserts the Commission's determination is not supported by substantial evidence. We disagree.

In determining that the milk equivalency claim was material to consumers, the FTC cited Kraft surveys showing that 71% of respondents rated calcium content an extremely or very important factor in their decision to buy Kraft Singles, and that 52% of female, and 40% of all respondents, reported significant personal concerns about adequate calcium consumption. The FTC further noted that the ads were targeted to female homemakers with children and that the 60 milligram difference between the calcium contained in five ounces of milk and that contained in a Kraft Single would make up for most of the RDA calcium deficiency shown in girls aged 9-11. Finally, the FTC found evidence in the record that Kraft designed the ads with the intent to capitalize on consumer calcium deficiency concerns.

Significantly, the FTC found further evidence of materiality in Kraft's conduct: despite repeated warnings, Kraft persisted in running the challenged ads. Before the ads even ran, ABC television raised a red flag when it asked Kraft to substantiate the milk and calcium claims in the ads. Kraft's ad agency also warned Kraft in a legal memorandum to substantiate the claims before running the ads. Moreover, in October 1985, a consumer group warned Kraft that it believed the Skimp ads were potentially deceptive. Nonetheless, a high-level Kraft executive recommended that the ad copy remain unaltered because the "Singles business is growing for the first time in four years due in large part to the copy." Finally, the FTC and the California Attorney General's Office independently notified the company in early 1986 that investigations had been initiated to determine whether the ads conveyed the milk equivalency claims. Notwithstanding these warnings, Kraft continued to run the ads and even rejected proposed alternatives that would have allayed concerns over their deceptive nature. From this, the FTC inferred—we believe, reasonably—that Kraft thought the challenged milk equivalency claim induced consumers to purchase Singles and hence that the claim was material to consumers.

With regard to the imitation superiority claim, the Commission applied a presumption of materiality after finding evidence that Kraft intended the challenged ads to convey this message. * * * It found this presumption buttressed by the fact that the challenged ad copy led to increased sales of Singles, even though they cost 40 percent more than imitation slices. Finally, the FTC determined that Kraft's consumer surveys were insufficient to rebut this inference and in particular criticized Kraft's survey methodology because it offered limited response options to consumers.

IV.

The Commission's cease and desist order prohibits Kraft from running the Skimp and Class Picture ads, as well as from advertising any calcium or nutritional claims not supported by reliable scientific evidence. This order extends not only to the product contained in the deceptive advertisements (Kraft Singles), but to all Kraft cheeses and cheese-related products, which include Cracker Barrel, Velveeta, and Philadelphia Brand Cream Cheese. Kraft contends this order is too broad and must be set-aside or modified because it (1) bans constitutionally protected commercial speech, and (2) is not rationally related to Kraft's violation of the Act.

A.

First amendment infirmities arise, according to Kraft, from the sweep of the order: by banning commercial speech that is only *potentially* misleading, the order chills some non-deceptive advertising deserving of constitutional protection. * * *

* * *

Kraft asserts that its advertisements are only potentially misleading … because the milk equivalency and imitation superiority claims are true and verifiable, there is no evidence that these claims actually misled

consumers, and the advertising medium is not inherently conducive to deception. Alternative remedial measures were readily available to the Commission, such as modifications to the ads or prominent disclosures, and thus, Kraft contends, the order is broader than reasonably necessary to prevent deception. * * *

We reject Kraft's argument. To begin with, the Commission determined that the ads were *actually* misleading, not *potentially* misleading, thus justifying a total ban on the challenged ads. Moreover, even if we were to assume the order bans some potentially misleading speech, it is only constitutionally defective if it is no "broader than reasonably necessary to prevent the [deception]." We conclude that it is sufficiently narrow to pass constitutional muster …. [T]he restriction at issue here is an administrative cease and desist order directed toward one company's cheese ads and predicated on a specific finding of past deceptive practices.

To reiterate, the FTC's order does two things: it prohibits the Skimp ads and the Class Picture ads (as *currently* designed) and it requires Kraft to base future nutrient and calcium claims on reliable scientific evidence. Kraft mischaracterizes the decision as a categorical ban on commercial speech when in fact it identifies with particularity two nutrient claims that the Commission found actually misleading and prohibits only those claims. It further places on Kraft the (minor) burden of supporting future nutrient claims with reliable data. This leaves Kraft free to use any advertisement it chooses, including the Skimp and Class Picture ads, so long as it either eliminates the elements specifically identified by the FTC as contributing to consumer deception or corrects this inaccurate impression by adding prominent, unambiguous disclosures. We note one additional consideration further alleviating first amendment concerns; Kraft, like any party to an FTC order, may seek an advisory opinion from the Commission as to whether any future advertisements comply with its order, and this procedure has been specifically cited by courts as one method of reducing advertiser uncertainty.

For these reasons, we hold that the specific prohibitions imposed on Kraft in the FTC's cease and desist order are not broader than reasonably necessary to prevent deception and hence not violative of the first amendment. * * * The *subject* of Kraft's ads (i.e., the milk and calcium content of Singles) is obviously a perfectly legitimate subject of commercial advertising. It is only the *manner* of presentation that needs rectification. Kraft is free to continue advertising the milk and calcium content in its cheese products, and it can avoid future violations by correcting the misleading elements identified in the FTC's decision. Kraft could, for example, redesign the Skimp and Class Picture ads so that calcium content is accurately presented (i.e., "each Kraft Single contains the calcium equivalent of 3.5 ounces of milk") or it could add prominent, unambiguous disclosures about calcium loss in processing, either of which would put it in full compliance with the order.

B.

Alternatively, Kraft argues that the scope of the order is not "reasonably related" to Kraft's violation of the Act because it extends to products that were not the subject of the challenged advertisements. The FTC has discretion to issue multi-product orders, so-called "fencing-in" orders, that extend beyond violations of the Act to prevent violators from engaging in similar deceptive practices in the future. Such an order must be sufficiently clear that it is comprehensible to the violator, and must be "reasonably related" to a violation of the Act. Kraft does not challenge the order's clarity or precision but only its reasonableness.

In determining whether a broad fencing-in order bears a "reasonable relationship" to a violation of the Act, the Commission considers (1) the deliberateness and seriousness of the violation, (2) the degree of transferability of the violation to other products, and (3) any history of prior violations. Here, the ALJ found that Kraft had not engaged in a long-term pattern of deceptive advertising, and that this was an isolated incident in response to significant competitive pressures on Kraft; hence, the ALJ opted for a narrow order. The FTC disagreed; it concluded that Kraft's violations were serious, deliberate, and easily transferable to other Kraft products, thus warranting a broad fencing-in order.

We find substantial evidence to support the scope of the order. The Commission based its finding of seriousness on the size ($15 million annually) and duration (two and one-half years) of the ad campaign and on the difficulty most consumers would face in judging the truth or falsity of the implied calcium claims. Although Kraft disputes the Commission's $15 million figure, arguing it covers many non-deceptive or unchallenged advertisements, that does not obviate the fact that this was an expensive, nationwide campaign with highly effective results. Moreover, the FTC properly found that it is unreasonable to expect most consumers to perform the calculations necessary to compare the calcium content of Kraft Singles with five ounces of milk given the fact that the nutrient information on milk cartons is not based on a five-ounce serving.

As noted previously, the Commission also found that Kraft's conduct was deliberate because it persisted in running the challenged ad copy despite repeated warnings from outside sources that the copy might be implicitly misleading. Kraft challenges this finding, arguing it responded to these warnings by acting in good faith to modify the ads, and further that it commissioned a post-dissemination survey to determine whether the complaints had any merit. This survey found that only an insignificant percentage of respondents detected the alleged claims. We reject these contentions. The deceptive claims were apparent from the face of the ad, but even if they somehow eluded Kraft, the Commission reasonably concluded that the steady stream of warnings should have put Kraft on notice that its surveys were somehow inadequate or defective. Kraft made three modifications to the ads, but two of them were implemented at the very end of the campaign, more than two years after it had begun. This dilatory response provided a sufficient basis for the Commission's conclusion.

The Commission further found that the violations were readily transferable to other Kraft cheese products given the general similarity between Singles and other Kraft cheeses. * * *

Finally, the FTC concluded that these factors outweighed Kraft's lack of prior violations. Kraft maintains that the Commission simply brushed aside its clean record even though prior violations are highly probative of propensity to commit future violations. This contention is also without merit because it is the circumstances of the violation as a whole, and not merely the presence or absence of any one of factor, that justifies a broad order. Hence, the FTC reasonably concluded that the seriousness, deliberateness, and transferability of the violations took precedence over the absence of any prior Kraft violations.

V.

For the foregoing reasons, Kraft's petition to set-aside the order is DENIED and the Commission's order is ENFORCED.

QUESTIONS FOR DISCUSSION FOR CASE 7.4

1. How is extrinsic evidence used in deceptive advertising cases brought under the FTC Act? In

deceptive advertising cases brought under the Lanham Act?

2. The packages containing cheese products have printed nutritional information that consumers can compare to other brands. Why does this not alleviate the FTC's concerns about consumers being misled by the advertisements?

3. What was untrue about Kraft's revised advertisements? Why didn't a disclaimer on the bottom of the advertisement correct any deficiencies?

4. What factors do you think prompt the FTC to act on allegedly deceptive advertising? How might a manager limit each factor's influence?

DISCUSSION QUESTIONS

1. Hot Wax, Inc., produces and markets car waxes to carwashes through the country. Its formula for car wax incorporates carnauba waxes at a considerable cost. Turtle Wax, Inc., entered the carwash supply industry, but it uses neither carnauba nor beeswax in its car waxes. Instead, it uses mineral seal oils or wax emulsions that are considerably cheaper than traditional wax ingredients. As a result, Turtle Wax has become a leader in the car wax industry. Hot Wax filed suit against Turtle Wax, alleging that Turtle Wax engaged in false advertising in violation of Section 43(a) of the Lanham Act by promoting its products as "wax" when the products did not actually contain wax. Turtle Wax responded that Hot Wax's definition of "wax" was overly formalistic and introduced consumer surveys that indicated that consumers got exactly what they expected from a wax when they purchased Turtle Wax products—polish, shine, and protection. Hot Wax filed for summary judgment. Should the court grant summary judgment to Hot Wax? Why, or why not?

2. Miramax Films Corp. released a movie in the United States called *Scream*, which had been directed by Wes Craven, an internationally renowned director of horror movies. A year later, Columbia Pictures released *I Know What You Did Last Summer* in the United States. Shortly before the release, Miramax discovered that Columbia was marketing *Summer* as "From the Creator of *Scream*." The only link between *Scream* and *Summer* is the screenwriter Kevin Williamson. Williamson wrote an original screenplay for "*Scream*" and adapted a novel by another author for the screenplay of *Summer*. In the advertisements, Williamson's name appeared in the small-print "credit block" of *Summer*, but he was never named or otherwise identified as the "creator" to whom the advertisements refer.

   Miramax filed suit against Columbia, alleging that Columbia was trying to profit from the popularity of *Scream* by inducing potential viewers of horror movies to see *Summer* in the false belief that it originated from the same source as *Scream*. Miramax seeks a preliminary injunction against further use of the advertising. Should the court grant the relief requested to Miramax? Why, or why not?

3. Abbott Laboratories makes and sells Ensure, a nutritional supplement beverage (NSB). Ensure has consistently held the greatest market share of all NSBs on the market. Gerber Products Co. reformulated a former product, Resource, into an NSB and launched an advertising campaign. The campaign asserted, among other things, that "America Prefers Resource Over Ensure" and "National Preference Winner Resource Beats Ensure." Abbot asserts that Gerber's claim is false because the tests that Gerber relied upon to support its claim were conducted as taste tests and not as tests indicating overall preference. Resource and Ensure are both used for medicinal or medical reasons and are substantially similar in nutritional value. Abbot filed suit under Section 43(a) of the Lanham Act, alleging that Gerber's advertising claims were literally false. Are they? Why, or why not?

4. Two Rivers, Wisconsin, enacted an extensive ordinance regulating the placement and nature of outdoor advertising. The preamble of the ordinance recognized "the need to protect the safety and welfare of the public; the need for well-maintained and attractive sign displays within the community; and the need for adequate business identification, advertising, and communication." Lavey is the president of the Lakeland Group, an advertising and public relations business. Lavey and the Lakeland Group have owned billboards for the last 15 years and have rented them to the public for the display of commercial and noncommercial messages. Two Rivers has frequently cited Lavey and the Lakeland Group for placing off-premises signs in areas where

the ordinance does not permit such signs. Lavey brought this action seeking a declaration that the ordinance violates his First Amendment rights. How should the court analyze this issue? What result should it reach?

5. The California Dental Association (CDA) is a voluntary nonprofit association of local dental societies to which about three-fourths of the dentists belong. The CDA lobbies and litigates in its members' interests and conducts marketing and public relations campaigns for their benefit. The dentists who belong to the CDA through the local associations agree to abide by a Code of Ethics (Code) that prohibits false and misleading advertising. The local associations enforce the code by denying membership to new dentists who refuse to withdraw or revise objectionable advertisements and by subjecting current members who violate the Code to censure, suspension, or expulsion from the CDA.

   The FTC brought a complaint against the CDA, alleging that it applied its guidelines so as to restrict truthful, nondeceptive advertising, and so violated Section 5 of the FTC Act. In particular, the FTC alleged that the CDA had unreasonably restricted price advertising, particularly about discounted fees, and advertising relating to the quality of dental services. Has the CDA violated the FTC Act? Why, or why not?

6. Sabal manufactured and sold of a line of over-the-counter topical hair loss products known as the "hair farming system." She claimed that these products work by cleaning out congested pores and allowing hair to escape that would otherwise be trapped beneath the scalp. Sabal entered into an exclusive marketing agreement with Mega Systems, Inc., to advertise her hair-farming products on a nationally broadcast radio infomercial. During the infomercial, she stated that her products "can deep clean underneath the surface of the scalp, and clean out all the debris that prevents the hair or blocks the hair from reaching the surface." She also stated: "I have a right to this theory, whether the medical community believes me or not, although they soon will because I'll be written up in most of the major medical journals around the world …. It's guaranteed to work on every human being …. And everyone should have their hair back in six months to a year, permanently, painlessly, and never have to purchase anything again." In addition to the infomercial, Sabal published similar claims on an Internet website and in a book she published.

The FTC charged her with deceptive advertising and fraudulent misrepresentation. How should the court rule on the FTC's motion for a preliminary injunction?

7. Novell, Inc., produces its NetWare networking software in two forms: original and upgrade. The upgrade version is substantially identical to the original in function; the primary difference is its lower price as the upgrade is available only to owners of previous versions of the software. Network Trade Center, Inc. (NTC) purchased older versions of the NetWare software in bulk at discounted prices, and ordered the cheaper upgrade of the newer software from authorized Novell distributors. (At no time was NTC an authorized distributor of Novell software.) NTC then advertised the "upgrade" as "New Retail" or as a "Special Novell Promotional Package" while showing pictures of the "original" NetWare box, and sold it to end users. Many end users expressed confusion to both NTC and Novell about the extent of the license they obtained: some thought that they had received the "original" retail version, and others thought that they could register the upgrade with Novell. Some became so frustrated that they returned their copies to NTC. Once Novell discovered NTC's practice, Novell ordered NTC to stop, but NTC continued to advertise the product. Novell has filed suit, alleging, among other claims, that NTC is in violation of the Lanham Act's prohibition against false advertising. Has NTC engaged in false advertising? Why, or why not?

8. Tommy Larsen, a Danish citizen, produces aesthetically pleasing functional objects, such as furniture. Larsen designed a compact disc holder called the "CD 25," which holds 25 CDs. At first, Larsen distributed his product only in Europe, but he soon began exporting the CD 25 to the United States. Soon thereafter, Larsen looked for a U.S. distributor for his product and entered into a limited distributorship with Terk Technologies Corp. Terk placed an order for 11,232 units at $1 per piece. Although the distribution agreement was not exclusive, Larsen treated it as though it were, allowing all orders in the United States to be fulfilled by Terk.

   Despite the success of the CD 25 in high-end retail stores, Terk did not place additional orders with Larsen, stating that demand did not warrant more units. In fact, however, Terk had placed an order with Allen Machine Products for 11,000 counterfeit units of the CD 25. Terk marketed these Allen-made CD 25s as the "TOMMY LARSEN" and "CD 25."

The counterfeit holders also had markings indicating that the design was Danish and the product was produced in Denmark. The counterfeits were actually produced in New York.

Larsen, suspicious about the lack of orders from Terk, examined several of the distributed products and discovered the counterfeiting. He sued Terk, arguing that Terk had engaged in passing-off in violation of the Lanham Act. Has Terk violated the Lanham Act? Why, or why not?

9. Synygy, Inc., produces Information Production and Distribution Systems, a software program that enables the user to integrate data from different sources. This software was targeted at companies in the pharmaceutical industry. Scott-Levin, Inc., compiles data for pharmaceutical companies that is used in computer programs such as those produced by Synygy. While working on a project for Bristol Meyers Squibb, Inc., Scott-Levin had disagreements with Synygy after Synygy changed file specifications without telling Scott-Levin and then blamed Scott-Levin for the conversion problems that ensued. In conversations with agents of Zeneca Pharmaceutical, Inc., a common customer of the two software companies, two Scott-Levin representatives discussed the problems they had working with Synygy in the past. Soon thereafter, Zeneca discontinued its relationship with Synygy. Zeneca claims that the discussions with the Scott-Levin representatives had no influence on that decision. In addition, during a client conference, Scott-Levin presented a slide show that contained the following slide: "simulate—to assume the outward qualities or appearance of, often with the intent to deceive." Simulate, Inc., was Synygy's name at the time of the client conference. Synygy sued Scott-Levin for commercial disparagement. Should Synygy prevail? Why, or why not?

10. Telebrands Corp. produces infomercials for television and distributes the products advertised on the commercials in retail stores. Telebrands became the exclusive licensee of the "SAFETY CAN," a can opener that cuts cans from the side and not from the top, thereby eliminating the sharp, jagged edge. On the packaging of the SAFETY CAN was the statement "AS SEEN ON TV" in bright red lettering. As a result of the $3 million advertising campaign, Telebrands received over 300,000 direct response orders from consumers and over 1.9 million retail orders. Wilton Industries, Inc., then began selling a hand-held can opener that produces no sharp edges, known as the Betty Crocker "Safe Touch™."

The packaging on the "Safe Touch™" also contained the "AS SEEN ON TV" logo. According to Wilton, it planned on showing an infomercial on national television, but it never did. The only television advertising that occurred for the "Safe Touch™" was small infomercials on cable preview channels in Chicago over a one-month time period. Telebrands alleged that the logo "AS SEEN ON TV" constitutes false advertising in violation of the Lanham Act. Telebrands asked the court to issue a preliminary injunction enjoining Wilton from using the logo. Should the court issue the preliminary injunction? Why, or why not?

11. Clorox Co. produces the top-selling brand of roach bait insecticide called Combat. United Industries is a smaller, relatively new entrant in the roach bait industry that sells the Maxattrax brand of roach insecticide. To promote the Maxattrax product, United produced and distributed a 15-second television commercial entitled "Side by Side." The commercial opened with two boxes sitting on kitchen countertops—one was Maxattrax and the other was the generic "Roach Bait" but was vaguely similar to packaging used in the Combat brand. A voice-over asked, "Can you guess which bait kills roaches in 24 hours?" The camera then panned to show two differing views of the kitchen. On the Maxattrax side, the kitchen was neat and orderly; on the generic brand's side, the room was dirty and disheveled, ostensibly as a result of the roach infestation. The words "Based on lab tests" appeared on the bottom of the screen, and another voice-over stated: "To kill roaches in 24 hours, it's hot-shot Maxattrax. Maxattrax, it's the no-wait roach bait."

Clorox asserted that this advertising campaign is not literally true and violates the Lanham Act's prohibition against false advertising because scientific tests conclude that Maxattrax (as well as all other roach bait products) can exterminate only those roaches that come into direct contact with the product during the 24-hour period. Clorox produced no evidence of consumer deception and therefore does not challenge the ad as being implicitly false or misleading. Clorox seeks a preliminary injunction enjoining United from using the ad in the future. Should the court issue the preliminary injunction? Why, or why not?

12. General Motors Corp. aired a commercial in which a voice was heard asking who held the record for being selected most frequently as most valuable player of the National Athletic Association's basketball

tournament. On the screen appeared the words "Lew Alcindor," former basketball star Kareem Abdul-Jabbar's name before his conversion to Islam. The ad went on to list the most valuable features of the Olds 88 as a "Definite First Round Pick." The current name, voice, signature, photograph, or likeness of Kareem Abdul-Jabbar did not appear in the ad. The trial court granted summary judgment to General Motors on Abdul-Jabbar's right-of-publicity claim. Was the trial court's decision correct? Why, or why not?

13. Dillard Department Stores ran a newspaper advertisement for a shirt known as a "henley." The ad featured a photograph of a man wearing a henley shirt with the words "This is Don" in large print beside the picture and an arrow pointing toward the man's head from the words. Underneath the words was the statement, "This is Don's henley" with a second arrow pointing toward the shirt. The ad also contained the name of the retailer, general information about the sale price of the shirts, the name of the shirts' manufacturer, the available sizes, and the following: "Sometimes Don tucks it in; other times he wears it loose—it looks great either way. Don loves his henley; you will too."

Don Henley is a popular rock-and-roll musician. He founded The Eagles in the 1970s and in the 1980s and 1990s pursued a successful solo career. He has sued Dillard for violating his right of publicity. How should the court rule on his claim? Why?

14. The Virginia legislature passed two regulations that prohibited the use of certain words in advertisements for alcoholic beverages generally and advertisements within college student publications specifically.

The first regulation, which applied to all advertisements, prohibited references to mixed beverages, except for the terms "Mixed Drinks," "Mixed Beverages," "Exotic Drinks," "Polynesian Drinks," "Cocktails," "Cocktail Lounges," "Liquor," and "Spirits." References to "Happy Hour" or similar terms were also prohibited.

The second regulation, which applied only to college student publications, limited advertising of beer, wine, and mixed beverages by restaurants in such publications to the use of the following words: "A.B.C. on-premises," "beer," "wine," "mixed beverages," "cocktails," or "any combination of these words." Reference to particular brands or prices was forbidden.

Educational Media at Virginia Tech, Inc., owns several print and broadcast media outlets, including a student-run newspaper at Virginia Tech. Almost 99 percent of its annual budget came from advertising revenue. It estimated that these regulations would cost it $30,000 in lost advertising revenue each year. Educational Media challenged the two regulations on First Amendment grounds.

Should these regulations be held valid or invalid under the *Central Hudson* test?

15. Sandoz Pharmaceuticals Corp. brought suit, alleging that representations by Richardson-Vicks, Inc. ("Vicks") regarding its product, Vicks Pediatric Formula 44, constituted false and deceptive advertising under Section 43(a) of the Lanham Act. Specifically, Sandoz challenged: (1) Vicks' assertion that Pediatric 44 starts to work the instant it is swallowed, and (2) Vicks' advertising claims that Pediatric 44 is superior to its competitors. Sandoz requested that the court issue a preliminary injunction against Vicks' advertising claims. What legal rules should the court consider in evaluating this request?

CHAPTER 8

Consumer Protection Law

In this chapter, we consider some of the major sources of consumer protection law. A *consumer* is any individual who purchases goods or services for personal or household consumption. Consumer protection laws arise at all levels of government, and involve numerous agencies. In addition, these laws may apply to very specific types of activities and often overlap. As a result, firms marketing to consumers face a very complex regulatory environment.

Overview

Consumer protection laws are found at the federal, state, and local levels of government. State laws are usually governed through the state attorney general's office or through an office of consumer affairs. State laws can be very comprehensive and may offer more protection than federal legislation in specific instances. However, we will focus our discussion here on federal law, which itself is very varied and is found in many different statutes and regulations.

"Consumer protection law" has no clear definition. The term encompasses a wide range of legislative and regulatory measures. Many of the topics that we discuss in Chapter 7, such as false or deceptive advertising or business practices and bait-and-switch tactics, can be viewed as consumer protection legislation. The Federal Trade Commission's (FTC's) *Policy Statement on Unfairness*, for example, which is discussed in the context of unfair advertisements in Chapter 7, applies equally to unfair business practices that adversely affect consumers (see Case Illustration 8.1).

In this chapter, we focus specifically on legislation addressing direct marketing, labeling and packaging regulation, health and safety regulation, and statutes relating to consumer credit transactions, such as the Truth-in-Lending Act and the Consumer Credit Protection Act.

Direct Marketing Activities

Direct marketing refers to marketing efforts designed to persuade consumers to make a purchase from their home, office, or other nonretail setting. Examples include direct mail, catalogs, telemarketing, and electronic retailing (including solicitations made via e-mail). Because operating costs are lower, direct marketing can be less expensive for retailers than selling through a retail outlet. Direct marketing can also be much more convenient for consumers.[1]

---

[1]Information about direct marketing activities is available at the website of The Direct Marketing Association, Inc., www.the-dma.org

CASE ILLUSTRATION 8.1

ORKIN EXTERMINATING CO. v. FTC, 849 F.2D 1354 (11TH CIR. 1988)

FACTS Between 1966 and 1975, Orkin Exterminating Company sold "lifetime" guarantees for extermination services. The contracts provided that the customer could renew his or her "lifetime" guarantee by paying an annual renewal fee in an amount specified in the contracts. The contracts did not provide for any increase in this fee.

By 1980, Orkin had determined that increasing costs and inflation rendered the contracts disadvantageous to Orkin. Orkin thus informed the customers that their annual renewal fees were going to be increased by 40 percent. Although many customers complained, they did not have any viable alternatives as switching to other competitors would have been no cheaper than paying Orkin's increased rates.

The FTC issued an administrative complaint that Orkin had committed an unfair act or practice in violation of Section 5 of the FTC Act. The ALJ agreed and issued an order requiring Orkin to roll back all fees in pre-1975 contracts to the levels specified in the contracts. Orkin appealed to the Commission, which affirmed the ALJ's decision. Orkin then appealed to the U.S. Court of Appeals.

DECISION The U.S. Court of Appeals noted that the FTC's *Policy Statement on Unfairness* provides:

> [T]o justify a finding of unfairness the injury must satisfy three tests. It must be substantial; it must not be outweighed by any countervailing benefits to consumers or competition that the practice produces; and it must be an injury that consumers themselves could not reasonably have avoided.

The court then reviewed the Commission's findings. The Commission had found that the first prong of the standard, requiring a finding of substantial injury to consumers, had been met. The Commission had stated: "The harm resulting from Orkin's conduct consists of increased costs for services previously bargained for and includes the intangible loss of the certainty of the fixed price term in the contract." In fact, Orkin's increase in annual fees generated more than $7 million in additional renewal fees.

In examining the second prong, the Commission had determined that the increase in annual fees did not result in any benefits to consumers, as it was not accompanied by an increase in the level or quality of the service provided.

Finally, with regard to the third prong, the Commission had found that the consumers could not have reasonably avoided the injury. The contracts had not given the consumers any indication that Orkin might raise the annual fees; thus "[a]nticipatory avoidance through consumer choice was impossible." Nor could consumers have avoided their injuries by switching their business to one of Orkin's competitors.

The Court of Appeals found no error in the Commission's findings and affirmed the Commission's cease-and-desist order.

These types of marketing techniques can also result in several types of abuses. Direct marketing thus tends to be fairly heavily regulated at the federal, state, and even local levels. The following discussion focuses on some of the more common forms of direct marketing regulation. Companies engaged in direct marketing should consult an attorney, however, to be certain that their proposed activities do not run afoul of any specialized laws, including any state or local laws, that might apply.

Telemarketing

Telemarketing refers to the selling of goods or services by telephone or fax machine. It can consist of either sales calls (usually unsolicited) by the marketer or orders placed by consumers, often through toll-free 800 numbers.

Telemarketing is regulated at both the federal and state levels. Not surprisingly, regulation of telemarketing has focused primarily on unsolicited sales calls, as opposed to customer-initiated sales orders.

Most states have statutes regulating telephone solicitation. State regulation may, in fact, impose more stringent requirements upon telemarketers than does federal regulation, such as requiring that the consumer give permission in writing before a telemarketing call may proceed or requiring telemarketers to create a "no-call list" of consumers who do not want to be contacted.

At the federal level, the *Telephone Consumer Protection Act* (TCPA),[2] which was passed in 1991, regulates telemarketing activities. This Act prohibits telephone solicitation using an automatic telephone dialing system or a prerecorded voice. The TCPA also regulates direct marketing via fax transmissions. Unlike "junk" mail, which can be easily thrown out, unsolicited fax advertisements impose costs upon the recipients in terms of paper, toner, and tied-up telephone lines. The TCPA thus makes it illegal to transmit fax ads without first obtaining the permission of the recipient.

The TCPA is enforced by the Federal Communications Commission (FCC). The TCPA also provides consumers with a private cause of action. Consumers sue in state court for violation of the TCPA and can recover either actual monetary damages resulting from a violation of the Act or $500 for each violation, whichever is greater. The court may treble the damage award if it determines that the defendant willfully or knowingly violated the TCPA.

The FTC also has a role to play in regulating telemarketers. Under the *Telemarketing and Consumer Fraud and Abuse Prevention Act*,[3] the FTC has authority to establish rules regarding telemarketing and to bring actions against fraudulent telemarketers. The FTC's *Telemarketing Sales Rule*[4] covers most types of interstate telemarketing calls to consumers, including calls to pitch goods, services, sweepstakes, prize promotions, and investment opportunities. It also applies to calls that consumers make in response to postcards or other materials that they receive in the mail (except catalogs), unless the materials contain the information that is required to be disclosed under the Rule. If a solicitation occurs via an e-mail inviting the sender to place an order via a telephone call, that call and any subsequent sale must comply with the Telemarketing Sales Rule requirements. The Rule does not apply to transactions that occur entirely online, however.

The Rule also does not apply to entities that are specifically exempted from FTC jurisdiction, including: (1) banks and other financial institutions; (2) long-distance telephone companies, airlines, and other common carriers; (3) nonprofit organizations; and (4) insurance companies that are otherwise regulated by state law. In addition, the Rule does not apply to certain types of calls, including: (1) 900-number calls; (2) calls placed by consumers in response to a catalog; (3) calls related to the sale of a franchise or certain business opportunities; (4) unsolicited calls from consumers; (5) calls that are part of a transaction involving a face-to-face sales presentation; (6) business-to-business calls that do not involve retail sales of nondurable office and cleaning supplies; and (7) most calls made in response to general media or direct mail advertising.

The Rule requires telemarketers, before they make their sales pitch, to inform the recipient that the call is a sales call and to identify the seller's name and the product or services being sold. The telemarketer must inform the recipient of the total cost and quantity of the product being sold; any material restrictions, limitations, or conditions on using or obtaining the goods; and whether the sale is final or nonrefundable. It is illegal for the telemarketer to misrepresent any information about the product, including cost, quantity, and other aspects or attributes of the product. Telemarketers are also

---

[2] 47 U.S.C. § 227.

[3] 15 U.S.C. §§ 6101 *et seq.*

[4] 16 C.F.R. §§ 310.1 *et seq.*, available at www.ftc.gov/os/2002/12/tsrfinalrule.pdf. See generally *Facts for Business: Complying with the Telemarketing Sales Rule*, available at www.ftc.gov/bcp/edu/pubs/business/marketing/bus27.shtm

prohibited from calling before 8 A.M. or after 9 P.M. and from calling customers who have previously indicated they do not want to be called.

Violations of the Telemarketing Sales Rule can result in civil penalties of up to $10,000 per violation, injunctions, and potential redress to injured consumers. The Rule is enforceable by the FTC and also by the state attorneys general, who can obtain nationwide injunctions against fraudulent telemarketers. Prior to the Rule, a state attorney general might have succeeded in closing down a fraudulent telemarketer within her own state but had no ability to prevent the telemarketer from relocating to a different state. The Rule has made it much more difficult for fraudulent telemarketers to simply relocate their operations. Private persons may also bring suit in federal court to enforce the Rule if they have suffered $50,000 or more in actual damages (see Case Illustration 8.2).

The FTC's *Mail or Telephone Order Merchandise Rule*[5] applies to the sale of merchandise that is ordered by mail, telephone, fax, or computer "regardless of the method used to solicit the order."[6] Under the Rule, the marketer must have a reasonable basis for stating or implying that it can ship within a certain time when it advertises mail or telephone order merchandise. If the marketer does not make a specific statement regarding shipping, it must have a reasonable basis for believing that it can ship within 30 days of the order. If the marketer later discovers that it cannot ship within the specified time period, it must obtain the customer's consent for the delayed shipment or refund all money paid. Online merchants may send delay notices via e-mail.

The FTC created the *National Do Not Call Registry*[7] in 2004 in an effort to assist consumers in reducing unwanted telemarketing calls. Once a consumer registers his or her residential phone number, the telemarketer must cease calling that number within 31 days. Cell phone numbers do not need to be included on the registry, as FCC regulations prohibit telemarketers from calling cell phone numbers with an automatic dialer. The registry does not apply to business lines and does not prohibit certain types of unsolicited nonmarketing calls, such as calls from political organizations and charities, or calls from companies with which the receiver has had a previous business relationship (such as purchase or inquiry).

Telemarketers and trade groups challenged this Registry as a violation of commercial free speech rights, but their challenge failed. Commercial free speech is discussed in more detail in Chapter 7.

➤ *See Discussion Case 8.1.*

Electronic Retailing and Advertising

Electronic retailing includes activities such as shop-at-home television networks and online retailing. Obviously, there has been tremendous growth in Internet-based retailing in recent years, as online retailers expand their operations and as consumers become more familiar and comfortable with this alternative method of purchasing goods and services.

While the Internet has opened up myriad new opportunities for retailing activities, it has also offered many possibilities for abusive retailing practices. Unsolicited commercial e-mail, also known as *junk e-mail* or *spam*, has proliferated in recent years. Many

---

[5] 16 C.F.R. Part 435. See generally *Facts for Business: A Business Guide to the Federal Trade Commission's Mail or Telephone Order Merchandise Rule*, available at http://www.ftc.gov/bcp/edu/pubs/business/adv/bus02.shtm

[6] 16 C.F.R. § 435.2(a).

[7] See www.donotcall.gov See generally *FTC Business Alert: Q&A for Telemarketers and Sellers about the Do Not Call Provisions of the FTC's Telemarketing Sales Rule*, available at www.ftc.gov/bcp/edu/pubs/business/alerts/alt129.shtm

CASE ILLUSTRATION 8.2

FTC v. GLOBAL MARKETING GROUP, INC., 594 F. SUPP. 2D 1281 (M.D. FLA. 2008)

FACTS This case arose out of the activities of eight Canadian advance-fee telemarketers, who would telephone consumers and induce them to purchase unsecured credit cards and credit card loss protection services. The consumers were charged fees, payable in advance, of up to $249. The consumers did not receive either the credit cards or the loss protection services they had paid for, however.

Ira Rubin was an owner or corporate officer of 24 corporations that assisted these Canadian telemarketers. The 24 corporations shared officers, employees, and office space, commingled funds, and were under common control. Rubin was actively involved in the day-to-day operations of these 24 corporations, including soliciting new telemarketer clients and managing existing clients; serving as the primary contact with the bank that provided the telemarketers with access to the Automated Clearing House Network (the electronic funds transfer system that provides for interbank clearing of electronic funds); reviewing, editing, and approving sales scripts used by the telemarketers; and handling law enforcement inquiries regarding the telemarketers. In the four-year period that Rubin and his corporations were involved with the eight telemarketers, he and his corporations netted over $8.6 million.

The FTC filed a complaint against Rubin, alleging that he personally violated the Telemarketing Sales Rule.

DECISION The court found that Rubin had violated the Telemarketing Sales Rule. The Rule provides, in relevant part:

It is a deceptive telemarketing act or practice and a violation of this Rule for a person to provide substantial assistance or support to any seller or telemarketer when that person knows or consciously avoids knowing that the seller or telemarketer is engaged in any act or practice that violates … this Rule.

The court determined first that the telemarketers had violated the Rule by making misleading statements to induce consumers to purchase goods or services. Although they promised consumers credit cards and loss prevention services in exchange for payment of advance fees, they never intended to follow through with providing such services, and in fact, never did. The court further found that Rubin assisted the telemarketers in this scheme by processing the more than $26 million in payments made by consumers; by reviewing, editing, and approving the sales scripts; and by handling customer complaints and law enforcement inquiries. Rubin also received periodic reports of the telemarketers' returns, which were as high as 71.5 percent.

The court concluded that "at a minimum, Rubin consciously avoided knowing the telemarketers were engaged in deceptive acts and practices given the extraordinary high return rate and Rubin's substantial involvement in the telemarketing scheme."

Moreover, the corporate form did not shield Rubin from individual liability. The court stated:

An individual may be held liable for corporate violations if the FTC can show "that the individual defendants participated directly in the practices or had authority to control them [and] that the individual had some knowledge of the practices." Authority is established by proof that the individual participated in corporate activities by performing the duties of a corporate officer. Knowledge may be proven by "evidence that the individual[] had … an awareness of a high probability of fraud along with an intentional avoidance of the truth."

Here, the telemarketer's sales scripts, which Rubin reviewed, clearly revealed an intent to engage in illegal conduct. Moreover, the periodic financial reports showing the unusually high returns, and Rubin's handling of law enforcement inquiries regarding the telemarketers' illegal activities, indicate that Rubin "either had actual knowledge of the illegal activity or that he was aware of a high probability of fraud and chose to avoid the truth."

The court issued a permanent injunction "restraining Rubin from engaging, directly or indirectly, in any and all future involvement with telemarketing operations." The court also issued a monetary judgment of $8,615,185 against Rubin.

Internet users are outraged at the use of spam, but it remains a common direct market-ing tool.

Firms who use unsolicited commercial e-mail as a marketing tool face a complex reg-ulatory environment. The states moved more quickly than the federal government on addressing the issue of spam, and several states, such as California, Nevada, and Wa-shington, passed their own regulations to control unsolicited commercial e-mail.

In 2003, the federal government enacted the *Controlling the Assault of Non-Solicited Pornography and Marketing Act* (CAN-SPAM),[8] which took effect on January 1, 2004. It regulates and criminalizes a number of unsolicited commercial e-mail activities, but allows the sending of bulk commercial e-mail, provided certain opt-out and other requirements are met. Unsolicited commercial e-mail that is subject to the Act must: (1) have accurate header information (i.e., the "to," "from," and routing information on the e-mail must accurately identify the sender); (2) contain an accurate "subject" line; (3) be labeled as an advertisement; (4) provide a valid physical postal address for the sender; and (5) conspicuously provide the recipient with an opportunity to opt out of any further communications from the sender. The Act is generally enforced by the FTC through regulatory actions, or by litigation in federal court brought by the FTC, state attorneys general, or other government officials. Violations are punishable by fines and/ or imprisonment of up to five years.

Because of the existence of state regulation of spam, the CAN-SPAM Act raises issues of preemption. The Act preempts any state statute, regulation, or rule that expressly reg-ulates commercial e-mail messages, except to the extent the state law prohibits falsity or deception in the e-mail, such as prohibiting fraud or computer crimes. Marketers who send unsolicited commercial e-mail thus must be very carefully to ensure that they com-ply not only with the federal law, but with the laws and regulations of all of the states to which they direct such e-mail. There have been several court challenges to state legisla-tion brought on preemption grounds, with mixed results.[9]

◆ *See Discussion Case 8.2.*

While the United States adopted an "opt-out" approach to unsolicited commercial e-mail, the European Union took the opposite approach. A 2002 European Directive requires that recipients must opt in before being sent unsolicited commercial e-mail.[10]

Home Solicitations

Home solicitation or *door-to-door sales* are regulated extensively at the state and federal levels. These are sales that are made at the buyer's home or in a place other than the seller's usual place of business. These types of sales are less likely to result in repeat transactions, so sellers have less incentive to seek to develop the goodwill of the customer and may engage in abusive or aggressive behavior.

The FTC's *Cooling-off Rule*[11] requires sellers to give consumers three days to cancel and receive a full refund on certain purchases of $25 or more made at the consumer's

---

[8]15 U.S.C. § 7701 *et seq.* See generally *Facts for Business: The CAN-SPAM Act: Requirements for Commercial Emailers*, available at www.ftc.gov/bcp/edu/pubs/business/ecommerce/bus61.shtm

[9]See *Asis Internet Services v. Vistaprint USA, Inc.*, 617 F. Supp. 2d 989 (N.D. Cal. 2009) (finding California anti-spam act was not preempted by CAN-SPAM); *Omega World Travel Inc. v. Mummagraphics Inc.*, 469 F.3d 348 (4th Cir. 2006) (Oklahoma spam statute was preempted by CAN-SPAM); *Free Speech Coalition, Inc. v. Shurtleff*, 2007 U.S. Dist. LEXIS 21556 (D. Utah 2007) (finding UTAH Child Protection Email Registry is not preempted by CAN-SPAM).

[10]Directive 2002/58 on Privacy and Electronic Communications.

[11]See www.ftc.gov/bcp/edu/pubs/consumer/products/pro03.shtm

home or at certain locations other than the seller's normal place of business, such as hotel or motel rooms, convention centers, and fairgrounds. The seller must provide the buyer with: (1) a summary of the right to cancel; (2) two copies of a cancellation form; and (3) a contract or receipt, which must be in the same language as that used in the sales transaction.

Most states also have cooling-off laws that allow the buyers of goods sold door-to-door to cancel the contract within a specified time period (usually 48 to 72 hours). While the federal Cooling-Off Rule does not apply to sales involving real estate, state statutes often do (see Case Illustration 8.3).

➤ *See Discussion Case 8.3.*

CASE ILLUSTRATION 8.3

KAMPOSEK v. JOHNSON, 2005 OHIO 344 (OHIO APP. 2005)

FACTS Phillip and Vickie Johnson operated a construction company. In response to an inquiry from Albin and Carol Kamposek, Vickie Johnson went to the Kamposeks' home and offered a proposal for construction work. The proposal included construction of a pole barn, an addition to the residence, new windows, conversion of a garage into living space, and siding of the entire house. The parties agreed upon a price of $28,800. The Johnsons did not provide the Kamposeks with a notice of their right to cancel this contract as required by the Ohio Home Solicitations Sales Act (HSSA).

The Kamposeks paid part of the contract price to the Johnsons, but were unhappy with the quality of the work, and refused to make the final payment. The Johnsons ceased work at that point.

The Kamposeks filed suit against the Johnsons for breach of contract. Seven months later (before the trial), the Kamposeks sent a letter to the Johnsons canceling the contract.

The trial court granted the Kamposeks' motion for summary judgment, finding that the contract was subject to the HSSA. The trial court ordered the Johnsons to return the $20,152.64 that the Kamposeks had paid toward the project.

DECISION The appellate court affirmed the outcome. The HSSA states, in relevant part:

(A) "Home solicitation sale" means a sale of consumer goods or services in which the seller or person acting for the seller engages in a personal solicitation of the sale at a residence of the buyer, including solicitations in response to or following an invitation by the buyer, and the buyer's agreement or offer to purchase is there given to the seller or a person acting for the seller, or in which the buyer's agreement

or offer to purchase is made at a place other than seller's place of business.***

Here, the contract was offered and accepted at the Kamposeks' residence, and previous case law had established that home improvement contracts generally fall within the HSSA. Thus, this contract was subject to the HSSA.

The HSSA further provides that a buyer in a home solicitation sale may cancel the sale within three days of signing the agreement. The seller must provide the buyer with notice of this right of cancellation, and the three-day period begins only when notice is given. The buyer may cancel the sale at any time prior to receiving notice of the right of cancellation. If the buyer cancels, the seller must return all payments to the buyer, and the buyer must, upon demand, allow the seller to reclaim the goods from the sale.

If the contract involves services, the HSSA does not permit the seller to begin performance of the contract until the three-day cancellation period has run. If the seller begins work before the expiration of the buyer's right to cancel, the seller bears the risk of loss should the buyer choose to cancel.

Home improvement contracts are classified as service contracts, and hence the Johnsons bore the risk of starting work prior to the end of the cancellation period. Moreover, the physical items involved in a home improvement contract are typically of little value to the seller if reclaimed, and removal of them often causes damage to the buyer's property that is difficult to restore without subjecting the buyer to additional hardship.

Thus, the court concluded, the Kamposeks were not liable for compensating the Johnsons for the partial work performed. Rather, the Kamposeks were entitled to a full return of all money paid to the Johnsons

(Continued)

because the Kamposeks exercised their right of cancellation in a timely fashion; nor were the Kamposeks required to return any materials received.

The appellate court explicitly noted that the "HSSA is intended to be a 'shield' for the consumer, not a 'sword.'" Where a consumer entered into a contract for the sole purpose of taking advantage of the seller's possible failure to provide adequate notice of the right of cancellation, the trial court would "have the discretion to make an equitable determination of damages." There was no evidence that the Kamposeks had misused the HSSA in this manner, however.

Unsolicited Merchandise, Merchandise on Approval, and Negative Option Plans

Legally, only two types of unsolicited merchandise may be sent through the mail: (1) free samples, which must be clearly and conspicuously marked; and (2) merchandise mailed by a charitable organization that is seeking contributions. In both instances, the recipient may treat the merchandise as a gift. Under the Postal Reorganization Act of 1970,[12] the mailing of any other type of unsolicited merchandise is considered an unfair trade practice and is illegal. The recipient of such merchandise is entitled to retain, use, discard, or otherwise dispose of the merchandise and is not obligated to either pay for it or return it. The recipient may also mark unopened packages "Return to Sender," and the Postal Service will return the packages with no additional postage charge to the recipient. In addition, a merchant who ships unordered merchandise knowing that it is unlawful to do so can be subject to civil penalties of up to $16,000 per violation.[13]

However, marketers may engage in *sales on approval* transactions under certain circumstances. Under the FTC Act, the marketer must obtain the customer's express agreement to send merchandise on approval. Under this sales mechanism, the customer may return merchandise, usually after a "no obligation" or "free trial" period, and does not have to pay for the merchandise until it is received and approved. Suppose, for example, that the marketer is selling a 30-volume set of encyclopedias with the understanding that a volume will be sent on approval to the customer each month. The marketer must explain the program in detail when soliciting the order and must obtain the customer's express agreement that a failure to return the cancellation document will be treated by both parties as a request to send the volume.

In addition, many music, book, and video club companies operate as *prenotification negative option plans.* Essentially, these marketers sell subscription plans to consumers who have agreed in advance to become subscribers. Under the FTC's *Prenotification Negative Option Rule,*[14] the marketer must provide certain information in the promotional materials, including how many selections the customer must buy, how and when the customer can cancel the membership, how and when to return the "negative option" form to cancel shipment of a selection, and how often a customer can expect to receive announcements and forms. Customers enrolled in the plan are then obligated to either return the negative option form within 10 days after receiving it or pay for the merchandise after receiving it.

---

[12] 39 U.S.C. § 3009.

[13] See generally *Facts for Business: A Business Guide to the Federal Trade Commission's Mail or Telephone Order Merchandise Rule,* available at www.ftc.gov/bcp/edu/pubs/business/adv/bus02.shtm

[14] 16 C.F.R. Part 425. See generally *Facts for Consumers: Prenotification Negative Option Plans,* available at www.ftc.gov/bcp/edu/pubs/consumer/products/pro09.shtm

900 Numbers

Providers of pay-per-call services (900 numbers) must comply with the FTC's *900-Number Rule*.[15] If the call to the 900 number costs more than $2, the provider must disclose the name of the 900-number company and the cost of the call in the introductory message of the call and must give the caller the opportunity to hang up without charge. Additional advertising disclosures must be made for services that promote sweepstakes or games of chance, provide information about a federal program but are not sponsored by a federal agency, or target children under the age of 18 years. Pay-per-call services and advertisements for them may not be targeted at children under the age of 12 years unless the advertisement is for a "bona fide educational service" as defined in the Rule.

Warranties and Guarantees

Under the FTC's *Rule on Pre-Sale Availability of Written Warranty Terms*,[16] sellers must make all written warranties on consumer products costing more than $15, whether extended by the manufacturer or by the seller, available to consumers before they purchase the product. If the marketer solicits orders for warranted consumer products through the mail or by telephone, it must either include the warranty in the catalog or advertisement or include a statement informing customers how they may obtain a copy. Door-to-door sales companies must offer the consumer a copy of the written warranty before the transaction is completed. Online merchants may use a clearly labeled hyperlink to lead to the full text of the warranty, but that text itself should be capable of being downloaded or printed so that the consumer can retain a copy. Warranties are discussed in more detail in Chapter 10.

Under the FTC Act, it is an unfair or deceptive practice for a marketer to fail to honor "satisfaction" and "money-back" guarantees fully and promptly. This requires return of the purchase price, shipping, handling, and other fees. Any limitations on the guarantee, such as requiring the customer to supply proof of purchase, requiring the return of the unused portion of the product, or time restrictions on the offer, must be stated clearly and conspicuously.[17]

Labeling and Packaging Regulation

Labeling and packaging issues are regulated heavily at both the state and federal levels. Generally, these laws are designed to ensure that accurate information is provided about the product and that adequate warnings are given regarding the dangers of use or misuse.

Among the major federal labeling statutes are: the *Fair Packaging and Labeling Act*,[18] which requires that labels on consumer goods identify the product, the net quantity of the contents, the manufacturer, and the packager or distributor; the *Flammable Fabrics Act*,[19] which sets safety standards for flammable fabrics and materials in clothing; the *Federal Cigarette Labeling and Advertising Act*,[20] which requires specific warnings on cigarette packaging and most related advertising and which bans advertising on television and radio;

---

[15]See generally *Facts for Business: Complying with the 900-Number Rule*, available at www.ftc.gov/bcp/edu/pubs/business/marketing/bus06.shtm; *Facts for Consumers: 900 Numbers*, available at www.ftc.gov/bcp/edu/pubs/consumer/telemarketing/tel04.shtm

[16]16 C.F.R. Part 702. See generally *A Businessperson's Guide to Federal Warranty Law*, available at www.ftc.gov/bcp/edu/pubs/business/adv/bus01.shtm

[17]16 C.F.R. Part 239 (*Guides for the Advertising of Warranties and Guarantees*).

[18]15 U.S.C. §§ 1451 *et seq.* See generally www.ftc.gov/os/statutes/flpa/outline.shtm

[19]15 U.S.C. § 1191 *et seq.*

[20]15 U.S.C. § 1331 *et seq.*

the *Smokeless Tobacco Health Education Act*,[21] which requires specific health warnings on chewing tobacco packaging and most related advertising and which bans advertising on television and radio; and the *Wool Products Labeling Act*,[22] which requires that most wool and textile products be labeled as to fiber content, country of origin, and identity of manufacturer or other business responsible for marketing or handling the item. Special labeling requirements also apply to food and drug products, as discussed below.

There are numerous other federal and state labeling requirements. A marketer should always check to see if any specific labeling regulations apply to the particular products it is producing or selling. Two particular issues arise in the labeling context: (1) the use of the "Made in USA" label and (2) "green" marketing claims.

"Made in USA" Labeling

United States content must be disclosed on automobiles and on textile, wool, and fur products. Most other products marketed in the United States are not required to disclose their amount of U.S. content. Many marketers choose to use the "Made in USA" label, however, as a way of distinguishing or marketing their goods.

The FTC, under its power to prevent deception and unfairness in the marketplace, requires that products advertised as "Made in USA" be "all or virtually all" made in the United States.[23] This means that all significant parts, processing, and labeling that go into the product must be of U.S. origin, with no or negligible foreign content. Products that contain a nonnegligible amount of foreign content should use a qualified "Made in USA" claim, such as "70% U.S. content" or "Made in USA of U.S. and imported parts" (see Case Illustration 8.4).

CASE ILLUSTRATION 8.4

UNITED STATES v. THE STANLEY WORKS, CIV. DOCKET 3: 06-CV-00883-JBA (D. CONN. JUNE 13, 2006), AVAILABLE AT WWW.FTC.GOV/OS/CASELIST/C3876/STANLEY_CON_DEC_1.PDF

FACTS The FTC alleged that The Stanley Works, a U.S. tool manufacturer, falsely claimed that its Zero Degree ratchets, made under Stanley's MAC Tools trademark, were Made in USA. The FTC alleged that the ratchets contained a substantial amount of foreign content.

DECISION The FTC and The Stanley Works entered into a Consent Decree in which The Stanley Works agreed to pay a $205,000 civil penalty. In addition, The Stanley Works agreed not to violate a 1999 FTC Order issued against it to resolve earlier claims that the company had made false Made in USA claims. The 1999 Order had prohibited The Stanley Works

from misrepresenting the extent to which any of its professional-grade hand tools were made in the United States. The expiration date of the 1999 Order was extended to 20 years from the date of the Complaint in the current action. (The Complaint was filed in June, 2008.)

In addition, for a period of 10 years, The Stanley Works must provide a copy of the Consent Decree and 1999 FTC Order to, and receive a signed acknowledgment of receipt from, all current or future officers and directors and all current or future employees, agents, or representatives responsible for "marking, labeling, packaging, advertising, or promoting any product covered" by the Consent Decree.

---

[21]15 U.S.C. § 4401 *et seq.*

[22]15 U.S.C. § 68 *et seq.*

[23]See *Facts for Business: Complying with the Made in the USA Standard*, available at www.ftc.gov/bcp/edu/pubs/business/adv/bus03.shtm

The requirement applies to any U.S. origin claims that appear on products, labeling, advertising, or other promotional materials, including online marketing efforts. The requirement also applies to both express claims of U.S. origin and implied claims that might arise through the use of U.S. symbols (such as an American flag or eagle) or geographic references.

The FTC enforces the "Made in USA" standard. The U.S. Customs Service has responsibility for enforcing requirements that imported goods be marked with their country of origin (e.g., "Made in China").

Many other countries have their own country-of-origin labeling requirements. Marketers must thus be aware of the rules applicable in the countries to which they intend to export their goods.

"Green" Marketing

It has become very common for marketers to claim that their products are "environmentally safe," "recyclable," "degradable," or "ozone friendly." Because many consumers place great weight on environmental claims and because these claims are often open to interpretation and abuse, the FTC, with the cooperation of the Environmental Protection Agency (EPA), has developed *Guides for the Use of Environmental Marketing Claims*[24] for advertisers to ensure that green-marketing claims do not mislead consumers. The FTC has issued documents entitled *Complying with the Environmental Marketing Guide*[25] and *Sorting Out "Green" Advertising Claims*[26] to assist businesses and consumers. Generally, marketers may not exaggerate the environmental benefits of their products or packaging. Claims regarding environmental benefits must be specific and substantiated.

The Guides apply to environmental claims, whether explicit or implicit, made in labeling, advertising, promotional materials, and all other forms of marketing, including marketing through the Internet or e-mail. The Guides are not enforceable regulations and do not have the force and effect of law. However, failure to comply with the Guides may result in FTC investigation, which can lead to corrective action under Section 5 of the FTC Act if the FTC determines that the marketer's behavior leads to unfair or deceptive acts and practices.

If a product or package is labeled "recycled," for example, unless the product is 100 percent recycled, it must state how much of that product or package is recycled. This helps ensure that consumers are not misled into buying a product that contains only minimal recycled content. Similarly, if a product is labeled "nontoxic," "essentially nontoxic," or "practically nontoxic," the manufacturer must have reason to believe that the product does not pose any significant risk to people or the environment.

In 2009, for example, the FTC charged Kmart Corp. and Tender Corp. with making false and unsubstantiated claims that certain of their paper products were "biodegradable." The Green Guides provide that marketers can make unqualified statements about the biodegradability of their products only if they have scientific evidence that their products will completely decompose within a reasonably short time frame under normal disposal conditions. The FTC alleged that Kmart's American Fare brand disposable plates and Tender Corp.'s Fresh Bath brand moist wipes are typically disposed of in landfills, incinerators, or recycling facilities, where it is impossible for them to biodegrade in a reasonably short time period. Both companies settled with the FTC, agreeing not to make deceptive claims regarding biodegradability of their products and agreeing to

[24]16 C.F.R. Part 260.

[25]See generally *Facts for Business: Complying with the Environmental Marketing Guides*, available at www.ftc.gov/bcp/edu/pubs/business/energy/bus42.shtm

[26]See generally www.ftc.gov/bcp/edu/pubs/consumer/genera;/gen02.shtm

obtain competent and reliable evidence to support their environmental claims about their products.[27]

International Labeling Considerations

Marketers who sell their products overseas need to be concerned with the labeling laws of each of the countries in which they market their products. First, marketers need to be certain that ingredient, promotional, and instructional information on labels is translated accurately and into the appropriate language or languages. Some countries, such as Belgium and Finland, require labeling to be bilingual. Second, failure to adhere to local requirements can have severe consequences. For example, an Italian judge banned the distribution of bottled Coca-Cola in Italy because the ingredients were listed on the bottle caps rather than on the bottles.[28] Finally, international marketers should be aware that laws vary substantially from country to country. Venezuela, for example, requires prices to be printed on the label while Chile prohibits this practice. Thus, the marketer must be certain to seek competent local counsel when making decisions about labeling in foreign countries.

Eco-labeling also raises numerous international issues. Eco-labeling is the practice of including information on the labels of goods regarding the environmental quality of the production process. The first environmental label was issued in Germany in 1978. Canada initiated a similar program in 1988 and Japan in 1989. The European Union adopted a Community Regulation authorizing its Member Countries to issue eco-labels in 1992. Agenda 21 of the Rio Earth Summit in 1992 urged governments to expand "environmental labeling ... to assist consumers to make informed choices." In addition, some developing countries, such as India, the Republic of Korea, and Singapore, have adopted eco-labeling programs.

Some forms of eco-labeling are voluntary and are undertaken by companies because of their appeal to consumers. The "dolphin-safe" label on canned tuna in the United States, for example, indicates that the company uses dolphin-safe methods of harvesting tuna—an issue of great interest and importance to many consumers.

While voluntary eco-labeling is seen as posing few, if any, serious trade implications, mandatory eco-labeling is a very controversial subject in the international arena, where it is often viewed as an illegal trade barrier. Many products can be produced with a variety of production processes, which may vary greatly from country to country. Eco-labeling, however, assumes that there is a global standard for production. Many developing countries argue that mandatory eco-labeling can be used as a trade barrier to keep such nations from participating in the global marketplace.

Countries that engage in mandatory eco-labeling need to be concerned about running afoul of the General Agreement on Tariffs and Trade (GATT). In 1992, for example, a GATT panel held that mandatory provisions of U.S. legislation regarding dolphin-safe tuna harvesting techniques were intended not only to protect dolphins but also to protect the U.S. fishing industry. The Panel found that the U.S. legislation was in violation of GATT Article III because it discriminated against imported products in favor of domestic products. The GATT Panel held that the primary goal of any environmental measures that affect trade must be to protect the environment rather than the domestic market. The Panel explained that if individual countries were allowed to impose their national environmental standards on other states:

> each contracting party could unilaterally determine the life or health protection policies from which other contracting parties could not deviate without jeopardizing their

---

[27]See www.ftc.gov/opa/2009/06/kmart.shtm

[28]See Information Bank Abstracts, *Wall Street Journal*, Nov. 18, 1977, at p. 35, col. 2.

rights under the General Agreement. The General Agreement would then no longer constitute a multilateral framework for trade among all contracting parties but would provide legal security only in respect of trade between a limited number of contracting parties with identical internal regulations.[29]

Thus, the Panel concluded, "a contracting party may not restrict imports of a product merely because it originates in a country with environmental policies different from its own."[30]

Efforts to create international standards for eco-labeling have been hampered by the fact that there is no obvious forum for setting such standards. The World Trade Organization, for example, is primarily a trade forum and lacks expertise in environmental issues. Governmental agencies and nongovernmental organizations (NGOs) that do have environmental expertise, on the other hand, often lack a trade focus.

Health and Safety Regulation

In addition to labeling requirements, specific laws govern consumer health and safety issues. The two major federal statutes in this area are the federal *Food, Drug and Cosmetic Act* (FDCA),[31] administered by the Food and Drug Administration (FDA),[32] and the *Consumer Product Safety Act* (CPSA),[33] administered by the Consumer Product Safety Commission (CPSC).[34] As the following discussion illustrates, however, a number of additional federal statutes address health and safety issues as well.

Food, Drug, and Cosmetic Laws

While the FTC regulates the *advertising* of food products, the FDA regulates the *safety* and *labeling* of such products. The federal FDCA governs the testing, manufacture, distribution, and sale of food, drugs, cosmetics, and medicinal products and devices. Under the FDCA, certain food additives, drugs, and medicinal devices may not be sold to the public unless they first obtain FDA approval.

The FDCA is administered by the FDA. The FDA is a large federal agency with extensive powers and is located within the Department of Health and Human Services. The FDA regulates over $1 trillion worth of products annually.

If the inspectors or investigators discover a violation of the FDCA, the FDA can encourage the firm to voluntarily correct the problem or to recall the product from the marketplace. However, the FDA has no authority to order recalls on its own initiative.

In the absence of voluntary cooperation, the FDA can seek legal sanctions. The FDA has broad powers to obtain search warrants and conduct inspections. It can also seek court orders for the seizure and destruction of products, injunctions, and criminal penalties (including imprisonment) against willful violators.

The CPSC and the FDA are the two agencies with primary responsibility for regulating the safety of imported consumer products. This international oversight role is becoming increasingly important. During fiscal year 2007, CPSC announced 472

---

[29]GATT Panel Report on United States—Restrictions on Imports of Tuna, Feb. 18, 1992, GATT B.I.S.D. (39th Supp.), at 199, para. 5.27 (1993).

[30]*Id.* at 204, para. 6.2.

[31]21 U.S.C. § 301 *et seq.*

[32]The FDA's home page is found at www.fda.gov

[33]15 U.S.C. § 2051 *et seq.*

[34]The CPSC's home page is found at www.cpsc.gov

recalls. Of those, 389 were recalls of imported products; 288 involved imports from China.[35]

Food   The FDCA establishes food standards, specifies safe levels of various food additives, and establishes classifications of food and food advertising. The Act prohibits the shipment, distribution, or sale of adulterated food, which is food that consists in whole or in part of any "filthy, putrid, or decomposed substance" or is otherwise "unfit for food." The Act does not require that food be pure or that it be completely free of any foreign substances. In a 1972 case, for example, a U.S. District Court concluded that a dairy corporation and its manager could not be held criminally liable for selling butter containing on average three miniscule particles of insect fragments per pound. The court concluded that "this contamination is a trifle, not a matter of concern to the law."[36] In fact, the FDA itself has set standards for the number of contaminants, or "defects," that are allowed in certain foods.[37]

On the other hand, substantial contamination of food can lead to civil and/or criminal liability for both the corporation and the corporate manager in charge. Thus, managers need to be aware of the potential for individual liability, as well as corporate liability, under the FDCA.

The FDCA also prohibits false and misleading labeling of food products. Most foods are required to carry nutrition labels as well, listing items such as total calories, calories from fat, total fat, saturated fat, cholesterol, sodium, total carbohydrates, dietary fiber, sugars, and certain vitamins.

States, too, may impose labeling requirements on food products in some instances. However, the ability of either the state or federal governments to impose such requirements is constrained by the First Amendment commercial speech doctrines discussed in Chapter 7 (see Case Illustration 8.5).

The federal regulatory regime addressing food products is expansive, and many agencies other than the FDA are involved in maintaining the safety and wholesomeness of the nation's food supply. For example, the Department of Agriculture (USDA)[38] inspects and grades meat and poultry that is to be consumed by humans, as well as administering various specific acts relating to agricultural marketing and inspection. The Centers for Disease Control and Prevention (CDC)[39] oversee issues relating to food-borne disease outbreaks. The EPA[40] oversees drinking water standards and regulates toxic substances and wastes to prevent their entry into the food chain, as well as regulating the use of pesticides. The Department of Commerce[41] inspects and certifies fishing vessels, seafood-processing plants, and retail facilities for federal sanitation standards. The Bureau of Alcohol, Tobacco, Firearms and Explosives (ATF)[42] regulates, among other things, alcoholic beverages (with the exception of wine containing less than 7 percent alcohol). U.S. Customs and Border Protection (CBP)[43] works with the various federal

---

[35]See CPSC, *Import Safety Strategy* (July 2008), available at www.cpsc.gov/BUSINFO/importsafety.pdf

[36]*United States v. Capital City Foods*, 345 F. Supp. 277, 279 (D. N.D. 1972).

[37]See 21 C.F.R. § 110.110.

[38]The USDA's home page is found at www.usda.gov

[39]The CDC's home page is found at www.cdc.gov

[40]The EPA's home page is found at www.epa.gov

[41]The Commerce Department's home page is found at www.commerce.gov

[42]The ATF's home page is found at www.aft.gov

[43]The CBP's home page is found at www.cbp.gov

CASE ILLUSTRATION 8.5

INTERNATIONAL DAIRY FOODS ASSOCIATION v. AMESTOY, 92 F.3D 67 (2D CIR. 1996)

FACTS In 1993, the FDA approved the use of recombinant Bovine Somatotropin (rBST), a synthetic growth hormone that increases milk production by cows. Because the FDA had found, "after exhaustive tests," that dairy products derived from herds treated with rBST were indistinguishable from products derived from untreated herds and that rBST posed no human safety or health concerns, the FDA declined to require labeling of products derived from cows treated with rBST.

In 1994, the state of Vermont enacted a statute requiring that milk or milk products derived from treated herds be labeled as such. The state imposed its requirement "to help consumers make informed shopping decisions."

International Dairy Foods Association, Milk Industry Foundation, International Ice Cream Association, National Cheese Institute, Grocery Manufacturers of America, Inc., and National Food Processors Association (collectively, the "plaintiffs") filed suit, arguing that the statute violated their First Amendment commercial free speech rights by compelling them to speak against their will. They requested a preliminary injunction. The trial court denied the injunction and the plaintiffs appealed.

DECISION The U.S. Court of Appeals determined that a preliminary injunction should issue because the plaintiffs had shown: (1) irreparable harm and (2) a likelihood of success on the merits. Although First Amendment claims usually center on the purposeful *suppression* of speech, the First Amendment also encompasses the right *not* to speak. The court concluded

that compelling the plaintiffs to label their products, albeit truthfully, caused them irreparable harm.

The appellate court also found that the plaintiffs had shown a likelihood of success on the merits. The court applied the Supreme Court's *Central Hudson* test for determining whether a restriction on commercial speech is constitutional: (1) whether the expression concerns lawful activity and is not misleading; (2) whether the government's interest is substantial; (3) whether the disputed regulation directly serves that asserted interest; and (4) whether the regulation is no more extensive than necessary.

The appellate court found that the Vermont regulation failed the second prong of the test. The trial court had found that Vermont "does not claim that, health or safety concerns prompted the passage of the Vermont Labeling Law," but instead defended the statute on the grounds of "strong consumer interest and the public's 'right to know' ...." The appellate court found these interests "insufficient to justify compromising protected constitutional rights." The court concluded that it was "aware of no case in which consumer interest alone was sufficient to justify requiring a product's manufacturers to publish the functional equivalent of a warning about a production method that has no discernable impact on a final product." Consumers interested in such information should, in the court's view, "exercise the power of their purses by buying products from manufacturers who voluntarily reveal it."

The appellate court thus remanded the case to the trial court for entry of a preliminary injunction enjoining enforcement of the statute.

agencies to ensure that food products entering or exiting the United States meet U.S. laws and regulations.

Dietary Supplements The line between food, drugs, and dietary supplements is blurring in the minds of many consumers, who are increasingly seeking health benefits from the foods they ingest. The regulatory line between these substances is blurring as well.

Traditionally, dietary supplements that made labeling claims for health or nutrition benefits were considered drugs by the FDA and were subject to rigorous preapproval, manufacturing, and labeling controls. Manufacturers who wished to avoid these expensive and time-consuming procedures could only inform the consumer of the product's contents but could not make any statements regarding possible or purported health benefits associated with the product.

Then Congress, believing that foods and dietary supplements do not raise the same risk as drugs and should not be held to the same substantiation standards, enacted the *Dietary Supplement Health and Education Act of 1994* (DSHEA).[44] The DSHEA allows a manufacturer to make certain statements, such as claims about the role of a nutrient or dietary ingredient with respect to the structure or function of the human body and statements of general well-being arising from consumption of a nutrient or other dietary ingredient, without first seeking permission of the FDA, provided that the manufacturer has substantiation for the statements. The label must contain a description of the product indicating that it is a "supplement," the name and address of the manufacturer, packer, or distributor, a complete list of ingredients, the net contents of the package, and a "Supplement Facts" panel containing nutritional labeling.

As a result of the DSHEA, most of the nutritional and safety labeling requirements that apply to food and drugs do not apply to the marketing of dietary supplements. Rather, under the DSHEA, the FDA's role in taking action against unsafe dietary supplements occurs after they are marketed.

The *Dietary Supplements and Nonprescription Drug Consumer Act*,[45] which took effect in December, 2007, requires manufacturers of nonprescription drugs and dietary supplements to report "adverse events" to the FDA.

Drugs and Medical Devices   The FDCA sets up an elaborate procedure under which drugs must be proven to be both safe *and* effective before they may be marketed to the public. Thus, the FDA has authority to regulate the testing, manufacture, distribution, and sale of drugs. The FDA does not conduct research on the efficacy or safety of new drugs but, rather, evaluates the results of studies done by the manufacturers. This evaluation process may take several years, although expedited processes are available for drugs that address incurable diseases, such as AIDS. It can be very expensive and time-consuming for a manufacturer to perform the necessary testing to show that a drug is safe and effective.

Under the FDCA, all prescription and nonprescription drugs must be labeled with proper directions for use and with warnings about potential side effects. The manufacture, sale, or distribution of adulterated or misbranded drugs is prohibited.

Under the 1976 *Medical Device Amendment* to the FDCA,[46] the FDA regulates medical devices, such as pacemakers; kidney dialysis machines; defibrillators; and other diagnostic, therapeutic, and health devices. Medical devices that are life supporting, life sustaining, or implanted must receive agency approval before they can be marketed. The mislabeling of medical devices is prohibited, and the FDA can remove ineffective devices from the marketplace. Even after a drug or medical device is approved for marketing, the FDA continues to collect and analyze reports on such products to monitor the products for any unexpected adverse reactions.

The *Food and Drug Administration Modernization Act of 1997*[47] (FDAMA) eliminated the existing prohibition on manufacturers disseminating information about unapproved uses of approved drugs, biologics,[48] and medical devices. When a drug or device manufacturer wants to market a new product, the manufacturer is required to submit the product, along with proposed labeling, to the FDA. The manufacturer is not required to submit labeling that indicates all possible uses of the drug or device. Rather, once the

---

[44]Pub. L. No. 103-147, 108 Stat. 4325 (1994).

[45]Pub. L. No. 109-462 (2006).

[46]21 U.S.C. § 360(c) *et seq.*

[47]Pub. L. No. 105-115, 111 Stat. 2296.

[48]*Biologics* include blood and blood products, vaccines, allergenics, and biological therapeutics.

FDA has approved a label stating one intended use, the manufacturer may market the product.

It is common for physicians to make "off-label" uses of drugs or devices, i.e., uses that are not described on the approved label; in fact, a 2009 research report found that 20 percent of outpatient prescriptions are for off-label use.[49] FDAMA allows manufacturers to disseminate off-label drug use information under prescribed conditions to health care practitioners, pharmacy benefit managers, health insurance issuers, group health plans, and federal and state government agencies. Manufacturers may not disseminate such information directly to patients. The Act illustrates the balancing that marketing managers must make when faced with new regulatory requirements. On the one hand, the FDAMA allows manufacturers to market their drugs for more purposes, thus potentially increasing sales and profits. On the other hand, the manufacturer must follow very strict requirements in marketing drugs for off-label uses or run the risk of incurring criminal or civil sanctions. In addition, the firm is likely to face increased products liability risks once it markets a drug for a use not approved by the FDA. Products liability issues are discussed in Chapter 10.

Cosmetics   Substances and preparations for cleansing, altering the appearance of, and promoting the attractiveness of a person are subject to FDA regulation. Ordinary household soap is exempted from such regulation.

The FDA may regulate cosmetics only *after* the products are released to the market. It has no authority to review or approve cosmetic products or ingredients prior to sale to the public. However, if a cosmetic product has drug properties (i.e., it cures, treats, mitigates, or prevents disease or affects the structure or function of the human body), it must be approved by the FDA as a drug.

The FDA also has no authority to require companies to do safety testing on their cosmetic products. If a product's safety has not been substantiated, however, it must bear a label stating: "Warning: The safety of this product has not been determined." The FDA also has no power to order recalls of a cosmetic product; rather, to remove a product from the marketplace, the FDA must prove in court that the product is unsafe, improperly labeled, or otherwise in violation of law.

Consumer Product Safety Law

The Consumer Product Safety Commission (CPSC) is an independent federal agency, created in 1972 and charged with the task of protecting "the public against unreasonable risks of injuries and deaths associated with consumer products." The CPSC consists of three commissioners, each nominated by the President and confirmed by the Senate, for a staggered seven-year term. Specifically, the CPSC: (1) conducts research on the safety of individual products; (2) maintains a clearinghouse on the risks associated with various consumer products; and (3) adopts rules and regulations to interpret and enforce the CPSA.

The CPSC regulates 15,000 types of consumer products used in the home or schools or for recreation, such as toys, clothing, appliances, furniture, and playground or sports equipment. It does not regulate products such as on-road motor vehicles, boats, aircraft, food, drugs, cosmetics, pesticides, alcohol, firearms, tobacco, or medical devices. The CPSC regulates every company, no matter how small, that manufactures, imports, distributes, or sells any type of consumer product covered by any law that the agency

---

[49]See Agency for Healthcare Research & Quality, *Developing Evidence-Based Research Priorities for Off-Label Drug Use*, available at http://effectivehealthcare.gov/healthInfo/

administers. It addresses only consumer product safety; issues relating to false advertising, fraud, and product quality are handled by the FTC.

The primary act that the CPSC administers is the *Consumer Product Safety Act* (CPSA).[50] Under the CPSA, the CPSC is authorized to set mandatory safety standards for consumer products and to ban the manufacture and sale of any product deemed by the Commission to pose an "unreasonable risk" to consumers. For example, the CPSC has set safety standards for bicycles and cigarette lighters and has banned the sale of lead-based paint. The CPSC also works with industry to develop voluntary industry standards.

The CPSC can require manufacturers of products it determines are "imminently hazardous" (i.e., products whose use can cause an unreasonable risk of death or serious injury or illness) to recall, repair, or replace the products or to take other corrective action.[43] The CPSC can seek injunctions, court orders to seize hazardous consumer products, and civil and/or criminal penalties. In addition, private parties can seek injunctions to prevent violations of the CPSA or of CPSC rules and regulations.

The CPSA imposes certain *reporting requirements* on businesses. First, any manufacturer, importer, distributor, or retailer of consumer products must notify the CPSA immediately if it concludes that one of its products: (1) has a defect that creates a substantial risk of injury to the public; (2) creates an unreasonable risk of serious injury or death; or (3) violates a consumer product safety standard or ban of the product.[51]

Second, a manufacturer must report to the CPSC when any of its products has been involved in three or more lawsuits in a two-year period, if such lawsuits allege death or grievous bodily injury and result in a settlement or court judgment in favor of the plaintiff. Third, a manufacturer, distributor, retailer, or importer of marbles, small balls, latex balloons, or toys or games containing such items must report to the CPSC any incidents of children choking on those items.

The CPSC also enforces several other consumer product safety laws, including the *Federal Hazardous Substances Act,*[52] which regulates household substances and children's products that might be toxic, flammable, or corrosive; the *Flammable Fabrics Act,*[53] which applies to clothing, mattresses, carpets, and similar products; the *Poison Prevention Packaging Act,*[54] which requires child-resistant packaging for certain drugs and other hazardous household substances; and the *Refrigerator Safety Act,*[55] which requires household refrigerator doors to be easily opened from the inside to minimize the possibility of children becoming trapped.

Various well-publicized product safety issues, such as lead paint on children's toys, has made consumer product safety a priority for Congress in recent years. The *Consumer Product Safety Improvement Act of 2008*[56] provides that all children's products manufactured after August 14, 2009, and their packaging, will be required to have permanent tracking labels that would allow manufacturers and consumers to track the product's source. The lead content limit children's products will be lowered at the same time. The Act carries significant penalties for violators, including civil fines of up to $100,000 for an individual violation and up to $15 million for a series of violations, as well as

---

[50]15 U.S.C. § 2051 *et seq.*

[51]15 U.S.C. § 2064.

[52]15 U.S.C. § 1261 *et seq.*

[53]15 U.S.C. § 1191 *et seq.*

[54]15 U.S.C. § 1471 *et seq.*

[55]15 U.S.C. § 1211 *et seq.*

[56]Pub. L. No. 110-314, 122 Stat. 3016 (2008).

criminal penalties of up to five years' imprisonment for directors, officers, and agencies of businesses dealing in consumer goods who knowingly and willfully violate the Act.

Consumer Credit Protection

The federal government has enacted several pieces of legislation designed to protect consumers from abuses by creditors. The primary statute in this area is the *Truth-in-Lending Act*[57] (TILA), which was passed in 1968 as part of the Consumer Credit Protection Act.[50] A number of additional acts have been added as amendments to TILA in the last 40 years. Most recently, the *Mortgage Disclosure Improvement Act*, which took effect July 30, 2009, made changes to TILA. TILA and some of its more important amendments are discussed below.

The Truth-in-Lending Act

TILA is administered by the Federal Reserve Board. The goal of TILA is to assure that creditors and advertisers engage in meaningful disclosure of consumer credit and lease terms so that consumers can shop around for the best financing arrangements. TILA's stringent disclosure requirements are intended to prevent creditors or advertisers from burying the cost of credit in the price of the goods sold. TILA does not set interest rates, but it does establish a uniform actuarial method for calculating consumer credit charges. TILA also establishes certain requirements for the advertisement of credit terms. The Act applies only to persons who, in the ordinary course of business, lend funds, sell on credit, or arrange for the extension of credit. Thus, loan transactions between two individuals are not regulated by TILA. In addition, TILA protects only *natural persons*, not artificial persons, such as corporations or other legal entities.

TILA's *disclosure* requirements are found in Regulation Z.[58] This regulation applies to any transaction governed by TILA involving an installment sales contract in which payment is to be made in more than four installments and the credit is primarily for personal, family, or household purposes. Generally, installment loans, retail and installment sales, car loans, student loans, home-improvement loans, and certain real estate loans are subject to Regulation Z. In particular, Regulation Z requires disclosure of the finance charge (defined as the interest charged over the life of the loan expressed as a dollar amount) and the annual percentage rate (APR), which is interest expressed as a percentage. Regulation Z also contains provisions regarding the *advertising* of credit. Any advertised specific credit terms must be available, and any credit terms mentioned in the advertisement must be fully explained. The FTC enforces these provisions of Regulation Z; consumers do not have a private cause of action to sue advertisers directly.

TILA sets forth very specific requirements regarding the procedures that must be followed in complying with the Act. If the creditor deviates from any of these procedures, the contract may be rescinded or canceled.

TILA also has specific provisions regarding credit cards. For example, the liability of a cardholder is limited to $50 per card for unauthorized charges made before the credit company is notified that a card has been lost or stolen. There are also provisions detailing procedures for the consumer and the credit card company to follow in resolving disputes about billing errors or withholding of payment for faulty purchases. In addition, while card issuers may send out unsolicited credit cards, the addressee is not liable for any charges made on an unsolicited card that is lost or stolen prior to receipt and

---

[57]5 U.S.C. § 1601 *et seq.*

[58]12 C.F.R. § 226.

acceptance by the addressee. If the addressee accepts the card, she becomes liable for any authorized charges made with it.

Finally, if advertising promotes consumer credit, the advertiser must comply with Regulation X. This provision applies to all advertisers, not merely to creditors, and so includes parties like manufacturers, real estate brokers, builders, and government agencies. It does not include the media in which the advertisements appear, however. This regulation requires disclosure of certain types of information, such as the APR, depending upon the type of credit being advertised. Advertisements promoting home equity lines of credit are subject to additional disclosure rules as well as Regulation X.

As already noted, TILA has been amended several times since its enactment. Some of these amendments are described below.

The Equal Credit Opportunity Act   The *Equal Credit Opportunity Act*[59] (ECOA) was enacted as an amendment to TILA in 1974. The ECOA prohibits the denial of credit solely on the basis of race, religion, national origin, color, gender, marital status, or age. (While the ECOA prohibits discrimination against older applicants, it does allow them to be afforded more favorable treatment.) The Act also prohibits discrimination on the basis of whether an individual receives certain forms of income, such as public assistance. Creditors may, of course, deny credit for valid reasons relating to creditworthiness, such as inadequate income, excessive debts, or poor credit history. Creditors must provide applicants with the reasons that credit was denied if the applicant so requests.

The ECOA applies to all creditors who extend or arrange credit in the ordinary course of their business, including banks, small loan and finance companies, retail and department stores, credit card companies, and credit unions. Unlike most provisions of TILA, the ECOA protects businesses as well as individuals. States may adopt equal credit opportunity acts that are more protective than the ECOA.

The Consumer Leasing Act   Consumer leases have become very popular in recent years, particularly automobile leases. The *Consumer Leasing Act*,[60] which was a 1988 amendment to TILA, and its accompanying Regulation M, offer protection to consumers who lease goods priced at $25,000 or less for personal, household, or family use, provided the lease term exceeds four months. The Act applies to anyone who advertises consumer leases and imposes specific disclosure requirements upon such parties. It does not apply to the media in which such advertisements appear.[55]

The Fair Credit Reporting Act   Congress enacted the *Fair Credit Reporting Act*[61] (FCRA) as part of TILA in 1970. The FCRA provides that consumer credit-reporting agencies may issue credit reports to users only for specific purposes, including the extension of credit, the issuance of insurance policies, employment evaluation, compliance with a court order, and compliance with a consumer's request for a copy of his own credit report. If a consumer is denied credit or insurance on the basis of the credit report or is charged more than others ordinarily would be for such credit or insurance, the consumer must be notified and must be given the name and address of the credit-reporting agency that issued the credit report.

In addition, consumers may request the source of any information being given out by a credit agency, as well as the identity of anyone who has received an agency report. Consumers are also entitled to access to the information about themselves contained

---

[59]15 U.S.C. § 1691 *et seq.* See www.ftc.gov/bcp/edu/pubs/consumer/credit/cre15.shtm

[60]15 U.S.C. §§ 1667 *et seq.* See www.ftc.gov/bcp/edu/pubs/business/adv/bus18.shtm

[61]15 U.S.C. § 1681 *et seq.* See www.ftc.gov/bcp/edu/pubs/consumer/credit/cre35.pdf

within a credit reporting agency's files. The agency is obligated, upon the consumer's written request, to investigate and delete any unverifiable or inaccurate information within a reasonable time period. If the agency does not find an error, the consumer is entitled to file a 100-word written statement of her version of the disputed information. Any subsequent credit reports must note the disputed item and must contain the consumer's statement.

A credit-reporting agency that negligently violates the provisions of the FCRA is potentially liable for actual damages, costs, and attorneys fees. An agency that willfully violates the FCRA may be liable for punitive damages as well. A credit-reporting agency is not liable under the FCRA for reporting inaccurate information, however, if it followed reasonable procedures to assure maximum possible accuracy.

The Fair Debt Collections Practices Act   Congress enacted the *Fair Debt Collection Practices Act*[62] (FDCPA) in 1977 in an attempt to prevent collection agencies from engaging in abusive, deceptive, and unfair practices. "Debt" is defined in the FDCPA as "any obligation or alleged obligation of a consumer to pay money arising out of a transaction in which the money, property, insurance, or services which are the subject of the transaction are primarily for personal, family, or household purposes ...."[63]

The FDCPA applies only to third-party debt collectors, i.e., to persons who routinely attempt to collect debts on behalf of other creditors (usually in return for a percentage of the amount owed), including specialized debt-collection agencies and attorneys. Creditors who attempt to collect their own debts are not covered by the FDCPA, unless they misrepresent to debtors that they are collection agencies.

In particular, the FDCPA prohibits collection agencies from:

- contacting the debtor at the debtor's place of employment if the employer objects;
- contacting the debtor during inconvenient or unusual times (the FDCPA provides that convenient hours are generally between 8 A.M. and 9 P.M. unless the debtor's particular circumstances, such as working the night shift, make those times inconvenient);
- contacting the debtor at inconvenient places, such as social events or worship services;
- contacting the debtor at all if the debtor is being represented by an attorney (the collection agency must deal with the attorney instead);
- using harassing or intimidating tactics (such as abusive language or threatening violence) or using false and misleading information (such as pretending to be a police officer); and
- any communication with the debtor after receiving written notice that the debtor is refusing to pay the debt or does not want to be contacted again, except to advise the debtor of further action to be taken by the collection agency (such as the filing of a lawsuit).

The FDCPA also requires collection agencies to provide a "validation notice" when they initially contact a debtor or within five days of that initial contact. The notice must indicate that the debtor has 30 days in which to dispute the debt and to request (in writing) a written verification of the debt from the collection agency. An agency that fails to comply with the Act is liable for actual damages, plus additional damages not to exceed $1,000, plus costs and attorneys fees. The FTC may also seek cease-and-desist orders against debt collectors.

 *See Discussion Case 8.4.*

---

[62]15 U.S.C. § 1692 *et seq.* See www.ftc.gov/bcp/edu/pubs/consumer/credit/cre27/pdf

[63]15 U.S.C. § 1692a(5).

The Fair and Accurate Credit Transactions Act Enacted in 2003, the *Fair and Accurate Credit Transactions Act*[64] is intended to ensure greater accuracy in consumer credit records. It enables consumers to obtain one free credit report a year from each of the credit reporting agencies,[65] and allows consumers to place fraud alerts in their credit files. It also has measures to prevent ID and credit theft.

DISCUSSION CASES

8.1 First Amendment Challenge to the Do-Not-Call Registry

Mainstream Marketing Services, Inc. v. Federal Trade Comm'n, 358 F.3d 1228 (10th Cir. 2004)

The four cases consolidated in this appeal involve challenges to the national do-not-call registry, which allows individuals to register their phone numbers on a national "do-not-call list" and prohibits most commercial telemarketers from calling the numbers on that list. The primary issue in this case is whether the First Amendment prevents the government from establishing an opt-in telemarketing regulation that provides a mechanism for consumers to restrict commercial sales calls but does not provide a similar mechanism to limit charitable or political calls. * * *

I. Background

In 2003, two federal agencies—the Federal Trade Commission (FTC) and the Federal Communications Commission (FCC)—promulgated rules that together created the national do-not-call registry. The national do-not-call registry is a list containing the personal telephone numbers of telephone subscribers who have voluntarily indicated that they do not wish to receive unsolicited calls from commercial telemarketers. Commercial telemarketers are generally prohibited from calling phone numbers that have been placed on the do-not-call registry, and they must pay an annual fee to access the numbers on the registry so that they can delete those numbers from their telephone solicitation lists. So far, consumers have registered more than 50 million phone numbers on the national do-not-call registry.

The national do-not-call registry's restrictions apply only to telemarketing calls made by or on behalf of sellers of goods or services, and not to charitable or political fundraising calls. Additionally, a seller may

call consumers who have signed up for the national registry if it has an established business relationship with the consumer or if the consumer has given that seller express written permission to call.[7] * * *

The national do-not-call registry is the product of a regulatory effort dating back to 1991 aimed at protecting the privacy rights of consumers and curbing the risk of telemarketing abuse. In the Telephone Consumer Protection Act of 1991 ("TCPA")—under which the FCC enacted its do-not-call rules—Congress found that for many consumers telemarketing sales calls constitute an intrusive invasion of privacy. Moreover, the TCPA's legislative history cited statistical data indicating that "most unwanted telephone solicitations are commercial in nature" and that "unwanted commercial calls are a far bigger problem than unsolicited calls from political or charitable organizations." The TCPA therefore authorized the FCC to establish a national database of consumers who object to receiving "telephone solicitations," which the act defined as commercial sales calls.

Furthermore, in the Telemarketing and Consumer Fraud and Abuse Prevention Act of 1994 ("Telemarketing Act")—under which the FTC enacted its do-not-call rules—Congress found that consumers lose an estimated $40 billion each year due to telemarketing

---

[7]The "established business relationship" exception allows businesses to call customers with whom they have conducted a financial transaction or to whom they have sold, rented, or leased goods or services within 18 months of the telephone call. Additionally, sellers can call consumers on the national do-not-call registry within three months after the consumer makes an inquiry or application. A seller who has an established business relationship with a consumer is still bound to comply with the company-specific rules if the consumer requests not to be called.

---

[64]15 U.S.C. §1681 *et seq.*

[65]See *Your Rights: Credit Reporting,* available at www.ftc.gov/bcp/menus/consumer/credit/rights.shtm

fraud. Therefore, Congress authorized the FTC to prohibit sales calls that a reasonable consumer would consider coercive or abusive of his or her right to privacy.

The FCC and FTC initially sought to accomplish the goals of the TCPA and the Telemarketing Act by adopting company-specific do-not-call lists, requiring sellers to maintain lists of consumers who have requested not to be called by that particular solicitor, and requiring telemarketers to honor those requests. Yet in enacting the national do-not-call registry, the agencies concluded that the company-specific lists had failed to achieve Congress' objectives. Among other shortfalls, the agencies explained that the large number of possible telephone solicitors made it burdensome for consumers to assert their rights under the company-specific rules, and that commercial telemarketers often ignored consumers' requests not to be called. Accordingly, the agencies decided to keep the company-specific rules as an option available to consumers, but to supplement them with the national do-not-call registry.

* * *

III. First Amendment Analysis

The national do-not-call registry's telemarketing restrictions apply only to commercial speech. Like most commercial speech regulations, the do-not-call rules draw a line between commercial and non-commercial speech on the basis of content. In reviewing commercial speech regulations, we apply the *Central Hudson* test. *Central Hudson Gas & Elec. Corp. v. Pub. Serv. Comm'n of N.Y.,* 447 U.S. 557, 566 (1980).

Central Hudson established a three-part test governing First Amendment challenges to regulations restricting non-misleading commercial speech that relates to lawful activity. First, the government must assert a substantial interest to be achieved by the regulation. Second, the regulation must directly advance that governmental interest, meaning that it must do more than provide "only ineffective or remote support for the government's purpose." Third, although the regulation need not be the least restrictive measure available, it must be narrowly tailored not to restrict more speech than necessary. Together, these final two factors require that there be a reasonable fit between the government's objectives and the means it chooses to accomplish those ends.

A. Governmental Interests

The government asserts that the do-not-call regulations are justified by its interests in 1) protecting the privacy of individuals in their homes, and 2) protecting

consumers against the risk of fraudulent and abusive solicitation. Both of these justifications are undisputedly substantial governmental interests.

* * * In *Frisby v. Schultz,* [487 U.S. 474 (1988)], the Court … stressed the unique nature of the home and recognized that "the State's interest in protecting the well-being, tranquility, and privacy of the home is certainly of the highest order in a free and civilized society." As the Court held in *Frisby*:

> One important aspect of residential privacy is protection of the unwilling listener …. [A] special benefit of the privacy all citizens enjoy within their own walls, which the State may legislate to protect, is an ability to avoid intrusions. Thus, we have repeatedly held that individuals are not required to welcome unwanted speech into their own homes and that the government may protect this freedom.

* * *

Additionally, the Supreme Court has recognized that the government has a substantial interest in preventing abusive and coercive sales practices.

B. Reasonable Fit

A reasonable fit exists between the do-not-call rules and the government's privacy and consumer protection interests if the regulation directly advances those interests and is narrowly tailored. In this context, the "narrowly tailored" standard does not require that the government's response to protect substantial interests be the least restrictive measure available. All that is required is a proportional response.

In other words, the national do-not-call registry is valid if it is designed to provide effective support for the government's purposes and if the government did not suppress an excessive amount of speech when substantially narrower restrictions would have worked just as well. These criteria are plainly established in this case. The do-not-call registry directly advances the government's interests by effectively blocking a significant number of the calls that cause the problems the government sought to redress. It is narrowly tailored because its opt-in character ensures that it does not inhibit any speech directed at the home of a willing listener.

1. Effectiveness

The telemarketers assert that the do-not-call registry is unconstitutionally underinclusive because it does not apply to charitable and political callers. First Amendment challenges based on underinclusiveness face an uphill battle in the commercial speech context. As a general rule, the First Amendment does not require that the government regulate all aspects of a problem before it can make progress on any front. * * * The underinclusiveness of a commercial speech regulation is relevant only if it renders the regulatory framework so irrational that fails materially to advance the aims that it was purportedly designed to further.

* * *

As discussed above, the national do-not-call registry is designed to reduce intrusions into personal privacy and the risk of telemarketing fraud and abuse that accompany unwanted telephone solicitation. The registry directly advances those goals. So far, more than 50 million telephone numbers have been registered on the do-not-call list, and the do-not-call regulations protect these households from receiving most unwanted telemarketing calls. According to the telemarketers' own estimate, 2.64 telemarketing calls per week—or more than 137 calls annually—were directed at an average consumer before the do-not-call list came into effect. Accordingly, absent the do-not-call registry, telemarketers would call those consumers who have already signed up for the registry an estimated total of 6.85 *billion* times each year.

To be sure, the do-not-call list will not block all of these calls. Nevertheless, it will prohibit a substantial number of them, making it difficult to fathom how the registry could be called an "ineffective" means of stopping invasive or abusive calls, or a regulation that "furnishes only speculative or marginal support" for the government's interests.[11]

Furthermore, the do-not-call list prohibits not only a significant *number* of commercial sales calls, but also a significant *percentage* of all calls causing the problems that Congress sought to address (whether commercial, charitable or political). The record demonstrates that a substantial share of all solicitation calls will be governed by the do-not-call rules.

The telemarketers asserted before the FTC that they might have to lay off up to 50 percent of their employees if the national do-not-call registry came into effect.

It is reasonable to conclude that the telemarketers' planned reduction in force corresponds to a decrease in the amount of calls they will make. Significantly, the percentage of *unwanted* calls that will be prohibited will be even higher than the percentage of all unsolicited calls blocked by the list. The individuals on the do-not-call list have declared that they do not wish to receive unsolicited commercial telemarketing calls, whereas those who do want to continue receiving such calls will not register.

Finally, the type of unsolicited calls that the do-not-call list does prohibit—commercial sales calls—is the type that Congress, the FTC and the FCC have all determined to be most to blame for the problems the government is seeking to redress. According to the legislative history accompanying the TCPA, "complaint statistics show that unwanted commercial calls are a far bigger problem than unsolicited calls from political or charitable organizations."

Additionally, the FTC has found that commercial callers are more likely than non-commercial callers to engage in deceptive and abusive practices. Specifically, the FTC concluded that in charitable and political calls, a significant purpose of the call is to sell a cause, not merely to receive a donation, and that non-commercial callers thus have stronger incentives not to alienate the people they call or to engage in abusive and deceptive practices. The speech regulated by the do-not-call list is therefore the speech most likely to cause the problems the government sought to alleviate in enacting that list, further demonstrating that the regulation directly advances the government's interests.

In sum, the do-not-call list directly advances the government's interests—reducing intrusions upon consumer privacy and the risk of fraud or abuse—by restricting a substantial number (and also a substantial percentage) of the calls that cause these problems. [T]he do-not-call list is not so underinclusive that it fails materially to advance the government's goals.

2. Narrow Tailoring

Although the least restrictive means test is not the test to be used in the commercial speech context, commercial speech regulations do at least have to be "narrowly tailored" and provide a "reasonable fit" between the problem and the solution. Whether or not there are "numerous and obvious less-burdensome alternatives" is a relevant consideration in our narrow tailoring analysis. A law is narrowly tailored if it "promotes a substantial government interest that would be achieved less

---

[11]It is unclear from the record exactly how many telemarketing calls will be blocked by the do-not-call regulations. Most significantly, we have not been provided with data as to how many of these unsolicited sales calls would be permissible under the established business relationship exception. In applying *Central Hudson*, however, we are entitled to rely on anecdotal evidence and make the common sense observation that the do-not-call list will apply to a substantial number of telemarketing calls.

effectively absent the regulation." Accordingly, we consider whether there are numerous and obvious alternatives that would restrict less speech and would serve the government's interest as effectively as the challenged law.

We hold that the national do-not-call registry is narrowly tailored because it does not over-regulate protected speech; rather, it restricts only calls that are targeted at unwilling recipients. The do-not-call registry prohibits only telemarketing calls aimed at consumers who have affirmatively indicated that they do not want to receive such calls and for whom such calls would constitute an invasion of privacy.

The Supreme Court has repeatedly held that speech restrictions based on private choice (i.e.—an opt-in feature) are less restrictive than laws that prohibit speech directly. * * *

Likewise, in rejecting direct prohibitions of speech (even fully protected speech), the Supreme Court has often reasoned that an opt-in regulation would have been a less restrictive alternative. * * *

* * *

[T]he national do-not-call registry does not itself prohibit any speech. Instead, it merely "permits a citizen to erect a wall ... that no advertiser may penetrate without his acquiescence." Almost by definition, the do-not-call regulations only block calls that would constitute unwanted intrusions into the privacy of consumers who have signed up for the list. Moreover, it allows consumers who feel susceptible to telephone fraud or abuse to ensure that most commercial callers will not have an opportunity to victimize them. Under the circumstances we address in this case, we conclude that the do-not-call registry's opt-in feature renders it a narrowly tailored commercial speech regulation.

The do-not-call registry's narrow tailoring is further demonstrated by the fact that it presents both sellers and consumers with a number of options to make and receive sales offers. From the seller's perspective, the do-not-call registry restricts only one avenue by which solicitors can communicate with consumers who have registered for the list. In particular, the do-not-call regulations do not prevent businesses from corresponding with potential customers by mail or by means of advertising through other media.

From the consumer's perspective, the do-not-call rules provide a number of different options allowing consumers to dictate what telemarketing calls they wish to receive and what calls they wish to avoid. Consumers who would like to receive some commercial sales calls but not others can sign up for the national do-not-call registry but give written permission to call to those businesses from whom they wish to receive offers. Alternatively, they may decline to sign up on the national registry but make company-specific do-not-call requests with those particular businesses from whom they do not wish to receive calls. Therefore, under the current regulations, consumers choose between two default rules—either that telemarketers may call or that they may not. Then, consumers may make company-specific modifications to either of these default rules as they see fit, either granting particular sellers permission to call or blocking calls from certain sellers.

Finally, none of the telemarketers' proposed alternatives would serve the government's interests as effectively as the national do-not-call list. Primarily, the telemarketers suggest that company-specific rules effectively protected consumers. Yet as the FTC found, "the record in this matter overwhelmingly shows the contrary ... it shows that the company-specific approach is seriously inadequate to protect consumers' privacy from an abusive pattern of calls placed by a seller or telemarketer."

First, the company-specific approach proved to be extremely burdensome to consumers, who had to repeat their do-not-call requests to every solicitor who called. In effect, this system gave solicitors one free chance to call each consumer, although many consumers find even an initial unsolicited sales call abusive and invasive of privacy. Second, the government's experience under the company-specific rules demonstrated that commercial solicitors often ignored consumers' requests to be placed on their company-specific lists. Third, consumers have no way to verify whether their numbers have been removed from a solicitor's calling list in response to a company-specific do-not-call request. Finally, company-specific rules are difficult to enforce because they require consumers to bear the evidentiary burden of keeping lists detailing which telemarketers have called them and what do-not-call requests they have made.

* * *

Finally, the telemarketers argue that it would have been less restrictive to let consumers rely on technological alternatives—such as caller ID, call rejection services, and electronic devices designed to block unwanted calls. Each of these alternatives puts the cost of avoiding unwanted telemarketing calls on consumers. Furthermore, as the FCC found, "although technology has improved to assist consumers in blocking unwanted calls, it has also evolved in such a way as to assist telemarketers in making greater numbers of calls and even circumventing such blocking technologies." Forcing consumers to compete in a technological arms race with the telemarketing industry is not an equally effective alternative to the do-not-call registry.

In sum, the do-not-call registry is narrowly tailored to restrict only speech that contributes to the problems the government seeks to redress, namely the intrusion into personal privacy and the risk of fraud and abuse caused by telephone calls that consumers do not welcome into their homes. * * *

* * *

D. Summary

For the reasons discussed above, the government has asserted substantial interests to be served by the do-not-call registry (privacy and consumer protection), the do-not-call registry will directly advance those interests by banning a substantial amount of unwanted telemarketing calls, and the regulation is narrowly tailored because its opt-in feature ensures that it does not restrict any speech directed at a willing listener. In other words, the do-not-call registry bears a reasonable

fit with the purposes the government sought to advance. Therefore, it is consistent with the limits the First Amendment imposes on laws restricting commercial speech.

* * *

QUESTIONS FOR DISCUSSION FOR CASE 8.1

1. Why does the Registry not apply to calls from political organizations or charities? Does this distinction make sense to you?
2. In footnote 7, the court states that it is relying upon "common sense" rather than data. Does this surprise you? Do you think that the court's practice creates any potential problems? Would requiring extensive data create any other types of problems?
3. Do you think the court struck the right balance here between the rights of consumers and the rights of telemarketers? Does the "established business relationship" exception provide sufficient protection for the commercial interests of telemarketers? Are there other ways that the federal government could have addressed the issue of unwanted solicitation calls?

8.2 CAN-SPAM, Preemption
Omega World Travel, Inc. v. Mummagraphics, Inc., 469 F.3d 348 (4th Cir. 2006)

Countless commercial email messages, known colloquially as "spam," pass through the Internet every day, inspiring frustration, countermeasures, and—as here—lawsuits. Based upon eleven commercial email messages, Mummagraphics, Inc., a provider of online services, seeks significant statutory damages from Omega World Travel, Inc., a Virginia-based travel agency ("Omega"); Gloria Bohan, Omega's president and founder; and Cruise.com, Inc., a wholly owned subsidiary of Omega (collectively, "appellees"). Mummagraphics alleges that Cruise.com sent the messages in violation of the Controlling the Assault of Non-Solicited Pornography and Marketing Act of 2003 ("CAN-SPAM Act"), as well as Oklahoma law.

* * *

I.

Appellant Mummagraphics, Inc., d/b/a Webguy Internet Solutions, is an Oklahoma corporation with its only

place of business in Oklahoma City. According to Mark Mumma, the company's president, Mummagraphics hosts web pages, registers domain names, designs web pages and logos, and sets up computer servers. Mummagraphics also operates websites devoted to opposing "spam" messages including "sueaspammer.com." * * * Mummagraphics owns the domain name webguy.net and uses the e-mail account inbox@webguy.net for company purposes.

Cruise.com operates a website selling cruise vacations and sends email advertisements—dubbed "E-deals" to prospective customers. It sent eleven "E-deals" containing travel offers to inbox@webguy. net between December 29, 2004 and February 9, 2005. Each message contained a line of text on which the recipient could click in order to be removed from future mailings, and each message also said that the recipient could opt-out of future e-mails by writing to a postal address contained in each message. Each message also contained a link to the Cruise.com website and a toll-free phone number for the company.

When Mark Mumma noticed the Cruise.com e-mails that inbox@webguy.net had received, he did not use the electronic opt-out link to remove the address from the Cruise.com e-mail list, but instead called John Lawless, Omega World Travel's general counsel, to complain. Mumma told Lawless that he had not asked to receive the "E-deal" messages. He told Lawless that he refused to use e-mail opt-out mechanisms because "only idiots do that," and he believed opt-out mechanisms just led to more unwanted messages. Mumma told Lawless that his preferred removal procedure was to sue for violations of Oklahoma law. Lawless asked Mumma for his e-mail address, but Mumma did not provide it. Instead, he asked Lawless to remove from all future mailings every address containing a domain name listed on Mummagraphics' "OptOutBy Domain.com" website. * * * On January 20, 2005, the day after speaking with Lawless, Mumma received another "E-deal" message at inbox@webguy.net. He sent a letter dated January 25, 2005 to Daniel Bohan of Omega World Travel, saying that he had received six unsolicited "E-deal" messages from Cruise.com, Omega's subsidiary, but again not specifying the email address at which he had received the messages. The letter claimed that the messages violated federal and state laws and said that Mumma intended to sue Bohan's company for at least $150,000 in statutory damages unless Bohan settled the matter for $6,250. * * * After Omega World Travel failed to pay Mumma, postings on one of Mumma's "anti-spam" websites accused Omega, Cruise.com, and Daniel and Gloria Bohan of being "spammers" who had violated state and federal laws. * * * On the basis of these postings, Omega World Travel, the Bohans, and Cruise.com sued Mumma and Mummagraphics in federal court, claiming [among other things] defamation …. Mummagraphics raised counterclaims against the appellees under Oklahoma and federal law, which are the only claims now before this court. Mummagraphics alleged, *inter alia*, that the Cruise.com e-mails contained actionable inaccuracies and that the appellees failed to comply with federal and state requirements that they stop sending messages to recipients who opted out through specified procedures. Both parties sought summary judgment on Mummagraphics' counterclaims, and the district court granted the appellees' motion. * * * Mummagraphics now appeals.

II.

A.

We turn first to the district court's determination that the CAN-SPAM Act preempted Mummagraphics'

claims under Oklahoma's statutes regulating commercial e-mail messages. The basic principles of preemption are well settled …. Our inquiry into the scope of a preemption clause is shaped by "two presumptions." First, under our federal system, we do not presume that Congress intends to clear whatever field it enters. Instead, we start from "the basic assumption that Congress did not intend to displace state law," and "that the historic police powers of the States were not to be superseded by the Federal Act unless that was the clear and manifest purpose of Congress." Second, from this departure point, we address preemption issues in accordance with the "oft-repeated comment … that '[t]he purpose of Congress is the ultimate touchstone' in every preemption case." Instead of imposing the narrowest possible construction on preemptive language when read in isolation, we seek "a fair understanding of congressional purpose," looking to "the language of the pre-emption statute and the statutory framework surrounding it," while also considering "the structure and purpose of the statute as a whole."

B.

Mummagraphics argues that it is entitled to damages because such damages are authorized by Oklahoma law and lie outside the CAN-SPAM Act's preemptive scope. The CAN-SPAM Act provides, in part,

> This chapter supersedes any statute, regulation, or rule of a State or political subdivision of a State that expressly regulates the use of electronic mail to send commercial messages, except to the extent that any such statute, regulation, or rule prohibits falsity or deception in any portion of a commercial electronic mail message or information attached thereto.

The principal Oklahoma provision under which Mummagraphics seeks damages provides:

> It shall be unlawful for a person to initiate an electronic mail message that the sender knows, or has reason to know:

> 1. Misrepresents any information in identifying the point of origin or the transmission path of the electronic mail message;
> 2. Does not contain information identifying the point of origin or the transmission path of the electronic mail message; or
> 3. Contains false, malicious, or misleading information which purposely or negligently injures a person.

* * * Congress did not intend "falsity" [as used in CAN-SPAM] to encompass bare error because such a reading would upset the Act's careful balance between preserving a potentially useful commercial tool and preventing its abuse. The Act's enacted findings make clear that Congress saw commercial e-mail messages as presenting both benefits and burdens. Congress found that "[t]he convenience and efficiency of electronic mail are threatened by the extremely rapid growth in the volume of unsolicited commercial electronic mail," but also that e-mail's "low cost and global reach make it extremely convenient and efficient, and offer unique opportunities for the development and growth of frictionless commerce." Congress noted that states had sought to regulate commercial e-mails, but it found that the resulting patchwork of liability standards had proven ineffective:

> Many States have enacted legislation intended to regulate or reduce unsolicited commercial electronic mail, but these statutes impose different standards and requirements. As a result, they do not appear to have been successful in addressing the problems associated with unsolicited commercial electronic mail, in part because, since an electronic mail address does not specify a geographic location, it can be extremely difficult for law-abiding businesses to know with which of these disparate statutes they are required to comply.

Congress implemented these findings by creating a national standard that would be undermined to the point of near-irrelevancy by Mummagraphics' interpretation of the preemption clause. Rather than banning all commercial e-mails or imposing strict liability for insignificant inaccuracies, Congress targeted only e-mails containing something more than an isolated error. The CAN-SPAM Act made it a crime to "materially falsif[y] header information in multiple commercial electronic mail messages and intentionally initiate[] the transmission of such messages," but it attached no criminal sanction to non-material errors. The Act created civil causes of action relating to error, but attached requirements beyond simple mistake to each of them. It permitted lawsuits based upon "*materially* false or *materially* misleading" header information. * * * In sum, Congress' enactment governing commercial e-mails reflects a calculus that a national strict liability standard for errors would impede "unique opportunities for the development and growth of frictionless commerce," while more narrowly tailored causes of action could effectively respond to the obstacles to

"convenience and efficiency" that unsolicited messages present. Mummagraphics' reading of the preemption clause would upend this balance and turn an exception to a preemption provision into a loophole so broad that it would virtually swallow the preemption clause itself. While Congress evidently believed that it would be undesirable to make all errors in commercial e-mails actionable, Mummagraphics' interpretation would allow states to bring about something very close to that result. The ensuing consequences would undermine Congress' plain intent. As we have noted, Congress found that because e-mail addresses do not specify recipients' physical locations, it can be difficult or impossible to identify where recipients live and hence to determine the state laws that apply. Moreover, commercial e-mails are a bulk medium used to target thousands of recipients with a single mouse-click, meaning that the typical message could well be covered by the laws of many jurisdictions. As a result, law-abiding senders would likely have to assume that their messages were governed by the most stringent state laws in effect. The strict liability standard imposed by a state such as Oklahoma would become a de facto national standard, with all the burdens that imposed, even though the CAN-SPAM Act indicates that Congress believed a less demanding standard would best balance the competing interests at stake. * * *

III.

We turn next to Mummagraphics' claims that the Cruise.com emails violated the CAN-SPAM Act. Mummagraphics first argues that the Cruise.com e-mails violated the Act's requirements concerning the accuracy of header information in commercial e-mails. The Act provides, "It is unlawful for any person to initiate the transmission, to a protected computer, of a commercial electronic mail message … that contains, or is accompanied by, header information that is materially false or materially misleading." The Act further explains,

> the term "materially", when used with respect to false or misleading header information, includes the alteration or concealment of header information in a manner that would impair the ability of an Internet access service processing the message on behalf of a recipient, a person alleging a violation of this section, or a law enforcement agency to identify, locate, or respond to a person who initiated the electronic mail message or to investigate the alleged violation, or the ability of a recipient of the message to

respond to a person who initiated the electronic message.

Mummagraphics alleges that the senders of the Cruise.com e-mails violated this provision because the messages' header information incorrectly indicated that the e-mails originated from the server "FL-Broadcast. net," and because the messages' "from" address read cruisedeals@cruise.com, although that e-mail address was apparently non-functional.

We agree with the district court that these inaccuracies do not make the headers "materially false or materially misleading." The e-mails at issue were chock full of methods to "identify, locate, or respond to" the sender or to "investigate [an] alleged violation" of the CAN-SPAM Act. Each message contained a link on which the recipient could click in order to be removed from future mailings, in addition to a separate link to Cruise.com's website. Each message prominently displayed a toll-free number to call, and each also listed a Florida mailing address and local phone number for the company. Several places in each header referred to the Cruise.com domain name, including one line listing Cruise.com as the sending organization.

These references come as little surprise, because the "E-deal" messages were sales pitches intended to induce recipients to contact Cruise.com to book the cruises that the messages advertised. Since the "E-deal" messages and their headers were replete with accurate identifiers of the sender, the alleged inaccuracies in the headers could not have impaired the efforts of any recipient, law enforcement organization, or other party raising a CAN-SPAM claim to find the company. If the alleged inaccuracies in a message containing so many valid identifiers could be described as "materially false or materially misleading," we find it hard to imagine an inaccuracy that would not qualify as "materially false or materially misleading." Congress' materiality requirement would be rendered all but meaningless by such an interpretation.

V.

We respect the fact that unsolicited commercial e-mail has created frustration and consternation among innumerable users of the Internet. The proper treatment of mass commercial e-mail has provoked controversy since perhaps the first such message was sent. Our role is not to determine the best way of regulating such messages, but merely to implement the balance that Congress struck. The CAN-SPAM Act prohibits some material misstatements and imposes opt-out requirements, but it does not make every error or opt-out request into grounds for a lawsuit. The e-mails in this case are not actionable under the Act. Nor can the messages be actionable under Oklahoma's statutes, because allowing a state to attach liability to bare immaterial error in commercial e-mails would be inconsistent with the federal Act's preemption text and structure, and, consequently, with a "fair understanding of congressional purpose." Since we agree that summary judgment was warranted on Mummagraphics' various claims, the judgment of the district court is *AFFIRMED*.

QUESTIONS FOR DISCUSSION FOR CASE 8.2

1. How does the court explain the role of preemption? What part of the Oklahoma statute does the court find is preempted by CAN-SPAM?

2. Do you agree with the court's findings that the inaccuracies in the e-mail at issue did not constitute a violation of CAN-SPAM? Does the court's ruling decrease the incentive for commercial e-mailers to ensure the accuracy of their e-mails, or do you think it has little effect on their behavior?

3. Do you think that Congress, when it passed CAN-SPAM, would have intended the result that the court reached in this case, or do you think that Congress intended a more stringent regulation of spam? What evidence can you point to in support of your argument?

8.3 Home Solicitations

Rossi v. 21st Century Concepts, Inc., 162 Misc. 2d 932, 618 N.Y.S. 2d 182 (City Ct. 1994)

The plaintiff, soon to be a new bride, attended the Great Bridal Expo. * * * Amongst the many exhibitors was the defendant, 21st Century Concepts, Inc. doing business as Royal Prestige ("Royal Prestige"). Royal Prestige, a direct marketing company, displayed a variety of knives, china, glassware, water filters and cookware. * * *

Royal Prestige sells its products through door-to-door sales. Royal Prestige became aware of the plaintiff and her bridal needs when she filled out a "lead" card at the Bridal Expo. Thereafter, Royal Prestige salesman Larry Kieffer called the plaintiff seeking to arrange a home sales visit. To induce the plaintiff to listen to his sales pitch, Mr. Kieffer offered plaintiff $100 in cash, a free facial and 100 rolls of free film.

Intrigued, the plaintiff agreed and on September 28, 1993 Mr. Kieffer knocked on the plaintiff's door, gave her $100 in cash, a free facial and one roll of free film. To obtain the remaining 99 rolls of "free" film the plaintiff had to use the first roll and have it processed by Royal Prestige's chosen film processor. After paying for her prints the plaintiff would be given one new roll of free film and so on. In addition, after the sale Mr. Kieffer offered plaintiff a reduced cost Caribbean vacation which plaintiff later rejected because of the poor quality and location of the offered hotels.

Once inside the plaintiff's home, Mr. Kieffer spent 2 1/2 hours extolling the alleged virtues of the entire line of Royal Prestige products. Most of that time (1 1/2 hours) was spent on selling plaintiff a set of pots and pans pretentiously identified as the Royal Prestige Health System (the "Health System"). The Health System consisted of several cooking pots which appeared to be small pressure cookers. These miniature pressure cookers were beautifully photographed and described in elegant terms as sauce pan, skillet, dutch oven and steamer/colander. The Health System was wildly expensive, e.g., the cost (including freight, handling and local sales tax) of the Royal Prestige "22 piece Health System" which consisted of seven pots plus accessories was $1,505.63 or nearly $200 a pot.

Mr. Kieffer pitched the Health System as a technically advanced means of retaining the nutritional value of cooked food. This claim was presented without any supporting documentation such as a Consumer Union Report or the like. * * * In addition, Mr. Kieffer tailored his pitch to the young expectant bride by suggesting a direct relationship between using the Health System pots and preventing heart disease and having healthier babies. The plaintiff relied upon Mr. Kieffer's representations about the benefits of the Health System, agreed to purchase the 22-piece Health System and gave Mr. Kieffer a check for the total cost of $1,505.63.

The front of the sales contract, dated September 28, 1993 contained the following: "You, the Purchaser, may cancel this transaction at any time prior to midnight of the third business day after the date of this transaction. See the attached notice of cancellation form for an explanation of this right." On the reverse side of the sales contract under the title of "Notice of Cancellation" there was extensive language regarding plaintiff's cancellation rights. The Notice of Cancellation contained blanks for the date, the name and address of the seller and the last possible day to cancel the contract. Mr. Kieffer failed to complete any of these blanks.

After receiving her ordered Health System on October 27, 1993, the plaintiff decided to cancel the sales contract and returned the pots with a letter demanding a full refund. Royal Prestige rejected plaintiff's cancellation of the sales contract and sent the purchased pots back to the plaintiff with a letter stating "[t]he quality of our cookware is considered by many experts to be the finest manufactured in the world today."

Discussion

* * *

The marketing of goods and services through door-to-door sales can be cost effective for manufacturers and distributors. Some manufacturers and distributors favor door-to-door sales for several reasons. *First*, the per unit cost of generating a sale is relatively low. This is because there is no retail store overhead such as rent, salaries, insurance and so forth. Instead a salesman working on a straight commission will use the consumer's living room to sell his wares and take his orders. *Second*, the selling price may be several times greater than that which would be obtainable in a more competitive environment where consumers compare different brands of the same product. * * * *Third*, consumers are less defensive and more comfortable in their own homes and because of this are especially susceptible to high pressure sales tactics.

Violation of Door-to-Door Sales Protection Act

Because of all of these factors door-to-door sales often lead to abuses, over-reaching, misrepresentations and fraud. As a consequence several States including New York have enacted remedial statutes which, within the limited context of retail sales made in the home, give consumers contractual rescission rights not otherwise available at common law. These statutes … have as their purpose "to afford consumers a 'cooling-off' period to cancel contracts which are entered into as a result of high pressure door-to-door sales tactics."

The contract between Royal Prestige and the plaintiff violated Personal Property Law § 428(l)(b). This section provides that with respect to the required notice of cancellation on the back of the contract, "the seller shall complete both copies by entering the name of the seller, the address of the seller's place of business, the date of the transaction, and the date, not earlier than the third business day following the date of the transaction ...." Mr. Kieffer failed to fill in the required information in the Royal Prestige sales contract. A failure to properly inform the plaintiff of her cancellation rights is a violation and allows the plaintiff to cancel her contract until a reasonable time after Royal Prestige has properly informed her of her cancellation rights. Royal Prestige has yet to complete the contract as required. Plaintiff timely cancelled her contract on October 27, 1993, demanded a refund of her contract payment of $1,505.63, returned the Health System to defendant (which she was not required to do [—] consumers may tender goods at residence), which refused to accept the rejected Health System returning it yet again to plaintiff.

The contract also violated Personal Property Law § 428 (4). This section provides that the sales contract "shall disclose conspicuously the seller's refund policy as to all goods ... subject to the door-to-door sales agreement." The Royal Prestige sales contract blissfully states that the "Seller promises you fair and honorable treatment." This statement is not only not true within the facts of this case, but also it is virtually meaningless and does not rise to the level of disclosing "seller's refund policy." Within twenty days after receiving the Health System the plaintiff timely notified Royal Prestige of her intent to cancel and demanded a full refund.

Demand for Rescission

Notwithstanding the statutory right of rescission afforded plaintiff by Personal Property Law § 428, the Royal Prestige sales contract should be rescinded based upon the application of several common-law doctrines. Whether viewed as a want of consideration or failure of consideration, it is clear that the plaintiff was grossly overcharged for the Health System she purchased.

Through high pressure sales tactics the plaintiff was induced to pay nearly $200 a pot for cookware of dubious and undocumented nutritional, medical or technical value. Royal Prestige misrepresented, implicitly or explicitly, that its Health System provided exceptional nutritional value, that it would prevent heart disease, that it would help the plaintiff have healthier babies and that many experts consider the Health System "to be the finest manufactured in the world today."

The Health System was grossly misrepresented, overpriced and the transaction was unconscionable.

Violation of General Business Law § 349

New York General Business Law § 349 prohibits deceptive business practices. General Business Law § 349 is a broad, remedial statute directed towards giving consumers a powerful remedy to right consumer wrongs. The elements of a violation of General Business Law § 349 are (1) proof that the practice was deceptive or misleading in a material respect, and (2) proof that plaintiff was injured. There is no requirement under General Business Law § 349 that plaintiff prove that defendant's practices or acts were intentional, fraudulent or even reckless. Nor is there any requirement under General Business Law § 349 that plaintiff prove that she relied upon defendant's misrepresentations and deceptive practices.

Initially, the failure of Royal Prestige to comply with the disclosure requirements of Personal Property Law § 428 regarding cancellation and refund rights also constitutes an unfair and deceptive business practice under General Business Law § 349.

Secondly, Royal Prestige's unsupported representations regarding the nutritional value of the Health System and its relationship to preventing heart disease and having healthier babies are misleading and deceptive.

Thirdly, the inducements used by Royal Prestige salesman Larry Kieffer to convince the plaintiff to open the door of her home and listen to his sales pitch were themselves misleading and deceptive. Mr. Kieffer promised plaintiff $100 and a free facial and he delivered these two inducements. Mr. Kieffer also promised 100 rolls of "free" film and delivered only one roll while the remaining 99 were available only if plaintiff spent monies on processing exposed film, one roll at a time. This "free" offer was misleading and deceptive. Mr. Kieffer promised a reduced price vacation which plaintiff rejected after discovering the poor quality and location of the hotels offered. This vacation offer was misleading and deceptive and failed to disclose material information regarding the actual value of the vacation package.

Damages

The court awards the following damages to the plaintiff.

First, damages will include the full contract price of $1,505.63 which includes freight, handling and local sales tax; the cost of mailing the Health System back to Royal Prestige of $49.70; and $100 because Royal Prestige refused to refund the contract price.

Second, … the Court finds that defendant willfully violated General Business Law § 349. Although the Court would like to treble plaintiff's actual damages of $1,555.33, this amount exceeds the maximum $1,000 permissible.

Third, pursuant to Personal Property Law § 429(3) and General Business Law § 349(h) the Court awards plaintiff attorney's fees and costs of $344.66. Considering plaintiff's counsel's vigorous efforts during trial and an excellent post-trial memorandum of law, the Court would have awarded greater fees and costs but at the time this lawsuit was filed the jurisdictional limit of this court was $2,000.

QUESTIONS FOR DISCUSSION FOR CASE 8.3

1. The court found that the defendant had violated the state cooling-off statute such that the plaintiff was permitted to cancel the contract one month after the sale had occurred. What should the defendant have done differently to have avoided this result?

2. The court also found that the defendant's actions violated the state's statute prohibiting deceptive business practices. Which actions of the defendant were deceptive?

3. What does the plaintiff ultimately recover? The court seems to feel that this amount is inadequate yet states that it is unable to award more to the plaintiff. Why?

8.4 Fair Debt Collections Practices Act
Gonzalez v. Kay, 577 F.3d 600 (5th Cir. 2009)

Plaintiff-Appellant Jose Gonzalez ("Gonzalez") allegedly failed to pay his Sprint PCS Wireless cell phone bills, totaling $448.97. Sprint turned the consumer debt over to US Asset Management Services, Inc. ("US Asset"), which in turn used the services of Defendants-Appellees Mitchell N. Kay ("Kay") and the Law Offices of Mitchell N. Kay, P.C. ("the Kay Law Firm") to collect the debt. The Kay Law Firm sent a collection letter to Gonzalez, which Gonzalez asserts violated the Fair Debt Collection Practices Act ("FDCPA or the Act"). * * *

I. Factual Background

* * * On November 21, 2007, the Kay Law Firm sent a collection letter to Gonzalez. The letter was printed on the Kay Law Firm's letterhead, but it was not signed. * * * The front of the letter states,

> Please be advised that your account, as referenced above, is being handled by this office.
>
> We have been authorized to offer you the opportunity to settle this account with a lump sum payment, equal to 65% of the balance due—which is $291.83!
>
> Unless you notify this office within 30 days after receiving this notice that you dispute the validity of this debt or any portion thereof, this office will assume this debt is valid.
>
> If you notify this office in writing within 30 days from receiving this notice, this office will: Obtain verification of the debt or obtain a copy of a

judgment and mail you a copy of such judgment or verification.

> If you request this office in writing within 30 days after receiving this notice, this office will provide you with the name and address of the original creditor, if different from the current creditor.

After a large white blank space, the bottom of the letter directs the recipient to "PLEASE ADDRESS ALL PAYMENTS TO" the "Law Offices of Mitchell N. Kay, P.C." Immediately below the payment information, the letter states, "Notice: Please see reverse side for important information." A box surrounds this notice. Below the notice box is a detachable payment stub.

On the back, the letter states, in the same font and typeface as the text on the front,

> This communication is from a debt collector and is an attempt to collect a debt. Any information obtained will be used for that purpose.
>
> Notice about Electronic Check Conversion: Sending an eligible check with this payment coupon authorizes us to complete the payment by electronic debit. If we do, the checking account will be debited in the amount shown on the check—as soon as the same day we receive the check—and the check will be destroyed.
>
> At this point in time, no attorney with this firm has personally reviewed the particular circumstances of your account.

Kay and the Kay Law Firm assert that this "disclaimer" language is sufficient to notify Gonzalez that lawyers were not involved in the debt collection. The parties agree that neither Kay nor any lawyers in his firm reviewed Gonzalez's file or were actively involved in sending the letter. Instead, Gonzalez asserted in his complaint that the letter was deceptive in that the Kay Law Firm "pretended to be a law firm with a lawyer handling collection of the Account when in fact no lawyer was handling the Account or actively handling the file." Gonzalez essentially contends that the Kay Law Firm is not actually a law firm at all but instead is a debt collection agency that uses the imprimatur of a law firm to intimidate debtors into paying their debts.

II. Jurisdiction and Standard of Review

* * *

When deciding whether a debt collection letter violates the FDCPA, this court "must evaluate any potential deception in the letter under an unsophisticated or least sophisticated consumer standard." We must "assume that the plaintiff-debtor is neither shrewd nor experienced in dealing with creditors." "At the same time we do not consider the debtor as tied to the very last rung on the [intelligence or] sophistication ladder." "This standard serves the dual purpose of protecting all consumers, including the inexperienced, the untrained and the credulous, from deceptive debt collection practices and protecting debt collectors against liability for bizarre or idiosyncratic consumer interpretations of collection materials."

III. Discussion

Congress enacted the FDCPA "to eliminate abusive debt collection practices by debt collectors, to ensure that those debt collectors who refrain from using abusive debt collection practices are not competitively disadvantaged, and to promote consistent State action to protect consumers against debt collection abuses." The FDCPA provides, "A debt collector may not use any false, deceptive, or misleading representation or means in connection with the collection of any debt." The statute then lists several activities that violate the FDCPA. Gonzalez claims that Kay and the Kay Law Firm violated subsections (3) and (10). Subsection (3) prohibits "[t]he false representation or implication that any individual is an attorney or that any communication is from an attorney." Subsection (10) prohibits "[t]he use of any false representation or deceptive means to collect or attempt to collect any debt or to obtain information concerning a consumer." There is no dispute that Gonzalez is a "consumer" under the FDCPA

and that Kay and the Kay Law Firm are "debt collectors" under the Act. A debt collector who violates the FDCPA is liable for actual damages, additional damages of up to $1,000, and attorneys' fees.

There are sound policy reasons for the FDCPA's prohibition on a debt collector sending a collection letter that is seemingly from an attorney. Judge Evans of the Seventh Circuit adroitly explained the intimidation inherent in this type of communication:

> An unsophisticated consumer, getting a letter from an "attorney," knows the price of poker has just gone up. And that clearly is the reason why the dunning campaign escalates from the collection agency, which might not strike fear in the heart of the consumer, to the attorney, who is better positioned to get the debtor's knees knocking.

A letter from a lawyer implies that the lawyer has become involved in the debt collection process, and the fear of a lawsuit is likely to intimidate most consumers. "Thus, if a debt collector (attorney or otherwise) wants to take advantage of the special connotation of the word 'attorney' in the minds of delinquent consumer debtors to better effect collection of the debt, the debt collector should at least ensure that an attorney has become professionally involved in the debtor's file." In the alternative, a lawyer acting as a debt collector must notify the consumer, through a clear and prominent disclaimer in the letter, that the lawyer is wearing a "debt collector" hat and not a "lawyer" hat when sending out the letter.

In [*Taylor v. Perrin, Landry, deLaunay & Durand*, 103 F.3d 1232, 1236 (5th Cir. 1997)], this court reversed the award of summary judgment to a defendant law firm under facts that were similar to those in the present case. The collection letter in question included a facsimile of the lawyer's signature under the law firm's letterhead, informed consumers that the creditor had retained the law firm to collect the debt, and stated that the creditor had instructed the law firm to file suit against the debtor if the debtor did not pay the debt within ten days. However, ... the lawyer and law firm were not at all involved in reviewing past due accounts or sending the letters. In reversing the award of summary judgment to the law firm/debt collector, we held that "a debt collector, who uses a mass-produced collection letter using the letterhead and facsimile signature of a lawyer who is not actually participating in the collection process, violates [the Act]."

In reaching this conclusion, we relied upon the Second Circuit's decision in *Clomon v. Jackson*, 988 F.2d 1314, 1321 (2d Cir. 1993). In *Clomon*, the Second

Circuit held that a lawyer violated the FDCPA when he "authorized the sending of debt collection letters bearing his name and a facsimile of his signature without first reviewing the collection letters or the files of the persons to whom the letters were sent." This court in *Taylor* quoted the following passage from *Clomon*:

> The use of an attorney's signature on a collection letter implies that the letter is 'from' the attorney who signed it; it implies, in other words, that the attorney directly controlled or supervised the process through which the letter was sent …. The use of an attorney's signature implies—at least in the absence of language to the contrary—that the attorney signing the letter formed an opinion about how to manage the case of the debtor to whom the letter was sent …. There will be few, if any, cases in which a mass-produced collection letter bearing the facsimile of an attorney's signature will comply with the restrictions imposed by [the Act].

The court in *Clomon* highlighted several factors that were important to its decision that the lawyer violated the FDCPA, e.g., that the letter was on the law firm's letterhead, included the lawyer's signature, and contained language stipulating that the lawyer had considered the individual debtors' files and had made judgments on how to collect the debts.

The Second Circuit more recently decided another FDCPA case that explains how a lawyer, acting as a debt collector, can avoid liability by including a clear and prominent disclaimer in the collection letter. In [*Greco v. Trauner, Cohen & Thomas, LLP*, 412 F.3d 260 (2d Cir. 2005)], the consumer received a letter printed on a law firm's letterhead but with no signature except for the firm's name in the signature block. The letter stated that the law firm represented the creditor for "collection and such action as necessary to protect our client." The letter also contained the following disclaimer: "At this time, no attorney with this firm has personally reviewed the particular circumstances of your account. However, if you fail to contact this office, our client may consider additional remedies to recover the balance due." The consumer filed suit, alleging that the letter violated … the FDCPA. The district court dismissed the case …, determining as a matter of law that the letter did not violate the FDCPA. The Second Circuit affirmed, concluding that the disclaimer explained the limited extent of any attorney involvement in collecting the debt. The court provided this important guidance:

> [A]ttorneys can participate in debt collection in any number of ways, without contravening the FDCPA, so long as their status as attorneys is *not misleading*. Put another way, our prior precedents demonstrate that an attorney can, in fact, send a debt collection letter without being meaningfully involved as an attorney within the collection process, so long as that letter includes *disclaimers* that should make clear even to the "least sophisticated consumer" that the law firm or attorney sending the letter is not, at the time of the letter's transmission, acting as an attorney.

* * *

Finally, the Middle District of Florida recently denied summary judgment to the Kay Law Firm after considering a letter that is virtually identical to the one in this case. The court determined that the use of the law firm's letterhead and the placement of the disclaimer on the back made the question of whether the letter was deceptive a factual dispute for the jury to decide. In particular, the court highlighted the contradiction between the law firm letterhead on the front and the disclaimer on the back of the letter. The court distinguished *Greco* by noting that the Second Circuit in *Greco* analyzed the language of the disclaimer, not its placement.

In sum, the main difference between the cases is whether the letter included a clear, prominent, and conspicuous disclaimer that no lawyer was involved in the debt collection at that time. There are some letters that, as a matter of law, are not deceptive based on the language and placement of a disclaimer. At the other end of the spectrum, there are letters that are so deceptive and misleading as to violate the FDCPA as a matter of law, especially when they do not contain any disclaimer regarding the attorney's involvement. In the middle, there are letters that include contradictory messages and therefore present closer calls. * * *

Here, the letter was printed on the law firm's letterhead, but it was unsigned. On the back, the letter indicated that it was from a "debt collector" and included the sentence, "At this point in time, no attorney with this firm has personally reviewed the particular circumstances of your account." This is the exact same disclaimer that the court in *Greco* found dispositive. However, the disclaimer in *Greco* was part of the body of the letter on the front page; a consumer who read the main text of the letter would necessarily learn that the law firm was sending the letter but that no attorneys had reviewed the file. In contrast, the "least sophisticated consumer" reading the letter from the Kay Law Firm would not learn that the letter was from a debt collector unless the consumer turned the letter over to read the "legalese" on the back. The disclaimer on the back of the letter completely contradicted the message on the front of the letter—that the creditor had retained the Kay Law Firm and its lawyers to collect the debt. That is, the disclaimer on the back may not have been *effective*. There was also ample room on the front of the letter to include this disclaimer so as to clearly articulate to the consumer the nature of the law firm's involvement. Accordingly, this letter falls in that middle ground in which the letter is neither deceptive as a matter of law nor not deceptive as a matter of law. Because the "least sophisticated consumer" reading this letter might be deceived into thinking that a lawyer was involved in the debt collection, the district court prematurely dismissed Gonzalez's complaint.

We acknowledge that this is a close case, which is why further inquiry at the district court is necessary. Based only on the allegations in the complaint and the letter itself, reasonable minds can differ as to whether this letter is deceptive. Although the mere presence of disclaimer language might be dispositive in certain circumstances, the context and placement of that disclaimer is also important. We do not construe the disclaimer in isolation but must analyze whether the letter is misleading as a whole. We caution lawyers who send debt collection letters to state clearly, prominently, and conspicuously that although the

letter is from a lawyer, the lawyer is acting solely as a debt collector and not in any legal capacity when sending the letter. The disclaimer must explain to even the least sophisticated consumer that lawyers may also be debt collectors and that the lawyer is operating only as a debt collector at that time. Debt collectors acting solely as debt collectors must not send the message that a lawyer is involved, because this deceptively sends the message that the "price of poker has gone up."

IV. Conclusion

We hold that the district court erred in concluding that Gonzalez failed to state a claim for relief that Kay and the Kay Law Firm violated the FDCPA. We therefore REVERSE the district court's judgment and REMAND for further proceedings.

QUESTIONS FOR DISCUSSION FOR CASE 8.4

1. What role does the doctrine of precedent play in this case? Which of the earlier cases discussed by this court are actually binding upon it?
2. Do you think that this outcome is fair, or do you think that it gives the debtor too much of an opportunity to avoid his debt? Who is this Act supposed to protect? Explain.
3. Procedurally, what will happen next in this case? Why can't this court simply resolve the case itself, instead of sending it back down to the lower court?

DISCUSSION QUESTIONS

1. Andrew Ladick brought suit against Gerald J. Van Gemert, an attorney, alleging that Van Gemert had sent him a letter on behalf of a California condominium association demanding payment of a past-due condominium assessment fee. He alleged that the letter violated the Fair Debt Collection Practices Act (FDCPA) because it failed to give a "validation notice" and did not expressly disclose that Van Gemert was attempting to collect a debt and that any information obtained would be used for that purpose. The trial court found that the condominium assessment that Van Gemert sought to collect was not a "debt" under the FDCPA and granted summary judgment to Van Gemert. Ladick appealed. On appeal, Van Gemert argued that a condominium assessment does not involve an extension of credit

and is more like a tax than a debt. Should the FDCPA apply to this transaction?
2. On November 9, 1997, Angel, a Spanish-speaking salesperson working for Credit Express Furniture, made a sales presentation at the home of the Spanish-speaking plaintiffs, Rigoberto and Pilar Filpo. The presentation was in Spanish as the Filpos spoke little or no English. Angel showed Pilar a catalog, from which she ordered six pieces of furniture for a total of $3,676. The contract signed by Rigoberto was in English and contained a provision stating that if the buyers cancelled their order or refused delivery, the buyers could pay 20 percent of the contract price as liquidated damages. The contract also stated that the merchandise could be exchanged only up to 30 days after delivery.

Under New York State's Door-to-Door Sales Protection Act, door-to-door sales contracts must contain, in the same language as the presentation and in 10-point type, the following notice:

You, the buyer may cancel this transaction at any time prior to midnight of the third business day after the date of this transaction see the attached notice of cancellation form for an explanation of this right

The Act also requires door-to-door sales contracts to have attached to them "a completed form in duplicate, captioned 'NOTICE OF CANCELLA-TION,'" also in the language of the oral presentation, informing consumers of their right to: (1) cancel the contract within three days; (2) demand a full refund; (3) receive a refund within three days; and (4) return the unwanted goods by making them available at the consumer's home.

Rigoberto paid for the furniture in cash when the furniture was delivered the following month. When Pilar arrived home several hours later and inspected the furniture, she found several nonconformities, including loose trim, holes in the fabric, and an incorrect fabric design and color. The next day, Pilar telephoned Credit Express Furniture, reported the damage, canceled the contract, and demanded a full refund. Credit refused to refund the purchase price but offered to exchange the furniture and to give the Filpos $300. Twice, a delivery person from Credit Express Furniture showed up at the Filpos' apartment with a replacement set of furniture and a check for $300, but both times the Filpos refused to accept the new furniture or the check, demanding instead that Credit Express Furniture take back the original set and return their $3,676 purchase price.

The Filpos filed suit against Credit Express Furniture. At this point, the Filpos have had the original set of furniture for two and one-half years. Should the court order Credit Express Furniture to accept the return of the furniture and to refund the Filpos' purchase price?

3. In November, 1988, Joyce Crystal purchased a waterfront home in Caroline County, Maryland. Soon afterward, she decided that a second-floor skylight should be removed for safety reasons. Her real estate agent brought a contractor named Callahan, from the firm of West & Callahan, Inc., over to the house. While Callahan was evaluating the skylight project, Crystal also asked him about remodeling her screened-in porch. She wanted the porch extended by six to eight feet and enclosed with windows and doors. The parties did not sign an agreement, and Callahan did not provide a notice of the right to cancel the agreement.

Crystal understood that the project would cost $10,000, while Callahan contends that he quoted a figure of approximately $10,000 for time and did not include materials. The final construction bill was $23,769.78, of which Crystal paid $2,000. She refused to pay the balance, arguing poor workmanship and defects, including problems such as incorrect paint color. She had not complained during the construction project, however.

West & Callahan, Inc., sued Crystal for nonpayment, and she counterclaimed, alleging Callahan violated the door-to-door sales act by failing to give her the notice of cancellation required by the Maryland Door-to-Door Sales Act and that she had the right to cancel the agreement at any point until proper notice was given. Thus, she stated in her counterclaim that she was canceling the entire agreement. May Crystal cancel the door-to-door transaction nearly one and one-half years after the work has been completed?

4. Prior to September 1, 1994, Richard Whiteside signed a lease with Park Towne Place Apartments in Philadelphia for an apartment to be leased from September 1, 1994, to March 31, 1997. Whiteside failed to pay the rent and voluntarily vacated the apartment in early March, 1997. Whiteside owed Park Town Place $4,342 for back rent. Park Town Place then retained National Credit Systems (NCS) to collect the back rent due.

During the first week of May, 1999, NCS telephoned Whiteside attempting to collect payment. On May 25, 1999, an NCS representative and Whiteside discussed on the telephone resolving the debt for less than the full amount owing but did not come to an agreement. Whiteside received one additional call from NCS after May 25, 1999. On June 9, 1999, NCS forwarded collection correspondence addressed collectively to Larry Hill (Whiteside's former roommate) and Whiteside to Hill and Whiteside.

Whiteside had also lost his job, had numerous other debts, and was forced to sleep on a friend's couch because of lack of money. He testified at trial that he experienced headaches and that his blood pressure increased because of these multiple problems.

Whiteside filed suit, alleging that NCS's debt collection practices violated the Fair Debt Collection Practices Act. Do they? Explain.

5. James Lee Anthony Jr. brought suit, arguing that the Top Tobacco Company negligently violated the Federal Labeling Act by failing to provide the Surgeon General's warning to purchasers of its loose-leaf tobacco products. The Federal Labeling Act provides that "it is unlawful for any person to manufacture, import, or package for sale or distribution within the United States any cigarettes, the package of which fails to bear the Surgeon General's warning." "Cigarette" is defined under the Federal Labeling Act as: (A) "any roll of tobacco wrapped in paper or in any substance not containing tobacco, and (B) any roll of tobacco wrapped in any substance containing tobacco which, because of its appearance, the type of tobacco used in the filler, or its packaging and labeling, is likely to be offered to, or purchased by, consumers as a cigarette described in subparagraph (A)."

Anthony indicated that he smoked products from Top Tobacco Company because there was no warning on the loose-leaf products. He claims he has numerous physical problems as a result of smoking Top Tobacco products. Should Top Tobacco Company be liable under the Federal Labeling Act for failure to put the Surgeon General's warning on loose-leaf tobacco products?

6. John Stevenson began receiving a number of phone calls from bill collectors about arrearages in accounts that were not his. He spoke with TRW, Inc., a credit-reporting firm, to try to correct the problem. In August, 1989, he wrote TRW and obtained a copy of his credit report. He discovered many errors, including some accounts that belonged to an individual of the same name living in a different location and some accounts that apparently belonged to his estranged son, John Stevenson Jr. In total, Stevenson disputed approximately 16 accounts, seven inquiries, and much of the identifying information.

Stevenson wrote TRW on October 6, 1989, requesting that his credit report be corrected. On November 1, TRW began a reinvestigation by contacting subscribers that had reported the disputed accounts. As a result of this investigation, TRW removed several of the disputed accounts by November 30. TRW retained one account on the record because the subscriber insisted that the information was accurate, and investigations on several other accounts were still pending. TRW also added a warning statement to Stevenson's account in December, indicating that his son had apparently used his

Social Security number without his consent to obtain credit. By February, 1990, TRW claimed that all disputed accounts with "negative" credit information had been removed. Inaccurate information continued to appear on Stevenson's report, however, and some of the disputed information was reentered after Stevenson had had it deleted.

Stevenson filed suit, alleging that TRW had violated the Fair Credit Reporting Act. Has TRW done so? Explain.

7. In July 1990, the Bartholomew Circuit Court in Columbus, Indiana, rendered a deficiency judgment against Jeff Henson in the amount of $4,075.54. The Clerk of the Court incorrectly recorded the judgment in the Judgment Docket, stating that a money judgment in that amount had been entered against both Jeff Henson and his brother Greg Henson.

Trans Union Corp. and CSC Credit Services, both credit-reporting agencies, listed the information on Greg Henson's credit report. Greg and his wife, Mary, filed suit against both companies, arguing that the companies had violated the Fair Credit Reporting Act by including this erroneous judgment in his account.

The agencies argued that the information that they had reported was accurate and that a judgment had been entered against Greg. Under Indiana law, the actual judgment entered by the court is the official act that renders the judgment legally binding; the entry of the judgment on the Judgment Docket is merely an administrative task undertaken by the Clerk.

While Greg alleged that he had contacted Trans Union twice in writing regarding the error and that no correction had been made, he did not allege that he had contacted CSC. Trans Union argued that it had no duty to investigate beyond the Judgment Docket to verify the accuracy of the reported information.

How should the court resolve this dispute?

8. On January 24, 1994, Frederick Hantske Jr. was telephoned at home by Paul Kallina, an employee of Brandenburger & Davis, Inc. Kallina told Hantske that he could possibly be an heir to an estate and arranged a meeting with him on the following day.

Kallina met with Hantske at his home in Charlottesville, Virginia, for one and one-half hours. Kallina explained that his firm searched official records for missing heirs. Kallina stated that the firm believed that Hantske was an heir to a certain estate and that the firm would undertake to prove Hantske's claim and would "fight for" Hantske to receive his inheritance. Kallina then presented a contract to Hantske under which Brandenburger & Davis would receive one-fourth of the inheritance received by Hantske in exchange for locating Hantske, notifying him, and proving his interests. If Hantske did not inherit anything, he would owe the firm nothing. Kallina estimated that Hantske's interest in the estate was approximately $30,000 and that the firm would receive a fee of $7,500. Hantske signed the written agreement that same day.

Hantske then went to court seeking to have the contract voided, arguing that under the Virginia Home Solicitation Sales Act of 1970 he had a right to cancel the contract after it was signed. The court found that the agreement between Hantske and Brandenburger & Davis fit the definition of a sale under the Virginia Act. Home solicitation statutes of this type normally provide a three-day "cooling off' time period in which the homeowner has an unwaivable right to cancel the sale. Because the agreement signed by Hantske did not include a right to cancel, the court found that it was unenforceable under the Act.

Should a homeowner such as Hanske be permitted to take advantage of information provided to him by a seller that he would not have easily learned about on his own? Should homeowners be allowed to cancel a signed agreement and retain the financial results? Is it ethical and fair to keep the benefits, cancel the agreement, and not pay for services and information provided? What interests is the Virginia Home Solicitation Sales Act trying to protect?

9. Laci Satterfield received a text message from Simon & Schuster, a publishing company, advertising a new Stephen King novel that it was publishing. Satterfield filed suit against Simon & Schuster for violation of the TCPA. Simon & Schuster argued that it had not violated the TCPA because an unsolicited text message is not a "call" for purposes of the TCPA. How should the court rule on this issue, and why?

10. David Wisniewski filed suit against Rodale, Inc., a publisher, alleging that Rodale had violated Section 3009 of the Postal Reorganization Act by sending him unsolicited books and then demanding payment. Rodale moved for summary judgment, arguing that Section 3009 does not create a private cause of action in consumers.

Section 3009 states:

(a) Except for (1) free samples clearly and conspicuously marked as such, and (2) merchandise mailed by a charitable organization soliciting contributions, the mailing of unordered merchandise or of communications prohibited by subsection (c) of this section constitutes an unfair method of competition and an unfair trade practice in violation of section 45(a)(1) of Title 15.

Section 45(a)(1) of Title 15 is part of the FTC Act, which gives enforcement power to the FTC, not to consumers.

Is Rodale correct in asserting that only the FTC, not consumers, may bring a case under Section 3009?

PART 5

Legal Issues Relating to Product Sale

Chapter 9
Contracts and Sales of Goods Law

Chapter 10
Warranties and Products Liability

Contracts and Sales of Goods Law

Although most people do not realize it, they form and execute contracts repeatedly during their daily lives. Every time you purchase gas, buy groceries, go to a movie, or visit a doctor or a dentist, you have formed a contract with the provider of the good or service you are acquiring.

Overview

In most instances, we do not even think about these informal contracts. They are typically oral, not written, transactions; they are formed and executed almost simultaneously; and, unless the goods or services purchased turn out to be defective, the transaction is complete almost immediately, with no lingering legal ramifications to worry about. Nonetheless, the law recognizes these transactions as creating legal relationships known as *contracts*.

Businesses likewise form frequent contractual relationships as they go about their normal, routine activities. Contract law issues arise at several stages in the marketing of goods and services. A manufacturer, for example, enters into purchase contracts with its suppliers and sales contracts with its distributors or retailers. The final sale to the consumer, whether the sale is made by the manufacturer itself, a retailer, or someone else in the chain of distribution, also creates a contractual relationship between the purchaser and the seller.

Businesses tend to pay more attention to their contractual relationships than do individuals. Nonetheless, many routine business transactions occur without the use of a formalized written contract or without the parties explicitly agreeing on the terms of their contract. The law provides default rules that control in the instances in which the parties have not negotiated their own contractual terms. Many of these default rules are discussed in this chapter. You should realize, however, that the law promotes freedom of contract. Explicit agreements of the parties, provided they are not illegal or against public policy, generally override the rules discussed here.

This chapter provides an overview of basic contract law principles, including both common law contracts and the special rules that apply to sales of goods. The law of contracts is considerably more detailed and complex than this necessarily brief description suggests, however, so managers should seek legal advice when confronted with these issues.

Sources of Contract Law

Contract law is a matter of state law. This raises an initial question, however, of *which* state law applies when the parties to the contract are located in two or more states. Many modern commercial transactions involve parties from different states or occur across state lines. If the parties enter into a written contract, they often include a *choice-of-law* provision that indicates which state's law is to govern the contract. Otherwise, the controlling law is the law of the state to which the substance of the contract and the parties are most closely related and the state that has the strongest governmental interest in having its law apply. There are specific *conflict-of-laws* rules that help courts make these determinations.

Two basic sources of law govern the sale of goods and services: the common law and the Uniform Commercial Code (UCC).

The Common Law of Contracts

The original source of contract law was the *common law*. As discussed in Chapter 1, common law refers to law that develops in the courts and that is primarily found in judicial decisions. Although state legislatures have passed statutes dealing with certain aspects of specific types of common law contractual relationships, such as employer-employee or landlord-tenant relationships, the common law is still the primary source of contract law. Today, the common law of contracts governs the sale of services (including employment and insurance contracts), intangible personal property (such as trade secrets), and real estate.

The American Law Institute (ALI) has compiled the *Restatement (Second) of Contracts*, which summarizes the generally accepted principles of the common law of contracts.[1] Each state has its own variations on the rules, however, so a marketer needs to be aware of the specific law that controls in the state or states in which it operates.

Uniform Commercial Code

The *Uniform Commercial Code* (UCC) is a model statute drafted by the National Conference of Commissioners on Uniform State Laws (NCCUSL)[2] and the ALI in the 1940s. It has several parts, called "Articles," which codify the law regarding certain types of commercial transactions.

Originally, commercial law varied from state to state. This imposed a very substantial burden on business, particularly as the economy grew and became national in scope and as businesses began operating across state lines. The UCC was intended to provide the states with a blueprint for commercial law that would standardize the rules across all the states and that would reflect the new legal issues raised by the growth in mass distribution of consumer goods in the early twentieth century.

Article 2 of the UCC, which was drafted in 1951 and which has been adopted in all of the states except Louisiana,[3] governs transactions involving sales of goods.[4] A *sale* is a contract by which title to goods is transferred from one party to another for a price. *Goods* are any tangible personal property. The law pertaining to the sale of goods still is not completely "uniform," as most states altered the UCC somewhat as they adopted it.

---

[1]For general information on the ALI, *see* www.ali.org

[2]For general information on the NCCUSL, see www.nccusl.org. For general information on the UCC, *see* www.law.cornell.edu/topics/sales.html

[3]Louisiana follows the civil law tradition of its French heritage rather than the common law system followed in the other 49 states.

[4]Article 2A governs the lease of goods. It was proposed by the drafters of the UCC in the late 1980s in response to uncertainty about how the provisions of Article 2 applied to the burgeoning business of the leasing of goods. Article 2A is substantially similar to Article 2. Some of the major distinctions between the two are that Article 2A contains no battle of the forms provision, the Statute of Frauds provision under Article 2A requires a writing for leases of $1,000 or more, and consumers are provided certain special protections in lease relationships. For general information on Article 2A, see www.law.cornell.edu/ucc/2A/overview.html

These alterations tend to be rather minor, however, so businesses can now engage in interstate business activities with a good deal more certainty and ease.

The UCC supplements the common law of contracts with regard to the sale of goods. If the UCC does not contain an explicit provision on a particular point, common law contract rules continue to apply. A marketer of goods thus needs to be aware of both sets of legal rules.

There are some fundamental distinctions between the UCC and the common law. First, the UCC is a lot less formalistic than the common law. This means that its rules are less rigid and that the UCC is more likely to find that an enforceable contract exists than is the common law, even if the parties have failed to agree on seemingly important terms. The UCC has specific "gap-filler" provisions (discussed below) that the courts use to supply certain missing terms.

Second, the common law applies equally to all parties. Under the UCC, by contrast, "merchants" are often subject to special rules. The UCC defines a *merchant* as a person who: (1) deals in goods of the kind being sold; (2) by his occupation holds himself out as having knowledge or skill peculiar to the practices or goods involved in the transaction; or (3) employs an agent or broker who holds himself out as having such knowledge or skill.[5] For example, the UCC imposes an obligation of good faith upon the parties to a contract.[6] A non-merchant seller is held to a subjective standard of "honesty in fact."[7] A merchant seller, on the other hand, is held to a higher objective standard that includes not only honesty in fact, but also the "observance of reasonable commercial standards of fair dealing in the trade."[8] Examples of other special merchant rules are provided later in the chapter.

Some contracts involve the sale of both goods and services. For example, if a buyer purchases new carpeting for his home, the sales contract may well also include installation of the carpet. If a dispute arises, should it be resolved under the UCC (because the sale of goods—carpet—is involved) or the common law (because the sale of a service—carpet installation—is involved)? In *hybrid contracts* involving both goods and services, the courts generally look to see whether the predominant focus of the contract is the sale of the goods or the sale of the service (see Case Illustration 9.1).

Elements of a Contract

A contract is a promise or set of promises for breach of which the law gives a remedy, or the performance of which the law in some way recognizes as a duty.[9]

A contract, in short, is a promise or set of promises that the courts will enforce. All contracts involve promises, but not all promises are contracts. For a contract to exist, four elements must be present: (1) mutual assent (i.e., offer and acceptance); (2) consideration; (3) legality; and (4) capacity.

Mutual Assent

Mutual assent requires a "meeting of the minds" between the two parties and is generally shown by a valid offer and acceptance. An *offer* is a statement by the *offeror* (person making the offer) that indicates a willingness to enter into a bargain. *Acceptance* occurs

---

[5]UCC § 2-104(1).

[6]UCC § 1-203.

[7]UCC § 1-201(19).

[8]UCC § 2-103(l)(b).

[9]Restatement (Second) of Contracts § 1 (1979).

when the *offeree* (person to whom the offer was made) indicates a willingness to enter into that proposed bargain. Only the intended offeror has the power to accept; third parties may not accept an offer and form a binding contract. Generally, the parties indicate their willingness through words, but conduct can also constitute an offer or acceptance. It is the objective, outward manifestation of the party's words or conduct that counts. The law will not recognize subjective or secret intentions of either party. In addition, offers usually cannot be accepted through *silence* of the offeree.

Offers are effective when received by the offeree. Under the *mailbox rule*, however, acceptances are effective when sent, even if never received by the offeror. This rule can create risks for the offeror. For example, if a properly addressed acceptance is lost in transmission, it is nonetheless effective and the offeror is bound to the contract even though it may be unaware of the acceptance. To avoid such a result, the offeror should expressly state in its offer that acceptance will be effective only upon receipt of the acceptance by the offeror.

Offers, once made, can be terminated in a number of ways. The offeree may *reject* it or issue a *counteroffer*. The offer may be explicitly *revoked* by the offeror or may expire after a *lapse of time*. The offeror may specify a time limit for acceptance in the offer; otherwise, the offer will automatically expire after a reasonable time period. Finally, the *death* or *incapacity* of either party will terminate the offer.

CASE ILLUSTRATION 9.1

THE PLANTATION SHUTTER CO. v. EZELL, 492 S.E. 2D 404 (S.C. CT. APP. 1997)

FACTS Ricky Ezell contracted to purchase specially-manufactured interior shutters for his home from The Plantation Shutter Company ("Plantation") for $5,985.75. Plantation was to manufacture and install the shutters. Ezell was not satisfied with 12 of the 37 panels after installation. Plantation agreed to remake the shutters. Ezell continued to complain about several aspects of the shutters, including their exposed hinges. Plantation agreed to specially-manufacture side strips to hide the hinges. Plantation made several attempts to schedule an appointment to install the hinges, but Ezell did not respond to its efforts. Finally, Plantation sent workers to the home to install the hinges, but Ezell refused them access. Plantation sued Ezell for breach of contract to collect the balance owing on the shutters. Ezell argued that the UCC did not apply to this contract because it was a contract for services.

DECISION The court disagreed, stating:

> In considering whether a transaction that provides for both goods and services is a contract for the sale of goods governed by the UCC courts generally employ the predominant factor test. Under this test, if the predominant factor of the transaction is the rendition of a service with goods incidentally involved, the UCC is not applicable. If, however, the contract's predominant factor is the sale of goods with labor incidentally involved, the UCC applies. In most cases in which the contract calls for a combination of services with the sale of goods, courts have applied the UCC.

> * * *

> Here, the contract does not provide for installation charges. The document is entitled "Terms of Sale." By signing the contract, however, the "customer" authorized the "sales representative" to do the "work" as specified. Although the term "work" sounds more like a service contract term, looking at the contract as a whole, it is predominantly a contract for the sale of goods; therefore, we must apply the UCC.

The court determined that Ezell was liable for breach of contract because he had accepted the shutters by failing to effectively reject them in accordance with UCC requirements.

Bilateral Versus Unilateral Contracts   Contracts can be either *bilateral* or *unilateral*, depending upon whether the offeror requested a promise or an act from the offeree. Most contracts are *bilateral* contracts in which a promise is given in exchange for another promise. If a hospital sends a purchase order for bandages to a medical supply company, for example, and the medical supply company sends back an acknowledgment form, the parties have formed a bilateral contract. The hospital has promised to pay for the bandages ordered, and the medical supply company has promised to provide the bandages in return for payment.

In a *unilateral contract*, a promise is given in exchange for an act (or a refraining from acting) by the other side. Acceptance of the contract occurs when the performance of the act is complete; no promise is requested of or made by the offeree (see Case Illustration 9.2).

CASE ILLUSTRATION 9.2

CIM INSURANCE CORP. v. CASCADE AUTO GLASS, INC., 660 S.E.2D 907 (N.C. APP. 2008)

FACTS Cascade Auto Glass, Inc., is an automobile glass replacement company. Between 1999 and 2004, Cascade repaired or replaced damaged windshields in at least 2,284 vehicles insured by GMAC-affiliated insurance companies.

Before 1999, GMAC administered its own glass repair or replacement program, and typically paid the full amount billed by Cascade for work performed for its insureds. In 1999, GMAC contracted with Safelite Solutions to serve as a third-party administrator of its auto glass program. Safelite informed Cascade that GMAC would now pay lower prices for Cascade's services.

Cascade disputed the Safelite prices. However, when an insured sought services, Safelite would send Cascade a confirmation fax stating the lower price that it would pay and including a statement that "[p]erformance of services constitutes acceptance of the above price." Although Cascade then would perform the services and bill GMAC a higher rate that it deemed "fair and reasonable," GMAC, through Safelite, paid Cascade at the lower prices quoted in its faxes. Cascade accepted these payments and deposited them into its bank accounts.

After Cascade threatened to sue GMAC for the additional sums it said were owing, GMAC filed suit seeking a declaration of the rights of the parties. The trial court entered summary judgment for GMAC, and the appellate court affirmed.

DECISION The appellate court began by explaining the nature of a unilateral contract:

> A unilateral contract is formed when one party makes a promise and expressly or impliedly invites the other party to perform some act as a condition for making the promise binding on the promisor.

Here, GMAC, through Safelite, informed Cascade of the prices it was willing to pay for services rendered by Cascade to its insureds through several means, including letters, telephone calls, confirmation faxes when claims were made but before work was done, and payment of invoices at GMAC's stated rate.

Although Cascade protested GMAC's prices, Cascade's own protests indicated that the faxes constituted offers from GMAC: "The purpose of this letter is to address [the confirmation faxes] and to dispel any notion that we are in agreement with the *offered pricing.*"

As the appellate court stated: "It is a fundamental concept of contract law that the offeror is the master of his offer. He is entitled to require acceptance in precise conformity with his offer before a contract is formed." Here, the offer stated that performance equaled acceptance. Thus, by performing the requested repairs or replacements, Cascade accepted the terms of GMAC's offers, and formed valid unilateral contracts at GMAC's stated prices.

Summary judgment for GMAC was affirmed.

Generally, businesses prefer to use bilateral contracts. In unilateral contracts, the offeror cannot be certain when or whether the offeree will perform the requested act and form the contract. For example, if the hospital fails to specify its intent regarding acceptance when it places its purchase order for bandages, the medical supply company may accept either by sending back an acknowledgment form promising to ship the bandages or by in fact shipping the requested bandages.[10] In the latter instance, the hospital will not know if the medical supply company has accepted the offer until the bandages actually arrive. For this reason, businesses often prefer to avoid issuing offers that result in unilateral contracts.

Where the language of the offer is ambiguous as to whether a unilateral or bilateral contract is proposed, both the UCC and the Restatement provide that the offeree may accept either by performance or by a promise.

Advertisements as Offers   Marketers often advertise the goods or services they have for sale. Does every such advertisement constitute an offer to every reader of the advertisement to enter into a contract?

Generally, no. Advertisements usually indicate that the marketer has goods or services for sale, describe those goods or services, and indicate prices. They operate as an invitation to the public to make an offer to purchase (which the seller may then accept or reject), but they generally do not rise to the level of an offer to sell. In addition, the courts generally view other sales materials, such as catalogs and price lists, as merely invitations to make an offer as well.

Advertisements that contain definite or specific language that clearly indicates a willingness on the part of the advertiser to be bound to a specific transaction may constitute an offer. For example, a court might interpret as an offer an advertisement to sell "13 SuperLite CoffeeMakers, Model 112B, for $39.95, First come, First served" because the advertiser has specified a definite number and definite type of coffeemaker to be sold.

◆ *See Discussion Case 9.1.*

Option Contracts and Firm Offers   As already stated, offers automatically expire after a reasonable time if they are not accepted. What is reasonable depends upon the circumstances of the offer and practices within the industry. In addition, offers may be revoked by the offeror at any time prior to acceptance. This is true even if the offer states that it will remain open for a certain time period.

However, the offeror can ensure that an offer will remain open if the offeree pays consideration (i.e., provides something of value), thus creating an *option contract*. This is a separate agreement that requires the offeree to provide consideration to the offeror in exchange for the offeror leaving the offer open for a specified time period. Option contracts are commonly used in the sale of real estate or businesses. Consideration is discussed further below.

The UCC provides a special rule for merchants called the *firm offer rule*. Under the UCC's firm offer rule,[11] an offer is not revocable if it is (1) made by a merchant (2) in a signed writing and (3) states that it will remain open for a certain time period. Firm offers do not require the payment of consideration. However, a firm offer cannot be made irrevocable for a period of time longer than three months unless consideration is paid.

Counteroffers and the Battle of the Forms   An offeree, of course, is under no obligation to accept an offer made to it. The offeree may *reject* the offer (which instantly

---

[10]UCC § 2-206(l)(b).

[11]UCC § 2-205.

terminates the offer) or may choose simply not to respond (which causes the offer to expire automatically after a reasonable time period).

What if the offeree is interested in the transaction presented to it but is not completely satisfied with the terms of the offer? The offeree may respond with a *counter-offer*. This has the legal effect of rejecting the original offer and putting a new offer on the table instead. Suppose that Amalgamated, Inc., contacts HR Consulting Co. and states that it is interested in having HR prepare new personnel manuals for its operations. Amalgamated has not made an offer at this point but is inviting HR to make an offer to it. HR (the offeror) then sends back a proposal, detailing the work product that it proposes to provide and stating a price of $50,000. Amalgamated (the offeree) believes that the price is too high and responds that it is willing to pay only $45,000 for HR's services.

Because Amalgamated has changed the terms of the offer sent to it, its response is a counteroffer (and Amalgamated is now the offeror). HR is the offeree and may decide whether to accept or reject the counteroffer that Amalgamated has put forth. No contract is formed between the parties unless and until HR agrees to the new terms proposed by Amalgamated.

Suppose HR rejects Amalgamated's counteroffer. May Amalgamated now go back and attempt to accept HR's original offer of $50,000? No. Amalgamated's counteroffer killed the original offer made by HR. At this point, all Amalgamated can do is issue a new offer for $50,000, which HR may choose to accept or reject.

Under the common law, the *mirror image rule* states that no contract is formed unless the offer and acceptance are identical in every respect. Suppose, for example, that Amalgamated, Inc., faxed a letter to Vendors Corp. offering to buy 100 widgets from Vendors, with delivery to occur on Tuesday, May 14. Vendors faxed back an acceptance, but the acceptance indicated that delivery was to occur on Monday, May 13. Under the common law mirror image rule, no contract has been formed and Vendors' purported acceptance is really just a counteroffer.

The common law's rigid mirror image rule does not mesh with the realities of modern-day business practice, where companies tend to use preprinted forms with boilerplate language. The buyer, for example, typically sends its purchase order form to the seller. The form contains preprinted provisions (that generally favor the buyer), with blanks where the buyer fills in terms such as price, quantity, and delivery requirements for the goods being ordered. The seller then sends back its preprinted acknowledgment form, which most likely has at least some differing preprinted terms (that generally favor the seller). Neither side typically reads the entire document sent by the other side but, rather, focuses on the terms critical to the immediate transaction, such as price, quantity, and delivery terms. Although the parties may not have reached agreement on all of the remaining terms, they clearly intend that a contract be formed. The mirror image rule frustrates this intention.

The UCC abandons the mirror image rule and focuses instead on the intent (or likely intent) of the parties to the transaction. UCC Section 2-207, known as the *Battle of the Forms* provision, tells the parties: (1) whether a contract has been created when the forms contain differing terms and, if so, (2) what terms control. The rules vary under this section depending upon whether both of the parties are merchants.

Under UCC Section 2-207, under most circumstances, a contract is formed even if the offer and acceptance contain differing terms. However, if the second document changes a *fundamental term* (for example, alters the quantity term), there is no acceptance and no contract is formed. In addition, if the second document *expressly states* that no contract will be formed unless the offeror agrees to the new or altered terms, no contract is formed. In both of these instances, the second document operates as a counteroffer.

If there is an acceptance and a contract has been formed, the second question is what terms will control? Different rules apply depending upon whether the second document contains *new* terms or *different* terms.

Whether *new* terms become part of the contract depends upon whether both parties are *merchants*. If *either* the buyer or the seller is *not* a merchant, a contract has been formed under the terms of the first document sent and any new terms in the second document are merely proposals for additions to that contract, which the other side may accept or reject.

If *both* the seller and the buyer *are* merchants, the new terms contained in the second document automatically become part of the contract unless: (1) the new terms materially alter the contract; (2) the other side objects within a reasonable time; or (3) the original offer stated that no new terms would be allowed. Material alterations include things such as disclaimers of warranties or clauses requiring arbitration in the event of a dispute. As a policy matter, the UCC takes the position that material alterations must be negotiated directly with the other side and may not be hidden in boilerplate language.

The UCC's position on *different* terms is much less clear. For example, suppose that the buyer's purchase order provides for one delivery date, but the seller's acknowledgment form states a different date. Some courts treat the different term in the same manner that they would treat a new term. Other courts find that the contract is formed but that the UCC's gap-filler provisions must be used to fill in the term on which the parties disagree. The outcome thus depends upon the state whose law controls the contract.

◆➤ *See Discussion Case 9.2.*

Consideration

The second required element for a contract is *consideration*—that is, a *bargained-for exchange*. Promises made without consideration are considered to be gratuitous or gift promises and are generally not legally enforceable as contracts.

Consideration consists of anything of value exchanged by the parties, such as money, property, services, a promise to do something the person is not otherwise legally required to do, or a promise to refrain from doing something the person is otherwise legally entitled to do. Courts do not inquire into the adequacy of consideration; thus, the exchange of anything of value, no matter how small, suffices, provided that the amount is not nominal or the transaction is not a sham (i.e., the agreement recites the payment of consideration, but no consideration in fact was paid). If a party fails to provide anything of value, however, its promise is *illusory* and no contract is formed (see Case Illustration 9.3).

Suppose the parties enter into a valid contract for 50 hours of bookkeeping services. One month later, the parties agree that the contract shall now be for 60 hours of such services, not 50. Must this *modification* of the original contract be supported by consideration? Under the common law, the answer is yes—modifications of contracts must be supported by consideration. The UCC, on the other hand, provides that while consideration is necessary for the initial contract, it is not necessary for a modification.[12] Thus, if the contract had been for goods rather than services, consideration would not have been required.

---

[12]UCC § 2-209(1).

CASE ILLUSTRATION 9.3

HARRIS v. BLOCKBUSTER, INC.,
622 F. SUPP. 2D 396 (N.D. TEX. APR. 15, 2009)

FACTS Blockbuster Online is a service that allows customers to rent movies through the Internet. Blockbuster entered into a contract with Facebook that caused the movie rental choices of Blockbuster customers to be disseminated on the customers' Facebook accounts to their Facebook friends.

Harris argued that this practice violated the Video Privacy Protection Act, which provides for liquidated damages of $2,500 per violation. In response to Harris' class action lawsuit, Blockbuster tried to invoke an arbitration provision in its "Terms and Conditions" document. This provision stated, in relevant part, that: "[a]ll claims, disputes or controversies ... will be referred to and determined by binding arbitration." The provision also provided that users of the service waived the right to file a class action. Before a customer could join Blockbuster Online, the customer was required to click on a box certifying that the customer had read and agreed to the Terms and Conditions.

Under Texas law, a contract must be supported by consideration. If there is no consideration, the contract is illusory and cannot be enforced. Harris argued that the arbitration clause was illusory because Blockbuster reserved the right to modify the Terms and Conditions, including the arbitration provision, "at its sole discretion" and "at any time," and provided that such modifications will be effective immediately upon being posted on the site. Under the heading "Changes to Terms and Conditions," the contract further stated:

> You agree to review these Terms and Conditions of Use periodically and your continued use of this Site following such modifications will indicate your acceptance of these modified Terms and Conditions of Use. If you do not agree to any modification of these Terms and Conditions of Use, you must immediately stop using this Site.

DECISION The court concluded that the Blockbuster arbitration provision was illusory because there was nothing in the Terms and Conditions that prevented Blockbuster from unilaterally changing any part of the contract other than providing that such changes would not take effect until posted on the website. In particular, the court noted, "there is nothing to suggest that once published the amendment would be inapplicable to disputes arising, or arising out of events occurring, *before* such publication." Thus, because Blockbuster had in no way limited its ability to unilaterally modify all rules regarding dispute resolution, the arbitration clause was illusory and unenforceable.

Legality/Unenforceability on Public Policy Grounds

Although contract law generally favors freedom of bargaining between the parties, the courts do not enforce certain types of bargains or agreements for public policy reasons. In those cases, they typically "leave the parties where they find them," which can be very harsh on a party who has fully performed its side of the bargain but has not yet received performance from the other side. There are two rationales behind this rule: (1) to discourage the illegal conduct in the future and (2) to avoid the inappropriate and unseemly sight of having the courts become involved in enforcing a socially undesirable activity.

Some agreements are unenforceable because they are statutory violations. For example, a person engaged in a trade or business required by law to be licensed may not be properly licensed or an individual or firm may be in violation of statutes prohibiting gambling or usury. In such an instance, the statute may well provide that any agreement entered into by such a person or firm is illegal and thus unenforceable. Other types of unenforceable agreements are not statutory violations but are nonetheless found to violate public policy. These would include contracts that attempt to improperly limit one party's liability for its own tortious conduct (*exculpatory clauses* are discussed more below) or contracts that unreasonably restrain trade.

Courts may also decline to enforce contracts they regard as *unconscionable* (i.e., unfair), including *contracts of adhesion*. Contracts of adhesion typically involve standardized documents drafted by a party with grossly disproportionate bargaining power in the relationship, who then presents the document to the other party on a "take it or leave it" basis.

Courts are reluctant to allow businesses to argue that a contract was unconscionable, although they readily use this doctrine to protect consumers.

Capacity

To form a contract, both parties must have *contractual capacity*. Most persons have full capacity to enter into a contract, but certain parties have only limited capacity. *Minors* (persons under the age of 18), for example, may enter into contracts. However, those contracts are often *voidable* at the option of the minor but not at the option of the other party to the contract. Thus, businesses need to use caution when contracting with minors, particularly as minors increasingly purchase expensive consumer items, such as electronics and automobiles. Businesses often require the minor's parent or another adult to co-sign the contract. Even if the minor is able to void the contract, the adult cosigner will remain bound.

Persons who have been placed under guardianship by a court as a result of incompetency have no capacity to enter into contracts. Persons who are mentally ill or mentally incompetent but who are not under guardianship and intoxicated persons may enter into contracts, but those contracts may be voidable at their option (but not by the other party to the contract).

Corporations make contracts through the acts of their officers, agents, and/or employees. Whether a particular individual has the authority to bind the corporation to a contract is determined by principles of agency or corporate law. The president generally has authority to enter into all contracts relating to business operations. If an individual other than the president is entering into the contract on behalf of the corporation, the other party to the contract would be wise to verify that that individual has the authority to do so.

Promissory Estoppel

There are instances in which a promise does not meet the required elements of a contract but a court nonetheless enforces it under the doctrine of *promissory estoppel*. The *Restatement (Second) of Contracts* defines this doctrine as follows: "A promise which the promisor should reasonably expect to induce action or forbearance on the part of the promisee or a third person and which does induce such action or forbearance is binding if injustice can be avoided only by enforcement of the promise."[13]

Generally, the doctrine of promissory estoppel requires four elements to be present: (1) a clear and unambiguous promise must have been made; (2) the party to whom the promise was made must have relied upon it; (3) that reliance must have been reasonable and foreseeable; and (4) the party relying on the promise must have been injured by that reliance. Under the Restatement (Second), however, reasonable reliance is not a required element. Rather, the promisee must show: (1) a promise; (2) that the promisor should have reasonably expected to induce action or forbearance; (3) that does induce such action or forbearance; and (4) that injustice can be avoided only through enforcement of the promise. The rationale behind the doctrine of promissory estoppel is to avoid the substantial hardship or injustice that would result if such a promise were not enforced.

◆ *See Discussion Case 9.3.*

---

[13] Restatement (Second) of Contracts § 90(a).

The Statute of Frauds

The law recognizes and enforces oral contracts in most instances. All states have adopted some form of a *Statute of Frauds*, however, that requires that certain types of contracts be in writing in order to be enforceable in court in the event of a dispute. These contracts include: (1) contracts that cannot be performed in one year; (2) contracts for the transfer of an interest in real property; and (3) contracts in which one person agrees to assume another's debts.

Under the UCC's Statute of Frauds provision,[14] contracts for $500 or more usually must be in writing in order to be enforceable in court. If a contract is initially for less than $500 (and thus not required to be in writing) but is modified to bring it over $500, the modification must be in writing.

Neither the common law nor the UCC requires that the writing be a formal document—even a handwritten note on a scrap of paper or the back of an envelope will suffice. Under the common law, the document must: (1) reasonably identify the subject matter of the contract; (2) indicate that a contract (as opposed to a lease or some other type of transaction) has been made between the parties; (3) state with reasonable certainty the essential terms of the contract; and (4) be signed by the party against whom enforcement is sought.

Returning to our example of Amalgamated, Inc., and HR Consulting, let us suppose that the parties negotiated and agreed on the terms orally. Amalgamated then sent a signed letter to HR, indicating that a contract had been formed and setting forth the terms of the agreement. The letter would be a sufficient writing to allow HR to enforce the contract against Amalgamated. Amalgamated would be unable to enforce the contract against HR, however, if HR failed to perform, because Amalgamated does not have a writing signed by HR.

The lesson for managers, of course, is to never sign a document unless the other side signs as well. Where the document is being exchanged through the mail, and one side necessarily has to sign before the other, the first signatory may be protected by inclusion of a clause to the effect: "This contract shall not be formed or take effect until signed by both parties."

Under the UCC, a writing satisfies the Statute of Frauds if it: (1) evidences a contract for the sale of goods; (2) is signed by the party against whom enforcement is sought; and (3) states the quantity.[15] In addition, the UCC has a special Statute of Frauds rule for merchants. Under the *reply doctrine*, if both parties are merchants, a written confirmation that: (1) indicates that a contract has been made; (2) has been signed by the sender; and (3) states the quantity is enforceable against the recipient as well as the sender unless the recipient objects in writing within 10 days after receipt.[16]

See Discussion Case 9.1.

Parol Evidence Rule and Contract Interpretation

The *parol evidence rule* provides that evidence of oral agreements and discussion prior to the signing of a writing that is intended to be the final expression of the parties' agreement may not be introduced to contradict that writing. The rule does not bar consideration of

---

[14]UCC § 2-201.
[15]UCC § 2-201(1).
[16]UCC § 2-201(2).

oral modifications of a contract made after the signing of the writing, however, unless the writing states that oral modifications are not allowed.

Most modern courts will allow parties to introduce extrinsic evidence to aid in the *interpretation* of an agreement. Thus, the parties can introduce evidence of what they thought the term in the writing meant. Three sources are particularly important to this interpretation role, particularly in UCC contracts. *Course of performance* refers to the manner in which the parties have conducted themselves with regard to the specific contract at issue.[17] *Course of dealing* refers to the manner in which the parties have acted with respect to past contracts.[18] *Usage of trade* refers to "any practice or method of dealing having such regularity of observance in a place, vocation or trade as to justify an expectation that it will be observed with respect to the transaction in question."[19] Although these sources cannot be used to contradict express terms in a written agreement, they can be used to interpret those terms. Where more than one source applies, the specific controls over the general. That is, an express contractual provision controls over a course of performance, which controls over a course of dealing, which controls over a usage of trade.[20]

Special UCC Rules

The UCC has a number of provisions relating to the sale of goods that differ significantly from the common law of contracts. Some of these special UCC rules are discussed here.

Definiteness and the UCC's "Gap-Filler" Provisions

Traditionally, the common law required a contract to be very definite in its terms, spelling out all of the material terms of the contract, such as the parties, the subject matter of the contract, the quantity, and the price, in order to be enforceable. Most modern courts have relaxed this requirement and will now supply a missing term where they can find a "reasonable" value for that term.

The UCC has codified this more liberal approach to definiteness of a contract. The UCC does not demand absolute certainty in an agreement in order for a contract to exist. Rather, the UCC requires only three elements to be present: (1) some sort of indication that an agreement exists; (2) the signature of the party against whom enforcement is sought; and (3) a statement of the quantity of goods being sold. The UCC has *gap-filler* rules that will fill in any terms left open or not addressed by the parties, such as price, performance, delivery or payment terms, or remedies.

The UCC will not fill in missing quantity terms—largely because there is no way to tell what the parties intended in terms of quantity if they failed to specify this themselves. The UCC will allow *output* contracts, however, where the buyer agrees to buy all that the seller produces, or *requirements* contracts, where the seller agrees to supply all that the buyer needs. In each case, however, the seller's production or the buyer's requirement is governed by norms of fair dealing and industry custom.

Performance of the Contract

Under the UCC, the basic obligation of the seller is to tender conforming goods to the buyer. The basic obligation of the buyer is to accept and pay for those goods in accordance with the contract terms.

---

[17]UCC § 2-208.

[18]UCC § 1-205(1).

[19]UCC § 1-205(2).

[20]UCC § 2-208(2).

Performance by the Seller   *Tender of delivery* requires the seller to: (1) put and hold conforming goods at the buyer's disposition and (2) give the buyer reasonable notification to allow the buyer to take delivery.[21] Tender of conforming goods by the seller entitles the seller to acceptance of them by the buyer and to payment of the contract price.[22]

The *perfect tender rule* requires the seller's tender to conform exactly to the terms of the contract. If the tender deviates in any way—say, the quantity delivered is insufficient, or the widgets are blue instead of green as called for under the contract—the buyer may: (1) reject the whole lot; (2) accept the whole lot; or (3) accept any commercial unit or units and reject the rest.[23] The parties can, of course, always contract around the perfect tender rule. For example, they can agree in the contract that the seller has the right to repair or replace any defective goods.

The UCC also creates a number of exceptions to the perfect tender rule. The most important of these is the seller's right to *cure*. The seller can cure—i.e., make a second delivery or substitute a different tender—in two circumstances: (1) when the time for performance under the contract has not yet expired or (2) if the seller reasonably believed that the tender would be acceptable to the buyer with or without a money allowance. If the buyer rejects the goods in this latter instance, the seller has a reasonable time period in which to cure provided the seller notifies the buyer of its intent to do so.[24]

Performance by the Buyer   The buyer's obligation under the UCC is to accept conforming goods and to pay for them. As previously noted, if the tender is nonconforming, the buyer may: (1) reject all of the goods; (2) accept all of the goods; or (3) accept any commercial unit or units and reject the rest. The buyer must pay at the contract rate for any units accepted but can recover damages for any nonconformity if the buyer notifies the seller of the breach.

Once the goods have been tendered, the buyer has a number of rights, including:

Inspection: Unless the parties agreed otherwise, the buyer has a right to inspect the goods before payment or acceptance. The buyer loses its right to reject the goods or to revoke its acceptance if it fails to inspect the goods within a reasonable time period. The buyer must pay the expenses of inspection but can recover those expenses from the seller if the goods are rightfully rejected as nonconforming.[25]

Acceptance: Acceptance occurs when the buyer, after a reasonable time to inspect: (1) signifies to the seller that the goods conform; (2) signifies to the seller that the buyer will take or retain the goods despite their nonconformity; or (3) fails to make an effective rejection of the goods.[26] Once the buyer has accepted the goods, the buyer may not reject them.

Revocation of acceptance: The buyer can revoke the acceptance of nonconforming goods if the nonconformity substantially impairs the value of the goods to the buyer, provided that the acceptance: (1) was premised on the reasonable assumption that the nonconformity would be cured by the seller, and it was not cured; or (2) was made without discovery of the nonconformity, and the acceptance was reasonably induced by the difficulty of discovery of the nonconformity before acceptance or by assurances of the seller.[27]

---

[21]UCC § 2-503(1).

[22]UCC § 2-507(1).

[23]UCC § 2-601.

[24]UCC § 2-508.

[25]UCC § 2-513.

[26]UCC § 2-606.

[27]UCC § 2-608(1).

Revocation is not effective until the buyer gives notification of it to the seller. The revocation must be made within a reasonable time after the buyer discovers or should have discovered the grounds for the revocation and before the goods have undergone any substantial change not caused by their defect.[28]

Rejection: Rejection must be made within a reasonable time after the goods are tendered or delivered. It does not take effect unless the buyer seasonably notifies the seller.[29] Rejection can be rightful or wrongful, depending upon whether the goods conform to the contract. The buyer has the right to reject nonconforming goods under the perfect tender rule, of course. The buyer may also reject conforming goods, although the buyer is then in breach of contract and is liable to the seller for damages as described below. Once the buyer has rejected the goods, the buyer cannot exercise any ownership interest in them but must hold the goods for a reasonable time to allow the seller to remove them.

Transfer of Title and Risk of Loss

Historically, under the common law, *title* (i.e., legal ownership) governed most aspects of the rights and duties of the buyer and seller arising out of a sales contract, including determining which party bore the risk of loss. Under the UCC, however, transfer of title and passage of risk of loss are considered separate issues. Two key questions thus arise: (1) When does *title* pass from the seller to the buyer? and (2) If the goods are damaged or destroyed before the buyer has accepted them, does the buyer or the seller bear the *risk of loss*?

Transfer of Title   Transfer of title is important for a variety of reasons. In addition to telling us who owns the goods, it tells us which party's creditors can reach the goods and which party is liable in the event that someone is injured by the goods.

Often, the parties specify in their contract at what moment title transfers from the seller to the buyer. For example, the parties may state: "Title and risk of loss in all goods sold hereunder shall pass to the buyer upon seller's delivery to carrier at shipping point." Under the UCC, the agreement of the parties controls.

If the parties fail to specify in their contract when transfer of title occurs, the UCC provides default rules that will control. These rules fall into two categories: (1) where the goods are to be physically delivered to the buyer and (2) where the goods are not to be moved.

Where the Goods Are to Be Physically Delivered If the goods are to be physically delivered from the seller to the buyer, the parties may use one of two types of contracts: (1) a shipment contract or (2) a destination contract.

A *shipment contract* requires the seller to turn the goods over to a carrier but does not require the seller to deliver them to a particular destination. Title passes to the buyer when the seller delivers the goods to the carrier for shipment to the buyer. Unless the parties state otherwise, or where the terms are ambiguous, sales contracts involving the transport of goods are presumed to be shipment contracts.

A *destination contract* requires the seller to deliver the goods to a particular destination (often, the buyer's place of business). Title passes to the buyer when the seller tenders the goods at the specified destination.

---

[28]UCC § 2-608(2).

[29]UCC § 2-602.

Where the Goods Are Not to Be Physically Moved If the contract provides that the seller is to transfer a *document of title* to the buyer, such as a warehouse receipt, bill of lading, or dock receipt, title transfers when the required document is delivered, even though the goods have not been physically moved.

In some instances, the parties may not intend either the goods or a document of title to be handed over. In such an instance, the title passes at the time of contracting, provided that the goods are identified to the contract; otherwise, title passes at the time of identification. *Identification* occurs when specific goods have been designated as the subject matter of the contract.

Passage of Risk of Loss   *Risk of loss* determines which party, buyer or seller, will bear the financial impact of the goods being damaged, lost, or destroyed before the buyer has accepted them. (It does not address the issue of whether the party bearing the loss might have a cause of action against a third party, such as a carrier or bailee, who caused the damage to the goods.) The parties to the contract can always agree on how risk of loss should pass. If they fail to do so, the risk of loss passes according to the UCC's default rules. Risk of loss passes differently depending upon whether neither party is in breach of contract or whether one party is in breach (see Case Illustration 9.4).

CASE ILLUSTRATION 9.4

SEMA CONSTRUCTION, INC. v. DIVERSIFIED PROD. INDUSTRIES, 2007 CAL. APP. UNPUB. LEXIS 8189 (CAL. APP. OCT. 10, 2007)

FACTS SEMA Construction, Inc., contracted to purchase steel beams from Diversified Product Industries, Inc. (DPI), a steel broker. Both parties understood that SEMA had not yet obtained necessary access to the construction site on which the steel would be used to stockpile the large beams. DPI recognized that SEMA did not want to take delivery of the steel at one site and then pay to transport it to the construction site later. Thus, on the purchase order prepared by SEMA and the invoice prepared by DPI, both parties included the words "will advise" inside the "ship to" box. SEMA paid in full for the steel within a week of the purchase order.

When, a month later, SEMA still did not have access to its construction site, it advised DPI to deliver the steel to an alternative storage site. An inventory of the steel after delivery revealed that 18 beams were missing (presumably stolen by an unknown party).

DPI informed SEMA that it would credit SEMA for the missing steel. SEMA responded in writing that because it had already paid DPI for the steel, SEMA expected immediate payment for the missing steel.

DPI replied in writing that payment would "be made in due course" and pointed out that when it received SEMA's purchase order, DPI had advised SEMA that the steel had to ship immediately because it had come off another job site where the contractor had no space or time to store the steel. DPI stated that it tried several times unsuccessfully to obtain delivery instructions from SEMA, and the loss of the steel was caused by SEMA's delay. DPI stated it was "not in the storage business" and it was "inappropriate for [SEMA] to insist that DPI take on the responsibility of guarding over steel reserved for SEMA in some other company's facility." It closed the letter by stating DPI would "take responsibility for the missing steel" but that "[t]his unfortunate circumstance ... should serve as a valuable lesson learned for us both."

SEMA bought replacement steel from another company for $ 0.065 per pound more than it contracted to pay DPI. When SEMA failed to receive a refund from DPI, SEMA filed a breach of contract claim against DPI. DPI countered that SEMA had breached the contract by failing to immediately provide a delivery date.

SEMA won $38,985.32 and DPI appealed.

(Continued)

DECISION The appellate court found that SEMA's delay in designating a time and place of delivery was consistent with the terms of the contract the parties had entered into. Under UCC 2-311, "An agreement for sale which is otherwise sufficiently definite … to be a contract is not made invalid by the fact that it leaves particulars of performance to be specified by one of the parties. Any such specification must be made in good faith and within limits set by commercial reasonableness." This contract contemplated that the delivery date would be specified at a later date by SEMA. SEMA did in fact request delivery within 30 days, which was a commercially reasonable time under the circumstances.

DPI was also incorrect in arguing that SEMA bore the risk of loss either after the date it paid for the steel or after DPI informed SEMA the beams were ready for delivery.

UCC 2-509 addresses risk of loss when there has been no breach of contract (as here). With a destination contract, the seller bears the risk of loss until the goods arrive at their specified destination. With a shipment contract, the risk of loss passes to the buyer when the goods are delivered to a carrier for shipment.

The court did not have to decide whether this was a destination or shipment contract. If it was a destination contract, the risk of loss was on DPI until the goods arrived at their destination. If it was a shipment contract, the risk of loss was on DPI until the goods were delivered to a carrier. Here, the evidence showed that the steel was missing "before any carrier had an opportunity to load it and deliver it." Thus, the risk of loss remained on DPI. The judgment of the trial court was affirmed.

In the Absence of a Breach In the *shipment* and *destination* contracts contexts already discussed, title and risk of loss pass at the same time, provided that neither party is in breach of contract.

In all other cases, title and risk of loss pass separately. Thus, if the seller sells goods to the buyer that are in the possession of a bailee (such as a warehouse), and they are not to be moved, the UCC sets forth three possibilities for transfer of risk of loss:

1. If the buyer receives a negotiable document of title covering the goods, the risk of loss passes at that time.
2. If the bailee acknowledges the buyer's right to take possession of the goods (for example, by sending a notice to the buyer that the goods are available), the buyer assumes the risk of loss upon receipt of the acknowledgment.
3. If the seller gives the buyer a nonnegotiable document of title or a written direction to the bailee to deliver the goods and the buyer has had a reasonable time to present the document or direction, the risk of loss passes to the buyer.[30]

The remaining cases usually involve a buyer who is to take delivery from the seller's premises. In such cases, we would expect that a merchant seller would keep insurance on goods under its control. A buyer, on the other hand, is unlikely to insure goods that are not in its possession. Thus, if the seller *is* a merchant, the risk of loss passes to the buyer only when the buyer receives the goods. If the seller is *not a* merchant, the risk of loss passes to the buyer only when the seller tenders delivery.

In the Event of a Breach If the seller tenders or delivers goods that do not conform to the contract, the risk of loss is on the seller until either the seller cures the breach or the buyer agrees to take the goods despite their nonconformity. Similarly, if the buyer wrongfully refuses to take the goods, the risk of loss rests on the buyer for a reasonable time period until the seller can fully insure the goods.[31]

---

[30]UCC § 2-509(2).
[31]UCC § 2-510.

Insurable Interest   Transfer of title and risk of loss are important issues because they help determine which party (or parties) has an *insurable interest* in the goods; i.e., which party (or parties) has the legal right to purchase insurance to protect the goods. The seller has an insurable interest as long as it retains title to or a security interest in the goods. The buyer has an insurable interest when goods are identified to the contract. In addition, any party who has the risk of loss with respect to the goods has an insurable interest in them.[32]

Breach of Contract and Contract Remedies

Actual and Anticipatory Breach

Breach of contract occurs when one party fails to perform its contractual obligations at the time performance is due. *Anticipatory breach*, also known as *anticipatory repudiation*, occurs when one party, through its conduct or words, indicates prior to the time when its performance is due under the contract that it intends to breach.

Under the common law, the nonrepudiating party may treat an anticipatory repudiation as a breach of contract and immediately sue for damages. Alternatively, that party may await the time of performance to see if the repudiating party will withdraw the repudiation and go forward with its performance. Under the UCC, however, the nonrepudiating party may await performance only for a commercially reasonable amount of time and then must undertake mitigation measures.[33] The repudiating party may retract its repudiation unless the nonrepudiating party has: (1) canceled; (2) materially altered its position; or (3) otherwise indicated that the repudiation is final.

Remedies Generally

Suppose that Buyer and Seller have entered into a contract, and Seller *breaches* (i.e., fails to perform its contractual duties). The law can respond to this in one of two ways: (1) it can permit Seller to breach and simply order Seller to pay Buyer for any damages Buyer may have suffered; or (2) it can treat a breach of contract as being such wrongful behavior that Seller should be punished for its actions.

Generally, contract law wants to promote economic efficiency and wants to put factors of production to their highest and best use. Thus, contract law will permit a breach of contract in most instances if it is more efficient (i.e., cheaper) for the breaching party to breach the contract and pay damages than to go through with performance. As a result, punitive damages are rarely awarded in breach of contract cases (although if the breach of contract also constitutes a tort, such as fraud, punitive damages may be available).

The objective of contract remedies, therefore, is to make the nonbreaching party "whole"—i.e., to put the nonbreaching party in as good a position economically as if the defendant had fully performed. In addition, remedies under contract law are generally *cumulative*, which means that the nonbreaching party can mix and match remedies until it has fully recovered for all of its losses.

Remedies for breach of contract may be *equitable* or *legal*. *Equitable remedies* are generally available only where monetary damages are inadequate to protect the nonbreaching party. Equitable remedies in contract cases usually involve either *specific performance* or issuance of an *injunction*. A decree for specific performance orders the promisor to render the promised performance. An injunction usually orders a party to refrain from a particular act. Specific performance is most commonly given for breach of a contract to

---

[32]UCC § 2-501.

[33]UCC § 2-610.

convey a piece of land and is never given for personal services contracts. The court cannot order an individual to work for a particular employer, although it may issue an injunction prohibiting the individual from working for a competitor. Specific performance is also granted when the goods involved in the contract are unique or where it would be difficult to fairly calculate monetary damages.

A court of equity can also order *rescission* (cancellation) of a contract where enforcing the contract would be unfair. When the courts order rescission, they generally order the parties to make *restitution* to each other as well; i.e., they order the parties to return any goods, property, or money that they have exchanged.

Legal remedies typically consist of monetary damages. The common law imposes a *duty to mitigate* upon the plaintiff. This means that if the plaintiff could have avoided a particular item of damage by reasonable effort but fails to do so, he will not be able to collect for that item of damage. The UCC also imposes a duty to mitigate upon plaintiffs who are buyers (but not upon seller-plaintiffs). If the seller fails to deliver or delivers nonconforming goods that the buyer rejects, the buyer must "cover" (i.e., obtain substitute goods in the marketplace) if she can reasonably do so, or she will be unable to recover for those damages that could have been prevented by cover.

Under the common law, if the injured party has fulfilled its duty to mitigate, it is entitled to receive *compensatory damages*, which are intended to put that party in as good a position economically as he would have occupied had the defendant not breached. The injured party generally can recover *consequential damages* as well, which are indirect damages that foreseeably flow from the breach.

Often, the parties to a contract place a *liquidated damages clause* in their written agreement. This is a provision that specifies what will occur and/or what remedies will be available in the event of a breach. Courts generally enforce such provisions provided they are satisfied that the clause is an attempt to estimate actual damages and not to penalize the party for breach of contract. Thus, courts generally require that to be enforceable, the liquidated damages clause must (1) be a reasonable estimate of the anticipated or actual loss in the event of breach and (2) address harm that is uncertain or difficult to calculate, even after the fact.

Some contracts also contain an *exculpatory clause*, which is a provision that attempts to excuse one party from liability for its own tortious conduct. Courts generally will not enforce exculpatory clauses that attempt to relieve a party of liability for intentional torts or for willful conduct, fraud, recklessness, or gross negligence but may enforce clauses that address liability for ordinary negligence or contractual breach, provided the clause is conspicuous and clear. Where the party attempting to benefit from the clause has substantially more bargaining power than the other party, the courts may find that the clause is unconscionable and so unenforceable. If the parties have equal bargaining power, however, the courts generally will allow them to allocate risk between themselves via an exculpatory clause.

Remedies in Sales Contracts

The UCC provides special remedies rules that differ from the common law rules. The remedies given will vary depending upon whether the buyer or the seller is the injured party and depending upon whether the goods have been accepted.

Where the Goods Have Not Been Accepted

Buyer's Remedies If the seller has breached the contract, the buyer has a variety of remedies from which to choose.[34] The more common remedies are discussed here.

---

[34]UCC §§ 2-711 to 2-717.

First, the buyer can *reject* the goods and *cancel* the contract. (This will be the preferred choice of a buyer who has entered into a losing bargain.) Second, the buyer can *cover*, i.e., buy commercially reasonable substitute goods from another seller in good faith and without delay and recover *the difference between the contract price and the cover price, less expenses saved*, from the breaching seller. Third, if the buyer is unable to cover or does not choose to do so, the buyer can recover the *difference between the contract price and the market price at the time the buyer learned of the breach, less expenses saved.*

The buyer may also recover *consequential damages* (e.g., injury to person or property resulting from a breach of warranty) and *incidental damages* (e.g., costs such as inspection, transportation, or storage expenses directly associated with the breach and the buyer's attempt to cover). If the buyer fails to cover, it cannot recover any consequential damages that were preventable by reasonable cover attempts.

Seller's Remedies   Where the buyer has breached, the seller also has a choice of remedies.[35] If the buyer has not accepted the goods, the seller has three options. First, if the seller resells the goods to a third party in good faith and in a "commercially reasonable" manner, the seller may recover the difference between the resale and the contract price, plus incidental damages. Second, the seller may recover the difference between the market price at the time and place for delivery and the unpaid contract price, plus incidental damages. Third, if either of these formulas will not make the seller whole, the seller may instead recover lost profits, plus incidental damages. This remedy is particularly important to a lost volume seller, i.e., a seller who had an adequate supply to have satisfied both the original contract and the resale, who probably would have made both sales in the absence of the breach, and who would have made a profit on both sales (see Case Illustration 9.5).

CASE ILLUSTRATION 9.5

VANDERWERFF IMPLEMENT, INC. v. McCANCE,
561 N.W.2D 24 (S.D. 1997)

FACTS Blaine McCance purchased a used farming disc from Vanderwerff Implement, Inc. for $2,575. After using the disc for one day, McCance found that the disc was leaving a six- to eight-inch ridge on one side. Within a day after purchase, McAfee telephoned Vanderwerff and informed the company of the problem. McCance stopped payment on his check and returned the disc two weeks later. Vanderwerff checked the disc but found no defect.

The trial court found that Vanderwerff had made an express warranty to McCance that the disc was "field ready," that this warranty had not been breached, and that McCance was in violation of an enforceable contract. The court also found that Vanderwerff was a lost volume seller and awarded damages to Vanderwerff in the amount of $2,575 plus interest.

McCance appealed the trial court's decision.

DECISION The appellate court stated that the normal measure of a seller's damages in the event of a breach is the difference between the market price and the contract price. A "lost volume seller," however, may seek damages for lost profits on the sales contract:

> To be a "lost volume seller," one must prove that "even though [it] resold the contract goods, that sale to the third party would have been made regardless of the buyer's breach," using the inventory on hand at the time. Furthermore, "the lost volume seller must establish that had the breaching buyer performed, the seller would have realized profits from two sales." The main inquiry is whether the seller had the ability to sell the product to both the buyer who breached and the resale buyer.

(Continued)

---

[35]UCC §§ 2-702 to 2-710.

The appellate court agreed with the trial court that Vanderwerff was a lost volume seller. Vanderwerff sold approximately 15 new and 15 used discs each year and typically carried about 10-12 discs in inventory. The "most compelling" evidence that Vanderwerff was a lost volume seller was that Vanderwerff actually resold the disc at issue.

The appellate court found that the trial court had awarded the wrong measure of damages, however.

A lost volume seller is entitled to the profit that the seller would have made had the buyer fully performed, plus interest. The trial court, however, awarded Vanderwerff the full contract price, including the profit, plus interest. The appellate court thus remanded the case for a correct determination of damages.

Finally, the seller may sue for the *contract price, plus incidental damages*, in a few specific situations (i.e., where the buyer has accepted the goods, where the risk of loss has passed to the buyer and the goods are lost in transit, or if the seller is unable to resell the goods because they are perishable or custom-made). Note that the seller can always recover incidental damages but cannot recover consequential damages (see Case Illustration 9.6).

CASE ILLUSTRATION 9.6

DETROIT RADIANT PRODS. CO. v. BSH HOME APPLIANCES CORP., 473 F.3D 623 (6TH CIR. 2007)

FACTS Detroit Radiant manufactures gas-fired infrared heaters for commercial and industrial applications. BSH Home Appliances Corporation manufactures home appliances under several well-known brand names.

BSH supplied Detroit Radiant with detailed specifications for a burner, known as the Pro 27 burner, and requested a price quote based on an annual estimated order of 30,000 units.

Once the parties had satisfactorily resolved their price negotiations, BSH sent first a purchase order for 15,000 units, followed by a purchase order for 16,000 units. Detroit Radiant began to make and ship the burners under "release schedules" provided by BSH.

Detroit Radiant shipped almost 13,000 burners to BSH over an eight-month span, which BSH accepted and paid for at the contract price. BSH then contracted with a different company, Solaronics, to be its supplier of Pro 27 burners (at a lower price), and stopped ordering from Detroit Radiant. BSH did not accept the remainder of the burners from Detroit Radiant. However, because BSH considered the Pro 27 burners in the hands of Detroit Radiant to contain proprietary technology, BSH did not want Detroit Radiant to sell the burners to competitors.

Detroit Radiant sued for breach of contract and claimed damages for the 18,114 units that BSH had not purchased. Detroit Radiant claimed $312,104 in

lost profits, plus $52,011 in unused inventory because the Pro 27 burners had been specially manufactured for BSH and could not be sold elsewhere.

The trial court awarded $418,216 to Detroit Radiant, and BSH appealed.

DECISION The appellate court affirmed the lower court decision. The court noted that the UCC provides alternative measures of damages when the buyer breaches, as here. The "default" measure of damages is "the difference between the market price at the time and place for tender and the unpaid contract price together with any incidental damages."

An alternative measure of damages, "lost profits," is most commonly available to a lost volume seller (which all parties agreed Detroit Radiant was not). However, lost profits damages are also available to a plaintiff who cannot adequately recoup under the default measure: "If the measure of damages provided in [UCC 2-708(1)] is inadequate to put the seller in as good a position as performance would have done then the measure of damages is the profit (including reasonable overhead) which the seller would have made from full performance by the buyer, together with any incidental damages."

Here, the Pro 27 were "specially manufactured" by Detroit Radiant to BSH's specifications. Moreover, because BSH prevented Detroit Radiant from selling the burners to any other party, there was no reasonably ascertainable or accessible market for the burners. The court concluded:

> *Detroit Radiant was left with a warehouse of burners and component parts that it could not unload, due both to the uniqueness of the Pro 27*

burner and to the fact that BSH itself did not want Detroit Radiant to share any secrets as to that burner. And Detroit Radiant was further left without its anticipated profits—i.e., the benefit of the bargain that it had entered into with BSH. Michigan contract law, not to mention common sense, dictates that BSH should pay up, and thus we AFFIRM the judgment of the district court.

Where the Goods Have Been Accepted   Where the buyer has accepted the goods but refuses to pay for them, the seller may sue for the *contract price, plus incidental damages*. If the accepted goods are nonconforming, however, the buyer may sue for *breach of warranty*. Warranties are discussed further in Chapter 10.

Contract Law and E-Commerce

On October 1, 2000, the Electronic Signatures in Global and National Commerce Act (E-SIGN Act)[36] took effect. This federal act provides that any transaction in or affecting interstate or foreign commerce will not be denied legal effect, validity, or enforceability solely because an electronic signature was used. Thus, this Act makes e-signatures as legally binding as handwritten signatures and removes legal barriers to the growth of electronic commerce. The Act does not address other issues relating to electronic contracting, however, such as how the holder of an electronic document can establish its authenticity.

The E-SIGN Act applies to a wide variety of legal transactions, including those arising under Article 2 of the UCC.[37] Thus, a buyer and seller may contract for a sale of goods over a website and be assured that the contract will not fail merely because it was signed electronically rather than formalized in a traditional paper-and-ink contract.

The E-SIGN Act preempts state laws that conflict with its provisions. The E-SIGN Act does not preempt state laws based on the Uniform Electronic Transactions Act (UETA), however. Almost all of the states have adopted UETA.[38] The UETA provides that: (1) a record or signature shall not be denied legal effect or enforceability just because it is in electronic form; (2) a contract shall not be denied legal effect or enforceability just because an electronic record was used in its formation; and (3) an electronic signature satisfies any legal requirement calling for a signature.

Many other countries have also passed electronic signature acts, including Germany in 1997[39] and Japan[40] and the United Kingdom in 2000.[41] The European Union enacted a Directive regarding the legal effect of electronic signatures in 1999.[42]

---

[36]15 U.S.C. §§ 7001-7006, 7021, and 7031.

[37]The E-SIGN Act applies to Article 2A as well.

[38]Information about the UETA, including a listing of the states that have adopted it, can be found on the NCCUSL's website at www.nccusl.org

[39]The Digital Signature Act can be viewed at www.ied.ox.ac.uk/gla/statutes/SIG.htm

[40]The Law Concerning Electronic Signatures and Certification Services can be viewed at/www.meti.go.jp/english/special/E-Commerce/index.html

[41]The Electronic Communications Act 2000 can be viewed at www.opsi.gov.uk

[42]Directive 1999/93/EC of the European Parliament and of the Council of 13 Dec. 1999 on a Community framework for electronic signatures, available at http://eur-lex.europa.eu

Contracts in the International Environment

When the contracting parties are from different countries, a number of special legal issues arise. A U.S. contracting party cannot automatically assume that U.S. law will apply to the transaction, nor can it automatically assume that the contract law of other countries will resemble the U.S. law with which it is familiar. In some countries, for example, title to goods may pass at the time of delivery; in others, it may pass as soon as an agreement is reached, preventing the seller from reclaiming the goods if the buyer fails to pay. Obviously, such distinctions can have profound effects upon the manner in which contractual relationships are formed and handled.

As of February, 2009, 73 countries (including the United States) had adopted the *United Nations Convention on the International Sale of Goods* (CISG).[43] The CISG applies to contracts for the sale of goods between parties whose places of business are in different countries but does not apply to sales of personal or consumer goods. Authentic texts of the CISG exist in six languages.[44] The CISG is roughly analogous to the American UCC. It represents, however, a compromise between the common law and civil law traditions of the various member countries.

The CISG automatically applies to relevant contracts between parties whose places of business are in different Contracting States unless the parties select otherwise. Thus, if the parties do not want the CISG to cover their international sales contract, they need to specifically so state and should select an alternative forum. In addition, parties whose contracts are not otherwise subject to the CISG may nonetheless elect to have the CISG apply to their contract.

Articles 1 through 6 of the CISG address its scope of application and general provisions. Articles 7 through 13 address the interpretation of contracts. Article 11 states that a sales contract does not have to be in writing, although several countries that have adopted the CISG have expressly excluded this provision. Articles 14 through 24 address contract formation, including offer and acceptance. Article 25 addresses enforcement issues.

There are some substantial differences between the UCC and the CISG. The UCC, for example, adopts the "mailbox" rule discussed earlier. The CISG, on the other hand, adopts the European principle that an acceptance is not effective until the offeror receives it. The CISG is also not as lenient as the UCC in finding the existence of a contract in battle of the forms situations; rather, most nonconforming acceptances under the CISG operate merely as counteroffers, not acceptances. The UCC supplies a price if necessary, as already discussed. The CISG, on the other hand, does not allow a contract to be formed unless the price term or a provision for determining the price is supplied in the agreement. The UCC requires a writing to satisfy the Statute of Frauds for contracts over $500, while the CISG does not require a writing to make a sales contract valid. The CISG also rejects the UCC's perfect tender rule, providing instead that the buyer may reject goods only where the nonconformity amounts to a fundamental breach of contract. This distinction reflects the longer shipping times and greater distances, costs, and complexities of international sales contracts.

◆ *See Discussion Case 9.4.*

Parties entering into international contracts should not rely solely upon the default rules that may apply under the CISG or other applicable laws but, rather, should have

---

[43]Information on the CISG, including its text, member countries, and cases decided under it may be found at www.cisg.law.pace.edu. The United States became a signatory effective January 1, 1988.

[44]Arabic, Chinese, English, French, Russian, and Spanish.

an express written agreement that addresses the special issues raised by international contractual relationships. The parties should consider including clauses such as a *forum clause* specifying the location and the court in which disputes are to be litigated; a *governing law clause* specifying which country's or state's law is to apply to the transaction; a *currency of payment clause* specifying the unit of currency that is to be the medium of exchange between the parties; a *force majeure clause* specifying what happens in the event of a war, natural disaster, strike, or extreme shortage; a *language clause* specifying the language in which agreements may be formed, notices sent, or enforcement pursued; and a *notice clause* specifying the manner in which notices are to be sent, taking into account delays caused by long distances, differing holidays, and other factors unique to the international setting. It is also often very important to have a *title passage clause*. The CISG does not address this aspect of international sales. Exporters often prefer to have title transfer outside the United States, so as to avoid adverse U.S. tax consequences.

Parties who enter into commercial contracts often consider including a provision requiring alternative dispute resolution in the event of a problem. Where the contracting parties are from different countries and neither wants to submit to the courts of the other's home country, arbitration clauses are particularly common. To be truly effective, arbitration clauses must be carefully drafted and must provide for a fair and efficient procedure. The clause should identity the arbitrators and the manner in which they are to be selected, the procedural rules that will govern the arbitration, the place of the arbitration, and the language in which it will be conducted.

DISCUSSION CASES

9.1 Advertisements as Offers, Statute of Frauds

Leonard v. PepsiCo., Inc., 88 F. Supp. 2d 116 (S.D. N.Y. 1999), *aff'd per curiam,* 210 F.3d 88 (2d Cir. 2000)

Plaintiff brought this action seeking, among other things, specific performance of an alleged offer of a Harrier Jet, featured in a television advertisement for defendant's "Pepsi Stuff" promotion. Defendant has moved for summary judgment .... [D]efendant's motion is granted.

I. Background

This case arises out of a promotional campaign conducted by defendant, the producer and distributor of the soft drinks Pepsi and Diet Pepsi. The promotion, entitled "Pepsi Stuff," encouraged consumers to collect "Pepsi Points" from specially marked packages of Pepsi or Diet Pepsi and redeem these points for merchandise featuring the Pepsi logo. * * *

A. *The Alleged Offer*

* * * The commercial opens upon an idyllic, suburban morning, where the chirping of birds in sun-dappled trees welcomes a paperboy on his morning route. As the newspaper hits the stoop of a conventional two-story house, the tattoo of a military drum introduces the subtitle, "MONDAY 7:58 AM." The stirring strains of a martial air mark the appearance of a well-coiffed teenager preparing to leave for school, dressed in a shirt emblazoned with the Pepsi logo, a red-white-and-blue ball. While the teenager confidently preens, the military drumroll again sounds as the subtitle "T-SHIRT 75 PEPSI POINTS" scrolls across the screen. Bursting from his room, the teenager strides down the hallway wearing a leather jacket. The drumroll sounds again, as the subtitle "LEATHER JACKET 1450 PEPSI POINTS" appears. The teenager opens the door of his house and, unfazed by the glare of the early morning sunshine, puts on a pair of sunglasses. The drumroll then accompanies the subtitle "SHADES 175 PEPSI POINTS." A voiceover then intones, "Introducing the new Pepsi Stuff catalog," as the camera focuses on the cover of the catalog.

The scene then shifts to three young boys sitting in front of a high school building. The boy in the middle is intent on his Pepsi Stuff Catalog, while the boys on either side are each drinking Pepsi. The three boys gaze in awe at an object rushing overhead, as the military march builds to a crescendo. The Harrier Jet is not yet visible, but the observer senses the presence of a mighty plane as the extreme winds generated by its flight create a paper maelstrom in a classroom devoted to an otherwise dull physics lesson. Finally, the Harrier Jet swings into view and lands by the side of the school building, next to a bicycle rack. Several students run for cover, and the velocity of the wind strips one hapless faculty member down to his underwear. While the faculty member is being deprived of his dignity, the voiceover announces: "Now the more Pepsi you drink, the more great stuff you're gonna get."

The teenager opens the cockpit of the fighter and can be seen, helmetless, holding a Pepsi. Looking very pleased with himself, the teenager exclaims, "Sure beats the bus," and chortles. The military drumroll sounds a final time, as the following words appear: "HARRIER FIGHTER 7,000,000 PEPSI POINTS." A few seconds later, the following appears in more stylized script: "Drink Pepsi—Get Stuff." With that message, the music and the commercial end with a triumphant flourish.

Inspired by this commercial, plaintiff set out to obtain a Harrier Jet. Plaintiff explains that he is "typical of the 'Pepsi Generation' ... he is young, has an adventurous spirit, and the notion of obtaining a Harrier Jet appealed to him enormously." Plaintiff consulted the Pepsi Stuff Catalog. The Catalog features youths dressed in Pepsi Stuff regalia or enjoying Pepsi Stuff accessories, such as "Blue Shades" ("As if you need another reason to look forward to sunny days."), "Pepsi Tees" ("Live in 'em. Laugh in 'em. Get in 'em."), "Bag of Balls" ("Three balls. One bag. No rules."), and "Pepsi Phone Card" ("Call your mom!"). The Catalog specifies the number of Pepsi Points required to obtain promotional merchandise. The Catalog includes an Order Form which lists, on one side, fifty-three items of Pepsi Stuff merchandise redeemable for Pepsi Points .... Conspicuously absent from the Order Form is any entry or description of a Harrier Jet. * * *

The rear foldout pages of the Catalog contain directions for redeeming Pepsi Points for merchandise. These directions note that merchandise may be ordered "only" with the original Order Form. The Catalog notes that in the event that a consumer lacks enough Pepsi Points to obtain a desired item, additional Pepsi Points may be purchased for ten cents each; however, at least fifteen original Pepsi Points must accompany each order.

Although plaintiff initially set out to collect 7,000,000 Pepsi Points by consuming Pepsi products, it soon became clear to him that he "would not be able to buy (let alone drink) enough Pepsi to collect the necessary Pepsi Points fast enough." Reevaluating his strategy, plaintiff "focused for the first time on the packaging materials in the Pepsi Stuff promotion," and realized that buying Pepsi Points would be a more promising option. Through acquaintances, plaintiff ultimately raised about $700,000.

B. *Plaintiff's Efforts to Redeem the Alleged Offer*

On or about March 27, 1996, plaintiff submitted an Order Form, fifteen original Pepsi Points, and a check for $700,008.50. Plaintiff appears to have been represented by counsel at the time he mailed his check; the check is drawn on an account of plaintiff's first set of attorneys. At the bottom of the Order Form, plaintiff wrote in "1 Harrier Jet" in the "Item" column and "7,000,000" in the "Total Points" column. In a letter accompanying his submission, plaintiff stated that the check was to purchase additional Pepsi Points "expressly for obtaining a new Harrier jet as advertised in your Pepsi Stuff commercial."

On or about May 7, 1996, defendant's fulfillment house rejected plaintiff's submission and returned the check, explaining that:

> The item that you have requested is not part of the Pepsi Stuff collection. It is not included in the catalogue or on the order form, and only catalogue merchandise can be redeemed under this program.

> The Harrier jet in the Pepsi commercial is fanciful and is simply included to create a humorous and entertaining ad. We apologize for any misunderstanding or confusion that you may have experienced and are enclosing some free product coupons for your use.

Plaintiff's previous counsel responded on or about May 14, 1996, as follows:

> Your letter of May 7, 1996 is totally unacceptable. We have reviewed the video tape of the Pepsi Stuff commercial ... and it clearly offers the new Harrier jet for 7,000,000 Pepsi Points. Our client followed your rules explicitly ....

This is a formal demand that you honor your commitment and make immediate arrangements to transfer the new Harrier jet to our client. If we do not receive transfer instructions within ten (10) business days of the date of this letter you will leave us no choice but to file an appropriate action against Pepsi.

This letter was apparently sent onward to the advertising company responsible for the actual commercial, BBDO New York ("BBDO"). In a letter dated May 30, 1996, BBDO Vice President Raymond E. McGovern, Jr., explained to plaintiff that:

I find it hard to believe that you are of the opinion that the Pepsi Stuff commercial ("Commercial") really offers a new Harrier Jet. The use of the Jet was clearly a joke that was meant to make the Commercial more humorous and entertaining. In my opinion, no reasonable person would agree with your analysis of the Commercial.

On or about June 17, 1996, plaintiff mailed a similar demand letter to defendant.

* * *

II. Discussion

* * *

B. *Defendant's Advertisement Was Not An Offer*

1. Advertisements as Offers

The general rule is that an advertisement does not constitute an offer. The Restatement (Second) of Contracts explains that:

Advertisements of goods by display, sign, handbill, newspaper, radio or television are not ordinarily intended or understood as offers to sell. The same is true of catalogues, price lists and circulars, even though the terms of suggested bargains may be stated in some detail. It is of course possible to make an offer by an advertisement directed to the general public, but there must ordinarily be some language of commitment or some invitation to take action without further communication.

Restatement (Second) of Contracts § 26 cmt. b (1979). Similarly, a leading treatise notes that:

It is quite possible to make a definite and operative offer to buy or sell goods by advertisement, in a newspaper, by a handbill, a catalog or circular or on a placard in a store window. It is not customary to do this, however; and the presumption is the other way .... Such advertisements are understood to be mere requests to consider and examine and negotiate; and no one can reasonably regard them as otherwise unless the circumstances are exceptional and the words used are very plain and clear.

1 Arthur Linton Corbin & Joseph M. Perillo, *Corbin on Contracts* § 2.4, at 116-17 (rev. ed. 1993). * * *

An advertisement is not transformed into an enforceable offer merely by a potential offeree's expression of willingness to accept the offer through, among other means, completion of an order form. * * * Under these principles, plaintiff's letter of March 27, 1996, with the Order Form and the appropriate number of Pepsi Points, constituted the offer. There would be no enforceable contract until defendant accepted the Order Form and cashed the check.

The exception to the rule that advertisements do not create any power of acceptance in potential offerees is where the advertisement is "clear, definite, and explicit, and leaves nothing open for negotiation," in that circumstance, "it constitutes an offer, acceptance of which will complete the contract." *Lefkowitz v. Great Minneapolis Surplus Store,* 86 N.W.2d 689, 691 (Minn. 1957). In *Lefkowitz,* defendant had published a newspaper announcement stating: "Saturday 9 AM Sharp, 3 Brand New Fur Coats, Worth to $100.00, First Come First Served $1 Each." Mr. Morris Lefkowitz arrived at the store, dollar in hand, but was informed that under defendant's "house rules," the offer was open to ladies, but not gentlemen. The court ruled that because plaintiff had fulfilled all of the terms of the advertisement and the advertisement was specific and left nothing open for negotiation, a contract had been formed.

The present case is distinguishable from *Lefkowitz.* First, the commercial cannot be regarded in itself as sufficiently definite, because it specifically reserved the details of the offer to a separate writing, the Catalog. The commercial itself made no mention of the steps a potential offeree would be required to take to accept the alleged offer of a Harrier Jet. The advertisement in *Lefkowitz,* in contrast, "identified the person who could accept." Second, even if the Catalog had included a Harrier Jet among the items that could be obtained by redemption of Pepsi Points, the advertisement of a Harrier Jet by both television commercial and catalog would still not constitute an offer. [T]he absence of any words of limitation such as "first come, first served," renders the alleged offer sufficiently indefinite that no contract could be formed. "A customer would not usually have reason to believe that the shopkeeper intended exposure to the risk of a multitude of acceptances resulting in a number of contracts exceeding the shopkeeper's inventory." There was no such danger in *Lefkowitz*, owing to the limitation "first come, first served."

The Court finds, in sum, that the Harrier Jet commercial was merely an advertisement. * * *

* * *

C. *An Objective, Reasonable Person Would Not Have Considered the Commercial an Offer*

Plaintiff's understanding of the commercial as an offer must also be rejected because the Court finds that no objective person could reasonably have concluded that the commercial actually offered consumers a Harrier Jet.

1. Objective Reasonable Person Standard

In evaluating the commercial, the Court must not consider defendant's subjective intent in making the commercial, or plaintiff's subjective view of what the commercial offered, but what an objective, reasonable person would have understood the commercial to convey.

If it is clear that an offer was not serious, then no offer has been made:

> What kind of act creates a power of acceptance and is therefore an offer? It must be an expression of will or intention. It must be an act that leads the offeree reasonably to conclude that a power to create a contract is conferred. This applies to the content of the power as well as to the fact of its existence. It is on this ground that we must exclude invitations to deal or acts of mere preliminary negotiation, and acts evidently done in jest or without intent to create legal relations.

Corbin on Contracts, § 1.11 at 30. An obvious joke, of course, would not give rise to a contract. On the other hand, if there is no indication that the offer is "evidently in jest," and that an objective, reasonable person would find that the offer was serious, then there may be a valid offer.

* * *

3. Whether the Commercial Was "Evidently Done In Jest"

Plaintiff's insistence that the commercial appears to be a serious offer requires the Court to explain why the commercial is funny.* * * The commercial is the embodiment of what defendant appropriately characterizes as "zany humor."

First, the commercial suggests, as commercials often do, that use of the advertised product will transform what, for most youth, can be a fairly routine and ordinary experience. * * * The implication of the commercial is that Pepsi Stuff merchandise will inject drama and moment into hitherto unexceptional lives. The commercial in this case thus makes the exaggerated claims similar to those of many television advertisements: that by consuming the featured clothing, car, beer, or potato chips, one will become attractive, stylish, desirable, and admired by all. A reasonable viewer would understand such advertisements as mere puffery, not as statements of fact, and refrain from interpreting the promises of the commercial as being literally true.

Second, the callow youth featured in the commercial is a highly improbable pilot, one who could barely be trusted with the keys to his parents' car, much less the prize aircraft of the United States Marine Corps. Rather than checking the fuel gauges on his aircraft, the teenager spends his precious preflight minutes preening. The youth's concern for his coiffure appears to extend to his flying without a helmet.

Finally, the teenager's comment that flying a Harrier Jet to school "sure beats the bus" evinces an improbably insouciant attitude toward the relative difficulty and danger of piloting a fighter plane in a residential area, as opposed to taking public transportation.

Third, the notion of traveling to school in a Harrier Jet is an exaggerated adolescent fantasy. * * * This fantasy is, of course, extremely unrealistic. No school would provide landing space for a student's fighter jet, or condone the disruption the jet's use would cause.

Fourth, the primary mission of a Harrier Jet, according to the United States Marine Corps, is to "attack and destroy surface targets under day and night vis'-ual conditions." * * * In light of the Harrier Jet's well-documented function in attacking and destroying surface and air targets, armed reconnaissance and air interdiction, and offensive and defensive anti-aircraft warfare, depiction of such a jet as a way to get to school in the morning is clearly not serious even if, as plaintiff contends, the jet is capable of being acquired "in a form that eliminates [its] potential for military use."

Fifth, the number of Pepsi Points the commercial mentions as required to "purchase" the jet is 7,000,000. To amass that number of points, one would have to drink 7,000,000 Pepsis (or roughly 190 Pepsis a day for the next hundred years—an unlikely possibility), or one would have to purchase approximately $700,000 worth of Pepsi Points. The cost of a Harrier Jet is roughly $23 million dollars, a fact of which plaintiff was aware when he set out to gather the amount he believed necessary to accept the alleged offer. Even if an objective, reasonable person were not aware of this fact, he would conclude that purchasing a fighter plane for $700,000 is a deal too good to be true.

Plaintiff argues that a reasonable, objective person would have understood the commercial to make a serious offer of a Harrier Jet because there was "absolutely no distinction in the manner" in which the items in the commercial were presented. Plaintiff also relies upon a press release highlighting the promotional campaign, issued by defendant, in which "no mention is made by [defendant] of humor, or anything of the sort." These arguments suggest merely that the humor of the promotional campaign was tongue in cheek. * * * In light of the obvious absurdity of the commercial, the Court rejects plaintiff's argument that the commercial was not clearly in jest.

* * *

D. *The Alleged Contract Does Not Satisfy the Statute of Frauds*

The absence of any writing setting forth the alleged contract in this case provides an entirely separate reason for granting summary judgment. Under the New York Statute of Frauds,

> a contract for the sale of goods for the price of $500 or more is not enforceable by way of action or defense unless there is some writing sufficient to indicate that a contract for sale has been made between the parties and signed by the party against whom enforcement is sought or by his authorized agent or broker.

N.Y.U.C.C. § 2-201(1). Without such a writing, plaintiff's claim must fail as a matter of law.

There is simply no writing between the parties that evidences any transaction. * * *

* * * Because the alleged contract does not meet the requirements of the Statute of Frauds, plaintiff has no claim for breach of contract or specific performance.

III. Conclusion

In sum, there are three reasons why plaintiff's demand cannot prevail as a matter of law. First, the commercial was merely an advertisement, not a unilateral offer. Second, the tongue-in-cheek attitude of the commercial would not cause a reasonable person to conclude that a soft drink company would be giving away fighter planes as part of a promotion. Third, there is no writing between the parties sufficient to satisfy the Statute of Frauds.

For the reasons stated above, the Court grants defendant's motion for summary judgment. * * *

QUESTIONS FOR DISCUSSION FOR CASE 9.1

1. Under what circumstances do advertisements constitute offers? Why did this advertisement not constitute an offer?

2. The court finds that an "objective, reasonable person" would interpret this advertisement merely as humor and not as a legitimate offer. Do you think that the line between jest and offer may be harder to draw in other advertisements? Can you think of any advertisements you have seen where the distinction was less clear than it was in this case?

3. The court also finds that PepsiCo was entitled to summary judgment under the Statute of Frauds. Why? Under what circumstances would a contract arising from an advertisement satisfy the Statute of Frauds?

9.2 UCC Battle of the Forms

Oakley Fertilizer, Inc. v. Continental Ins. Co., 276 S.W.3d 342 (Mo. App. 2009)

Introduction

Oakley Fertilizer, Inc. ("Seller") appeals from the judgment of the Circuit Court of St. Louis County granting summary judgment in favor of Continental Insurance Company. * * * We reverse and remand.

Background

In mid-2005, Continental issued an insurance policy to Seller. The policy covered shipments of goods made in the course of Seller's business. Specifically, the policy provided:

To cover all shipments for the Assureds [sic] own account or for the account of Owners of the cargo transported by the Assured which the Assured agrees to insure, such agreement to be made prior to any known or reported loss, or prior to or simultaneous with the sailing of the vessel.

The Continental policy also stated that coverage did not extend to shipments insured by other parties and required Seller to notify Continental of each shipment covered by the policy.

In July 2005, Seller entered into negotiations with Ameropa North America ("Buyer") for the sale of approximately 3000 short tons of fertilizer ("the cargo") to be shipped to Buyer in Caruthersville, Missouri from New Orleans on barges operated by a third party carrier ("Carrier"). Subsequently, Seller sent a "sales contract" to Buyer, which Buyer received but did not sign or return. The sales contract memorialized the terms discussed during the parties' negotiations. The contract also included a term providing that the cargo's title and risk of loss would transfer from Seller to Buyer after Seller received "good funds" from Buyer and that "Buyer assumes responsibility of product insurance at [that] point."

In response to Seller's sales contract, Buyer emailed an electronically signed agreement to purchase the cargo ("purchase agreement") to Seller. The purchase agreement did not mention the sales contract and included the term, "$200.00/ ST FOB BARGE EX NEW ORLEANS, LA".

Between August 23 and 24, 2005, the cargo was loaded onto the barges in New Orleans. On August 29, Hurricane Katrina and/or its related storms damaged the barges. Initially, Seller advised Buyer that the cargo was not damaged. Relying on this advice, Buyer tendered full payment to Seller on September 8, 2005. However, when, shortly thereafter, the cargo arrived at its destination, Buyer rejected it due to "crusty wet product." Seller later sold the damaged cargo at salvage value and issued a credit to Buyer for a partial amount of the purchase price and provided substitute fertilizer in lieu of a refund on the remaining purchase price.

After reimbursing Buyer, Seller demanded coverage under the Continental policy for the loss to the cargo. Continental denied coverage on the grounds that the cargo's title and risk of loss transferred from Seller to Buyer at the time the cargo was loaded in New Orleans, prior to the damage, and, therefore, Buyer, not Seller, was responsible for the loss.

Following the denial of coverage, Seller brought suit against Continental alleging breach of its insurance contract. Both parties filed motions for summary judgment. The trial court granted Continental's motion .... Seller appeals.

* * *

Discussion
A. Did the Trial Court Correctly Apply Section 2-207 of the Uniform Commercial Code

In its sole point, Seller contends that the trial court erred in granting summary judgment for Continental because genuine issues of material fact precluded the finding that Buyer, and not Seller, held the risk of loss when the cargo was damaged. Continental maintains that title and risk of loss passed to Buyer at the time the barges were loaded, and, therefore, the insurance policy does not cover the loss at issue. Simply stated, Continental's entitlement to summary judgment turns on whether the trial court correctly applied the Uniform Commercial Code when it held that: (1) there was no agreement between the parties as to transfer of title and risk of loss, and therefore (2) the title and risk of loss transferred from Seller to Buyer when the barges were loaded.

Both parties agree that Seller's sales contract and Buyer's purchase agreement are the only two documents evidencing the terms of Buyer and Seller's agreement. The two contractual documents, however, contain different terms concerning the transfer of title and risk of loss. Seller's sales contract expressly provided that Seller retained title and risk of loss until Seller received payment from Buyer. The "F.O.B. New Orleans" term in Buyer's purchase agreement denoted that risk of loss transferred to Buyer when the cargo was loaded aboard the barges at the place of shipment in New Orleans.[2] The cargo sustained storm damage

---

[2] The designation "F.O.B" means "free on board" and is a term of art defined by the Uniform Commercial Code. In relevant part, the Code provides that "when the term is F.O.B. the place of shipment, the seller must at that place ship the goods in the manner provided in this article ... and bear the expense and risk of putting them into the possession of the carrier[.]" Section 2-319(1)(a). Both Seller and Continental agree that the F.O.B. shipment term used in Buyer's purchase agreement is consistent with the Code's definition to the extent that it would operate to transfer the risk of loss at the time the cargo was loaded onto barges in New Orleans.

after the barges were loaded, but before Seller received payment from Buyer. As such, title and risk of loss transferred to Buyer *after* the loss under the sales contract's term, and *before* the loss under the purchase agreement's term.

To determine which term controlled Buyer and Seller's contract, we apply Section 2-207 of the Uniform Commercial Code, which governs transactions for the sale of goods and "provides the workable rule of law addressing the problem of the discrepancies in the independently drafted documents exchanged between the two parties."

Section 2-207 provides:

(1) A definite and seasonable expression of acceptance or a written confirmation which is sent within a reasonable time operates as an acceptance even though it states terms additional to or different from those offered or agreed upon, unless acceptance is expressly made conditional on assent to the additional or different terms.

(2) The additional terms are to be construed as proposals for addition to the contract. Between merchants such terms become part of the contract unless:

(a) the offer expressly limits acceptance to the terms of the offer;

(b) they materially alter it; or

(c) notification of objection to them has already been given or is given within a reasonable time after notice of them is received.

(3) Conduct by both parties which recognizes the existence of a contract is sufficient to establish a contract for sale although the writings of the parties do not otherwise establish a contract. In such case the terms of the particular contract consist of those terms on which the writings of the parties agree, together with any supplementary terms incorporated under any other provisions of this chapter.

When applying this provision, this Court has noted that Section 2-207 is "one of the most important, subtle and difficult in the entire Code" and that to correctly apply it, "the facts presented must be reconciled, step-by-step, with various provisions of U.C.C. s. 2-207." Accordingly, we assess Seller and Buyer's sales agreement under each subsection of Section 2-207 to determine when the cargo's title and risk of loss transferred from the Seller to the Buyer.

First, we determine whether Buyer and Seller formed a valid contract under Section 2-207(1). Continental impliedly argues, and the trial court apparently agreed, that there was no valid written contract or agreement within the meaning of Section 2-207(1), thus triggering application of Section 2-207(3). We disagree. Applicable case law supports a finding that Seller's sales contract and Buyer's purchase agreement formed a valid sales contract through written offer and acceptance, thus triggering application of Section 2-207(2).

Seller's sales contract constituted an offer. Because the Code does not define the term "offer," the common law definition applies. "An offer is made when the offer leads the offeree to reasonably believe that an offer has been made." Seller's sales contract, which described, among other things, the goods to be shipped, the quantity, the price, and the shipment date, was sufficient to apprise Buyer of Seller's offer to contract.

Buyer's purchase agreement constituted a valid acceptance of Seller's offer. Section 2-207(1) provides that "[a] definite and seasonable expression of acceptance … operates as an acceptance even though it states terms additional to or different from those offered or agreed upon, unless acceptance is expressly made conditional on assent to the additional or different terms." Buyer's unconditional purchase agreement, which agreed to the same essential terms stated in Buyer's sales contract was a "seasonable expression of acceptance" forming a binding contract. The fact that the purchase agreement contained a risk of loss term different from that of the offer does not preclude the purchase agreement from constituting a valid acceptance.

Having identified the sales contract and purchase agreement as the parties' respective offer and acceptance, we proceed to Section 2-207(2). Under Section 2-207(2), additional or different terms in an acceptance "are to be construed as proposals for addition to the contract." U.C.C. § 2-207(2). Between merchants, such additional or different terms become part of a contract unless "(a) the offer expressly limits acceptance to the terms of the offer; (b) they materially alter it; or (c) notification of objection to them has already been given or is given within a reasonable time after notice of this is received." The record reveals that Seller's sales contract did not limit acceptance to its terms and Seller did not object to the different risk of loss term in Buyer's purchase agreement. As such, the risk of loss term in Buyer's purchase agreement became part of the contract unless the term "materially altered" the contract.

Under … Section 2-207(2), an acceptance's different or additional term will "materially alter" the contract when it "result[s] in surprise or hardship if incorporated without express awareness by the other party." The burden of proving that a term is a "material alteration" falls on the party opposing the inclusion of the additional or different term.

Though no Missouri court has expressly addressed the issue, a majority of courts have held that the question of materiality, under Section 2-207(2), is generally a question of fact determined by the expectations of the parties and the particular facts of the case.[7] In holding that materiality is a fact question, these courts have also recognized that the question of materiality is not suitable for summary judgment.

Applying the approach advanced by the majority of courts, we agree that the question of materiality under U.C.C. § 2-207(2) is generally a question of fact and is not appropriate for summary judgment. Thus, at this stage in the litigation, we do not determine whether Buyer's different risk of loss term "materially altered" the parties' contract, and are therefore unable to conclude, as a matter of law, whether Seller held the cargo's title and risk of loss at the time the cargo was damaged. Accordingly, the trial court erred when concluding that "[p]ursuant to applicable U.C.C. Rules and evidence presented, the title and risk of loss transferred at the time of loading [Carrier's] barges and before the loss herein occurred[,]" and summary judgment in favor of Continental cannot be affirmed on this basis.

As noted above, Continental argues for the application of Section 2-207(3), which provides that terms to which the parties do not agree will be supplemented by the default provisions of the Code. Section 2-207(3) reads:

> Conduct by both parties which recognizes the existence of a contract is sufficient to establish a contract for sale *although the writings of the parties do not otherwise establish a contract.* In such case the terms of the particular contract consist of those terms on which the writings of the parties agree, together with any supplementary terms incorporated under any other provisions of this chapter.

U.C.C. § 2-207(3) (emphasis added).

Section 2-207(3) expressly provides that its application is limited to instances where the writings of the parties do not establish a valid contract and the parties nevertheless act as if a contract exists. In such cases, courts will apply Section 2-207(3) to enforce the sales contract and use the supplementary provisions of the Code to supply the terms not agreed upon by the parties. In this case, however, Section 2-207(3) is inapplicable because, as discussed above, Seller's sales contract and Buyer's purchase agreement established a valid written contract under Section 2-207(1). Accordingly, Continental's reliance on—and the trial court's apparent application of—Section 2-207(3) is misplaced and does not support summary judgment in favor of Continental.[8]

* * *

Conclusion

Because summary judgment in favor of Continental cannot be sustained on the grounds articulated by the trial court …, we reverse the trial court's judgment and remand for proceedings consistent with this opinion.

QUESTIONS FOR DISCUSSION FOR CASE 9.2

1. Why was it necessary for the court to apply UCC Section 2-207 here? On what term or terms did the parties' documents disagree?
2. Did the court determine that the parties had a contract? If so, did the court determine what the terms of that contract were?
3. Was UCC Section 2-207(3) relevant to this dispute? Why or why not?
4. Does this decision fully resolve the dispute between the parties? Procedurally, what happens next in this case?

---

[7]Some courts have recognized that certain contract terms—e.g., warranty, arbitration, and indemnity clauses—result in such "surprise or hardship" that they "materially alter" a contract as a matter of law. However, we have found no cases which held that the type of title and risk of loss term in this case materially altered a contract within the meaning of Section 2-207(2) as a matter of law.

[8]We note that Continental, in addition to arguing for the application of Section 2-207(3), also argues at length about the Code's presumption for "F.O.B. shipment" contracts, which, like the terms in the purchase agreement, would shift the risk of loss to Buyer at the time the cargo was loaded upon the barges in New Orleans. Specifically, Continental claims that because the Buyer and Seller's contractual documents do not agree as to when risk of loss transferred, the Code's presumption for "F.O.B. shipment" contracts is applicable. Continental's argument, however, reflects a misunderstanding of the Code's presumption for "F.O.B. shipment" contracts. A contract will be construed as a F.O.B. shipment contract unless the parties "expressly specify" otherwise. In other words, the F.O.B. presumption is only applicable in instances where the terms of the contract fail to expressly address the transfer of risk of loss. Under the instant facts, both Seller's sales contract and Buyer's purchase agreement "expressly specified" when the risk of loss transferred, and consequently, those express terms will not be superseded by the Code's presumption for F.O.B. shipment contracts.

9.3 Promissory Estoppel, Contract Remedies
Tour Costa Rica v. Country Walkers, Inc.,
758 A.2d 795 (Vt. 2000)

Defendants Country Walkers, Inc. (CW) and Robert Maynard (Maynard) appeal from the superior court's denial of their ... motion for judgment as a matter of law, following a jury verdict for plaintiff, Tour Costa Rica (TCR), on its promissory estoppel claim. The jury awarded plaintiff, a company that runs tours in Costa Rica, damages after finding that defendant had breached a promise of a two-year commitment to use TCR to develop, organize and operate Costa Rican walking tours for defendant during that period. We affirm.

* * *

CW is a Vermont business, owned by Maynard and his wife, that sells guided tours at locations around the world. In 1994, Leigh Monahan, owner of TCR, contacted Maynard and offered to design, arrange and lead walking tours in Costa Rica for defendant. During negotiations, Monahan explained to Maynard that she had just incorporated the tour company and, because the company had limited resources, she could not afford to develop specialized tours for defendant unless she had a two-year commitment from CW to run its Costa Rican tours through TCR. In the summer of 1994, the parties entered into a verbal agreement under which plaintiff was to design, arrange and lead customized walking tours in Costa Rica for CW from 1995 through 1997. * * *

In March and April 1995, plaintiff conducted two walking tours for CW.

* * * Between the end of April and June of 1995, the parties discussed the details of, and scheduled the dates for, approximately eighteen walking tours for 1996 and 1997. Due to limited resources, plaintiff could not conduct tours for anyone else while working with defendant and, therefore, stopped advertising and promoting its business, did not pursue other business opportunities and, in fact, turned down other business during this period. In August 1995, a few weeks before the next tour was to occur, defendant informed plaintiff that it would be using another company for all of its future tours in Costa Rica. When challenged by plaintiff with its promised commitment, Maynard responded: "If I did and I certainly may have promised you a two year commitment, I apologize for not honoring it."

Notwithstanding this apology, defendant went on to operate tours in Costa Rica using a rival company. * * * Due to the suddenness of the break with CW, plaintiff was left without tours to run during a prime tourist season, and without sufficient time to market any new tours of its own.

Plaintiff filed suit against defendant, alleging ... promissory estoppel .... * * *

* * *

* * * The case went to the jury, and the jury found for ... plaintiff on the promissory estoppel claim, and awarded expectation damages in the amount of $22,520.00. * * * This appeal followed.

I.

Defendant first argues that plaintiff failed to make out a prima facie case of promissory estoppel. Under the doctrine of promissory estoppel: "A promise which the promisor should reasonably expect to induce action or forbearance on the part of the promisee or a third person and which does induce such action or forbearance is binding if injustice can be avoided only by enforcement of the promise." The action or inaction taken in reliance on the promise must be "of a definite and substantial character." In other words, the promisee must have detrimentally relied on the promise. Defendant does not seriously dispute that there was a promise or that plaintiff did take action based on the promise. Rather, defendant argues that plaintiff's reliance was not reasonable or detrimental, and that this is not a case where injustice can be avoided only by enforcement of the promise. We first address defendant's argument that plaintiff's reliance was not reasonable.

A.

In determining whether a plaintiff reasonably relied on a defendant's promise, courts examine the totality of the circumstances. Here, plaintiff presented evidence that it relied on defendant's promise of a two-year exclusive commitment by (a) ceasing to advertise and promote the business, failing to pursue other business opportunities, and turning down other business; (b) making hotel and restaurant reservations and arranging for transportation for the tours it was to operate for CW; and (c) making purchases related to the tours it was to operate for CW. Plaintiff suggests that this reliance was reasonable because, in negotiations with Maynard, plaintiff made clear that it required a two-year commitment due to its limited resources, the time it would have to devote to develop specialized tours for CW, and the ongoing communication between the parties as to future dates and requirements for tours.

Defendant argues that plaintiff's reliance was not reasonable based solely on standard industry practice that permits the cancellation of tours upon thirty to sixty days' notice.

While there was no dispute that tours could be canceled with appropriate notice, there was evidence that this industry practice did not apply to the parties' two-year commitment. Monahan testified that she and Maynard specifically agreed to the two-year time frame because she wanted a measure of security for her fledgling company. She further testified that it was her understanding, from negotiations with Maynard, that the two-year commitment was unaffected by the possibility that some scheduled tours might be canceled if, for example, too few people signed.

* * *

[W]e find that plaintiff presented sufficient evidence to enable the jury to conclude that plaintiff's reliance on defendant's promise was reasonable.

B.

Defendant next argues that plaintiff's reliance on defendant's promise was not detrimental. Defendant suggests that the only evidence of detriment offered by plaintiff was Monahan's testimony concerning expenses for a few minor equipment purchases. Plaintiff disagrees.

Plaintiff maintains that its reliance was detrimental because (1) it lost business due to the fact that (a) it stopped advertising and promoting the business, did not pursue other business opportunities, and turned down other business in reliance on the parties' agreement, and (b) after defendant breached the agreement, plaintiff had no money to advertise or conduct other tours; (2) it spent money in preparation for the tours it was to operate for defendant; and (3) its reputation in the industry suffered because it had to cancel two-years' worth of reservations it had made on behalf of defendant.

Defendant does not dispute that plaintiff stopped advertising and promoting the business, did not pursue other business opportunities and turned down other business, or that plaintiff's reputation was harmed.

Instead, defendant contends that (1) plaintiff would have had to arrange for transportation and make reservations at hotels and restaurants for any tours it arranged for CW, whether or not the tours were part of an exclusive two-year arrangement, and (2) the money plaintiff spent in preparation for the tours is not, in and of itself, sufficient to show detrimental reliance.

Defendant's first argument is flawed because, as noted above, Monahan testified that she told Maynard that plaintiff could not afford to arrange tours for CW without an exclusive two-year agreement. There was no evidence that plaintiff would have prepared tours for CW if the parties did not have an exclusive two-year agreement. Defendant's second argument is flawed because it overlooks the facts that plaintiff stopped advertising and promoting the business, did not pursue other business opportunities, and in fact turned down other business. In reliance on a two-year commitment, plaintiff stopped soliciting business from other sources and declined other bookings, a substantial change in position for a fledgling tour business. Further, plaintiff's reputation in Costa Rica's tourism industry was damaged.

The evidence shows that, as a result of defendant's breach of the parties' agreement, plaintiff suffered significant harm for each of the above-mentioned reasons. Accordingly, the jury could reasonably conclude that plaintiff's reliance on defendant's promise was detrimental.

C.

Whether injustice can be avoided only by enforcement of the promise is a question of law informed by several factors, including:

(a) the availability and adequacy of other remedies, particularly cancellation and restitution;

(b) the definite and substantial character of the action or forbearance in relation to the remedy sought;

(c) the extent to which the action or forbearance corroborates evidence of the making and terms of the promise, or the making and terms are otherwise established by clear and convincing evidence;

(d) the reasonableness of the action or forbearance; [and]

(e) the extent to which the action or forbearance was foreseeable by the promisor.

Restatement (Second) of Contracts § 139(2) (1981).

* * * Damages available in a promissory estoppel action depend upon the circumstances of the case. * * *

Expectation damages, which the jury awarded in this case, provide the plaintiff with an amount equal to the benefit of the parties' bargain.

One potential component of expectation damages is loss of future profits.

The purpose of expectation damages is to "put the nonbreaching party in the same position it would have been [in] had the contract been fully performed." Restitution damages seek to compensate the plaintiff for any benefit it conferred upon the defendant as a result of the parties' contract. The purpose of restitution damages is to return the plaintiff to the position it held before the parties' contract. Reliance damages give the plaintiff any reasonably foreseeable costs incurred in reliance on the contract. As with restitution, the purpose of reliance damages is to return the plaintiff to the position it was in prior to the parties' contract. Restitution damages are inapplicable in the instant case because there is no evidence that plaintiff conferred any benefit on defendant as a result of defendant's promise. Further, cancellation is inapplicable, as defendant had already breached its promise, and cancellation would provide no remedy for plaintiff. Reliance damages are also inappropriate because the majority of the harm plaintiff suffered was not expenditures it made in reliance on defendant's promise, but rather, lost profits from the tours it had scheduled with defendant, lost potential profits because it failed to pursue other business opportunities, and harm to its reputation.

Therefore, an award of expectation damages is the only remedy that adequately compensates plaintiff for the harm it suffered.

As to the other factors considered, plaintiff's actions and inactions were of a definite and substantial character. * * * As previously discussed, plaintiff's reliance on defendant's promise was reasonable, and plaintiff's actions and inactions were foreseeable by defendant. Defendant expected plaintiff to take specific actions on defendant's behalf and to design and conduct tours to defendant's specifications. Further, defendant was aware that plaintiff was a new company without a lot of capital, and that it was spending much of that capital preparing tours for defendant.

Taking the above factors into consideration, there was sufficient evidence to allow the jury to conclude that, in this case, injustice could be avoided only by enforcement of the promise through an award of monetary damages.

* * *

The jury's damage award was not clearly erroneous. Affirmed.

QUESTIONS FOR DISCUSSION FOR CASE 9.3

1. Why is this a promissory estoppel case and not a breach of contract case?
2. What are the elements of promissory estoppel? Which of those elements are at issue in this case?

9.4 Convention on the Sale of Goods

Zhejiang Shaoxing Yongli Printing & Dyeing Co., Ltd. v. Microflock Textile Group Corp., 66 U.C.C. Rep. Serv. 2d (Callaghan) 716 (S.D. Fla. May 19, 2008)

THIS MATTER came before the Court on the Plaintiffs' Motion for Summary Judgment …. As more fully explained below, the plaintiff is entitled to judgment as a matter of law.

Procedural Background

The plaintiff filed an action against the defendant for breach of contract for failing to make full payment for goods delivered and accepted. The plaintiff and the defendant had an on-going business relationship between 2002 and 2004, whereby, pursuant to purchase orders placed by the defendant, the plaintiff sold and shipped various polyester dyed fabric ("Goods") from China to the defendant in the United States.

The action involves eight (8) separate orders and shipments of the Goods, which had an agreed total contract price in the amount of $316,797.78. Between August 27, 2002, and March 5, 2004, the defendant made eight (8) partial payments that totaled $204,954.24. The balance remaining is $111,843.54. The plaintiff claims that it is entitled to statutory interest at the rate of six percent (6%) per year from the due date of each unpaid invoice.

* * *

Analysis

* * *

II. The United Nations Convention on Contracts for the International Sale of Goods (1980) ("CISG") Governs

The parties in this action are from the United States of America and the People's Republic of China. Both countries are signatories to the United Nations Convention on Contracts for the International Sale of Goods (1980) ("CISG"). The CISG "applies to contracts of sale of goods between parties whose places of business are in different States when the States are Contracting States." CISG, Art. 1(a). The CISG governs "the formation of the contract of sale and the rights and obligations of the seller and the buyer arising from such a contract." CISG, Art. 4. The CISG automatically applies to international sales contracts between parties from different contracting states unless the parties agree to exclude the application of the CISG, as stated in Article 6 of the CISG. Because the parties did not agree to exclude the application of the CISG, the CISG provides the substantive law governing this contractual dispute. Domestic law, including the Uniform Commercial Code as incorporated in Fla. Stat. §§ 670.101 − 680.532, does not govern the parties' contractual relationship.

Article 12 of the CISG gives Contracting States the right to require that the parties' intention to be bound by an agreement be evidenced exclusively in writing, when a Contracting State makes an Article 96 declaration:

> Any provision ... of part II of this convention that allows a contract of sale or modification or termination by agreement or any offer, acceptance or other indication of intention to be made in any form other than in writing does not apply where any party has his place of business in a Contract State which has made a declaration under Article 96 of this Convention. The parties may not derogate from or vary the effect of this article.

CISG, Art. 12. China has made such a declaration under Article 96. The plaintiff's principal place of business is in the People's Republic of China. The Chinese Declaration requires all agreements to be in writing to be enforceable.

Under the CISG, a "contract is concluded at the moment when an acceptance of an offer becomes effective." CISG, Art. 23. The defendant provided via facsimile or e-mail written orders for various goods from the plaintiff. The purchase orders constitute offers under the CISG. The plaintiff filled the orders presented by the [defendant], shipped the orders, and submitted written invoices and packing lists to the defendant. The invoices and packing lists constitute acceptance under the CISG. The eight contracts between the plaintiff and the defendant satisfy the CISG requirements for an enforceable contract under the CISG.

III. There Is No Genuine Issue of Material Fact.
A. There Are No Written Documents to Show that the Plaintiff Agreed to Modify or Waive the Defendant's Obligation to Pay the Full Amount of the Eight Invoices.

* * *

It is undisputed that at no time after delivery of the Goods did the plaintiff, in writing, change, modify, waive, or in any way agree in writing to modify the defendant's obligation to pay the outstanding balance of $111,843.54 owed pursuant to the eight invoices. There is no evidence in the record to reflect a written modification of the parties' eight contracts to permit less than full payment. Any negotiations, if they occurred or to what extent they occurred, between the parties for modified payments on the eight invoices were not made in writing, are not evidenced by a writing, and do not satisfy the requirements of the Chinese Declaration under Article 96 of the CISG. Without any evidence of a written modification, the CISG requires this Court to enforce the invoices as stated. The balance owed on the subject invoices totals $111,843.54. There being no genuine issue as to any material fact, the plaintiff is entitled to judgment as a matter of law in its favor against the defendant in the amount of $111,843.54.

* * *

C. The Plaintiff Is Not Entitled to Pre-judgment Interest.
The plaintiff also seeks pre-judgment interest under Florida law. The CISG is silent on the issue of interest. Because substantive domestic law does not apply, the

plaintiff is not entitled to any interest. The plaintiff is not entitled to pre-judgment interest.

Accordingly, it is

ORDERED AND ADJUDGED that the Plaintiffs' Motion for Summary Judgment is GRANTED. A judgment in the amount of $111,843.54 will be entered in favor of the plaintiff and against the defendant.

QUESTIONS FOR DISCUSSION FOR CASE 9.4

1. Why does the CISG, and not the UCC, govern this contract?
2. Why does the court find that the parties' agreement must be in writing?
3. What constituted the offer in this contract? What constituted the acceptance?

DISCUSSION QUESTIONS

1. From 1988 to 1992, Dennis McInerney served as a sales representative for Charter Golf, Inc., a company that manufactures and sells golf apparel and supplies. McInerney's sales territory originally covered Illinois but was later expanded to include Indiana and Wisconsin. In 1989, Hickey-Freeman, which manufactures a competing line of golf apparel, offered McInerney a position as an exclusive sales representative that included an 8 percent commission. McInerney contacted Jerry Montiel, Charter Golf's president, to notify him of his intention to accept Hickey-Freeman's offer. Montiel wanted McInerney to continue to work for Charter Golf and offered McInerney a 10 percent commission on sales in Illinois and Wisconsin "for the remainder of his life" in a position where he could be discharged only for dishonesty or disability. McInerney then refused the Hickey-Freeman offer and continued working for Charter Golf. The working relationship between McInerney and Charter Golf deteriorated, and Charter Golf fired McInerney. McInerney sued for breach of contract. In response, Charter Golf argued that: (1) McInerney's promise to forgo the Hickey-Freeman job was not sufficient consideration to turn an existing employment-at-will contract into a contract for lifetime employment; and that, (2) if there was a contract, the Statute of Frauds requires that a lifetime employment contract be in writing. How should the court rule on these two claims, and why?

2. In August 1995, Carl Merritt contacted RxP Prods., Inc. ("RxP") about selling "RxP Gas Kicker," a fuel additive, as a private-label product. The parties entered into an agreement, which stated, in its entirety:

> This agreement is made on this 28th day of September, 1995, between RxP Products, Inc., hereafter referred to as RxP, and Merritt-Campbell, Incorporated, hereinafter referred to as Merritt-Campbell.

In consideration of the sum of ten dollars ($10.00), the receipt of which is acknowledged, RxP agrees to sell to Merritt-Campbell the product marketed as "RxP Gas Kicker" under the following terms:

1. RxP guarantees the following price to Merritt-Campbell for a period of five (5) years from the date of first order.
   a. RxP Gas Kicker bottled in 2.5 ounce quantities—$1.25 per bottle (excluding labels).
   b. RxP Gas Kicker in 55 gallon drum quantity—$1,280,00 (sic) per drum.
   Said pricing may be increased only in the case of documented price increases to RxP for raw materials.
2. RxP will bottle RxP Gas Kicker in either green or black bottles, as provided as samples, upon request for Merritt-Campbell.
3. RxP guarantees shipment within fourteen (14) days from receipt of order from Merritt-Campbell.
4. Both RxP and Merritt-Campbell agree unconditionally to maintain confidentiality regarding the relationship between the two companies. This confidentiality includes, but is not limited to, any disclosure of the source product market by RxP and Merritt-Campbell. The scope of this confidentiality includes, but is not limited to, any director, officer, employee, or agent of both RxP and Merritt-Campbell.
5. It is understood by RxP that it is the intention of Merritt-Campbell to market the product heretofore referred to as "RxP Gas Kicker" under a private label.

A dispute arose between the two parties. Merritt-Campbell filed suit against RxP alleging that RxP had breached a requirements contract entered into by the parties. Merritt-Campbell sought specific performance as a remedy. RxP responded that the contract did not satisfy the UCC Statute of Frauds because it failed to state a quantity term. Who is correct?

3. Gary Trimble placed a written order for advertising for his business in Ameritech's 1994–95 PAGES-PLUS Directory. Ameritech failed to publish Trimble's advertisement. The contract that Trimble had signed provided:

> if publisher should be found liable for loss or damage due to a failure on the part of the publisher or its directory, in any respect, regardless of whether customer's claim is based on contract, tort, strict liability, or otherwise, the liability shall be limited to an amount equal to the contract price for the disputed advertisement, or that sum of money actually paid by the customer toward the disputed advertisements, whichever sum shall be less, as liquidated damages and not as a penalty, and this liability shall be exclusive. In no event shall publisher be liable for any loss of customer's business, revenues, profits, the cost to the customer of other advertisements or any other special, incidental, consequential or punitive damages of any nature, or for any claim against the customer by a third party.

Trimble was not charged for the advertisement. He filed suit for damages arising from loss of business. The trial court granted Ameritech's request for summary judgment and Trimble appealed. Is the clause in the parties' contract limiting Ameritech's liability valid and enforceable?

4. Kathleen F. Liarikos purchased a 1984 Jaguar XJS from Pine Grove Auto Sales in 1988. She asserted that Pine Grove made various representations about the car's low mileage. In 1990, after the car had had a variety of mechanical problems, Liarikos discovered that the Jaguar's odometer had been turned back. She then sent a letter to Pine Grove that she asserted was a revocation of her acceptance of the Jaguar. Liarikos received no response from Pine Grove. Liarikos continued to use the vehicle as she needed a car in order to conduct her business. Did Liarikos negate her revocation of acceptance by continuing to use the Jaguar?

5. Bertha Jamison contracted to purchase a set of encyclopedias from Encyclopedia Britannica for $1,652.08. She made a $100 down payment and signed a document entitled "Britannica Revolving Credit Agreement—Retail Installment Contract," in which she agreed to pay $57 per month until the purchase price was fully paid. The contract specified Jamison's street address as the location to which the encyclopedias were to be shipped. Soon thereafter, Encyclopedia Britannica assigned the contract to Merchants Acceptance, Inc.

Jamison never received the encyclopedias. A United Parcel Service (UPS) tracking slip revealed the encyclopedias were shipped to Jamison's post office box, not to her street address. Jamison refused to make any of the payments on her account. Merchants sued for payment of the outstanding balance. How should the court rule, and why?

6. Sunset Trails, Inc., provides private recreational facilities, entertainment, and catering for large corporate groups, conventions, and other private parties. On March 25, 1996, Nortex Drug Distributors, Inc., signed a contract reserving Sunset Trails' facilities and catering for a company picnic on July 7, 1996. The contract provided for a minimum of 400 persons at $17.50 per person, for a total of $7,000. The contract contained the following cancellation damages provision:

> Due to the exclusive nature of the CIRCLE R RANCH for group bookings only, the Client will be responsible for payment of the full contract … in the event that this function is cancelled.

On July 2, 1996, five days before the scheduled event, Nortex informed Sunset Trails that it was canceling the picnic. Because of the late notice, Sunset Trails was unable to rebook the facilities for July 7. Sunset Trails sent Nortex a bill for $7,000. Nortex refused to pay the bill and contended that the cancellation provision in the contract was an unlawful penalty provision. Sunset Trails argued that the provision was a valid liquidated damages provision. How should the court rule, and why?

7. On August 21, 1992, Miguel A. Diaz Rodriguez ("Diaz") contracted with Learjet, Inc., to purchase a model 60 aircraft. The contract called for a $250,000 deposit to be made upon execution of the contract; $750,000 to be paid on September 18; $1 million to be paid 180 days before the delivery date of July 30, 1993; and the balance to be paid on delivery. Learjet anticipated making a profit of $1.8 million on the sale to Diaz.

Diaz paid the $250,000 deposit on August 21, but made no further payments. At the end of September 1992, Diaz called Learjet, indicated he did not want the aircraft, and requested a return of his deposit. Learjet indicated that it would not return the deposit but, rather, would retain it as liquidated damages in accordance with the express terms of the contract, which provided for the retention of such payments in the event of breach.

Learjet then contracted with Circus Circus Enterprise, Inc., for sale of the aircraft. Learjet realized a $1,887,464 profit on the sale of the aircraft to Circus Circus, which was larger than the profit it would have made on the sale to Diaz. Diaz filed suit for return of the $250,000 deposit, alleging that the retention of the deposit was an unreasonable and unenforceable penalty. At the time that Diaz breached the contract, Learjet was operating at 60 percent capacity. Learjet would have been able to accelerate its production schedule to produce more model 60 planes during any given year. How should the court rule?

8. Frigidaire, which manufactures freezers, contacted McGill Manufacturing Co. about purchasing an electrical switch that McGill had advertised as "water resistant." McGill sent Frigidaire some samples of the switches and a price quotation that contained the conditions of sale on its reverse side. Among those conditions was a statement that limited McGill's warranty obligations to either repayment of the purchase price or replacement of the returned parts. The samples were not completely water resistant, so the parties agreed upon a slight redesign of the switches, with a corresponding increase in price.

Frigidaire then sent McGill a blanket purchase order for the redesigned switches. The purchase order set forth Frigidaire's terms and conditions of purchase, which included express warranties of merchantability and fitness for a particular purpose. The purchase order also stated:

> This Purchase Order is to be accepted in writing by Seller by signing and returning promptly to Buyer the Acknowledgment Copy, but if for any reason Seller should fail to sign and return to Buyer the Acknowledgment Copy, the commencement of any work or performance of any services hereunder by Seller shall constitute acceptance by Seller of this Purchase Order and all its terms and conditions.

> Acceptance of this Purchase Order is hereby expressly limited to the terms hereof. Any terms proposed by Seller which add to, vary from, or conflict with the terms herein shall be void and the terms hereof shall govern. If this Purchase Order has been issued by Buyer in response to an offer the terms of which are additional to or different from any of the provisions hereof, then the issuance of this Purchase Order by Buyer shall constitute an acceptance of such offer subject to the express condition that the Seller assent that this Purchase Order constitutes the entire agreement between Buyer and Seller with respect to the subject matter hereof and the subject matter of such offer.

The purchase order stated the original price of the switches, not the increased price that reflected the agreed-upon redesign.

The next day, McGill sent a computer-generated acknowledgment form, which set forth terms similar to the terms on the original price quotation but which included additional limitations and exclusions of warranties. Ten days later, McGill's sales representative changed the incorrect price on the purchase order form, signed it, and returned it to Frigidaire.

Frigidaire produced several thousand freezers containing McGill's switches. The switches began to fail within a matter of months. Frigidaire filed suit, alleging breach of contract and breach of express and implied warranties and seeking in excess of $1.5 million in damages. Frigidaire argues that the terms found in its blanket purchase order should control; McGill argues that the terms found in its acknowledgment form should control. Which party is correct, and why?

9. On April 14, 1993, Saint Switch, Inc., offered to sell fuel pumps to Norca Corp., stating that its offer was firm until July 31, 1994. On August 18, 1993, Saint Switch forwarded to Norca a new offer stating different price terms for the fuel pumps. On November 4, 1993, Norca attempted to accept the original offer made on April 14, 1993. Is Norca permitted to accept that original offer? Why or why not?

10. Carol Poole began working as a travel agent for Incentives Unlimited in April 1992. Four years later, Incentives asked Poole to sign an "Employment Agreement" that contained a covenant not to compete. The covenant prohibited Poole from competing directly with Incentives within a four-county

area for one year after ceasing her employment with Incentives. Poole signed the Agreement.

Poole soon left Incentives and began working at a competing travel agency. Incentives sued to enforce the covenant not to compete. The trial court awarded summary judgment to Poole. Incentives appealed. Is the covenant not to compete enforceable? Why or why not?

11. In March 1998, McDonald's Corp. began the "1998 McDonald's Monopoly Game" to promote sales of its food items. Customers could win by collecting the entire series of official "Collect to Win" stamps or by obtaining an "Instant Win" stamp. The official rules of the promotion game were posted at all participating McDonald's locations. The official rules stated in part:

> All game materials are subject to verification at a participating McDonald's or the Redemption Center, whichever is applicable. Game materials are null and void and will be rejected if not obtained through authorized, legitimate channels, or if they are mutilated or tampered with in any way (except for the signed initials of the potential winner), or if they contain printing, typographical, mechanical, or other errors. All decisions of McDonald's and the Redemption Center are final, binding and conclusive in all matters.

The official rules also stated: "You are not a winner of any prize until your official game stamp(s) has been verified at the Redemption Center or a participating McDonald's, whichever is applicable."

On April 2, Vernicesa Barnes ordered hash browns at a McDonald's restaurant. The container had a game piece attached that stated: "$200,000 Dream Home Cash—Stamp 818—Need Stamps 818, 819, & 820 to Win—Instant Winner!" Interpreting this to mean that she had an "Instant Win" Stamp, Barnes filled out the forms to begin the redemption process and mailed the stamp and signed forms to McDonald's Redemption Center.

On May 1, Barnes received a letter from the Redemption Center notifying her that the game stamp was a miscut "Collect to Win" stamp and would not be honored. Barnes filed suit, alleging breach of contract. How should the court rule on her claim?

12. Jordan Systems, Inc., a construction subcontractor, contracted to purchase custom-made windows from Windows, Inc., a fabricator and seller of windows located in South Dakota. The purchase contract provided: "All windows to be shipped properly crated/packaged/boxed suitable for cross country motor freight transit and delivered to New York City."

Windows, Inc., constructed the windows and arranged to have them shipped to Jordan by a common carrier, Consolidated Freightways Corp. During the course of shipment, however, approximately two-thirds of the windows were damaged as a result of "load shift." The damage resulted from the windows being improperly loaded on the truck by Consolidated's employees.

Jordan sued Windows to recover incidental and consequential damages based on Windows' alleged breach of contract. How should the court rule on this claim?

13. Tacoma Fixture Company, Inc. (TFC), a cabinet manufacturer, regularly ordered paint and varnish products from Rudd over a period of several years. In a typical transaction, TFC would place its order with Rudd by telephone or fax, and Rudd would arrange shipment of the products. Neither party would issue a written confirmation order, but Rudd would mail an invoice to TFC after the goods were shipped and delivered. These invoices included several terms that TFC did not specifically agree to, such as a warranty disclaimer, a remedy limitation, a forum selection clause, and an attorney fee clause.

TFC experienced several problems with Rudd's products, which caused the cabinet finishes to crack and discolor. TCF sued for breach of express and implied warranties, but Rudd argued that the warranty disclaimers and remedy limitations contained on its invoices shielded it from liability. How should the court rule on TCF's claims?

14. Reynold Williams Jr., purchased a 2004 GMC Yukon SLT from Spitzer Autoworld Canton, L.L.C. According to the written purchase agreement, Williams was to receive a trade-in allowance of $15,500 for his 2003 Ford Explorer. The purchase agreement also had a statement indicating that this was the entire agreement between the parties. Williams subsequently sued Spitzer, stating he and Spitzer had reached a prior oral agreement that he would receive a trade-in allowance of $16,500 and that this agreement should have been incorporated in the purchase agreement. Williams stated that he had failed to notice the difference when signing the contract because he was focused on the monthly payment amount. He stated that the error only became apparent to

him when he found out that his financing had been declined and that he owed an additional $2,000 to pay off the loan secured by the Explorer. How should the court rule on Williams' claim, and why?

15. In October, 2003, Mountain Camo, Inc. entered into a contract with Wendall and Janet Mills in which Mountain Camo sold the Mills a number of items of "close-out inventory." According to the contract, payment for the goods was due on March 30, 2005. The Mills picked up the inventory personally in November, 2004, but put the goods straight into warehouse storage without inspecting them. The Mills made no payments on the goods and eventually returned them to Mountain Camo in May or early June, 2005. Mountain Camo sold the goods to another buyer for $45,000, and sued the Mills for $94,771.54, which is the difference between the $139,771.54 value of the goods and the $45,000 Montana Camo received for sale of the goods to a third party. The Mills argue that they were not in breach of contract because they had rejected the goods because of defects and odd sizing that would render the goods difficult to sell, and thus had returned them to Mountain Camo. How should the court rule, and why?

CHAPTER **10**

Warranties and Products Liability

This chapter addresses (1) warranties and (2) products liability law. The first topic arises under contract law (which is the topic of Chapter 9), the second under tort law. We are concerned here with the civil liability that manufacturers and sellers of goods incur to buyers, users, and bystanders for damages or injury caused by defective goods. This is an area in which proactive management, such as careful planning during the design, manufacturing, and labeling processes, can substantially reduce, though not eliminate, the likelihood of litigation and the potential liability that a company might face. Liability for product defects can extend beyond manufacturers to a number of additional parties in the supply chain (including retailers, wholesalers, and suppliers of raw materials and component parts), so marketers of goods, as well as manufacturers, need to be aware of the law regarding products liability and warranties.

Overview

Originally, the law provided little protection for purchasers when goods turned out to be defective in some manner. In the nineteenth century, product sales were governed by the notion of *caveat emptor* ("let the buyer beware"). Sellers and manufacturers were not held liable for product defects unless they had behaved wrongfully toward or had breached a specific promise made to the buyer with whom the manufacturer had contracted to sell goods. This state of affairs evolved for a number of reasons, including the general notions of laissez-faire and economic individualism that prevailed at that time. Because buyers and sellers typically were of relatively equal size and bargaining ability, courts believed that the parties should be permitted to negotiate the transaction themselves, without interference from the law. The buyer often purchased directly from the manufacturer, and the long lines of distribution that we see today did not exist. Goods were typically uncomplicated, and purchasers could more easily examine them for defects prior to purchase. Finally, the courts wanted to promote the industrialization process by protecting infant industries from lawsuits.

By the twentieth century, however, commerce had changed dramatically. Lines of distribution had become long, and buyers seldom dealt directly with manufacturers. Large corporations evolved, which meant that sellers often had far more bargaining power than buyers. The increased complexity of the goods being sold made it more difficult for consumers to identify defects in products they were about to purchase, and the growth in consumer goods was accompanied by a growth in consumer injuries. Ultimately, as a matter of public policy, the courts determined that sellers and manufacturers could best bear the costs of product defects because they could spread those costs throughout society by increasing prices if necessary. There was a rapid growth in products liability law in the 1960s and the 1970s, and some commentators now argue that the governing rule is *caveat venditor* ("let the seller beware").

Today, the law seeks to protect consumers and purchasers, who are typically the weaker parties in the sales relationship. This goal is accomplished through *warranties*, which are contractual obligations created and enforced under the Uniform Commercial Code (UCC), and through *products liability law*, which imposes tort liability upon manufacturers and sellers of defective products for the injuries caused by their products. Warranties and products liability law protect not only buyers who are individual consumers but also buyers who are businesses. Thus, companies involved in business-to-business sales must be aware of these legal rules as well as those involved in consumer sales.

This chapter first examines the contractual obligations of warranty law, then turns to the tort liabilities created by products liability law.

Warranties

A *warranty* is a contractual promise by a seller or lessor that the goods that he sells or leases conform to certain standards, qualities, or characteristics. Warranties are primarily governed by state law—in particular, by the UCC. Warranties are made to purchasers and users of the product and possibly to third parties injured in their person or property by the goods. The UCC applies to the sale of goods, but does not extend to the sale of services, real estate transactions, or bailments.

Sellers of goods are generally not required to warrant their goods and may disclaim or modify warranties provided they undertake the necessary steps in doing so. Article 2 of the UCC recognizes four types of warranties: (1) warranties of title; (2) express warranties; (3) implied warranties of merchantability; and (4) implied warranties of fitness for a particular purpose. The last three are known as warranties of quality. All of these warranties (or any combination thereof) may arise in a single sale. Under the UCC, all warranties are to be construed as cumulative and consistent to the extent possible.

Warranty of Title

Under UCC Section 2-312, the seller of goods automatically warrants that: (1) the title conveyed is good; (2) the seller has the right to convey the title; and (3) the goods are free from any security interest or other lien upon them of which the buyer was not aware at the time of the sale. This warranty arises automatically in most sales; no special action by the seller or buyer is required to create it (see Case Illustration 10.1). If the seller is a *merchant*,[1] the seller also automatically warrants that the goods are free from any rightful claims of patent, trademark, or similar infringement by any third party. If the buyer provided the specifications to the seller for the goods, however, the buyer must hold the seller harmless for any infringement claims arising out of the seller's compliance with those specifications.

---

[1]Recall from Chapter 9 that a "merchant" is defined under UCC Section 2-104 as "a person who deals in goods of the kind or otherwise by his occupation holds himself out as having knowledge or skill peculiar to the practices or goods involved in the transaction or to whom such knowledge or skill may be attributed by his employment of an agent or broker or other intermediary who by his occupation holds himself out as having such knowledge or skill."

CASE ILLUSTRATION 10.1

CURRAN v. CIARAMELLI, REPORTED IN *NEW YORK LAW JOURNAL,* NOV 10, 1998, P. 25.

FACTS In March 1998, Plaintiff purchased a Corvette from Defendant for the sum of $8,500 in cash. In April, 1998, after consulting with the local police department, he discovered that the car's vehicle identification number had been altered and that the vehicle had been reported stolen in March, 1992. The car was seized by the police and Plaintiff brought suit against Defendant for breach of the warranty of title.

Defendant testified that she did not know of the alleged theft at the time she sold the car to Plaintiff. She had purchased the car from Vincent Garofala in July, 1997, who in turn had purchased the car from Bright Bay Lincoln Mercury in June, 1994. Garofala had a copy of a Retail Certificate of Sale and a copy of a New York title issued to Gail M. DiFede by the New York Department of Motor Vehicles, which was apparently Bright Bay's source of title to the car. Defendant argued she was not liable for breach of warranty of title because she had received good title from Garofala, who had received good title from Bright Bay, who had received good title from DiFede.

DECISION The court rejected Defendant's argument, stating:

> [A] thief cannot pass title to stolen goods and mere delivery of the goods does not relieve the seller of the obligation of warranty of title. By transferring a stolen vehicle to the Plaintiff, irrespective of whether or not she had knowledge of the theft, the Defendant breached the warranty of title codified in section 2-312(1)(a) of the Uniform Commercial Code. One who sells a stolen automobile is liable to the buyer thereof for breach of warranty of title.

The court thus awarded the Plaintiff the purchase price of $8,500 plus $709.68 he had spent on repairs on the car.

Express Warranties

If the seller expressly represents that her goods have certain qualities and the goods do not have those qualities, the buyer may sue for breach of *express warranty*. This is true even if the seller believed that the representation was true and had no way of knowing that it was not true and even if the seller had no intention of creating an express warranty. Express warranties may be written or oral and may be formed by the conduct of the seller as well as by words.

UCC Section 2-313 states two requirements for creating an express warranty. First, the seller must: (1) make an affirmation of fact or promise regarding the goods; or (2) provide a description of the goods; or (3) furnish a sample or model of the goods. Second, that statement or promise, description, or sample or model must be "part of the basis of the bargain" that the buyer made. All statements by a seller are considered to be part of the basis of the bargain unless the seller can demonstrate that the buyer did not rely upon them (see Case Illustration 10.2).

Only statements of fact create an express warranty; statements of opinion do not. Sellers are permitted to "puff their wares." Thus, the statement "this computer is capable of running any software program in the marketplace" creates an express warranty, but the statement "this is an excellent computer" does not. It is often hard to tell whether a particular statement is one of fact or opinion, e.g., "this computer is well designed." In such instances, the courts often consider the relative knowledge of the parties involved. If the buyer is not knowledgeable about the seller's goods, the courts are more likely to treat the statement as one of fact that creates an express warranty. If the buyer knows as much or almost as much about the goods as the seller, the courts are more likely to treat the statement as one of opinion that does not create an express warranty.

See Discussion Case 10.1.

CASE ILLUSTRATION 10.2

KOLARIK v. CORY INT'L CORP., 721 N.W.2D 159 (IOWA 2006)

FACTS Plaintiff fractured a tooth while biting down on an olive from a jar of pimento-stuffed green olives that had been imported and sold at wholesale by Defendant.

Plaintiff sued, arguing that the words "minced pimento stuffed" on the label of the jar of olives created an express warranty that the olives had been pitted. The trial court granted summary judgment for Defendants, and Plaintiff appealed.

DECISION The appellate court affirmed the trial court's ruling. UCC§ 2-313 provides that an express warranty can be created by a description of the goods. However, comment 7 to UCC§ 2-313 qualifies this provision by stating:

> Of course, all descriptions by merchants must be read against the applicable trade usages with the general rules as to merchantability resolving any doubts.

Defendant's vice president of quality control testified in his deposition that olives must be pitted in order to be stuffed. He further testified:

> [T]here's a reasonable expectation that most of the pits would be removed, and there's some expectation that it's not a perfect world, and some of the pits or fragments may not be removed .... When the olives go into those machines, the machines do very well,

but, you know, the olives have different shapes. And the reason they don't get pitted right all the time is because of the different shapes of the olives.

Because pitted olives are processed and received in bulk, no practical method of inspection exists. The United States Department of Agriculture standards for pitted olives allow 1.3 pits or pit parts per 100 olives.

The appellate court thus concluded:

> "[E]xpress warranties ... must be read in terms of their significance in the ... trade and relative to what would normally pass in the trade without objection under the contract description." Given the evidence of how the defendants receive and resell these olives, it is unrealistic to impart to the description "minced pimento stuffed" the meaning that defendants are guaranteeing that the olives in the jar are entirely free of pits or pit fragments. It is much more realistic to interpret the description as only warranting that the particular jar of olives contains pimento-stuffed, green olives that would pass as merchantable without objection in the trade. Plaintiff has provided no evidence that the contents of the jar, taken as a whole, did not live up to this warranty.

The trial court's decision was affirmed.

Implied Warranty of Merchantability   Under UCC Section 2-314, a seller who is a merchant in the type of goods being sold impliedly warrants that the goods are of merchantable quality, i.e., that they are fit for the ordinary purpose for which they are being sold. The *implied warranty of merchantability* would apply, therefore, to sales of bicycles by a bike shop owner but not to sales of furniture by that same individual at a yard sale. Similarly, an individual selling even a brand-new bike at a yard sale would not create an implied warranty of merchantability because he would not be a merchant of bicycles. The implied warranty of merchantability arises automatically in every sale of goods by a merchant unless expressly disclaimed by the seller as discussed below.

Any merchant seller of goods, including a retailer or wholesaler, impliedly warrants the merchantability of goods, even if the seller did not manufacture the goods. For goods to be "merchantable," they must: (1) pass without objection in the trade under the contract description; (2) in the case of fungible goods, be of fair, average quality; (3) be fit for the ordinary purpose for which such goods are sold; (4) be of even kind, quality, and quantity within each unit and among all units; (5) be adequately contained, packaged, and labeled; and (6) conform to any promises or affirmations of fact made on the container or label. For example, Toys "R" Us was held liable for breach of the implied warranty of merchantability when the right pedal snapped off of a fully assembled bicycle it had sold to an individual, causing the rider to fall and be injured. Expert testimony established that the pedal had been improperly threaded onto the crank arm, and that the pedal would not have dislodged had it been properly threaded.[2]

Under UCC Section 2-314(1), the implied warranty of merchantability extends explicitly to "the serving for value of food or drink to be consumed either on the premises or elsewhere." It is not clear whether this warranty extends to used goods, however, even where the seller deals regularly in goods of that kind (e.g., used car dealers or second-hand merchandise stores).

➡ *See Discussion Cases 10.1, 10.2.*

Implied Warranty of Fitness for a Particular Purpose   Under UCC Section 2-315, an implied warranty of fitness for a particular purpose arises when: (1) the seller has reason to know of the particular purpose for which the buyer intends to use the goods; (2) the seller has reason to know that the buyer is relying upon the seller's skill or judgment to select or furnish suitable goods; and (3) the buyer actually relies upon the seller's skill or judgment in selecting or furnishing the goods. The seller does *not* have to be a merchant for this implied warranty to arise, although the seller must have some sort of expertise in the goods.

The distinction between the implied warranty of merchantability and the implied warranty of fitness for a particular purpose is an important one. Suppose that a buyer informs an appliance store that she is seeking an oven for use in her commercial bakery. The store sells her a nondefective oven that is designed for residential use but is not capable of handling commercial baking applications. The appliance store has not breached the implied warranty of merchantability because the oven is fit for its ordinary purpose—residential baking. The store has breached the implied warranty of fitness for a particular purpose, however.

➡ *See Discussion Cases 10.1, 10.2.*

Privity

Privity of contract is a requirement that the plaintiff demonstrate that he contracted directly with the defendant in order to bring a cause of action. Historically, the doctrine of privity was applied in warranty actions in such a way as to prevent plaintiffs from suing manufacturers or other parties within the chain of distribution with whom the plaintiff had not directly contracted. Rather, the "vertical" privity requirement limited the plaintiff to suing his immediate seller. Similarly, only the buyer who had purchased the goods could sue the seller; family members, guests, and bystanders who were injured by the product had no right to recover for breach of warranty because they lacked "horizontal" privity.

The 1960 decision of the New Jersey Supreme Court in *Henningsen v. Bloomfield Motors, Inc.,* radically changed the law regarding privity in warranty actions (see Case Illustration 10.3).

---

[2] *Hyatt v. Toys "R" Us, Inc.,* 2007 Del. Lexis 300 (Del. July 9, 2007).

CASE ILLUSTRATION 10.3

HENNINGSEN v. BLOOMFIELD MOTORS, INC., 161 A.2D 69 (N.J. 1960)

FACTS Chrysler Corporation manufactured a car with a defective steering mechanism. Claus Henningsen purchased the car from Bloomfield Motors, a Chrysler dealer, and gave the car to his wife, Helen. Helen Henningsen was injured when the steering mechanism failed with 468 miles on the odometer. She sued both Bloomfield Motors and Chrysler Corp. for breach of the implied warranty of merchantability.

DECISION Helen Henningsen clearly was not in privity with Chrysler Corp. because: (1) the actual purchase was made by her husband, Claus, and (2) he had purchased the car from Bloomfield Motors, a dealer, and not Chrysler Corp. directly. Nonetheless, the New Jersey Supreme Court held that as a matter of public policy, the doctrine of privity ought not to be allowed to act as a bar to Helen Henningsen's recovery from Chrysler. The court stated:

The limitations of privity in contracts for the sale of goods developed their place in the law when marketing conditions were simple, when maker and buyer frequently met face to face on an equal bargaining plane and when many of the products were relatively uncomplicated and conducive to inspection by a buyer competent to evaluate their quality. With the advent of mass marketing, the manufacturer became remote from the purchaser, sales were accomplished through intermediaries and the demand for the product was created by advertising media. In such an economy it became obvious that the consumer was the person being cultivated. Manifestly, the connotation of "consumer" was broader than that of "buyer." He signified such a person who, in the reasonable contemplation of the parties to the sale, might be expected to use the product.

The court thus concluded: "[W]here the commodities sold are such that if defectively manufactured they will be dangerous to life or limb, then society's interests can only be protected by eliminating the requirement of privity between the maker and his dealers and the reasonably expected ultimate consumer." Because Helen Henningsen was "a person who, in the reasonable contemplation of the parties to the warranty, might be expected to become a user of the automobile," she was protected by the warranty.

Today, UCC Section 2-318 offers states a choice of three positions regarding privity (with the result that the UCC is not particularly uniform in this regard). *Alternative A* provides that if the final purchaser is a beneficiary of a warranty, express or implied, any member of her household and any houseguest are also covered by the warranty "if it is reasonable to expect that such person may use, consume or be affected by the goods" and if such person is personally injured as a result of the breach. Most states have officially adopted this alternative, although in many states the courts have interpreted the language more broadly in their case law.

Alternative B provides that warranty protection extends "to any natural person who may reasonably be expected to use, consume or be affected by the goods and who is injured in person by breach of the warranty." Thus, this alternative gives a cause of action for breach of warranty to parties such as employees or passersby who suffer personal injury as a result of the breach. Even if a state has not officially adopted Alternative B, its products liability case law may well provide for the same result that would be reached under this statutory language.

Alternative C extends breach of warranty protection even further by allowing artificial persons (such as corporations) to recover as well as natural persons and by allowing recovery for property damage as well as personal injury.

Warranty Disclaimers

Warranty disclaimers are permitted, but not favored, under the UCC. The courts also tend to be hostile to attempts by manufacturers or sellers to disclaim express or implied warranties. Any ambiguities as to whether a disclaimer was made generally are construed against the seller. As a general rule, sellers should make their disclaimers explicit, unequivocal, and conspicuous.

The UCC imposes specific requirements for disclaiming each of the warranties described above. It is easier for the parties to disclaim or limit implied warranties than it is to disclaim or limit express warranties. The UCC specifically notes, for example, that implied warranties can be excluded or modified by course of dealing or course of performance or usage of trade.[3] This means that if the parties actually do or reasonably should understand as a result of their prior dealings with each other or as a result of common knowledge within the trade that no implied warranties are contemplated by the transaction, none arise.

Warranty disclaimers limit only the plaintiff's warranty claim, which arises in contract. Disclaimers do not affect any claims that the plaintiff might have in tort (e.g., negligence or strict products liability claims) for personal injury or property damage that might have occurred as a result of the product defect. These tort actions are discussed below.

Warranty of Title   A warranty of title can be disclaimed only by specific language in the contract or by special circumstances surrounding the transaction that clearly indicate to the buyer that the seller is not claiming title or is only purporting to sell whatever title the seller might have. For example, a statement such as "I convey only such right and title as I have in the goods" would suffice to disclaim the warranty of title. The buyer could not later complain if it turns out that the seller did not have good title to convey. Similarly, goods sold pursuant to a judicial sale carry no warranty of title, as the circumstances of the sale should make it clear to the buyer that the seller has no way of knowing or guaranteeing whether title is good.

Express Warranty   It is difficult to disclaim an express warranty. Sellers are better off simply not creating such a warranting in the first place rather than attempting to disclaim it after the fact. Express warranties can be excluded or modified but only by clear and unambiguous language of the parties. The courts do not like sellers giving a warranty with one hand and then taking it back with the other through a disclaimer, so they tend to view disclaimers of express warranties with a harsh eye.

Implied Warranty of Merchantability   Under UCC Section 2-316(2), disclaimers of the implied warranty of merchantability must mention the word "merchantability." The disclaimer may be oral, but, if it is made in writing, it must be conspicuous (e.g., capital letters, larger type, contrasting typeface or color) (see Case Illustration 10.4).

◆ *See Discussion Case 10.2.*

Implied Warranty of Fitness for a Particular Purpose   The implied warranty of fitness for a particular purpose can be disclaimed only in writing, and the disclaimer must be conspicuous. The disclaimer need not mention the word "fitness." In fact, the UCC notes that the statement that "[t]here are no warranties which extend beyond

---

[3]UCC § 2-316(3)(c).

CASE ILLUSTRATION 10.4

BAKER v. BURLINGTON COAT FACTORY, 175 MISC. 2D 951, 673 N.Y.S.2D. 281 (1998)

FACTS Plaintiff Catherine Baker purchased a fake fur coat for $127.99 from defendant Burlington Coat Factory Warehouse in Scarsdale, New York. She returned the coat two days later after it began shedding profusely. She demanded a refund of her $127.99 cash payment. Burlington offered either a store credit or a new coat of equal value, but refused to issue a cash refund. Baker filed suit, alleging, among other things, breach of contract, and breach of the implied warranty of merchantability.

Burlington noted that it displayed several large signs in its store, which stated: "Warehouse policy: Merchandise, in New Condition, May be Exchanged Within 7 Days of Purchase for Store Credit and Must Be Accompanied by a Ticket, and Receipt. No Cash Refunds or Charge Credits." In addition, the front of Baker's sales receipt stated: "Holiday Purchases May Be Exchanged Through January 11th, 1998 In House Store Credit Only No Cash Refunds or Charge Card Credits." The back of the receipt stated: "We Will Be Happy to Exchange Merchandise In New Condition Within 7 days When Accompanied By Ticket and Receipt. However, Because Of Our Unusually Low Prices: No Cash Refunds or Charge Card Credits Will Be Issued. In House Store Credit Only." Baker stated that she had not read this language and was not aware of Burlington's "no cash refunds" policy.

DECISION The court found for Baker, stating:

Under most circumstances retail stores in New York State are permitted to establish a no cash and no credit card charge refund policy and enforce it.

Retail store refund policies are governed, in part, by General Business Law § 218-a, which requires conspicuous signs on the item or at the cash register or on signs visible from the cash register or at each store entrance, setting forth, its refund policy

*including whether it is "in cash, or as credit or store credit only". * * ***

* * * Although plaintiff professed ignorance of defendant's refund policy; the court finds that defendant's signs and the front and back of its sales receipt reasonably inform consumers of its no cash and no credit card charge refund policy.

Notwithstanding its visibility the defendant's no cash and no credit card charge refund policy as against the plaintiff is unenforceable. Stated, simply when a product is defective as was the plaintiff's … shedding Fake Fur, the defendant cannot refuse to return the consumer's payment whether made in cash or with a credit card.

UCC§ 2-314(2)(c) mandates that "a warranty that the goods shall be merchantable is implied in a contract for their sale if the seller is a merchant with respect to goods of that kind …. (2) Goods to be merchantable must be … (c) … fit for the ordinary purposes for which such goods are used."

Should there be a breach of the implied warranty of merchantability then consumers may recover all appropriate damages including the purchase price in cash. The court finds that defendant sold plaintiff a defective and unwearable Fake Fur and breached the implied warranty of merchantability. The plaintiff is entitled to the return of her purchase price of $127.99 in cash and all other appropriate damages.

The court specifically noted that the UCC's provisions regarding the implied warranty of merchantability preempt any contrary provisions in General Business Law Section 218-a permitting a no-cash-refund policy. If the coat had not been defective and Baker had simply had a change-of-heart about her purchase, Section 218-a would have applied and Baker would not have been entitled to a refund. Because the coat was defective, however, the limitations in the exchange policy did not apply.

---

the description on the face hereof" is sufficient to disclaim all implied warranties of fitness.[4]

"As Is"   Selling goods "as is" or "with all faults" (or with "other language which in common understanding calls the buyer's attention to the exclusion of warranties and

---

[4]UCC § 2-316(2).

makes plain that there is no implied warranty"[5]) disclaims *all* implied warranties, including the implied warranty of merchantability, even if the word "merchantability" is not used. This language does not disclaim any express warranties that the seller might have made, however, nor does it relieve the seller of products liability based in tort. A number of states will not allow consumer products to be sold "as is."

The Buyer's Obligations in Warranty Actions

As mentioned in Chapter 9, the UCC gives the buyer the right to inspect the goods. If the buyer refuses to examine the goods, or if the buyer actually examines the goods (or a sample or model) as fully as the buyer desires before entering into the contract, there is no implied warranty with respect to defects that a reasonable examination would disclose. Refusal or failure to inspect does not affect any express warranties that might have been made.

In addition, the buyer must give the seller written or oral notice of a breach of warranty within a reasonable time after the breach should have been discovered. If the buyer fails to provide notice of the breach, the buyer will not be permitted to recover from the seller in a warranty action. The requirement of notice protects the seller's right to cure, if cure is appropriate or possible under the circumstances. "Cure" is discussed in Chapter 9.

Remedies and Defenses

If the breach of warranty occurs before the buyer has accepted the goods, the buyer's remedies are the same as they would be in any other breach of contract situation: the buyer may reject the goods, demand specific performance, cover, or recover damages in accordance with various UCC formulas. These remedies are discussed in Chapter 9.

If the buyer has accepted the goods, the buyer's damages for breach of warranty are generally calculated as *the difference between the value of the goods as warranted and the value of the goods as accepted, plus consequential and incidental damages.*[6] Recall from Chapter 9 that *incidental damages* include any costs or expenses directly associated with the seller's delay or delivery of defective goods, such as storage or inspection charges, costs of return shipping, or costs of cover. *Consequential damages* include personal or property damage arising from the breach of warranty. The seller is liable for consequential damages for economic losses, such as loss of profits from the anticipated resale of the goods or loss of goodwill or business reputation, only where the seller at the time of the contract had reason to know of such losses. This foreseeability requirement does not apply to consequential damages claims for noneconomic losses, such as personal injury (including medical expenses and recovery for pain and suffering) and property damage. Punitive damages generally are not available in breach of warranty claims.

The seller may raise a number of defenses to warranty actions, including misuse or abuse of the product by the plaintiff, failure to follow instructions, improper maintenance, or ordinary wear of the product. These defenses often arise in the products liability context as well and are discussed more fully below.

It is very common for sellers to try to limit their liability for the quality of their goods by limiting the remedies that are available to the buyer in the event of a breach. The UCC permits the parties to specify the remedy available in the event of the breach and

---

[5]UCC § 2-316(3)(a).

[6]UCC § 2-714(2) and (3).

to make that remedy exclusive.[7] Sellers often use a contractual provision that limits the seller's liability to the repair or replacement of the defective goods. The UCC does not permit the limitation of consequential damages where the plaintiff has suffered personal injury as a result of defective consumer goods. Limitation of "commercial" damages (i.e., economic losses in a business setting) is permitted. State or federal legislation (such as the Magnuson-Moss Federal Warranty Act, discussed below) may also restrict the ability of sellers to limit the remedies available in the event of a breach of warranty. Warranty actions have been on the decline in recent years, as plaintiffs have increasingly turned to the strict liability cause of action discussed below under Products Liability Law.

◆ See Discussion Case 10.1.

The Magnuson-Moss Federal Warranty Act

The UCC's provisions regarding warranty protection for buyers of consumer goods have been supplemented by both federal and state legislation. The *Magnuson-Moss Federal Warranty Act*[8] applies to *written* warranties on *consumer products*. The Act does not address oral warranties, nor does it apply to products sold for resale or for commercial purposes. Congress' goals in passing the Act were to: (1) ensure that consumers could get complete information about warranty terms and conditions; (2) ensure that consumers could compare warranty coverage prior to purchase; (3) promote competition on the basis of warranty coverage; and (4) strengthen incentives for companies to perform their warranty obligations and resolve consumer disputes quickly and without unnecessary expense to consumers.

The Act does not require sellers to make any warranties on consumer products. It does provide, however, that, if a seller makes a written warranty on a consumer product, that warranty must be conspicuously labeled as either a *full warranty* or a *limited warranty* and must contain specific information. The Act also provides that if the seller makes any written warranty, the seller is prohibited from disclaiming the implied warranties of merchantability and fitness for a particular purpose. The warranty information must be provided in a single, easy-to-read document and must be available to consumers prior to purchase.

A *full warranty* entitles the consumer to free repair of the product within a reasonable time period or, after a reasonable number of failed attempts to fix the product, entitles the consumer to choose either a full refund or replacement of a defective product. A full warranty also prevents the warrantor from placing any time limit on the warranty's duration; rather, full warranties last for a reasonable time period. (What is reasonable is a question of fact.) Finally, a full warranty prevents the warrantor from excluding or limiting consequential damages for breach of warranty unless such exclusions are conspicuous on the face of the warranty.

A *limited warranty* is anything less than a full warranty. Under a limited warranty, liability for implied warranties cannot be disclaimed altogether but may be limited in duration if the time period stated is reasonable and if the limitation is conspicuously disclosed.

Under rules promulgated by the Federal Trade Commission (FTC) under the Act, all warranties must answer five basic questions: (1) What does the warranty cover or not cover? (2) What is the period of coverage? (3) What will the company do to correct

---

[7]UCC § 2-719(l)(b).

[8]15 U.S.C. §§ 2301 *et seq.* The Act took effect in 1975. The Federal Trade Commission's (FTC's) "A Business person's Guide to Federal Warranty Law" is available online at www.ftc.gov/bcp/conline/pubs/buspubs/warranty.shtm

problems? (4) How can the customer obtain warranty service? and (5) How will state law affect consumers' rights under the warranty?[9] Because of the difficulty that national sellers of goods could have in answering the last question, the FTC permits companies to use the following "boilerplate" language:

> This warranty gives you specific legal rights, and you may also have other rights which vary from state to state.

Consumers who successfully sue for breach of the Magnuson-Moss Act may recover legal and equitable relief and may receive costs and reasonable attorney's fees.

Several states also have consumer protection statutes that provide additional protection to purchasers of consumer goods. This legislation may prohibit or limit the use of disclaimers, specify that warranties last for a reasonable time period, require that the seller provide reasonable service and repair facilities, or expand the remedies available to consumers. Marketers thus need to inform themselves of the specific laws that apply in each state in which they market their goods.

Note that a consumer uses the Magnuson-Moss Act and implied and/or express warranties to obtain satisfaction when the good purchased disappoints the consumer and is not worth the price paid. In such a situation, both the seller and the consumer are bound by whatever limitations or disclaimers exist, provided such limitations or disclaimers are allowed by the law. When a product causes physical injury, however, the injured party turns to products liability law and many of the rules discussed above do not apply.

◆ *See Discussion Case 10.2.*

Products Liability Law

Products liability refers to the liability incurred by a seller of goods when the goods, because of a defect in them, cause personal injury or property damage to the buyer, a user, or a third party. In recent years, products liability has been stretched to reach beyond tangible goods to include items such as electricity, natural gas, pets, and real estate.

Products liability is based in tort law, while warranties are based in contract law. Although products liability claims can be brought under a number of different tort theories, including misrepresentation and fraud, this chapter focuses on the two most common theories: negligence and strict liability.

Products liability law is state, not federal, law. Although it originally started out as a form of common law, several states have enacted comprehensive products liability statutes that supplement or supplant various aspects of the common law.

Negligence

Many products liability claims are based in negligence. The basic notion behind *negligence* is a failure on the part of the defendant to exercise "due care." If the defendant's conduct imposes an unreasonable risk of harm to another person that results in an injury to that person or to his property, the defendant is liable for negligence. The Delaware Supreme Court described the difference between warranty and negligence actions as follows: "A claim for breach of warranty, express or implied, is conceptually distinct from a negligence claim because the latter focuses on the manufacturer's conduct, whereas a breach of warranty claim evaluates the product itself."[10]

---

[9]The FTC has issued a document, "Writing Readable Warranties," which is available online at www.ftc.gov/bcp/conline/pubs/buspubs/writwarr.shtm

[10]*Bell Sports, Inc. v. Yarusso,* 759 A.2d 582 (Del. 2000).

Generally, to prove negligence, the plaintiff must show that: (1) the defendant owed a legal duty to the plaintiff; (2) the defendant failed to comply with this legal duty (i.e., failed to exercise due care); (3) the defendant's failure to exercise due care was the "proximate" (legal) cause of plaintiff's harm; and (4) the plaintiff suffered actual damages as a result of the defendant's actions. In judging whether the defendant's behavior posed an unreasonable risk of harm, the courts apply the "reasonable person" standard: Would a reasonable person of ordinary prudence behave as the defendant did under the circumstances?

◆ See Discussion Case 10.3.

Historically, a manufacturer's duty was limited to those who were in privity of contract with the manufacturer; i.e., an injured plaintiff could sue in negligence only if she had contracted directly with the manufacturer for the purchase of the good. In a famous 1916 case, *MacPherson v. Buick Motor Co.*,[11] the New York Court of Appeals rejected the notion of privity in cases where negligently made products caused personal injury. All of the other states have since adopted the holding of *MacPherson*, and it is now the rule that a party who has negligently manufactured a product is liable for personal injuries proximately caused by her negligence, regardless of whether privity is present. A manufacturer's duty now extends to remote purchasers of products, as well as to users and bystanders, provided they are foreseeable plaintiffs. Moreover, a manufacturer can be liable in negligence for property damage as well as for physical injury.

The range of potential defendants is broad. Manufacturers of component parts, assembly manufacturers, wholesalers, retailers, bailors, and other suppliers all potentially may be held liable in negligence for product defects if it can be shown that they acted carelessly toward the plaintiff. The *manufacturer* owes the broadest duty of care of any category of potential defendant. The manufacturer of a product must exercise "due care" in making the product so that it is safe to be used as intended. This means that the manufacturer must exercise due care in: (1) designing the product; (2) selecting the materials; (3) using the appropriate production processes; (4) assembling, testing, and inspecting the product; (5) placing adequate warnings on the label informing the user of the dangers of which an ordinary person might not be aware; (6) packaging, handling, and shipping the product; and (7) inspecting and testing component parts used in the final product.

Plaintiffs often find it difficult to hold a wholesaler or retailer liable for negligence. The wholesaler or retailer is not held liable for merely selling a negligently designed or manufactured product, as that party might have no duty to inspect or might have no reasonable opportunity to discover the defect even upon inspection. The seller has no duty to inspect goods packaged in sealed containers that are not to be opened before sale to the consumer, for example. The seller may be held liable for negligence, however, if the defect is obvious or if the seller has received other defective goods from the manufacturer in the past and has failed to inspect the current goods. The seller may also be liable for negligence if he knows or should know that the product is dangerous and fails to warn his customers; if the seller fails to use due care in selling the product to a person incapable of using it safely (e.g., selling explosives to a child); or if the seller has done something negligent with the product, such as carelessly assembling it or otherwise preparing it for final sale.

Sellers and manufacturers have a duty to warn buyers and users of *foreseeable* risks of harm associated with their products, but they do not have duty to warn of every risk that might be associated with a product. For example, a Louisiana appellate court held that

---

[11] 111 N.E.1050 (N.Y. 1916).

the manufacturer and the seller of a portable propane tank were not liable for failure to warn when a teenager died after filling a plastic bag with propane and sniffing it with the expectation of getting high. The court found that the teenager's use of the product was neither reasonable nor reasonably anticipated by the manufacturer and seller.[12]

Strict Products Liability

Since the 1960s, the courts have been fashioning a new kind of relief for plaintiffs in products liability actions—*strict liability*. The objective of strict products liability is to encourage manufacturers and sellers to produce and sell safer products and to spread the costs of injuries caused by defective products among all consumers, rather than forcing random victims to bear the full cost of their injuries. Strict liability is the leading legal theory in products liability actions today.

How does strict liability differ from negligence in products liability cases? First, strict liability focuses on the product itself: Was the product unreasonably dangerous? If so, the seller may be held liable even if the seller was as careful as possible in the preparation and sale of the product. Negligence, on the other hand, focuses on the defendant's behavior: Did the defendant fail to exercise its duty of care? Second, under strict liability, the injured plaintiff has a claim against anyone in the chain of distribution, including the immediate seller, the wholesaler, the manufacturer, and the manufacturer of component parts, regardless of fault. Under negligence, the plaintiff has a claim only against the party or parties whose lack of due care caused the injury.

The Restatements As discussed in Chapter 1, a Restatement is a compilation of common law principles drafted by the American Law Institute (ALI), which is a group of distinguished scholars and practitioners. Restatements are not legally binding law, although courts often adopt the principles contained within the various Restatements as binding rules within their jurisdictions.

Strict products liability law was originally based upon the *Restatement (Second) of Torts*, which was adopted in 1965. In the decades since then, virtually all states have accepted the theory of strict liability for dangerously defective products, and most have incorporated some form of Section 402A as part of their common law. In 1997, the ALI adopted the Restatement (Third) of Torts: Products Liability as part of its periodic review and updating process. Although some courts have adopted the Restatement (Third), so far Section 402A of the Restatement (Second) remains the prevailing legal rule on strict products liability.

The Restatement (Second) of Torts The foundation for modern strict products liability is Section 402A of the Restatement (Second) of Torts, which provides:

§ *402A. Special Liability of Seller of Product for Physical Harm to User or Consumer.*

(1) One who sells any product in a defective condition unreasonably dangerous to the user or the consumer or to his property is subject to liability for physical harm thereby caused to the ultimate user or consumer, or to his property, if
   (a) the seller is engaged in the business of selling such a product, and
   (b) it is expected to and does reach the user or consumer without substantial change in the condition in which it is sold.
(2) The rule stated in Subsection (1) applies although
   (a) the seller has exercised all possible care in the preparation and sale of his product, and

---

[12] *Kelley v. Hanover Insurance Co.*, 722 So.2d 1133 (La. App. 1998).

(b) the user or consumer has not bought the product from or entered into any contractual relation with the seller.[13]

Section 402A of the Restatement (Second) thus provides that a seller engaged in the business of selling a particular product is liable for physical harm or property damage suffered by the ultimate user or consumer of that product *if* the product was in a defective condition unreasonably dangerous to the user or the consumer or to her property. Section 402A applies to all commercial sellers of products, whether manufacturers, wholesalers, or retailers, but does not apply to casual, onetime sellers (see Case Illustration 10.5).

In addition, the strict liability doctrine does *not* make the seller an insurer of the product. Sellers are held liable only for products that are both defective and unreasonably

---

CASE ILLUSTRATION 10.5

McANANY v. CASE, INC., 2007 PA. DIST. & CNTY. DEC. LEXIS 384, 83 PA. D. & C.4TH 449 (PENN. CT. COMMON PLEAS 2007)

FACTS Defendant, a paving company, traded in a skid steer loader to Southeastern Equipment Co., Inc., for a new loader. Shortly after the trade-in, Plaintiff's employer, Cade Paving, purchased the used loader from Southeastern "as is." Plaintiff, an experienced loader operator, was severely injured while using the loader to remove excess gravel and debris from a driveway.

The trial court granted Defendant summary judgment on Plaintiff's strict liability claim. Plaintiff appealed.

DECISION The appellate court affirmed the grant of summary judgment to Defendant.

The Restatement (Second) of Torts § 402A provides:

(1) *One who sells any product in a defective condition unreasonably dangerous to the user or consumer or to his property is subject to liability for physical harm thereby caused to the ultimate used or consumer, or to his property, if*
  (a) *The seller is engaged in the business of selling such a product, and*
  (b) *It is expected to and does reach the user or consumer without substantial change in the condition in which it is sold.*

The court explained the rationale behind strict liability: "public policy demands that liability be fixed where it will be most effective at reducing the peril to life and health which arise from the selling of defective products." Specifically, "[t]he policy behind strict liability is to ensure costs of injuries sustain[ed from]

purchasing defective products are paid by the manufacturers who put the products on the market and not by the injured persons themselves."

The appellate court found that Defendant was not a "seller engaged in the business of selling such a product." There are situations in which a seller of used goods can be liable for selling defective merchandise, such as where the seller not only sold both new and used motorcycles produced by the same manufacturer but the seller and the manufacturer maintained a close business relationship. Here, however:

Defendant merely traded-in the used loader to purchase a new one. Although, Defendant has done this a number of times in the past, selling skid steer loaders or any other equipment remains outside of Defendant's business.... Defendant clearly does not deal in selling items created by one manufacturer. Although Defendant has made 12 transactions either selling or trading in equipment, it does not sell equipment on a normal basis; it is in the business of paving.

* * * It is apparent that Defendant merely trades-in its equipment to get new equipment in order to render a service, not as an act of selling or distributing them as a business venture. Defendant is not engaged in the business of selling paving equipment and should not be expected to assume liability injuries sustained by equipment they previously owned.

Thus, Defendant was not strictly liable for Plaintiff's injuries.

---

[13]Restatement (Second) of Torts § 402A.

dangerous; they are not held liable for every injury to a user of a product. Under Section 402A, the plaintiff must show that the defect existed at the time that the product left the defendant's hands and that the defect was not the result of a subsequent modification or alteration by another party. It can be hard for a plaintiff to show this against a manufacturer if the product passed through several intermediate suppliers before reaching the plaintiff.

Courts applying Section 402A generally use either the consumer expectations test or the risk-utility test to determine whether a product is defective. Comment i of Section 402A states that a product is considered to be "in a defective condition unreasonably dangerous" if it is "dangerous to an extent beyond that which would be contemplated by the ordinary consumer who purchases it, with the ordinary knowledge common to the community as to its characteristics."[14] Under this *consumer expectations test*, if a plaintiff, applying the knowledge of an ordinary consumer, sees a danger and can appreciate that danger, the plaintiff cannot recover for any injury she incurs as a result of that danger.

Most courts have moved away from the consumer expectations test and have embraced the *risk-utility test* instead. Under this test, a product is "unreasonably dangerous" if a reasonable person would conclude that the danger, whether foreseeable or not, outweighs the utility of the product. However, if a product is *unavoidably unsafe* but its benefits outweigh its dangers, the seller is not held strictly liable for any injuries that occur. The Restatement recognizes, for example, that the rabies vaccine carries a risk of severe side effects. The Restatement also notes, however, that "since the disease itself invariably leads to a dreadful death, both the marketing and the use of the vaccine are fully justified, notwithstanding the unavoidable high degree of risk which they involve. Such a product, properly prepared, and accompanied by proper directions and warning, is not defective, nor is it unreasonably dangerous."[15]

◆ *See Discussion Cases 10.3, 10.4.*

The Restatement (Third) of Torts: Products Liability The Restatement (Second) focused primarily on products with manufacturing defects and did not directly address two other major categories of defects: defective warnings and defective design. Many commentators argued that strict liability was inappropriate for these two categories of defects because it was unfair that manufacturers should be held liable for failure to warn of unknowable risks or failure to make their products safer than was technologically feasible.

The Restatement (Third) sets forth 21 black-letter rules for products liability. In particular, Section 2 of the Restatement (Third) provides explicit rules for the three categories of product defects: (1) manufacturing defects; (2) design defects; and (3) inadequate warnings. The Restatement (Third) maintains the strict liability standard for manufacturing defects adopted in the Restatement (Second) but moves toward a fault-based (i.e., negligence) standard for design and warning defects. Section 2 provides:

Section 2 Categories of Product Defect

A product is defective when, at the time of sale or distribution, it contains a manufacturing defect, is defective in design, or is defective because of inadequate instructions or warnings. A product:

(a) contains a manufacturing defect when the product departs from its intended design even though all possible care was exercised in the preparation and marketing of the product;

[14]Restatement (Second) of Torts § 402A, comment i.
[15]Restatement (Second) of Torts § 402A, comment k.

(b) is defective in design when the foreseeable risks of harm posed by the product could have been reduced or avoided by the adoption of a reasonable alternative design by the seller or other distributor, or by a predecessor in the commercial chain of distribution, and the omission of the alternative design renders the product not reasonably safe;

(c) is defective because of inadequate instructions or warnings when the foreseeable risks of harm posed by the product could have been reduced or avoided by the provision of reasonable instructions or warnings by the seller or other distributor, or a predecessor in the commercial chain of distribution, and the omission of the instructions or warnings renders the product not reasonably safe.[16]

CASE ILLUSTRATION 10.6

MATHEWS v. UNIVERSITY LOFT CO., 903 A.2D 1120 (N.J. SUPER. CT. 2006)

FACTS Plaintiff, a 21-year-old college senior at Stockton State College, lived in a campus apartment. He slept in a new "loft bed," which was six feet off the floor. About a month after he began sleeping on the loft bed, Plaintiff was startled awake, fell off the bed, and injured his shoulder.

Plaintiff continued sleeping in the loft bed, but made a point of sleeping "all the way against the wall," as far as possible from the open edge of the bed. There were no warning labels on the bed, and Plaintiff testified that it had never "cross[ed his] mind" or "occurred to" him that he could fall or that the bed was dangerous in any way. He stated that if he had seen a warning, he would have been "aware of the hazard that was present" and would have slept closer to the wall in the first place.

Plaintiff was awarded $179,001 at trial on a claim "based on lack of warning." Defendant University Loft Co., the manufacturer of the bed, appealed.

DECISION The appellate court ruled that Plaintiff's failure-to-warn claim should have been dismissed, and reversed the judgment for Plaintiff.

Under the New Jersey Products Liability Act, a plaintiff can prove a product was defective by showing it was: (1) defectively manufactured; (2) defectively designed; or (3) "failed to contain adequate warnings or instructions." A manufacturer can avoid product liability caused by failure to warn by showing that the product has an adequate warning or instruction.

As the court noted, however, adequacy of a warning becomes an issue only where there is duty to warn in the first place. Here, Defendant had no duty to warn against the danger of falling from the loft bed because the danger was "open and obvious." Under the Restatement (Third) of Torts: Products Liability § 2, a product

is defective because of inadequate instructions or warnings when the foreseeable risks of harm posed by the product could have been reduced or avoided by the provision of reasonable instructions or warnings by the seller or other distributor, or a predecessor in the commercial chain of distribution, and the omission of the instructions or warnings renders the product not reasonably safe.

The court went on to quote Comment j of the Restatement:

In general, a product seller is not subject to liability for failing to warn or instruct regarding risks and risk-avoidance measures that should be obvious to, or generally known by, foreseeable product users. When a risk is obvious or generally known, the prospective addressee of a warning will or should already know of its existence. Warning of an obvious or generally known risk in most instances will not provide an effective additional measure of safety. Furthermore, warnings that deal with obvious or generally known risks may be ignored by users and consumers and may diminish the significance of

(Continued)

---

[16]Restatement (Third) of Torts: Products Liability § 2.

warnings about non-obvious, not-generally-known risks. Thus, requiring warnings of obvious or generally known risks could reduce the efficacy of warnings generally ... (emphasis added).

Thus, the appellate court held that:

the obviousness of the danger is an absolute defense to plaintiff's failure to warn action in this case. [W]arnings would lose their efficacy and meaning if they were placed on every instrument known to be dangerous, such as a knife, scissor, glass, bat, ball, bicycle, or other product that poses a generally-known risk of injury if misused, dropped, or fallen from.... The risks are so obvious here that we fail to see what a college student would or could have done differently while asleep to protect himself from falling, or what a warning could have advised in addition to the obvious.

Perhaps the most controversial provision of the Restatement is the requirement that a plaintiff suing a manufacturer over a defectively designed product must show that a reasonable alternative design (RAD) would have prevented the harm, a standard that many commentators believe tilts the law in favor of the manufacturer and away from the consumer. Section 402A of the Restatement (Second) did not require the plaintiff to show the existence of a RAD but, rather, found that a product that is "unreasonably dangerous to the user or consumer or to his property" is defective even if there is no way to eliminate that danger.

Issues Raised by Strict Products Liability   Strict products liability raises a number of unique legal issues.

Subsequent Remedial Design   Plaintiffs often try to show that the defendant redesigned the product after the plaintiff's injury in order to make it safer, arguing that the redesign indicates that the original design was defective and that a safer design was available and should have been used. Traditionally, most courts have not allowed this evidence in to prove that the product was defective on the public policy grounds that admitting such evidence would discourage manufacturers from engaging in redesign and from producing safer products.

Latent Defects   Plaintiffs in several mass products liability class actions have attempted to argue that the product has some sort of latent defect such that it might fail under certain circumstances and cause injury, even though no plaintiff has suffered actual injury yet. Most of these claims have involved automotive defects, such as child seats, passive restraints, tires, and transmissions, but cases have also been brought involving cell phones and heart valves.

The heart valve cases illustrate the conflicting policy concerns that such cases can raise. Shiley, Inc., a subsidiary of Pfizer, Inc., had manufactured and sold the Bjork-Shiley Concavo-Convex heart valve from 1979 to 1986. The heart valves had been marketed in several sizes worldwide. The heart valves were withdrawn from the market in 1986 after a number of recipients died from sudden failure of the valves. The valves failed without warning and seemingly at random, making it impossible for doctors to pinpoint which patients would be likely to incur a problem with the valves. Unless the patient received open heart surgery to replace the valve within several hours of the failure, the patient would die.

A study indicated that the overall cumulative failure rate for the size of valve sold in the United States was 4.2 percent over eight years. Over 500 failures had occurred worldwide, killing about two-thirds of the patients involved. Removal and replacement of the valves entails open heart surgery, which itself carries a mortality risk of 5 percent, which is higher than the failure rate associated with the valves.

In a settlement of a class action suit brought against it, Pfizer agreed to pay $75 million to a patient fund; $80 million to $130 million for medical and psychological consultations, depending upon the number of claims; $500,000 to $2 million to each recipient whose heart valve breaks; and $10 million to patients' spouses.[17]

A number of heart valve recipients who had not suffered valve failure attempted to bring suits based upon the latent defects in the valves and their fears that their valves might fail in the future. The courts uniformly rejected their claims.[18] In *Farsian v. Pfizer*,[19] for example, the plaintiff, who had had a Bjork-Shiley heart valve implant in 1981, sued Pfizer, arguing that the manufacturer had engaged in fraudulent conduct by marketing the valve even though the manufacturer knew of serious manufacturing problems that directly related to the fracture problem in the valve. Although the plaintiff's heart valve was functioning properly at the time of suit, he argued that the higher rate of fracture and risk of death associated with the valve reduced the value of the valve and that he had suffered mental anguish and emotional distress since he learned of the fraud. The Alabama Supreme Court rejected his claim, finding that the plaintiff had no cause of action where he had not suffered an injury-producing malfunction of the product. *A fear* of failure of a product, absent a failure itself, is insufficient to support a products liability claim.

Liability for Misrepresentations   Section 9 of the Restatement (Third) also imposes liability upon commercial product sellers and distributors for harm to persons or property caused by misrepresentations of material fact, whether fraudulent, negligent, or innocent. Thus, a seller could be held liable for written or oral statements about a product made by salespersons or advertisements. Moreover, under this section, it does not matter if the product was nondefective, if the seller honestly believed that the representation was accurate, or if the plaintiff did not actually see or rely upon the misrepresentation.

Section 402B of the Restatement (Second) contains a similar provision, though it requires that the plaintiff show that he had "justifiably" relied upon the misrepresentation.

Marketers should be alert to the liability created by these sections and should take care to ensure that salespersons and advertising agencies do not make inaccurate representations about their products.

Market Share Liability   Generally, the plaintiff bears the burden of showing that the defendant caused the plaintiff's injury. Causation can be difficult to show in many instances, however. For example, many women who suffered injury as result of their mothers' taking the drug DES during their pregnancies 20 or more years earlier were unable to demonstrate which of over 300 manufacturers made the precise pills that their mothers took.[20] Each manufacturer used the identical formula in producing the drug.

In such instances, where several manufacturers produced a similar product with a common defect and where the plaintiff is unable to demonstrate which manufacturer in particular was the cause of her injury, many (but not all) courts are willing to impose *market share liability*. Under this approach, liability is apportioned among all of the

---

[17]See generally Ben L. Kaufman, "Flat-Rate Fees Denied for Class-Action Lawyers," *The Cincinnati Enquirer*, Jan. 11, 1998, p. B04; Milt Freudenheim, "Pfizer Settles Suit Over Heart Valve," *The New York Times*, Late Edition-Final, Sept. 3, 1993, sec. D, p. 3; "FDA Suggests Removal of Heart Valve," *Facts on File World News Digest*, Apr. 2, 1992, p. 233; Gina Kolata, "Heart Valve Called So Risky Its Removal Must Be Considered," *The New York Times*, Late Edition-Final, Mar. 13, 1992, Sec. A, p. 1.

[18]See *Angus v. Shiley, Inc.*, 989 F.2d 142 (3d Cir. 1993); *Walus v. Pfizer, Inc.*, 812 F. Supp. 41 (D.N.J. 1993); *Spuhl v. Shiley, Inc.*, 795 S.W.2d 573 (Mo. App. 1990); *Brinkman v. Shiley, Inc.*, 732 F. Supp. 33 (M.D. Pa.), *aff'd without op.*, 902 F.2d 1558 (3d Cir. 1989).

[19]682 So. 2d 405 (Ala.), *dismissed*, 97 F.3d 508 (11th Cir. 1996).

[20]See *Sindell v. Abbott Laboratories*, 607 P.2d 924 (Cal. 1980).

firms in the industry that might have produced the product that caused the plaintiff's injury. In such an instance, most courts give each defendant the opportunity to prove that it did not produce the product that injured that particular plaintiff. Some courts, however, do not permit defendants to exculpate themselves in this way. For example, the New York Court of Appeals stated in a 1989 case: "[B]ecause liability here is based on the over-all risk produced, and not causation in a single case, there should be no exculpation of a defendant who, although a member of the market producing DES for pregnancy use, appears not to have caused a particular plaintiff's injury."[21]

Successor Liability   A corporation that purchases or acquires the assets of another corporation may well find it has purchased or acquired liability for product defects as well. Traditionally, a corporation purchasing or acquiring the assets of another may be held liable for the obligations and liabilities of the seller if: (1) the purchaser expressly or impliedly agreed to assume such obligations or liabilities; (2) the transaction is in effect a consolidation or merger of the seller and the purchaser; (3) the purchaser is merely a continuation of the seller; or (4) the transaction is a fraudulent attempt to escape liability for such obligations or debts.

Some modern courts also impose liability on the acquiring corporation where: (1) the purchaser continues the manufacture of the product line of the seller; or (2) the purchaser continues the enterprise of the seller. The Restatement (Third) rejects these new theories of successor liability and adopts only the four traditional categories.[22]

Remedies   In most states, a plaintiff must suffer an "economic loss" in order to recover in tort. This doctrine requires that the product defect cause personal injury or physical damage to property other than the defective product itself. Remedies available in products liability actions include recovery for personal injury, property damage, and possibly punitive damages. Indirect economic loss (such as lost profits and loss of business goodwill) and basis-of-the-bargain damages are difficult to recover in tort but are available in breach of warranty actions.

Thus, the type of remedy that the plaintiff wishes to recover often guides the plaintiff's decision as to which theory (warranty or tort liability) to sue under. Plaintiffs need not necessarily choose a single cause of action, however. A plaintiff may, and usually does, sue for breach of warranty, negligence, and strict liability all arising out of a single sale and injury, for example.

Manufacturers and sellers frequently try to limit the remedies available to purchasers of their products, often by excluding recovery for consequential damages or by limiting recovery to repair or replacement of the defective good. The courts are unlikely to uphold such limitations in tort actions involving ordinary consumers but may well do so in actions involving buyers who are businesses or other sophisticated consumers of relatively equal bargaining power.

Similarly, manufacturers or sellers often insert a disclaimer of liability for negligence or strict liability within their sales contracts. The courts are reluctant to allow manufacturers or sellers to disclaim their liability for their own negligence or strict liability in consumer cases, however, and rarely give effect to such disclaimers in that setting. The courts are more likely to allow such disclaimers when the parties are of equal bargaining power, as in a business-to-business transaction.

Defenses to Products Liability Actions   There are several defenses that a defendant may attempt to raise in a products liability action: (1) contributory or comparative

---

[21]*Id.* at 1072.

[22]Restatement (Third) of Torts: Product Liability § 12.

negligence; (2) voluntary assumption of risk; (3) misuse or abuse of product; (4) the state-of-the-art defense; (5) compliance with government standards; and (6) the learned intermediaries and sophisticated purchasers rules. Each is discussed below.

Contributory/Comparative Negligence *Contributory negligence* was once the majority rule but today applies only in a minority of states, and even then often only in limited circumstances. This doctrine provides that if both the plaintiff and the defendant were negligent and the plaintiff's negligence is *a* (though not necessarily the *sole*) proximate cause of her injuries, the plaintiff receives no recovery. Some states apply this doctrine in some types of strict liability cases, such as those involving product misuse or abuse, as well as in negligence cases.

Comparative negligence (also known as comparative fault) applies in the majority of states. This doctrine provides that if the plaintiff and the defendant were both negligent, plaintiff's recovery will be reduced by his relative degree of fault. Thus, if the plaintiff was 30 percent at fault and the defendant 70 percent at fault, the plaintiff will recover 70 percent of his damages but will not recover for the 30 percent of his damages attributable to his own lack of due care. In a *pure* comparative fault system, the plaintiff will always recover for the portion of the injury attributable to the defendant. In a *mixed* comparative fault system, the plaintiff will recover nothing if the plaintiff is more than 50 percent at fault for his injuries. As you can imagine, it can be very difficult factually to assign relative degrees of fault to the plaintiff and defendant. Typically, much time and effort are devoted to this issue during the trial stage of the litigation.

In jurisdictions that have adopted comparative negligence, the defense always applies in negligence actions, and some courts apply it in strict liability actions as well.

➤ *See Discussion Case 10.4.*

Voluntary Assumption of Risk *Voluntary assumption of risk* occurs when the plaintiff knew of the risk of harm presented and voluntarily and unreasonably chose to encounter it. Historically, voluntary assumption of risk operated as a complete bar to the plaintiff's recovery. However, the doctrine has fallen into disfavor with many courts. Where it is still followed, this defense may apply in both strict liability and negligence cases, as well as in warranty actions.

The defense typically applies only where it is clear beyond question that the plaintiff voluntarily and knowingly proceeded in the face of an obvious and dangerous condition and only where it is clear from the circumstances that the plaintiff willingly accepted the risk. Mere contributory negligence does not show a voluntary assumption of risk.

In addition, many courts reject the doctrine in the employment context, finding that "an employee does not voluntarily and unreasonably assume the risk of danger during the course of employment because 'the competitiveness and pragmatism' of the real world workplace compels employees to either perform risky tasks or suffer various adverse employment consequences, ranging from termination to more subtle sanctions."[23] These courts generally continue to apply comparative negligence in such cases, however, so that an employee cannot completely abdicate responsibility for her own safety.

Misuse or Abuse of Product *Misuse or abuse of product* differs from voluntary assumption of risk in that misuse or abuse includes actions that the injured party did not know to be dangerous, while assumption of risk does not. This defense is only available to the seller where the misuse or abuse is not reasonably foreseeable. If it is foreseeable, the seller must take reasonable actions to guard against the misuse or abuse. Where the

---

[23]*Staub v. Toy Factory, Inc.*, 749 A.2d 522, 532 n.11 (Pa. Super. Ct. 2000) (citation omitted).

defense is available to the seller, however, it is a defense to both negligence and strict liability actions, as well as warranty actions (see Case Illustration 10.7).

State-of-the-Art Defense and Post-Sale Duties to Warn Generally, in determining whether a product is "in a defective condition unreasonably dangerous" to the consumer or user or to his property, the courts consider the state of human knowledge at the time that the product was sold, not at the time that products liability case is heard. The seller should be held liable only for what it reasonably could have known at the time the product was sold. Many states have statutes that specifically provide that a product is not defective if it is designed and sold in a manner consistent with industry customs or the state of the art at the time of sale[24] (see Case Illustration 10.8).

Some states that apply the state-of-the-art defense require only that the manufacturer conform to industry standards.[25] The problem with such an approach, of course, is that

---

CASE ILLUSTRATION 10.7

MECURIO v. NISSAN MOTOR CORP., 81 F. SUPP. 2D 859 (N.D. OHIO 2000)

FACTS Roy Mercurio drove his Nissan Altima into a tree at a speed of between 30 and 40 miles per hour. At the time, his blood alcohol content was at least .18 percent. When the car struck the tree, the passenger compartment collapsed and Mercurio suffered a severe closed head injury. Mercurio's wife brought a products liability action against Nissan, the car's manufacturer, claiming that the car was not crashworthy.

DECISION The defendant first argued that evidence of Mercurio's blood alcohol content should be admitted into court to show that Mercurio had engaged in unforeseeable misuse of the car. The court rejected the defendant's argument, stating that "[t]he fact that a collision may have been caused by the driver's intoxication, as opposed to another form of negligence, does not reduce the manufacturer's duty to provide a reasonably safe vehicle."

The court noted that "although the intended purpose of automobiles is not to participate in collisions, it is foreseeable that the collisions do occur, and an automobile manufacturer is under an obligation under Ohio law to use reasonable care in the design of its vehicle to avoid subjecting the user to an unreasonable risk of injury in the event of a collision." The court concluded that "[r]egardless of the cause of Mercurio's

accident, the type of accident that is at issue in this case—a frontal collision with a stationary object at thirty to forty miles per hour—is foreseeable." Thus, evidence of Mercurio's blood alcohol content was not admissible to demonstrate unforeseeable misuse of the car.

The defendant next argued that by driving under the influence of alcohol, Mercurio voluntarily assumed the risk of whatever injuries he suffered. Under Ohio law, a plaintiff assumes the risk of an unreasonably dangerous condition when: (1) he knows of the condition; (2) the condition is patently dangerous; and (3) he voluntarily exposes himself to the condition.

Here, the court found, the dangerous condition that Mercurio allegedly assumed was the alleged uncrashworthiness of the car, not the risk of an accident generally. The defendant had not alleged, however, that Mercurio knew that the vehicle's subfloor posed a risk of buckling or that the subfloor was patently dangerous, or that Mercurio voluntarily exposed himself to the dangers of driving in a vehicle that was not crashworthy. Under these facts, the defendant could not raise the defense of assumption of risk.

Thus, the court granted the plaintiff's motion to exclude any reference to Mercurio's consumption of alcohol on the night of his automobile accident.

---

[24]See, e.g., Ariz. Rev. Stat. Ann. § 12-681 *et seq.;* N.H. Rev. Stat. Ann. § 507:8-g; Tenn. Code Ann. §§ 29-28-104-105.

[25]See, e.g., *Beech v. Outboard Marine Corp.*, 584 So.2d 447 (Ala. 1991).

CASE ILLUSTRATION 10.8

ANDERSON v. OWENS-CORNING FIBERGLAS CORP., 810 P.2D 549 (CAL. 1991)

FACTS Carl Anderson filed a suit in strict liability against Owens-Corning Fiberglas Corp. and other manufacturers of products containing asbestos, alleging that he had contracted asbestosis and other lung ailments through exposure to asbestos and asbestos products while working at a naval shipyard from 1946 to 1976. His complaint alleged that the defendants were liable in strict liability for failing to warn the users of the risk of danger associated with asbestos and asbestos-containing products. The defendants responded by raising the state-of-the-art defense; i.e., "that even those at the vanguard of scientific know ledge at the time the products were sold could not have known that asbestos was dangerous to users in the concentrations associated with defendants' products."

DECISION The California Supreme Court ruled that: "Exclusion of state-of-the-art evidence, *when the basis of liability is a failure to warn*, would make a manufacturer the virtual insurer of its product's safe use, a result that is not-consonant with established principles underlying strict liability." The court stated that public policy grounds supported such an outcome: "[I]f a manufacturer could not count on limiting its liability to risks that were known or knowable at the time of manufacture or distribution, it would be discouraged from developing new and improved products for fear that later significant advances in scientific knowledge would increase its liability."

Thus, the court held that "a defendant in a strict products liability action based upon an alleged failure to warn of a risk of harm may present evidence of the state of the art, i.e., evidence that the particular risk was neither known nor knowable by the application of scientific knowledge available at the time of manufacture and/or distribution."

an entire industry may be lax in requiring safety devices or in developing safer technologies. Other states go to the opposite extreme, requiring that the manufacturer conform to cutting-edge technology within its industry.[26] An intermediate, third approach, which was adopted in the Restatement (Third),[27] requires the manufacturer to act reasonably in keeping up with technological advances within its industry and in including safe components and safety devices.[28] In a few states, the manufacturer is held liable for the harm caused by a defect even if discovery of the defect was scientifically and/or technically impossible at the time the product was marketed.

In some instances, the manufacturer may have no reason to know of a defect at the time of sale but may later discover a defect. The state-of-the-art defense would not have required a warning at the time of sale. The question then becomes whether the manufacturer must issue a warning at the time the defect is discovered.

---

[26]See *Fibreboard Corp. v. Fenton*, 845 P.2d 1168 (Colo. 1993).

[27]Restatement (Third) of Torts: Products Liability § 2(b) and (c). These subsections provide that a product:
- (b) is defective in design when the foreseeable risks of harm posed by the product could have been reduced or avoided by the adoption of a reasonable alternative design by the seller or other distributor, or a predecessor in the commercial chain of distribution, and the omission of the alternative design renders the product not reasonably safe;
- (c) is defective because of inadequate instructions or warnings when the foreseeable risks of harm posed by the product could not have been reduced or avoided by the provision of reasonable instructions or warnings by the seller or other distributor, or a predecessor in the commercial chain of distribution, and the omission of the instructions or warnings renders the product not reasonably safe.

[28]See *Vassallo v. Baxter Healthcare Corp.*, 696 N.E.2d 909 (Mass. 1998).

Many states, through their common law or statutes, require manufacturers to provide a *post-sale warning* in such instances. The Restatement (Third) also imposes such a duty on manufacturers. Section 10 states:

(a) One engaged in the business of selling or otherwise distributing products is subject to liability for harm to persons or property caused by the seller's failure to provide a warning after the time of sale or distribution of a product if a reasonable person in the seller's position would provide such a warning.

(b) A reasonable person in a seller's position would provide a warning after the time of sale if

    (1) the seller knows or reasonably should know that the product poses a substantial risk of harm to persons or property; and

    (2) those to whom a warning might be provided can be identified and can reasonably assume to be unaware of the risk of harm; and

    (3) a warning can be effectively communicated to and acted on by those to whom a warning might be provided; and

    (4) the risk of harm is sufficiently great to justify the burden of providing a warning.[29]

Other states reject a post-sale duty to warn if the product met standards of reasonableness when it was sold.[30]

Does a seller have a duty to monitor products post-sale to discover defects? Comment c to the Restatement (Third) says no, because such monitoring would be too burdensome for manufacturers. Rather, "[a]s a practical matter, most post-sale duties to warn arise when new information is brought to the attention of the seller, after the time of sale, concerning risks accompanying the product's use or consumption.[31]

In addition, there is no general duty to *recall* defective products. The Restatement (Third) imposes liability for a post-sale failure to recall a product upon commercial product sellers and distributors only if: (1) a government directive has been issued specifically requiring the recall or (2) the seller or distributor voluntarily undertakes such a recall but then does not act reasonably in recalling the product.[32] This limited duty to recall is not as broad as the duty to provide post-sale warnings of defects; i.e., there are situations in which a manufacturer has a duty to issue post-sale warnings but does not have a duty to undertake a recall.

Manufacturers, distributors, and retailers of consumer products who discover information that a product violates applicable consumer product safety rules or contains a defect that would create a substantial hazards have a duty to immediately inform the Consumer Product Safety Commission. This topic is discussed further in Chapter 8.

Compliance with Government Standards Suppose that the seller's product is regulated and that the state or federal government has set standards for it. If the seller is in compliance with those standards, does the seller have an automatic defense for products liability actions? The answer is no. Government standards generally set *minimum* requirements, and compliance with those standards does not automatically shield the manufacturer or seller from liability, though it may be considered as evidence by the judge or jury that the product is not defective. Several states do have statutes that make

---

[29]Restatement (Third) of Torts: Products Liability § 10.

[30]See, e.g., *Campbell v. Gala Indus., Inc.*, 2006 U.S. Dist. Lexis 26606 (D.S.C. Apr. 20, 2006); *Flax v. Daimler Chrysler Corp.*, 2006 Tenn. App. Lexis 822 (Dec. 27, 2006).

[31]Restatement (Third) of Torts: Product Liability § 10 comment c.

[32]Restatement (Third) of Torts: Product Liability § 11 comment c.

regulatory compliance a defense in certain situations. New Jersey, for example, has such a statute for FDA-approved drugs and drug labels.

The Restatement (Third) creates a rule of absolute liability for *noncompliance* with safety statutes or regulations, stating that where the person injured is in the class of persons whom the statute or regulation was intended to protect and the danger is one against which the statute or regulation was intended to protect, the noncompliance renders the product defective.[33]

The Learned Intermediaries and Sophisticated Purchaser Rules In some instances, a manufacturer or supplier may satisfy its duty to warn by providing warnings to a "learned intermediary," as opposed to the end user of the product. For example, drug manufacturers may provide doctors with adequate information of the risks and hazards associated with drugs; the prescribing or treating physician then intervenes between the manufacturer and the consumer.[34] This rule has also been used to shield a cobalt manufacturer who informed an employer (who was a sophisticated cobalt user) but not the employee of the risks of dust inhalation,[35] and a supplier of naphtha who warned an employer of the chemical's combustibility but did not warn the worker who was ultimately injured in an explosion.[36] The theory behind this defense is that the learned intermediary or sophisticated user is better able to make an "informed choice" and to tailor the warnings to meet the end user of the product.

The doctrine has come under fire in recent years, however, as drug manufacturers increasingly advertise their products to consumers. For example, the New Jersey Supreme Court ruled that if a manufacturer markets its products directly to consumers, it has a duty to warn consumers directly of the foreseeable risks associated with the drug.[37]

Statutes of Limitation/Statutes of Repose *Statutes of limitation* require that a cause of action be brought within a certain time period (usually measured in a matter of a few years). Thus, if the plaintiff delays too long in filing the suit, she will be prevented by law from doing so. Breach of warranty actions are subject to the statute of limitations for contract claims. Generally, breach of warranty actions must be brought within four years after the cause of action has accrued, which is ordinarily the date at which the seller delivers the goods to the buyer.

In tort actions, the statute of limitations is usually two or three years. It does not begin to run, however, until the time of the injury or until the defect was or should have been discovered by the plaintiff. This may be many years after the purchase of the product. Thus, despite being shorter, the tort statute of limitations can actually be more favorable to the plaintiff than the breach of warranty statute of limitations in many instances.

Statutes of repose are state statutes that limit manufacturer and/or seller liability for defective goods to a specific time period. Most such statutes provide that the seller or manufacturer cannot be held liable for defects that manifest themselves after a certain time period, usually 10 to 12 years after purchase of the goods by the consumer. Thus, these statutes relieve sellers and manufacturers of liability for defects in older goods.

Products Liability Reform Tort reform in general, and products liability reform in particular, have been hot topics before state and federal legislatures for the past several years. In virtually every legislative session for the past two decades, a products liability

---

[33]Restatement (Third) of Torts: Products Liability § 4.

[34]Restatement (Second) of Torts § 402A.

[35]*Tasca v. GTE Prods. Corp.*, 438 N.W.2d 625 (Mich. App. 1988).

[36]*Whitehead v. Dycho Co.*, 775 S.W.2d 593 (Tenn. 1989).

[37]*Perez v. Wyeth Laboratories, Inc.*, 734 A.2d 1245 (N.J. 1999).

reform bill has been introduced in Congress, though none has been successful. These bills would reform existing products liability law by providing for measures such as:

- making it more difficult to obtain punitive damage awards;
- capping the amount of punitive damages awarded in any one case; and
- shielding sellers from liability for manufacturing defects.

Many states have passed their own tort reform measures. These state laws generally limit recoveries (often by capping them at $250,000 or $500,000) for non-economic losses, such as pain and suffering or mental or emotional distress. About two-thirds of the states restrict or limit the recovery of punitive damages. Some states also have statutes limiting the liability of non-manufacturers.

International Products Liability Laws Products liability laws typically develop in nations with economies marked by both mass production and mass consumption. In such settings, older, more traditional negligence standards cease to function well because they impose a difficult burden of proof on injured consumers. In the United States, with its common law tradition, the inequities that resulted from the negligence standard were reformed primarily through judicial decisions and the development of an extensive body of case law of products liability, including strict liability. In civil law nations, the movement from a products liability system based on negligence to one based on strict products liability has developed more commonly through legislation.

DISCUSSION CASES

10.1 Warranties—Express and Implied, Warranties—Remedies
Dunleavey v. Paris Ceramics USA, Inc., 57 U.C.C. Rep. Serv. 2d (Callaghan) 653 (Super. Ct. Conn. 2005)

On three separate occasions during the year of 2001, the plaintiff, Anne Dunleavey d/b/a Unique Interiors, an interior designer, ordered a combined total of 3,280 square feet of French Antique Bourgogne stone from the Bourgogne region of France from the defendant, Paris Ceramics USA, Inc., a stone retailer, at a cost of $124,693.33. The stone was needed to renovate the deck area around the outdoor pool of Dunleavey's client, Terrance McClinch. Paris Ceramics' agent represented to Dunleavey that the stone was suitable for exterior use in Fairfield, Connecticut.

Dunleavey resold the stone to McClinch at a markup of $50,900. The stone was installed by C.A. Sanzaro, Inc., the contractor hired by John Desmond Builders, Inc., McClinch's general contractor. The installation of the stone was completed around September 2001. Between November 2001 and January 23, 2002, approximately 40–50% of the stone had flaked and broken off rendering the entire deck area unsuitable for use. On January 23, 2002, a meeting was held

between Dunleavey, Richard Abbot (Paris Ceramics' vice-president of operations), McClinch, Desmond, and Caesar Sanzaro (C.A. Sanzaro, Inc.'s principal), in which all agreed that the stone had to be completely replaced. Abbott stated that Paris Ceramics would do whatever was necessary to correct the situation at its own cost. Following the meeting, Dunleavey asked Paris Ceramics for a refund of $124,693.33. Paris Ceramics requested for an opportunity to remedy the situation by supplying the replacement stone. During the Spring of 2002, however, the patio stone was replaced at the McClinch residence with stones supplied by another stone retailer. Subsequently, Dunleavey was informed that McClinch would no longer be using her services.

On August 26, 2002, Dunleavey filed a complaint against Paris Ceramics alleging ... breach of warranty .... * * *

* * *

II. Breach of Warranty

Dunleavey ... claims that Paris Ceramics breached (1) an implied warranty for a particular purpose, (2) an implied warranty of merchantability, and (3) an express warranty created by a description of the goods, by a sample or by a model.

"Where the seller at the time of contracting has reason to know any particular purpose for which the goods are required and that the buyer is relying on the seller's skill or judgment to select or furnish suitable goods, there is unless excluded or modified under [UCC § 2-316] an implied warranty that the goods shall be fit for such purpose." "To establish a cause of action for breach of the implied warranty of fitness for a particular purpose [therefore], a party must establish (1) that the seller had reason to know of the intended purpose and (2) that the buyer actually relied on the seller."

"A warranty of merchantability is implied in any sale of goods by a merchant seller; the statutory standards for merchantability include, under [UCC § 2-314(2)(c)], that the goods be fit for the ordinary purpose for which such goods are used." "[UCC] § 2-314 imposes warranty liability for the protection of buyers. The purpose behind ... § 2-314 is to hold a merchant seller responsible when inferior goods are passed along to an unsuspecting buyer. Thus, whether or not the defects could, or should, have been discovered by the merchant seller, the merchant seller is liable to the buyer whenever the goods are not, at the time of delivery, of a merchantable quality .... The Uniform Commercial Code is designed to protect the buyer from bearing the burden of loss where merchandise does not live up to normal commercial expectations ...."

"In the case of the implied warranty of merchantability, there is liability without fault. Although the goods must be nonconforming [for a breach to occur], no distinction is made in terms of the fault of the defendant. The implied warranty of merchantability is breached whether or not the seller could have prevented the nonconformity.... The only practical and logical conclusion is that the warrantor is made liable, although free from moral or personal fault, because society for one reason or another wants to place the burden of harm resulting from nonconforming products upon the warrantor rather than upon the buyer...."

[UCC § 2-313] provides that "(1) express warranties by the seller are created as follows: (a) Any affirmation of fact or promise made by the seller to the buyer which relates to the goods and becomes part of the basis of the bargain creates an express warranty that the goods shall conform to the affirmation or promise. (b) Any description of the goods which is made part of the basis of the bargain creates an express warranty that the goods shall conform to the description. (c) Any sample or model which is made part of the basis of the bargain creates an express warranty that the whole of the goods shall conform to the sample or model."

It is an uncontested fact that Paris Ceramics knew that Dunleavey ordered French Antique Bourgogne stone to be installed on the exterior patio of the McClinches' residence. The evidence also shows that Dunleavey relied on the expertise of Paris Ceramics' agent in making her decision to use French Antique stone for the project, and that the stone failed for its particular purpose within a few months of its installation. Dunleavey ... has established that Paris Ceramics knew of her intent to use the stone for an exterior patio, and that she relied on Paris Ceramics' agent in choosing an appropriate stone for the job. Dunleavey has, therefore, established that Paris Ceramics breached an implied warranty for a particular purpose as to Dunleavey's purchase of the French Antique Bourgogne stone.

The court also finds that Paris Ceramics breached an implied warranty of merchantability and an express warranty when it sold the French Antique stone to Dunleavey. Dunleavey ordered the stone to be used on the exterior of the McClinches' residence. As mentioned above, the evidence shows that the stone was not fit for exterior use. It is also an uncontested fact that Paris Ceramics is a stone retailer that has been in the business for more than ten years. Whether or not the defect of the stone could have been discovered by Paris Ceramics is irrelevant as to whether or not it should be held responsible for breaching an implied warranty of merchantability. In addition, the evidence shows that Paris Ceramics' agent explicitly told Dunleavey that the stone would be suitable for exterior use. The court, therefore, finds that Paris Ceramics breached an implied warranty of merchantability and an express warranty.

1. Mitigation of Damages

The Supreme Court has often held that "in the contracts and torts contexts ... the party receiving a damage award has a duty to make reasonable efforts to mitigate damages.... What constitutes a reasonable effort under the circumstances of a particular case is a question of fact for the trier.... Furthermore, [the court has] concluded that the breaching party bears the burden of proving that the nonbreaching party has failed to mitigate damages."

Paris Ceramics claims that Dunleavey failed to mitigate her damages. In her defense, Dunleavey claims that she had no control or authority over the McClinches' residence. The court finds that although Paris Ceramics was willing to replace the stone at its own expense, the decision to allow Paris Ceramics to replace the stone was not Dunleavey's decision to make, but rather McClinch's decision. Although Dunleavey may not have done her best in order to try to convince McClinch to take up Paris Ceramics' offer to replace the patio stone, the evidence shows that McClinch was aware that Paris Ceramics was willing to replace the failed stone. Because McClinch did not accept Paris Ceramics' offer and decided to use another stone supplier, the court finds that Dunleavey should not be held responsible for McClinch's decision. Accordingly, the court finds that Dunleavey did not fail to mitigate her damages.

* * *

IV. Damages

"The measure of damages for breach of warranty is the difference at the time and place of acceptance between the value of the goods accepted and the value they would have had if they had been as warranted, unless special circumstances show proximate damages of a different amount." [UCC § 2-714.] "In a proper case any incidental and consequential damages under the next section [UCC § 2-715] may also be recovered." "The UCC provides remedies to one who purchases defective goods, including incidental and consequential damages caused by a seller's breach. Such remedies are defined in [UCC § 2-715."][8]

---

[8](1) Incidental damages resulting from the seller's breach include expenses reasonably incurred in inspection, receipt, transportation and care and custody of goods rightfully rejected, any commercially reasonable charges, expenses or commissions in connection with effecting cover and any other reasonable expense incident to the delay or other breach.

(2) Consequential damages resulting from the seller's breach include (a) any loss resulting from general or particular requirements and needs of which the seller at the time of contracting had reason to know and which could not reasonably be prevented by cover or otherwise; and (b) injury to person or property proximately resulting from any breach of warranty.

[UCC § 2-715.]

Dunleavey paid Paris Ceramics $114,636 for the stone and $10,327.33 for shipping. As evidenced by her invoice, she charged McClinch $50 per square foot, which yields $49,364 in profit. She also charged McClinch $9,840 in taxes. As per Dunleavey and McClinch's mediation agreement, she also had to pay him back $74,536 for the installation of the patio and McClinch's general contractor's overhead cost and profit. In addition, the cost of removing the damaged patio was $11,543.40. Wherefore, Dunleavey is owed $270,246.73 for Paris Ceramics' breach of warranty.[10]

* * *

QUESTIONS FOR DISCUSSION FOR CASE 10.1

1. What types of warranties were formed here? What behavior on the part of the defendant led to the creation of each of those types of warranties?

2. The defendant's argument that the plaintiff failed to meet her duty to mitigate her damages failed. Why? Do you think this outcome was fair to the defendant?

3. How does the court calculate the damages owing to the plaintiff? Do you feel the plaintiff was fully compensated for her losses? Why or why not?

---

[10] * * * In addition, she claims that she is owed an extra $395,071.10, which allegedly represents money the McClinches owe her. She claims that Paris Ceramics should pay her for that amount because if it wasn't for the failure of the stone, McClinch would not have fired her and would have given her at least two more projects. In his deposition testimony presented at trial, however, McClinch testified to having other disputes with Dunleavey besides the failing of the stone. He also testified that he probably would not have continued to use Dunleavey's services even if the problem with the stone had never happened. The court finds, therefore, that Dunleavey did not prove beyond a preponderance of the evidence that "but for" Paris Ceramics' breach, McClinch would have paid her the $395,071.10.

10.2. Warranties—Disclaimers, Magnuson-Moss Federal Warranty Act
Thomas v. Micro Center, 875 N.E.2d 108 (Ohio App. 2007)

Plaintiff-appellant C. Douglas Thomas appeals from a summary judgment rendered in favor of defendant-appellee Micro Center, Inc. on his claims for breach of warranties relating to a defective laptop computer he purchased from Micro Center. * * * We affirm in part and reverse in part. * * *

I

* * *

Appellant purchased a Toshiba computer from Micro Center on January 2, 2004. The Micro Center purchase receipt stated that "NOTEBOOK/LAPTOP COMPUTERS *** MAY BE RETURNED OR EXCHANGED WITHIN 7 DAYS OF PURCHASE ***."

Toshiba provided a one-year, limited warranty against defects in materials and workmanship, and further warranted that the computer would conform to the factory specifications in effect at the time the computer had been manufactured.

Appellant also purchased a three-year, "TechSaver Protection Plan." The plan specifically stated that "coverage begins on the date of purchase of the covered equipment and is inclusive of the manufacturer's warranty. During the manufacturer's warranty period, any parts and labor covered by that warranty are the sole responsibility of the manufacturer." The plan stated that it was an agreement between Butler Financial Solutions, LLC and the purchaser.

The computer began to malfunction just three weeks after purchase. Appellant spoke with Toshiba's customer service, and then brought the computer back to Micro Center. Appellant stated that the problem had "something to do with the programming." Micro Center accepted the computer back and reinstalled the operating system to get the computer working.

The computer worked correctly for only one month after that. Sometime in March or April 2004, the computer began malfunctioning. Appellant said that he called Toshiba customer service about eight times at that point. He could not recall the exact nature of the problems he experienced, but said that Toshiba "carried me through and it started working again." These fixes lasted for only two or three weeks, though. Toshiba told appellant that he had a broken "recovery disk." It sent him a new disk and the computer began working again.

In July 2004, the computer again stopped working. Toshiba diagnosed the problem as a "hard drive problem" and replaced the hard drive. Appellant received the computer back in August 2004, but it would not "boot." Toshiba told appellant to take the computer to a local repair facility. That facility again replaced the hard drive along with some other components, but these repairs did not fix the problems. It told appellant that it could not repair his computer. Appellant again contacted Toshiba and said that he wanted a replacement computer. Toshiba told appellant to contact Micro Center because it was "not their policy to replace computers." Micro Center told appellant that it had no obligation to replace the computer because the computer was still under warranty with Toshiba. Appellant contacted Toshiba's legal department by mail to demand a replacement computer, but his letter went unanswered.

Appellant filed a complaint against both Toshiba and Micro Center that asserted three claims: (1) breach of contract based on the express warranty issued by Toshiba and the TechSaver Protection Plan extended warranty purchased through Micro Center, (2) breach of implied warranties of merchantability and fitness …, and (3) violation of the Magnuson-Moss Warranty Act. Micro Center filed a motion for summary judgment on all three claims, arguing that it did not issue any warranties to appellant, that appellant's claims related to a time period in which Toshiba has warranted the computer, and that the Magnuson-Moss Act was inapplicable to commercial transactions …. The court granted summary judgment without opinion.

II

Appellant first argues that Micro Center is liable to him [under UCC § 2-314] because it imposes implied warranties of merchantability and fitness for a particular purpose. He maintains that, regardless of what Toshiba may have disclaimed, these implied warranties applied to Micro Center.

[UCC § 2-314] states in pertinent part:

(A) Unless excluded or modified as provided in [UCC § 2-316], a warranty that the goods shall be merchantable is implied in a contract for their sale if the seller is a merchant with respect to goods of that kind.

The implied warranty of fitness for a particular purpose is set forth in [UCC § 2-315], which states:

Where the seller at the time of contracting has reason to know any particular purpose for which the goods are required and that the buyer is relying on the seller's skill or judgment to select or furnish suitable goods, there is unless excluded or modified under [UCC § 2-316] an implied warranty that the goods shall be fit for such purpose.

[UCC § 2-316] governs the exclusion of implied warranties. That section states:

(B) Subject to division (C) of this section, to exclude or modify the implied warranty of merchantability or any part of it the language must mention merchantability and in case of a writing must be conspicuous, and to exclude or modify any implied warranty of fitness the exclusion must be by a writing and conspicuous. Language to exclude all implied warranties of fitness is sufficient if it states for example, that 'There are no warranties which extend beyond the description on the face hereof.'

Micro Center is a "merchant" as defined by [UCC § 2-104(1)].

The record contains no evidence to show that Micro Center excluded its warranties under [UCC § 2-316]. The sales receipt shows that Micro Center limited the return or exchange of laptop computers to seven days after purchase, but this did not constitute a valid exclusion of warranties. To be effective, the exclusion of a warranty must mention merchantability and, in the case of fitness for a particular purpose, must be conspicuous. The receipt offered into evidence contained none of these requirements.

* * *

Toshiba's exclusion of implied warranties does not apply to Micro Center. In *Barazzotto v. Intelligent Sys., Inc.* (1987), 40 Ohio App.3d 117, 119-120, 532 N.E.2d 148, the [court stated]:

When the manufacturer sells the goods to a dealer who resells the goods to the ultimate purchaser, the latter cannot sue the manufacturer if the manufacturer ha[s] made a disclaimer of warranties that satisfies UCC § 2-316. The fact that the manufacturer is thus protected from liability does not protect the dealer who resells without making this [sic] own disclaimer of warranties. That is, the manufacturer's disclaimer of warranties does not run with the goods

so as to protect any subsequent seller of them. To the contrary, each subsequent seller must make his own independent disclaimer in order to be protected from warranty liability.

* * *

Micro Center presented no evidence to show that it excluded any warranties when it sold the computer to appellant. We therefore find that the court erred by granting summary judgment to Micro Center on appellant's claims for breach of implied warranties of merchantability and fitness for a particular purpose.

III

Appellant based his second claim under the Magnuson-Moss Warranty Act.

The Act requires manufacturers and sellers of consumer products who provide written warranties to consumers to give detailed information about their warranty coverage. In addition, it affects both the rights of consumers and the obligations of warrantors under written warranties. It is important to understand that the Act applies only to written warranties. [The Act] states in part:

Full and conspicuous disclosure of terms and conditions; additional requirements for contents. In order to improve the adequacy of information available to consumers, prevent deception, and improve competition in the marketing of consumer products, any warrantor warranting a consumer product to a consumer by means of a written warranty shall, to the extent required by rules of the Commission, fully and conspicuously disclose in simple and readily understood language the terms and conditions of such warranty. ***

There is no evidence that Micro Center offered any warranties on the Toshiba computer. The only evidence of a written warranty consists of the Toshiba warranty and the TechSaver extended warranty. Micro Center did state its return policy on the receipt that it printed at the time of the transaction. That policy, however, is not required by law and does not constitute a written warranty for purposes of the Act. The receipt did not contain any written information relating to the performance or workmanship of the computer. The return policy is nothing more than a courtesy to its customers and not a warranty.

It follows that with no written warranty issued by Micro Center, appellant could not, as a matter of law, prevail on any Magnuson-Moss warranty claim directed against Micro Center. The court did not err by granting summary judgment to Micro Center on appellant's Magnuson-Moss warranty claim.

* * *

IV

This cause is affirmed in part, reversed in part and remanded to the lower court for further proceedings consistent with this opinion.

10.3 Products Liability—Negligence, Strict Liability

Gaines-Tabb v. ICI Explosives, USA, Inc., 160 F.3d 613 (10th Cir. 1998)

Individuals injured by the April 19, 1995, bombing of the Alfred P. Murrah Federal Building ("Murrah Building") in Oklahoma City, Oklahoma, filed suit against the manufacturers of the ammonium nitrate allegedly used to create the bomb. * * * The district court dismissed the complaint for failure to state a claim upon which relief may be granted, and the plaintiffs appealed. We affirm.

* * *

Background

On April 19, 1995, a massive bomb exploded in Oklahoma City and destroyed the Murrah Building, causing the deaths of 168 people and injuries to hundreds of others. On May 10, 1995, plaintiffs filed this diversity action, on behalf of themselves and all persons who incurred personal injuries during, or may claim loss of consortium or wrongful death resulting from, the bombing, against ICI Explosives ("ICI"), ICI's parent company, Imperial Chemical Industries, PLC, and another of Imperial Chemical's subsidiaries, ICI Canada.

ICI manufactures ammonium nitrate ("AN"). Plaintiffs allege that AN can be either "explosive grade" or "fertilizer grade." According to plaintiffs, "explosive-grade" AN is of low density and high porosity so it will absorb sufficient amounts of fuel or diesel oil to allow detonation of the AN, while "fertilizer-grade" AN is of high density and low porosity and so is unable to absorb sufficient amounts of fuel or diesel oil to allow detonation.

Plaintiffs allege that ICI sold explosive-grade AN mislabeled as fertilizer-grade AN to Farmland Industries, who in turn sold it to Mid-Kansas Cooperative Association in McPherson, Kansas. Plaintiffs submit that a "Mike Havens" purchased a total of eighty 50-pound bags of the mislabeled AN from Mid-Kansas. According to plaintiffs, "Mike Havens" was an alias used either by Timothy McVeigh or Terry Nichols, the two men tried for the bombing. Plaintiffs further allege that the perpetrators of the Oklahoma City bombing used the 4000 pounds of explosive-grade AN purchased from Mid-Kansas, mixed with fuel oil or diesel oil, to demolish the Murrah Building.

* * *

Analysis

* * *

I. Negligence

Plaintiffs allege that ICI was negligent in making explosive-grade AN available to the perpetrators of the Murrah Building bombing. Under Oklahoma law, the three essential elements of a claim of negligence are: "(1) a duty owed by the defendant to protect the plaintiff from injury, (2) a failure to properly perform that duty, and (3) the plaintiff's injury being proximately caused by the defendant's breach." The district court held that ICI did not have a duty to protect plaintiffs and that ICI's actions or inactions were not the proximate cause of plaintiffs' injuries. Although causation is generally a question of fact, "the question becomes an issue of law when there is no evidence from which a jury could reasonably find the required proximate, causal nexus between the careless act and the resulting injuries." Because we determine that there is a failure of causation as a matter of law, we need not discuss whether under Oklahoma law defendants owed plaintiffs a duty of care.

* * * Under Oklahoma law, "the causal nexus between an act of negligence and the resulting injury will be deemed broken with the intervention of a new, independent and efficient cause which was neither anticipated nor reasonably foreseeable." Such an intervening cause is known as a "supervening cause." To be considered a supervening cause, an intervening cause must be: (1) independent of the original act; (2) adequate by itself to bring about the injury; and (3) not reasonably foreseeable. "When the intervening act is intentionally tortious or criminal, it is more likely to be considered independent."

"A third person's intentional tort is a supervening cause of the harm that results—even if the actor's negligent conduct created a situation that presented the opportunity for the tort to be committed—unless the actor realizes or should realize the likelihood that the third person might commit the tortious act." If "the intervening act is a reasonably foreseeable consequence of the primary negligence, the original wrongdoer will not be relieved of liability." * * *

Oklahoma has looked to the Restatement (Second) of Torts § 448 for assistance in determining whether the intentional actions of a third party constitute a supervening cause of harm. Section 448 states:

> The act of a third person in committing an intentional tort or crime is a superseding cause of harm to another resulting therefrom, although the actor's negligent conduct created a situation which afforded an opportunity to the third person to commit such a tort or crime, unless the actor at the time of his negligent conduct realized or should have realized the likelihood that such a situation might be created, and that a third person might avail himself of the opportunity to commit such a tort or crime.

Comment b to § 448 provides further guidance in the case before us. * * * [U]nder comment b, the criminal acts of a third party may be foreseeable if (1) the situation provides a temptation to which a "recognizable percentage" of persons would yield, or (2) the temptation is created at a place where "persons of a peculiarly vicious type are likely to be." There is no indication that a peculiarly vicious type of person is likely to frequent the Mid-Kansas Co-op, so we shall turn our attention to the first alternative.

We have found no guidance as to the meaning of the term "recognizable percentage" as used in § 448, comment b. However, we believe that the term does not require a showing that the mainstream population or the majority would yield to a particular temptation; a lesser number will do. Equally, it does not include merely the law-abiding population. In contrast, we also believe that the term is not satisfied by pointing to the existence of a small fringe group or the occasional irrational individual, even though it is foreseeable generally that such groups and individuals will exist.

We note that plaintiffs can point to very few occasions of successful terrorist actions using ammonium nitrate, in fact only two instances in the last twenty-eight years—a 1970 bombing at the University of Wisconsin-Madison and the bombing of the Murrah Building. Due to the apparent complexity of manufacturing an ammonium nitrate bomb, including the difficulty of acquiring the correct ingredients (many of which are not widely available), mixing them properly, and triggering the resulting bomb, only a small number of persons would be able to carry out a crime such as the bombing of the Murrah Building. We simply do not believe that this is a group which rises to the level of a "recognizable percentage" of the population.

As a result, we hold that as a matter of law it was not foreseeable to defendants that the AN that they distributed to the Mid-Kansas Co-op would be put to such a use as to blow up the Murrah Building. Because the conduct of the bomber or bombers was unforeseeable, independent of the acts of defendants, and adequate by itself to bring about plaintiffs' injuries, the criminal activities of the bomber or bombers acted as the supervening cause of plaintiffs' injuries. Because of the lack of proximate cause, plaintiffs have failed to state a claim for negligence.

* * *

III. Manufacturers' Products Liability

Plaintiffs assert that ICI is strictly liable for manufacturing a defective product. We read their complaint as alleging both that the AN was defectively designed because, as designed, it was more likely to provide explosive force than an alternative formula, and that ICI failed to issue adequate warnings to Mid-Kansas that the AN was explosive grade rather than fertilizer grade so that Mid-Kansas could take appropriate precautions in selling the AN.

"In Oklahoma, a party proceeding under a strict products liability theory—referred to as manufacturer's products liability—must establish three elements: (1) that the product was the cause of the injury, (2) that the defect existed in the product at the time it left the manufacturer, retailer, or supplier's control, and (3) that the defect made the product unreasonably dangerous." "Unreasonably dangerous" means "dangerous to an extent beyond that which would be contemplated by the ordinary consumer who purchases it, with the ordinary knowledge common to the community as to its characteristics." A product may be unreasonably dangerous because it is defectively designed or manufactured, or because it is not accompanied by the proper warnings regarding use of the product.

As the basis of their defective design claim plaintiffs contend that ICI could have made the AN safer by using an alternate formulation or incorporating additives to prevent the AN from detonating. Plaintiffs' suggestion that the availability of alternative formulas renders ICI strictly liable for its product contradicts Oklahoma law. "Apparently, the plaintiff would hold the manufacturer responsible if his product is not as safe as some other product on the market. That is not the test in these cases. Only when a defect in the product renders it less safe than expected by the ordinary consumer will the manufacturer be held responsible." The "ordinary consumer" is "one who would be foreseeably expected to purchase the product involved." As plaintiffs acknowledge, the ordinary consumer of AN branded as fertilizer is a farmer. There is no indication that ICI's AN was less safe than would be expected by a farmer.

Similarly, plaintiffs have failed to state a claim regarding ICI's alleged failure to warn Mid-Kansas that the AN was explosive grade rather than fertilizer grade. "Under Oklahoma law, a manufacturer may have a duty to warn consumers of potential hazards which occur from the use of its product." If the manufacturer does not fulfill this duty, the product may be unreasonably dangerous. Interpreting Oklahoma law, this court has held that the duty to warn extends only to "ordinary consumers and users of the products." Under this rationale, defendants had no duty to warn the suppliers of its product of possible criminal misuse.

Conclusion

We AFFIRM the dismissal of plaintiffs' complaint for failure to state a claim upon which relief may be granted.

QUESTIONS FOR DISCUSSION FOR CASE 10.3

1. Products liability typically arises under state law. Why is this case being heard in federal court? What law does the court apply—federal or state?
2. The court determines that the defendant is not liable in negligence because there is no proximate causation between the plaintiff's injury and the defendant's breach. Explain.
3. The court also determines that the defendant is not strictly liable for the plaintiff's injuries. Why?
4. What two types of strict liability claims does the plaintiff allege?
5. If the use of a fertilizer as an explosive device is widely published on the Internet, do you think that such a use would then be reasonably foreseeable? If a manufacturer's product is used by a third party in a way that was unforeseen and someone is injured as a result, do you think that the manufacturer loses the defense that the use was unforeseeable in future lawsuits involving similar conduct by other third parties?

10.4 Strict Liability—Consumer Expectations, Risk-Utility Test
Higgins v. Intex Recreation Corp., 99 P.3d 421 (Wash. Ct. App. 2004)

This is a suit for personal injury damages based on product liability. To make a case, the plaintiffs had to show that the product was not reasonably safe as designed. Ultimately our disposition here turns on whether the plaintiffs' showing at trial was sufficient to send the question of the product's (a snow tube) safety to the jury. The plaintiffs submit that the snow tube went too fast, had no means for the rider to control it, and turned the rider into a fixed backward position. The product distributor responds essentially that this is what the tube was designed to do and therefore the product performed as designed and was not defective, as a matter of law. We conclude that the plaintiffs' showing was sufficient to submit the question whether the snow tube was *not* reasonably safe as designed to the jury. And we therefore affirm the judgment for the plaintiffs.

Facts

Intex Recreation Corporation distributes a vinyl, inflatable tube called Extreme Sno-Tube II. Dan Falkner bought one and used it sledding that same day. He described his first run with the tube as fast. And the tube took him farther than other sliding devices he had used. During Mr. Falkner's second run, the tube rotated him backward about one-quarter to one-third of the way down the hill. A group of parents, including Tom Higgins, stood near the bottom of the hill. Mr. Higgins heard a noise, looked, and saw seven-year-old Kyle Potter walking in the path of Mr. Falkner's speeding Sno-Tube:

> The size of the person on the sled and the little boy walking, I could see that their heads were going to hit so I took off as fast as I could and I grabbed him and, as I grabbed him to lift him, the tube, I misjudged the speed of the tube. It was going a lot faster than I thought, and it clipped me in the ankle, and I threw Kyle and my feet went straight up into the air and I landed on my forehead and snapped my head back.

The impact severed Mr. Higgins's spinal cord and left him a quadriplegic.

Mr. Higgins and his family sued Intex Recreation Corporation for damages based on negligence and strict liability. He also sued Dan Falkner, Curt Potter, and Kyle Potter for negligence. Curt Potter is Kyle's father; he was present at the hill at the time of the accident.

Much of the testimony at trial focused on the design of the Sno-Tube and specifically its speed and the lack of any way to direct it. Before Mr. Higgins's accident, Intex had prepared a hazard inventory. It evaluated hazards for each Intex product, and classified them by likelihood of the hazard and severity of any injury. Intex ranked the Sno-Tube 1-A, that is, most likely to involve collisions with severe injuries resulting. Intex recognized that a problem with the Sno-Tube is that

"[u]sers may believe that these products have a steering mechanism and [may] misjudge their ability to control them." Speed is a function of the Sno-Tube. Intex's Sno-Boggan goes just as fast but does not rotate. The only way to stop the Sno-Tube is to bail out. Competitors sell inflatable sledding devices with ridges that assist the rider in directing them. But the general position of Intex was that if the Sno-Tube did not go fast and rotate it would not be a Sno-Tube.

The plaintiffs put on ample expert testimony that Sno-Tubes in general carry a higher risk of injury because the rider can easily wind up going over 30 miles per hour downhill backwards with no way to direct or stop the tube. Those same experts concluded that ridges on the bottom of the Sno-Tube would have stopped the rotation and assisted the rider in directing it.

Intex moved for directed verdict at the close of the plaintiffs' case and for judgment as a matter of law following the jury's verdict. It predicated both motions on its view that the plaintiffs had not presented sufficient evidence of a design defect—essentially the Sno-Tube performed as designed. The court denied both motions.

A jury found Dan Falkner not negligent. It found Curt Potter negligent and responsible for 60 percent of the plaintiffs' damages. It found Kyle Potter negligent and responsible for 5 percent. And it found the Sno-Tube was not reasonably safe as designed and held Intex strictly liable for 35 percent of the damages.

Intex appeals.

Discussion
Product Liability—Design Defect
Washington's Product Liability Act—RCW 7.72.030

(a) A product is not reasonably safe as designed if, at the time of manufacture, the *likelihood that the product would cause the claimant's harm* or similar harms, *and the seriousness of those harms, outweighed the burden on the manufacturer to design a product that would have prevented those harms and the adverse effect that an alternative design that was practical and feasible would have on the usefulness of the product* ....

    ....

(3) In determining whether a product was not reasonably safe under this section, the trier of fact shall consider whether the product was *unsafe to an extent beyond that which would be contemplated by the ordinary consumer.*

RCW 7.72.030(1)(a), (3) (emphasis added). There are two tests then for determining whether a product is defective.

The *risk-utility test* requires a showing that the likelihood and seriousness of a harm outweigh the burden on the manufacturer to design a product that would have prevented that harm *and* would not have impaired the product's usefulness. RCW 7.72.030(1)(a). The *consumer-expectation test* requires a showing that the product is more dangerous than the ordinary consumer would expect. RCW 7.72.030(3). This test focuses on the reasonable expectation of the consumer. A number of factors influence this determination including the intrinsic nature of the product, its relative cost, the severity of the potential harm from the claimed defect, and the cost and feasibility of minimizing the risk.

Intex argues that the Sno-Tube did exactly what it was designed to do and exactly what consumers expected it to do—go fast and rotate. So any design that eliminated the tube's ability to rotate and go fast eliminated the characteristics that differentiate the Sno-Tube from other sledding products. Intex also argues that sledding—on *any* device—carries the risk of severe injury. And the reasonable consumer understands or should understand this.

We are passing upon the court's denial of a directed verdict and its refusal to grant judgment as a matter of law. Both decisions turn on whether we find substantial evidence in this record to support the jury's finding that this product is unreasonably dangerous under the two tests set out in the statute.

Risk-Utility Test

We look first at the arguments Intex advances under the risk-utility test. Intex argues that under the risk-utility test, the Sno-Tube, as a matter of law, was reasonably safe as designed. In its view, there is no feasible alternative design with this function—a function sought by the consumer.

A plaintiff can satisfy its burden of proving an alternative design by showing that another product "more safely serve[s] the same function as the challenged product." There is evidence in this record from which a jury could conclude that the placement of ribs or ridges on the bottom of the Sno-Tube, like those used on Intex's Sno-Boggan, would keep the rider facing downhill. The rider could then see obstacles and direct the tube. All this could be done without significantly sacrificing speed. This is enough … to prove an alternative safer design.

Intex argues essentially that some products are unavoidably and inherently unsafe. And while that may be true, [a previous case] suggests some guidelines for evaluating when that is an excuse: "[T]he … manufacturer of a challenged product would have to demonstrate that an inherently dangerous product is also 'necessary regardless of the risks involved to the user.'" The focus is on the product and its relative value to society.

Now, the ride down a snow-covered hill backward at 30 miles per hour may be a thrill. But it has very little social value when compared to the risk of severe injury. We do not think the Sno-Tube is a product that is "'necessary regardless of the risks involved to the user.'"

Intex relies on our case of *Thongchoom v. Graco Children's Products, Inc.*, 71 P.3d 214 (2003), for the proposition that a design change would result in a product that does not do what this one does and, therefore, it would be a fundamentally different product. *Thongchoom* is distinguishable. The function of the product there (a baby walker) was baby mobility. And the only proposed alternative eliminated that essential function—mobility. The product could not be described as inherently unsafe. It simply enabled a baby to move about.

The evidence here was of the obvious—speeding backward at 30 miles per hour down a crowded snow-covered hill is not safe, at least according to this jury. Again, reasonable inferences here are that the user cannot watch for others in his or her path. And, bystanders cannot always move fast enough to avoid the tube. There was ample evidence that an alternative design would permit the user to see what is in his or her path and avoid collisions by either bailing out or by using some minimal steering.

We find ample evidence to support this verdict, applying the risk-utility test.

Consumer-Expectation Test

We next take up Intex's assertion that the tube was not "unsafe to an extent beyond that which would be contemplated by the ordinary consumer." RCW 7.72.030(3). Again, we find ample evidence in this record to support the plaintiffs' assertion to the contrary.

Intex's Vice President, William Frank Smith, testified that Sno-Tube users "may believe that these products have a steering mechanism and [may] misjudge their ability to control them." And a reasonable jury could easily infer that the average consumer may expect the Sno-Tube to rotate. But he or she might not expect that it would continue in a backward position.

The trier of fact was instructed on and was entitled to consider a number of factors:

> In determining the reasonable expectations of the ordinary consumer, a number of factors must be considered. The relative cost of the product, the gravity of the potential harm from the claimed defect and *the cost and feasibility of eliminating or minimizing the risk may be relevant in a particular case. In other instances the nature of the product or the nature of the claimed defect may make other factors relevant to the issue.*

Here, the Sno-Tube is inexpensive. But so is Intex's Sno Boggan. And the Sno-Boggan provides a fast ride but not a blind high-speed ride. A jury could then find that a reasonable consumer would expect that a snow

sliding product would not put him or her in a backward, high-speed slide.

We find ample evidence in favor of the plaintiffs applying the consumer-expectation test.

* * *

We affirm the judgment.

QUESTIONS FOR DISCUSSION FOR CASE 10.4

1. Why does the court apply both the risk-utility test and the consumer expectation test in this case?
2. How should the manufacturer alter its behavior in response to this case?
3. If the manufacturer has to alter its product as a result of this case, it may end up producing a product that is less attractive to potential consumers. Does the court view this as a problem? Why or why not?

DISCUSSION QUESTIONS

1. Donald Josue Jr. was rendered paraplegic as a result of a single-vehicle accident in which he was ejected from the bed of an Isuzu pickup truck. Josue sued Isuzu, the manufacturer of the truck, asserting, among other things, that Isuzu was liable for (1) negligent failure to warn and (2) strict liability for failure to warn. Both claims were based on the allegation that the pickup truck was defectively designed because it did not contain a warning label informing users of the truck of the dangers associated with riding in the bed of the truck. How does negligent failure to warn differ from strict liability failure to warn? How should the court rule in this case?

2. David Weiner was transporting a 54-inch long, 180-pound canister of nitrous oxide (to use in inflating balloons), which he took to rock concerts in his girlfriend's two-door, hatchback Acura. Weiner flipped down the back of the rear seats to make room for the canister. He suffered personal injuries when he hit a guardrail and the unrestrained canister slid into the back of the driver's seat, pinning him between the seat and the shoulder harness. Weiner sued the manufacturers and sellers of the Acura on two strict liability theories: (1) design defect (because the front seats could not withstand the impact of a 180-pound object and because no restraints were provided to secure the cargo) and (2) failure to warn. How should the court rule on these claims?

3. Werner Co. manufactures an eight-foot aluminum stepladder, which passed the safety standards of the ANSI and the Underwriter's Laboratory, two independent organizations that evaluate stepladders. Daniel Gawenda was injured when he fell from one of these ladders. He sued Werner, alleging that Werner's failure to build more rigid rear rails into the stepladder constituted negligent design. Gawenda offered no evidence of a stepladder that used more rigid rear rails than Werner's, nor did his expert present evidence describing the feasibility of alternative designs. How should the court rule on Werner's negligence claim?

4. Mr. and Mrs. Holowaty, a Canadian couple, stopped at McDonald's for breakfast while traveling through Rochester, Minnesota. Mr. Holowaty purchased a cup of coffee containing the warnings "HOT!" and "CAUTION: CONTENTS HOT" on both the lid and the cup. McDonald's requires its franchises to serve their coffee at between 175 and 185 degrees in containers carrying such warnings. Mrs. Holowaty sat in the passenger seat with the beverage tray on her lap. While exiting the parking lot, the coffee tipped and spilled half its contents on Mrs. Holowaty, causing second-degree burns to her thighs and permanent scars. Mr. and Mrs. Holowaty sued McDonald's as the franchisor, alleging that the coffee was defective because it was excessively hot

and because McDonald's failed to provide adequate warnings about the severity of burns that could result. Although the Holowatys admitted that they knew that the coffee would be hot and could cause burns, they argue that reasonable consumers would not anticipate second-degree burns. How should the court rule on their claim?

5. K2 Corporation, a subsidiary of Anthony Industries, marketed the "Dan Donnelly XTC," a snowboard without predrilled holes for bindings. Without such a pattern, purchasers could install their choice of any bindings by simply screwing them into a fiberglass retention panel in the snowboard's core. Hyjek purchased this model and was injured in March 1991 when his binding came loose from the snowboard, striking him inside his left ankle. In 1993, he sued Anthony Industries, claiming that the design was not reasonably safe and the system of threaded screws was a foreseeably inadequate and unsafe binding retention method. In 1992, K2 had begun to design a new system involving "through-core inserts" molded into the snowboard. Fine threaded screws were then screwed into the inserts to hold the bindings in place. Hyjek sought to enter into evidence K2's subsequent change in design to support his claim for design defect. Should the judge allow the evidence into trial?

6. Larry Moss purchased a Crosman 760 Pumpmaster BB gun from a local Kmart store for his seven-year-old son Josh. Larry saw a warning on the box that stated "May cause death or injury" but thought that it might refer just to birds or small animals. The box also contained the following warning, which Larry did not read:

> WARNING: NOT A TOY. ADULT SUPERVISION REQUIRED. MISUSE OR CARELESS USE MAY CAUSE SERIOUS INJURY OR DEATH. MAY BE DANGEROUS UP TO 475 YARDS (435 METERS). THIS AIR GUN IS INTENDED FOR USE BY THOSE 16 YEARS OF AGE OR OLDER. FOR COMPLETE OPERATING INSTRUCTIONS, REVIEW OWNERS MANUAL INSIDE BOX BEFORE USING THIS AIR GUN.

Additional warnings and flyers were contained inside the box, but Larry did not read them before allowing Josh to use the gun. Larry's instructions to Josh on the proper use of the gun indicated that Larry was aware that the gun could be dangerous if misused, however.

Josh and his cousin Tim were playing with the gun in the woods. Josh hid behind a tree about 15 feet in front of Tim and stuck his head out from behind the tree just as Tim fired. The BB pierced Josh's eye, entered his brain, and killed him. Josh's parents brought a suit against Crosman Corp. and Kmart Corp., alleging that the defendants caused Josh's death by failing to provide adequate warnings detailing the dangers associated with the gun. How should the court rule on this claim?

7. Greg Presto's mental illness was being treated with Clozaril, an antipsychotic medication manufactured by Sandoz Pharmaceuticals Corp. Because Clozaril can damage a patient's immune system, pharmacists and nurses at Caremark, Inc., a distributor of the drug, dispensed the medicine, drew Greg's blood each week, monitored the results of those tests, and provided the results to Dr. Warren, the prescribing physician. The Clozaril helped Greg's condition, but it had undesirable side effects. Greg and his mother requested that Greg be taken off the medication, and Dr. Warren allegedly agreed. In August, 1991, Greg stopped taking the medication, but he failed to heed the warning included in the drug's packaging to gradually reduce the dosage over a one- or two-week period lest the patient's psychotic symptoms recur. Greg committed suicide. The Prestos sued Sandoz, alleging that the manufacturer failed to warn Greg of the dangers he faced if he discontinued use of the drug suddenly. What defense might Sandoz raise? How should the court rule on this claim?

8. In early October, 1989, Sandra Ruffin purchased "Compelling Everglade" carpet, manufactured by Salem Carpet Mills, Inc. The store manager told Ruffin that the carpet "was a higher quality carpet than what she brought in [to the store]" and that she was getting "a very good grade of material." Ruffin alleges that shortly after she purchased the carpet and had it installed, she and her minor daughter began experiencing physical symptoms such as nosebleeds, rashes, extreme sweating, chills, sleeplessness, and racing of the heart. After repeated complaints, the store removed the carpet from her home less than a month after its installation. Ruffin alleges that she and her daughter have suffered severe toxic injuries as a result of the chemicals in the carpet installed in her house and asserts a claim for breach of express warranty. Has an express warranty been created?

9. Skip Wright, a firefighter with 13 years' experience, was operating a Stang deck gun attached to a fire engine while extinguishing a fire. During the course of the fire, the water reaching the water cannon had to be routed from the hydrant through the truck's water pump. The extreme pressure created an unusual force, called a "water hammer," where the force of the water is four to six times greater than normal, detaching the water cannon from the truck and throwing Wright into the air. He landed on the ground with the water cannon falling on top of him. Wright brought suit under a failure-to-warn theory. Stang argued that anyone familiar with fire apparatus would recognize the risk of a water hammer. Stang did not produce evidence to the court that it had provided any warnings regarding the potential hazards of a water hammer. How should the court resolve this dispute?

10. The Black Talon bullet, designed and manufactured by Olin Corp., is a hollow-point bullet designed to bend upon impact into six, ninety-degree-angle, razor-sharp petals or "talons" that increase the wounding power of the bullet by stretching, cutting, and tearing tissue and bone. On December 7, 1993, Colin Ferguson opened fire on the passengers of a commuter train departing from New York City. Ferguson, using the Black Talons in a 9mm semi-automatic handgun, killed six people, including Dennis McCarthy, and injured nineteen, including Kevin McCarthy. Their injuries were enhanced because the bullets performed as designed. Kevin McCarthy and the estate of Dennis McCarthy sued Olin Corp. under design-defect theories based in negligence and strict liability. How should the court resolve this dispute?

11. Ronald Anderson Jr. is a self-employed construction contractor from New York. While working on a project in Connecticut, Anderson purchased lumber from a Home Depot in Danbury, Connecticut. Wishing to protect the lumber from the rain, Anderson also purchased a tarp and bungee stretch cords to cover the lumber that sat in the bed of his pickup. The bungee cords came in an assortment pack of various lengths. Anderson purchased the cords after examining the package, noticing two statements: "Made in the U.S.A. We Make Our Products Where We Make Our Home[s]—America" and "Premium Quality." He failed, however, to read the warnings on the package regarding proper use, including the importance of wearing protective eye wear while using the cords, the maximum stretching capacity of the cords, and admonitions against stretching the cords toward or away from one's body.

After Anderson strapped the tarp over the bed of his truck, one of the hooks on the cords became dislodged, hitting him in the left eye. Anderson alleges that the manufacturer, Bungee Int'l Mfg. Corp., breached an express warranty created by the "Made in the U.S.A." and "Premium Quality" statements as well as the drawings showing proper usage. Anderson alleged that the "Made in the U.S.A." and the "Premium Quality" labeling on the packaging, along with the five drawings showing recommended uses, caused him to believe that the cord was "a good, strong, top notch American-made product suitable for numerous uses." The hooks on the cord were made in Taiwan, but the product was assembled in the United States and under federal regulations could be advertised as "Made in the U.S.A." Has there been a breach of express warranty?

12. In 1994, Daniel Scoggin hired Broward Marine for $5,000 to perform a "bottom job" on his 77-foot sailboat, the "Jubilem." A "bottom job" is a final paint job involving sandblasting the hull to the bare metal and applying a protective coat that prevents barnacles from attaching to the hull of the ship. New Nautical Coatings, Inc., manufactured the paint used on the Jubilem. New Nautical's products contained an express warranty that, if used properly, the paint would protect the hull for one year, and a booklet contained detailed instructions as to use.

Three months after the paint job, the coating began to peel. New Nautical determined that this was because Broward had not properly sandblasted the boat, as prescribed by the detailed instructions, and supplied replacement paint at no cost. Once again, the boat was not sandblasted because Scoggin did not want to pay the extra cost. Broward applied a test patch to the boat, and a representative of Nautical approved the new paint job, saying "yeah, go ahead and apply it and [Nautical] would warranty it." The coating did not last. Scoggin sued for breach of an express warranty. Has there been a breach of express warranty?

13. In an attempt to save on utility costs, Metro National Corp. decided to construct a thermal-energy-storage system to replace its central-air-conditioning system at Memorial City Medical Center. Metro contacted Morris & Associates about purchasing three of its ice harvesters (which are

essentially industrial icemakers). Dunham-Bush manufactured a specially engineered compressor, the 1216SE, for use in the Morris harvesters. Hoping to enter this burgeoning market, Dunham-Bush assured Morris that the compressors were specially designed, reliable, and suitable for use under the predicted field conditions. In addition, Dunham-Bush extended its usual one-year warranty to a five-year one on the 1216SE. On several occasions, Morris assured Metro that the compressors were extremely reliable, and Dunham-Bush quickly replaced a compressor that immediately failed. Metro ordered two more units later that year. The compressors experienced a 70 percent failure rate. Metro gave up on the Morris systems and purchased instead a new 200-ton central-air-conditioning system. If Metro were to sue Dunham-Bush for breach of warranty, what warranties should they allege were breached? Should the court find that the warranties had been breached?

14. Reliance Granite Company, run by James R. Noggle, manufactures gravestone monuments for monument dealers. Willis Mining, Inc., quarries granite, cuts it into blocks, and sells it to such manufacturers. Noggle purchased blocks from Willis, created monuments, and sold them. Within 18 months, the monuments sold by Noggle became discolored, forcing Noggle to replace them. When Noggle sought reimbursement from Willis, Willis refused to pay. Noggle brought this suit against Willis alleging, among other claims, breach of an implied warranty of merchantability. Willis claims that no breach occurred because Noggle inspected the blocks and selected them with monument manufacturing in mind. How should the court resolve this dispute?

15. Scott Gebo's hand was crushed at work in the rollers of a paper embossing machine when a protective guard system failed. Gebo filed a products liability suit against Filtration Sciences, Inc. Filtration Sciences had originally purchased the embosser in 1966 and it had modified the machine by designing and installing the guard system. Three years prior to Geho's injury, Filtration Science sold its paper mill and all the machinery contained therein, including the embosser, to Knowlton Specialty Papers, Inc.

Should Filtration Sciences be held strictly liable for Gebo's injuries? What public policy implications does this case raise?

Glossary

Ab initio from the beginning.

Abrogate recall or repeal; make void or inoperative.

Absolute liability liability for an act that causes harm even though the actor was not at fault.

Acceptance unqualified assent to the act or proposal of another; as the acceptance of a draft (bill of exchange), of an offer to make a contract, of goods delivered by the seller, or of a gift or deed.

Accident an event that occurs even though a reasonable person would not have foreseen its occurrence, because of which the law holds no one responsible for the harm caused.

Accord agreement to a different performance other than what was originally specified in the contract.

Accord and satisfaction an agreement to substitute a different performance for that called for in the contract and the performance of this substitute agreement.

Acknowledgment an admission or confirmation, generally of an instrument and usually made before a person authorized to administer oaths, such as a notary public; the purpose being to declare that the instrument was executed by the person making the instrument, or that it was a voluntary act or that that person desires that it be recorded.

Action a proceeding to enforce any right.

Action in personam an action brought to impose liability upon a person, such as a money judgment.

Action in rem an action brought to declare the status of a thing, such as an action to declare the title to property to be forfeited because of its illegal use.

Action of assumpsit a common law action brought to recover damages for breach of a contract.

Act of God a natural phenomenon that is not reasonably foreseeable.

Act-of-state doctrine the doctrine whereby every sovereign state is bound to respect the independence of every other sovereign state, and the courts of one country will not sit in judgment of another government's acts done within its own territory.

Actual the physical delivery of an agreement.

Administrative agency a governmental commission or board given authority to regulate particular matters.

Administrative law the law governing administrative agencies.

Administrative Procedure Act (APA) a federal law governing the operations and process of federal administraaive agencies.

Administrative regulations rules made by state and federal administrative agencies.

Advisory opinion an opinion that may be rendered in a few states when there is no actual controversy before the court and the matter is submitted by private persons, or in some instances by the governor of the state, to obtain the court's opinion.

Affidavit a statement of facts set forth in written form and supported by the oath or affirmation of the person making the statement setting forth that such facts are true on the basis of actual knowledge or on information and belief. The affidavit is executed before a notary public or other person authorized to administer oaths.

Affirmative covenant   an express undertaking or promise in a contract or deed to do an act.

Agency   the relationship that exists between a person identified as a principal and another by virtue of which the latter may make contracts with third persons on behalf of the principal. (Parties—**principal, agent, third person**)

Agent   one who is authorized by the principal or by operation of law to make contracts with third persons on behalf of the principal.

Airbill   a document of title issued to a shipper whose goods are being sent via air.

Aktiengesellschaft   German version of the société anonyme, very similar to the U.S. corporate form of business organization.

Alteration   any material change of the terms of a writing fraudulently made by a party thereto.

Ambiguous   having more than one reasonable interpretation.

Amicus curiae   literally, a friend of the court; one who is approved by the court to take part in litigation and to assist the court by furnishing an opinion in the matter.

Answer   what a defendant must file to admit or deny facts asserted by the plaintiff.

Anticipatory breach   the repudiation by a promisor of the contract prior to the time that performance is required when such repudiation is accepted by the promisee as a breach of the contract.

Anticipatory repudiation   the repudiation made in advance of the time for performance of the contract obligations.

Antitrust acts   statutes prohibiting combinations and contracts in restraint of trade—notably, the federal Sherman Antitrust Act of 1890.

Apparent authority   appearance of authority created by the principal's words or conduct.

Appeal   taking a case to a reviewing court to determine whether the judgment of the lower court or administrative agency was correct. (Parties—**appellant, appellee**)

Appellate jurisdiction   the power of a court to hear and decide a given class of cases on appeal from another court or administrative agency.

Arbitration   the settlement of disputed questions, whether of law or fact, by one or more arbitrators by whose decision the parties agree to be bound.

Article 2   section of Uniform Commercial Code that governs contracts for the sale of goods.

Article 2A   the portion of the UCC that governs the lease of goods.

Assignee   a third party to whom contract benefits are transferred.

Assignment   transfer of a right. Generally used in connection with personal property rights, as rights under a contract, commercial paper, an insurance policy, a mortgage, or a lease. (Parties—**assignor, assignee**)

Assumption of risk   the common law rule that an employee could not sue the employer for injuries caused by the ordinary risks of employment on the theory that the employee assumed such risks by undertaking the work. The rule has been abolished in those areas governed by workers' compensation laws and most employers' liability statutes.

Attorney in fact   a private attorney authorized to act for another under a power of attorney.

Attorneys   counselors at law who are officers of the court.

Authenticate   make or establish as genuine, official, or final, such as by signing, countersigning, sealing, or performing any other act indicating approval.

Bailee   person who accepts possession of a property.

Bailment   the relationship that exists when personal property is delivered into the possession of another under an agreement, express or implied, that the identical property will be returned or will be delivered in accordance with the agreement. (Parties—**bailor, bailee**)

Bailment for hire   a contract in which the bailor agrees to pay the bailee.

Bailor   the person who turns over the possession of a property.

Battle of the forms   merchants' exchanges of invoices and purchase orders with differing boiler plate terms.

Bilateral contract   an agreement under which one promise is given in exchange for another.

Bill of lading   a document issued by a carrier reciting the receipt of goods and the terms of the contract of transportation. Regulated by the federal Bills of Lading Act or the UCC.

Bill of sale   a writing signed by the seller reciting that the personal property therein described has been sold to the buyer.

Bona fide   in good faith; without any fraud or deceit.

Boycott   a combination of two or more persons to cause harm to another by refraining from patronizing or dealing with such other person in any way or inducing others to so refrain.

Breach   the failure to act or perform in the manner called for in a contract.

Cancellation   a crossing out of a part of an instrument or a destruction of all legal effect of the instrument, whether by act of party, upon breach by the other party, or pursuant to agreement or decree of court.

Carrier   an individual or organization undertaking the transportation of goods.

Case law   law that includes principles that are expressed for the first time in court decisions.

Cause of action   the right to damages or other judicial relief when a legally protected right of the plaintiff is violated by an unlawful act of the defendant.

Caveat emptor   Let the buyer beware. This maxim has been nearly abolished by warranty and strict tort liability concepts and consumer protection laws.

Cease and desist order   an order issued by a court or administrative agency to stop a practice that it decides is improper.

Certiorari   a review by a higher court of the regularity of proceedings before a lower court. Originally granted within the discretion of the reviewing court. The name is derived from the language of the writ, which was in Latin and directed the lower court to certify its record and transfer it to the higher court. In modern practice, the scope of review has often been expanded to include a review of the merits of the case and, also, to review the action of administrative agencies.

CF   cost and freight.

Choice-of-law clause   a clause in an agreement that specifies which law will govern should a dispute arise.

C.I.F.   cost, insurance, and freight.

Circumstantial evidence   relates to circumstances surrounding the facts in dispute from which the trier of fact may deduce what has happened.

C.I.S.G.   uniform international contract code contracts for international sale of goods.

Civil action   in many states a simplified form of action combining all or many of the former common law actions.

Civil court   a court with jurisdiction to hear and determine controversies relating to private rights and duties.

Clayton Act   a federal law that prohibits price discrimination.

COD   cash on delivery.

Comity   a principle of international and national law that the laws of all nations and states deserve the respect legitimately demanded by equal participants.

Commerce clause   that section of the U.S. Constitution allocating business regulation.

Commercial impracticability   when costs of performance rise suddenly and performance of a contract will result in a substantial loss.

Commercial unit   the standard of the trade for shipment or packaging of a good.

Commoncarrier   a carrier that holds out its facilities to serve the general public for compensation without discrimination.

Common law   the body of unwritten principles originally based upon the usages and customs of the community that were recognized and enforced by the courts.

Comparative negligence   a defense to negligence that allows plaintiff to recover reduced damages based on his level of fault.

Compensatory damages   a sum of money that will compensate an injured plaintiff for actual loss.

Complaint   the initial pleading filed by the plaintiff in many actions, which in many states may be served as original process to acquire jurisdiction over the defendant.

Condition   an event that affects the existence of a contract or the obligation of a party to a contract.

Condition precedent   event that if unsatisfied would mean that no rights would arise under a contract.

Condition subsequent   an event whose occurrence or lack thereof terminates a contract.

Conflict of interest   conduct that compromises an employee's allegiance to that company.

Conflict of laws   the body of law that determines the law of which state is to apply when two or more states are involved in the facts of a given case.

Consent decrees   informal settlements of enforcement actions brought by agencies.

Consequential damages   damages the buyer experiences as a result of the seller's breach with respect to a third party.

Consequential loss   a loss that does not result directly from a party's act but from the consequences of that act.

Consideration   the promise or performance that the promisor demands as the price of the promise.

Consignee   person to whom goods are shipped.

Consignment   a bailment made for the purpose of sale by the bailee. (Parties—**consignor, consignee**)

Consignor   person who delivers goods to the carrier for shipment.

Conspiracy   an agreement between two or more persons to commit an unlawful act.

Constitution   a body of principles that establishes the structure of a government and the relationship of the government to the people who are governed.

Constitutional law   the branch of law that is based on the constitutions in force in a particular area or territory.

Consumer credit   credit for personal, family, and household use.

Consumer credit transaction   a transaction referred to by the FTC rule limiting the rights of a holder in due course in this type of transaction to protect consumers of goods or services for personal, family, or household use.

Consumer goods   goods used or bought primarily for personal, family, or household use.

Consumer lease   lease of goods by a natural person for personal, family, or household use.

Contract   a binding agreement based upon the genuine assent of the parties, made for a lawful object, between competent parties, in the form required by law, and generally supported by consideration.

Contract of adhesion   a contract offered by a dominant party to a party with inferior bargaining power on a take-it-or-leave-it basis.

Contractual capacity   the ability to understand that a contract is being made and to understand its general meaning.

Contributory negligence   negligence of the plaintiff.

Cooperative   a group of two or more persons or enterprises that acts through a common agent with respect to a common objective, such as buying or selling.

Copyright   a grant to an author or artist of an exclusive right to publish and sell the copyrighted work for the life of the author or artist and fifty years thereafter. For a "work made for hire," a grant of an exclusive right to publish and sell the copyrighted work for 100 years from its creation or 75 years from its publication, whichever is shorter.

Costs   the expenses of suing or being sued, recoverable in some actions by the successful party and, in others, subject to allocation by the court. Ordinarily, costs do not include attorney's fees or compensation for loss of time.

Counterclaim   a claim that the defendant in an action may make against the plaintiff.

Counterfeiting   manufacturing, with fraudulent intent, of a document or coin that appears genuine.

Counteroffer   a proposal by an offeree to the offeror that changes the terms of, and thus rejects, the original offer.

Course of dealing   pattern of performance between two parties to a contract.

Court   a tribunal established by government to hear and decide matters properly brought to it.

Covenants   obligations of parties in a lease.

Creditor   person (seller or lender) who is owed money; also may be a secured party.

Crime   a violation of the law that is punished as an offense against the state or government.

Cross complaint   a claim that the defendant may make against the plaintiff.

Cross-examination   the examination made of a witness by the attorney for the adverse party.

Customary authority   authority of an agent to do any act that, according to the custom of the community, usually accompanies the transaction for which the agent is authorized to act.

Cybersquatters   the term for those who register and set up domain names on the Internet for resale to the famous users of the names in question.

Damages   a sum of money recovered to redress or make amends for the legal wrong or injury done.

Debtor   a buyer on credit, i.e., a borrower.

Declaratory judgment   a procedure for obtaining the decision of a court on a question before any action has been taken or loss sustained. It differs from an advisory opinion in that there must be an actual, imminent controversy.

De facto   existing in fact as distinguished from as of right, as in the case of an officer or a corporation purporting to act as such without being elected to the office or having been properly incorporated.

Defamation   libel, the attacking of someone's reputation.

Defendant   party charged with a violation of civil or criminal law in a proceeding.

Delegated powers   powers expressly granted the national government by the Constitution.

Delegation   the transfer to another of the right and power to do an act.

Demurrer   a pleading that may be filed to attack the sufficiency of the adverse party's pleading as not stating a cause of action or a defense.

Deposition   the testimony of a witness taken out of court before a person authorized to administer oaths.

Design patents   patents that protect new and nonobvious ornamental features that appear in connection with an article of manufacture.

Detrimental reliance   see **reliance** and **promissory estoppel**.

Dicta   see obiter dictum.

Direct damages   losses that are caused by breach of a contract.

Directed verdict   a direction by the trial judge to the jury to return a verdict in favor of a specified party to the action.

Direct examination   the asking of witnesses about details pertinent to a case.

Directors   the persons vested with control of the corporation, subject to the elective power of the shareholders.

Discharge of contract   termination of a contract by performance, agreement, impossibility, acceptance of breach, or operation of law.

Discovery   procedures for ascertaining facts prior to the time of trial in order to eliminate the element of surprise in litigation.

Dismiss   a procedure to terminate an action by moving to dismiss on the ground that the plaintiff has not pleaded a cause of action entitling the plaintiff to relief.

Disparagement of goods   the making of malicious, false statements as to the quality of the goods of another.

Dispute Settlement Body   a means, provided by the World Trade Organization, for member countries to resolve trade disputes rather than engage in unilateral trade sanctions or a trade war.

Distributor   the entity that takes title to goods and bears the financial and commercial risks for the subsequent sale of the goods.

Domicile   the home of a person or the state of incorporation, to be distinguished from a place where a person lives but does not regard as home, or a state in which a corporation does business but in which it was not incorporated.

Donee   recipient of a gift

Donor   person making a gift.

Draft   see **bill of exchange**.

Due care   the degree of care that a reasonable person would exercise to prevent the realization of harm, which under all the circumstances was reasonably foreseeable in the event that such care was not taken.

Due process   the constitutional right to be heard, question witnesses, and present evidence.

Due Process Clause   the process of checking the environmental history and nature of land prior to purchase.

Dumping   selling goods in another country at less than their fair value.

Duress   conduct that deprives the victim of free will and that generally gives the victim the right to set aside any transaction entered into under such circumstances.

Duty   an obligation of law imposed on a person to perform or refrain from performing a certain act.

Economic duress   threat of financial loss.

Effects doctrine   the doctrine that states U.S. courts will assume jurisdiction and will apply antitrust laws to conduct outside of the United States where the activity of business firms has direct and substantial effect on U.S. commerce.

Electronic funds transfer (EFTA)   any transfer of funds (other than a transaction originated by a check, draft, or similar paper instrument) that is initiated through an electronic terminal, telephone, computer, or magnetic tape so as to authorize a financial institution to debit or credit an account.

Employment-at-will doctrine   doctrine in which the employer has historically been allowed to terminate the employment contract at any time for any reason or for no reason.

En banc   the term used when the full panel of judges on the appellate court hears a case.

Equity   the body of principles that originally developed because of the inadequacy of the rules then applied by the common law courts of England.

Estoppel   the principle by which a person is barred from pursuing a certain course of action or of disputing the truth of certain matters.

Ethica   a branch of philosophy dealing with values that relate to the nature of human conduct and values associated with that conduct.

European Union (EU)   name used to describe the union of the fifteen member countries of Europe who seek to unify their economic, monetary, and political policies.

Evidence   that which is presented to the trier of fact as the basis upon which the trier is to determine what happened.

Exculpatory clause   a provision in a contract stating that one of the parties shall not be liable for damages in case of breach; also called limitation-of-liability clause.

Execute   to carry out a judgment.

Executed contract   an agreement that has been completely performed.

Executive branch   the branch of government (e.g., the president) formed to execute the laws.

Executory contract   an agreement by which something remains to be done by one or both parties.

Exemplary damages   damages, in excess of the amount needed to compensate for the plaintiff's injury, that are awarded in order to punish the defendant for malicious or wanton conduct; also called "punitive damages."

Exhaustion of administrative remedies   the requirement that an agency make its final decision before the parties can go to court.

Existing goods   goods that physically exist and are owned by the seller at the time of a transaction.

Expert witness   one who has acquired special knowledge in a particular field as through practical experience or study, or both, whose opinion is admissible as an aid to the trier of fact.

Export sale   a direct sale to customers in a foreign country.

Express authority   authority of an agent to perform a certain act.

Express contract   an agreement of the parties manifested by their words, whether spoken or written.

Express warranty   a statement by the defendant relating to the goods, which statement is part of the basis of the bargain.

Ex-ship   the obligation of a seller to deliver or unload goods from a ship that has reached its port of destination.

Fair use   a principle that allows the limited use of copyrighted material for teaching, research, and news reporting.

FAS   free alongside the named vessel.

FCPA   Foreign Corrupt Practices Act; prohibits bribery by U.S.-based companies in their international operations.

Federal district court   a general trial court of the federal system.

Federal Register   a government publication issued five days a week that lists all administrative regulations, all presidential proclamations and executive orders, and other documents and classes of documents that the president or Congress direct to be published.

Federal sentencing guidelines   federal standards used by judges to determine mandatory sentencing terms for convicted criminals.

Federal supremacy   declared by constitution for use when direct conflict between state and federal statutes exist.

Federal system   the system of government in which a central government is given power to administer to national concerns while individual states retain the power to administer to local concerns.

Federal Trade Commission Act   a statute prohibiting unfair methods of competition in interstate commerce.

Fifth Amendment   constitutional protection against self incrimination which also guarantees due process.

Firm offer   an offer stated to be held open for a specified time, which must be so held in some states even in the absence of an option contract, or under the UCC, with respect to merchants.

FOB   free on board, indicating a seller is providing for the shipping of goods to the buyer.

FOB place of destination   general commercial language for delivery to the buyer.

FOB place of shipment   a 'ship to' contract.

Food, Drug, and Cosmetic Act   a federal statute prohibiting the interstate shipment of misbranded or adulterated foods, drugs, cosmetics, and therapeutic devices.

Forbearance   refraining from doing an act.

Foreign corporation   a corporation incorporated under the laws of another state.

Forgery   the fraudulent making or altering of an instrument that apparently creates or alters a legal liability of another.

Formal contracts   written contracts or agreements whose formality signifies the parties' intention to abide by the terms.

Forum   a court in which any lawsuit should be brought.

Franchise   a privilege or authorization, generally exclusive, to engage in a particular activity within a particular geographic area, such as a government franchise to operate a taxi company within a specified city, or a private franchise as the grant by a manufacturer of a right to sell products within a particular territory or for a particular number of years.

Franchise agreement   sets forth rights of franchisee to use trademarks, etc., of franchisor.

Franchisee   person to whom franchise is granted.

Franchising   the granting of permission to use a trademark, trade name, or copyright under specified conditions.

Franchisor   party granting the franchise.

Fraud   the making of a false statement of a past or existing fact, with knowledge of its falsity or with reckless indifference as to its truth, with the intent to cause another to rely thereon, and such person does rely thereon and is harmed thereby.

Fraud in the inducement   is fraud in the obtaining of a promise to an instrument, not fraud as to the nature of the instrument itself.

Freedom of Information Act   federal law permitting citizens to request documents and records from administrative agencies.

Freight insurance   insures that shipowner will receive payment for transportation charges.

Full warranty   the obligation of a seller to fix or replace a defective product within a reasonable time without cost to the buyer.

Funds transfer   communication of instructions or requests to pay a specific sum of money to the credit of a specified account or person without an actual physical passing of money.

Fungible goods   goods of a homogeneous nature of which any unit is the equivalent of any other unit or is treated as such by mercantile usage.

Future goods   goods that exist physically but are not owned by the seller as well as goods that have not yet been produced.

Gambling   making a bet with a chance for profit and similar to a lottery in that there are the three elements of payment, prize, and chance.

General agent   an agent authorized by the principal to transact all affairs in connection with a particular kind of business or trade or to transact all business at a certain place.

General damages   damages that in the ordinary course of events follow naturally and probably from the injury caused by the defendant.

General jurisdiction   the power to hear and decide all controversies involving legal rights and duties.

Gift   the title to an owner's personal property voluntarily transferred by a party not receiving anything in exchange.

Good faith   the absence of knowledge of any defects in or problems.

Goods   anything movable at the time it is identified as the subject of a transaction.

Gray market goods   foreign-made goods with U.S. trademarks brought into the United States without the consent of the trademark owners to compete with these owners.

Guarantor   one who undertakes the obligation of guaranty.

Guaranty   an undertaking to pay the debt of another if the creditor first sues the debtor and is unable to recover the debt from the debtor or principal. (In some instances the liability is primary, in which case it is the same as suretyship.)

Horizontal price fixing   a violation of antitrust law whereby competitive businesses—manufacturers, for example—agree on the price they will charge for a good or service.

Identification   point in the transaction when the buyer acquires an interest in the goods subject to the contract.

Identified   term applied to particular goods selected by either the buyer or the seller as the goods called for by the sales contract.

Illusory promise   a promise that in fact does not impose any obligation on the promisor.

Immunity   not being subject to liability ordinarily imposed by law.

Implied contract   a contract expressed by conduct or implied or deduced from the facts. Also used to refer to a quasi contract.

Implied warranty   a warranty that was not made but is implied by law.

Imputed   vicariously attributed to or charged to another; for instance, the knowledge of an agent obtained while acting in the scope of authority is imputed to the principal.

Incidental authority   authority of an agent that is reasonably necessary to execute express authority.

Incidental damages   incurred by the nonbreaching party as part of the process of trying to cover or sell; includes storage fees, commissions and the like.

Incorporation by reference   a contract consisting of both the original or skeleton document and the detailed statement that is incorporated in it.

Indemnity   the right of a person secondarily liable to require that a person primarily liable pay for loss sustained when the secondary party discharges the obligation that the primary party should have discharged; the right of an agent to be paid the amount of any loss or damage sustained without fault because of obedience to the principal's instructions; an undertaking by one person for a consideration to pay another person a sum of money to indemnify that person when a specified loss is incurred.

Indemnity contract   an undertaking by one person, for a consideration, to pay another person a sum of money in the event that the other person sustains a specified loss.

Independent contractor   a contractor who undertakes to perform a specified task according to the terms of a contract but over whom the other contracting party has no control except as provided for by the contract.

Informal contract   a simple oral or written contract.

Infringement   the violation of trademarks, patents, or copyrights by copying or using material without permission.

Injunction   an order of a court of equity to refrain from doing (negative injunction) or to do (affirmative or mandatory injunction) a specified act. Its use in labor disputes has been greatly restricted by statute.

In pari delicto   equally guilty; used in reference to a transaction as to which relief will not be granted to either party because both are equally guilty of wrongdoing.

Instructions   summary of the law given to jurors by the judge before deliberation begins.

Insurable interest   an interest in the nonoccurrence of the risk insured against, generally because such occurrence would cause financial loss, although sometimes merely because of the close relationship between the insured and the beneficiary.

Insurance   a plan of security against risks by charging the loss against a fund created by the payments made by policyholders.

Insured   person to whom the promise in an insurance contract is made.

Insurer   promisor in an insurance contract.

Integrity   the adherence to one's values and principles despite the costs and consequences.

Intellectual property rights   Trademark, copyright, and patent rights protected by law.

Intentional tort   a civil wrong that results from intentional conduct.

Interlineation   a writing between the lines or adding to the provisions of a document, the effect thereof depending upon the nature of the document.

Interpleader   a form of action or proceeding by which a person against whom conflicting claims are made may bring the claimants into court to litigate their claims between themselves, as in the case of a bailee when two persons each claim to be the owner of the bailed property, or an insurer when two persons each claim to be the beneficiary.

Interrogatories   written questions used as a discovery tool that must be answered under oath.

Invasion of privacy   tort of intentional intrusion in to the private affairs of another.

Inventory   goods held primarily for sale or lease to others; raw materials, work in progress, materials consumed in a business.

Investigative consumer report   a report on a person based on personal investigation and interviews.

Ipso facto   by the very act or fact in itself without any further action by anyone.

Irrebuttable presumption   a presumption that cannot be rebutted by proving that the facts are to the contrary; not a true presumption but merely a rule of law described in terms of a presumption.

Joint and several contract   a contract in which two or more persons are jointly and separately obligated or under which they are jointly and separately entitled to recover.

Joint contract   a contract in which two or more persons are jointly liable or jointly entitled to performance under the contract.

Judge   primary officer of the court.

Judgment   the final sentence, order, or decision entered into at the conclusion of the action.

Judgment n.o.v.   a judgment that may be entered after verdict upon the motion of the losing party on the ground that the verdict is so wrong that a judgment should be entered the opposite of the verdict, or non obstante veredicto (notwithstanding the verdict).

Judgment on the pleadings   a judgment that may be entered after all the pleadings are filed when it is clear from the pleadings that a particular party is entitled to win the action without proceeding any further.

Judicial branch   the branch of government (courts) formed to interpret the laws.

Jurisdiction   the power of a court to hear and determine a given class of cases; the power to act over a particular defendant.

Jury   a body of citizens sworn by a court to determine by verdict the issues of fact submitted to them.

Laches   the rule that the enforcement of equitable rights will be denied when the party has delayed so long that rights of third persons have intervened or the death or disappearance of witnesses would prejudice any party through the loss of evidence.

Last clear chance   the rule that a defendant who had the last clear chance to have avoided injuring the plaintiff is liable even though the plaintiff had also been contributorily negligent. In some states also called the humanitarian doctrine.

Law   the order or pattern of rules that society establishes to govern the conduct of individuals and the relationships among them.

Law of the case   matters decided in the course of litigation that are binding on the parties in the subsequent phases of litigation.

Law of the forum   the law of state in which the court is located.

Legislative branch   the branch of government (e.g., Congress) formed to make the laws.

Letter of credit   a written agreement by which the issuer of the letter, usually a bank, agrees with the other contracting party, its customer, that the issuer will honor drafts drawn upon it by the person named in the letter as the beneficiary. Domestic letters are regulated by the UCC, Article 5; international letters, by the Customs and Practices for Commercial Documentary Credits. Commercial or payment letter: the customer is the buyer of goods sold by the beneficiary and the letter covers the purchase price of the goods. Standby letter: a letter obtained instead of a suretyship or guaranty contract requiring the issuer to honor drafts drawn by the beneficiary upon the issuer when the customer of the issuer fails to perform a contract between the customer and the beneficiary. Documentary letter: a letter of credit that does not obligate the issuer to honor drafts unless they are accompanied by the documents specified in the letter.

Libel   written or visual defamation without legal justification.

Licensing   the transfer of technology rights to a product.

Limitation-of-liability clause   a provision in a contract stating that one of the parties shall not be liable for damages in case of breach; also called "exculpatory clause."

Limited jurisdiction   a court's power to hear and determine cases within certain restricted categories.

Limited warranty   any warranty that does not provide the complete protection of a full warranty.

Liquidated damages   a provision stipulating the amount of damages to be paid in the event of default or breach of contract.

Liquidation of damages clause   the specification of exact compensation in case of a breach of contract.

Lis pendens   the doctrine that certain kinds of pending action are notice to everyone so that if any right is acquired from a party to such action, the transferee takes that right subject to the outcome of the pending action.

Lottery   any plan by which a consideration is given for a chance to win a prize; it consists of three elements: (1) there must be a payment of money or something of value for an opportunity to win, (2) a prize must be available, and (3) the prize must be offered by lot or chance.

Mailbox rule   timing for acceptance tied to proper acceptance.

Majority   of age, as contrasted with being a minor; more than half of any group, as a majority of stockholders.

Mark   any word, name, symbol, or device used to identify a product or service.

Market power   the ability to control price and exclude competitors

Mask work   the specific form of expression embodied in a chip design, including the stencils used in manufacturing "semiconductor chip products."

Mediation   the settlement of a dispute through the use of a messenger who carries to each side of the dispute the issues and offers in the case.

Merchant   a seller who deals in specific goods classified by the UCC.

Minor   at common law anyone under 21 years of age, but now any person under 18 in most states, and 19 in a few.

Misdemeanor   a criminal offense that is neither treason nor a felony.

Misrepresentation   a false statement of fact although made innocently without any intent to deceive.

Money   a medium of exchange.

Most-favored-nation clause   a clause in treaties between countries whereby any privilege subsequently granted to a third country in relation to a given treaty subject is extended to the other party to the treaty.

Motion for summary judgment   request that the court decide case on basis of law only because there are no material issues disputed by the parties.

Motion to dismiss   a pleading that may be filed to attack the sufficiency of the adverse party's pleading as not stating a cause of action or a defense.

Natural law   a system of principles to guide human conduct independent of, and sometimes contrary to, enacted law and discovered by man's rational intelligence.

Necessaries   things indispensable or absolutely necessary for the sustenance of human life.

Negligence   the failure to exercise due care under the circumstances in consequence of which harm is proximately caused to one to whom the defendant owed a duty to exercise due care.

Negligence per se   an action that is regarded as so improper that it is declared by law to be negligent in itself without regard to whether due care was otherwise exercised.

Negotiable warehouse receipt   a receipt that states the covered goods will be delivered 'to the bearer' or 'to the order of.'

Nominal damages   a nominal sum awarded the plaintiff in order to establish that legal rights have been violated although the plaintiff in fact has not sustained any actual loss or damages.

Nonnegotiable bill of lading   see 'straight bill of lading.'

Nonnegotiable warehouse receipt   a receipt that states the covered goods received will be delivered to a specific person.

Obiter dictum   that which is said in the opinion of a court in passing or by the way, but which is not necessary to the determination of the case and is therefore not regarded as authoritative as though it were actually involved in the decision.

Objective intent   the intent of parties to an agreement that is manifested outwardly and will be enforced.

Offer   the expression of an offeror's willingness to enter into a contractual agreement.

Offeree   person to whom an offer is made.

Offeror   person who makes an offer.

Operation of law   the attaching of certain consequences to certain facts because of legal principles that operate automatically, as contrasted with consequences that arise because of the voluntary action of a party designed to create those consequences.

Option contract   a contract to hold an offer to make a contract open for a fixed period of time.

Order   designates payment to a particular person or entity for their further direction.

Ordinary contract defenses   any defense that a party to an ordinary contract may raise, such as a lack of capacity of parties, absence of consideration, fraud, concealment, or mistake.

Original jurisdiction   the authority to hear a controversy when it is first brought to court.

Output contract   the contract of a producer to sell its entire production or output to a given buyer.

Parol evidence rule   the rule that prohibits the introduction in evidence of oral or written statements made prior to or contemporaneously with the execution of a complete written contract, deed, or instrument, in the absence of clear proof of fraud, accident, or mistake causing the omission of the statement in question.

Past consideration   something that has been performed in the past and which, therefore, cannot be consideration for a promise made in the present.

Patent   the grant to an inventor of an exclusive right to make and sell an invention for a nonrenewable period of 20 years.

Patentable   a term used to describe an invention that is new and not obvious to a person of ordinary skill and knowledge in the art or technology to which the invention is related.

Per se   in, through, or by itself.

Person   a term that includes both natural persons, or living persons, and artificial persons, such as corporations which are created by act of government.

Personal property   property that is movable or intangible, or rights in such things.

Physical duress   threat of physical harm to person or property.

Plant patents   patents that protect the developers of a sexual reproduction of new plants.

Pleadings   the papers filed by the parties in an action in order to set forth the facts and frame the issues to be tried, although, under some systems, the pleadings merely give notice or a general indication of the nature of the issues.

Postdate   to insert or place on an instrument a later date than the actual date on which it was executed.

Power of appointment   a power given to another, commonly a beneficiary of a trust, to designate or appoint who shall be beneficiary or receive the fund after the death of the grantor.

Power of attorney   a written authorization to an agent by the principal.

Precedent   a decision of a court that stands as the law for a particular problem in the future.

Preempt   to take precedence over.

Preemption   the federal government's superior regulatory position over state laws on the same subject area.

Presumption   a rule of proof that permits the existence of a fact to be assumed from the proof that another fact exists when there is a logical relationship between the two or when the means of disproving the assumed fact are more readily within the control or knowledge of the adverse party against whom the presumption operates.

Price   the consideration for sale of goods.

Prima facie   evidence that, if believed, is sufficient by itself to lead to a particular conclusion.

Principal Register   a federal register maintained for recording trademarks and service marks.

Private carrier   a carrier owned by the shipper, such as a company's own fleet of trucks.

Privity   a succession or chain of relationship to the same thing or right, such as privity of contract, privity of estate, privity of possession.

Privity of contract   the relationship between a promisor and the promisee.

Procedural law   the law that must be followed in enforcing rights and liabilities.

Product disparagement   false statements made about a product or business.

Product liability   liability imposed upon the manufacturer or seller of goods for harm caused by a defect in the goods, comprising liability for (a) negligence, (b) fraud, (c) breach of warranty, and (d) strict tort.

Promisee   a person to whom a promise is made.

Promisor   a person who makes a promise.

Promissory estoppel   the doctrine that a promise will be enforced although it is not supported by consideration when the promisor should have reasonably expected that the promise would induce action or forbearance of a definite and substantial character on the part of the promised and injustice can be avoided only by enforcement of the promise.

Proximate cause   the act that is the natural and reasonably foreseeable cause of the harm or event that occurs and injures the plaintiff.

Proximate damages   damages that in the ordinary course of events are the natural and reasonably foreseeable result of the defendant's violation of the plaintiff's rights.

Punitive damages   damages, in excess of those required to compensate the plaintiff for the wrong done, that are imposed in order to punish the defendant because of the particularly wanton or willful character of wrongdoing; also called "exemplary damages."

Pur curiam opinion   an opinion written by the court rather than by a named judge when all the judges of the court are in such agreement on the matter that it is not deemed to merit any discussion and may be simply disposed of.

Quantum meruit   an action brought for the value of the services rendered the defendant when there was no express contract as to the purchase price.

Quasi   as if, as though it were, having the characteristics of; a modifier employed to indicate that the subject is to be treated as though it were in fact the noun that follows the word quasi, as in quasi contract, quasi corporation, quasi-public corporation.

Quasi contract   a court-imposed obligation to prevent unjust enrichment in the absence of a contract.

Quasi-judicial proceedings   forms of hearings in which the rules of evidence and procedure are more relaxed but each side still has a chance to be heard.

Quid pro quo   literally 'what for what.' An early form of the concept of consideration by which an action for debt could not be brought unless the defendant had obtained something in return for the obligation sued upon.

Reasonable care   the degree of care that a reasonable person would take under all the circumstances then known.

Rebuttable presumption   a presumption that may be overcome or rebutted by proof that the actual facts were different from those presumed.

Reformation   a remedy by which a written instrument is corrected when it fails to express the actual intent of both parties because of fraud, accident, or mistake.

Remand   decision of appellate court to send a case back to trial court for additional hearings or a new trial.

Remedy   the action or procedure that is followed in order to enforce a right or to obtain damages for injury to a right.

Repudiation   the result of a buyer or seller refusing to perform the contract as stated.

Requirements contract   a contract to buy all requirements of the buyer from the seller.

Rescission by agreement   the setting aside of a contract by the action of the parties as though the contract had never been made.

Rescission upon breach   the action of one party to a contract to set the contract aside when the other party is guilty of a breach of the contract.

Res ipsa loquitur   the permissible inference that the defendant was negligent in that the thing speaks for itself when the circumstances are such that ordinarily the plaintiff could not have been injured had the defendant not been at fault.

Respondeat superior   the doctrine that the principal or employer is vicariously liable for the unauthorized torts committed by an agent or employee while acting within the scope of the agency or the course of the employment, respectively.

Reverse   the term used when the appellate court sets aside the verdict or judgment of a lower court.

Right   legal capacity to require another person to perform or refrain from an action.

Right of privacy   the right to be free from unreasonable intrusion by others.

Right to cure   the second chance for a seller to make a proper tender of conforming goods.

Risk   the peril or contingency against which the insured is protected by the contract of insurance.

Risk of loss   in contract performance is the cost of damage or injury to the goods contracted for.

Robinson-Patman Act   a federal statute designed to eliminate price discrimination in interstate commerce.

Sale of goods   a present transfer of title to movable property for a price.

Sale on approval   term indicating that no sale takes place until the buyer approves or accepts the goods.

Seasonable   timely.

Service mark   any word, name, symbol, or device that identifies a service.

Several contracts   separate or independent contracts made by differerent persons undertaking to perform the same obligation.

Sherman Antitrust Act   a federal statute prohibiting combinations and contracts in restraint of interstate trade, now generally inapplicable to labor union activity.

Shop right   the right of an employer to use in business without charge an invention discovered by an employee during working hours and with the employer's material and equipment.

Slander   defamation of character by spoken words or gestures.

Sovereign immunity doctrine   the doctrine that states that a foreign sovereign generally cannot be sued unless an exception to the Foreign Sovereign Immunities act of 1976 applies.

Special agent   an agent authorized to transact a specific transaction or to do a specific act.

Special damages   damages that do not necessarily result from the injury to the plaintiff but at the same time are not so remote that the defendant should not be held liable therefor provided that the claim for special damages is properly made in the action.

Special jurisdiction   a court with power to hear and determine cases within certain restricted categories.

Specific performance   an action brought to compel the adverse party to perform a contract on the theory that merely suing for damages for its breach will not be an adequate remedy.

Statute of frauds   a statute that, in order to prevent fraud through the use of perjured testimony, requires that certain kinds of transactions be evidenced in writing in order to be binding or enforceable.

Statute of limitations   a statute that restricts the period of time within which an action may be brought.

Statutory law   legislative acts declaring, commanding, or prohibiting something.

Stop delivery   the right of an unpaid seller under certain conditions to prevent a carrier or a bailee from delivering goods to the buyer.

Straight (or nonnegotiable) bill of lading   a document of title that consigns transported goods to a named person.

Strict liability   a civil wrong for which there is absolute liability because of the inherent danger in the underlying activity, for example, the use of explosives.

Strict tort liability   a product liability theory that imposes liability upon the manufacturer, seller, or distributor of goods for harm caused by defective goods.

Subjective intent   a secret intent of a person.

Subject matter jurisdiction   judicial authority to hear a particular type of case.

Substantial impairment   material defect in a good.

Substantial performance   the equitable doctrine that a contractor substantially performing a contract in good faith is entitled to recover the contract price less damages for noncompletion or defective work.

Substantive law   the law that defines rights and liabilities.

Substitution   discharge of a contract by substituting another in its place.

Sui generis   in a class by itself, or its own kind.

Sui juris   legally competent, possessing capacity.

Summary judgment   a judgment entered by the court when no substantial dispute of fact is present, the court acting on the basis of affidavits or depositions that show that the claim or defense of a party is a sham.

Summons   a writ by which an action was commenced under the common law.

Tariff   domestically a government-approved schedule of charges that may be made by a regulated business, such as a common carrier or warehouser. Internationally a tax imposed by a country on goods crossing its borders, without regard to whether the purpose is to raise revenue or to discourage the traffic in the taxed goods.

Tender   an offer of money as part of a contract.

Tender of goods   to present goods for acceptance.

Tender of payment   an unconditional offer to pay the exact amount of money due at the time and place specified by the contract.

Tender of performance   an unconditional offer to perform at the time and in the manner specified by the contract.

Testimony   the answers of witnesses under oath to questions given at the time of the trial in the presence of the trier of fact.

Theory of the case   the rule that, when a case is tried on the basis of one theory, the appellant in taking an appeal cannot argue a different theory to the appellate court.

Third party beneficiary   a third person whom the parties to a contract intend to benefit by the making of the contract and to confer upon such person the right to sue for breach of contract.

Tie-in sale   the requirement imposed by the seller that the buyer of particular goods or equipment also purchase certain other goods from the seller in order to obtain the original property desired.

Toll the statute   stop the running of the period of the Statute of Limitations by the doing of some act by the debtor.

Tort   a civil wrong that interferes with one's property or person.

Tortious interference   see "contract interference."

Trade dress   a product's total image including its overall packaging look.

Trade libel   written defamation about a product or service.

Trademark   a name, device, or symbol used by a manufacturer or seller to distinguish goods from those of other persons.

Trade name   a name under which a business is carried on and, if fictitious, it must be registered.

Trade-secrets   secrets of any character peculiar and important to the business of the employer that have been communicated to the employee in the course of confidential employment.

Transferee   buyer or vendee.

Transferor   seller or vendor.

Treble damages   three times the damages actually sustained.

Trespass   an unauthorized action with respect to person or property (Party—**trespasser**).

Trial de novo   a trial required to preserve the constitutional right to a jury trial by allowing an appeal to proceed as though there never had been any prior hearing or decision.

Trier of fact   in most cases a jury, although it may be the judge alone in certain classes of cases (as in equity) or in any case when jury trial is waived, or when an administrative agency or commission is involved.

Trust   a transfer of property by one person to another with the understanding or declaration that such property be held for the benefit of another; the holding of property by the owner in trust for another, upon a declaration of trust, without a transfer to another person. (Parties—**settlor, trustee, beneficiary**)

Trust agreement   instrument creating a trust.

Unconscionable   unreasonable, not guided or restrained by conscience and often referring to a contract grossly unfair to one party because of the superior bargaining powers of the other party.

Undisclosed principal   a principal on whose behalf an agent acts without disclosing to the third person the fact of agency or the identity of the principal.

Undue influence   the influence that is asserted upon another person by one who dominates that person.

Unfair competition   the wrong of employing competitive methods that have been declared unfair by statute or an administrative agency.

Unilateral contract   a contract under which only one party is obligated to perform.

Universal agent   an agent authorized by the principal to do all acts that can lawfully be delegated to a representative.

Usage of trade   language and customs of an industry.

Usury   the lending of money at greater than the maximum rate of interest allowed by law.

Utility patents   the patents that grant inventors of any new and useful process, machine, manufacture, or composition of matter or any new useful improvement of such devices the right to obtain a patent.

Vacating of judgment   the setting aside of a judgment.

Valid   legal.

Valid contract   an agreement that is binding and enforceable.

Value   consideration or antecedent debt or security given in exchange for the transfer of a negotiable instrument.

Verdict   the decision of the trial or petty jury.

Vertical price fixing   an agreement by a retailer with a producer, for example, not to resell below a stated price, which is a violation of antitrust law.

Vicarious liability   imposing liability for the fault of another.

Void   of no legal effect and not binding on anyone.

Voidable   a transaction that may be set aside by one party thereto because of fraud or similar reason but which is binding on the other party until the injured party elects to avoid.

Voidable contract   an agreement that is otherwise binding and enforceable but may be rejected at the option of one of the parties as the result of specific circumstances.

Voidable title   title of goods that carries with it the contingency of an underlying problem.

Void agreement   an agreement that cannot be enforced.

Voir dire examination   the preliminary examination of a juror or a witness to ascertain fitness to act as such.

Volenti non fit injuria   the maxim that the defendant's act cannot constitute a tort if the plaintiff has consented thereto.

Waiver   the release or relinquishment of a known right or objection.

Warehouser   a person engaged in the business of storing the goods of others for compensation.

Warehouse receipt   a receipt issued by the warehouser for stored goods. Regulated by the UCC, which clothes the receipt with some degree of negotiability.

Warranties of seller of goods   warranties consisting of express warranties that relate to matters forming part of the basis of the bargain; warranties as to title and right to sell; and the implied warranties that the law adds to a sale depending upon the nature of the transaction.

Warranty   a promise either express or implied about the nature, quality, or performance of the goods.

Warranty of title   implied warranty that title to the goods is good and transfer is proper.

Willful   intentional, as distinguished from accidental or involuntary. In penal statutes, with evil intent or legal malice, or without reasonable ground for believing one's act to be lawful.

World Trade Organization (WTO)   agency responsible for administering the objectives of the General Agreement on Tariffs and Trade (GATT).

Writ of certiorari   ordered by the U.S. Supreme Court granting a right of review by the court of a lower court decision.

Index

900 numbers, 283

A

Abandonment, 206
Abuse of product, 374–375
Acceptance, 317, 327
Access plus similarity test, 44
Accounting of profits, 212
Actual breach, 331
Actual damages, 206, 212, 214
Adhesion, contracts of, 324
Administrative agency rules
    and regulations, 6
Adversary system, 7
Advertisements, as offers, 320, 337–341
Advertising
    agreements to restrict, 119, 123
    bait-and-switch, 247
    comparative, 249
    corrective, 243
    of credit, 293
    deceptive, 264–271
    electronic retailing, 278–280
    false, 237–241, 259–264
    international issues, 252
    Internet and, 250–251
    online banner, 214–215
    regulation of, 231–274
    substantiation of, 246
*Advertising and Marketing on the Internet: Rules
    of the Road* (FTC), 251
Affirm the decision, 8
Agent, 163, 165

Agriculture, Department of (USDA), 288
Alcohol, Tobacco, Firearms and Explosives
    (ATF), 288
Amended Sentencing Guidelines, 118
American Inventors Protection Act of 1999, 27,
    31, 35
American Law Institute (ALI), 6, 316
American legal system, 7–10
    common law, 6–7
    court structure, 8–10
    equity, 7–8
    jurisdiction. *See* Jurisdiction
Anglo-American law, 7
Anticipatory breach, 331
Anticipatory repudiation, 331
Anticybersquatting Consumer Protection Act
    (ACPA), 213
*Antitrust Guidelines for Collaborations Among
    Competitors* (FTC), 124
Antitrust Guidelines for International Operations
    (FTC), 136
Antitrust law, 109–154
    cases, 137–150
    Clayton Act, 112–113, 116, 124,
        127, 132
    common law contracts in restraint of trade,
        110–111
    concerted refusals to deal, 122–123
    federal statutes, 111–118
    franchising and, 165–168, 182–184
    group boycotts, 119, 122–123
    horizontal market allocations, 119, 123,
        137–138
    horizontal restraints among competitors, 118–124

Antitrust law (*continued*)
  international issues, 136–137
  Internet and, 135
  monetary damages, 111
  monopolization, 128–131
  overview of, 109–110
  price-fixing, 119, 121–122
  remedies for violations, 116–118
  Robinson-Patman Act, 114, 131–132, 133
  rule of reason vs. *per se* violations,
      115–116, 118
  Sherman Act, 111–112, 120, 122, 124,
      127–128, 133
  state enforcement, 135–136
  statistics, 117
  vertical restraints against competition, 124–128
  See also Federal Trade Commission Act
Apparent agent theory, 165
Appeal of right, 9
Appellant, 8
Appellate court of last resort, 9
Appellate jurisdiction, 8
Arbitrary marks, 193
Attempted monopolization, 131, 145–147,
      148–150
Attorney fees, 35, 49, 78, 206, 212, 237
Attribution, right of, 40
Automobile Dealers' Franchise Act, 160

B

Bait-and-switch advertising, 247
Banner advertising, 214–215
Bargained-for exchange, 322
Battle of the Forms, and counteroffers, 320–322,
      341–344
BBBOnLine, 252
Berne Convention, 37, 40, 41–42, 50
Beyond a reasonable doubt, 8
Bidding, predatory, 130
Bid-rigging, 119, 122
Bilateral contracts, 319–320
Blocking patent, 32
Blurring, 211
Bond, 243
Boycotts, 119, 122–123
Breach, absence of, 330
Breach, actual, 331
Breach, anticipatory, 331
Breach of contract, 234, 330
Broker's discount, 114

Business format franchise, 156
Business methods, 27
Business opportunity statutes, 162
Business strategies
  contractual agreements, 82–86
  intellectual property audits, 86–88
  Internet and, 215–216
Buyer, performance by, 327–328
Buyer's obligations, 363

C

Capacity, and contracts, 324
Caveat emptor, 355
Caveat venditor, 356
Cease-and-desist order, 243
Centers for Disease Control and Prevention
      (CDC), 288
Certification mark, 193
Children's Advertising Unit (CARU), 246
Children's Online Privacy Protection Act
      (COPPA), 251
Circumstantial evidence, 119
Civil law, 4, 7
Civil penalties, 243
Claim, implied, 246
Claims, 30
Clayton Act, 112–113, 116, 124, 127, 132
Co-branding, 168
Cofranchise, 168
Collective mark, 193
Collective membership mark, 193
Collective service mark, 193
Collective trademark, 193
Commerce, Department of, 288
"Commercial" damages, 364
Commercial disparagement, 241
Commercial free speech. *See* Commercial speech
Commercial speech, 231–274
  cases, 253–271
  commercial disparagement, 241
  common law causes of action, 234–236
  false advertising, 237–241, 259–264
  Federal Trade Commission Act, 241–243
  FTC regulation, general principles of, 243–247
  overview of, 231–234
  right of publicity, 234–236
  statutory causes of action, 236–250
Common law, 6–8, 316
Common law causes of action, and
      commercial speech, 234–236

Company's perspective, unsolicited ideas, 81–82

Comparative advertising, 249

Comparative negligence, 374

Compensatory damages, 332

Competition, meeting, 133

Competition, meeting in good faith
    defense, 135

Competitive intelligence activities, 77

*Complying with the Environmental
    Marketing Guide* (FTC), 285

Concerted refusals to deal, 119, 122–123

Concurrent jurisdiction, 11

Confidentiality, duty of, 75–76

Conflict of laws rules, 12

Confusion, likelihood, 203–204

Conscious parallelism, 120

Consent order, 242

Consequential damages, 332, 333, 363

Consideration, 322–323

Constitution, state, 6

Constitution, U.S., 5

Consumer credit protection, 293–296

Consumer expectations test, 369, 386–389

Consumer Leasing Act, 294

Consumer Product Safety Act (CPSA),
    287, 292

Consumer Product Safety Commission (CPSC), 287,
    291–293

Consumer Product Safety Improvement Act of
    2008, 292

Consumer protection law, 275–312
    cases, 296–309
    consumer credit protection, 293–296
    direct marketing activities, 275–283
    health and safety regulation, 287–293
    labeling and packaging regulation, 283–287
    overview of, 275

Consumer redress, 243

Contests, 249–250

Contracts and sales of goods law, 315–353
    bilateral contracts, 319–320
    breach of contract, 234, 330–332
    capacity and, 324
    cases, 337–349
    common law, 316
    death and, 318
    definiteness, 326
    destination contracts, 328, 330
    e-commerce and, 335
    elements of a contract, 317–324
    incapacity, 318

    international issues, 336–337
    interpretation of, 326
    legality of, 323–324
    overview of, 315
    parol evidence rule, 325–326
    performance of, 326–328
    privity of, 359–360
    promissory estoppel, 324, 345–347
    public policy and, 323–324
    remedies for breach, 331–335, 345–347
    in restraint of trade, 110–111
    sources of contract law, 315–317
    special UCC rules, 326
    statute of frauds, 325, 337–341
    unconscionable contracts, 324
    unenforceability, 323–324
    unilateral contracts, 319–320
    unreasonable contracts, 110

Contracts of adhesion, 324

Contractual agreements, 82–86

Contributory infringement, 33, 44, 204

Contributory negligence, 374

Controlling the Assault of Non-Solicited
    Pornography and Marketing Act (CAN-SPAM),
    280, 300–303

Convention filing, 36

Convention for the Protection of Industrial
    Property, 36

Cooling-off Rule (FTC), 280–281

Copying, 43

Copyright Act of 1976, 38, 88

Copyright law, 37–51
    cases, 55–65
    creation of copyright, 41
    defenses to infringement, 45–47
    deposit and registration, 42–43
    duration of copyright, 43
    infringement, 43–45, 58–61
    international issues, 50–51
    on the Internet, 49–50
    overview of, 88
    ownership of, 41
    procedures, 41–43
    remedies for infringement, 47–49
    rights provided by, 40–41
    sources of, 37–38
    subject matter of, 38–40, 58–61

Copyright notice, 41–42

Corrective advertising, 243

Cosmetics, 291

Cosmetics laws, 287–291

Cost justification, 133
Council of Better Business Bureaus (CBBB), 246
Counterfeiting, 209
Counteroffer, 318, 320–322, 341–344
Course of dealing, 326
Course of performance, 326
Court structure, 8–10
Courts of Appeal, U.S., 10
Covenant not to compete, 75, 82–83, 96–100
Covenants, naked, 110
Credit, advertising of, 293
Credit cards, 293–294
Criminal law, 3–4
Criminal penalties, 49
Criminal prosecution, 78–79
Criminal sanctions, 117
Cure, 327
Currency of payment clause, 337
Customs Service, U.S., 202–203
Cybersquatting, 171–172, 213–214

D

Damages, 116
    actual, 206, 212, 214
    commercial, 364
    commercial speech and, 237
    compensatory, 332
    consequential, 332, 333, 363
    double, 78
    incidental, 333–334, 363
    punitive, 236, 237
    statutory, 214
    treble, 35, 206, 237
    See also Monetary damages
Database Directive, 40
Dealing, course of, 326
Death, and contracts, 318
Deceit, 234
Deception, 245–247
Deceptive advertising, 264–271
Deceptive marks, 197
Deceptive pricing, 247–248
Deep linking, 215
Defective product recall, 377
Defendant, 8
Defenses
    for copyright infringement, 45–47
    fair use, 45, 61–65, 204
    for patent infringement, 34

price discrimination, 133–135
for product liability, 373–378
state-of-the-art, 375–377
for trademark infringement, 204–206, 211, 221–224
warranties and product liability, 363–364
Definiteness, and contracts, 326
Deposit and registration, of copyright, 42–43
Descriptive marks, 194
Design patents, 26, 29, 88
Destination contract, 328, 330
Dietary Supplement and Nonprescription Drug Consumer Act, 290
Dietary Supplement Health and Education Act of 1994 (DSHEA), 290
Dietary supplements, 289–290
Dilution, 203, 209–212, 221–224
Direct evidence, 119
Direct franchising, 172
Direct infringement, 33, 43–44
Direct marketing activities, 275–283
    900 numbers, 283
    electronic retailing and advertising, 278–280
    home solicitation, 280–282, 303–306
    merchandise on approval, 282
    negative option plans, 282
    telemarketing, 276–278
    unsolicited merchandise, 282
    warranties and guarantees, 283
Direct Marketing Association, The, 252
Disclaimer, 246, 361–363, 382–384
Disclosure, 246, 293
Disclosure rules, for franchises, 161–162
Discriminatory pricing, 114
Disparagement, commercial, 241
Distinctiveness, 193
District Courts, U.S., 10
Diversity cases, 11
"Dolphin-safe" label, 286
Do-Not-Call registry. *See* National Do Not Call Registry
Dot Com Disclosures: Information about Online Advertising (FTC), 251
Double damages, 78
Drug laws, 287–291

E

Eco-labeling, 286–287
E-commerce, 335
Economic Espionage Act, 77, 78–79, 88

Economic rights, 40

Electronic retailing and advertising, 278–280

Electronic Signatures in Global and National Commerce Act (E-SIGN Act), 335

Employees, trade secrets and, 74–75

En banc, 10

Encroachment, 168–170

Endorsements, 248

Environmental Protection Agency (EPA), 285

Equal Credit Opportunity Act (ECOA), 294

Equitable relief, 116

Equitable remedies, 331

Equity, 7–8

Espionage, industrial, 76

Essential facilities doctrine, 131, 148–150

European Commission's Consumer Affairs website, 252

European Patent Convention, 36

European Union, 40

European Union Persona Data Directive, 252

Exclusive dealing agreements, 127

Exculpatory clauses, 323, 332

Experimental use defense, 34

Express claim, 246

Express warranties, 357–359, 361

F

Fair and Accurate Credit Transaction Act, 296

Fair Credit Reporting Act (FRCA), 252, 294–295

Fair Debt Collections Practices Act (FDCPA), 294, 306–309

Fair Packaging and Labeling Act, 283

Fair use defense, 45, 61–65, 204

False advertising, 237–241, 259–264

Fanciful marks, 193

Federal Cigarette Labeling and Advertising Act, 283

Federal Communications Commission (FCC), 277

Federal court structure, 9–10

Federal disclosure rules, 161–162

Federal government, 4–5

Federal Hazardous Substances Act, 292

Federal law, primary sources of, 5–6

Federal question, 8, 11

Federal Reserve Board, 293

Federal Trade Commission Act
    antitrust law, 113–114
    cases, 264–271
    commercial speech, 241–243
    false advertising, 237

    overview of, 249
    regulation, general principles of, 243–247

Federal Trade Commission (FTC), 364–365

Federal Trademark Dilution Act of 1995, 210

Financial Privacy Rules (FTC), 252

Firm offers, 320

First Amendment, 221–224, 231, 296–300

First to invent, 29

Fixation, 40

Flammable Fabrics Act, 283, 292

Food, Drug and Cosmetic Act (FDCA), 287

Food, drug, and cosmetic laws, 287–291

Food and Drug Administration (FDA), 287, 291

Food and Drug Administration Modernization Act of 1997 (FDAMA), 290–291

Force majeure clause, 337

Foreign patents, 35–37

Foreseeable risks, 366

Forms, and counteroffers, 320–322

Forum clause, 337

Framing, 215

Franchise, 155
    business format, 156
    cofranchise, 168
    creation of, 159–160
    definition of, 156–158
    direct, 172
    international issues, 172–173
    Internet and, 170–172
    location restrictions, 173–175
    offering on the Internet, 171
    types of, 156
    See also Franchisor-Franchisee relationship

Franchise Disclosure Document (FDD), 161

Franchise Disclosure Rule, 157, 161–162, 170

Franchisor-Franchisee relationship, 155–188
    antitrust issues, 165–168, 182–184
    cases, 173–184
    co-branding, 168
    control of Internet activities, 171–172
    disclosure, 161–162
    encroachment, 168–170
    existence of, 163, 175–179
    legal issues arising from, 162–170
    multi-level marketing, 170
    overview of, 155–156
    regulation of, 160–162
    termination issues, 170
    vicarious liability of franchisor, 163–165, 179–182
    See also Franchise

Fraud, 234
Fraudulent misrepresentation, 234
Full warranty, 364
Fundamental term, 321

G

Gap-filler rules, 326
General Agreement on Tariffs and Trade
    (GATT), 286
Generic terms, and marks, 194
Geographic markets, 118, 129
Geographic terms, and marks, 194
Goodwill, 192
Governing law clause, 337
Government standards, compliance with, 377–378
Gray markets, 207–209
"Green" marketing, 285–286
Group boycotts, 119, 122–123
Guides Against Bait Advertising (FTC), 247
Guides Against Deceptive Pricing (FTC), 247
*Guides concerning use of Endorsements and
    Testimonials in Advertising* (FTC), 248
Guides for the Use of Environmental Marketing Claims
    (FTC), 285

H

Health and safety regulation, 287–293
Home solicitation, 280–282, 303–306
Horizontal market allocations, 119, 123, 137–138
Horizontal price-fixing, 121, 137–138
Horizontal restraints among competitors, 118–124
Hybrid contracts, 317
Hyperlinking, 215

I

Identification, 329
Illegal conduct, 76
Illinois Franchise Disclosure Act, 156
Immoral marks, 197
Implied claim, 246
Implied covenant of good faith, 169
Implied warranty of fitness for particular purpose,
    359, 361–362
Implied warranty of merchantability, 358–359, 361
Importation, parallel, 207–209
Impoundment, 47
In rem jurisdiction, 12, 214
Incapacity, and contracts, 318

Incidental damages, 333–334, 363
Indemnification clauses, 165
Inducement to infringement, 33
Industrial espionage, 76
Inequitable conduct, 34
Inevitable disclosure rule, 75
Infringement
    contributory, 33, 44, 204
    on copyright, 43–45, 58–61
    direct, 33, 43–44
    on patent, 32–35
    on trademark, 203–209, 221–227
Inherently distinctive marks, 193
Injunctions
    antitrust law, 111
    breach of contract, 331
    commercial speech and, 237
    copyright infringement and, 47
    covenants not to compete and, 83
    definition of, 7
    false advertising, 239
    under Lanham Act, 214
    patent infringement and, 34
    preliminary, 34, 116, 206, 236, 237
    trade secret misappropriation and, 77–78
Inquisitorial system, 7
Inspection, 327
Insurable interest, 331
Integrity, right of, 40
Intellectual property assets, protection of. *See* Business
    strategies; Contractual agreements; Copyright law;
    Patent law; Trade secret law
Intellectual property audits, 86–88
Intellectual property law, categories of, 23–25
Intent to use application, 201
Interbrand competition, 127
Intermediate appellate courts, 9
International issues
    antitrust law, 136–137
    contracts and, 336–337
    copyright law and, 50–51
    franchising and, 172–173
    labeling and packaging regulation, 286–287
    trade secret law, 80
International products liability laws, 379
International Trade Commission (ITC), 51
Internet
    advertising and, 250–251
    antitrust law, 135
    copyright law and, 49–50
    covenants not to compete and, 83

encroachment issues, 172
franchising and, 170–172
junk e-mail, 278
offers on, 171
strategies for business, 215–216
trademarks on, 213–216
Internet, jurisdiction on, 12–13
Internet Corporation for Assigned Names and
     Numbers (ICANN), 213
Interpretation, of contracts, 326
Intrabrand competition, 127
Invention, ownership of, 29
Invention assignment agreement, 75, 86, 87
Inventor, 29
Inventor's perspective, unsolicited ideas, 80–81

J

Joint ventures, 119, 123–124, 172
Judicial review, 6
Junior user, 200
Junk e-mail, 278
Jurisdiction, 11–13
   appellate, 8
   cases, 13–20
   concurrent, 11
   on the Internet, 12–13
   original, 8
   over the parties, 12
   permanent, 34, 206, 212, 236, 237
   personal, 12
   personam, 12
   in rem, 12, 214
   subject matter, 11–12

L

Labeling and packaging regulation, 283–287
   "Green" marketing, 285–286
   international issues, 286–287
   "Made in USA" labeling, 284–285
Language clause, 337
Lanham Act
   cases, 259–264
   commercial speech and, 237–241
   Internet and, 214
   overview of, 249
   trademark law and, 88, 192, 200, 202,
      203, 206
Lapse of time, 318
Latent defects, 371–372

Law
   classifications of, 3–5
   primary sources of, 5–6
   secondary sources of, 6–7
   sources of, 5–7
Learned intermediaries rule, 378
Legal environment of marketing activities, 3–20
   American legal system, 7–10
   classifications of the law, 3–5
   introduction to, 3
   jurisdiction. *See* Jurisdiction
   sources of the law, 5–7
Legal system, American, 7–10
   common law, 6–8
   court structure, 8–10
   equity, 7–8
   jurisdiction. *See* Jurisdiction
Legality, of contracts, 323–324
Lever Rule, 208
Liability, strict, 367–379, 384–389
Likelihood of confusion, 203–204
Limited warranty, 364
Linking issues, 215
Liquidated damages clause, 332
Local governments, 5
Location restrictions, and franchises, 173–175
Long-arm statutes, 12
Loss, risk of, 329–330
Lost profits, 35, 78
Lost sales, 49

M

"Made in USA" labeling, 284–285
Madrid Protocol, 212
Magnuson-Moss Federal Warranty Act, 364–365,
      382–384
Mail or Telephone Order Merchandise Rule
      (FTC), 278
Mailbox rule, 318
Market conditions defense, 135
Market conditions, response to, 133
Market power, 128
Market share liability, 372–373
Marketing
   green marketing, 285–286
   See also Legal environment of marketing activities
Marks. *See* Trademark law
Master franchise agreement, 172
Matrix marketing, 170
Maximum price, 125

Maximum price-fixing, 167
Medical Device Amendment, 290
Medical devices, 290–291
Meng, Xiadong Sheldon, 79
Merchandise on approval, 282
Merchants, 322, 356
Metatags, 215, 224–227
Microsoft, 215
Minimum contacts, 12
Minimum price, 124
Mirror image rule, 321
Misrepresentation, liability for, 372
Misuse of product, 374–375
Mitigate, duty to, 332
Mixed comparative fault system, 374
Mock-ups, 248–249
Modification, 322
Modify the decision, 8
Monetary damages
    antitrust law, 111
    breach of contract, 234, 330–332
    commercial speech and, 236
    copyright infringement and, 49
    covenants not to compete and, 83
    false advertising, 239
    patent infringement and, 34–35
    trade secret misappropriation and, 78
Monopolization
    attempted, 131, 145–147, 148–150
    conspiracy to, 131
    by a single firm, 128–131
Monopoly power, 128–131
Monopsony power, 128, 131
Moral rights, 40
Mortgage Disclosure Improvement Act, 293
Multi-level marketing, 170
Multiple brand product market, 129–130
Mutual assent, 317–322

N

Naked covenants, 110
National Advertising Division (NAD), 250
National Conference of Commissioners on Uniform
    State Laws (NCCUSL), 6, 316
National Cooperative Research Act, 123
National Do Not Call Registry, 278, 296–300
Negative option plans, 282
Negligence, 163–164, 364–367, 384–386
    comparative, 374
    contributory, 374

Network marketing, 170
Noncompete agreement, 75, 82–83, 92–96
Nondisclosure agreement (NDA), 75, 83–85
Nonobviousness standard, 28
Nonprice agreements between manufacturer and
    dealer, 125, 127
Notice clause, 337
Notice to the public, 35
Novelty, 28, 53–55

O

Offer, 317
Offeree, 318
Offeror, 317
Offers
    acceptance of, 317, 327
    advertisements as, 320, 337–341
    consideration and, 322–323
    counteroffer, 318, 320–322, 341–344
    firm, 320
    forms, 320–322
    rejection of, 320–321
    revocation of, 318
    revocation of acceptance, 327–328
Office of Harmonization of the Internal Market, 212
Official Gazette, 31, 200–201
Off-label use of drugs or devices, 291
On-line advertising, 250–251
Online Privacy Alliance, The, 252
On-sale bar, 53–55
Option contracts, 320
Organization for Economic Co-operation and
    Development (OECD), 209
Original jurisdiction, 8
Originality, 38–40
Ornamental features, 29
Output contracts, 326

P

Package design, 197
Packaging regulation. *See* Labeling and packaging
    regulation
Palming off, 237
Parallel importation, 207–209
Parallelism, conscious, 120
Paris Convention, 36
Parodies, 45, 47
Parol evidence rule, 325–326
Passing off, 237

Patent, definition of, 25
Patent Act, 25, 33, 88
Patent and Trademark Office (PTO), 25
Patent Cooperation Treaty, 36–37
Patent invalidity, 34
Patent law, 25–37
   application procedures, 30–31
   blocking patents, 32
   cases, 51–55
   foreign patents, 35–37
   infringement, 32–34
   overview of, 88
   ownership, 29 30
   prosecution procedure, 32
   rights granted by, 31–32
   standards for issuance, 26–29
   statistics, 26
   v. trade secret law, 73–74
Patent misuse, 34
Patents, types of, 26–29, 88
Per se rule, 128
Per se violations, 115–116, 118
Perfect tender rule, 327
Performance
   by buyer, 327–328
   of contracts, 326–328
   course of, 326
Permanent injunction, 34, 206, 212,
   236, 237
Personal jurisdiction, 12
Personal names, and marks, 194
Personam jurisdiction, 12
Petitioner, 8
Petroleum Marketing Practices Act, 160
Plaintiff, 8
Plant patents, 26
Plus factors, 120
Poison Prevention Packaging Act, 292
Policy Statement on Deception (FTC), 245
Policy Statement on Unfairness (FTC), 244, 275
Policy Statement Regarding Advertising Substantiation
   (FTC), 247
Ponzi schemes, 170
Portals, 214–215
Postal Lottery Statute, 170
Post-sale duties to warn, 375–377
Precedent, doctrine of, 7
Predatory bidding, 130
Predatory pricing, 130
Preliminary injunction, 34, 116, 206,
   236, 237

Prenotification Negative Option Rule
   (FTC), 282
Preponderance of evidence, 8
Presumption of validity, 31
Price, maximum, 125
Price, minimum, 124
Price discrimination, 114, 131–135
   defenses to, 133–135
   elements of, 132–133
Price restraints, 138–142, 143–144, 167–168
Price-fixing, 119, 121–122, 137–138, 167
Pricing
   deceptive, 247–248
   discriminatory, 114
   predatory, 130
Primary-line price discrimination, 132
Principal Register, 192
Prior art search, 30
Prioritizing Resources and Organization for
   Intellectual Property Act of 2008 (PRO-IP),
   49, 209
Privacy issues, 251–252
Private law, 4
Privity of contract, 359–360
Procedural law, 4
Process, in infringement, 33
Product, abuse of, 374–375
Product, appearance of, 197
Product, misuse of, 374–375
Product and trade name franchise, 156
Product demonstrations, 248–249
Product design, 197
Product disparagement, 241
Product liability law. See Warranties and
   product liability
Product liability reform, 378–379
Product markets, 118, 129
Products, in infringement, 33
Profits, 206, 212
PRO-IP Act of 2008, 49, 209
Promissory estoppel, 324, 345–347
Proprietary information agreement, 83
Prosecution, 30, 78–79
Prosecutor, 8
Protocol Relating to the Madrid Agreement
   Concerning the International Registration of
   Trademarks, 212
Public law, 4
Public policy, and contracts, 323–324
Publicity, right of, 234–236
Puffing, 241

Punitive damages, 236, 237
Pure comparative fault system, 374
Pyramid schemes, 170

R

Reason, rule of, 115–116, 138–144
Reasonable alternative design (RAD), 371
Reasonable royalty, 35, 49, 78
Recall of defective products, 377
Record, 8
Refrigerator Safety Act, 292
Refuse to deal, 131
Rejection, 328
Rejection of offer, 320–321
Remand cases, 8
Remedies
　for antitrust law violations, 116–118
　attorney fees, 35, 49, 78, 206, 212, 237
　for breach of contract, 331–335,
　　345–347
　for copyright infringement, 47–49
　for misappropriation, 77–79
　for patent infringement, 34–35
　sales contracts, 332–335
　for trademark dilution, 211–212
　for trademark infringement, 206,
　　224–227
　warranties and product liability, 363–364, 373
Reply doctrine, 325
Reporting requirements, 292
Requirements contracts, 326
Resale price maintenance agreements, 124–126
Rescission, 332
Respondent, 8
Restatement (Second) of Contracts, 37, 110, 169,
　316, 324
Restatement (Second) of Torts, 367–369
Restatement (Third) of Torts, 367,
　369–371
Restatements of the Law, 6
Restitution, 332
Restraint of trade, 110–111
Reverse passing off, 237
Reverse the decision, 8
Reverse-engineering, 72
Revocation, of offer, 318
Revocation of acceptance, 327–328
Rio Earth Summit, 286
Risks, foreseeable, 366

Risk-utility test, 369, 386–389
Robinson-Patman Act, 114, 131–132, 133
Rockefeller, John D., 111
Rule of reason, 115–116, 138–144
Rule on Pre-Sale Availability of Written Warranty
　Terms (FTC), 283

S

Sales contracts, remedies in, 332–335
Scandalous marks, 197
Scientific evidence, 247
Secondary liability, 44
Secondary meaning, 194
Secondary-line price discrimination, 133
Seller, performance by, 327
Senior user, 200
Service mark, 192
Sherman Act, 111–112, 120, 122, 124, 127,
　128, 133
Shipment contract, 328, 330
Shop rights, 75
Signaling behavior, 119
Small claims court, 9
Smokeless Tobacco Health Education
　Act, 284
Sonny Bono Copyright Term Extension
　Act, 43
Sophisticated purchaser rule, 378
Sorting Out "Green" Advertising Claims (FTC), 285
Sovereign immunity doctrine, 136
Spam e-mail, 278
Specialty tribunals, 10
Specific performance, 7, 331
Standard Oil Trust, 111
Stare decisis, 7
State court structure, 8–9
State disclosure rules, 162
State governments, 5
State law, primary sources of, 6
Statement of Policy Regarding Comparative Advertising
　(FTC), 249
State-of-the-art defense, 375–377
Statute of frauds, 325, 337–341
Statutes, 6
Statutes of limitation, 378
Statutes of repose, 378
Statutory causes of action, commercial speech and,
　236–250
Statutory damages, 214

Strict liability, 367–379, 384–389
Strict products liability, 367–379
Subfranchise, 168
Subject matter jurisdiction, 11–12
Subsequent remedial design, 371
Substantial injury, 244
Substantiation of advertising, 246
Substantive law, 4
Successor liability, 373
Suggested retail prices, 125
Suggestive marks, 193–194
Supplemental Register, 202
Supreme Court, U.S., 10
Sweepstakes, 249–250

T

Tarnishment, 211
Telemarketing, 276–278
Telemarketing and Consumer Fraud and Abuse
    Prevention Act, 277
Telemarketing Sales Rule (FTC), 277
Telephone Consumer Protection Act (TCPA), 277
Tender of delivery, 327
Termination issues, franchise, 170
Tertiary-line price discrimination, 133
Testimonials, 248
Ticketmaster, 215
Tie-in sales, 127
Time, lapse of, 318
Title, document of, 329
Title, transfer of, 328–329
Title passage clause, 337
Trade dress, 194–195
Trade secret law, 71–80
    acquisition of competitor's, 76
    cases, 89–96
    definition of, 71–73
    international issues, 80
    misappropriation of, 75–77
    overview of, 88
    ownership of, 74–75
    patent protection vs., 73–74
    protection of, 79–80
    remedies for misappropriation, 77–79
Trademark, 191
    arbitrary marks, 193
    cancellation of, 201–202
    color as, 216–217
    creation and ownership of, 199–202

distinctiveness of, 193–194
    overview of, 88
    protection of, 218–220
    registration of, 200–201
    searches, 197–199
    U.S. Customs Service assistance, 202–203
    what may constitute, 194–197
    See also Trademark law
Trademark Dilution Revision Act (TDRA), 210
Trademark law, 191–229
    blurring, 211
    cases, 216–227
    counterfeiting, 209
    creating and protecting a mark, 193–203
    deceptive trademarks, 197
    defenses to infringement, 204–206, 221–224
    dilution, 203, 209–212, 221–224
    gray markets, 207–209
    infringement, 203–209, 221–227
    international issues, 212
    Internet, 213–216
    origins of, 192
    overview of, 191–192
    parallel importation, 207–209
    remedies for infringement, 206, 224–227
    remedies under Dilution Act, 211–212
    tarnishment, 211
    types of, 192–193
Trade-Related Aspects of Intellectual Property Rights
    (TRIPS), 37, 80
Treaty, 5–6
Treble damages, 35, 206, 237
Trials courts, 9–10
TRUSTe, 252
Truth-in-Lending Act (TILA), 293–296
Tying arrangements, 125, 127–128, 165–167
Typopiracy, 214
Typosquatting, 214

U

Unavoidably unsafe, 369
Unconscionable contracts, 324
Unenforceability, of contracts, 323–324
Unfair competition, 234
Unfairness, 244–245
Uniform Commercial Code (UCC), 7, 236, 316–317,
    326, 356
Uniform Deceptive Trade Practices Act
    (UDTPA), 238, 241

Uniform Domain Name Dispute Resolution Policy
    (UDRP), 214
Unilateral contracts, 319–320
United Nations Convention on the International Sale
    of Goods (CISG), 336, 347–349
United States Trade Representative
    (USTR), 51
Universal Copyright Convention of 1952
    (UCC), 50
Unjust enrichment damages, 78
Unreasonable contracts, 110
Unsolicited ideas, law of, 80–82, 100–103
Unsolicited merchandise, 282
Usage of trade, 326
Usefulness standard, 29
Utility patents, 26–29, 88

V

Valid cost justification, 133, 135
Vertical minimum price restraints, 168
Vertical price restraints, 138–142, 143–144, 167–168
Vertical restraints, 118
Vertical restraints against competition, 124–128
Vicarious liability, 44
Voluntary assumption of risk, 374

W

Warranties and product liability,
    355–392
  "as is," 362–363
  breach of warranty, 335
  buyer's obligations, 363

  cases, 379–389
  defenses to product liability, 373–378
  direct marketing and, 283
  disclaimers, 246, 361–363, 382–384
  express warranties, 357–359, 361
  full warranty, 364
  implied warranty of fitness for
    particular purpose, 359,
    361–362
  implied warranty of merchantability,
    358–359, 361
  limited warranty, 364
  Magnuson-Moss Federal Warranty Act,
    364–365, 382–384
  negligence, 364–367, 384–386
  overview of, 355–356
  privity of contract, 359–360
  products liability law, 365–379
  remedies and defenses, 363–364
  remedies for product liability, 373
  strict product liability, 367–379
  warranty of title, 356–357, 361
Wholesaler's discount, 114
Wool Products Labeling Act, 284
Works for hire, 41, 55–58
World Intellectual Property Organization
    (WIPO), 50
World Trade Organization (WTO), 51
Writ of certiorari, 10

X

Xerox Corporation, 196